The Politics and Economics of the European Union, Second Edition

An Introductory Text

By

Robert A. Jones
Senior Lecturer in European Studies
Sheffield Hallam University, UK

Edward Elgar
Cheltenham UK • Northampton, MA, USA

Published by
Edward Elgar Publishing Limited
Glensanda House
Montpellier Parade
Cheltenham
Glos GL50 1UA
UK

Edward Elgar Publishing, Inc.
136 West Street
Suite 202
Northampton
Massachusetts 01060
USA

A catalogue record for this book
is available from the British Library

Library of Congress Cataloguing in Publication Data

Jones, Robert A., 1946–
        The politics and economics of the European Union : an introductory
text / by Robert A. Jones — 2nd ed.
            p. cm.
        Includes bibliographical references and index.
        1. European Union. I. Title.

JN30 .J57 2001
341.242'2—dc21   2001031362

ISBN 1 84064 082 0 (cased)
         1 84064 110 X (paperback)
Printed and bound in Great Britain by MPG Books Ltd, Bodmin, Cornwall

Contents

SECTION 2 INSTITUTIONS, POLICY PROCESSES AND THE BUDGET

SECTION 3 THE POLICIES OF THE EUROPEAN UNION

List of Figures, Maps and Tables

Figures

Maps

Tables

List of Abbreviations and Acronyms

ACP	African, Caribbean and Pacific countries
ACUSE	Action Committee for a United States of Europe
ADAPT	adaptation of the workforce to industrial change
ALTENER	promotion of renewable energy sources
AP	accession partnership
APEC	Asia-Pacific Economic Co-operation Forum
ARION	programme of study visits for educational specialists
ASEAN	Association of South-East Asian Nations
BEUC	European Bureau of Consumers' Unions (Bureau Européen des unions de consommateurs)
BSE	Bovine spongiform encephalopathy ('mad cow disease')
CACM	Central American Common Market
CAP	Common Agricultural Policy
Caricom	Caribbean Community
CCP	Common Commercial Policy
CE	Council of Europe
CEDEFOP	European Centre for the Development of Vocational Training
CEECs	Central and East European countries
CEFTA	Central European Free Trade Area
CERN	European Centre for Nuclear Research
CET	Common external tariff
CFCs	Chlorofluorocarbons
CFI	Court of First Instance
CFP	Common Fisheries Policy
CFR	Charter of Fundamental Rights
CFSP	Common foreign and security policy
CIS	Commonwealth of Independent States
CJTF	Combined Joint Task Force
CMEA	Council for Mutual Economic Assistance (Comecon)
CoA	Court of Auditors
Comecon	See CMEA
COMESA	Common Market for Eastern and Southern Africa

COMETT	Community Action Programme in Education and Training for Technology
COPA	Committee of Professional Agricultural Organisations (Comité des organisations professionnelles agricoles)
CoR	Committee of the Regions
CORDIS	Community Research and Development Information Service
COREPER	Committee of Permanent Representatives
COST	European co-operation on scientific and technical research
CSF	Community support framework
CTP	Common Transport Policy
DG	Directorate-General of the European Commission
DIANE	Direct Information Access Network for Europe
EA	Europe Agreement
EAGGF	European Agricultural Guidance and Guarantee Fund
EBRD	European Bank for Reconstruction and Development
EC	European Community
ECB	European Central Bank
ECHO	European Community Humanitarian Office
ECIP	European Community Investment Partners
ECJ	European Court of Justice
ECOFIN	Council of Economic and Finance Ministers
ECOWAS	Economic Community of West African States
ECSC	European Coal and Steel Community
ECT	European Community Treaty
ECU	European currency unit
EDC	European Defence Community
EDF	European Development Fund
EEA	European Economic Area
EEB	European Environmental Bureau
EES	European Employment Strategy
EFTA	European Free Trade Association
EIB	European Investment Bank
EIF	European Investment Fund
EMCF	European Monetary Co-operation Fund
EMI	European Monetary Institute
EMS	European Monetary System
EMU	economic and monetary union
EP	European Parliament
EPC	European political co-operation (later CFSP)
EPU	European political union
ERA	European Research Area

ERASMUS	European action scheme for the mobility of university students
ERDF	European Regional Development Fund
ERM	exchange rate mechanism
ESA	European Space Agency
ESC	Economic and Social Committee
ESCB	European System of Central Banks
ESDI	European Security and Defence Identity
ESDP	European Security and Defence Policy
ESF	European Social Fund
ESP	European social policy
ETUC	European Trade Union Confederation
EU	European Union
Euratom	European Atomic Energy Community
EUREKA	European Research Co-ordination Agency
EURES	European Employment Services Agency
Eurodac	European Automated Fingerprint Recognition System
Eurofer	European Confederation of the Iron and Steel Industry
Europol	European Police Office
Eurostat	EC Statistical Office
EUROTECNET	action programme in the field of vocational training and technological change
EURYDICE	Programme to promote information exchanges on education systems
EUSP	EU social policy
FAWEU	Forces Answerable to the WEU
FDI	Foreign direct investment
FEU	full economic union
FIFG	Financial Instrument for Fisheries Guidance
FORCE	action programme for the development of continuing vocational training
GAC	General Affairs Council
G7	Group of Seven leading industrial nations (the US, Canada, Japan, France, Germany, Italy, the UK)
G24	Group of twenty-four industrial nations (members of the OECD: the OECD is now the 'G30').
GATT	General Agreement on Tariffs and Trade
GDP	Gross domestic product
GNP	Gross national product
GSP	Generalised System of Preferences
IBRD	International Bank for Reconstruction and Development (World Bank)

IEGP	Independent European Programme Group
IGC	Intergovernmental conference
IGO	International governmental organisation
IMF	International Monetary Fund
IMPEL	EU network for the implementation and enforcement of environmental law.
INGO	International non-governmental organisation
Interpol	police co-operation centre
INTERREG II	initiative concerning cross-border co-operation and energy networks
ISPA	Instrument for structural policies for pre-accession
IT	information technology
JET	Joint European Torus
JHA	Justice and Home Affairs
KALEIDOSCOPE	programme to support artistic and cultural events having a European dimension
KAROLUS	training officials in the enforcement of EC regulations
KONVER	programme to assist areas affected by the rundown of defence industries and of military installations
LEADER II	initiative for rural development
LEONARDO	action programme for the implementation of a European Community vocational training policy
LIFE	financial instrument for the environment
LINGUA	programme to promote the teaching and learning of foreign languages in the European Community
MAGP	multiannual guidance programme
MATTHAUS	specific common programmes for the vocational training of customs officials
MCA	monetary compensation amount
MEDIA	action programme to promote the development of the European audiovisual industry
MEP	Member of the European Parliament
Mercosur	a customs union, Argentina, Brazil, Paraguay and Uruguay
MFA	multifibre agreement
MLG	multilevel governance
MNC	Multinational corporation
MRA	Mutual recognition agreements
NACC	North Atlantic Co-operation Council
NAFTA	North American Free Trade Association
NATO	North Atlantic Treaty Organisation
NCB	National central bank
NGO	non-governmental organisation

NICs	newly industrialised countries
NOW	New Opportunities for Women
OCTs	overseas countries and territories
ODIHR	Office of Democratic Institutions and Human Rights
OECD	Organisation for Economic Co-operation and Development
OEEC	Organisation for European Economic Co-operation
Official Journal	Official Journal of the European Communities (note: the Treaty of Nice will change its name to Official Journal of the European Union)
OLAF	Office de la Lutte Anti-Fraude (Anti-Fraud Office)
OPEC	Organisation of Petroleum Exporting Countries
OSCE	Organisation for Security and Co-operation in Europe (formerly CSCE)
PACT	Pilot Actions for Combined Transport
PCA	partnership and co-operation agreement
PDB	preliminary draft budget
PESCA	initiative aimed at solving the problems caused by the restructuring of the fisheries sector
PETRA	action programme for the vocational training of young people and their preparation for adult and working life
PFP	Partnership for Peace
PHARE	Poland and Hungary: Aid for Economic Restructuring
PJCCM	Police and judicial co-operation in criminal matters
PPEWU	Policy planning and early warning unit
QMV	qualified majority voting
RACE	R&D in Advanced Communications Technologies in Europe
RAPHAEL	cultural heritage programme
RECHAR II	initiative concerning the economic conversion of coalmining areas
REGIS II	initiative concerning the most remote regions
RESIDER II	programme to assist the conversion of steel areas
RETEX	initiative for regions heavily dependent on the textiles and clothing sector
RRF	rapid reaction force
RTA	Regional trading agreement
RTD	research and technological development
SAA	stabilisation and association agreement
SAPARD	Special access programme for agriculture and rural development
SAVE	special action programme for vigorous energy efficiency

SCA	Special Committee on Agriculture
SEA	Single European Act
SEM	Single European Market
SIS	Schengen information system
SLIM	Simpler legislation for the Internal Market
SME	small and medium-sized enterprise
SOCRATES	programme for the development of quality education and training and of a European dimension in studies
SPC	Social Protection Committee
STABEX	system for the stabilisation of export earnings
SYSMIN	system for the stabilisation of export earnings from mining products
TAC	total allowable catch (of fish)
TACIS	Technical Assistance to the CIS
TBA	Trade barrier agreement
TCN	Third country national
TEMPUS	Trans-European Mobility Programme for University Studies
TENs	trans-European networks
TEU	Treaty on European Union
TREVI	Terrorisme, Radicalisme, Extrémisme, Violence Internationale
ToA	Treaty of Amsterdam
ToN	Treaty of Nice
TOR	Traditional own resources
UCLAF	Unité de coordination de la lutte Anti-Fraude (Unit for the Co-ordination of Fraud Prevention – now OLAF)
UNCTAD	United Nations Conference on Trade and Development
UNESCO	United Nations Educational, Scientific and Cultural Organisation
UNHCR	United Nations High Commission(er) for Refugees
UNICE	Union of Industrial and Employers' Confederations of Europe
UNIDO	United Nations Industrial Development Organisation
UNRWA	United Nations Relief and Works Agency
URBAN	initiative for urban areas
VAT	value-added tax
WEU	Western European Union
WTO	World Trade Organisation
YOUTHSTART	programme to assist the integration of young people into the labour market

Preface to the Second Edition

In preparing the second edition of this book, I have endeavoured to stay faithful to the aims of the first edition, that is to produce a textbook on the European Union (EU) which is accessible, comprehensive and topical. I have therefore retained as far as possible the style and format of the first edition. The contents of the book have been extensively revised and updated, to take account of many recent changes affecting the Union's institutions, policies and prospects. I have also given more weight to certain topics, such as enlargement, economic and monetary union, justice and home affairs, security and defence policy, European 'fundamental rights' and to the Union's 'constitutional development'. These topics are not only of considerable current importance, but are also likely to figure prominently on the list of subjects students are likely to encounter on courses in EU studies.

Since the first edition of this book appeared, some key questions relating to the future of the EU have been at least partially answered. For example, in the mid-1990s, some analysts were questioning whether EMU (the economic or monetary union project) would get off the ground, that is, whether EMU was a bird which would actually fly. The euro was launched in 1999 and the changeover to euro notes and coin within the eurozone is set for completion by 28 February 2002. Similarly, in some quarters there were doubts about the seriousness of the Union's commitment to expanding eastwards. Since then, the EU has launched an accession process, which is now well advanced, for 12 candidate countries. However, in the case of both EMU and enlargement, key questions remain to be answered, in particular how the euro will perform in the long term and the implications for the Union of the next enlargements. In EU studies, it remains true that there are more questions than there are answers, and even the answers are likely to give rise to further questions.

Students of the European Union are likely to discover very quickly that the European Union project, however, interpreted, is by no means static; that the Union's structures, processes and policies are continuing to evolve; and that, if there is an end point to the process of European integration, it has not yet been reached. Therefore, the second edition of this book, like the first, seeks to equip students with the knowledge and conceptual tools with which to better understand a dynamic and increasingly complex phenomenon.

Robert A. Jones   June 2001

Map 1 Membership of the European Union (EU15)

year of entry

| Original Members | 1973 | 1981 | 1986 | 1995 |

B = Belgium; N = Netherlands

Note: see Chapter 20 for details of future and potential members.

The Purpose and Plan of the Book

This book seeks to provide students with a clear and topical introduction to the aims, institutions and policies of the European Union (EU) in the post-cold war era. The EU is currently undergoing rapid change, rendering it impossible to provide a 'cut and dried' exposition of its characteristics or future prospects. Therefore, the book will seek throughout to enhance the reader's understanding of the main issues and controversies surrounding the Union's development.

The first section comprises an introduction to various historical and theoretical perspectives on European integration. By the end of the section, the reader should have a good understanding of the reasons for the formation of the EU and of the principal factors shaping its development. The section also seeks to identify the EU's distinctive features, by means of a comparative analysis of post-war integration projects. The second section examines the EU's institutional machinery and policy processes. It also seeks to shed light upon the dynamics of institutional change within the Union. The third section examines the main EU policies. The following ten key points should provide the reader with a preliminary perspective on the Union:

- **it is unique**. The reader should beware of false and misleading analogies. Although the EU shares some characteristics with federal states, with international organisations and with other post-war regional integration projects, it has features which differentiate it from any other political or economic formation;
- **it is unfinished**. The integration process in the EU has frequently been described as a journey to an unknown destination. Although there is general agreement that the EU is by no means complete, there is no agreement concerning its ultimate purpose, size or shape;
- **it has been an exercise in partial integration**. For much of its history, the EU project has been confined to Western Europe. The end of the cold war resulted in qualitative changes in the Union's agenda for enlargement and in its relationships with Central and Eastern Europe. The Union has already committed itself to a southward and eastward expansion. Cyprus, Malta and ten former communist countries in Central and Eastern Europe are currently undergoing an accession process. Turkey has also been accepted as a

candidate country and several countries in the Western Balkans have been offered the 'perspective' of future membership. The West European focus of Union integration is also being challenged by the collaborative links the Union is developing with European countries outside its borders. These links, embracing activities in diverse fields (including trade, energy, the environment, transport, research and education) are examples of an emerging trend towards the 'pan-Europeanisation' of European integration;

- **its development has been very uneven**. Far from being a smooth, linear process, the Union's growth has been by 'fits and starts' (with periods of relatively rapid development and of inertia). The range and depth of the Union's policy responsibilities are also very uneven. The strength of the 'integration impulse', as a key factor in the development of the Union, should not, however, be underestimated;

- **it has been an elite project**. Levels of citizen participation in the European Union project have generally been very low (as shown most clearly, but by no means only, by low turnouts in elections to the European Parliament). The problem of the Union's 'democratic deficit' surfaces in various forms throughout this book;

- **the intertwining of political and economic objectives**. Although for much of its history the European Union has been widely interpreted as being primarily an economic formation, its development has been inspired by a combination of political and economic objectives. For example, the political dimension of projects such as the Single European Market programme and Economic and Monetary Union (EMU) should not be underestimated;

- **it is a product of many influences**. The lack of clarity, coherence or 'tidiness' which have frequently been observed in relation to the Union's goals and institutional structure is due in no small measure to the multiple influences shaping the Union's development. It is therefore probably futile to search for the 'essence' or 'true nature' of the Union;

- **its central concepts are 'fuzzy'**. Many of the ideas which are regarded as central to an understanding of the Union (such as 'integration', 'federalism', 'subsidiarity' and indeed the term 'Union' itself) are interpreted in many different ways. Indeed, the development of the Union has owed much to the tolerance of ambiguity concerning the interpretation of the Union's goal of an 'ever closer union';

- **the tension between 'intergovernmentalist' and 'supranational' influences** – that is, between the conception of the Union as essentially a 'club of sovereign states' and as a project involving the surrender of state sovereignty to non-state institutions. This tension has crucially influenced the Union's institutional framework and operational characteristics;

- **it is the world's most advanced project in regional integration.** Although many other attempts have been made to forge regional economic and political formations, both within and outside Europe, most have either stalled or failed and none has achieved the degree of integration attained by the EU. Arguably, this degree of success is due to a combination of historical, political and economic circumstances peculiar to post-war Western Europe.

○ 'European Community' or 'European Union'?

Any study of European integration must deal with the problem of nomenclature. Following the entry into force of the Treaty on European Union (the 'Maastricht Treaty' or 'TEU') on 1 November 1993, the term 'European Union' has gained wide currency as a description of what was formerly referred to as the 'European Community'. However, although the treaty brought into being the 'European Union', it neither abolished the 'European Community' nor explicitly sanctioned the general substitution of the term 'Union' for 'Community'. Nor did it bestow upon the Union a legal personality. The subsequent confusion surrounding correct usages is a consequence of various compromises and fudges made at the European Council meeting in Maastricht (at which the TEU was agreed) in December 1991 and subsequently at the European Council meeting in Amsterdam in June 1997, which agreed the Treaty of Amsterdam (ToA). Far from resolving the EU/EC nomenclature problem, if anything the ToA made the distinction between the EU and EC even fuzzier in some respects.

The nomenclature problem is by no means due solely to the TEU. Until 1967 (when the 1965 Merger Treaty came into force), there were three separate 'Communities': the European Economic Community (EEC), the European Coal and Steel Community (ECSC) and the European Atomic Energy Community (Euratom). As a result of this merger, these Communities together officially became the 'European Communities'. However, the term 'European Community' has been widely used as a general description of the three Communities. The TEU changed the name of the 'European Economic Community' to 'European Community', the 'EEC Treaty' thereby becoming the 'EC Treaty'. Despite this change, 'European Community' is still used as a general description of the three Communities. When the ECSC treaty expires in July 2002, the ECSC will be absorbed into the European Community.

The 'European Union' established by the TEU has a 'temple' structure, comprising three co-existing pillars: prior to the ratification of the Treaty of Amsterdam, these were firstly, the 'European Communities' pillar, comprising the 'European Community' (formerly known as the European Economic Community), the ECSC and Euratom; secondly, the 'Common Foreign and Security Policy' (CFSP), or second, pillar; and thirdly, the 'Justice and Home Affairs', or third, pillar. The Treaty of Amsterdam retained the three-pillar structure but not only changed the name of the third pillar to 'Police and Judicial Co-operation in Criminal Matters' (PJCCM) but also substantially altered its content, primarily by moving asylum and immigration policy from the third to the first pillar. The 'roof' of the temple consists of 'common provisions' setting out the Union's broad objectives (Title I). The temple's 'plinth' consists of final provisions outlining relationships with existing EC treaties, arrangements for ratification and other matters (Title VIII). In the treaty, the aims and structure of the Union are set out in various 'titles', as shown in Figure 1 below. Title VII, which is not shown in the diagram, deals with enhanced co-operation between member states (also known as 'closer' or 'reinforced' co-operation) and its provisions apply to both the TEU and the EC Treaty (see Chapter 4).

Figure 1 The Three Pillars of the European Union

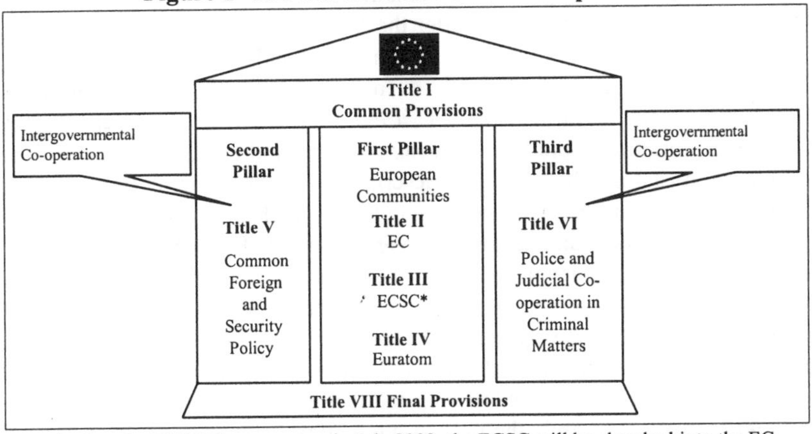

Note: * when the ECSC Treaty expires in July 2002, the ECSC will be absorbed into the EC.

The second pillar primarily involves forms of *intergovernmental co-operation*, due to the unwillingness of most member states to place the core area of CFSP within the decisionmaking framework of the European Community. However, the pillar is not entirely separate from the Community pillar: decisions on matters within the ambit of the second pillar are made by the Council of the European Union (formerly known, and still widely referred to, as the 'Council of Ministers'), the key decision-taking body within the Community. The Commission is 'fully associated' with the work of the Council in relation to CFSP, even though its implementation roles in relation to Community policy do not fully extend to areas covered by these pillars.

The third pillar, prior to the entry into force of the ToA, was very similar in institutional and legal form to the second pillar. As a result of the ToA, not only were major areas of justice and home affairs policy shifted from the third to the Community pillar, but also some of the remaining elements of the third pillar were partly made subject to Community institutional and legal procedures. In other words, the boundary between the first and third pillars is somewhat fuzzier than it was prior to the entry into force of the ToA. For example, the European Court of Justice, a Community institution, also now has important roles in the third pillar. The third pillar can therefore no longer be described without qualification as an intergovernmental pillar: it remains primarily intergovernmental in character, but with 'Communitarised' aspects.

Strictly speaking, when matters relating solely to the European Community are being discussed, the term 'European Community' should still be used. Again strictly speaking, the term 'Union' should be used when referring to all three pillars collectively, or to matters specific to the second and third pillars. This distinction was confirmed by the UK government in a reply to a parliamentary question put by the leading 'Eurosceptic' MP Bill Cash in December 1993. However, soon after the Maastricht Treaty came into force, the Council of Ministers took a decision to formally describe itself as 'the Council of the European Union', even when it is discussing European Community affairs. In November 1993, the secretary-general of the Commission issued a note to all directors-general and heads of service of the Commission stating that the full description of the Commission remains 'Commission of the European Communities', which must be used for legal acts decided by the Commission, although the term 'European Commission' could be used in non-legal documents. The tendency of the EU institutions seems to be to use the term 'Union' in preference to 'Community', except where legal precision is required or when a particular phrase has entered into general usage (for example, the term 'Community preference' rather than 'Union preference' is still used to refer to the principle underlying the Union's policies of protectionism in the field of international trade).

Some opponents of 'deeper' European integration still view the term 'Union' with suspicion, because of its 'federalist' overtones. However, the Union title has already widely displaced the term 'European Community' in the media and is also now used extensively in Commission publications. The Treaty of Nice contains a provision which will change the title of the *Official Journal of the European Communities* to *Official Journal of the European Union*. In recognition of this powerful incoming tide, and for reasons of consistency, the term 'Union' is used in this study for current and general references to what was formerly referred to as the Community, even though some of these usages may be technically incorrect.

In both official and non-official publications, readers may encounter the terms 'European Union law' and 'European Community law' being used, sometimes interchangeably. EU law is a broad category, embracing EC law (by far the most substantive and wide-ranging); the law of the second pillar (very largely intergovernmental); and the law of the third pillar (now a mixture of intergovernmental and EC elements). But most references to EU law are in fact references to EC law. Similarly, what is frequently referred to as the EU budget is strictly speaking the budget of the European Communities, since there is no reference to an 'EU budget' in the treaties. The TEU provides for administrative and (subject to unanimous decision by the Council) operational expenditure relating to the second and third pillars to be charged to the budget of the European Communities. However, the terms 'Union law' and 'Union budget' are gaining wide currency and therefore are also used in this study, even though some usages may be technically incorrect.

The term 'Community' will be used to describe events relating to the three Communities after the 1967 merger until 1 November 1993, when the Union formally came into existence. In references to events prior to the merger, the Communities will be referred to by their separate names. Although both the EEC and Euratom treaties were signed in Rome in 1957, this study follows conventional usage in referring to the EEC Treaty as 'the Treaty of Rome'.

O The New Numbering System

The Treaty of Amsterdam (ToA) introduced a new numbering system for both the TEU and the EC Treaty. The re-numbering exercise was made necessary by the deletion of some, and the insertion of new, provisions into the treaties. But it was also intended to make the treaties simpler and more comprehensible. However, this laudable objective was by no means fully achieved. Each treaty article was given a new number and a table of equivalencies between the new and previous numbers was included as an annex to the ToA. However, the subjects of the new treaty articles do not correspond in all cases to the 'old' articles: this is due to the fact that some new provisions were added and others deleted from the treaties prior to the renumbering exercise. For example, because new treaty articles were added to Title VI of the TEU, Article 42 is listed as ex K.14, but relates to Article K.9 in the original numbering. Similar anomalies can be found in the EC Treaty.

In the TEU, the articles are now referred to by numbers rather than letters (so that, for example, Article A is now Article 1). The TEU and the EC Treaty are numbered separately. When the new numbering system was introduced (following the entry into force of the ToA in May 1999), a common practice in publications was to refer to both sets of numbers. For example, the article referring to subsidiarity in the EC Treaty might be referred to as Article 5, ex 3b. However, it is now over two years since the new numbering system came into effect and its usage has become well-established in official and non-official texts. Therefore, to avoid cluttering the text with references to two sets of numbers, or alternatively including a long list of equivalencies, in this book I have decided to use the new numbering exclusively, except for certain historical references to specific articles in the treaties (when reference will be made to both sets of numbers). A list of the equivalencies between the current and previous numbering can be found on the EU's main website at: www.europa.eu.int/eur-lex/en/treaties.

A further potential source of confusion is the division of the treaties into 'titles'. The TEU has eight titles. Title II refers to the EC treaty. But the EC treaty itself is also divided into titles and chapters. In this book, the name of the title and treaty is given alongside that of the article if it is thought that there could be confusion between the TEU titles and those of the EC Treaty.

◯ The ECU and the Euro

Before the launch of the single European currency on 1 January 1999, financial data emanating from European Union institutions was denominated in ECU (European currency units). After this date, they have been denominated in euros (€). As the conversion rate used on 1 January 1999 was 1 ECU for 1 euro, the € symbol will be used for the Union's financial statistics, regardless of whether these relate to the period before or after this date. This will avoid switching back and forth between the two when presenting financial data.

◯ The Treaty of Nice

This book was completed after the Treaty of Nice (ToN) was negotiated and signed but before it has been ratified. All references to the ToN therefore carry the crucial proviso that this treaty has not entered into force.

The importance of this proviso was reinforced by the 'no' vote in the Irish referendum on the treaty held on 7 June 2001. The treaty was agreed by the European Council meeting as an Intergovernmental Conference in Nice on 11 December 2000 and was signed by the governments of all member states on 26 February 2001. It has to be ratified by all member states before it can come into effect. The target date for ratification is the end of 2002. The treaty provides the institutional framework for a Union of up to 27 members. Although the ToA allows for an enlargement of up to five countries, it is widely acknowledged that failure to ratify the ToN would at the very least complicate, and might even slow down, the enlargement process.

With the exception of Ireland, ratification in member states is being sought by means of a parliamentary vote rather than through a referendum. The referendum in Ireland was necessary because the Irish constitution requires it. On 7 June 2001, Irish voters rejected the treaty by 53.87% to 46.13% (on a very low turnout of 34.79%). Although the treaty was supported by all three main political parties, by the trades unions and by the Catholic church, it was opposed by a coalition which included the Greens, Sinn Féin, pacifist groups and the anti-abortion lobby. Various specific explanations have been put forward to explain the 'no' vote, such as the very low turnout; the poor campaign of the 'yes' side; the complexity of the treaty (polls taken before the vote showed that over half of voters said they did not understand it); concern that the treaty could jeopardise Ireland's neutrality and the fear that it could jeopardise the amount of aid Ireland receives from the structural funds. Others have argued that it could represent a more generalised public opposition to – or at least a lack of enthusiasm for – deeper European integration which goes far beyond the borders of Ireland. It might also be rooted in the failure of the EU's political elites to communicate effectively with their citizens on European issues and of a tendency of these elites to take public support for their EU deliberations for granted. Shortly after the 'no' vote, the Irish Prime Minister Bertie Ahern acknowledged that there was a 'widespread sense of disconnection' between the EU's political establishment and EU citizens.

There is clearly no enthusiasm for a re-negotiation of the treaty among the governments of member states (with fresh memories of the gruelling negotiations at Nice). Shortly after the result, the Commission president, Romano Prodi, and the president of the Council, the Swedish Prime Minister, Göran Persson, issued a joint statement affirming that the EU would work with the Irish government to find a way forward, without changing the substance of the treaty. On 11 June in Luxembourg, the foreign ministers of member states, meeting as the General Affairs Council, agreed a statement excluding any reopening of the text of the ToN and reaffirming that the ratification process would continue on the basis of this text and in accordance with the agreed timetable. This was reaffirmed by the Gothenburg European Council a few days later. The Irish government intends to hold a second referendum, after an extensive period of reflection in order to find out why Irish voters rejected the ToN. Other member states intend to proceed with ratification. Less than a week after the Irish referendum, the French National Assembly approved the treaty by 407 votes to 27, with 113 abstentions.

At the time of writing, various possible solutions to the problem of Ireland's 'no' vote were being mooted. A widely discussed idea is that Ireland may be offered certain opt-outs and clarifications in order to make the treaty more palatable to Irish voters in a second referendum. For example, a protocol might be added to the ToN, explicitly excluding Ireland from the defence aspects of the treaty. A similar solution was used in 1992 following the rejection by Danish voters of the Maastricht treaty. The Danes voted for the treaty in a second referendum. The ratification process for the ToN underlines the point made in the preface about the dynamic and increasingly complex nature of the EU. It also demonstrates that studies of the EU are snapshots of a moving and unpredictable target.

Section 1

Perspectives on the European Union's Development

Chapter 1

The Origins and Development of the European Union

● POST-WAR 'NEW THINKING' ON EUROPEAN CO-OPERATION

○ 'Never Again'

In May 1995, the commemorative ceremonies marking the 50th anniversary of the end of the Second World War in Europe provided moving insights into the origins of the European Union (EU). The 'never again' mood which inspired the ceremonies had also inspired the founders of the Union at the end of the war. The war had once again demonstrated Europe's inability to resolve its disputes peacefully. It had devastated Western Europe's industries and infrastructure. It left Western Europe fearful of Soviet aggression and economically and militarily dependent upon the United States. Although the human and physical destruction wrought by the war was even greater in Eastern Europe, enforced communisation of the Soviet-occupied countries effectively ended any meaningful debate concerning post-war reconstruction in this region. Western Europe, however, was fermenting with radical ideas for reconstruction. By destroying and discrediting the pre-war political and economic order, the war created a fertile climate for fresh approaches to the problem of conflict between West European countries.

The idea which perhaps received the most widespread acceptance in continental Western Europe was that European countries would need to engage in new forms of co-operation in order to achieve their goals of reconstruction. Although each country had its own special motives for seeking co-operation, some reasons were common to all, such as fear of another war in Europe, fear of Soviet aggression and fear of economic collapse. The United States gave both verbal and practical encouragement to European co-operation, notably by insisting that US economic aid for European reconstruction (Marshall Aid) be administered on a Europe-wide basis. The war therefore inspired *new thinking* on approaches to European co-operation. Some variants of this new thinking went beyond ideas for co-operation between the governments of sovereign states and embraced 'supranational' notions for transferring elements of state sovereignty to new European institutions.

○ Rebuilding the West European States System

In relation to the reform of the West European states system at the end of the war, there were wide differences of view concerning the form 'European co-operation' should take. A rough distinction might be made between *system transformers* and *system menders* (although these labels were not used at the time and need to be applied with caution). The transformers, inspired by supranationalist ideas (of which federalism and functionalism are major forms), regarded the states system as dangerous, outmoded and doomed: for them, the war was no accident, but was a direct consequence of the division of Europe into nation-states. The transformers therefore sought to replace, or at the very least fundamentally modify, the system of independent sovereign states (federalist transformers favoured a frontal assault on the state through the creation of a European government and parliament, whereas functionalist transformers favoured the gradualist strategy of transferring some state functions to supranational authorities). Menders wanted to make the states system work better, through mechanisms of intergovernmental co-operation.

As will be seen, in the buzzing, booming confusion of the real world, the distinction between system menders and system transformers is by no means easy to apply, not least because the participants in European co-operation processes have often been unclear about their ultimate aims. Menders, as well as transformers have used the term 'European integration' in preference to the less radical term 'European co-operation'. Moreover, menders have frequently larded their speeches with the language of transformation (in current terminology, 'Euro-rhetoric'). Similarly, the pursuit of national interest by European governments has often been cloaked in the language of 'Euro-federalism'. Nevertheless, the transformer/mender distinction may still be useful as a means of identifying the main approaches to the reshaping of post-war Western Europe.

It was the system menders who were to have the biggest influence on the shape and character of the new order in early post-war Western Europe, not least because the mending approach found greater favour with West European governments. The inadequacy of the nation-state system was recognised by many menders, but their preferred solution was to seek to make the system less inadequate rather than replace it. Far from leading to the demise of the sovereign state, both world wars led to the creation of more states and to the creation of international institutions designed to bolster rather than undermine the states system. The West European institutions created in the late 1940s – for example, the Organisation for European Economic Co-operation (or OEEC, the body established to administer Marshall Aid) and the Council of Europe were intergovernmental organisations. The North Atlantic Treaty Organisation (NATO), the Euro-Atlantic security alliance, was also founded on 'intergovernmentalist' principles.

The institutional foundations of the European Union were laid in the 1950s, with the creation of the European Coal and Steel Community (ECSC), the European Economic Community (EEC) and Euratom. Although each of these organisations has some supranational features, in their aims and structure they also reflect the powerful influence of intergovernmentalism. Milward, a contemporary economic historian, has argued that the new institutional architecture of post-war Western Europe was largely created to make the states system work better, not as part of a grand design for a federal Europe. In his view, intergovernmental co-operation rescued the European nation-state, by providing a means by which it could perform its security and welfare functions (Milward, 1992). However, the price of this rescue has been an erosion of the ability of states to make independent decisions, because they have been drawn into an expanding and tightening web of co-operation. Moreover, although transformers by no means fully achieved their goals in the early post-war years, their ideas constituted a resilient intellectual current, powerful enough to survive setbacks and to exert a distinctive influence upon the development of the Union.

● CONTENDING APPROACHES TO EUROPEAN UNITY

○ Precursory Ideas

Although, as a geographical concept, the term Europe can be traced back to the writings of the Greek historian Herodotus in the 5th century BC, Europe as a cultural concept – that is, as a distinct civilisation, with a history – began to emerge clearly only in the 18th century (den Boer, 1995). By scraping the barrel of history, some nascent ideas for a 'united Europe' can be discerned, for example, in the writings of Maximilien Sully (1559–1641), Emmanuel

Kant (1724–1804), William Penn (1644–1718), Jeremy Bentham (1748–1841), Jean Jacques Rousseau (1712–68) and Comte Saint-Simon (1760–1825). However, these writers espoused widely different conceptions of European unity: for example, for Sully it meant a union of European sovereigns, for Kant a unity of states and for Saint-Simon a unity of peoples. This confusion about what is meant by a united Europe is as relevant today.

As a powerful political force, the idea of a united Europe emerged only in the 20th century, as a byproduct of the two world wars. In the late 19th century, this idea gained support among some European intellectuals, but was hardly part of mainstream political thinking in any European state: other political ideas, for example nationalism and socialism, had far greater popular appeal. The danger of the international anarchy of the states system had been exposed by the horrors of the Great War (1914–18), which provided the stimulus for radical, if often unrealistic, thinking on the recurring problem of European conflict. A Pan-European Union was launched in 1923 by an Austrian count, Richard Coudenhove-Kalergi, but, despite holding a pan-European congress in 1926 and opening branches in most European countries, it never achieved more than fringe group status.

More promisingly for pan-Europeanists, a proposal for a Federal Union of European States was put before the League of Nations by the French foreign minister, Aristide Briand, in 1929. Briand was inspired by the aim of closer co-operation between France and Germany. Although this proposal was made by the representative of a major European government, it was rather vague on detail and in prevailing political conditions stood little chance of adoption (it was referred to a League committee and shelved). In this period, the ideologies of nationalism, and in some countries fascism, were far more potent than pan-Europeanism. Although Fascist movements espoused pan-European ideas, these were based on ideas of dominance and national antagonism. The Versailles Treaty signed in the aftermath of the Great War had reaffirmed the principle of sovereignty and led to the creation of many new states. The League of Nations, established to maintain international peace through collective security, was a club of states not a supranational body. Although European powers played the dominant role in the League, it was designed as a global, not a European, organisation.

○ European Federalism and Its Alternatives

In the 1930s, neither collective security nor resort to traditional balance of power alliance systems prevented remilitarisation and the slide to another war in Europe. The Second World War gave a boost to federalist ideas in Western Europe, by creating bonds between opponents of fascism, by discrediting aggressive nationalism and by increasing the receptiveness of European elites to new ideas. Federalist groups were active during the Second World War in resistance movements in various occupied countries in Europe. In 1941, Altiero Spinelli and Ernesto Rossi, who were political prisoners confined by Benito Mussolini on Ventotene island in Italy, issued a federalist programme known as the Ventotene Manifesto. In 1944, the European representatives of resistance movements issued a declaration calling for a 'federal union of the European peoples' after the war. The federalist vogue in continental Europe at the end of the war led to the formation of a European Union of Federalists in December 1946. For over four decades after the war Spinelli was a tireless, if often frustrated, champion of federalist ideas.

To what extent were these ideas shared by those in government in this period? Various schemes for Anglo-French union were mooted in the early war years. Jean Monnet, often referred to as the founding father of the European Union, was a French civil servant and businessman who spent the war years in London and the United States. He served as an economic planner in the US during the Second World War and made many contacts with influential US policymakers. In 1940, he drafted a plan for a Franco-British Union, which would have included a common parliament and a common citizenship. The plan was supported by the British Cabinet under Winston Churchill, although for Churchill, this was probably meant as a morale booster rather than a serious proposal. Ideas for federal union gained support among governments in exile in London: a plan for close economic links between Belgium, the Netherlands and Luxembourg (Benelux) was agreed in 1943, leading to the Benelux customs union agreement of September 1944.

Support for European federalism again appeared to come from Winston Churchill in September 1946, when he made a speech in Zurich advocating 'a kind of United States of Europe'. However, he was referring to co-operation between states in continental Europe (with the British role limited to that of benevolent sponsor), as a means of reconciling France and Germany. In Churchill's view, Britain's future lay in strong links with the United States and the Empire. In the immediate post-war years, Britain was in a better position than her continental neighbours, both economically and politically: it was the only West European state with representation at the Yalta and Potsdam conferences. It had survived the war with its institutions intact. It had a substantially higher GDP per capita than the continental average. The bulk of its exports went outside Europe. Britain saw itself as a world power, with world responsibilities. From the early 19th century, Britain had a foreign policy tradition of splendid isolation from continental entanglements (due largely to preoccupation with its Empire). In relation to Europe, it saw its role as a balancer, preventing any one European power from becoming too powerful but avoiding long-standing commitments. The British also had a dislike of grandiose schemes, and preferred pragmatic solutions to practical problems. Prime ministers Clement Attlee and Winston Churchill, and their foreign ministers Ernest Bevin and Anthony Eden, were all opposed to British participation in European integration projects.

In May 1948, a committee of European federalists (the International Committee of the Movements for European Unity) organised a Congress in The Hague, with the aim of forging a united Europe. The Congress was attended by 750 delegates from 16 countries, including many prominent statesmen and politicians, such as Winston Churchill, Anthony Eden and Harold Macmillan. The sheer diversity of the membership of the Congress (as well as staunch federalists, it also included staunch anti-federalists, such as Churchill and Eden) ensured that there could be no agreed model of a united Europe. The Congress was to prove a great disappointment to the federalists. It did not lead to the creation of a European parliament with strong powers, as they had wanted. Instead, negotiations between European governments after the Congress resulted in the creation of a very weak body, the Council of Europe, in May 1949. The Council's institutional structure comprised a Consultative Assembly of members of parliament (MPs), appointed by national parliaments and with no legislative powers, plus a Committee of Ministers of member states. The UK government adamantly opposed any scheme which would erode national sovereignty, and insisted that the Consultative Assembly be subordinate to the Committee of Ministers. The Council, based in Strasbourg, has subsequently achieved prominence through its Court of Human Rights, but otherwise has remained a rather obscure body. Like most regional and global international organisations created in this period the Council is essentially a form of *intergovernmental co-operation*.

The most significant move towards supranationalism in relation to European co-operation in this period did not come from the 'big bang' approach to the redesign of Europe favoured by the federalists, which required a frontal assault on sovereignty. The outcome of the 1948 Congress showed clearly that the governments of Europe were unwilling to surrender sovereignty to a supranational parliament. The federalist approach was undermined by two elementary political realities: governmental power and the loyalties of citizens to their own nation-states. An alternative approach, developed by Monnet and manifested in the European Coal and Steel Community in 1952, aimed to create a united Europe in a piecemeal, *ad hoc*, way by encouraging technical co-operation between European countries in specific functional areas (known as the *functionalist* or *sectoral integration* approach). This was expected to lead to a gradual erosion of sovereignty and to a gradual shift of loyalties from the national to the European level.

In Eastern Europe, various schemes for regional federations (for example, for a Balkan Union or a Trans-Danubian Federation) were advanced in the early post-war years by Yugoslavia, Bulgaria and other communist regimes.

However, these did not receive Joseph Stalin's imprimatur and by January 1948 all federal and confederal plans were being denounced by the Soviets. Stalin's divide and rule policy discouraged collaboration between communist countries, thereby creating a set of 'mini Iron Curtains' within the Soviet bloc. A Soviet inspired and dominated form of *socialist economic integration* was nevertheless created. The Council for Mutual Economic Assistance (CMEA), better known as 'Comecon', was formally established in 1949, to promote economic collaboration between communist countries. It remained largely a paper organisation until the late 1950s, when it was revived by Nikita Khrushchev as a means of strengthening the cohesion of the Soviet bloc. A central objective of the CMEA was the promotion of interstate trade, nominally based on the principle of the socialist international division of labour. From the outset, it was described in communist propaganda as a superior alternative to the EEC, which was demonised as an exploitative capitalist organisation. Four sets of ideas for European unity in the post-war period can therefore be identified (see Table 1.1).

Table 1.1 Approaches to European Unity

The intergovernmental co-operation approach, involving economic and political co-operation between sovereign governments (the degree to which 'intergovernmentalism' constitutes a threat to sovereignty depends upon the extent to which states can opt out of collective decisions).

The federalist approach, involving the creation of powerful institutions (an executive, a parliament and a court) above the level of the nation-state. A substantial degree of state sovereignty would be transferred to these supranational institutions.

The functionalist (sectoral integration) approach, involving the transfer of elements of sovereignty to supranational institutions in specific fields of policy (for example, coal and steel).

Socialist integration, involving economic collaboration between communist states, based on the principle of the 'socialist international division of labour'.

It will be useful at this point to consider the relevance of these ideas to the three rival economic formations which were to emerge in post-war Europe: the European Community (the main pillar of the European Union); the European Free Trade Association (EFTA); and Comecon. The Community's development has been influenced (by no means in equal measure) by intergovernmentalist, federalist and functionalist ideas. EFTA was founded in Stockholm in November 1959 as a free trade club firmly based on intergovernmentalist principles and with no supranational aspirations. Its seven members (Austria, Britain, Denmark, Norway, Portugal, Sweden and

Switzerland) favoured free trade in industrial goods but not the model of integration pursued by the Community. Despite the exaggerated claims made on behalf of Comecon in communist propaganda, following its revival in the late 1950s it operated on the basis of intergovernmentalism. The Soviet Union was much bigger in size than the other member states, which tended to be suspicious of Moscow's motives in promoting Comecon. To assuage these fears, the Soviet Union insisted that Comecon was not a supranational organisation and posed no threat to the sovereignties of member states. In practice, the sovereignties of these countries were already limited by Soviet political and military dominance. Comecon, wound up in 1991, never had major institutions like the Commission, the European Parliament or the European Court of Justice. Nor did it have a convertible currency and therefore most goods were traded through barter arrangements.

● LAYING THE INSTITUTIONAL FOUNDATIONS

○ The European Coal and Steel Community (ECSC)

Although the primary impetus for European integration was the need to prevent conflict between the European states, from the outset it also had a strong economic rationale. Jean Monnet, who had been appointed by General Charles de Gaulle in 1946 to mastermind France's economic recovery, was the principal architect of the plan for a European Coal and Steel Community. Monnet's ultimate aims in pursuing European co-operation remain a subject of controversy, not least because he was a pragmatist who emphasised that Europe could not be built all at once. He strongly favoured Franco-German co-operation and European links with the US. He favoured projects which went beyond 'mere co-operation' between governments and embraced the idea of a 'fusion of interests' of the European peoples as a long-term goal. But he admitted that he did not know what kind of Europe would emerge. Although he favoured the establishment of a 'United States of Europe' he took no part in the federalist movement of 1945–48, being more at home in the corridors of power than at federalist rallies.

The idea of the Monnet plan was to establish a system of joint regulation of the coal and steel industries of participating states. Cross-border trade barriers would be abolished and the industries would be regulated by a 'supranational' authority. The plan offered practical economic benefits for the participants, by providing coal and steel producers with a larger market for their goods. The initial idea was to link the French and German coal and steel industries, but the Benelux countries and Italy also expressed a desire to participate. The ECSC plan was approved and presented by Robert Schuman, the French foreign minister, in an announcement subsequently known as the Schuman Declaration. Schuman came from the province of Lorraine, which for centuries had been the subject of a territorial dispute between France and Germany. He was strongly committed to Franco-German co-operation. In the early post-war years, the aim of France had been to contain Germany rather than to co-operate with it. However, for various reasons (not least US influence) French policy soon shifted to one of seeking co-operation with its dangerous neighbour. The plan was enthusiastically supported by West Germany's Chancellor Konrad Adenauer and received the backing of the US. From the outset, there was explicit acknowledgement of the political objectives of the ECSC plan. The Schuman Declaration sought to make the possibility of war between the participants unthinkable and impossible, by creating a *de facto* solidarity between them. It was a functionalist experiment, but its stated objectives reflected federalist aspirations as a long-term goal. Thus the plan was described in the declaration as a first step towards 'a European federation indispensable to the preservation of peace'.

The plan was designed to serve both national and wider European interests. The six original members had their own objectives in pursuing co-operation: for example, without it France feared that its steel industry would not be able to compete with its German counterpart. It reduced the likelihood of German *revanchism* and provided France with an opportunity to play a leading role in European developments. For West Germany, it offered the prospect of gaining full acceptance by the international community. It also offered the German coal and steel industries bigger markets. It gave the Benelux countries a leverage on policy developments which they might otherwise not have had. Some other European countries were primarily agricultural and therefore the ECSC held little interest for them. Some West European countries, including Britain, favoured measures to promote co-operation between states, but opposed 'supranationalist' schemes such as the ECSC and therefore declined to participate. In any case, Britain expected the ECSC to fail.

The ECSC was established by the Treaty of Paris (April 1951) for 50 years. It came into existence in 1952, with Monnet as the first president. The treaty eliminated trade barriers (duties, quotas and dual pricing) on coal, steel and iron ore. It created a supranational authority (the High Authority). It also had a Council of Ministers, a European Assembly, a Court of Justice and a consultative committee comprising producer, worker and other interests. The High Authority, deriving from French administrative ideas, was an appointed, technocratic executive, with the power to prohibit subsidies and to impose fines. Monnet was adamant that the High Authority should be independent of governments, in other words that it was supranational. But the fact that the ECSC also had a Council of Ministers showed that governments were not willing to surrender full sovereignty over these functions to a supranational authority. The Assembly was not to be directly elected (delegates were designated by national parliaments) and was given only very weak powers. Indeed, the Assembly was added almost as an afterthought.

The establishment of the ECSC demonstrated the feasibility of functional integration, that is, the integration of specific sectors of policy previously controlled by national governments. In its early years it was widely regarded as a great success, although national interests later blocked the emergence of fully integrated coal and steel industries. According to Monnet, the ECSC proposals were revolutionary and constituted 'the abnegation of sovereignty in a limited but decisive field'. He saw it as the forerunner of a broader united Europe, because what had been done in the case of coal and steel could be applied to other sectors. The ECSC's structure served as the prototype for the institutional structure of the European Economic Community established five years later (except that the EEC's Commission was given less power than the High Authority and its Council of Ministers more power than that of its ECSC counterpart). In both cases, however, parliamentary control was very weak. Featherstone (1994) has argued that the EU's 'democratic deficit' has its roots in the technocratic model of integration first manifested in the ECSC.

O   European Defence Co-operation

The issue of defence was the cause of considerable disagreement between West European governments in the early post-war years. Four contentious security questions required urgent answers: firstly should West Germany be allowed to rearm (and if so under what conditions); secondly, how could Western Europe be effectively defended against a possible Soviet attack; thirdly, what was to be the role of the US in the defence of Western Europe; and fourthly, what was to be the *form* of defence co-operation between European countries? Would co-operation take the form of a conventional alliance system, or would it involve a pooling of defence resources?

The Brussels Treaty signed in 1948 by the UK, France and Benelux, was a conventional alliance and was directed against the prospect of a resurgent Germany. But the most immediate threat to European security came from the Soviet Union. West Europeans were clearly not capable of defending themselves against a Soviet attack without US support. The Soviet threat led to the creation of NATO, a transatlantic rather than a purely European alliance. Neither the Brussels Treaty nor the NATO Treaty involved a loss of control of member countries' armed forces to a supranational organisation. But some West Europeans were still thinking about how Western Europe could organise its own defence: moreover, some of their ideas went beyond proposals for a conventional alliance, to embrace the prospect of the pooling of military resources. In October 1950, the French Premier René Pleven put forward a plan for the creation of a 'European Defence Community', on similar lines to the ECSC (see Table 1.2). The EDC would have been directed by a European Political Community, embracing a Council of Ministers and a directly elected parliament. A key aim of the plan was to lock Germany into a European defence system in order to limit its capacity for independent action.

Table 1.2 Timeline 1: 1946–54

1946	**September:** Winston Churchill's speech in Zurich advocating 'a kind of United States of Europe'.
1947	**March:** Belgium, the Netherlands and Luxembourg agree to set up a customs union.
	June: Marshall Plan proposed.
	October: creation of Benelux economic union.
1948	**March:** Brussels Treaty signed by UK, France and Benelux.
	April: OEEC created, to effectuate the Marshall Plan.
	May: Congress of Europe held in The Hague.
1949	**Spring:** Berlin blockade by Soviet forces.
	April: NATO created.
	May: Council of Europe created , with ten members.
1950	**May:** Schuman Declaration, proposing that French and German coal and steel be placed under a common authority.
	October: Pleven Plan for an EDC.
1951	**April:** Treaty of Paris, establishing the ECSC signed by six states.
1952	**May:** EDC Treaty signed by the six ECSC states.
	July: ECSC High Authority begins work.
1954	**August:** EDC Treaty rejected by the French parliament.
	October: Western European Union formed.
	December: UK and ECSC sign an association agreement.

A draft EDC treaty was drawn up by Monnet and by the same team which had drafted the Schuman plan. The plan was signed by the six members of the ECSC in May 1952. It was ratified by four national parliaments, but was rejected by the French parliament in August 1954. France was not ready to relinquish control over its armed forces. Britain had no intention of subordinating its forces in a European army and would have no truck with the Pleven plan. Eden, the British foreign secretary, put forward a counter-proposal for the creation of a conventional alliance, to be known as the Western European Union. The WEU was created in 1954: it was simply an expanded version of the Brussels Treaty and was an indirect way of allowing West Germany into the NATO alliance. It also provided legitimation for German rearmament. The WEU was given its own Parliamentary Assembly and Council, but was clearly based on intergovernmental co-operation, not supranationalism. However, NATO was a far more credible defence organisation than the WEU. Western Europe was not ready for integration in the field of defence. Whether or not it is any readier now, almost half a century later is a question which will be examined in Chapter 19.

O   Relaunching the European Unity Idea

Following the failure of the EDC, Monnet and others were seeking ways to maintain the impetus of integration by applying the ECSC model to other sectors, such as atomic energy and transport. Monnet favoured atomic energy as the next sector to be pooled, along the lines of the ECSC. In February 1955, Monnet left the presidency of the ECSC High Authority to become head of the Action Committee for a United States of Europe (ACUSE), a small supranationalist pressure group. The governments of the six members of the ECSC were interested in further economic co-operation, particularly in the area of trade. For example, the Benelux countries had created their own customs union and wished to extend it.

In June 1955, the foreign ministers of the six states of the ECSC met in Messina in Sicily to discuss proposals for a customs union. The chairman was Paul-Henri Spaak, the foreign minister of Belgium. The British sent an official from the Board of Trade rather than a minister to the talks: when discussion at the talks went beyond the idea of co-operation between governments, the official was withdrawn. The British foreign minister, Sir Anthony Eden, made many anti-federalist pronouncements and showed no interest in involving Britain in either the ECSC or in a European customs union. Britain preferred co-operation to take place within the OEEC and within the Council of Europe. The British put forward an alternative scheme for a free trade area as a way of killing off the customs union idea, but without success. Spaak's report on the Messina conference, presented at a foreign ministers' meeting in Venice in May 1956, proposed the creation of a common market and an Atomic Energy Community. This led to the signing of the European Economic Community and European Atomic Energy Community (Euratom) treaties in Rome in March 1957.

The EEC Treaty (commonly referred to as the Treaty of Rome) was not solely about economics: for example, its preamble contained a reference to a determination 'to lay the foundations of an ever closer union among the peoples of Europe'. The treaty's main thrust, however, was towards the pursuit of concrete economic objectives: that is, the creation of a common market, a customs union and of various Community policies (see Table 1.3 below). Its provisions on economic policy reflected a dual influence of free trade principles and of a belief that economic problems could not be solved by market forces alone. The latter influence was manifested for example in the creation of the European Social Fund (ESF), the European Investment Bank (EIB) and the Common Agricultural Policy (CAP). France insisted that agriculture be included as an integral part of the treaty, as a means of providing a bigger market for its agricultural exports. The Euratom Treaty sought to promote collaboration between member states and a common market in the nuclear energy sector. Member states were unwilling to relinquish control of their nuclear industries and therefore the treaty contains various get-out clauses.

Table 1.3 The Main Objectives of the EEC Treaty

- a common market and progressive approximation of economic policies of member states;
- promotion of harmonious economic development and higher living standards;
- closer relations between member states;
- removal of all tariffs and quantitative restrictions on imports and exports between member states;
- a common external tariff and a common commercial policy towards third countries;
- free movement of goods, services, capital and labour;
- common policies for agriculture and transport;
- a European social fund;
- a European investment bank to finance investment projects in the signatory states.

The institutional structures of the EEC and Euratom were both modelled on that of the ECSC: the EEC and Euratom were given four main institutions: a Commission (equivalent to the ECSC High Authority); a Council of Ministers; an Assembly; and a Court of Justice. The main difference was that the EEC and Euratom treaties were more intergovernmental than the ECSC Treaty in that in each case the Council of Ministers had more power and the Commission somewhat less than its ECSC counterpart. The Assembly and Court were common to all three institutions. The Assembly was to be eventually directly elected, but governments were reluctant to invest it with too much power. The 1965 Merger Treaty (in force in 1967) created a single Council and Commission for all three Communities.

In the 1950s and 1960s, West European integration rode on the back of a post-war economic boom. Between 1945 and 1968, Western Europe enjoyed high productivity and low unemployment. Post-war recovery in Western Europe was rapid, due to factors such as high investment rates, US capital and

ts. After 1958, there was a big leap in intra-Community trade.
for the removal of cross-border tariffs and for the setting of a
al tariff were completed before schedule.

○ Forms of Economic Integration

Britain was by no means the only West European country reluctant to commit itself to a customs union. Several favoured the formation of a free trade area, based on a *customs association*, a looser form of organisation which requires neither a common external tariff nor a common external trade policy. Following the signing of the Stockholm Convention in July 1959, a customs association known as the European Free Trade Association was formed between Britain, Denmark, Norway, Sweden, Austria, Switzerland and Portugal, aimed at achieving free trade in industrial goods by 1970. It was conceived as an alternative to the model of economic integration espoused in the Treaty of Rome. The scale below (sometimes viewed as an economic integration continuum) moves from loose to tight economic relationships between states. It should be noted, however, that in the real world these categories have fuzzy boundaries and that it is also possible for participating countries to jump stages.

• **A customs association:** barriers to trade, such as customs duties and quotas, between members are removed, but members retain the right to determine their own trade restrictions in relation to non-members. A potential flaw in the customs association idea stems from the freedom it allows members to have different trade policies in relation to non-members. If, for example, member A imposes a 10% tariff on agricultural goods entering its borders from outside the free trade area, whereas member B has only a 5% tariff on the same goods, then there would be a clear incentive for people in country B to import goods for export to country A. To overcome this problem, common rules need to be formulated and enforced.

• **A customs union** involves the removal of customs duties and quotas between members, and the introduction of a common external tariff in relation to non-members. It involves a tighter relationship between members than a customs association, because members lose their individual ability to set their own external tariffs.

• **A common market** involves the removal of all impediments to the mobility of factors of production across the borders of member states. Since it is likely to develop from a customs union, it focuses on the removal of non-tariff barriers to trade. An example is the Single European Market, designed to achieve free movement of goods, services, people and capital across the borders of member states. It requires more extensive intergovernmental collaboration than a Customs Union.

- **Economic and monetary union (EMU):** its most tangible feature is the harmonisation of monetary and fiscal policies and the replacement of the currencies of the member states by a common currency or by fixed exchange rates (see Chapter 11).
- **Full economic union (FEU):** it would involve the merging of large elements of the national economic policies of participating countries into a single economic policy. Some analysts, in particular those opposed to 'deeper' European integration, argue that the implications of EMU are likely to be so profound that EMU and FEU would virtually amount to the same thing. Others, however, argue that EMU still leaves national governments in control of some major economic policies.

○ From Rapid Development to Inertia

After the rapid progress of the 1950s and early 1960s, the Community entered a relatively fallow period. There was a long lull in integration activity which lasted for well over two decades. Many aims of the Treaty of Rome (for example, for a full common market and a common transport policy) existed only on paper. A change in political leadership in France weakened the prospects for rapid integration. Schuman was replaced as French foreign minister by the 'non-federalist' Georges Bidault. De Gaulle, who became president in 1958, was opposed to European federalism and favoured a 'Europe of States', not a 'United States of Europe' or a Europe of 'myths, fictions and pageants'. But although he disliked the supranationalist aspects of the ECSC and Euratom, he was not opposed to political and economic co-operation between European states, especially if France could play a leading role. Moreover, the CAP offered substantial benefits for French agriculture.

Within the EEC, a major crisis developed in 1965, arising from attempts to increase the powers of the Commission and the Council of Ministers. The Commission wanted the EEC to have its own budget, a move strongly opposed by de Gaulle, who also opposed a proposal for majority voting in the Council of Ministers (meaning that states would have to accept the decisions of the majority). France refused to attend Council meetings in this period (the policy of the 'empty chair'). In 1966, this deadlock was ended by the Luxembourg compromise, an agreement which allowed a member state to veto a proposal if it considered it a threat to its vital national interests. The Luxembourg compromise, however, is not enshrined in any Union treaty and has no legal force (see Chapter 5). The ECSC, Euratom and the EEC were amalgamated on 1 July 1967 to form the 'European Communities'.

Proposals to relaunch the Community had to await the end of de Gaulle's presidency. De Gaulle's abrupt departure from government in April 1969 enhanced the prospects of an agreement on key issues concerning the

Community's development, not least in relation to Britain's prospects of entry. De Gaulle's successor as president, Georges Pompidou, soon announced his support for British entry. The Hague summit of December 1969 (see Table 1.4) approved several major measures: the Community was to be given its own budget; the European Parliament's powers were to be increased; foreign ministers were to examine the prospects for economic and monetary union; and negotiations for the entry of new members were to begin. But apart from the decision on enlargement, the summit produced few immediate results.

Table 1.4 Timeline 2: 1955–72

1955	**June:** Messina Conference on integration attended by the foreign ministers of the six ECSC states. Spaak Committee established to examine options for further integration.
1957	**March:** Rome treaties signed, establishing the EEC and Euratom.
1958	**January:** Rome treaties come into force.
1959	**November:** EFTA convention signed in Stockholm.
1961	**July:** the six EEC members issue the 'Bonn Declaration' aimed at political union. **August:** Ireland applies, and the UK and Denmark request negotiations for EEC membership. **December:** Austria, Sweden and Switzerland apply for association with EEC.
1962	**January:** framework of CAP agreed. **April:** Norway requests negotiations aimed at membership of EEC.
1963	**January:** EEC negotiations on entry suspended, following opposition by de Gaulle to UK entry.
1965	**April:** treaty merging executives of the three Communities (in force 1 July 1967). **July:** French boycott of institutions begins, over disagreements on budgetary and institutional issues.
1966	**January:** the 'Luxembourg compromise' ends French boycott.
1967	**May:** UK, Ireland, Denmark and Norway reapply for membership.
1968	**July:** EEC Customs Union completed.
1969	**December:** Hague summit.
1970	**June:** new negotiations for accession of UK, Ireland, Denmark and Norway.
1972	**January:** signing of treaties of accession for UK, Ireland, Denmark and Norway. Norwegian referendum leads to withdrawal of Norway's application.

● BRITAIN'S SLUGGISH AND AMBIVALENT SHIFT TOWARDS MEMBERSHIP

The events leading to Britain's applications for membership of the Community in the 1960s is a story of diminishing options. In the 1950s, it put its faith in the special relationship with the US and in the emerging British Commonwealth. Only when British illusions about these relationships had been shattered did the British seek closer links with the Community. By the early 1960s, the idea of membership had become more attractive to the UK, for several reasons: the Suez crisis dented British faith in the 'special relationship' with the US. The Commonwealth link was not proving as valuable to the UK as its proponents hoped. Trade with EFTA was unbalanced, because whereas the UK had a large market, the other EFTA countries had only small markets to offer UK exporters. Britain's economic performance in the late 1950s was poor in comparison with that of 'the Six'. From the late 1950s, GNP per capita of the Six was substantially higher than the corresponding figure for Britain.

The UK first applied for entry in 1961. It sought special deals to protect its agriculture and its partners in EFTA and the Commonwealth. However, at this time de Gaulle was sceptical of the UK's motives. He vetoed Britain's application in 1963 and again in 1967, on the grounds that Britain was not sufficiently European in outlook (meaning that it was too close to the US and to the Commonwealth) and would, if admitted, be a Trojan horse for the US. Both the Labour and Conservative parties were divided on the issue, which meant that they were reluctant to dwell on it at election times. For much of the post-war period, the official Labour Party position on European integration veered between hostility and ambivalence. Although a Labour government under Harold Wilson sought entry into the Community in the late 1960s, a powerful group within the Labour Party continued to oppose membership. A Conservative government, returned to office in 1970, negotiated Britain's entry. Following tortuous negotiations, a treaty of accession for membership of the UK, Denmark, Norway and Ireland was signed in Brussels in 1972. After a referendum, Norway opted not to join.

Although various transitional arrangements were agreed (for example, the UK got a five-year transition to the CAP) the 1973 entrants were forced to accept the Community as it was, including its budgetary and agriculture policies, neither of which were advantageous to the UK. The Heath government which negotiated Britain's entry possibly hoped that the costs of membership, such as higher food prices and high budgetary contributions, would be offset by increased trade and economic growth. Ironically, the UK entered when the Community's economic boom years had ended. Britain's budgetary contributions were high because, as a large importer, it paid substantial amounts in customs levies. Because it had a relatively small, but efficient, farm sector its contributions were not offset by receipts from the CAP (by far the largest item in the Community budget). The Labour government returned in 1974 sought to renegotiate the entry terms, and held a referendum on entry in June 1975, which resulted in a 67% vote in favour of continued UK membership. Following her victory in the 1979 General Election, Margaret Thatcher (who had replaced the pro-European Edward Heath as Leader of the Conservative Party in 1975) demanded 'Britain's money back' from the Community. Britain received a series of rebates in the early 1980s, but these by no means corrected the imbalance. In 1979 the UK's net budgetary contribution was almost £1 billion. At the European Council in Fontainebleau in June 1984, Mrs Thatcher negotiated a budget rebate for the UK, but even after the deal Britain remained a substantial net contributor.

It is clear that Britain's troubled relationship with Europe cannot be solely attributed to specific and transient causes such as the 'anti-European' attitudes of particular leaders or disputes about specific issues. It does not explain the longevity of Britain's position as an 'awkward partner' (George, 1990), which has survived several changes of government, or why the Union has had low public support in Britain. More fundamental (and less easily correctable) reasons of the difficulties have been suggested. For example, Britain is geographically separate from her European partners – but then so are Ireland and Greece. In the case of these countries, however, their governments could point to tangible material benefits from membership, in the form of substantial net gains from the Union budget. Despite its loss of empire and the declining importance of the Anglo-American special relationship, Britain has continued to view itself as being more than a European power. It has a long and unbroken tradition of parliamentary sovereignty (unlike most other member states). It has an unwritten constitution and tends to dislike the continental 'treaty bound' approach to integration.

The negotiating style of British governments with other member governments has frequently been confrontational and couched in 'us and them' terms. Britain has also perhaps tended to overestimate its importance to other member states and on several crucial occasions has wrongly assumed that integration initiatives could not proceed without British support. Britain has also been accused by other member states of adopting spoiling tactics to impede progress towards deeper integration: for example, in the 1950s, it played a key role in setting up EFTA as a rival to the EEC; at the negotiations leading to the Treaty on European Union (TEU or Maastricht Treaty) in December 1991, it put forward its 'hard ECU' plan as an alternative to the plan for a single European currency; in the 1990s it favoured rapid enlargement of the Union in preference to rapid deepening of integration.

It is now widely recognised that it would have been better for Britain to have participated in the development of the European Union from the start, in order to have shaped this development in a way more in keeping with British preferences. Despite the fact that Britain has been an awkward partner within the Union, it is now so firmly embedded into the Union's political and economic structures that the idea of withdrawal now appears almost unthinkable. The mainstream British debate on Europe now centres on what kind of relationship Britain should develop with its European partners, despite proposals from certain 'Eurosceptic' circles for the UK to leave the EU and re-join EFTA, or even join NAFTA (the North American Free Trade Association), and despite the election of three members of the UK Independence Party to the European Parliament in June 1999.

In 1998, George argued that the differences between British governments in their approach to Europe is often exaggerated and that the British approach has tended to be marked by consistency rather than by sharp discontinuous change (George, 1998). The election of a Labour government in May 1997 was seen by many as marking such a sharp change. The Labour Party has shed the 'anti-Europe' image it acquired in the 1970s and 1980s. In 1988, it abandoned its policy to take Britain out of the Union. In the 1990s, as the Conservative Party became increasingly riven by in-fighting over the UK's relationship with Europe, the Labour Party presented a united, pro-Europe stance. But in George's view, the new Labour government's fundamental objectives with regard to Europe were not very different from those of their Conservative predecessors, with the exception of social policy, and he argued that even in this policy field, the differences were not as great as they might seem. At his first meeting with other EU leaders in Noordwijk in May 1997, British Prime Minister Tony Blair stated his opposition to new social policy measures which would harm competitiveness and emphasised the importance of flexible labour markets. The Blair government has adopted a cautious approach to the possible entry of the UK into the eurozone; it has refused to agree to the UK's participation in the Schengen system, concerned with removal of remaining restrictions on freedom of movement across EU borders; it has flatly refused to countenance the removal of the UK's budget rebate; it has rejected the idea of an EU savings tax, favoured by most other EU governments and by the Commission. Although it has played a major role in developing new ideas on European defence, it rejected the inclusion of defence as a subject for 'enhanced co-operation' in the Treaty of Nice (ToN).

However, the Conservative party, led by William Hague between June 1997 and June 2001, sought to emphasise the sharp differences between the two main parties on European issues, particularly on the single European currency (see Chapter 11). This strategy did not pay electoral dividends for the Conservatives in the June 2001 general election: voters appear to accord European issues lower priority than other issues, such as education, health and the economy. The relationship between the UK, led by the current Labour government, and her European partners is certainly less fraught and awkward than it was during recent Conservative governments. One reason for this is that the Labour governments elected in May 1997 and June 2001 are closer ideologically to most other EU governments than were Conservative governments (most of the 15 member states currently have social democratic governments). Moreover, there is little enthusiasm among most member states for pursuit of a federalist agenda, as was shown in the negotiations for the Amsterdam and Nice treaties. Although in the Nice negotiations, Blair drew 'red lines' around certain topics (for example, refusing to countenance extension of qualified majority voting to taxation and social affairs), several member states showed that they were just as capable of digging in their heels in defence of perceived national interests. Nor is it a case of 'Britain versus the rest' in Council decisionmaking. For example, in 1998–99, of the 85 qualified majority votes in the Council, Britain voted against or abstained on only five occasions (less than either France or Germany). Nevertheless, British governments have to contend with a domestic press which is generally more hostile to the EU than elsewhere. The British public remains unenthused by the EU project: only 23% of the British electorate voted in the 1999 European Parliament (EP) elections, compared to an EU average of 49% and the vast majority of UK citizens are opposed to the UK adopting the euro.

● THE DEVELOPMENT OF THE SINGLE EUROPEAN MARKET AND THE EUROPEAN UNION: THE 'SECOND RELAUNCH'

A host of factors in the 1970s and early 1980s inhibited the Community's development. A long economic recession, exacerbated by the oil crises of 1973–74 and 1979–80, meant that domestic economic concerns loomed larger than the issue of deeper European integration. The absorption of three new members, and the vexatious issue of Britain's budgetary contributions, also deflected attention away from this issue. The fact that each country had an effective veto on institutional reform was also a major impediment to the launch of new initiatives. This is not to say that the Community was completely 'comatose' in this period. The European Regional Development Fund (ERDF) was set up in 1975. In 1979, the European Monetary System (EMS), including the Exchange Rate Mechanism (ERM) was established (see Chapter 11) and the first direct elections to the European Parliament were held. In 1970, member states established a system of 'European political co-operation', essentially a forum for intergovernmental consultation on foreign policy issues. One of the most significant developments in relation to the institutional balance within the Community was the emergence of the European Council, comprising formal summit meetings of European leaders. These were not provided for in the Treaty of Rome, but came into existence as an offshoot of Council of Ministers' meetings. The European Council came into being in December 1974 and has continued to grow in importance.

In the 1970s and early 1980s, there were many attempts to kick-start the European Community's institutional development: in 1972, the Werner plan for economic and monetary union by 1980 was agreed in principle by the member states. The Tindemans report on European Union in 1975 advocated many measures, such as direct elections to the European Parliament, a 'Citizens' Europe' and extension of majority voting in the Council of Ministers, which have subsequently been adopted. A proposal for European Union was launched by the foreign ministers of Germany and Italy in 1981 (the Genscher–Colombo initiative). The European Council in Stuttgart in June 1983 agreed a 'solemn declaration' on European Union. In the early 1980s the 'Crocodile Club' and the 'Kangaroo group', both comprising members of the EP, sought to accelerate the integration process (the Crocodile Club had radical federalist objectives, whereas the Kangaroo group favoured pursuit of a 'single market' programme). The EP approved a 'draft treaty on European Union' in 1984, but had no power to achieve its aspirations. Although a quantum leap towards European Union did not appear likely, by the mid-1980s a majority of member governments nevertheless supported further integration. The European Council in Fontainebleau in June 1984 established two committees (referred to as the Dooge and Adonnino committees, after their chairmen) to examine the possibilities for further development of the Community. James Dooge focused on institutional questions and Pietro Adonnino on the problem of the Community's democratic deficit. The Dooge Committee produced a majority and a minority report which were presented to the European Council in Milan in June 1985. The majority report favoured the strengthening of EC institutions and the establishment of a single European market. The Adonnino Committee developed many proposals for a Citizens' (or People's) Europe.

Most reform proposals in this period fell by the wayside because they were too radical and contentious for the time. Others, such as that of a Citizens' Europe were perhaps too fuzzy to catch on. But the idea of a single European market programme commanded a broad measure of support among national governments and business groups, for several reasons: it offered a practical solution to the perceived common problem of 'Eurosclerosis' (manifested in widening gaps in the Community's economic performance relative to those of Japan and the US). Even opponents of further integration, such as Mrs Thatcher, could not object to a programme designed to remove barriers to trade between member states. The election of market-oriented governments in several member states in the 1980s also increased the possibility that the Single European Market (SEM) programme would be adopted. Moreover, the aims of the programme were hardly new, since they sought to fulfil objectives set out in the Treaty of Rome. The rapport between President François Mitterrand of France and Chancellor Helmut Kohl of West Germany provided a favourable political climate for further integration. The appointment of Jacques Delors to the presidency of the Commission in 1984 was also a significant factor, because of his dynamism and determination to achieve a great leap forward in integration. The institutional and policy implications of the SEM programme were not widely appreciated at the time. Mrs Thatcher viewed the programme as about removing trade barriers, not as a means to deeper integration. But the logic of the programme required that national policies in many sectors be 'harmonised'. Institutional reform was also required in the interests of effective implementation. At the European Council in Milan in 1985, Mrs Thatcher agreed to an extension of majority voting in the Council of Ministers (meaning that on many key issues, members would have to accept majority decisions) and also to an extension of the powers of the European Parliament.

The SEM programme provided the momentum for further attempts at integration, against stiff opposition from Mrs Thatcher, a staunch opponent of proposals for 'ever closer union'. In a speech in Bruges in October 1988, Thatcher outlined her preferred model of the European Community (which was remarkably similar to de Gaulle's vision of a *Union des Patries*) and attacked the idea of a European 'superstate'. Her opposition to Euro-federalism, the CAP and the ERM had strong ideological roots. She opposed policies which would diminish sovereignty or which would lead to more government intervention. She was increasingly at odds with her counterparts in the Community on a wide range of issues, but especially in relation to ideas for a single European currency, for a 'Social Charter' and for a common foreign and security policy (CFSP). The European Council in Strasbourg in December 1989 set up an intergovernmental conference (IGC) on economic and monetary union, despite Mrs Thatcher's objections. In June 1990, the European Council in Dublin established a parallel intergovernmental conference on political union. The results of the two IGCs, which opened at the European Council in Rome in December 1990, formed the basis of the negotiations on European political and monetary union at the European Council in Maastricht in December 1991 (Table 1.5 below) There was little domestic interest in the IGCs. Ordinary citizens' lack of involvement or interest in integration developments prior to Maastricht has been referred to as a *permissive consensus*. This allowed the policymaking elites (governments, parties, bureaucrats and pressure groups) to set reform agendas and to make decisions without taking too much account of citizens' reactions.

At Maastricht, John Major, who had replaced Margaret Thatcher as British prime minister in October 1990, negotiated 'opt-outs' for the UK on monetary union and on the Social Chapter (see Chapter 3). An increasingly bitter rift on Europe developed within the Conservative Party, reminiscent of the conflicts over Europe which almost tore the Labour Party apart in the 1960s and 1970s. The referenda on the TEU held in Denmark, France and Ireland exposed the extent of public concern about the implications of deeper European integration. In Denmark, 50.7% voted against the treaty. Ireland and France voted in favour by 69% and 51%, respectively. The referenda provided a jolt to governments which had got used to taking decisions on Europe without considering the views of 'ordinary' Europeans. They provided evidence that the era of permissive consensus might be coming to an end. By securing opt-outs and clarification of various issues, the Danish government made the treaty more palatable to the Danes, who approved it by a narrow majority in a second referendum. In the UK, parliamentary ratification was delayed until after the second Danish referendum. But the ERM crises of 1992 and 1993 (see Chapter 11) raised serious doubts about the feasibility of the Maastricht blueprint for EMU.

Table 1.5 Timeline 3: 1973–93

1973	**January:** the UK, Denmark and Ireland join the Community.
1975	**June:** Greece applies to join.
1977	**March:** Portugal applies to join.
	July: Spain applies to join.
1979	**March:** the EMS established.
	June: first direct elections to the EP.
1981	**January:** Greece joins the Community.
1985	**June:** Commission White Paper on the completion of the SEM.
1986	**January:** Portugal and Spain join Community.
1987	**July:** Single European Act (SEA) comes into force.
1989	**April:** Delors committee presents report on EMU.
	Autumn: revolutions in Eastern Europe.
1988	**June:** European Council convenes IGCs (commencing December) on EMU and political union.
1990	**November:** German reunification.
1991	**December:** IGCs culminate in agreement on TEU at Maastricht.
1992	**May:** European Economic Area Treaty signed.
	June: Danish referendum narrowly rejects TEU.
	September: withdrawal of UK and Italy from ERM.
	December: SEM programme 'completed'.
1993	**August:** *de facto* suspension of ERM (move to 15% bands).
	November: TEU comes into force.

An important side-effect of the SEM programme was the effect it had upon EFTA countries, fearful of the effects of the programme upon their trade with the Community. They therefore sought guaranteed access to the SEM through a closer formal link between EFTA and the Community. The Community responded by offering EFTA the opportunity to participate in a 'European Economic Area', a free trade zone embracing the EC and EFTA. Although a European Economic Area (EEA) Treaty was agreed, negotiations proved so tough that four EFTA countries – Austria, Finland, Norway and Sweden – decided to go the whole hog and apply for membership of the Community (or European Union, after the entry into force of the TEU). With the exception of Norway, whose voters rejected a firm offer of EU membership for the second time, these countries acceded to the Union in January 1995. The Swiss people rejected the EEA Treaty in a referendum in December 1992.

But the most important development with regard to enlargement was the EU's decision to accept the applications for membership of ten former communist countries, plus Cyprus and Malta, even though it was made clear that the applicant states were required to meet strict entry criteria before they would be allowed to enter the Union. The Commission's *Agenda 2000* document, published in July 1997 (see Chapter 20), set out a detailed plan for the admission of these countries into the EU, although it left many key issues unanswered, in particular regarding the budgetary and institutional implications. Largely because of the SEM programme and the TEU, new members are forced to make stronger commitments to the EU than previous applicants. Even so, there is no shortage of eager candidates for entry. The enlargement issue has intensified the debate in the EU about the speed and direction of integration (that is, should the EU concentrate on deepening integration among existing members or on absorption of new members?). Turkey was added to the list of candidate countries in December 1999.

In the late 1990s, attention turned to whether or not member states would meet the Maastricht 'convergence criteria' for entry into the final stage of the EMU. In May 1998, the Council, meeting in the composition of heads of state or of government decided in Brussels that 11 countries had met these conditions. The UK, Sweden and Denmark decided not to participate in this stage and Greece did not meet the criteria for entry. On 1 January 1999, the euro project was launched, amid much fanfare and optimism about its prospects. The resignation of the Commission in March 1999, following allegations of financial mismanagement and nepotism, dampened the mood of 'euro-phoria' surrounding the euro's launch. The mood was further dampened by the euro's decline in value against the dollar, deflating predictions that it would soon rival the dollar as a reserve currency (see Chapter 11).

The TEU was the first Union treaty to contain a reference to its future revision. A new intergovernmental conference on Union reform was established in 1996 and concluded its work at the Amsterdam European Council in June 1997, at which the Treaty of Amsterdam (ToA) was negotiated. Although the issue of enlargement was expected to loom large in the IGC and in the subsequent treaty, decisions on enlargement were largely postponed. Instead, the ToA, which came into force in March 1999, introduced major changes in the fields of justice and home affairs, employment and also considerably strengthened the powers of the European Parliament, notably by extending the co-decision procedure. Another IGC on Union reform was established at the Cologne European Council in June 1999 and completed its work in time for the Nice European Council in December 2000, where a new treaty (the ToN) was negotiated (see Table 1.6). The IGC focused on the institutional questions posed by impending enlargement. A parallel conference, known as a Convention, was established with the task of preparing a draft European Charter of Fundamental Rights in time for the Nice European Council. Although the Charter was approved by member states at Nice, it was not incorporated into the ToN, largely because of doubts about bestowing a legally binding status on its provisions.

Table 1.6 Timeline 4: 1994–2000

1994	**February:** Austria, Finland, Norway and Sweden agree entry terms. **June:** elections to the EP. Austrian referendum in favour of entry. **Autumn:** Sweden and Finland vote for entry, Norway against.
1995	**January:** Austria, Sweden and Finland enter the Union. **December:** Madrid European Council agrees name of single European currency and affirms 1 January 1999 as the launch date.
1996	**March:** IGC on EU reform opens in Turin.
1997	**June:** IGC agrees the ToA. **July:** Commission presents *Agenda 2000*. **December:** *Agenda 2000* agreed by Luxembourg European Council.
1998	**May:** the Council in the composition of heads of state or government decides which countries qualify for the final stage of EMU.
1999	**January:** launch of the euro, with 11 countries participating. **March:** Resignation of the Commission. **May:** ToA in force. **June:** elections to EP. **December:** Helsinki European Council accepts Turkey as a candidate for EU entry; agrees proposal for a European rapid reaction force.
2000	**March:** New IGC launched. **September:** Danish voters reject Danish entry into the eurozone. **October:** Charter of Fundamental Rights completed. **December:** IGC agrees ToN. Nice European Council accepts the Charter of Fundamental Rights.

● A PRELIMINARY EVALUATION

○   The EU in Comparative Perspective

Two waves of regional integration in the post-war period can be identified: from the 1950s, many attempts were made to forge free trade areas or common markets in Europe, Africa, Latin America, the Caribbean and Asia. *First-wave regionalism* largely failed outside Europe. If judged against other attempts at integration in post-war Europe (Comecon and EFTA), the EU must be regarded as a success. Following the departure of Sweden, Austria and Finland, EFTA now comprises four countries with a combined population of only 11 million. Comecon was part of communism's 'grand failure' in Eastern Europe. Even before the cold war officially ended, several Comecon members had announced their intention to leave the organisation and to seek closer links with its flourishing Western rival. *Second-wave regionalism* (commencing in the 1990s) is more extensive than the first wave, and has possibly been precipitated by increasing international economic inter dependence and advances in communications. The second wave involves various attempts to forge regional trading pacts, customs associations, customs unions and common markets.

Of the 214 regional trade agreements (RTAs) notified to GATT (General Agreement on Tariffs and Trade) or to its successor the World Trade Organisation (WTO) between 1948 and 2000, 90 have been concluded since 1995. However, these second-wave projects (some of which involve attempts to restart stalled experiments) are still at a fragile stage of development and none approach the level of integration achieved by the EU. Of the 214 RTAs, 134 were still in force in 2000. Various regional economic groupings have emerged in post-communist Central and Eastern Europe. The Commonwealth of Independent States (CIS) was formed following the collapse of the Soviet Union in 1991. Several of its members have signed a charter for economic co-operation, although the main thrust of the economic policies of CIS countries seems to be towards increasing national autonomy. Eleven states in the Black Sea region (with a total population of 350 million) have formed the Black Sea Economic Co-operation Organisation, which has a permanent secretariat and a trade and development bank. The 'Visegrad Group' (Hungary, Poland, the Czech Republic and Slovakia) have agreed to the mutual elimination of tariffs and have formed the Central European Free Trade Area (CEFTA), which also now includes Slovenia and Romania and has a combined population of 90 million. But all of the CEFTA countries have reoriented their trade towards Western Europe and have been accepted for entry into the EU.

The North American Free Trade Association embraces the US, Canada and Mexico. It aims to eliminate virtually all restrictions on trade and investment between the three countries over 15 years (from 1994). The trilateral relationship is obviously unequal. Canada has a slightly lower GNP per capita than the US, but a much smaller population. Mexico's GNP per capita is about one-tenth that of the US. There is a significantly higher proportion of intraregional trade within the EU than between NAFTA countries. NAFTA is a free trade area, not a customs union and does not prescribe common tariffs on goods from outside the NAFTA area. It allows for free movement of goods, services and capital and limited free movement of business persons within NAFTA. Unlike the European Community, it has neither a legal personality nor 'supranational' institutions. In April 2001, 34 countries in the Americas, with a combined population of 750 million, reached an agreement on a 'Free Trade Area of the Americas' (FTAA) by 2005. But the diversity of the group is likely to hamper its development.

In Latin America, 'Mercosur'(*Mercado Comun del Sur* or the 'Common Market of the South') is a customs union and common market comprising Brazil, Paraguay, Argentina and Uruguay. Chile and Bolivia became associate members in 1996 and 1997. Mercosur accounts for about 45% of Latin America's population, for a third of its foreign trade and for half of its GDP. The 'Andean Pact' of 1969 aimed to forge links between Venezuela, Colombia, Ecuador, Peru and Bolivia, although a free trade area was not formed until 1991. In 1960, the Central American Common Market (CACM) was established (Guatemala, El Salvador, Honduras, Nicaragua, Costa Rica and Panama), but made little progress until its revival in the 1990s. The Caribbean Community and Common Market (Caricom), formed in 1973, has 15 members and is seeking a single market and economy, although progress has been slow. In Africa, the two most well-known formations are ECOWAS (the Economic Community of West African States), with 16 members, and COMESA (the Common Market for Eastern and Southern Africa), with 20 members. So far they have promised far more than they have delivered.

In East Asia, the success of 'individualist' economic strategies in recent years has meant that countries have seen little advantage in pursuing deep economic integration. Regional co-operation in Asia has tended to focus on measures to increase or safeguard market share. The members of ASEAN – the Association of South-East Asian Nations (Singapore, Malaysia, Thailand, Indonesia, the Philippines and Brunei, Vietnam, Laos, Myanmar and Cambodia) – have agreed to set up a free trade area by 2003, although the bulk of their trade is with other regions. The Asia-Pacific Economic Co-operation Forum (APEC) is a consultative forum founded in 1989 and aims to increase multilateral economic co-operation between countries in the Pacific rim. Its diverse membership comprises 21 countries in Asia, the Americas and Australasia. Although there is a plan for a free trade and investment zone by 2020, APEC's policies are not yet based on legally binding commitments.

○   **Why Has EU Integration Advanced so Far?**

The SEM, the TEU, the ToA and the ToN are manifestations of another period of accelerated development. What causes these sudden spurts in integration? In the 1950s, the conditions for integration are widely regarded as having been favourable: these included the stimulus of the war, receptive elites, the homogeneity of the original members, US support and economic growth. But deeper integration also moved ahead in the economically less favourable conditions of the late 1980s. Table 1.7 sets out some possible reasons for the relatively high degree of integration achieved by the EU.

Table 1.7 Factors Conducive to EU Integration

- the impetus for change deriving from the trauma of WW2;
- rapid economic growth in Western Europe in the early post-war years meant that the EU got off to a good start;
- the shared characteristics of members: for example, geographical proximity; similar economic and political systems (all are liberal democracies and have market economies); a relatively high level of economic development; perception of a common 'European' identity;
- until German reunification, no one member was much larger than the second largest;
- personalities: at various points, 'change agents' such as Monnet and Delors, have given the Union integration process a powerful boost;
- the pace of enlargement has so far been relatively slow, and therefore the entry issue has not crowded out the issue of internal development;
- the perception of the economic benefits to be derived from integration;
- vested interests (that is, the beneficiaries of the CAP and of certain other EU policies) have provided the 'cement', binding member states;
- members have been prepared to tolerate ambiguity and incoherence concerning the ultimate aims of integration. The potentially divisive effects of 'crunch' issues has thereby been muted to some degree;
- the Union has developed crisis management and conflict resolution strategies which have helped to prevent disintegration.

Although many specific causes of 'integration spurts' can be identified, two general factors seem to be at work: firstly, they occur when governments become more receptive to the logic of integration, in that they perceive that positive benefits (not necessarily the same benefits) will flow to their countries from deeper collaboration. Secondly, the logic of integration is given force and urgency by perception of a common threat (of war, invasion and economic weakness in the early post-war years and of economic stagnation in the 1980s and 1990s). These theoretical issues will be explored in the next chapter. It might be argued that, since the end of the cold war, many of the factors which have been conducive to EU integration no longer apply. For example, the prospect of a war between Western European countries now appears unthinkable. Germany is now significantly larger and more powerful than the second-largest member. Enlargement is increasing the diversity of the Union's membership and is diminishing the importance of the factor of geographical proximity. Some analysts even detect a decline in US support for European integration, in particular with regard to the area of defence and security (see Lundestad, 1998). Moreover, the pursuit of political, economic and monetary union is rendering it increasingly difficult to sweep crunch issues concerning the depth of integration under the carpet.

○ The Union's Achievements and Failures

Any attempt to assess the successes and failures of the Union so far depends very much on the criteria used and the perspective adopted. From small beginnings, the Union has made substantial progress in integration. It has made a major contribution to the healing of Franco-German conflict. It has had a dynamic effect on trade between members. It has launched both a single European market and a single European currency. It is currently seeking to develop a military capability, in the form of a rapid reaction force. If judged solely against the progress made by other post-war regional formations, the EU must be regarded as a success. But serious questions can be raised about the 'successes' of the EU outlined in Table 1.8 below.

It would also be easy to advance a counter-case, that the Union's economic performance has failed to match that of its main competitors in recent decades. For example, the economic performance of the EFTA states has been at least as good for much of the post-war period; that of the US has been even better. The Union has high unemployment relative to the US and Japan. It has a relatively poor record for developing new high-tech industries. Moreover, despite the 'hype' of the Single European Market programme, the aims of the programme are still far from being fully realised. Protectionist policies, notably the CAP, have restricted international trade and arguably have not been to the general benefit of EU citizens. Nor has the European integration project succeeded in exciting, or to any great degree involving, 'ordinary' citizens. Nor does the Union yet have a fully developed portfolio of policies: for example, education, health, welfare and law and order remain very largely national responsibilities. The civil wars in ex-Yugoslavia damaged the Union's credibility in foreign affairs. The development of a common foreign and security policy remains at a nascent stage, despite the changes to CFSP in the ToA and recent initiatives in security and defence.

Table 1.8 Some Indicators of the Union's Success

- there is a long queue of countries keen to join. Any club which has a waiting list of would-be entrants must be doing something right;
- no member has withdrawn (compare this to EFTA or to the now defunct Comecon);
- it has a strong institutional and policy base;
- it has achieved a deeper level of integration than any other post-war grouping;
- it has launched the single European currency;
- it is very much alive: many of its counterparts are dead, dying or at a nascent stage;
- it is an international actor in its own right (for example, the Commission negotiates trade agreements on behalf of all member states);
- it is the largest regional bloc in the world and has by far the highest level of intraregional trade.

○ **Challenges Facing the Union**

Both externally and internally, the Union faces major challenges. The increased size and diversity of the Union is creating major institutional and policy problems. The next enlargements of the Union will not only substantially increase the Union's membership but will also result in a substantial increase in the number of small member states. This is likely to mean that the Union will be much harder to manage than in the past (despite the institutional changes designed to address this problem in the ToN). The Union's sluggish record on employment, when judged against those of its major global competitors, is also an issue of vital current importance. Despite the increased powers of the European Parliament, the problem of the Union's democratic deficit remains as great as ever. The rejection of the ToN by Irish voters in June 2001 (see p. xxviii) may reflect a wider, underlying 'disconnection' between the EU's decisionmaking elites and EU citizens. It remains to be seen if the EU rapid reaction force is an effective military instrument or merely an exercise in political symbolism. Although the United States has for most of the post-war era been strongly supportive of the European integration project, in recent years it has tended to be more openly critical of the Union and its policies: for example, the US and the EU are currently at loggerheads on several trade issues and the US has been suspicious of the implications for NATO of the Union's plans to develop a military capability of its own. It seems clear that transatlantic links need to be managed more sensitively by both sides than in the recent past. The capacity of the Union to rise to these challenges will be examined in later chapters.

● CONCLUSION

This chapter has sought to show that there was nothing inevitable about the way the European Union has developed. Moreover, growing international interdependence and the emergence of second-wave regionalism suggests that analyses of the Union's development have to be considered in the context of broader structural changes taking place in the global economy. But in some respects the Union remains unique. Various approaches might be adopted to shed light on the dynamics of change in relation to European integration: for example, we could adopt an *heroic perspective* and focus on the influence of key personalities, such as Monnet, Schuman, Spaak and Delors (as accelerators) and de Gaulle and Thatcher (as would-be decelerators) of integration; we might adopt an *ideological perspective* and attribute European integration to the influence of ideas (such as functionalism, federalism or supranationalism); we could opt for *a situational perspective*, and focus on circumstances and events (such as Europe's parlous situation at the end of the war). In practice, however, these one-dimensional approaches are more misleading than enlightening, because European integration is a product of a dynamic mix of influences, deriving from people, ideas and circumstances.

FURTHER READING

Arter, P. (1993), *The Politics of European Integration in the Twentieth Century*, Dartmouth, Aldershot.

den Boer, P. (1995), 'Europe to 1914: The Making of an Idea', in Wilson, K. and Van Der Dussen, J., *The History of the Idea of Europe*, Routledge, London.

Dinan, D. (1994), *Ever Closer Union?*, Macmillan, London.

Featherstone, K. (1994), 'Jean Monnet and the "Democratic Deficit" in the European Union', *Journal of Common Market Studies*, vol. 32, no. 2, pp. 147–70.

George, S. (1990), *An Awkward Partner, Britain in the European Community*, Oxford University Press, Oxford.

George, S. (1998), 'Britain and the European Union', *European Access*, no. 6, pp. 12–13.

Greenwood, S. (1992), *Britain and European Co-operation Since 1945*, Blackwell, Oxford.

Lieshout, R.H. (1999), *The Struggle for the Organisation of Europe*, Edward Elgar, Cheltenham and Northampton, MA.

Lundestad, G. (1998), *'Empire' by Integration: The United States and European Integration, 1945-1997*, Oxford University Press, Oxford.

Milward, A.S. (1992), *The European Rescue of the Nation-State*, Routledge, London.

Stirk, P. (1989), *European Unity in Context: The Inter-war Period*, Pinter, London.

Vanthoor, W.F.V. (1999), *A Chronological History of the European Union*, Edward Elgar, Cheltenham and Northampton, MA.

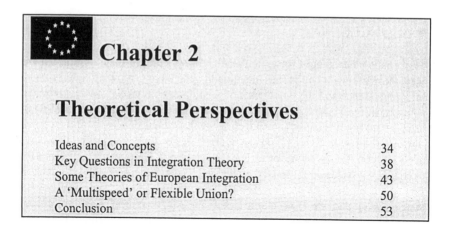

Chapter 2

Theoretical Perspectives

● IDEAS AND CONCEPTS

○ The Importance of Ideas

There is no 'single currency' of ideas in relation to European integration. Indeed, the subject has inspired a remarkably diverse range of ideas and theories, some of which are *prescriptive* (the authors approve of integration and seek to prescribe integration strategies) and some *descriptive* (the authors are primarily concerned to understand and explain the 'why' and 'how' of integration). In practice, it is difficult to classify integration theories into these two categories, because even the most prescriptive theory has to be supported by description and explanation, and even the most determinedly objective student of integration will make value judgements. Nor does the subject have a 'common language', in that many key terms used in discussions on European integration (such as sovereignty or federalism) are capable of very different interpretations. Two striking features of European integration as a subject of study have been the inability of theory to keep up with events and the ability of events to confound even the most elaborate theory.

The European Union (EU) is difficult to theorise about, for two fundamental reasons: firstly, the Union is a dynamic phenomenon and therefore explanatory theories are attempting to hit a moving target. Even if scholars could agree on an explanatory theory (a most unlikely prospect), developments in the Union would be likely to render this consensus view out of date before very long. Secondly, the EU is not only highly dynamic, but is becoming increasingly complex. Indeed, the EU is now so complex that a theory which seeks to explain everything is likely to be so general as to be capable of explaining little. As the EU has become more complex and multidimensional, there is far more to theorise about. Therefore, any explanation of a set of events or circumstances in the EU may match only one part of the EU's system. Put bluntly, attempts to explain the EU are likely to have limited shelf lives and are likely to offer only partial answers. Nevertheless, neither the origins nor the subsequent development of the Union can be understood without reference to the corpus (more accurately, clash) of ideas which have given direction and shape to European integration processes and to perceptions of these processes.

O **Definitions**

Dictionary definitions of integration can never fully encapsulate the various shades of meaning that can be given to this word. In broad terms, it means the coming together of separate units to form a whole. This implies that it goes beyond 'interstate co-operation' (where arguably there is no whole) although the boundary between co-operation and integration is very fuzzy and the two terms are often used as synonyms. Definitions by economists and by political scientists naturally have different emphases. The economist Jovanovic (1992, p. 8) defines international economic integration as 'a process by which the economies of separate states merge in large entities'. Political scientists tend to focus on the implications of integration for national sovereignty and for the behaviour of political actors. From this perspective the integration process involves (1) the voluntary relinquishment by nation-states of the power to make independent decisions in certain policy areas (decisionmaking is shared by the governments of participating states or is transferred to new central institutions) and (2) the shifting of the loyalties, expectations and activities of national political actors to a new centre (see Lindberg, 1963, Chapter 1).

A fundamental distinction is between *voluntary* and *involuntary* integration. There are many examples in history of the involuntary form, such as the forcible incorporation of many newly independent states into the Soviet Federation after the Bolshevik revolution. Similarly, regional economic integration in Eastern Europe during the communist period was by no means fully voluntarist, because of the coercive power exercised over the East European 'People's Democracies' by the Soviet Union. The EU is founded on *voluntarist* principles (no country is forced to join, and no country would be prevented from leaving it). Another fundamental feature of the EU integration process is that, from its inception, it has had explicitly political, as well as economic, goals. Many other distinctions between types of integration can be made. For example, *positive integration* involves the *building* of common institutions and policies, whereas *negative integration* refers to the *removal* of cross-border barriers of various kinds. In practice, however, this distinction between 'building things up' and 'knocking things down' is difficult to sustain: for example, the Single European Market (SEM) programme was nominally about knocking down barriers to trade, but entailed major institutional and policy changes amounting to the most significant exercise in positive integration since the 1950s (a fact that at least one of the signatories to the Single European Act, Mrs Thatcher, did not realise until it was too late!). We could also distinguish between *integration 'width'* (the range of subjects covered by integration agreements) and *integration 'depth'* (the extent to which there is a pooling of sovereignty in a particular policy area).

○ Sovereignty

We have already noted the centrality of the sovereignty principle in discussions on European integration. Sovereignty has two principal aspects: firstly an *internal* aspect, meaning supremacy, or authoritative decision-making power, within a state (for example, we speak of the sovereignty of parliament, the supreme lawmaking body within the UK). Secondly, an *external* aspect, meaning the independence of states in international affairs. The sovereign state is still generally regarded as the chief actor in the international system. It has shown remarkable ability to adjust to new realities, such as increasing international interdependence and the rise of 'non-state actors', such as multinational corporations (MNCs), international governmental organisations (IGOs, such as the International Monetary Fund (IMF)) and international non-governmental organisations (INGOs, such as Oxfam). However, in an increasingly interdependent world, the meaning of sovereignty has to be continually reassessed and redefined. For example, the internationalisation of modern business, manifested in copious flows of trade, investment, technology and information across state boundaries, means that the old 'billiard ball' model of the state (in which states are assumed to have hard, impenetrable surfaces), is clearly out of date. Sovereignty is not an all-or-nothing condition and therefore it can be gained or lost by degrees.

Integration has also been at least partly inspired by the belief that sovereignty is a malign and dangerous force. According to its critics, it divides humanity into separate units and encourages selfish and insular behaviour. Because it is regarded as a means of uniting human beings, integration tends to be perceived by its proponents as being morally superior to 'non-integration'. But the drive towards integration has also been motivated and justified by perceived welfare and security benefits of 'going it with others': according to the proponents of integration, these benefits outweigh trade-off costs in terms of the erosion of sovereignty. They argue that in an increasingly interdependent world, national sovereignty is being eroded anyway and that countries joining together are likely to have more 'clout' in the international arena. Conversely, opposition to integration generally reflects a desire to defend state sovereignty (which tends to be equated with national independence). Its defenders argue that it enables peoples to govern themselves; that it protects smaller countries against domination by larger ones; and that it remains a focus of national loyalties.

What are the principal integration mechanisms through which the sovereignties of participating states may be eroded?

Firstly, elements of decisionmaking power may be *transferred* from national governments to 'supranational' authorities (see the example in Figure 2.1). The word 'supra' means 'above', and so literally supranationalism means above the level of nation-states. The High Authority of the European Coal and Steel Community (ECSC), the European Commission, the European Parliament (EP), the European Court of Justice (ECJ) and the European Central Bank (ECB) are often referred to as supranational, in that they perform functions on behalf of the Union as a whole and do not specifically represent the interests of the individual governments of member states. European governments have not, however, been prepared to commit suicide by transferring power wholesale to supranational authorities. For example, the Single European Act (SEA), the Treaty on European Union (TEU) and the ToA increased the powers of the EP, but the European Council and the Council of the European Union (both 'intergovernmental' institutions) are, respectively, the key guiding and decisionmaking bodies in the Union. Some analysts (for example, Keohane and Hoffman, 1991, p. 16) deny that the Commission is a supranational entity, because it is not an authoritative decision*maker* above the nation-state, although it clearly has supranational characteristics in the sense referred to above. Many key policy areas, such as foreign affairs, defence, domestic justice and responsibility for direct taxation remain in the hands of the governments of member states.

Secondly, governments of states may participate in shared decisionmaking, in which they agree to be bound by collective decisions. Shared decisionmaking by national governments is often referred to as 'intergovernmentalism'. But distinctions which place supranationalism and intergovernmentalism at opposite ends of a spectrum are misleading, because collective decisionmaking by governments is also literally supranational (that is, it takes place above the level of individual national governments). Shared decisionmaking in its minimalist form (*loose intergovernmentalism*) constitutes no appreciable threat to sovereignty, because individual governments can veto decisions they find unacceptable. But in its maximalist form (*tight intergovernmentalism*), based on the principle of binding majority voting, it imposes limits on sovereignty, because member states are forced to accept majority decisions. Within the Union, binding majority voting (an example of tight intergovernmentalism) constitutes a greater threat to state sovereignty than the transfer of functions to 'supranational' authorities. Its *raison d'être* is that it enables the Union to move forward, by preventing decisions favoured by the majority from being vetoed.

However, as long as membership of the Union remains voluntary, then it can be argued that sovereignty has been 'lent' rather than lost. The TEU explicitly confirmed the right of any member state to withdraw from the Union. Although the principle that Union law has primacy over national law is well established, this principle is ultimately based on the willingness of national parliaments to accept this. Eurosceptics would retort that, because the issue of withdrawal is not on the political agendas of member states, lent sovereignty is as good as lost (a circular argument!).

Figure 2.1 Two Means of Eroding Sovereignty

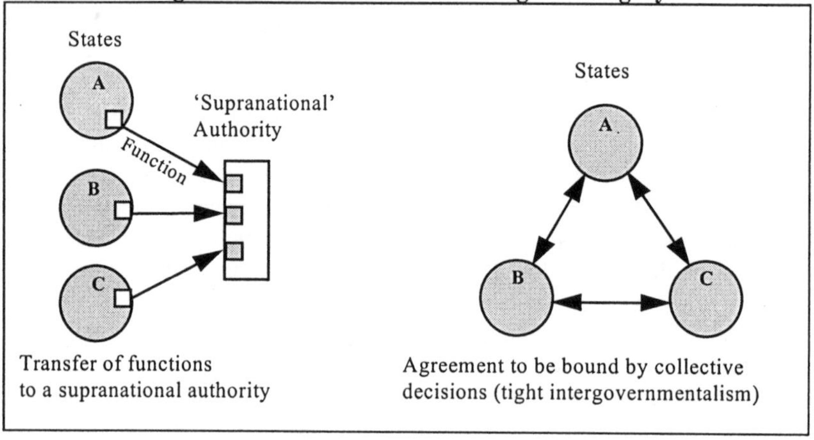
States
A
'Supranational'
Authority
Function
B
C
Transfer of functions
to a supranational authority
States
A
B
C
Agreement to be bound by collective
decisions (tight intergovernmentalism)

● KEY QUESTIONS IN INTEGRATION THEORY

❍ Key Questions

Table 2.1 below seeks to provide a preliminary overview of EU integration theory by breaking down the questions theoreticians ask into broad categories. On this basis, the corpus of EU integration theory might be crudely divided into 'what', 'why', 'who' and 'how' questions, focusing respectively on: *what* the EU is; *why* it has developed in the way it has; *who* has power in the EU system; and *how* the EU's institutional machinery actually works. This categorisation provides a preliminary insight into the substance of the debates in integration theory. But as actual theories tend to address several of these questions (although not necessarily according them equal importance) it is too crude to be used as a means of classifying specific theories.

Table 2.1 Key Questions in Integration Theory

- **'What'** questions seek to explain the nature of the EU: for example, by comparing it to states, confederations or international organisations.
- **'Why'** questions seek to identify and explain the causal factors which have shaped and are shaping the Union's development. Some 'why' theorising seeks to provide a general explanation of the Union's development whereas other types seek only to explain a set of specific events or circumstances.
- **'Who'** questions seek to identify the key actors in EU affairs and policy processes. They seek to examine how power is distributed in the system, for example between national, supranational and subnational actors.
- **'How'** questions examine how the EU's institutional and policy machinery works, for example by analysing the EU's working methods and styles of policymaking.

○ **The Nature of the EU**

The question 'what is the EU?' has exercised integration theorists throughout the Union's history. Answers are normally sought by comparing the Union to other political formations in the international system.

- **Is the EU a type of state?** Accepting the conventional model of the 'Westphalian' state as a basis of comparison, the Union is not a state and seems unlikely to develop into one in the foreseeable future. It does not have a monopoly of 'legitimate coercion'; it has limited tax and spend functions; it has a weak centre, in that there is no central governing authority; nor is it recognised as a state by other international actors. International relations scholars tend to view the EU as fundamentally different from a state whereas comparative government theorists tend to argue that, although the Union may not be a state, it nevertheless has some state-like features and therefore can be analysed using concepts and theories derived from the comparative study of states. For some writers, the resemblance between the EU and a state is such that they are prepared, although usually with elaborate qualifications, to attach the label 'state' to the Union. Thus it has been described as a 'regulatory state' (Majone, 1994), a 'post-modern state' (Caporaso, 1996), and a 'nascent federal European state' (Pinder, 1995). However, closer analyses of the thinking of these writers shows that the perceived 'state-like' qualities of the Union do not embrace the attributes required for a fully developed state.

  - The *regulatory state* conception of the Union is based on the assumption that the Union has state-like regulatory characteristics, such as rulemaking mechanisms, commitment to the rule of law and to legal processes, even thought it does not yet perform certain key 'traditional' state functions, such as control of taxation and spending, foreign affairs or defence. The

EU does of course have redistributive policies (principally agriculture, regional development, social funds and development assistance) as well as regulatory policies. But member states retain control of the bulk of redistributive policies, such as taxation and welfare. According to Majone, regulation is at the core of EU policymaking and has developed for two main reasons: firstly, because of the inadequacy of intergovernmental solutions to common problems; and secondly because in some policy fields a high level of technical and administrative discretion is required. Moreover, EU regulatory rules are the product of a very elaborate and frequently protracted process of negotiation and bargaining, involving networks of formal and informal actors.

- The *post-modern state* conception is based on the premise that states are changing their role and functions, to the extent that the Union can be fitted into the state category, following reassessment of the distinctive features of modern statehood. The debate about whether or not the EU will at some point metamorphose into a state may well hinge on conceptions of statehood which are already out of date. Elazar (1995) has argued that the state is acquiring new characteristics, in that it is involved in a network of economic and military commitments which limit state sovereignty and result in various forms of shared rule, both with other states and with international organisations. This means that modern states are far removed from the old 'billiard ball' model of states in the international system. Kohler-Koch (1996) has argued that the way states are governed has changed, so that the EU may not be fundamentally different from the new governance within states.

- The '*embyronic federal state*' conception views the Union as a state in the making, or as a form of integration which could develop into a state (that is, a 'could be' state). This conception tends to regard the Union as an emerging federation. Because many countries have federal systems of government, federalism is perhaps the most easily understood (and by the same token misunderstood) of all concepts in integration theory. In a federal system, there is a formal distribution of power between central and regional levels of government. These powers (together with the rights of citizens) are usually defined in a constitutional document. There is usually a federal supreme court to adjudicate in disputes on constitutional issues. The central level invariably has responsibility for foreign and security policy, but many functions are shared with the regional level. In continental Europe, federal systems tend to be associated with *decentralisation* and are viewed as a means by which the powers of the central government can be kept in check, whereas in the UK (lacking a federal tradition) federalism is often viewed as a *centralising* doctrine, designed to wrest power from national governments and parliaments.

Some commentators believe that the Union is already a federation in all but name (Begg, 1993, p. 162) or is on the way to becoming one (Pinder, 1995, p. 22). The Union already has many federal characteristics – for example: a Union title, some supranational institutions, including an increasingly powerful Parliament, a Court of Justice and a seemingly ever-widening range of common policies. However, there are several major differences between the Union and a 'typical' federation. Firstly, the EU does not have a written constitution and is based upon treaties negotiated by governments. Secondly, the power exercised by member states in EU decisionmaking has no parallel in any existing federation. For example, state governors in the US federal system are not key decisionmakers at central level. Nor, in contrast with EU governments, do they play any significant role in foreign and defence policy. According to Caporaso, it is possible that the Union may never acquire the full range of functions performed by states (Caporaso, 1996). There are several reasons why the EU is unlikely to develop into a federal 'United States of Europe' on the US model: the peoples in the American colonies were more homogeneous than are contemporary Europeans (they had a common language and culture and were largely of British ancestry); the colonies were not fully formed nation-states; nor were their economies fully developed. An American scholar, Larry Siedentop, after comparing EU integration with the development of US federalism in the late 18th century, concludes that 'Europe is not yet ready for federalism' (Siedentop, 2000, p. 231).

• **Is the Union a 'confederation'?** A confederation is a looser arrangement than a federation, in that the participating units retain a higher degree of independence. The participating states see benefit in combining together, but not too closely and do not wish to merge into a single state. Confederations tend to have more limited powers than federations, although they may have some supranational institutions. The states are likely to be geographically close. Normally there is a right of secession. A confederation is a voluntary union of states rather than peoples. In 1981, Forsyth argued that the EU was essentially a confederation, in that it was a voluntary and contractual union of states: although it involved the creation of supranational institutions, states were the main decisionmakers. However, it might be argued that deepening of EU integration in the last two decades has shifted the Union somewhat away from the confederal towards the federal model.

The Union is clearly more than a confederation, but is less than a full federation. Kincaid (1999) refers to the Union as a form of 'confederal federalism', that is, as a confederal system with some federal features (others would argue that it is a federal system with confederal features!). Others view the Union as essentially a *consociation*, which is a form of integration pursued by national governments in order to better achieve their policy objectives and thus consolidate their power rather than relinquish it to supranational organisations. According to Taylor (1996), the building of consensus between governments is the primary characteristic of consociations. Chryssochoou (1997) views the EU as a consociation with confederal elements, in that it involves co-operative joint decisionmaking at the Union level. However, in both 'consociationalism' and 'confederal consociationalism', the national governments play the key roles and therefore these models view the EU as essentially an arrangement between states rather than as a type of state.

- **Is the Union an international organisation?** If the Union is not a state, can it be classified as an international governmental organisation, a category which includes a diverse range of bodies such as the United Nations, the World Trade Organisation and the North Atlantic Treaty Organisation (NATO)? The answer must be no. The EU is far more 'supranational' than any of the organisations referred to above, which are essentially intergovernmental clubs; it has a much greater degree of institutional and policy integration between its members and also a much broader policy range than any international governmental organisation.

- **The 'betweenness' of the EU.** Probably the nearest we can currently get to the answer to the question as to whether the Union most resembles a state or an international organisation is that it has features of but differs from both, lying somewhere between these two categories (in this sense, Laffan (1998) refers to the 'betweenness' of the EU), although arguably the depth and breadth of integration in the Union is such that the Union now resembles a state more than it does an international organisation. Bulmer (1994) argues that the Union occupies a grey area between intrastate and interstate relations, which he refers to as 'governance without government', that is, the exercise of governmental functions without government. Thus, although the EU does not have a government as such, it has a system of governance and must be regarded as a political system, meaning that it has decisionmaking institutions and rules; citizens and groups seek to achieve their aims through the system; decisions of the system have significant impacts; and there is feedback between the system's outputs and citizens' demands (Hix, 1998).

- **The uniqueness of the EU.** As we noticed in the previous chapter, in recent years there has been a tremendous growth in the number and variety of other regional formations, such as the North American Free Trade Association (NAFTA) or the Asia-Pacific Economic Co-operation Forum (APEC). This raises the question as to whether the development of the Union is part of a much broader process affecting other regions of the world. Is EU integration merely the most advanced form of the regional integration which according to some analysts is driven by globalisation? 'Globalisation' is generally described as a process in which national borders decline in significance; in which global industries and firms are replacing national industries; in which global markets are replacing national markets; and in which flows of capital and other factors of production are no longer confined within national boundaries, leading to a massive increase in cross-border trade and investment. It is certainly the case that increased competition in global markets was a major factor in pushing forward economic integration in the EU, for example through development of the Single European Market. It might also be argued that it reflected the perceived failure of national governments to cope with the consequences of globalisation. In other words, the increased pace of European integration since the mid-1980s might be seen as a response to threats deriving from globalisation. Similarly, the growth of international migration pressures and international crime is forcing member states to co-ordinate their efforts to deal with these problems. Globalisation may explain why states co-operate with each other, but it does not explain why EU integration has proceeded so much further than other regional formations. Nor does it explain its peculiar form. The EU is unique in the degree and form of integration it has achieved. Clearly, globalisation has been a factor in, but is not the only driving force of European integration.

● SOME THEORIES OF EUROPEAN INTEGRATION

Anyone looking for a definitive explanatory theory of European integration will be disappointed. The trend in integration theory is towards less dogmatic explanations of integration events and processes. Recent approaches tend to disclaim the view that the Union's path of development was inevitable, or that its future can be confidently predicted. They tend to lay greater stress than earlier theories upon the *choices* available to governments and upon the influence of international events and circumstances. Newer theories are also more eclectic than the old, drawing upon various schools of thought. Not surprisingly, theorists are likely to use conceptual 'lenses' derived from their own disciplines. International relations scholars have had a major influence on EU theorising. More recently, specialists in the study of comparative government and politics have made major contributions to integration theory, principally by utilising conceptual lenses developed in the study of national political systems in their analyses of the Union. Newer theories naturally tend to build upon and recast old ideas (in some cases, it is a case of old wine in new terminological bottles). Grand theories, which seek to provide a comprehensive explanation of the EU's nature and development, have tended to be replaced by 'middle range' theories which focus on specific questions. There are an increasing number of these theories, meaning that the study of the EU is becoming increasingly fragmented. The sections below outline some of the most widely discussed theories of European integration.

○ Functionalism

As noted in Chapter 1, 'functionalists' favour the strategy of gradually undermining state sovereignty, by encouraging technical co-operation in specific policy areas across state boundaries. The founding father of the functionalist school was David Mitrany, a Romanian-born scholar who taught for many years at the London School of Economics. He regarded nationalism as the biggest threat to world peace and favoured a shift in human loyalties from the national to the international level through mutually beneficial international co-operation in sectors such as transport, agriculture, science and health. Mitrany's ideas rest on the assumption that governments are less able to meet the welfare needs of their citizens than 'non-political' international authorities. He favoured what he called *technical self-determination* over national self-determination and believed that human loyalties would shift from the nation-state to supranational authorities because of the tangible material benefits these authorities would provide. People would therefore become more committed to transnational co-operation and less nationalistic (Mitrany, 1966). Mitrany envisaged the emergence of a spreading web of supranational authorities, to undertake tasks formerly performed by national governments. According to Mitrany, there would be many such agencies, and therefore international power would be diffused rather than centralised. Mitrany thought that these authorities would have a strong managerialist ethos and would be 'above' politics. Mitrany was interested in global rather than regional co-operation (whereas Monnet's ideas had a strong regional focus). For Mitrany, regional integration was nationalism writ large. Therefore, he was opposed to a 'continental union' in Europe, and to the creation of institutions which in his view mirrored those of sovereign states.

The weaknesses of the functionalist approach seem glaring in the light of post-war history: for example, it assumes that functional co-operation can be separated from politics. However, the decisions of technical agencies are often highly political: several, such as the United Nations Educational, Scientific and Cultural Organisation (UNESCO) and the International Labour Organisation, have been torn by political disputes. These agencies have been created by states for their mutual benefit: they remain under the ultimate control of sovereign states and are dependent upon them for their resources. Moreover, the creation of functional authorities has arguably made the states system work better rather than undermining it. There is also scant evidence that loyalties are shifting from the state level to international organisations. Functionalism also left many key questions unanswered, such as how co-ordination of functional authorities would work or how disputes between them would be resolved. It nevertheless provided a corpus of ideas upon which theorists of European integration would later build.

○ Neo-functionalism

This approach is far more realistic than the older functionalism, and less prescriptive: it was developed in the 1950s and 1960s to explain integration processes in the European Community. It is therefore based on intensive study of an actual case. Haas, Nye and Lindberg (all, incidentally, American scholars) are generally acknowledged to be the founders of this approach. Haas (1958) viewed integration as a developing and expanding process involving bargaining and compromise, like other forms of politics. He argued that there could be a learning curve of co-operation between governments, in which the experience of co-operation in some fields could lead of co-operation in others: co-operation was likely to begin in the field of *low politics* (such as coal and steel) and might then be extended to *high politics* (such as foreign and defence policy). In other words, there could be a *spillover* effect from co-operation in one policy area to another. Haas did not believe this spillover process to be automatic or inevitable, not least because it would depend upon choices made by governments and other actors. The main differences between neo-functionalism and older type functionalism are:

- In neo-functionalism, the political dimension and the role of governments in integration processes are fully accounted for. A central assumption of this approach is that functional co-operation will take place at the behest of governments. Unlike the older functionalism, neo-functionalism accepts the importance of political conflict and the existence of competing interests. It emphasises the importance of elites and elite bargaining rather than mass support for integration in its early stages.
- Neo-functionalism has a stronger empirical foundation and seeks to explain in some detail how a specific integration process actually works.
- It focuses upon integration between groups of countries in specific regions of the world ('regional integration') rather than upon global integration.

After Haas wrote his first book on the subject, there was a lull or plateau in European integration which seemed to undermine the neo-functionalist case. Setbacks in the process of European integration led to the incorporation of the concept of *spillback* (that is, reverse integration) into neo-functionalist theories. In his later writings, Haas acknowledged that the conditions which had provided the driving force for integration in the early period had run out of steam. He noted that there had not been spillover to other areas besides agriculture. He also argued that the power of nationalism and the influence of external factors (international events) had both been underestimated. In addition, he recognised that European integration was too complex to fit neatly into any theoretical model.

Since the mid-1980s, there has been a period of accelerated development of the Union, manifested in the Single European Market programme and the

TEU. Was this the result of 'spillover'? Keohane and Hoffman (1991, p. 19) deny that spillover was primarily responsible for the SEM – rather, they attribute it to a combination of factors, in particular to the convergence of national interests, to developments in the global economy and to concern about the poor competitiveness of European industry. Nevertheless, it seems unlikely that recent deepening of integration within the EU could have occurred without a learning curve of collaborative experience. For example, the SEM programme may well have provided the momentum for the TEU's provisions on economic and monetary union. The impact of SEM has also frequently been cited as a major contributory factor to the development of the Union's justice and home affairs (JHA) policies.

○ **Federalism**

The influence of federalist ideas on European integration processes is difficult to gauge. In Chapter 1 we noted that early post-war federalist groups were essentially fringe movements which had no discernible influence upon the key policymakers in this period. But many of the prime movers in the development of the Union have espoused federalist ideas at some point. In terms of the influence of the federalist movement, parallels might be drawn with the 'environmentalist' movement, which has seen some of its ideas absorbed in a less radical form into mainstream political discourse. 'Euro-federalism' is still regarded as a laudatory idea in many parts of continental Europe. Contemporary federalists (often referred to as *neo-federalists*) tend to be more realistic about the prospects of realising their goals than their predecessors and are prepared to build a federal union in incremental steps rather than all at once (Monnet also espoused an 'incrementalist' approach).

The aim to transform the EU into a fully fledged federation, with its own government and parliament, was espoused by the German foreign minister Joshka Fischer in a speech entitled 'From Confederacy to Federation – Thoughts on the Finality of European Integration' in Berlin in May 2000. Although Fischer made it clear that he was speaking in a personal capacity, it is clear that the federal dream is very much alive in some parts of continental Europe, including in some high places in Germany. In April 2001, German President Johannes Rau and German Chancellor Gerhard Schröder put forward separate proposals for an EU federal constitution (*Financial Times*, 30 April 2001). European federalist groups are also very active in promoting the idea of an EU constitution (see Chapter 4). In May 2001, Schröder's ideas were challenged by the French Prime Minister Lionel Jospin, who espoused a different vision on the EU's constitutional future based on a 'federation of nation states' (*Le Monde*, 28 May 2001) – arguably a more realistic proposal, as Fischer has subsequently acknowledged (*Der Standard*, 26 June 2001).

O Intergovernmentalism

This approach stresses the role of governments in European integration processes. We have already noted that the term 'intergovernmentalism' tends to be used rather loosely. In addition to the distinction made earlier between tight and loose forms, a further distinction needs to be made between *prescriptive intergovernmentalism* (the view that governments *should* be the dominant actors in the Union) and *descriptive intergovernmentalism* (the view that governments *are*, for good or ill, the key actors in the Union). The Union is clearly different from purely intergovernmental bodies, such as the Organisation for Economic Co-operation and Development (OECD) or NATO, because it contains 'supranational' institutions of considerable importance. The extensive use of binding majority voting in the Council also differentiates the Union from most other international organisations.

Proponents of prescriptive intergovernmentalism seek to oppose attempts to enhance the powers of the Union's 'supranational' institutions. In its maximalist form (for example, espoused by British Eurosceptics), prescriptive intergovernmentalism favours a 'club of states' conception of the Union. Proponents of descriptive intergovernmentalism downplay the role of supranational institutions and cite the important role played in EU policymaking by the Council, the European Council and a support network of intergovernmental committees. According to this approach, which emphasises the importance of intergovernmental bargaining, developments in integration only occur when they coincide with the interests of the governments of member states. For example, it has been argued that the election of more market-oriented governments in member states in the 1980s, and the consequent convergence of 'national interests', was a major factor in the development of the Single European Market programme (Moravcsik, 1991). Descriptive intergovernmentalist theories have frequently emphasised the importance of Franco-German co-operation as the driving force or motor of European integration. An influential and controversial example of descriptive incrementalism is the theory of *liberal intergovernmentalism*, developed by Moravcsik (1998). Moravcsik, who bases his ideas on detailed empirical investigations of some specific policies, argues that the EU policy process is largely centred on intergovernmental bargaining and that the influence of supranational actors is generally marginal and limited to situations where they have strong allies amongst member states, that is, supranational actors are not strong in their own right. He furthermore argues that the preferences of governments are shaped primarily by economic interests and are dynamic (because governments can change).

Arguably, intergovernmental bargaining theories need to be qualified and supplemented, by reference to the important roles played by the Commission, the European Court of Justice, the European Parliament, interest groups and domestic politics in the EU policy system. The role of domestic politics in intergovernmental bargaining also needs to be acknowledged (Bulmer, 1983). The *domestic politics* approach emphasises the interplay between the national politics of member states and 'European' politics. It assumes that the behaviour of governments at the European level is explicable in terms of their need to take account of both domestic and European pressures and 'audiences'. Thus, in negotiations at European level, governments will seek to protect and foster domestic interests (and thereby bolster their domestic image and standing), but in dealings with their counterparts (the governments of other member states) will not wish to appear to be 'anti-European'. For governments, domestic interests also embrace considerations of party unity. Balancing domestic and European pressures is not always possible: the fact that the UK government headed by John Major was frequently out of step with other member states on European issues has been partly attributed to its need to appease a large and voluble group of Eurosceptic Conservative MPs.

○ Policy Networks

A 'policy network' has been defined as 'an arena for the mediation of the interests of governments and interest groups' (Peterson, 1995, p. 391). It is a network because it involves the interaction, in the form of bargaining, negotiation and collaboration, between groups of actors in the policy process, although these actors do not have equal power. The actors are not only governments and Union institutions, but also interest groups of various kinds, such as agricultural or business lobbies. Keohane and Hoffman (1991, p. 13) view the EU as having a 'network' form of organisation. EU policy is viewed as the outcome of bargaining and coalition formation between diverse actors, including governments, EU institutions and interest groups: interactions take place within a framework of *mutual interdependency*, although national governments are still considered to play the dominant role in decisionmaking.

The 'network' approach combines elements of intergovernmentalist and neo-functionalist perspectives. It derives from the study of 'pluralist' policy processes in liberal democracies, where government organisations and organised interests form policy communities in order to achieve their aims. In the policy community model, many organised interests work so closely with governmental organisations in formulating and delivering policy that they are inside the policymaking process rather than seeking to exert pressure from without. Governmental institutions allow organised interests into the policy process, because the latter have resources of use to them, such as knowledge and expertise, or because they may cause trouble if they are left out. In other words, the actors depend on one another in order to achieve their policy goals.

No study of how policy in the Union is made would be complete without consideration of the role played by organised interests in policymaking. Both the Commission and the Council are reliant for information, expertise and advice on these interests. There are both formal and informal channels through which groups seek to influence EU policy. As is true of policy networks within states, organised interests tend to be much more populous and influential in some areas of EU policy (for example, agriculture and business) than in others (such as consumer policy or foreign affairs).

The principal value of the policy networks approach is that it seeks to provide a comprehensive and accurate picture of how and who by EU policies are made, taking into account both formal and informal policy processes and the roles of both institutional actors and of organised interests. Whereas other approaches tend to focus on the roles of governments and of supranational bodies in the EU policy process, the policy networks approach seeks to give organised interests their due importance. However, as an explanatory theory of EU policymaking, it perhaps promises more than it delivers: its critics argue that it merely tells us that EU policy is shaped by numerous formal and informal actors in a policymaking 'arena'. Moreover, there are formidable problems in identifying an analysing EU policy networks, given the complexity and dynamic nature of the EU.

○ Multilevel Governance

The multilevel governance (MLG) approach developed by Marks (1996) focuses on the interrelationships between levels of government in the EU (supranational, national and subnational) and upon how the actors at these levels interact. The MLG hypothesis views the Union as a political system, in which the governments of member states are by no means the only important actors in EU policymaking, because the influence of supranational actors, in particular the Commission, the EP and the ECJ, and also of subnational actors, that is, local and regional governments, must also be taken into account. MLG is therefore less state centred than intergovernmentalism although it does not assume that power in the EU decisionmaking process is equally distributed between the levels. Marks acknowledges that the national level remains the most important. MLG differs from federalism, which also involves multiple layers of government, in that it does not assume that the system has a formal constitutional basis, or that the powers of the levels are clearly defined. In MLG, the power exercised by the different levels is less clear cut and more dynamic. The debate concerning the validity of the MLG hypothesis has centred on the extent to which the 'supranational' and subnational levels are powerful in their own right or whether they reflect, or are controlled by, the national level.

○ **The New Institutionalism**

The study of government used to be largely confined to an examination of the role of formal institutions in the policy process. This 'institutionalist' approach went out of fashion in the 1970s, following the emergence of 'behaviourist' approaches which emphasised the role of both formal and informal actors and processes in policymaking. The 'new institutionalism' defines the term 'institution' much more broadly than before, to embrace both formal and informal institutions and incorporating values, cultural norms, conventions, symbols, ways of doing things and many other characteristics. 'New institutionalist' approaches seek to explain how 'institutions' (defined in the broad sense above) influence the behaviour of policymakers and serve to shape policy outcomes (Puchala, 1999). Applied to the study of the EU, the new institutionalism, according to its advocates, helps to explain why policymakers behave in the way they do and why specific policy choices are made. The new institutionalism can be categorised into at least three types, namely historical, rational choice and sociological institutionalism. The historical type is based on the assumption that institutions have a history which influences the behaviour of actors. Rational choice institutionalists assume that actors in the decisionmaking process are self-interested and that institutions set limits on, and also shape, their behaviour. Sociological institutionalists emphasise the role of institutional conventions and norms which provide actors with guidance as to how to act. A criticism of the new institutionalism is that its proponents tend to define the term 'institution' so broadly that it can embrace almost anything. Nevertheless, according to its proponents it provides a framework of analysis which enables us to look beyond surface events and relationships.

● A 'MULTISPEED' OR FLEXIBLE UNION?

Multispeed concepts do not constitute a comprehensive theory, but focus on the problem of how European integration processes can proceed, given the increasingly heterogeneous nature of the Union's membership. The central idea of a multispeed Europe is that there will (or should) be variations in the pace of integration pursued by member states. The terms *Europe à la carte* (which was first developed by the German academic and ex-Commissioner Ralf Dahrendorf), *flexi-Europe* or *variable geometry* are often used to express the same idea. But there is a crucial difference between 'multispeed' and *à la carte* concepts. In a multispeed Europe, member states will be expected eventually to arrive at the same destination. In an *à la carte* Europe, there would always be scope for countries to opt out of specific areas of policy –

that is, there would be no common destination. The Commission, in a report prepared for the 1996/97 Intergovernmental Conference, accepted the multispeed principle, but firmly opposed *à la carte* Europe (see Chapter 4).

Yesterday's heresy is often tomorrow's conventional wisdom. The multispeed idea is still viewed with hostility by those who regard it as a cynical ploy to impede the pace of integration. The idea found support amongst opponents of deeper integration. In May 1994, at a Euro-election rally at Ellesmere Port, John Major outlined a vision of Europe in which the EU's functions 'should be carried out in different ways, often involving different groups of states'. This vision of a 'multitrack, multispeed, multilayered' Europe was attacked by critics as tantamount to consigning the UK to the slow lane of a two-speed Europe and as incompatible with Major's erstwhile aim to place the UK at the heart of Europe.

However, the multispeed idea has also been adopted by those anxious to ensure that rapid progress towards deeper integration is not impeded by 'laggard' countries: a multispeed Europe has fast lanes as well as slow ones. It had been espoused in a limited form in the Tindemans Report on European Union in 1975, but received a generally adverse reaction. In April 1994, Alain Lamassoure, France's European Affairs minister, proposed a 'hard core' of EU members, comprising countries applying all Union policies provided for in the Union treaties. He suggested that this might initially comprise the founder members and would be linked by a political declaration rather than by a new treaty. A similar proposal was put forward in Germany by Karl Lamers in a policy report for the Christian Democratic Union in the summer of 1994, fuelling suspicions in some parts of the Union that Germany and France were seeking to create a Union 'premier league'. In November 1994, the French prime minister, Edouard Balladur, proposed a 'concentric circles' model of integration, with three tiers, a hard core of EU members at the centre (France, Germany and perhaps the four other original EU members); a second tier of EU countries not ready or willing to pursue deeper integration; and a third tier of partner countries outside the EU.

Although these specific ideas were not taken up, the idea that groups of EU countries should be allowed to pursue deeper integration in specific fields continued to gain ground. A joint declaration on 'reinforced co-operation' was issued by the French and German foreign ministers in October 1996. The Treaty of Amsterdam formally sanctioned the idea of 'flexible integration', by introducing provisions (known as 'closer co-operation') which would allow groups of EU states to pursue integration projects, under strict conditions. However, no projects under these provisions have yet been undertaken (arguably because the conditions are so strict or, more cynically, because support for such co-operation by most member states amounts to posturing). In June 2000, French President Jacques Chirac gave a speech in the German parliament calling for France and Germany to set up a 'pioneer group' of EU countries to pursue deeper integration. The Treaty of Nice (ToN) will introduce measures to make it easier for groups of countries to engage in such co-operation (re-titled 'enhanced co-operation' in the treaty (see Chapter 4)). Table 2.2 provides a snapshot of these concepts.

Table 2.2 EU Flexible Integration Concepts

- **Multispeed**: EU countries pursue the same integration path, but at different speeds (in some versions, the metaphor used is of fast and slow trains travelling along a single track; in others of fast and slow tracks).
- **Europe à la carte**: EU countries are allowed to pick and choose from a menu of integration projects.
- **Concentric circles**: states are placed in different integration rings, depending on the degree of integration they are able or willing to pursue (the central ring would contain a core group of states).
- **Core or Pioneer** groups: countries most committed to, and capable of pursuing, deeper integration engage in vanguard integration projects and set examples for the rest.
- **Closer co-operation**: the term for flexible integration in the ToA (groups of member states can pursue deeper integration projects in defined fields under strict conditions).
- **Enhanced co-operation**: the term for closer co-operation in the ToN (which will make the conditions for co-operation somewhat easier). Interestingly, in the French language version of the ToN, the term 'coopérations renforcées' (reinforced co-operation) is used.

But even before the ToA and the emergence of 'pioneer' or 'hard-core' concepts, in significant ways European integration was already proceeding at multispeed, albeit in an *ad hoc*, piecemeal way rather than as part of a grand design. For example, the agreements reached at Maastricht implicitly sanctioned the multispeed approach in several ways: the UK was allowed to opt out of key aspects of monetary and social policy; Maastricht's intergovernmental pillars provide scope for member states to opt out of joint actions in the fields of foreign and security policy and justice and home affairs; the principle of subsidiarity widens the scope for differences in policy between member countries. Five member countries now participate in the *Eurocorps* (which in 2001 began transforming itself into a European rapid reaction corps, to serve as a crisis management tool of the EU's European Security and Defence Policy: see Chapter 19). Implicit in the Eurocorps project is the assumption that it is legitimate for a group of member states to pursue deeper integration outside the Union framework, providing that the project is compatible with the Union's goals. Prior to its formal incorporation into the Union framework, the Schengen Agreement fitted into this category. Not all EU countries currently participate in the single currency project (see Chapter 11) or in the Schengen Agreement. Denmark is unenthusiastic about participation in the EU's rapid reaction force, scheduled for 2003.

A flexible EU is by no means an unmixed blessing. It increases the complexity of EU institutional structures, rendering them more difficult for ordinary citizens to understand. There is a danger that it could solidify into an *à la carte* Europe, which could lead to the unravelling of the Union. It could lead to the creation of several classes of EU membership. Conversely, it provides a flexible framework for future integration and may be the only way in which an increasingly heterogeneous Union can be held together.

● CONCLUSION

There is no shortage of contending theories to explain the nature and development of the EU. In recent years, the dominance of EU theorising by International Relations scholars has been challenged by scholars from other disciplines, in particular from comparative government and politics. The sheer number and variety of theoretical approaches to the Union is likely to be confusing to those new to EU studies. Moreover, none of these theories is broad and subtle enough to capture the essence of the Union, or explain why it has developed in the way it has. Arguably, all of the contending theories have something to offer in providing insights and perspectives as we struggle to understand what is an increasingly complex phenomenon. However, none is capable of telling the whole story.

Finally, there is a type of theory which is as yet largely absent, at least in an explicitly developed form, from the integration theory literature. This might be termed 'end-point' or 'journey's end' theory. Unless it is assumed that member states can go on integrating forever, it seems reasonable to assume that there must be some point at which the EU project can be regarded as largely complete. There are several possible reasons why little work has been done on 'end-point theory': firstly, integration has been widely regarded as a process rather than as an end as such; secondly, it is widely recognised that the integration process is as yet far from complete and therefore speculation about its ultimate end point is premature; thirdly, the success of the EU integration project has been partly due to a certain ambiguity about the ends of integration. But recent developments – for example, the launch of an official debate on the future of Europe (http://www.europa.eu.int/futurum); acceptance of the idea of flexible integration, the 'no' vote in the Irish referendum on the ToN and growing interest in the idea of a Union constitution – may stimulate theorising about the Union's final destination.

FURTHER READING

Begg, D. (1993), *Making Sense of Subsidiarity*, Centre for Economic Policy Research, London.

Bulmer, S. (1983), 'Domestic Politics and European Community Policy Making', *Journal of Common Market Studies*, vol. 21, no. 4, pp. 349–63.

Bulmer, S. (1994), 'The Governance of the EU: A New Institutionalist Approach', *Journal of Public Policy*, vol. 14, no. 4, pp. 351–80.

Caporaso, J. (1996), 'The European Union and Forms of State', *Journal of Common Market Studies*, vol. 34, no.1, pp. 29–52.

Chryssochoou, D. (1997), 'New Challenges to the Study of European Integration', *Journal of Common Market Studies*, vol. 35, no. 4, pp. 521–42.

Elazar, D.J. (1995), 'From Statism to Federalism. A Paradigm Shift', *Publius*, vol. 25, no. 2, pp. 5–18.

Forsyth, M. (1981), *Union of States: The Theory and Practice of Confederation*, Leicester University Press, Leicester.

Haas, E.B. (1958), *The Uniting of Europe*, Stanford University Press, Stanford, CA.

Hix, S. (1998), 'The study of the EU II: The "New Governance" Agenda and Its Rival', *Journal of European Public Policy*, vol. 5, no. 1, pp. 38–65.

Jovanovic, M.N. (1992), *International Economic Integration*, Routledge, London.

Keohane, R.O. and Hoffman, S. (eds.) (1991), *The New European Community*, Westview Press, Boulder, CO.

Kincaid, J. (1999), 'Confederal Federalism and Citizen Representation in the EU', *West European Politics,* vol. 22, no.2, pp. 34–58.

Kohler-Koch, B. (1996), 'Catching up with Change: The Transformation of Governance in the EU', *Journal of European Public Policy*, vol. 3, no. 3, pp. 359–380.

Laffan, B. (1998), 'The European Union: a distinctive model of internationalization', *Journal of European Public Policy*, vol. 5, no. 2, pp. 235–53.

Lindberg, L.N. (1963), *The Political Dynamics of European Economic Integration*, Stanford University Press, Stanford, CA.

Majone, G. (1994), 'The Rise of the Regulatory State', *West European Politics*, vol. 17, no. 3, pp. 77–101.

Marks, G., Scharpf, F., Schmitter, P. and Streeck, W. (1996), *Governance in the European Union*, Sage, London.

Mitrany, D. (1966), *A Working Peace System*, Quadrangle Books, Chicago.

Moravcsik, A. (1991), 'Negotiating the Single European Act', in Keohane and Hoffman, *op. cit.*, pp. 41–84.

Moravcsik, A. (1998), *The Choice for Europe: Social Purpose and State Power from Messina to Maastricht*, Cornell University Press, Ithaca, NY.

Peterson, J. (1995), 'Decision-making in the European Union: Towards a Framework for Analysis', *Journal of European Public Policy*, vol. 2, no. 1, pp. 69–93.

Pinder, J. (1995), *European Community*, Oxford University Press, Oxford.

Puchala, D.J. (1999), 'Institutionalism, Intergovernmentalism and European Integration', *Journal of Common Market Studies*, vol. 37, no.2, pp. 317–31.

Siedentop, L. (2000), *Democracy in Europe*, Allen Lane, London.

Taylor, P. (1996), *The European Union in the 1990s*, Oxford University Press, Oxford.

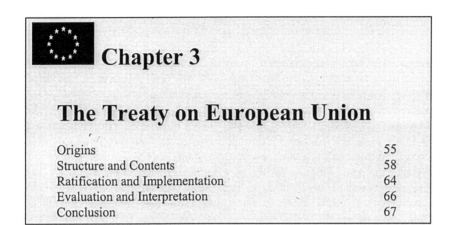

Chapter 3

The Treaty on European Union

● ORIGINS

The Treaty on European Union (TEU) – better known as the Maastricht Treaty – was agreed at the European Council in Maastricht in December 1991 and signed in February 1992. The Maastricht summit is widely acknowledged to be a landmark event in the European integration process. All of the issues examined in this book have been affected in some way by the decisions reached at Maastricht. The treaty is broader in scope, open to a wider range of interpretations and has sparked more controversy than any other Union treaty.

The Preamble to the Treaty of Rome refers to the determination to 'lay the foundation of an ever closer union of the peoples of Europe'. Until the 1980s this lofty (and undefined) aspiration remained dormant but not entirely forgotten. In 1983, the European Council in Stuttgart agreed a rather vague 'Solemn Declaration on European Union'. In February 1984, the European Parliament (EP) passed a 'Draft Treaty on European Union', although it lacked the power to transform this proposal into reality. The preamble to the Single European Act (SEA) (signed in February 1986) refers to the 'will to transform relations as a whole among their states into a European Union'. At the time there seemed no certainty that this aspiration would be pursued any more seriously than the 'ever closer union' goal contained in the Treaty of Rome. However, the Single European Market (SEM) programme, launched at the European Council in Milan in June 1985, provided the momentum for further integration in three principal ways: it demonstrated the feasibility of a leap forward in integration; the creation of a 'level playing field for business' had very broad-ranging institutional and policy implications; Euro-federalists, inspired by the launch of the SEM, were determined to keep the integration ball rolling.

The progression from the SEA to the TEU provides some support for the 'spillover' theory that integration in one area of activity leads to integration in others. Monetary union and the creation of a 'European social space' were the most obvious next targets for integration, not least because a true level playing field for business could not be fully realised without them. 'One market one money' became a Commission catchphrase in this period. At the European Council in Hanover in June 1988, Commission President Jacques Delors was asked to chair a committee to examine the practical measures needed to achieve economic and monetary union (EMU). The Committee reported in April 1989 in favour of a three-stage transition to EMU. The European Council in Madrid in June 1989 agreed that stage 1 would commence on 1 July 1990. In December 1989, the European Council in Strasbourg agreed that an intergovernmental conference (IGC) would outline the next two stages. At this meeting all member states except the UK adopted the 'Social Charter', in order to develop a 'social space' to match the 'economic space' being created by the SEM. The European Council in Dublin in June 1990 agreed to convene an IGC on EMU in December.

Despite the fact that the SEM programme provided an important impetus for the agreements reached at Maastricht, spillover theory provides only a partial explanation of the events leading to the TEU. Spillover is by no means an inevitable consequence of integration activity. Nor can spillover theory fully explain the peculiar form and content of the TEU. Other possible influences must also therefore be examined. External events are one obvious source of influence. The crumbling of communism in Eastern Europe and the crisis in the Gulf gave added urgency to the need for greater co-operation in the fields of foreign and security policy. The end of the cold war opened up a debate on defence issues, focused on the future of NATO and the Western European Union (WEU). German reunification altered the power balance within the Community, forcing urgent consideration of how potential problems arising from Germany's additional weight could best be dealt with.

The development of the TEU also demonstrates the pivotal role of governments as accelerators and decelerators of integration. A proposal jointly formulated by President Mitterrand and Chancellor Kohl for political union was discussed at the special European Council in Dublin in April 1990. The proposal sought a reduction in the democratic deficit, improved institutional efficiency and the development of a common foreign and security policy (CFSP), all to come into force on the same day as the completion of the SEM. It became clear that Kohl in particular was keen to link the goals of monetary union and political union. The Mitterrand–Kohl proposal did not meet with the approval of the UK or Portugal and the decision was postponed until the next European Council in Dublin in June. Discussions at the June summit exposed wide divisions on what political union would mean. Whereas

Mitterrand stated that the Union should have a 'federal finality', Mrs Thatcher favoured a 'Europe of states' model quite at variance with federalist schemes for European Union. At the summit Thatcher expressed strong opposition to political union initiatives. Nevertheless, the Dublin summit in June 1990 approved a decision to establish an intergovernmental conference on European political union (EPU) to run in parallel with the EMU conference. It should be noted that these were *intergovernmental* conferences, meaning that neither the EP nor the Commission were full participants in the discussions (although the Commission was a *de facto* participant, without voting rights, and the EP was allowed to make its views known).

Far less preparatory work had been done on EPU than on EMU. The Commission produced an opinion on political union in October 1990, which advocated the creation of European Union leading to 'a federal type organisation', to prevent the Community from degenerating into a 'mere free trade area'. It favoured many of the ideas presented in the Mitterrand–Kohl proposals. In this period, the issue of the institutional architecture of a future Union focused on two alternative models, known as the 'temple' and 'tree' structures. The temple would divide the Union into separate pillars, some of which would be the domain of governments. The tree would give the Union a single, integrated structure. Like a tree it would form an organic unity, with a trunk and various branches. The tree is generally regarded as the more supranationalist option, because unlike the temple it does not restrict or exclude the involvement of Community institutions in key policy areas (notably foreign and security policy and justice and home affairs). It is hardly surprising therefore that the Commission's opinion favoured a tree structure. The IGCs on EMU and EPU opened at the European Council in Rome in December 1990. The European Council asked the conference on EPU to focus on five areas: democratic legitimacy; foreign and security policy; European citizenship; extension and strengthening of Community action; and Community effectiveness and efficiency.

In 1991, the six-month Council presidency was held first by Luxembourg and then by the Netherlands. The Luxembourg presidency produced a draft treaty on political union in June. This was expected to form the basis for a final draft, to be signed in Maastricht in December. The Luxembourg presidency favoured a temple structure, which was disliked by the Commission and parliament and also by some governments. The initial draft favoured giving the EP powers of 'co-decision' with the Council in some policy areas. Some countries, notably Germany, Belgium, the Netherlands, Luxembourg and Italy, wanted an even stronger role for the EP. France strongly supported monetary union but was lukewarm about political union. The four poorest members pushed for stronger policies on economic and social cohesion (that is, policies to narrow the disparity in wealth between rich and poor regions and countries). A reference to the Union's 'federal vocation' was inserted into the draft at the suggestion of the Commission.

The Dutch presidency put forward its own ideas, in a 96-page 'federalist' document. It favoured a tree structure and considerably enhanced powers for the EP. These federalist proposals were rejected by ten EC foreign ministers in September 1991 (only Holland and Belgium supported them) in favour of a draft based on the less radical Luxembourg proposals. To further complicate matters, other member states also put forward alternative proposals on specific issues. For example, there were British–Italian and Franco–German proposals on defence, reflecting a difference in emphasis between 'Euro–Atlanticist' and 'Europeanist' approaches to European defence structures. Given these conflicting pressures, it is perhaps surprising that a treaty was agreed at all.

The treaty covers so many subjects and is so vague and contradictory in places as to be open to various interpretations. The intergovernmental bargaining models of decisionmaking referred to in Chapter 2 may shed light on why the treaty lacks clarity. Each government came to Maastricht with a shopping list of requirements. No government wanted to be blamed for a breakdown in negotiations. However, each had to keep an eye on its domestic audience (meaning domestic political elites rather than the general public). A deal was only made possible by fudging some contentious issues through liberal use of vague and equivocal formulae, by watering down parts of the draft text and by conceding opt-outs to the UK on monetary union and the Social Chapter.

Although John Major, who had replaced Mrs Thatcher in October 1990, was viewed as more 'pro-European' than his predecessor, this proved to be more a matter of style than of substance. He was resolutely opposed to a single currency and to the Social Chapter, both of which were on the Maastricht agenda. The British opt-outs negotiated on these subjects showed that member states were prepared to countenance a multispeed Europe in preference to a breakdown of negotiations. Major also threatened to reject the draft unless references to federalism were removed. The reference to the Union's federal goal was dropped on the first day of the Maastricht summit.

● STRUCTURE AND CONTENTS

○ Structure

The treaty agreed at Maastricht comprised seven titles, 17 protocols and 33 declarations. The protocols were appended to and formed part of the treaty and were justiciable by the European Court of Justice (ECJ). The most important of these were on social policy, operational aspects of EMU and economic and social cohesion. The 33 declarations covered a broad range of subjects. For example, there were declarations on the role of national parliaments in the European Union and on the right to access to information. The declarations were appended to, but separate from the treaty and had no legal force. They were nevertheless part of its context and could be used by the ECJ for interpretation. The titles, forming the main body of the text, are outlined in Table 3.1.

Table 3.1 The Seven TEU Titles
(Prior to the Treaty of Amsterdam's (ToA's) Amendments)

Title I: Articles A–F. Common Provisions. Articles A and B set out the Union's tasks and objectives. Articles C, D and E dealt with the institutional framework and the powers of the major EU institutions. Article F committed the Union to respect for the national identities of member states and of fundamental rights.

Title II: Article G. Provisions amending the EEC Treaty, with a view to establishing the European Community. The term European Economic Community was replaced by European Community. This title covered the broadest range of subjects (indeed, it constituted a 'treaty within a treaty'). It contained 238 articles, including provisions on the powers of Community institutions and the Community's policy responsibilities. Economic and monetary policy is covered under this title.

Title III: Article H. Provisions relating to the ECSC.

Title IV: Article I. Provisions amending the European Atomic Energy Community (Euratom).

Title V: Articles J–J11. Provisions on CFSP.

Title VI: Articles K–K9. Provisions on co-operation in the fields of justice and home affairs (intergovernmental co-operation on immigration, asylum, drugs, terrorism, fraud, civil and criminal matters).

Title VII: Articles L–S. Final provisions, dealing with various institutional and legal issues. Article O stated that any European state may apply to join the Union.

○ Contents

Article A of the treaty's common provisions established a Union and stated that the treaty 'marks a new stage in the process of creating an ever closer union among the peoples of Europe, in which decisions are taken as closely as possible to the citizen'. The term Union was only vaguely described. The Union is not a distinct organisation. With the exception of the European Council, it has no institutions of its own and no legal powers. Nor does it replace the EC: indeed, Article A stated that the Union was founded on the European Communities (the three Communities are often collectively referred to as the 'European Community'). Most of the treaty deals with matters falling within the ambit of the Communities. Article B set out the Union's objectives, namely:

- to promote economic and social progress which is balanced and sustainable, in particular through the creation of an area without internal frontiers, through the strengthening of economic and social cohesion and through the establishment of economic and monetary union, ultimately including a single currency in accordance with the Treaty's provisions;
- to assert its identity on the international scene, in particular through the implementation of a common foreign and security policy, including the eventual framing of a common defence policy, which might in time lead to a common defence;
- to strengthen the protection of the rights and interests of the nationals of member states through the introduction of a citizenship of the Union;
- to develop close co-operation on justice and home affairs;
- to maintain in full the *acquis communautaire* (that is, Community treaties, legislation, declarations, resolutions, and international agreements) and build on it.

Most of Title II deals with Community policies: for example, economic and monetary policy, social policy, education, vocational training, culture, public health, consumer protection, trans-European networks, industry, economic and social cohesion, the environment, research and technological development (RTD) and development co-operation. These references collectively constituted a significant extension of the Community's policy responsibilities. The provisions and protocols on EMU arguably constituted the most important single element of the treaty and are examined in Chapter 11. Article 8 of Title II stated that all citizens of member states were citizens of the Union and outlined the rights pertaining to this citizenship.

The treaty also included important institutional provisions, reflecting the desire to tackle the democratic deficit and to enhance the effectiveness and efficiency of the Union. It gave the EP more power, although far less than it would have liked. Thus the EP was given powers of co-decision with the Council in some policy areas. The range of subjects covered by the co-operation procedure was extended. The 'assent procedure', giving the EP powers of veto on some decisions, was also extended. The EP was also given the power to veto the appointment of the Commission and the power to appoint an ombudsman. The use of qualified majority voting in the Council was extended. The ECJ was given power to impose fines on states which had not complied with its earlier judgments. The Court of Auditors was upgraded to a full Community institution. The treaty established a Committee of the Regions. These institutional changes are discussed in detail in Chapter 5. The main elements of the treaty are outlined in Table 3.2.

Table 3.2 The Main Elements of the TEU Agreed at Maastricht

- it created a European Union;
- it established 'European citizenship';
- it established a three-pillared structure for the Union;
- it set out a procedure for economic and monetary union;
- it set out procedures for intergovernmental co-operation in foreign and security policy and in justice and home affairs;
- it deepened and extended the EC's policy portfolio (in some cases this involved the deepening of existing policy and in other cases new policy areas are introduced);
- it established the principle of subsidiarity;
- the European Council was identified as responsible for providing the Union with the impetus for development and for defining the Union's general political guidelines;
- it extended the use of qualified majority voting in the Council;
- it increased the powers of the European Parliament;
- it created a Committee of the Regions;
- it upgraded the Court of Auditors to a full Community institution.

○ Subsidiarity

The treaty sought to clarify the boundaries between national and Community levels of responsibility for policy, by stating that Community action will be in accordance with the principle of 'subsidiarity'. Subsidiarity is now widely regarded as one of the most important of all principles relating to European integration. It is not mentioned in any of the previous treaties, although there is one implicit reference to it in the SEA (Article 11). It was first given prominence in the preamble to the EP's Draft Treaty on European Union in 1984. It was defined in the following way in the TEU:

> The Community shall act within the limits of the powers conferred upon it by this Treaty and of the objectives assigned to it therein. In areas which do not fall within its exclusive competence, the Community shall take action, in accordance with the principle of subsidiarity, only if and in so far as the objectives of the proposed action cannot be sufficiently achieved by the member States and can therefore, by reason of the scale or effects of the proposed action, be better achieved by the Community. Any action by the Community shall not go beyond what is necessary to achieve the objectives of this Treaty (Article 3b, now Article 5, EC Treaty).

Each of the above three sentences has been subject to intense scrutiny. The definition is of crucial importance because of its implications for the distribution of power between regional, national and European levels of government. It is a broad principle rather than a clear guide and is open to many different interpretations. A common interpretation is that decisions should be taken at the lowest possible level (that is national, regional or local) rather than at 'European' level, unless there is good reason to do otherwise – that is, it involves the search for the best level of government. It could mean that the EU should not have its finger in every pie and should only do what states cannot do well for themselves. UK Prime Minister John Major seized on the principle as a kind of talisman against 'federalism', viewing it as moving decisionmaking back towards the member states in areas where Union law need not, and should not apply. But it has also been interpreted as fitting into the logic of federalism, by allowing for division of responsibilities between levels of government (European, national and regional). Indeed, it has been argued that it only makes sense within a federal context.

But some federalists view the principle with suspicion, fearing that it might be used by national governments as a fig leaf to avoid their commitments. The principle could run counter to the Union's attempts to introduce common standards in many policy areas. Arguably, many EU policies, such as the Common Agricultural Policy (CAP) and social and regional policy, conflict directly with the principle. The European Council in Lisbon in June 1992 favoured the strict application of the subsidiarity principle to legislation and institutions and commissioned studies of how this could be achieved. From September 1992, the Commission implemented a new procedure for reviewing proposals on the grounds of subsidiarity. The Commission's paper on subsidiarity in October 1992 stated that 'a first consequence of the subsidiarity principle is that national powers are the rule and the Community's the exception'. The special European Council in Birmingham in November 1992 called for 'subsidiarity tests' when legislation was being prepared. This led to a set of guidelines, agreed at the European Council in Edinburgh in December 1992, which require the following questions to be put in relation to any proposal:

- Can the Community act? Does it have a legal basis to do so?
- Should the Community act? Can it be achieved by member states, or will it be better achieved by the Community?
- How much should the Community do? Is it using the lightest possible form of legislation, leaving as much as possible for national decision?

The European Council in Edinburgh also agreed procedures to ensure that these questions were addressed at all stages of the Community's legislative process. Thus all Commission proposals where appropriate would include a subsidiarity declaration and all proposals would be examined by the Council in relation to Article 3b. Any member state could insist that proposals which raise subsidiarity issues be put on a Council agenda. An interinstitutional agreement on subsidiarity was reached between the Council, the EP and

Commission in October 1993. The institutions undertook to ensure that they applied 'subsidiarity checks' to their internal procedures. The Commission was required to include a subsidiarity justification in its explanatory memoranda on draft legislation and to produce an annual report on compliance with subsidiarity. The Council and parliament were required to justify amendments to Commission proposals which involved more intensive or extensive Community intervention. Despite these developments, the mechanism for allocating responsibilities between the European and the national (or regional) levels remained rather unclear and the issue of subsidiarity was re-examined by the 1996/97 IGC. The ToA includes an attempt to define subsidiarity in more detail (see next chapter).

⊙ The Intergovernmental Pillars

Titles V and VI created two intergovernmental pillars, excluding the subjects of these pillars from the EC's normal decisionmaking processes. Title V stated that general foreign and security policy guidelines would be decided by the European Council. The Council of the European Union would then define and implement the CFSP on the basis of these general guidelines. The Council would take common positions on issues and would decide matters to be taken by joint action by unanimous vote, although it could decide to use qualified majority voting (QMV) in respect of decisions on implementation. The Commission may refer questions on CFSP to the Council. The EP's role was confined to the rights to be consulted, to make recommendations and to be kept regularly informed. The CFSP pillar was outside the jurisdiction of the ECJ. Article J.4 stated that the eventual framing of a common defence policy 'might in time lead to a common defence'. The Western European Union was to be developed as the defence component of the Union, working in co-operation with NATO. Table 3.3 outlines the contents of the JHA pillar.

Table 3.3 The JHA Pillar: 'Matters of Common Interest'

- asylum policy;
- rules governing the crossing of external borders of the member states;
- immigration policy;
- combating drug addiction;
- combating fraud on an international scale;
- judicial co-operation in civil matters;
- judicial co-operation in criminal matters;
- customs co-operation;
- police co-operation to prevent and combat terrorism, drug trafficking and other serious forms of international crime.

Title VI on co-operation in the fields of justice and home affairs (JHA) identified nine matters which members were to regard as of common interest (Table 3.3). Member states were required to inform and consult one another within the Council on these areas with a view to adoption of joint positions and joint actions. Article K.4 established a co-ordinating committee of senior officials (the 'K.4' Committee, now the Article 36 committee) to co-ordinate and prepare the Council's work and to give opinions on JHA matters.

○ Social Policy

Because of British objections to the Social Charter, the seven social policy articles formed a special protocol. Eleven of the 12 member states stated their wish to implement the Charter on the basis of the *acquis communautaire* (using Community institutions to make policy in the areas covered by the protocol). The UK did not take part in deliberations or decisions on these areas. But the social provisions contained in the EC Treaty were still applicable to the UK. The TEU therefore caused two legal bases to coexist: the social provisions of the EC Treaty applicable to all member states and the protocol on social policy under which acts could be adopted for all member states excluding the UK (this situation was ended by the ToA, which incorporated the protocol into the EC Treaty).

● RATIFICATION AND IMPLEMENTATION

○ A Rough Passage

The treaty was expected to come into force on 1 January 1993 (following ratification by national parliaments and by the EP) but its passage into law proved unexpectedly troublesome. With hindsight, the architects of the treaty have only themselves to blame, because they had made little effort to engage ordinary citizens in the debates concerning 'European Union'. Public opinion polls exposed widespread ignorance about the content of the treaty. Moreover, these polls also showed that a substantial proportion of European citizens were at best lukewarm about the goal of European Union.

The 'temple' structure added additional layers of complexity on to an already highly complex institutional structure. The vagueness and, in places, contradictory nature of the Treaty meant that virtually anything could be read into it. It could be interpreted as either a defeat or victory for Euro-federalist ideals. In a phrase widely attributed to John Major (who subsequently denied saying it) a UK government spokesman described the outcome of the summit as 'game, set and match for Britain' (*The Times*, 11 December 1991), because it supposedly halted the centralising trend. Many Conservative MPs came to different conclusions. An increasingly vocal and well-organised opposition to Maastricht emerged in several member states. Three countries (Denmark, France and Ireland) held referenda on the treaty. The referenda exposed an unexpected degree of public opposition to the treaty. The treaty was narrowly rejected in a Danish referendum in June 1992 (50.7% voted against it). The votes in Ireland in June (69% in favour) in France in September (only 51.05% in favour) showed the extent of hostility to the treaty. In debates on the referenda, issues directly relating to the treaty became mixed up with other issues, such as abortion in Ireland and CAP reform in France.

The credibility of the treaty was also undermined by internal and external events. The crises in the Exchange Rate Mechanism (ERM) from the summer of 1992 onwards jeopardised the prospects of rapid progress towards monetary union. There were increasing doubts in Germany as to whether Germans really wanted to exchange their solid Deutschmark for the untried ECU. The inability of the member states to develop a coherent and effective strategy to cope with the civil war in ex-Yugoslavia raised grave doubts about the feasibility of the common foreign and security policy. The Danish government sought to make the treaty more palatable to the Danish electorate by seeking clarification of certain issues (that it could opt out of the final stage of monetary union; that it was not committed to participation in a common defence policy and that Union citizenship did not replace Danish citizenship). These assurances were given at the European Council in Edinburgh in December 1992, without need for a treaty revision. The second Danish referendum held in May 1993, resulted in a 'yes' vote of 56.8%.

In the UK, the treaty was not a major issue in the April 1992 General Election and was supported by the three main parties (the Labour and Liberal Democratic parties criticised the government for not accepting the full Maastricht package). After the election, the UK government's presentation of the treaty as a victory for the intergovernmentalist, decentralising tendency came under attack from a powerful backbench group of Eurosceptic Conservative MPs, who fought a long rearguard action against ratification. The UK government finally ratified the treaty in August 1993. It was ratified by Germany in October 1993, following a ruling by the German Constitutional Court. The treaty came into force on 1 November 1993. Even after ratification, the future of the treaty (if viewed as a blueprint for the Union's development) remained in doubt: key policy provisions, for example in relation to EMU, social policy, CFSP and justice and home affairs, proved far more difficult to put into practice than was envisaged at Maastricht. In many respects, the treaty was a rather insular document, which gave insufficient weight to current international circumstances (in particular, to the impact of the end of the cold war upon the structure of Europe).

● EVALUATION AND INTERPRETATION

○ The Case For and Against the TEU Agreed At Maastricht

The main arguments in this debate are summarised in Table 3.4.

Table 3.4 The Case For and Against the TEU Agreed at Maastricht

For
- it constituted a logical stage on the road to European integration;
- it set out a comprehensive approach to European integration;
- it laid a foundation for economic and monetary union;
- it narrowed the EU's democratic deficit, giving more power to the EP;
- it contained many benefits for ordinary people, such as extra voting rights and additional social, diplomatic and consular protection;
- co-ordinated action is required to tackle issues of mutual concern to member states (such as economic policy, crime and foreign policy);
- it complemented the SEM, by seeking to remove barriers to cross-border trade not dealt with by SEM provisions (notably currency differences);
- without further development, the integration process would stall (bicyclists who stop peddling fall off).

Against
- it involved a huge loss of national sovereignty, removing major areas of policy from the control of national governments and parliaments;
- it was a 'ragbag' of vague commitments and compromises. Virtually anything could be read into it;
- it was a treaty too soon. The SEM process was by no means finished. Enlargement should have taken priority over further deepening;
- monetary union was by no means a necessary requirement of European integration;
- it was a treaty too far: as the three referenda and subsequent opinion polls have shown, the people of Europe do not want it;
- public knowledge and understanding of the treaty remains low:
- there is no evidence that the extension of the EP's powers has narrowed the 'democratic deficit';
- it was unworkable: many provisions were too ambitious and proved very difficult to achieve;
- deeper European integration has made it more difficult for other European countries to enter the Union;
- the fact that two subsequent treaties have been negotiated proves its shortcomings.

◯ Was the TEU Agreed at Maastricht a Federal Treaty?

The Maastricht TEU was open to too many interpretations for this question to be definitively answered. It was easy to seize on a particular statement in the Treaty in order to justify the worst fears of the anti-federalists. Neither the word 'federal' nor the word 'supranational' occurred anywhere in the Treaty. Prior to the Maastricht summit, the Commission published a discussion paper which favoured the creation of a Union 'of a federal type'. However, the word 'federalism' was deliberately omitted from the Treaty, at British insistence. The general thrust of the treaty was towards closer integration (perhaps 'federalising' rather than 'federalist'): its provisions have given the Union some of the major features of a federal state, such as a common currency, a central bank and a common foreign and security policy. The EP's report on the Treaty viewed it as 'a step forward, albeit an insufficient one, on the road to a European Union of federal type' (EP, 1992, p. 25).

Conversely, the Treaty could be viewed as an essentially *inter-governmentalist* treaty, which kept power firmly in the hands of national governments. The UK government presented the TEU as constituting a defeat for Euro-federalist ideas, because it confirmed the role of governments in Union decisionmaking processes and affirmed the 'anti-centralising' doctrine of subsidiarity. The key policy areas of foreign and security policy and justice and home affairs remained largely outside Community decisionmaking structures. Union citizenship was both vaguely defined and limited. British Eurosceptics, however, remained unconvinced and viewed it as a federalist document which, if fully implemented. would reduce the sovereignties of member states to mere ciphers. The treaty could also be interpreted as providing a blueprint for a multispeed Europe, in that it effectively sanctioned opt-outs on EMU, defence and aspects of social policy.

● CONCLUSION

Although the TEU was never meant to be the last word on the subject of Union reform, the fact that two other Union treaties were negotiated within a decade of the Maastricht agreement is testimony to its many flaws. The TEU was the first Union treaty to contain an article requiring certain of its provisions to be revised (Article N (2)). This requirement was initially viewed as a fine-tuning clause rather than as a means to a further major revision of the treaties. However, throughout the 1990s, the issue of enlargement loomed ever more important, meaning that two IGCs launched in this decade were to have a somewhat different focus to those which led to Maastricht. Of the three Union treaties negotiated since 1991 (that is, of Maastricht, Amsterdam and

Nice), the former is arguably the most significant in terms of its impact on the Union: not only did it provide the blueprint for monetary union, but also introduced many institutional and policy changes which were to be further developed by the subsequent treaties.

Before moving on to the next chapter, it should be remembered that the ToA not only made changes to the substance of the TEU but also renumbered its provisions. The ToA also renumbered the provisions in the EC Treaty (see pp. xxvii–xxviii and p. 73). In this chapter, which has examined the aims, structure and content of the TEU agreed at Maastricht, for the sake of clarity reference has been made to the original numbering. Table 3.5 provides an insight into the 'equivalences' between the previous and new numbering. For the reason mentioned on p. xxvii, the new numbers do not correspond in every case to the previous numbers.

Table 3.5 The Renumbering of the TEU's Provisions in the ToA

Previous numbering		New numbering	
Title 1	Articles A–F.1	Title 1	Articles 1–7
Title II	Article G	Title II	Article 8
Title III	Article H	Title III	Article 9
Title IV	Article I	Title IV	Article 10
Title V	Articles J.1–J.18	Title V	Articles 11–28
Title VI*	Articles K.1–K.14	Title VI	Articles 29–42
Title VIa+	Articles K.15–K.17	Title VII	Articles 43–45
Title VII	Articles L–S	Title VIII	Articles 46–53

Note: *: restructured by ToA; +: introduced by ToA.

FURTHER READING

Baum, M. (1996), *An Imperfect Union: The Maastricht Treaty and the New Politics of European Integration*, Westview Press. Boulder, Colo.

Begg, D. (1993), *Making Sense of Subsidiarity*, Centre for Economic Policy Research, London.

Church, C.H. and Phinnemore, D. (1994), *European Union and European Community*, Harvester Wheatsheaf, London.

Commission (1992), *Treaty on European Union,* Brussels.

European Parliament (1992), *Maastricht: The Position of the EP*, Luxembourg.

Dyson, K. and Featherstone, K. (1999), *The Road to Maastricht: Negotiating Economic and Monetary Union*, Oxford University Press, Oxford.

Laursen, F. and Vanhoonacker, S. (eds) (1992), *The Intergovernmental Conference on Political Union*, Martinus Nijhoff, Dordrecht.

Lynch, P., Neuwahl, N. and Rees, W. (eds) (2000), *Reforming the European Union: From Maastricht to Amsterdam*, Pearson Education, London.

Monar, J. et al. (1993), *The Maastricht Treaty on European Union*, European Interuniversity Press, Brussels.

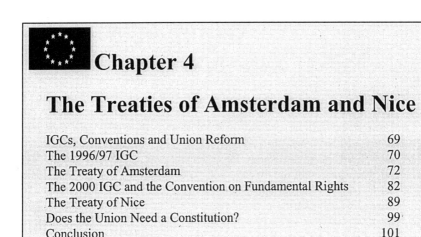

Chapter 4

The Treaties of Amsterdam and Nice

● IGCS, CONVENTIONS AND UNION REFORM

Within a decade of the signing of the Treaty on European Union (TEU), two further Union treaties (of Amsterdam and Nice) were negotiated. All three treaties were preceded by intergovernmental conferences (IGCs). IGCs are formal mechanisms for preparing or revising EU treaties. Use of IGCs as vehicles for the development of the Union indicates two things: firstly, the determination of the governments of member states to control the process of treaty change (thereby in practice relegating the Commission, the European Parliament (EP) and other Union institutions to the sidelines); and secondly, the preference for piecemeal change rather than for a once and for all reform. Since the Union's formation, there have been seven IGCs. The IGC launched in 2000 was the fourth within a decade, which suggests that the pace of Union reform is increasing (see Table 4.1). In December 2000, the Nice European Council agreed that another IGC will be launched in 2004 in order to examine the future of the EU, with particular reference to constitutional issues.

Table 4.1 Intergovernmental Conferences

Dates	Main Subjects	Results
1950–51	Coal and steel community	ECSC Treaty
1955–57	Trade/agriculture/atomic energy	EEC and Euratom Treaties
1985	Single European Market	Single European Act
1990–91	Economic and monetary union	Treaty on EU
1990–91	Political union	Treaty on EU
1996–97	Institutional and policy reform	Treaty of Amsterdam
2000	Enlargement-related institutional reform	Treaty of Nice
2004	The future of the EU	

The increased frequency of IGCs also indicates the inability of member states to agree on a definitive blueprint for the Union's institutional arrangements, procedures and policies and of a tendency for difficult issues to be shelved for reconsideration at a later date. Moreover, in the spring of 2000, the European Council also launched a 'convention' to run parallel with IGC 2000, with the task of drafting a Charter of Fundamental Rights for the Union. IGC 2000 and the convention were described as two 'reform trains' heading towards the same destination, that is, the Nice European Council in December 2000, at which a new Union treaty was to be negotiated. The principal difference between an IGC and a convention is that the latter is a more inclusive body (comprising representatives from Union institutions and national parliaments as well as from the governments of member states). But the convention is also a less authoritative body than an IGC, because ultimately the governments of member states negotiate Union treaties. It is no surprise that those of a federalist persuasion would prefer the convention rather than the IGC to be the main vehicle for constitutional change in the Union. However, as was clearly shown by the rampant intergovernmentalism of the Nice summit in December 2000, the governments of most member states have no intention of relinquishing control of this process.

● THE 1996/97 IGC

Every IGC takes place against a background of domestic and international events. The 1996/97 IGC took place when a large group of countries had applied for EU membership; when fighting in the Balkans exposed the weaknesses of the Union as an international actor; when unemployment in the Union remained unacceptably high, and when several member states were experiencing major influxes of refugees and asylum seekers. The chastening experience of the Maastricht ratification process was also fresh in the minds of those responsible for the IGC. There was no desire for an exercise on the scale of Maastricht. Moreover, little effort had been made during the IGCs preceding Maastricht to keep the public informed about the reform process, let alone to canvass public opinion on reform.

The 1996/97 IGC was not only more widely publicised than previous IGCs, but was also more inclusive, in that a wide variety of institutions and groups were invited to put forward their views on reform. It was the first IGC to formally involve the EP (two Members of the European Parliament (MEPs) served as non-voting members). It therefore resulted in a wider debate concerning the EU's future than took place prior to Maastricht (although this debate hardly engaged ordinary EU citizens). The TEU required an IGC to be convened in order to examine a range of specific provisions – for example, in relation to civil protection, energy, tourism, common foreign and security policy (CFSP), justice and home affairs (JHA), the powers of the EP and the scope of the co-decision procedure. Other topics were later added to the list by the European Council, so that the IGC considered a much broader range of subjects than was originally envisaged. In December 1993, the Brussels European Council agreed that the IGC would consider many specific institutional reform issues, including the legislative role of the EP, the number of commissioners and the weighting of votes in the Council. The wider brief of the IGC was confirmed by the European Councils held in Corfu (June 1994) and in Essen (December 1994). The Essen summit agreed on the formation of a *Reflection Group* to prepare for the 1996 IGC. The summit instructed the Group to consider the Union's options in the light of future enlargement and improvements to institutional efficiency. The Group, chaired by the Spanish minister Carlos Westendorp, commenced its work in June 1995. It had 18 members (representatives of the foreign ministers of each member state, a Commission representative plus two MEPs). The Group's report, published in December 1995, provided the basis for the IGC's mandate, agreed at the Turin European Council in March 1996. The three principal themes of the mandate were: to consider how the Union could be brought closer to its citizens; to examine how the Union institutions could be made more democratic and efficient, in the context of future enlargement; to examine how the Union's capacity for external action could be strengthened.

This meant a wide-ranging review of the functioning of the Union, although it excluded economic and monetary union (EMU), which had been thoroughly dealt with in the TEU. The first theme embraced consideration of specific policies directly affecting EU citizens, such as employment, environmental and consumer protection, visa asylum and immigration and so on; the second focused on legislative procedures and institutional powers; the third focused on the common foreign policy and the coherence of the Community's external economic relations. The deliberations of the IGC exposed deep divisions between member states, and also between the institutions, on a wide range of reform issues. Some member states were keen to pursue reforms which would lead to a major deepening of EU integration, whereas others resisted this. Each EU country had its shopping list of concerns for consideration by the IGC. For example, Germany was concerned to pursue common policies on asylum and immigration. Countries in the Mediterranean sought to strengthen the EU's role in tourism. Nordic countries sought a stronger environmental policy. Most governments sought some kind of formal commitment to employment generation, with the newly elected French socialist government being the most enthusiastic. Some favoured stronger integration in foreign policy, whereas others were at best lukewarm about a stronger CFSP. Germany, the Benelux countries and Italy favoured an extension of qualified majority voting (QMV) and greater powers for the EP. France proposed a redistribution of Council votes, reduction of the number of commissioners and a greater role for national parliaments. The diversity of opinion on many issues was so great that several major questions relating to institutional reform had to be shelved, leading to a provision in the Treaty of Amsterdam (ToA) for a new IGC to be convened prior to the next enlargement. Despite these differences, all EU governments were keen to avoid a breakdown of negotiations and agreement on a new treaty was reached at the Amsterdam European Council in June 1997. Ratification by member states was achieved either through a referendum (in the case of Denmark and Ireland) or through a parliamentary vote. The treaty was fully ratified by March 1999 and came into force the following May.

● THE TREATY OF AMSTERDAM

○ A Snapshot of the Treaty

● **Objectives.** Because the ToA lacks a grand theme (unlike for example the TEU, which set out a blueprint for EMU) it is difficult to explain its purpose in a nutshell. Broadly speaking, it is about rectifying some of the perceived deficiencies of the TEU and about adapting the Union's institutions and policies to cope with a broad range of pressing problems and issues (for example, enlargement, migration and cross-border crime, unemployment, the Union's capacity to take decisions, differences between member states regarding the pace of integration, the relationship between the Union and its citizens and the Union's capacity for external action).
● **Structure and Key Elements.** The ToA essentially consists of revisions to four treaties, that is, the TEU, the European Community (EC) Treaty, the European Coal and Steel Community (ECSC) Treaty and the Euratom Treaty. It is not therefore separate from earlier treaties. It includes amendments to the existing treaties set out in 15 articles plus 13 protocols and 59 declarations (51 adopted by all, and eight by some, member states). The articles are divided into three parts: part 1 (Articles 1–5) concern major amendments to the TEU and EC treaties incorporated into the text of these treaties; part 2 (Articles 6–11) is concerned with simplification of the treaties; part 3 (Articles 12–15) consists of general and final provisions.

The new treaty deletes more than 56 obsolete articles from the treaties and renumbers the rest. It changes the name and substantially alters the content of Title VI of the TEU (that is, the 'third pillar') and adds a new title on Closer Co-operation (Title VII) into this treaty. The ToA seeks to simplify and consolidate the treaties. There is a difference between simplification and consolidation. *Simplification* means deleting lapsed provisions and as a consequence adapting certain other provisions. *Consolidation* refers to an attempt to rationalise the treaties into a coherent whole. The articles, titles and sections of the TEU and the EC are renumbered, in accordance with a table of equivalencies set out in an annex to the ToA. The ToA brought the ECSC and Atomic Energy treaties in line with the EC Treaty. A declaration appended to the treaty states that the work begun on consolidation would continue, with the aim of drafting a consolidation of all relevant treaties. Most readers of the ToA are likely to form the view that the aim of simplification has by no means been achieved. The ToA is not a tidy or user-friendly document. It comprises amendments to existing treaties rather than a treaty in its own right and is likely to be confusing to those unfamiliar with the format, content and language of the earlier EU treaties. The structure and key elements of the treaty are shown in Tables 4.2 and 4.3.

Table 4.2 The TEU Titles, as Amended by the ToA

		Articles
Title I	Common Provisions	1–7
Title II	European Community Treaty	8
Title III	European Coal and Steel Community Treaty	9
Title IV	European Atomic Energy Community Treaty	10
Title V	Common Foreign and Security Policy	11–28
Title VI	Police and Judicial Co-operation in Criminal Matters	29–42
Title VII	Closer Co-operation	43–45
Title VIII	Final Provisions	46–53

Table 4.3 Key Elements of the ToA

- it introduces some institutional reforms (e.g. extension of QMV; extension and reform of co-decision; clarification of 'subsidiarity');
- it establishes an 'area of freedom, security and justice';
- it makes major changes to 'justice and home affairs' policy;
- it incorporates the Schengen Agreement into the EU;
- it reforms CFSP, aiming to make it more coherent and effective;
- it incorporates the social protocol into the treaty;
- it introduces a stronger policy on employment;
- it includes stronger provisions on environmental protection;
- it strengthens and extends other policies, such as consumer policy, public health and cultural policy;
- it includes explicit provisions regarding respect for human rights;
- it allows for flexibility in integration;
- it seeks to simplify and consolidate the treaties.

Perhaps the most important elements of the ToA are the shifting of visa, immigration and asylum policy from the third pillar to the first (Community) pillar; the attempt to make CFSP more coherent and effective; the extension of co-decision; the extension of QMV; the incorporation of the Schengen Agreement into the treaty; the incorporation of the Maastricht Social Chapter; and the new chapter on employment. These elements are explained briefly below and in more detail in other chapters of this book.

○ Institutional Reforms in the ToA

• **Decisionmaking.** The main changes to decisionmaking introduced by the ToA were the extension and streamlining of the co-decision procedure (thereby enhancing the role of the EP) and the extension of QMV in the Council (thereby reducing the possibility of national vetoes). The treaty extended the co-decision procedure to 14 existing treaty areas and to eight new responsibilities, meaning that this procedure now covers about 80% of Council decisions. Co-decision is now firmly established as the main legislative procedure. Five years after ratification, the ToA also allows for co-decision to apply to some cross-border asylum issues, such as visas. The ToA also makes important changes to the procedure for co-decision, by enabling proposals to be adopted after a single reading in the EP if certain conditions are met and by imposing time limits on other stages of the procedure (for details, see Chapter 5). The co-operation procedure, under which the EP's powers are weaker, applies now only to four areas of monetary union.

The treaty gives the EP one new power of assent, that is, sanctions in the event of a serious and persistent breach of fundamental rights by a member state. It gives the EP the right to approve the nominee for Commission president (previously, the EP had the right only to be consulted). It also has the right to be consulted on third-pillar intergovernmental co-operation arrangements on justice and home affairs. It introduces more open and clearer communications between the EP and national parliaments. There is now a mandatory six-week consultation time which gives national parliaments the opportunity to review and react to all Commission proposals.

• **Subsidiarity and proportionality.** As was shown in Chapter 3, the TEU's provisions on subsidiarity were open to diverse interpretations and led to various attempts by the Commission to spell out their meaning and practical significance more precisely. It was not surprising, therefore that the 1996/97 IGC revisited the issue of subsidiarity, or that it would be addressed in the ToA. A protocol to the ToA seeks to define authoritatively these principles and how they should be applied. The ToA confirms that the principles must be considered together. 'Proportionality', as defined by the Commission, seeks to ensure that the impact of Union law on national law does not go beyond what is necessary to achieve the objectives of the treaty. The protocol states that each institution is required to ensure that it complies with the principle of subsidiarity when exercising its powers; the principle must respect in full the *acquis communautaire* and the institutional balance; it must not call into question the powers conferred on the European Community by the Treaty, as interpreted by the European Court of Justice (ECJ); for any proposed Community legislation, the reasons on which it is based must be stated, to justify compliance with the principles of subsidiarity and proportionality; for Community action to be justified, the objectives of the action cannot be sufficiently achieved by member states and can therefore be better achieved by the Community; the form of Community action must be as simple as possible, consistent with achievement of the objective and effective enforcement; the Community shall legislate only to the extent necessary; and Community measures should leave as much scope for national decision as possible, consistent with the aims of the measure and treaty requirements.

The protocol also requires the Commission to consult widely before proposing legislation and, wherever appropriate, publish consultation documents; it must justify its proposals with regard to the principle of subsidiarity and explain the financial implications, which must be proportionate to the objective. It also requires the Commission to submit an annual report to the European Council, the EP and the Council on the application these principles. The report is also sent to the Committee of Regions (CoR) and to the Economic and Social Committee (ESC). The protocol also put forward guidelines to be used in examining whether the above conditions were fulfilled, namely: the issue under consideration must have transnational aspects which cannot be satisfactorily regulated by action by member states; actions by member states alone or lack of Union action would conflict with the requirements of the treaty or would otherwise significantly damage member states' interests; and that action at Union level would produce clear benefits compared with action at member state level.

• **Closer co-operation.** The treaty formally sanctions integration initiatives involving groups of member states within the Union framework, although under stringent conditions. The notion of 'closer co-operation' (also known as 'flexible integration', 'enhanced co-operation' or 'reinforced co-operation') was not on the original IGC agenda, but emerged as a result of the desire of several member states to pursue 'vanguard projects', even if not all member states participated. In the 1996/97 IGC there were significant differences concerning how much, and under what conditions such projects should be allowed (see Table 4.4 below for an outline of the main arguments for and against closer co-operation). In December 1995, President Chirac and Chancellor Kohl published a letter stating that they intended to propose the idea of 'reinforced co-operation' to the IGC and that the objection of one member state should not be allowed to impede further integration. The UK argued that such policies should only become Union policies when this is agreed by all. The idea of Europe *à la carte*, whereby individual member states could pick and choose from a comprehensive menu of integration projects, was strongly opposed by the Commission, which nevertheless favoured a form of flexible integration providing it was open to all and compatible with the *acquis communautaire*. The Reflection Group favoured a multi speed approach and temporary 'opt-outs' ('derogations'). The election of a new UK government in May 1997 reduced the conflict between the UK and other member states over flexible integration, although at the IGC the new government insisted that flexibility should require the consent of all member states. This view was reflected in Article 11 of the EC Treaty as revised by the ToA, which included a provision enabling a member state, for important and stated reasons of national policy, to block a vote on closer co-operation (a stipulation subsequently removed by the Treaty of Nice: ToN).

Table 4.4 Arguments For and Against 'Closer Co-operation'

For
• it is a practical solution to the increasing diversity of the Union;
• it is a safety valve to defuse conflicts concerning the pace of integration;
• it allows for groups of states to test specific policies.
Against
• it adds additional layers of complexity onto an already complex Union;
• it renders the Union more difficult to understand;
• it will create resentment by leading to a two-tier Union.

The ToA introduced a framework whereby member states wishing to establish closer co-operation among themselves may make use of the institutions, procedures and mechanisms laid down by the TEU and the EC Treaty, providing the intended co-operation: is aimed at furthering the objectives of the Union and at protecting and serving its interests; respects the principles of the treaties and the Union's single institutional framework; is used as a last resort; concerns a majority of member states; does not affect the *acquis communautaire*; does not affect the competencies, rights, obligations and interests of non-participating states; is open to all member states; and complies with the specific additional criteria laid down in Article 11 of the EC Treaty and Article 40 of the TEU. Article 11 stipulates that the intended co-operation must not concern areas falling within the exclusive competence of the Community; it must not affect Community policies, actions or programmes; it must not concern Union citizenship or discriminate between nationals of member states; it must not constitute a discrimination or a restriction of trade between member states and must not distort the conditions of competition between the latter. It must also remain within the limits of the powers conferred upon the Community by the treaty. Article 40 is concerned with closer co-operation in the fields of police and judicial co-operation There was no provision for closer co-operation in CFSP, although the treaty does provide for 'constructive abstention', which is a form of flexibility. The term 'flexibility' was removed from the treaty signed by member states on 2 October in favour of 'closer co-operation'. The closer co-operation provisions allowed for a multi speed Europe under very stringent conditions, but not a Europe *à la carte.*

Although insertion of 'closer co-operation' provisions in the ToA constituted a victory for those favouring vanguard projects, the provisions were hedged with so many conditions that in some respects it was a hollow victory. It is little wonder therefore that this issue was added to the 2000 IGC agenda or that the ToN revised these provisions (see below).

◯ Changes to Specific Policies

• **An area of freedom, security and justice.** In the mid-1990s, a host of problems involving migration and cross-border crime served to ensure that justice and home affairs issues received high priority in the treaty negotiations. The treaty seeks to transform the Union into an area of freedom, security and justice. It transfers much of the content of the third (Justice and Home Affairs) pillar into the first (Community) pillar. It thus brings issues such as asylum, visas, immigration and controls at external borders under Community rules and procedures, although it stipulates that for a five-year period major legislation in this field has to secure the agreement of all member states. After this time, EU leaders can choose to use QMV for specific measures, providing all member states agree. The Schengen Agreement is incorporated into the framework of the Union.

The third pillar is retained, but is renamed 'Police and Judicial Co-operation in Criminal Matters'. In addition to providing for common action in police and judicial co-operation, the new third pillar includes provisions for common action to combat racism and xenophobia. The boundaries between the Community and the third pillars are also made less distinct, in that the ECJ and the EP are given roles (albeit limited) in the new third pillar. These changes, although significant, are in the nature of interim rather than final solutions. For example, the treaty did not establish a common asylum and immigration policy. Moreover, the Schengen system now straddles both the first and third pillars, which could be a source of considerable confusion. The fuzzier boundaries between the first and third pillars adds an additional layer of complexity onto an already complex Union.

- **The common foreign and security policy (CFSP).** There was widespread agreement that the Maastricht formula for CFSP had not worked well and that changes had to be made to the second pillar. However, there was little enthusiasm for radical CFSP reform among member states and therefore the ToA's changes to the second pillar are largely concerned with making CFSP more effective and consistent. For example, the ToA changes CFSP decisionmaking procedures to allow a member state to abstain without blocking an otherwise unanimous decision; it introduces 'common strategies', to co-ordinate external policies; it seeks to give CFSP a higher profile, through the creation of a 'high representative'; it creates a policy planning and early warning unit (PPEWU), to anticipate and analyse crisis situations; it redefines the EU's CFSP tasks: thus the EU is now able to carry out peacekeeping, humanitarian and rescue tasks and crisis management tasks. The effects of the changes to CFSP could be significant or superficial, depending on the will of member states to make them work. As with the changes made to the third pillar, changes to the second pillar were also interim measures, as the treaty left many issues unresolved. Since ratification of the ToA, there is some evidence of a stronger determination on the part of the EU to develop a more effective CFSP and defence capability, but this could be attributed to other factors, such as the EU's poor performance in the Kosovo conflict rather than to the treaty as such.
- **Social and employment policy.** The treaty incorporates the agreement on social policy which previously applied to all except the UK. It also strengthens the chapter on social policy, particularly with regard to the combating of social exclusion. It adds two other important amendments: the inclusion of non-discrimination and greater equality of men and women at work. The formal abolition of the UK opt-out on social policy was made possible by the election of a Labour government in the UK in May 1997. The removal of the opt-out should at least enhance the coherence of this important field of EU policy. The treaty specifies promotion of high employment as a Union objective, through the co-ordination of the employment policies of the member states and the development of a common strategy for employment. (Article 3, ECT) and establishes a co-ordination process on employment policy at Union level, including the adoption of guidelines for employment and annual assessments of national measures. The employment chapter has been viewed as a counterweight to the heavy emphasis on EMU in the TEU. Again, whether or not it has a significant effect depends to a large degree on the willingness of member states to make it work.
- **Bringing the EU closer to its citizens.** The treaty seeks to make the Union more 'citizen friendly' by, for example giving citizens the right to petition the EP and to apply to the ombudsman, and allowing them to write to any European institution and have a reply in the same language; by allowing

citizens the right to take the European institutions to the ECJ over any action considered a breach of their fundamental rights; and by improving citizens' access to the EP, Council and Commission documents. The ToA stipulates that any citizen of the Union, and those residing or having a registered office in a member state, has a right of access to documents of the EU institutions. The Council, when acting in its legislative capacity, is required to make votes and explanations of vote public. The treaty seeks to clarify the meaning of Union citizenship, by stating explicitly that 'citizenship of the Union shall complement and not replace national citizenship' (Article 17, ECT). Although laudable, in practical terms these changes are hardly earth-shaking. The vast majority of EU citizens remain unaware of these rights and so far it appears doubtful whether they have had much practical effect on the aim of bringing the EU 'closer to the citizen'.

• **Human rights and non-discrimination.** Several factors contributed to the inclusion of specific references to human rights in the TEU as amended by the ToA: for example, the attention given to extensive human rights abuses in the Balkans and the belief that the Union needed to set a good example, not least to applicant countries from Central and Eastern Europe. The treaty states explicitly that the Union is 'founded on the principles of liberty, democracy, respect for human rights and fundamental freedoms, and the rule of law, principles which are common to member states' (Article 6). It adds references to respect for human rights as a criterion for membership of the Union. The statement is particularly relevant to the enlargement process, because no applicant state would be admitted to the Union if it did not observe these principles. Any member state in serious and persistent breach of these principles may be penalised, by having certain of its membership rights, including voting rights, suspended (Article 7). An article on the principle of non-discrimination is introduced, allowing the Union to adopt measures to combat discrimination on grounds of sex, racial or ethnic origin, religion or belief, disability, age or sexual orientation (Article 13). Article 136 of the EC Treaty requires the Union's social policy objectives to be in accordance with the fundamental social rights set out in the 1961 European Social Charter and the Community Charter of the Fundamental Social Rights of Workers (1989).

Again, although undoubtedly laudable, the references to human rights and non-discrimination in the treaty could be little more than moral padding, aimed more at making the Union look virtuous, rather than a serious attempt to deal with discrimination and human rights abuses. But these references were significant in that they reflected a desire to explicitly link human rights considerations to the nature and objectives of the Union. It seems unlikely that the 'Charter of Fundamental Rights', declared at the Nice European Council, would have been possible without these references.

- **Other substantive policies.** The treaty makes changes to many other policies. For example, with regard to the environment, it makes achievement of sustainable development an EU objective Article 2, TEU). Article 6 of the EC Treaty requires environmental protection requirements to be integrated into the definition and implementation of Community policies (known as 'mainstreaming', this requirement also applies to research and technological development). It introduces measures to improve and safeguard human health and clarifies the objective to promote a high level of consumer protection. The extension of co-decision also has implications for specific policies.

○ Evaluation

The ToA was another stage in the continuing process of Union reform. It came into force in the same year that the euro was launched and arguably was overshadowed by the attention given to monetary union. Most ToA reforms are incremental rather than spectacular, but could nevertheless prove to be of crucial importance to the future development of the Union. One way of assessing the impact of the ToA on the Union's institutional structure is to ask: who were the institutional gainers and losers? Overall, the EP was an institutional gainer, in that the treaty extends co-decision (although not as much as the EP had hoped); the ECJ was a gainer, in that its powers are extended in relation to the safeguarding of fundamental rights, asylum and immigration policy and to aspects of police and judicial co-operation in criminal matters; the Court of Auditors also had its competencies increased.

Another way of assessing the ToA is to consider what it left out or failed to do (see Table 4.5). For example, it did not abolish the EU's pillars structure. It did not give the EU a legal personality. Although Italy, Luxembourg, Germany, Austria, the Netherlands and Portugal favoured this proposal, it was not adopted at Amsterdam. The implications of not having a legal personality are: the EU may not act in its own right and can act only through the Community institutions (the EC does have a legal personality); it has no budget of its own, but is dependent on the Community budget. Nor did the treaty integrate the Western European Union (WEU) into the Union, or give the EP more power in CFSP. The fact that another IGC was launched so soon after the ratification of the treaty is indicative of the failure of the ToA to provide comprehensive and definitive answers to the problem of EU reform. Because of disagreements between member states on a host of issues, the ToA reflected a search for a lowest common denominator (a text all could agree on) rather than a search for a 'perfect' solution to the EU's problems. It was also indicative of the EU's habit of shelving difficult questions and of its penchant for hiding disagreements in a fog of vague and ambiguous language. Many contentious issues were therefore sidelined or left for the next IGC.

Table 4.5 Strengths and Weaknesses of the ToA

Strengths

- it gives the EP more power (in particular, by extending co-decision);
- it simplifies legislative procedures;
- it extends the use of QMV in the Council to 14 new cases;
- it improves transparency in decisionmaking;
- it improves communication between the EP and national parliaments;
- it gives the Committee of the Regions greater administrative autonomy;
- it simplifies and consolidates the previous Union treaties;
- it 'Communitarises' asylum and immigration policy;
- it incorporates the Schengen system into the Union;
- it establishes an area of freedom, security and justice within the EU;
- it gives CFSP greater coherence and visibility and may lead to more effective external action;
- it strengthens the Union's commitment to combat unemployment;
- it strengthens social policy;
- it spells out the principle of subsidiarity.
- it allows for groups of states to pursue closer co-operation;
- it includes tougher measures on public health and consumer protection.

Weaknesses

- it lacks a central theme and has no coherence;
- it fudged the issue of institutional reform;
- the pillars structure is maintained;
- co-decision is not applied to all legislative acts;
- assent of the EP is not extended to amendments to treaties;
- it does not give the Union an international legal personality;
- the EP is not given rights of consultation in CFSP;
- it is written in an unclear and frequently ambiguous manner;
- it does not address adequately the implications of Union enlargement;
- it postponed a decision on the issue of the size of the Commission;
- the ECJ's jurisdiction, although extended, remains incomplete;
- the role of the EP in the third pillar remains limited;
- the EP was not granted a right of assent to the treaty;
- the incorporation of Schengen is done in an extremely complicated way;
- CFSP is not incorporated into the Community pillar;
- the Western European Union is not incorporated into the Union;
- no defence or military policy was adopted as part of the Treaty;
- it did not simplify budgetary procedures;
- the fact that another IGC was launched in 2000 proves its shortcomings.

● THE 2000 IGC AND THE CONVENTION ON FUNDAMENTAL RIGHTS

○ The 2000 IGC

A protocol on the institutions attached to the ToA required a new IGC to be convened at least a year before the membership of the EU exceeded 20, in order to carry out a comprehensive review of the composition and functioning of the institutions. Although in some quarters (notably the Commission and parliament) there was enthusiasm for a radical and broad IGC agenda, this enthusiasm was not shared by the majority of member states. Most member states viewed the IGC as primarily a vehicle for dealing with a limited number of institutional questions left over from the 1996/97 IGC and the ToA. But as had been the case with previous IGCs, there were pressures towards 'mission creep' (that is, expansion of the IGC's original agenda). Mission creep pressures included the fallout from the resignation of the Commission; the poor turnout at the EP elections in June 1999; and growing awareness of the magnitude of the institutional implications of the next enlargements.

The urgency of the need for further institutional reform became apparent in March 1999, following the forced resignation of the Commission. The new Commission president, Romano Prodi, vowed to put forward far-reaching reform proposals. In September 1999, Prodi established a 'committee of wise men' led by Jean-Luc Dehaene, to examine the institutional problems which needed to be addressed by the next IGC. The Dehaene Committee presented its report the following month. The Dehaene report called for the IGC to be given an ambitious and radical agenda. It argued that Council decisionmaking was sluggish and that there was lack of co-ordination between Councils. It criticised the performance of the Commission and the lack of impact of the EP upon public opinion. It favoured a major extension of QMV, with parallel extension of the co-decision procedure, and a reassessment of voting weights. It favoured an extension of the powers of the Commission president, for example by giving him a bigger say in the nomination and selection of commissioners and the power to sack individual commissioners. It called for changes to 'closer co-operation' provisions, to make it easier for groups of EU states to pursue deeper integration. It argued that the next IGC should start with a draft treaty on the table and favoured a reorganisation of treaty texts, to avoid constant treaty revisions. It noted that in an enlarged Union, the existing ratification process would become increasingly tortuous. It therefore favoured changing the process by which EU treaty revisions were ratified, so that revisions would not in all cases require the approval of national parliaments. This would be achieved through dividing the treaty into two parts: a basic treaty, which could only be modified through an IGC and ratification by each member state; and secondly, a separate text or texts, which could be modified by the Council, with the assent of the EP. This would reduce the need for constant modifications of the treaties and would make them more readable, understandable and accessible to the public. It also favoured the extension of the Union's defence capabilities. The report received a generally unfavourable reaction from the governments of member states. The Cologne European Council had decided that the next IGC should concentrate on matters left unresolved by the ToA, for example, the Council's voting system and the size of the Commission, that is, a 'minimalist' agenda. Not surprisingly the Dehaene report received a warmer welcome from the Commission and the EP.

In its own proposals for the 2000 IGC (Commission, 2000), the Commission saw merit in the Dehaene report's idea for the treaties to be divided into two parts: the basic texts and implementing texts of less fundamental importance. It favoured the election of some MEPs on Europe-wide lists, to encourage the development of Europe-wide parties and constituencies. It favoured abolition of national vetoes, with the exception of institutional matters, international agreements and tax and social security decisions unrelated to the single market. It suggested two options for the composition of the Commission: firstly, that the number of commissioners should be limited to 20, regardless of the future number of member states, with a rotation system; and secondly, that a Commission should comprise one member from each member state, conditional on a major reorganisation of the Commission. It argued that if groups of states wished to pursue closer co-operation, they should be able to do so with the support of a third of the member states rather than a majority as specified in the ToA. It recommended abolition of the right of a member state to block such co-operation. It also favoured extension of closer co-operation to CSFP in certain circumstances. It favoured the replacement of unanimity by QMV as a general rule and introduction of a double majority voting system, whereby a decision would be adopted if supported by a simple majority of member states and a simple majority of the total population of the EU. It also proposed reforms to the ECJ, CoA and Economic and Social Committee (ESC).

Reform proposals for consideration by the IGC were also to be put forward by other EU institutions, by non-governmental organisations and by the governments of member states. In December 1999, the Helsinki European Council declared that the EP would be closely associated and involved in the work of the conference and that the Council presidency would take steps to ensure that candidate countries were regularly briefed on the progress of discussions and would have the opportunity to put their viewpoints. The Helsinki European Council required the IGC to be convened in February

2000 and to complete its work by December 2000. The IGC opened on 14 February and held nine meetings at ministerial level, 19 at the level of representatives of the preparatory group and three ministerial conclaves. The EP president took part in the ministerial level meetings and attended official and informal meetings of the preparatory group. The Cologne and Helsinki European Councils determined that it would address the following themes:

- the size and composition of the Commission;
- weighting of votes in the Council;
- possible extension of qualified majority voting in the Council;
- other necessary amendments to the treaties in connection with the above issues and in implementing the ToA;
- any other matters that the presidency may propose for the agenda.

At the Feira European Council in June 2000, and again at the informal European Council in Biarritz in October, EU leaders were divided on the key issues relating to voting in the Council and the size of the Commission. Of the 73 articles subject to national vetoes in the Council, about 30 were deemed constitutional in nature and would be left untouched. This left over 40 which might be made subject to QMV (the number of items is greater if certain sub-articles are counted as separate provisions). But each member state had its own 'no go' areas with regard to extension of QMV. For example, the UK government sought retention of unanimity for treaty change and accession; taxation, border controls, social security, defence and 'own resources'. In the spring of 2000, the Portuguese presidency had drawn up a list of 25 articles which it believed should be transferred from unanimity to QMV. The list included rules on state aid, culture and the free movement of self-employed workers but excluded most aspects of direct and indirect taxation, except for combating fraud, tax evasion and environmental taxation. In the autumn of 2000, the French presidency also sought to persuade other member states to extend QMV to a range of new areas, including social policy. The issue of the future size of the Commission also remained unresolved. At the Biarritz European Council in October, there was a stronger measure of agreement on easing the ToA's stringent conditions on closer co-operation, thereby making it easier for groups of states to pursue deeper integration.

○ The Charter of Fundamental Rights of the EU

The idea for such a charter had been put forward by the EP in 1989. Although the original EU treaties do not deal with human rights, such rights have been adopted as general principles in EU law and are referred to in the Single European Act (SEA), the TEU and (more explicitly) in the ToA (that is, Articles 6 and 7 of the TEU as revised by the ToA). These articles entrench the principles of liberty, democracy, respect for human rights and fundamental freedoms as fundamental features of the Union. The Union now produces an annual report on human rights. A standard clause is now included in the EU's trade and co-operation agreements on respect for human rights.

In June 1999, the Cologne European Council set up an *ad hoc* body, to be known as the Convention, to draw up a draft charter of fundamental rights of the EU, to make the overriding importance and relevance of these rights more visible to the Union's citizens. The European Council would then propose to the EP and to the Commission that, together with the Council, they should issue a solemn proclamation of a European Charter of Fundamental Rights. They would then consider the possibility of integrating the Charter into the EU treaties. In addition to the fundamental rights and freedoms guaranteed by the European Convention on Human Rights (which is under the auspices of the Council of Europe), the European Council also required the Charter to include the fundamental rights pertaining only to the Union's citizens and also to take account of fundamental social rights as contained in the 1961 Turin European Charter and the 1989 European Social Charter (Article 136, ECT).

The composition of the Convention was determined by the Tampere European Council in October 1999. At Tampere it was decided that the Convention would comprise 62 members: 15 representatives of the governments of member states, 16 MEPs, 30 members of national parliaments and a representative from the Commission, plus two observers from the ECJ and two from the Council of Europe. Other bodies were invited to give their views. The Convention was also required to engage in an exchange of views with the candidate countries. The Convention's proceedings were public and all preparatory proceedings were made available on the internet. The Convention held its first meeting in December 1999 and adopted a draft charter in October 2000, in time for consideration by the Biarritz European Council, which unanimously accepted it. The Charter contains a preamble and 54 articles, divided into seven chapters. The preamble states that:

> The peoples of Europe, in creating an ever closer union among them, are resolved to share a peaceful future based on common values. Conscious of its spiritual and moral heritage, the Union is founded on the indivisible, universal values of human dignity, freedom, equality and solidarity; it is based on the principles of democracy and the rule of law. It places the individual at the heart of its activities, by establishing the citizenship of the Union and by creating an area of freedom, security and justice.

The titles of the seven chapters of the Charter are: 1. **Dignity** (Articles 1–5); 2. **Freedoms** (Articles 6–19); 3. **Equality** (Articles 20–26); 4. **Solidarity** (Articles 27–38); 5. **Citizens' Rights** (Articles 39–46); 6. **Justice** (Articles 47–50); and 7. **General Provisions** (Articles 51–54).

The Charter's 54 articles are shown in Table 4.6 below.

Table 4.6 The European Charter of Fundamental Rights

Article	Subject
1	Human dignity
2	Right to life
3	Right to the integrity of the person
4	Prohibition of torture and inhuman or degrading treatment or punishment
5	Prohibition of slavery and forced labour
6	Right to liberty and security
7	Respect for privacy and family life
8	Protection of personal data
9	Right to marry and right to found a family
10	Freedom of thought, conscience and religion
11	Freedom of expression and information
12	Freedom of assembly and of association
13	Freedom of the arts and sciences
14	Right to education
15	Freedom to choose an occupation and right to engage in work
17	Right to property
18	Right of asylum
19	Protection in the event of removal, expulsion or extradition
20	Equality before the law
21	Non-discrimination
22	Cultural, religious and linguistic diversity
23	Equality between men and women
24	The rights of the child
25	The rights of the elderly
26	Integration of persons with disabilities
27	Worker's right to information and consultation within the undertaking
28	Right of collective bargaining and action
29	Right of access to placement services
30	Protection in the event of unjustified dismissal
31	Fair and just working conditions
32	Prohibition of child labour and protection of young people at work
33	Family and professional life
34	Social security and social assistance
35	Health care
36	Access to services of general economic interest
37	Environmental protection
38	Consumer protection
39	Right to vote and to stand as a candidate at elections to the EP
40	Right to vote and to stand as a candidate at municipal elections
41	Right to good administration
42	Right of access to documents
43	Right to refer to ombudsman of the Union
44	Right to petition EP
45	Freedom of movement and of residence
46	Diplomatic and consular protection
47	Right to an effective remedy and to a fair trial
48	Presumption of innocence and right of defence
49	Principles of legality and proportionality of criminal offences and penalties
50	Right not to be tried or punished twice for same criminal offence
51	Scope
52	Scope of guaranteed rights
53	Level of protection
54	Prohibition of abuse of rights

The status and content of the Charter remain highly controversial (see Table 4.7). The *status* issue concerns whether it should be a declaration or showcase of existing rights (a position favoured for example by the UK) or whether it should enshrine new, legally enforceable, rights. Germany Italy and Belgium favour incorporating the Charter into EU law, whereas the UK and Ireland do not. It remains to be seen how the Charter might be integrated into the treaties. Inclusion into the treaties is likely to make the Union's legal framework more complex and arguably is no substitute for a comprehensive constitutional document. The *content* was controversial largely because of the wide-ranging nature of the 'rights' (economic, social and cultural) included in the Charter. For example, the Charter's 'social rights' embrace various entitlements, such as entitlement to social security benefit and social services and entitlement to preventative health care and housing assistance. Social rights are not generally regarded as fundamental rights in all member states; they are specified in the laws of some member states but not others. Moreover, even in the former case, they are not necessarily enforceable. A related issue concerned whether the ECJ should monitor such rights, or whether a new court should be created for the purpose.

Table 4.7 The Case For and Against the Charter of Fundamental Rights

For
• the EU now affects most areas of citizens' lives and therefore it is essential that citizens have rights commensurate with the extension of the EU's powers and responsibilities;
• it will strengthen the ECJ's jurisdiction in the field of human rights and will provide citizens with clearer judicial remedies;
• it will provide a benchmark when EU legislation is being drafted;
• it will provide EU citizens with clear information as to their rights;
• it will serve to educate EU citizens about their rights;
• references to rights as scattered in various EU documents and it makes sense to codify them into a single, accessible text;
• it will enhance the EU's credibility when demanding that other countries respect human rights;
• it underpins the need for acceding countries to respect human rights.
Against
• there are already enough formal references to rights in the EU treaties and therefore a charter of rights is unnecessary;
• the EU is not a state and references to rights are contained in the constitutions of most member states;
• it will be difficult to enforce and therefore far from enhancing the credibility and profile of the EU, it is likely to diminish both.

The charter idea is vociferously opposed by UK Eurosceptics, who see it as yet another attempt to push the Union in a federalist direction and to encroach on state sovereignty and domestic law. It is also opposed by the UK Conservative Party and the Confederation of British Industry. In response to criticisms for agreeing to the Charter, the UK Labour government argued that the Charter is in large measure a codification of existing rights and is a symbolic declaration rather than a legally binding document. However, its opponents view it as the thin end of a federalist wedge, fearing that the Charter may be built into the premises of the ECJ's decisions and that it may be used as a preamble to an EU constitution. The Charter was adopted by the EP by 410 votes to 93 and was unanimously approved by member states at the Biarritz European Council. At the Nice European Council in December, the Charter was 'declared' by member states, but was not incorporated into the Nice treaty. Ironically, in the period when the Charter was drafted, the EU had a potential human rights issue to deal with involving Austria (Table 4.8).

Table 4.8 Why 14 Member States Imposed Sanctions on Austria

In January 2000, the far-right Freedom Party entered into a coalition government in Austria. This led to the imposition of sanctions against Austria by the other member states the following month. Although a ToA provision allows for the suspension of certain treaty rights of a member state for serious and persistent breaches of human rights, it was not claimed that Austria had yet violated this provision. Sanctions were therefore imposed by the other member states individually and not in accordance with EU treaty obligations. These involved suspending various bilateral communications. The issue of sanctions was criticised on various grounds: it was generally acknowledged that the elections which had given the Freedom Party sufficient seats to enter the coalition had been free and fair. Countries imposing sanctions on Austria were therefore accused of interfering with democratic processes in another member state. In some countries (notably in Finland and Denmark) there was disquiet that member states had questioned the right of electors to choose their government. At the time sanctions were applied, the new government had not been in office long enough to perpetrate a serious breach of human rights.

In September 2000, a 'committee of wise men' appointed by the Commission published a report which advocated the lifting of sanctions against Austria on the grounds that they were counterproductive. The committee found no fault with the Austrian government's human rights record or with the status of minorities. By this time, several member states were looking for a face-saving formula to lift the sanctions, not least because of threats from Austria to veto important future decisions, including on enlargement and treaty reform. The sanctions were lifted on 12 September 2000.

● THE TREATY OF NICE

○ Arguments at the Nice European Council

The Nice summit was not only the longest in the Union's history (taking 41 hours over five days), it was also probably the most fraught, with arguments taking place between the participants in both public and private. Most of these arguments centred on the issue of national voting weights in the Council and representation in the Commission and the EP. The summit therefore was largely about member states defending and promoting their institutional interests rather than about the pursuit of 'deeper' Union integration. All member states drew 'red lines' over sensitive issues on which they would not make concessions (in particular over the extension of qualified majority voting to specific policies). Various battle lines and entrenched positions emerged during the summit. There was a 'big-state–small-state' split over voting weights and representation (with the smaller states accusing the larger ones of ganging together to selfishly pursue their national interests); tensions emerged also between France and Germany over the latter's claim to more votes and seats in consideration of its population size. The poorer member states were concerned to ensure that no decision would be taken which could result in a reduction of their aid from the structural funds.

The Nice summit has been described as a gruelling game of 15-hand poker, in that the participants were loath to disclose how much they were prepared to concede. French President Jacques Chirac and Prime Minister Lionel Jospin held 'confessionals' with each head of government in order to gauge their positions and also to encourage them to make concessions. However, Chirac was accused by some of the other participants of riding roughshod over the other delegations and of refusing to make concessions himself (for example, on the issues of French voting parity with Germany and extension of QMV to certain aspects of trade). In these negotiations, national interests appeared to be paramount. By holding bilateral talks with other leaders, Chirac sidelined the Commission. It is little wonder therefore that the Commission and the EP were deeply dissatisfied with the outcome of Nice. Given the diversity of national positions on a wide range of issues, it is remarkable that a deal, however messy and incomplete, was done at all. But the governments of member states were well aware that a new treaty embracing major institutional reforms was essential to cope with the next enlargements. The Nice 'showdown' led to widespread criticism of the method used to reviewing and changes the treaties. Tony Blair stated that EU business could not be conducted like this in the future. However, as long as member states remain the main parties to treaty negotiations, it is difficult to see how the negotiation process could be radically altered.

○   **A Snapshot of the Treaty of Nice**

•   **Objectives.** The Treaty of Nice (ToN) has a specific and practical purpose: to prepare the Union's institutions for enlargement. The preamble to the treaty states that the contracting parties:

> Recalling the historic importance of the ending of the division of the European continent, desiring to complete the process started by the Treaty of Amsterdam of preparing the institutions of the European Union to function in an enlarged Union; determined on this basis to press ahead with the accession negotiations in order to bring them to a successful conclusion, in accordance with the procedure laid down in the TEU, have resolved to amend the TEU, the treaties establishing the European Communities and certain related acts.

•   **Structure.** The ToN comprises changes to various articles in the TEU and the EC treaties, with specific emphasis on institutional provisions and decisionmaking procedures. It is divided into two parts, the first dealing with substantive amendments and the second with transitional and final provisions. It includes four legally binding protocols (A: on enlargement; B: on the statute of the ECJ; C: on the financial consequences of expiry of the ECSC treaty; and D: on Article 67 of the EC Treaty, to introduce QMV on certain migration issues from May 2004). It also includes 24 declarations adopted by the IGC (for example, on European security and defence policy; on enlargement; on the QMV threshold; and on the future of the EU) and three others by specific member states, of which the IGC took note. The key elements of the ToN are outlined in Table 4.9 below.

Table 4.9 Key Elements of the Treaty of Nice

• it stipulates institutional arrangements for an enlarged Union;
• it extends QMV to a substantial number of provisions;
• it introduces new requirements for the blocking threshold in QMV;
• it changes voting weights in the Council (from 2005);
• it allocates voting weights and seats for a Union of 27;
• it extends co-decision to several new areas;
• it sets limits on the future size of the Commission;
• it changes procedures for selection of the Commission;
• it sets a new limit on the future size of the EP;
• it introduces new procedures to facilitate enhanced co-operation;
• it introduces new rules and regulations governing operation of the ECJ;
• some provisions will be introduced when the ToN comes into force, whereas others will be introduced gradually or at a later date;
• it preserves vetoes on subsidies to poorer member states until 2007.

○ **Institutional Reforms**

• **Qualified majority voting.** If the current voting arrangements in the Council were to remain unchanged the accession of a large number of small states would have two unacceptable consequences: firstly, it would severely limit the ability of the Council to make decisions, as it would increase the number of possible vetoes; secondly, it could mean that decisionmaking would be dominated by the smaller states, as these would have a voting strength collectively disproportionate to their population size (in an EU of 27, the 14 smallest states will have only 12% of the EU's population). Negotiations on QMV centred on three issues: (1) extension of QMV to new subjects; (2) the form of QMV to be used; (3) the distribution of votes.

1. *The extension of QMV:* About 80% of the Council's legislative decisions are already taken under QMV. At Nice, member states continued to haggle over which aspects of the remaining 20% should be subject to QMV. The UK's 'red lines' (that is, issues which they would not agree to be subject to QMV) were taxation (a position shared by Luxembourg and Ireland), social security, defence, treaty changes, EU funding and border controls. Germany opposed extending QMV to asylum and immigration. France drew red lines over aspects of trade policy. Spain sought and won agreement that national vetoes over provision of subsidies to poorer countries will continue to 2007. Following tortuous negotiations, QMV was extended to about 35 provisions (the 'precise' number depends upon definitions of what constitutes a provision in its own right, hence the differences in the figures given in various commentaries on this subject). Thus QMV is extended to industrial policy; economic relations with non-EU countries; judicial co-operation in civil matters (excluding aspects relating to family law); measures to facilitate freedom of movement of EU citizens; approval of the regulations and general conditions governing the performance of the duties of MEPs; the statute of European political parties; the rules of procedure of the ECJ and CFI; decisions on appointments to internal posts, including special representatives for the CFSP; and international agreements on trade in services and intellectual property (excluding the television and film industries, health, social and educational services). The provisions pertaining to the subjects mentioned above will be subject to QMV as soon at the ToN is ratified. In other cases, extension of QMV is deferred until specified dates or until certain conditions are met (for example, various provisions on asylum and immigration (see Chapter 16); cohesion – from 2004; and financial regulations on the responsibility of financial controllers, authorising and accounting officers – from 2007).

2. *The form of QMV to be used:* Three main forms of QMV were considered during the 2000 IGC: firstly, a simple reweighting of votes,

based on population size; secondly, a simple dual majority (requiring the votes of a majority of member states plus a minimum population threshold); and thirdly, a weighted dual majority (requiring a majority of the weighted votes of member states, plus a minimum population threshold). France rejected the Commission's proposal for a simple double majority system, whereby any EU decision would need the support of a majority of states and a second majority of countries making up over 50% of the EU population. It would have weakened France's voting power and increased Germany's, because of its large population.

A complex compromise was eventually agreed, involving a weighted double majority system, plus the possibility that a third majority may be required for some votes (amounting to a weighted 'triple majority' in these cases). The two majorities which are *definitely* required are: (1) a majority of weighted votes; and (2) a majority of the member states. The third majority which *may* be required involves a population threshold: the treaty allows a member of the Council to request verification that the qualified majority comprises at least 62% of the total population of the Union – the 'demographic filter' or verification clause. The new system will be introduced from 1 January 2005. Until the next enlargements, QMV decisions will require for their adoption at least 169 (71.31%) of votes out of 237 cast by at least a majority of members where the treaty requires them to be adopted following a Commission proposal. In other cases, acts will require at least 169 votes cast by at least two thirds of the members. As new members are admitted, the threshold will rise gradually but will not exceed 73.4%. When EU membership rises to 27, the QMV threshold will increase to 73.91%. A Union of 27 will have a total of 345 weighted votes in the Council. Acts will require 255 votes in favour cast by a majority of members on a proposal from the Commission, or two thirds when there is no Commission proposal.

3. *The distribution of votes.* This issue led to a 'big-state–small-state' dispute. The largest member states were willing to give up their right to appoint two commissioners in return for improvements in their relative voting strengths. Several countries had specific axes to grind. Chancellor Gerhard Schröder argued strongly for an increase in Germany's votes to take account of its population size. President Chirac strongly opposed this on the grounds that it would upset the balance between France and Germany. Belgium sought to retain its voting parity with the Netherlands, even though the latter has a 50% larger population. Spain also sought an increase in its voting weight. Although candidate countries were not at the negotiating table, post-accession voting allocations were agreed for them.

The result of these negotiations was a series of rough compromises: the big four states had their voting weights increased from 10 to 29. Spain's total increased from eight to 27. Poland (with roughly the same population size as Spain) will also have 27 votes after accession. The agreement contained several glaring anomalies. For example, Belgium lost its voting parity with Netherlands whereas France kept its parity with Germany. Romania will be awarded only one vote more than Netherlands, even though it has 7 million more people. In the negotiations, the Belgian prime minister, Guy Verhofstadt, cast himself in the role of champion of the smaller states: although he failed in his attempts to maintain Belgian voting parity with the Netherlands, his protests won two extra seats for Belgium in the EP and also extra votes for Lithuania and Romania. The new weightings will not take effect until 1 January 2005.

The result of these various compromises on QMV is that the Council decisionmaking process will become more complicated. But extension of QMV to new areas will reduce the possibility of decisions being blocked through vetoes. The new weightings and the 62% population majority criterion favour the bigger states, in that by voting together they can block proposals. But the 'majority of states' criterion favours the smaller states.

• **The size, composition and selection of the Commission.** There would be obvious practical problems if the number of commissioners increased with every enlargement. However, member states disagreed as to what should replace the current arrangements. The key issues in the negotiations concerning the Commission were: the ceiling at which the size of the Commission should be capped; the basis upon which commissioners would be chosen, in the event of the number of member states exceeding the number of commissioners; and the voting method used to choose commissioners.

Several member states, the UK, France, Germany and Spain, and also the Commission, favoured capping the size of the Commission. However, smaller countries were keen to ensure that they did not lose their right to choose a Commissioner. The solution offered was a compromise. The big countries will give up their second Commissioner from 1 January 2005 and a 'deferred ceiling' arrangement will be introduced, whereby there will be one Commissioner per country up to 2010 or when the EU reaches a certain size. When the EU grows to 27 members, the number of members of the Commission is to be less than the number of member states. The actual number will be decided by unanimous vote. A rotation system will be introduced, based on the principle of equality, the implementing arrangements for which will also be decided by unanimous vote. Until this time, any acceding state will be entitled to have one of its nationals as a member of the Commission. The entire Commission will be chosen and approved by QMV. The Council meeting in the composition of heads of state or of government and acting by QMV will nominate the person it intends to appoint as president of the Commission, subject to the approval of the EP. The Council acting by QMV and by common accord of the president will adopt a list of the others it intends to appoint to the Commission, The president and other Commission members nominated are then subject as a body to a vote of approval in the EP. They are then appointed by the Council acting by QMV. To deal with the problems of co-ordination resulting from the increase in the number of Commissioners, the powers of the Commission president will be strengthened. The president will decide on the Commission's internal organisation and will appoint the vice-presidents after obtaining the collective approval of the Commission. The president is also given power to dismiss Commissioners: a Commissioner will be required to resign if the president so requests, after obtaining the collective approval of the Commission.

- **Other Institutional Changes**
  - *Size and composition of the EP.* For the 2004–09 term the maximum number of MEPs will be 732. However, it may temporarily exceed 732 in the event of the entry into force of accession treaties after the adoption of a Council decision on the change. The numbers of MEPs allocated to member states ranges from 99 for Germany to five for Malta (see Chapter 5). The treaty provides a legal basis for a statute for political parties at European level. The EP, after seeking an opinion from the Commission and with the approval of the Council acting by QMV, will lay down the regulations and general conditions governing the performance and duties of its members.
  - *The European Court of Justice.* The treaty includes important changes to the structure and operation of the ECJ (see Chapter 5), primarily to enable the Court to cope with its increasingly heavy workload. The Court of First Instance (CFI) is given powers to hear direct actions and may be given the right to deliver preliminary rulings in certain areas. A third tier of courts (known as judicial panels) is added to relieve the CFI of certain cases.
  - *European Council.* The treaty states that from 2002 one European Council per Presidency will be held in Brussels and that when the Union comprises 18 members, all European Council meetings will be held there.
  - *Economic and Social Committee (ESC) and the Committee of the Regions (CoR).* The treaty set a ceiling of 350 seats for both the ESC and COR. It states that the ESC must in future comprise representatives of the various economic and social groups in civil society and that each representative of the CoR shall either hold a regional or local authority electoral mandate or are politically accountable to an elected body.
  - *European Coal and Steel Community.* Assets and liabilities of the ECSC as they exist on 23 July 2002 to be transferred to the European Community.
  - *The Official Journal* to be titled 'the Official Journal of the European Union'.
  - *Appointments.* For example, members of the ESC, CoR and Court of Auditors will be appointed by the Council acting by QMV.

- **Enhanced co-operation** (referred to in the ToA as 'closer co-operation'). Enhanced co-operation was not on the original 2000 IGC agenda, but was added to it at the Feira European Council in June 2000. No measures under closer co-operation had been adopted since ratification of the ToA, partly because the criteria for co-operation were so stringent. Thus any member state had a right to veto such co-operation, even if it did not wish to participate in it. Pressure for change came from Germany, Italy and (more ambiguously) France, which favoured the idea of a pioneer or core group of states pushing the integration process forward. Some member states sought to extend co-operation, whereas the UK was adamant that it should not extend to defence.

Changes to enhanced co-operation are set out in some detail in the ToN (in amendments to Articles 27, 40, 43 and 44 of the TEU and in Article 11 of the EC Treaty). These changes remove the veto mechanism from the first and third pillars; introduce enhanced co-operation to aspects of CFSP (formerly it applied only to the first and third pillars); outline procedures whereby a member state wishing to join an established enhanced co-operation may apply to do so; and specify the requirements for enhanced co-operation. For example, it must be aimed at furthering the objectives of the EU and the Community; it must respect the EU treaties and the EU's single institutional framework; it must respect the *acquis communautaire*; it must remain within the limits of the powers of the EU and Community; it must not concern areas within the exclusive competence of the Community; it must not undermine the internal market; it must not constitute a barrier to trade, or distort competition, between member states; it must involve a minimum of eight member states; it must respect the competences, rights and obligations of non-participating member states; it must not affect the provisions of the protocol integrating the Schengen *acquis* into the EU; it must be open to all member states; it may be undertaken only as a last resort.

  - *First pillar procedures.* Member states intending to establish enhanced co-operation in the EC pillar address a request to the Commission, which may then submit a proposal to the Council or alternatively will inform the states concerned of reasons for not doing so. Authorisation is granted by the Council acting by QMV on a proposal from the Commission after consulting the EP, except in areas covered by co-decision, where the EP's assent is required. A member state may refer the matter to the European Council, but has no veto. The Council takes the final decision by QMV.

  - *Second pillar procedures.* Enhanced co-operation under the CFSP pillar relates to implementation of a joint action or a common position but not to matters having military or defence implications. Member states intending to establish such co-operation address a request to the Council, which is forwarded to the Commission and to the EP for information. The Commission gives an opinion, particularly on whether the proposal is consistent with Union policies. A right of veto is built in to these procedures. Although the Council decides by QMV on enhanced co-operation under CFSP, each member state may ask for the matter to be referred to the European Council for a unanimous decision.

- *Third pillar procedures.* Member states seeking enhanced co-operation under the PJCCM pillar address a request to the Commission, which may submit a proposal to the Council, or provide reasons for not doing so. The Council grants authorisation by QMV after consulting the EP. Although any member state may refer a matter to the European Council, it has no veto, because the Council takes the final decision by QMV.

○ Implications for Specific Policies

The treaty was primarily concerned with institutional change rather than substantive policy reform. Indeed, some urgent policy issues, such as the reform of the CAP or structural funds, were discreetly avoided. But many of the institutional reforms have implications for specific policies, namely:

- **Justice and home affairs.** It allows for the extension of QMV and co-decision to some aspects of visas, asylum, immigration and other policies relating to the free movement of persons (excluding passports) although it defers application of most of these changes until a later date and lays down conditions before they can come into effect. It seeks to foster co-operation in JHA, through the European Judicial Co-operation Unit ('Eurojust') (Article 29, TEU). Eurojust comprises national prosecutors and magistrates (or police officers of equivalent competence) detached from each member state, having the task of facilitating co-ordination between national prosecuting authorities and supporting investigations into cross-border organised crime.

- **Defence.** The treaty excises most references to the Western European Union from the TEU. A declaration annexed to the final act of the IGC concerning European Security and Defence policy (ESDP) requires the European Council to take a decision as soon as possible in 2001 to make ESDP operational quickly. Defence is explicitly excluded from enhanced co-operation. QMV is extended to the appointment of CFSP representatives.

- **Social policy.** The French presidency was initially keen to promote a radical social agenda in the IGC. However, the UK was adamantly opposed to a blanket extension of QMV and of co-decision to social policy. The treaty nevertheless contains various changes to social policy. It inserts references to combating of social exclusion and the modernisation of social protection systems into Article 137 of the EC Treaty. By unanimous agreement the Council may decide to extend co-decision to protection of workers, condition of employment for third country nationals, representing collective defence of workers and so on. A new article (144, ECT, replacing the previous article), establishes a *Social Protection Committee* (SPC), to monitor the social situation and development of social protection policies in member states and the Community and to promote exchanges of information, experience and good practice between member states and the Commission and to prepare reports or opinions at the request of the Council or Commission. Each member state and the Commission will appoint two members of the SPC.

• **The environment**. It inserts a declaration on Article 175 of the EC Treaty, asserting member states' determination to see the EU play a leading role in promoting environmental protection in the EU and in international efforts at global level. It requires full use to be made of all possibilities offered by the treaty to promote this objective, including use of market-oriented incentives.

• **Trade**. A new text of Article 133 of the EC Treaty extends QMV to negotiation and conclusion of international agreements on trade in services and trade-related aspects of intellectual property, but excludes educational, health and social services and also culture. It makes the Council and Commission responsible for ensuring that agreements are compatible with internal policies and rules. The Commission is required to report regularly to a special committee appointed by the Council on the progress of negotiations.

• **Fundamental rights**. Following the chastening experience of the sanctions imposed on Austria, it sets out procedures (Article 7, TEU) to determine a clear risk of a serious breach by a member state of fundamental rights, as mentioned in Article 6(1) of the same treaty. On a proposal by a third of member states, by the EP or the Commission, the Council, acting on a four-fifths majority of its members, and after obtaining the EP's assent (requiring a two-thirds majority) may determine that a clear risk exists and will make appropriate recommendations to that state, after hearing the state concerned.

○ Evaluation

At first sight, it is easy to characterise the ToN as a modest treaty, concerned with tying up loose ends or leftovers from Amsterdam. However, although it lacks a grand vision, it addresses the institutional implications of enlargement more specifically and explicitly than any previous treaty. Although criticised by the EP and receiving only a luke warm endorsement from the Commission president, the ToN contains a number of specific changes of major importance. On the other hand, it ducked the issues of the Common Agricultural Policy and the allocation of structural funds, and made little progress on cohesion, tax regulation or social legislation. Nor did it simplify the treaties. Decisionmaking in the Council will be even more complex and cumbersome than before. Some analysts see the outcome of Nice as marking the end of the federalist dream, in that the treaty negotiations focused on the assertion of national interests. Others view Nice as signalling a shift in power towards the big countries (Germany, France, Britain, Italy, Spain and, when acceded, Poland). On the whole, the treaty received a positive welcome in the candidate countries (excluding Turkey) because it addressed some of their concerns. The EP passed a resolution expressing disappointment. It stated that the treaty fell far short of what is necessary to strengthen the EU's capability for enlargement and its democratic legitimacy. It regretted that most governments gave priority to short-term national interests; that no automatic link was made between QMV and co-decision; and that the Charter of Fundamental Rights is neither incorporated nor even mentioned in the treaty. Despite misgivings, the EP voted to support the Treaty by 338 votes to 98 in May 2001 (it had no power to block its ratification).

The treaty was signed in Brussels on 26 February 2001. As was the case with previous treaties, it must be ratified by all member states. With the exception of Ireland, ratification will not involve a referendum and is being sought through parliamentary processes. However, the process of ratification received a setback on 7 June 2001, when the people of Ireland voted against the Treaty in a referendum (see pp. xxviii–xxix).

Table 4.10 Strengths and Weaknesses of the Treaty of Nice

Strengths

- it addresses the issue of enlargement directly and explicitly;
- extension of QMV enhances the ability of the Council to take decisions;
- it sets future limits on the size of the Commission;
- unlike the two previous treaties, it does not duck institutional reform.

Weaknesses

- it ducks key issues, such as reform of the CAP and structural funds;
- the reforms to QMV will make decisionmaking more complex;
- it does not extend QMV to certain key areas (e.g. taxation and welfare);
- it does not make a link between QMV and co-decision;
- the limit of 732 on the number of MEPs is arbitrary;
- it does not give the Union a legal personality;
- it reflects the interests of big states rather than smaller ones;
- it does nothing to bring the Union closer to the people;
- it does not incorporate the Charter of Fundamental Rights;
- it is not couched in user-friendly terms;
- another IGC is to be launched in 2004, proving the ToN's shortcomings.

O   The Post-Nice Agenda. Yet Another IGC?

The declaration on the future of the Union included in the final act of the conference states that 'with ratification of the Nice Treaty, the EU will have completed the institutional changes necessary for the accession of new member states'. But it is clear that this statement does not herald the end of the EU reform process. In July 2000, German Chancellor Gerhard Schröder informed leaders of the German regions that he favoured a new IGC in 2003– 04 to define the division of competencies between the different levels of government in the EU. Schröder was under pressure from regional governments in Germany to address their concern about their lack of influence in the EU. For example, the head of the Bavarian government has expressed dissatisfaction that 12 million Bavarians have less influence in the EU than 429,000 Luxembourgers. The proposal for yet another IGC before IGC 2000 had been concluded arguably undermined the prospect that the Nice treaty would provide definitive answers to the Union's institutional problems, by providing negotiators with excuses to shelve decisions. The declaration on the future of the Union requires the European Councils to be held in Gothenburg in June 2001 and in Laeken (Belgium) in December 2001 to agree a declaration on appropriate initiatives with regard to:

- establishing and monitoring a more precise delimitation of competencies between the EU and member states, reflecting the subsidiarity principle;
- the status of the Charter of Fundamental Rights of the EU;
- a simplification of the treaties with a view to making them clearer and better understood, without changing their meaning;
- the role of national parliaments in the European architecture;
- improving and monitoring the democratic legitimacy and transparency of the Union and its institutions, to bring them closer to citizens.

The declaration stated that a new IGC will be convened in 2004, to consider these items. Finnish Prime Minister Paavo Lipponen has suggested that IGCs might be replaced with a convention modelled on that which drafted the Charter of Fundamental Rights. Conventions are more inclusive bodies than the IGCs and arguably might reduce the inter state haggling and obsession with national interests so evident at Nice. The convention idea is supported by the EP, Belgium, the Netherlands, Germany, Italy, Luxembourg and Sweden. It is currently opposed by other states, in particular by the UK and Denmark, not least because it would dilute the influence of governments.

● DOES THE UNION NEED A CONSTITUTION?

The piecemeal approach to reform of the Union, using IGCs and treaty revisions as the main vehicles for change, has resulted in institutional and procedural arrangements of labyrinthine complexity. The four basic treaties (EC, TEU, ECSC and Euratom) contain over 700 articles and 38 protocols. Various reform measures for reducing this complexity have been suggested, such as the consolidation of EU treaties into a single, shorter, more readable treaty and a clearer demarcation between areas of responsibility between the various EU institutions and between the Union and member states.

An alternative would be to formulate a Union constitution. A constitution is a set of principles and rules contained in a document. A constitution would be likely to provide a clearer definition of Union purposes and a clearer, more comprehensible institutional framework. Some analysts believe that the EU already has a constitution in all but name. It operates according to a set of rules, many of which are enshrined in law. It has a set of values which are also set down in legal texts. It has a law applicable in member states which is more like domestic law than international law. As the EU policy portfolio has expanded, so has the applicability of the doctrine of supremacy, which is a key feature of written constitutions. Like a formal constitution, the EU grants citizens certain rights; it sets out the powers of the institutions and the relationship between these institutions. The revisions of the treaties can be regarded as a form of creeping constitutionalisation of the Union. However, this treaty-based constitutional framework is becoming more complex and difficult to fathom, despite attempts at simplification and consolidation. What the EU does not have is a single document, similar to the US constitution.

Various proposals for a Union constitution have been mooted, emanating mainly from European Federalist groups and the EP. In February 1994, the EP adopted a resolution endorsing a 'draft constitution on the European Union'. In 1999, the Union of European Federalists launched a campaign for a European constitution. Following a request by the Commission to produce a report on the reorganisation of the treaties, in May 2000 the Florence University Institute proposed a 'Fundamental Treaty of the European Union', with less than 100 articles setting out provisions on the foundations of the Union, fundamental rights, citizenship, the institutional framework, operating rules and policy objectives. This 'treaty' resembles a constitutional document.

In May 2000, German Foreign Minister Joschka Fischer advocated the creation of a European federation with a written constitution, a government and a two-chamber parliament. He argued that a limited number of EU countries should sign a new 'treaty of Europe', which would be the foundation of a European federation. In April 2001, a call by German president Johannes Rau for an EU federal constitution was followed by proposals by German chancellor Gerhard Schröder for a European federation in which the Commission would become the central government. There would be a two-chamber parliament, with the Council and EP respectively forming the upper and lower chambers, and an EU police force (*Der Spiegel*, 30 April, 2001). But this plan (which at the time of writing had yet to be approved by Schröder's own party) appears far too radical to gain EU-wide acceptance.

In 2000, for the first time, the Commission's survey of EU public opinion included a question on support for a European constitution. It found that 70% of EU citizens supported the idea, with only 6% against (*Eurobarometer*, no. 53, 2000). In his address to the German Bundestag in June 2000, President Chirac proposed a European constitution within a few years. In October 2000, the EP accepted a report by 395 votes to 105 calling for a European constitution before the 2004 EP elections. But adoption of a written constitution would antagonise those opposed to a federalist future for the EU. It could impose a framework which would be too rigid to cope with the pressures for change resulting from future enlargement. It remains to be seen whether current political and academic exercises in EU 'constitution mongering' are any more successful than those of the past. The only certainty about the EU's institutions and processes is that they will continue to evolve.

● CONCLUSION

Both the ToA and the ToN have been widely viewed as 'tidying up' exercises, dealing with 'leftovers' from the previous treaty. In both cases, however, the agenda for the treaties contain far more than 'leftover' provisions. In 2004 another IGC will be launched to consider the future of the Union. A common thread linking the ToA and the ToN (and which will also link these to the next Union treaty) is the issue of enlargement. Neither treaty fully addressed the institutional and policy challenges of enlargement. It remains to be seen whether the next treaty will provide definitive answers to the perplexing questions of governance in an increasingly diverse Union.

FURTHER READING

Commission (2000), *Adapting the Institutions to Make a Success of Enlargement*, europa.eu.int/igc 2000.

Fischer, O. (2000), *From Confederacy to Federation – Thoughts on the Finality of EU Integration*, German Embassy website, http://www.german-embassy.org.uk.

Florence University Institute (2000), *Report on the Reorganisation of the Treaties. A Basic Treaty for the EU*, COM (2000) 434.

Galloway, D. (2001), *The Treaty of Nice and Beyond*, Sheffield Academic Press, Sheffield.

Neunreither, K. and Wiener, A. (2000), *European Integration After Amsterdam*, Oxford University Press, Oxford.

Treaty of Amsterdam (1997), *Official Journal*, C340, November.

Treaty of Nice (2001), *Official Journal*, C80, March.

Secretary-General of the Commission (2001), *Memorandum to the Members of the Commission, Summary of the Treaty of Nice*, SEC (2001) 99.

Section 2

Institutions, Policy Processes and the Budget

 **Chapter 5**

Institutions and Policy Processes

● THE EU'S INSTITUTIONAL STRUCTURE

○ The Structure is Unique

The unique character of the European Union (neither a state nor an international organisation, but with features of both) is reflected in its institutional structure. A key feature of a state is that it has a government with an identifiable head. Within the EU there is no clearly defined 'government' or 'opposition' as such. Nor does the Union's institutional structure fit the conventional model of the three branches of government (executive, legislative and judicial) within a state. Elements of each of the above features of governance can be discerned in the Union's institutional structure, but analogies can be misleading. Perhaps the most misleading analogy of all would be to liken the Union to a smoothly running, elegantly-designed machine comprising neatly fitting interlocking parts and constructed by a single engineer at a particular point in time. The Union system of governance is more like a contraption with many rough and fuzzy edges, consisting of a set of machines with roughly interacting parts designed by many hands, inspired by different ideas, frequently adapted and roughly tuned. The system comprises a network of interdependent institutions, none of which can function (or indeed makes sense) without reference to others.

○ The Influence of Treaties

Perhaps the single most important feature of the Union is that it is founded on treaties. In the absence of a written constitution, treaties provide the legal foundation of the Union's institutional framework. For example, the roles of the Union's principal institutions are set out (by no means fully or unambiguously) in the treaties. The institutions are required to act within the powers conferred upon them by the treaties. The treaties also impose legal obligations upon member states. The institutional complexity of the Union is exacerbated by the fact it is not based on a single treaty (the Single European Act (SEA), the Treaty on European Union (TEU), the Treaty of Amsterdam (ToA) and the Treaty of Nice (ToN) amended, but did not replace, the earlier treaties). Nor do the treaties provide a comprehensive and up-to-date guide to the Union's actual institutional structure or activities. For example, one of the Union's most important institutions, the European Council, operated for over a decade before it was even mentioned in a treaty.

○ An Evolving Structure

The Union's somewhat ramshackle structure exemplifies the Union's *ad hoc* approach to institutional change. Unlike many state constitutions, which have a quality of finality about them, the Union's treaties were never meant to be the last word on the Union's institutional arrangements. The Union's 'institutional balance' (the distribution of power between institutions) has undergone significant changes in recent years and is continuing to evolve. For example, the power of the European Parliament (EP) has significantly increased in the last decade. The European Council, although not established until 1974 and deriving from informal 'fire-side chat' meetings between governmental heads, is a body of first-rank importance. The TEU established a three-pillared institutional framework and also created several new Union bodies, most notably the European Central Bank (ECB). The ToA also made changes to the Union's institutional balance, in particular by extending the EP's legislative powers of co-decision with the Council. The ToN is largely concerned with the formulation of practical solutions to the institutional problems posed by the impending accession into the Union of a large number of (mostly small) countries. An intergovernmental conference (IGC) scheduled for 2004 will examine additional institutional questions, such as the delimitation of competencies between the EU and member states.

O   The Influence of Competing Values and Interests

Both 'intergovernmental' and 'supranational' institutions co-exist (not always harmoniously) within the Union. The Council and the European Council are intergovernmental bodies, comprising ministerial representatives from member states, whereas the Commission, the Court of Justice, the European Parliament, the Court of Auditors and the European Central Bank have supranational characteristics, designed to reflect a European interest which transcends the specific interests of member states. This hybrid structure reflects the conflicting influences of intergovernmentalist and supranationalist pressures on the Union's development.

O   A Highly Complex Institutional Framework

Article 3 of the TEU states that the Union shall be served by 'a single institutional framework'. But this statement needs to be qualified. As Figure 5.1 overleaf shows, the framework does not fit neatly into the three-pillared Union structure created by the TEU. The Union does not (with the exception of the European Council) have institutions of its own but utilises those of the European Community. With the exception of the Council, the role of EC institutions in the second and third pillars is limited. The Commission is 'fully associated' with the work of the CFSP (common foreign and security policy) (second) and PJCCM (police and judicial co-operation in criminal matters) (third) pillars, but does not have sole right of policy initiative under these pillars, being forced to share this with member states. The EP's role in the second and third pillars is very limited: it has a right to ask questions of, and to make recommendations to, the Council; it must be consulted and have its views considered by the Council presidency; it is kept informed by the Council presidency and by the Commission of developments in the second and third pillars. The European Court of Justice (ECJ) has no role in relation to the second pillar and a very limited role in the third pillar.

The second pillar remains very largely intergovernmental. However, CFSP administrative and operational expenditure (excluding expenditure with military or defence implications) is now charged to the EU budget (which, as previously explained, is strictly speaking the budget of the European Communities). The ToA transferred some areas formerly located within the third pillar to the first pillar and also granted the ECJ jurisdiction to give preliminary rulings on framework decisions and conventions established under this pillar (Article 35, TEU). Therefore, although intergovernmental arrangements still predominate in the third pillar, it has to a limited degree been partly 'Communitarised'. The TEU introduced a 'bridge' procedure allowing for the possibility of some third-pillar areas to be transferred to the first pillar (and therefore to be subject to Community decisionmaking procedures). Under Article 42 of the revised TEU, any area within Article 29 covering third-pillar subjects may be transferred to Title IV of the EC Treaty. This procedure requires unanimity in the Council and ratification by all member states. It has yet to be used.

Figure 5.1 The Union's Institutional Framework

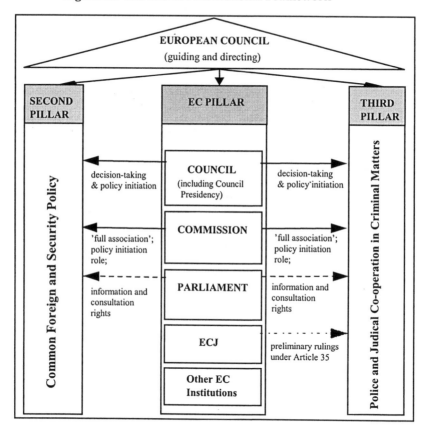

○ The Principle of 'State Entitlement'

The principle of state entitlement is woven into the institutional fabric of the Union. The rules governing member states' entitlements to votes, seats or nomination rights in EU institutions give smaller member states greater institutional weight than their population sizes would justify. Member states are allocated votes in the Council, seats in the EP and nomination rights in relation to appointed bodies (although those selected are required to serve the interests of the EU as a whole and do not take orders from any government).

The principle also extends to language: with the entry of Finland and Sweden, the number of official languages rose from nine to 11. In 2000, the translation service translated 1,252,400 pages of documents and the joint interpreting and conference service provided 141,781 interpreter days. The EP alone spends about 30% of its budget on translation. There are currently 110 possible language combinations for EU translators and interpreters to cope with, a figure which would rise to 380 if six additional official languages are introduced following enlargement. Even if the number of official languages were reduced to five, it would still mean 20 translation combinations. It is unlikely that agreement could be reached on replacing this babel of tongues with one official language. The three main candidates for this role, English, French and German, all have their drawbacks: although English is now the most widely spoken second language in the EU, it is the first language of only 63 million EU citizens, compared with 90 million for German. French is a traditional language of diplomacy and the EU's main institutions are based in predominantly French-speaking cities. But both French and German are now easily outmatched as a second language by English. An alternative might be to reduce the number of official languages to three. For practical reasons, EU institutions already tend to use 'working languages', that is, English, French and, to a lesser degree, German. But designation of these as the only official languages would rankle with some other member states, not least Italy and Spain, which would complain about the exclusion of their own languages.

The issue of state entitlement was addressed, but largely 'ducked', by the 1996–97 IGC and by the ToA due to fierce disagreements between member states concerning how the application of this principle should be amended. Impending enlargement virtually forced member states to make concrete decisions on issues such as the right of every member state to nominate a commissioner, the weighting of Council votes and the allocation of seats in the EP in an expanded Union. As was shown in Chapter 4, the 2000 IGC found it impossible to find solutions to these issues which satisfied all member states (or indeed all candidate countries). The key problem lies in finding a system of entitlement which is acceptable to both large and small states (thereby avoiding accusations of big or small state dominance) and which does not impede the Union's operational efficiency.

Table 5.1 lists the entitlements in EU15 and Table 5.2 the entitlements for an EU of 27 members, as contained in the Treaty of Nice. The abbreviations in the tables are: EP: European Parliament; Comm.: Commission; ECJ: European Court of Justice; ESC: Economic and Social Committee; CoR: Committee of the Regions; CoA: Court of Auditors; Pop: Population; and App.: Appointed (as distinct from elected).

Table 5.1 State Entitlement in EU15

	Pop.	Council	EP	Comm.	ECJ	ESC	CoR	CoA
	(1000s)	Votes	Seats	App.	App.	App.	App.	App.
Austria	8,082	4	21	1	1	11	11	1
Belgium	10,213	5	25	1	1	12	12	1
Denmark	5,313	3	16	1	1	9	9	1
Finland	5,160	3	16	1	1	9	9	1
France	58,966	10	87	2	1	24	24	1
Germany	82,038	10	99	2	1	24	24	1
Greece	10,533	5	25	1	1	12	12	1
Ireland	3,744	3	15	1	1	9	9	1
Italy	57,612	10	87	2	1	24	24	1
Lux.	429	2	6	1	1	6	6	1
Neth.	15,760	5	31	1	1	12	12	1
Portugal	9,980	5	25	1	1	12	12	1
Spain	39,394	8	64	2	1	21	21	1
Sweden	8,854	4	22	1	1	11	11	1
UK	59,247	10	87	2	1	24	24	1
Total	**376,325**	**87**	**626**	**20**	**15**	**220**	**220**	**15**

Table 5.2 The Nice Formula for State Entitlement in EU27

	Pop.	Council	EP	Comm.	ECJ	ESC	CoR	CoA
	(1000s)	Votes	Seats	App.	App.	App.	App.	App.
Austria	8,082	10	17	1	1	12	12	1
Belgium	10,213	12	22	1	1	12	12	1
Bulgaria	8,230	10	17	1	1	12	12	1
Cyprus	752	4	6	1	1	6	6	1
Czech R.	10,290	12	20	1	1	12	12	1
Denmark	5,313	7	13	1	1	9	9	1
Estonia	1,446	4	6	1	1	7	7	1
Finland	5,160	7	13	1	1	9	9	1
France	58,966	29	72	1	1	24	24	1
Germany	82,038	29	99	1	1	24	24	1
Greece	10,533	12	22	1	1	12	12	1
Hungary	10,092	12	20	1	1	12	12	1
Ireland	3,744	7	12	1	1	9	9	1
Italy	57,612	29	72	1	1	24	24	1
Latvia	2,439	4	8	1	1	7	7	1
Lithuania	3,701	7	12	1	1	9	9	1
Lux.	429	4	6	1	1	6	6	1
Malta	379	3	5	1	1	5	5	1
Neth.	15,760	13	25	1	1	12	12	1
Poland	38,667	27	50	1	1	21	21	1
Portugal	9,980	12	22	1	1	12	12	1
Romania	22,489	14	33	1	1	15	15	1
Slovakia	5,393	7	13	1	1	9	9	1
Slovenia	1,978	4	7	1	1	7	7	1
Spain	39,394	27	50	1	1	21	21	1
Sweden	8,854	10	18	1	1	12	12	1
UK	59,247	29	72	1	1	24	24	1
Total	**482,181**	**345**	**732**	**27**	**27**	**344**	**344**	**27**

● CLASSIFICATION OF UNION INSTITUTIONS

The Union now contains so many institutions that some attempt at classification is necessary. The most obvious classification is on the basis of what they do and the roles they perform, as shown in Table 5.3.

Table 5.3 The Main Functions and Roles of the Institutions

Institution	Main Functions and Roles
European Commission (appointed)	Policy initiation; implementation; guardian of treaties; drafting budget; monitoring; troubleshooting; external relations; 'motor' of integration.
Council of the European Union (ministers)	Main legislative and decision taking arm; adoption of budget; external relations.
European Council (heads of government or state)	Guidance and strategic direction; decision-taking.
European Parliament (directly elected)	Legislative scrutiny, amendment and 'co-decision'; assent; supervision; adoption of budget; discussion forum; redress of grievances.
European Court of Justice & Court of First Instance (appointed)	Judicial interpretation and enforcement.
Economic and Social Committee (appointed)	Advice and representation.
Committee of the Regions (appointed)	Advice and representation.
Court of Auditors (appointed)	Financial auditing.
European Investment Bank (appointed)	Financing development projects.
European Central Bank (appointed)	Monetary policy (see Chapter 11)
Other Institutions (appointed)	See below for details.

The treaties do not provide detailed and comprehensive descriptions of institutional functions and roles. Moreover, the functions and roles of several institutions overlap. A common distinction is between the five 'principal' institutions' (Commission, Council, European Council, Parliament, Court of Justice) and the rest. The principal institutions are regarded as indispensable to the operation of the EU in its present form, although several other institutions form an integral part of the EU's institutional framework. The European Central Bank is also a major EU institution. The institutions will now be examined in more detail.

● THE COMMISSION

○ Main Functions and Roles

The Commission is at the heart of the EU's activities and performs major political, executive, legislative, administrative and monitoring tasks. The Commission is sometimes referred to as a 'civil service' but this is misleading. It has considerably more formal power and a much broader range of responsibilities, than, say, the British civil service. It also performs functions which are more directly and overtly political than a public bureaucracy. The Commission was originally conceived as an apolitical, 'technocratic' body, but its guiding, energising and monitoring roles are clearly political (as is its strong impulse towards deeper EU integration). It is headed by a formidable team of career politicians and is at the centre of most new initiatives in the EU.

It is useful to divide the Commission into two categories: the executive Commission and the administrative Commission. The executive Commission (generally referred to as the 'College of commissioners') performs roles somewhat similar in *certain* respects to those of ministers in a government whereas the administrative Commission (known as the 'Services') provides support functions, similar to those of a civil service. The executive Commission currently comprises 20 high-ranking appointees, serving for the same term of five years, whereas the administrative Commission is made up of employees in permanent posts. Most appointees to the executive Commission are prominent career politicians (in the 1999–2005 Commission, only one commissioner, Mario Monti, was not a politician). Those appointed tend to be prominent in their own countries. Most have held senior rank in a government, although few have achieved the highest positions of prime minister or foreign minister. The current and last presidents of the Commission, however (Romano Prodi and Jacques Santer), both achieved the rank of prime minister in their home countries before being appointed. The 1999–2005 Commission includes five women, more than any previous Commission. The Commission's principal functions and roles are as follows.

● **Policy initiation and development.** The EC, Euratom and European Coal and Steel Community (ECSC) treaties bestow upon the Commission primary responsibility for initiating and formulating policy proposals. This responsibility extends to both general and specific proposals, ranging from fundamental ideas concerning the future direction of the Union to technical legislation. In relation to the Union's CFSP and PJCCM pillars, the Commission shares rights of policy initiative with the Council. There is an important distinction between the Commission's role in non-legislative and in legislative initiatives. Whereas its role in non-legislative initiatives is shared with the Council, it has sole responsibility for initiating and drafting legislative initiatives (Article 211, ECT). Although the Council and the EP can request the Commission to produce legislative proposals, they cannot initiate or draft them. Amendments to Commission proposals by the Council require the Commission's approval, except where the Council puts forward an amendment by unanimous vote.

We have noted that the Council and the European Council also generate policy initiatives and the Commission is frequently instructed by them to develop concrete proposals or ideas in pursuit of these initiatives. It has therefore been argued that the Commission's 'policy initiative' role has been weakened. But it is still the source of many major proposals. The Commission engages in an extensive network of consultations with Union institutions, governments, and pressure groups prior to the submission of proposals. It is advised by a network of committees, principally by consultative committees (representatives of sectional interests nominated by industry, unions, consumer groups and so on and appointed by the Commission) and by committees of experts nominated by national governments. The 'expert' committees tend to meet more regularly than the consultative committees and also tend to be more influential.

The Commission draws up a legislative programme for each year, which is published in the *Official Journal*. The Commission's annual work programme is presented to the EP by the president of the Commission. About 35% of the Commission's legislative proposals are the result of international agreements; between 25 and 30% concern amendment of existing EU law; and about 20% result from an express request from other Union institutions (in particular the Council and the EP), member states and economic operators, although it is not legally bound to respond to requests from other institutions. It is for the Commission to decide whether or not to put forward a proposal. The European Council often asks the Commission to undertake studies or initiatives (it made about 80 requests between 1995 and 1998). About 10% of legislative initiatives are required by EU law (for example, fixing agricultural prices). The Commission itself launches initiatives, after consulting relevant groups. The total number of Commission proposals has tended to fall in recent years. In 2000, the Commission sent 594 proposals, recommendations or draft instruments for adoption by the Council or by the EP and Council together (48 directives, 193 regulations, 252 decisions) and presented 304 communications, memorandums and reports.

• **Implementation.** The Commission's implementation tasks are primarily concerned with rulemaking, monitoring and co-ordinating rather than actually delivering policies. It is responsible for ensuring that policies are carried out and provides guidance on implementation to a wide range of organisations in the public and private sectors. It operates the Common Agricultural Policy and is in charge of the administration of Union funds (including aid programmes for Eastern Europe and developing countries). Its implementation powers derive either directly from the treaties or from powers conferred on it by the Council. It has its own powers under the EC Treaty in relation to competition policy and the control of government subsidies. The treaties give the Commission some direct legislative powers, mainly in relation to the ECSC and the operation of the common external tariff. The Council has conferred upon the Commission some legislative powers in specific and technical policy areas, mainly to do with agriculture and the completion of the internal market. The Commission's implementation role is constrained by the fact that most policies are implemented by national, regional and local authorities of member states.

- **'Guardian of the treaties'.** It has a major responsibility to ensure that the provisions of the Treaties and the decisions of Community institutions are properly applied. Its watchdog role gives it the power to supervise the day-to-day running of Community policies and to investigate breaches of Community rules. It can investigate possible breaches on its own initiative or as a result of complaints from governments, firms or individuals. It can and does take member states to the ECJ for failing to fulfil their treaty obligations. It has well-developed procedures for dealing with breaches of policy or failure to implement policy. It informs the state concerned before initiating infringement proceedings. It sends a letter of formal notice, requiring a reply within two months. If no satisfactory explanation is forthcoming, it issues an opinion stating why the member is in breach of its treaty obligations. Again there is normally a two-month period to reply. This is usually the end of the matter. If no satisfactory reply is forthcoming, the Commission may refer the matter to the ECJ. Infringement proceedings are mainly commenced because directives had not been properly incorporated into national law, although the vast majority of these will be settled without resort to the court. In November 1999, the Commission threatened France with a referral to the ECJ if it failed to lift its ban on beef exports from the UK. In 2000, the Commission commenced 1317 infringement proceedings, issued 460 reasoned opinions and referred 172 cases to the ECJ.

The TEU gave the Commission power to recommend that a fine be imposed by the ECJ on a member state that has failed to comply with an earlier judgment of the court. It can impose fines on firms in breach of EU law on restrictive trade practices. It can require firms breaching rules on 'state aids' (state subsidies for industry) to pay back moneys. It has the power to block large cross-border mergers. It also administers 'safeguard clauses' in the treaties, which allow treaty requirements to be waived in certain circumstances. The ToA extended the Commission's 'guardian' role to the 'Communitarized' matters of free movement, asylum and immigration.

- **Financial responsibilities.** Each year the Commission draws up a draft EU budget and is involved at each further stage of the EU budgetary process. It manages the budget and is involved in management of various programmes which are funded jointly by the EU and other countries or organisations (for example, pan-European research programmes and the PHARE programme for Central and Eastern Europe, which it administers on behalf of the Organisation for Economic Co-operation and Development: OECD).

- **Inter-institutional brokerage and troubleshooting.** The Commission performs vitally important mediation and conciliation roles, for example by seeking to find compromise formulae acceptable to all member governments in disputes within the Council and by seeking to broker deals between the Council and parliament in relation to legislation.

- **External relations**. The Commission has acquired an increasingly prominent international role as a negotiator on behalf of the Union, although the agreements it reaches with other countries and with international organisations are subject to the approval of the Council and in some cases of the EP. It negotiates a wide variety of external agreements. It is a representative or participant on behalf of the EU in meetings of several major international organisations, including the World Trade Organisation (WTO), the OECD and the United Nations. The Commission president attends 'G8' summits of the world's leading industrial countries. The Commission maintains delegations in many parts of the world and is the focal point of contact for the diplomatic missions which most countries maintain with the EU. It is 'fully associated' with the work of the CFSP pillar, although in a role subordinate and supportive to the Council.

○ Limits on the Commission's Powers

Despite its formidable range of functions, the Commission is not the vast, all-powerful bureaucracy of popular legend. It has a weaker claim to a democratic mandate than the Council, the European Council or the EP: whereas the Commission is an appointed body, the Council and European Council are made up of the representatives of democratically elected governments and the EP of directly elected members. It must operate within the powers granted to it by the treaties. For example, although it has the power of policy initiation, its proposals can be, and often are, rejected or amended. It has no power to force the Council, the European Council or the EP to accept its proposals. It formulates budgetary proposals, but these are subject to the approval of the Council and the EP. Moreover, the Council, and the European Council exercise directing roles which effectively place limits on the Commission's roles as policy initiator and 'motor' of the Union.

Although the Commission plays the key role in formulating rules and procedures for policy implementation, policies are largely carried out by the national, regional and local bureaucracies of member states. Devolved policy implementation in the Union is no unmixed blessing. It has resulted in serious problems of uneven and patchy implementation, through non-compliance and foot-dragging. There is considerable scope for policies to be washed out, diluted or delayed at the implementation stage. The Commission's legislative powers are largely of a delegated kind and therefore in this regard the Commission is dependent on what the Council is prepared to delegate to it (mainly regulatory policies, such as the Common Commercial Policy and agriculture). Its role is limited in relation to the second and third pillars. It also has a limited role in Union reform: whilst it may play an important role in developing proposals for reform, it is the member states which ultimately take the key reform decisions and agree Union treaties.

○   The Commissioners

Collectively known as the 'college', the commissioners are required to be chosen on the basis of their general competence by common accord of member states. Their independence must be beyond doubt and they are required to give an undertaking neither to seek nor take instructions from any government or from any other body (Article 213, ECT). During their term of office they may not engage in any other occupation, gainful or not. The complexion of the Commission is, however, determined by national governments, because they choose commissioners on the basis of criteria more specific than general competence. commissioners from smaller member states (which each nominate one commissioner) are usually associated with the governing party. Governments of states nominating two tend to choose one from the governing party and one from the opposition, although this is not a legal requirement. In the UK a convention has developed that one commissioner is chosen from the governing party and one from the opposition. Commissioners serve for a renewable term of five years. Governments can choose not to appoint commissioners to a second term. Lord Cockfield was not reappointed by Mrs Thatcher, after a series of disagreements with her about the Single European Market (SEM) Programme. Although commissioners are appointed to serve the 'general interest', they nevertheless bring with them valuable national perspectives, which helps to ensure that the Commission is not divorced from national thinking. The fact that commissioners may wish to return to national politics serves as an incentive for them not to completely disregard national interests, but it would be unwise for them to push the latter too overtly (in August 2000, the commissioner for Enlargement, Gunter Verheugen, was accused of attempting to foster his future career in German politics by appearing to call for a

German referendum on the next enlargements, an accusation he vigorously denied).

The Treaty of Nice introduces qualified majority voting (QMV) into the processes by which people are selected to serve as commissioners. The pre-Nice arrangements (which are still technically in force pending ratification of the ToN but which will probably not be used again) are as follows: the governments of member states are required to collectively choose a nominee for president of the Commission by unanimous agreement. The Council's nominee then has to be approved by the EP. Member states then, by common accord with the presidential nominee, nominate the other persons who they intend to appoint to the Commission. Nominees are then subject as a body to a vote of approval by the EP. Following the EP's approval, the Commission is then appointed by common accord of the governments of member states (Article 214, ECT). The ToN revises Article 214 as follows: the Council, meeting in the composition of heads of state or government and acting by QMV, will nominate the person it intends to appoint as president. The nominee must then be approved by the EP. The Council, acting by QMV and in common accord with the nominee for president, will adopt the list of other persons it intends to appoint as commissioners, drawn up in accordance with proposals made by each member state. The president and other commissioners will then be subject as a body to a vote of approval by the EP. The president and other commissioners will then be appointed by the Council acting by QMV.

What criteria determine the choice of president? Although the selection process is by no means fully open, it is possible to identify some key factors shaping choices. Candidates are likely to have held high rank: possible candidates to succeed Delors included four serving prime ministers (Jean-Luc Dehaene, Filipe Gonzáles, Ruud Lubbers, Jacques Santer), a former head of GATT (Peter Sutherland) and a serving commissioner and former cabinet minister (Leon Brittan). Only three presidents, however (Prodi, Santer and Gaston Thorn), have held prime ministerial office. Many issues surfaced during the selection process for the new president in 1994. The UK government suspected that France and Germany were seeking to foist their preferred candidate (Dehaene, the Belgian prime minister) on other members. At the Corfu European Council in June 1994, the UK government vetoed the nomination of Dehaene on the grounds that he was a federalist and a supporter of 'big government'. Brittan's chances were handicapped by his strong views on free trade and his background as a former member of a Thatcher cabinet. Following deadlock on the issue at Corfu, a special summit meeting in July chose Santer as a compromise candidate. Santer had been nobody's first choice. The EP threatened to reject his nomination on the grounds that they had been excluded from the selection process, but endorsed it by 260 votes to 238, with 23 abstentions. The president-designate was questioned at a plenary session of the EP before the vote. By introducing QMV for the selection of the president, the ToN will prevent repeat of the circumstances which denied Dehaene the presidency.

The performance of the current holder is another factor shaping preferences. In 1994, there seemed to be wide agreement that the nominee should not be another 'philosopher king' like Delors. Santer was thought to be more of a conciliator and team player than Delors (who was accused of running an 'imperial presidency'). Unlike Delors, Santer did not come from a centralising administrative tradition. The selection of Romano Prodi in March 1999 was made under the unprecedented circumstances of the Santer Commission's resignation, following scathing criticisms of the Commission in the first report of a Committee of Independent Experts (1999) – also known as the Middelhoek Committee, after its chairman – established by the EP to inquire into allegations of fraud, mismanagement and nepotism in the Commission. Although only a small number of commissioners were specifically criticised for errors and none were personal beneficiaries of fraud, the report contained a blanket condemnation of the refusal of commissioners to take responsibility. The Santer Commission as a whole resigned on 16 March, but remained in office until a new Commission was in place. There was wide agreement that the next president would have to be a strong, authoritative figure, capable of pushing through urgent Commission reforms. Prodi was chosen as presidential nominee at the Berlin European Council in March 1999 with remarkably little disagreement among member states, He was prime minister of Italy when financial reforms were implemented to enable Italy to qualify for entry into the eurozone. The nomination was approved by a large majority in the EP (392 in favour, 72 against, with 41 abstentions).

Table 5.4 Commission Presidents

Period	President	Country	Party	Prior Position
1958–67	W. Hallstein	Germany	Christian Dem.	Foreign minister
1967–70	J. Rey	Belgium	Liberal	Finance minister
1970–72	F. Malfatti	Italy	Christian Dem.	Public works minister
1972–73	S. Mansholt	Netherlands	Liberal	Agriculture minister
1973–77	F. Ortoli	France	Cons.	Finance minister
1977–81	R. Jenkins	UK	Labour	Finance minister
1981–85	G. Thorn	Luxembourg	Liberal	Prime minister
1985–94	J. Delors	France	Socialist	Finance minister
1995–99	J. Santer	Luxembourg	Christian Dem.	Prime minister
1999–2005	R. Prodi	Italy	Socialist	Prime minister

Table 5.4 above shows that presidents have·tended to be chosen from big

and small countries in rotation (whether by accident or design), although not invariably so. It has also been suggested that an additional pattern of alternation, in terms of political affiliation, can be discerned: for example, of the last three incumbents, the socialist Delors was followed by the Christian Democrat Santer, who was followed by the socialist Prodi. But again, these 'patterns' can be misleading. Of the ten Commission presidents so far, only one, Roy Jenkins, has come from a state which was not amongst the original six members of the Union. Two of the original six members have had two of their nationals serve as Commission president.

Under the ToA, the 19 designated commissioners are agreed between the governments of the member states and the nominee for president. The EP holds confirmation hearings with each commissioner and then votes on the new team. The hearings take place before parliamentary committees. Nominees are required to make a statement and answer questions. In respect of the appointment of the 1999–2005 Commission, questionnaires were sent out by the EP's committees to the proposed commissioners in July 1999 and replies were received by 15 August. The hearings were held in the EP buildings in Brussels, between 30 August and 7 September. The hearings were in public and transcripts were made available on the internet. Even if the performances of some commissioners are judged by Members of the European Parliament (MEPs) to have been unsatisfactory, the EP has no power to reject individual nominees. The president of the EP may request the president-elect of the Commission to make alterations to prospective portfolios, in the light of the hearings. It may also comment on the proposed structure of the Commission. If approved, the new Commission is then formally appointed by the governments of member states. Prospective commissioners must then swear the oath of office before the ECJ.

The EP's role in the selection and de-selection of the Commission has increased, although the crucial role of nominating people for posts still lies firmly with the Council. The EP remains dissatisfied with the dominant role played by governments in the selection process and is seeking to exert a much stronger influence. commissioners can only be removed collectively by the EP. Individual commissioners can be removed by the ECJ, on application by the Council or Commission, for failing to fulfil conditions for performance of their duties or for serious misconduct. No individual commissioner has ever been removed from office, although the Santer Commission as a whole resigned in 1999, following a threat by the EP to dismiss them if they did not do so. The ToN will grant the president the power to effectively sack individual commissioners (see below). Ten commissioners in the 1993–95 Commission were retained from the previous Commission, but only seven in the 1995–99 (Santer) Commission and only 4 in the 1999–2005 Prodi Commission. Table 5.5 below provides details of the Prodi Commission.

Table 5.5 The 1999–2005 European Commission

Name and Role	Background	Responsibilities
Romano Prodi President	Italian (60), prime minister; socialist	Secretariat-General; Legal Service; Media & Communication Service
Neil Kinnock* VP for Administrative Reform	British (57), party leader; socialist	Overall co-ordination of administrative reform; Personnel & Admin. DG; Inspectorate-General; Interpreting & Conference Service; Translation Service
Loyola De Palacio VP for relations with the EP; Transport & Energy	Spanish (49), F, minister, Conservative	Relations with EP, CoR, ESC, and the ombudsman; Transport and Energy DG
Mario Monti* Competition	Italian (56), academic/ journalist; Conservative	Competition DG
Franz Fischler* ' Agriculture and Fisheries	Austrian (53), minister, Christian Democrat	Agriculture DG; Fisheries DG; Rural Development
Erkki Liikanen* Enterprise, Inf. Society	Finnish (49), minister, socialist.	Competitiveness; Innovation Enterprise DG; Information Society DG
Frits Bolkestein Internal Market	Dutch (66),minister, Centre-right	Internal Market DG Financial Services; Customs &Taxation DG
Philippe Busquin Research	Belgian (58),minister, socialist	Research DG Science, R&D; Joint Research Centre
Pedro Solbes Mira Ec. & Monetary Affairs	Spanish (57), minister, socialist	Ec. & Financial Affairs DG; Statistical Office
Poul Nielson Development, Humanitarian Aid	Danish (56), minister, Social Democrat	Development DG; Humanitarian Aid Office
Günter Verheugen Enlargement	German (55), minister, Social Democrat	Enlargement process including the pre-accession strategy Enlargement Service
Chris Patten External Relations	British (55), minister, ex-governor of Hong Kong, Conservative	External Relations DG; CFSP; Delegations in non-member countries; Common Service for External Relations
Pascal Lamy Trade	French (52), head of Delor's cabinet, socialist	Trade DG; Trade policy and instruments
David Byrne Health, Consumer Prot'n	Irish (52), minister, Conservative	Public Health; Health and Consumer Protection DG
Michel Barnier Regional Policy	French (48), minister, Conservative	Regional Policy DG; Cohesion fund; Inter-governmental Conference
Viviane Reding Education and Culture	Luxembourguese (48), F, MEP/journalist, Christian Democrat	Education & Culture DG Citizens' Europe; Transparency; Publications Office
Michaele Schreyer Budget	German (48), F, parliamentarian, Greens	Budget DG, Financial Control DG; Fraud Prevention Office
Margot Wallström Environment	Swedish (45), F, minister, Social Democrat	Environment DG; Nuclear Safety
António Vitorino Justice & Home Affairs	Portuguese (42), deputy prime minister, CD	Justice and Home Affairs DG; Freedom, Security and Justice
Anna Diamantopoulou Employment & Social Affairs	Greek (40), F, minister, socialist	Employment and Social Affairs DG; Equal opportunities

Notes: * member of previous Commission; age on appointment in brackets; F = female.

○ The President's Roles

He (always a 'he' so far) distributes Commission portfolios; he performs a guiding and co-ordinating role in relation to the Commission as a whole; he is the main spokesman of the Commission; he is the chief representative of the Commission in its dealings with other EU institutions and other bodies; he sets out the Commission's annual programme each January in the EP. But the president is by no means all-powerful. He is not elected and therefore does not have a democratic mandate. Although he must approve member states' choices, he does not choose his fellow commissioners. Moreover, treaties prior to the ToN did not give the president the power to sack commissioners. However, before they were formally approved, each prospective commissioner of the 1999–2005 College gave a personal undertaking to Romano Prodi that he or she would resign if asked by the president to do so. The ToN requires a member of the Commission to resign if the president so requests, after obtaining the collective approval of the Commission (Article 217, ECT).

In accordance with Declaration 32 of the ToA (and new provisions in the ToN), the president now enjoys broad discretion in the allocation of tasks within the College of Commissioners as well as in any reshuffling of those tasks during a Commission's term of office. This effectively gives the president the power to reshuffle portfolios and to deprive a commissioner of a portfolio. The ToN states that the president shall decide on the Commission's internal organisation 'in order to ensure that it acts consistently, efficiently and on the basis of collective responsibility'. The treaty also requires the president to structure and allocate the responsibilities incumbent upon the Commission and allows the president to reshuffle allocation of these responsibilities. In addition, it requires the president to appoint vice-presidents, after obtaining the collective approval of the Commission (Article 217, ECT). However, it has been the practice for commissioners to stay in the posts to which they are assigned at the outset for the duration of their terms. Selections for Commission portfolios have in the past tended to be heavily influenced by the preferences of national governments. Larger member states expect that one of their nominees will be given a big portfolio. Nominees naturally have their own preferences and also seek to influence the selection process. 'Big' Commission portfolios also tend to go to reappointed commissioners.

Santer sought to break up portfolios, to prevent the 'personal fiefdoms' which developed under Delors and to improve co-ordination between commissioners. He also decided to have a share in responsibility for CFSP, monetary affairs and institutional questions. In the Santer Commission, there was more geographical demarcation (that is, responsibility for relations with particular regions or countries). Prodi also introduced major changes to Commission portfolios. For example, he divided external relations by subject rather than geographical region, with one commissioner (Patten) having an overall co-ordination role. He created new departments for enterprise, justice and home affairs, health and consumer protection, education and culture, media and communications services, mainly through the amalgamation of existing departments. The enterprise department brings together the portfolios for industry, small and medium-sized enterprises (SMEs), and innovation policy. The transport and energy portfolios were merged in January 2000.

○ **The Organisation of the Commission**

The Commission is a 'college', meaning that Commission decisions are taken on a collective basis. The College takes decisions (where necessary) by simple majority vote, usually by show of hands, with the president holding the deciding vote when votes are tied. commissioners are required to observe the principle of collective responsibility, in that they are expected to present a united front. The Commission meets weekly to decide on Commission business. From January 1995, the term of office of the Commission was extended from four to five years, to make it co-terminous with that of the EP. The TEU gave the Commission the right to designate from its members one or two vice-presidents. Prior to this, no less than six commissioners were so designated. The new system therefore upgraded the vice-presidential role. In 1999, Prodi appointed Neil Kinnock and Loyola de Palacio to the vice-presidencies.

Each commissioner has his or her own private office or cabinet, headed by a *chef de cabinet*. They are the personal staff of the commissioners and perform advisory, co-ordinative, supervisory and gatekeeping roles. Until the appointment of the Prodi Commission, they were normally chosen from the commissioner's home country (from the civil service, a political party or interest group). Prodi introduced smaller and more multinational cabinets, with around six members from three different nationalities in each cabinet. The *chefs de cabinet* meet to prepare proposals for the weekly meeting of the commissioners. A major part of the Commission's business is agreed by the Cabinets, leaving unresolved issues and broader questions to the commissioners themselves. There is a network of inter-Cabinet committees to facilitate co-ordination. The most important cabinet is that of the president. The Commission's weekly agenda is prepared by the President's *chef de cabinet* and by the secretary-general of the Commission. The cabinet, currently comprising nine members, frees up time for the president, deflects conflict from him and feeds him with ideas and information. Most Commission business is conducted in French or English.

Below cabinet level, the Commission is organised into units with specific policy or support responsibilities. The basic unit is the *Directorate-General* (DG), within which are directorates and divisions. There are currently 24 DGs; between one and eight directorates within each DG and between five and 36 Divisions in each directorate. The Prodi Commission introduced various changes to the organisation of the administrative Commission: directorates were given names rather than numbers (so that, for example, DG1 became the Trade DG). From 1 October 1999, the number of Commission departments (that is, DGs, plus various special services) was reduced from 42 to 36 (24 DGs and 12 special services). The special services include a Secretariat-General, a Legal Service, a Press Service, a Statistical Office, a Translation Service, a European Community Humanitarian Office (ECHO), an Office for Official Publications and a European Anti-Fraud Office. The secretary-general, who takes the minutes of the Commission, is the president's main advisor on appointments. The Legal Service plays a key role in approving major policy initiatives and monitoring breaches of Community law. The Commission is also responsible for overseeing EU agencies, such as the European Environment Agency and the European Training Foundation.

Table 5.6 Directorates and Special Services (Prodi Commission)

Directorates	**Special Services.**
Agriculture	Secretariat-General
Budget	Common Service for External
Competition	Relations
Development	EuropeAid-Co-operation Office
Economic and Financial Affairs	European Anti-Fraud Office – OLAF
Education and Culture	Humanitarian Aid Office - ECHO
Employment and Social Affairs	Joint Interpreting and Conference
Energy and Transport	Service
Enlargement	Joint Research Centre
Enterprise	Legal Service
Environment	Office for Official Publications
External Relations	Press and Communication Service
Financial Control	Statistical Office (Eurostat)
Fisheries	Translation Service
Health and Consumer Protection	
Information Society	
Internal Market	
Justice and Home Affairs	
Personnel and Administration	
Regional Policy	
Research	
Taxation and Customs Union	
Trade	

As is true of most large organisations, there are 'turf disputes' and conflicts over policy and resources within the Commission. These occur between commissioners and also within and between DGs. The Commission has frequently been criticised for lacking organisational coherence, in that each DG has to a large degree tended to function independently of other DGs, leading to inconsistencies in overall Commission policy. Various mechanisms for ensuring effective co-ordination between DGs have been adopted. There are regular meetings of members of the different cabinets and many inter-DG committees, but the degree of co-ordination between DGs is still widely thought to be insufficient, making it one of Prodi's first reform targets. For example, he has sought to encourage mobility of staff between DGs.

○   **The Staff of the Commission**

Excluding the members of the cabinets and the commissioners, the staff are known as 'the Services'. These are career officials recruited mainly by open competitive examination from all member states and are mainly located in Brussels, although about 2000 work in Luxembourg. In 2000, there were 16,409 administrative posts and 3704 research posts. In addition, 522 people were employed in the Publications Office; 224 at the Anti-Fraud Office; 45 at the European Centre for the Development of Vocational Training and 85 at the European Foundation for the Improvement of Living and Working Conditions. About 15% of staff are engaged in translation services. Commission staff work in three main languages, English, French and German, although legislative proposals must be presented in all official languages.

Commission staff are appointed from all member states and there are open competitions for all staff categories, comprising pre-selection tests, a written examination and an oral examination, which is normally held in Brussels. Staff are divided into four grades, from A to D (although if current plans to reform the Commission go ahead, these will be abolished). Within each grade, there are various levels (for example, the top grade, A, reserved for university graduates, ranges from A8 to A1). 'B' officials are junior administrators; 'C' officials are typists, secretaries and so on; 'D' officials are manual and service staff. B, C and D staff can apply for promotion to the next grade. Most Commission staff will change department more than once during their careers. Until recently, the criterion of 'national balance' as well as merit has been an important a factor in the promotion of Commission staff. For example, there has been an informal national quota system for senior Commission posts. From the outset of his presidency, Prodi sought to ensure that posts were awarded on merit and experience rather than nationality (so that 'national flags' were no longer assigned to senior positions). He has been keen to rotate senior officials, so they do not remain too long in the same job. The top officials (directors-general and directors) are now required to change posts at regular intervals, so that by 2002, no director-general will have been in post for more than seven years. Prodi also introduced a rule that directors-general should not be of the same nationality as the commissioners to whom they are responsible. He also sought to increase the number of women occupying senior management positions. Some DG posts are now advertised publicly and directors-general are given performance targets to fulfil.

○ Evaluation and Reform Prospects

Arguably, if the Commission did not exist, it would have to be invented, because no other institution is capable of holding the Union together. It has played a powerful role in each major development of the Union. It takes a broader (Union-wide) view on affairs than national governments. It can also take a longer view, because it is less likely to be affected by political short-termism than elected officials. The Commission is a frequent target for criticism. In popular mythology, it is regarded as synonymous with 'Brussels', a shorthand term for bloated, overcentralised, rule-obsessed bureaucracy. It has been argued that the Commission has too much power for an unelected body; that it combines too many roles; that its political and administrative functions are inherently incompatible; that there are too many commissioners, with too many overlapping responsibilities; that it has insufficient resources to achieve its formidable range of tasks; and that it places too much emphasis on policy formulation and too little on managerial ability and implementation.

As early as 1979, an official report on the reform of the Commission (the Spierenburg report) had recommended a raft of reforms to the organisation and functioning of the Commission. The report had been requested by the Commission president, in the light of future enlargement. However, the report's key recommendations (for example, for a reduction in the number of commissioners and improvements in co-ordination) were never implemented. There are several possible reasons why the Commission has proved difficult to reform: for example, it might be argued that the Commission has been too busy doing things to have the time to reform itself; secondly, reform of the college raised politically sensitive issues, such as the right of all member states to nominate at least one commissioner; thirdly, until recently, the impetus for radical change was lacking (weak systems of accountability meant that commissioners and their staff were able to shrug off criticism without major repercussions). The enforced resignation of the Commission in March 1999 gave a powerful boost to demands for radical reform. It should be noted that the current reform process was virtually forced on the Commission by a 'whistleblower' (Paul van Buitenen, a Dutch assistant auditor in the financial control directorate of the Commission) who forwarded a damning report on financial irregularities, fraud and nepotism to the EP, which then ordered the Middelhoek Committee's inquiry (see p. 118).

Attempts to modernise the administrative Commission had begun in 1995, following the accession of Sweden, Finland and Austria. Two modernisation initiatives, based on a Scandinavian model, were introduced, that is, MAP 2000, concerned with reforms in the area of staff policy and administration, and SEM 2000, concerned with reforms in the management of resources. In October 1997, the Commission launched an internal screening exercise, designed to assess its own operation, known as 'Designing Tomorrow's Commission'. In April 1998, the Commission combined these three initiatives into a single measure, known as 'Tomorrow's Commission', with the aim of changing the Commission's management culture and preparing it for the future. But these reforms proved to be too little, too late. Given the circumstances of Prodi's appointment, it is little wonder that reform of the Commission is now accorded high priority. The two reports of the Middelhoek Committee in 1999 were scathing in their criticism of many aspects of the functioning of the Commission. For example, the second report criticised personnel policies which encouraged favouritism based on nationality; lack of penalties for poor performers; the Commission's weak control of agricultural and regional aid funds, which they described as 'vulnerable to fraud'; and over-reliance on external sources of administrative and technical support. The report put forward 90 recommendations, including the appointment of an EU prosecutor, with powers to investigate EU officials.

Suggestions for reform of the Commission have tended to focus on two aspects: firstly, reform of the executive Commission, embracing issues such as the size and cohesion of the college and the roles and accountability of the commissioners; and secondly upon reform of the administrative Commission, embracing issues such as administrative efficiency and the management of staff. The two reform themes prioritised by Prodi when taking office were definition of the role of the Commission in relation to the Council and the EP and a clearer definition of the relationship between politics and administration in the workings of the Commission.

In the spring of 2000, the Commission launched a review of its activities, to ensure that it focuses on its core tasks. At the beginning of his Commission, Prodi requested Vice-President Kinnock to present a wide-ranging report on reform, taking into account reports by the Middlehoek Committee and other contributions. In January 2000, Kinnock produced an 84-point action plan for a thorough and comprehensive reform of the Commission. The plan included proposals to ensure merit-based promotion, tighter disciplinary procedures, performance assessments and improved management skills. It favoured 'activity-based management', meaning that objectives and activities would be directly linked to available human and financial resources. A 'service culture' would be promoted, based around the four principles of accountability, responsibility, efficiency and transparency. These would be accompanied by specific measures, such as a code of conduct for good administrative behaviour, rules to give citizens greater access to EU documents, a code of conduct for relations with the EP and shortening of time periods for payment of bills. It recommended that procedures for 'whistleblowers' should be introduced. The plan was attacked by the staff unions, who not surprisingly were concerned about threats to their security and perks. It was also criticised for being jargon-ridden and unclear in many places. Nevertheless, Kinnock continued to develop his reform plans. In February 2001, he launched specific plans for staff reforms, including a plan to replace the division of work into four categories (A-D) with 20 promotion steps; the introduction of annual appraisal for most staff; promotion on merit points; personal training maps to indicate staff needs; encouragement of staff mobility; more competitive systems of recruitment and selection; and appraisal systems to detect underperformance. The target date for completion of these reforms is 2003, although they are currently the subject of negotiations with the staff unions.

In the past, the Commission has shown itself to be remarkably resistant to radical reform and it remains to be seen whether the current reform drive will have the desired transformative effect. Pessimists might point out that the current reforms do not really get to grips with the problem of the imbalance between the Commission's tasks and available resources, that organisations have cultures which are difficult to change and that public images of organisations are also difficult to change quickly.

● THE COUNCIL OF THE EUROPEAN UNION (widely referred to as the Council of Ministers, or 'the Council')

○ Main Functions and Roles

The Council is an intergovernmental institution, comprising ministerial representatives of member states. It is the EC's legislative body, although it now exercises legislative power in co-decision with the EP. It takes decisions and confers power on the Commission to act. Together with the EP, it adopts the budget. It is responsible for putting the guidelines of the European Council into effect (see below). It is responsible for co-ordinating member states' economic policies (Article 202, ECT). It is playing an increasingly important role in policy initiation: policy ideas from the Council feed into the Commission through the various contacts between the two institutions. It may request the Commission to undertake studies for the achievement of common objectives, and to submit to it any appropriate proposals (Article 208, ECT).

The Council has responsibility for intergovernmental co-operation in relation to the CFSP and PJCCM pillars.

The Council meets mainly in Brussels, in its own purpose-built headquarters. In practice, there are many 'Councils' (over 20), because the ministerial composition of Council meetings depends on the subject matter. For example, meetings on agriculture or transport are attended by transport or agriculture ministers, respectively. Meetings of finance ministers are known as ECOFIN; those of foreign ministers are known as the General Affairs Council (GAC). The number of meetings for each Council varies from once or twice a year to every month (excluding August). The General Affairs, ECOFIN and Agriculture councils each meet monthly. At Council meetings ministers are supported by a small team of officials. Large numbers of officials (for example, foreign ministry advisors, permanent representatives, plus other advisors) attend meetings of the GAC, which is at the pinnacle of the Council 'hierarchy' in that items not resolved in other Councils may be referred to it. In December 1999, the Helsinki European Council confirmed the GAC's central responsibility for co-ordinating the work of the Council. Unresolved issues may also be discussed by the European Council, but this meets only two or three times a year. In December 1992 the European Council agreed that the Council will continue to be based in Brussels, with meetings in April, June and October in Luxembourg. Meetings take place behind closed doors. They are chaired by ministers from the country holding the six-month presidency of the Council. At least one commissioner attends these meetings, which usually last for one day. In 2000, the Council held 87 meetings, enacting 43 directives, 182 regulations and 30 decisions and making seven recommendations.

○ Council Voting Methods

Before discussing Council voting methods, it should be noted that there is an underlying 'culture of consensus' within the Council. This means that where possible Council members seek to avoid conflict and therefore only a small number of acts are actually adopted with negative votes being cast. But without some resort to binding voting procedures, the Council's decision-making process would be severely handicapped. The three methods are prescribed in the treaties, namely:

• **Unanimity.** This used to be the main voting method, but the SEA, the TEU and the ToA narrowed the range of subjects to which it applies (as, if ratified, will the ToN). There are nevertheless a large number of specific decisions which still require unanimity. Within the first (Community) pillar, it is still used for decisions in certain sensitive fields, such as taxation, social security and migration. Certain constitutional matters also require unanimity, as do some legislative procedures (see below). There are still three treaty articles (42, 47 and 151, ECT) where the co-decision procedure is linked with unanimity. Unanimity is also required if the Council amends a Commission proposal when the Commission opposes this. Unanimity is still the principal voting method within the second (CFSP) and third (PJCCM) pillars. However, in both of these pillars, the Council can decide by unanimity that implementing measures in joint actions can be decided by QMV.

The main problem with unanimity is that it gives each member state a veto over decisions. Each enlargement increases the number of possible vetoes where unanimity applies. But member states are reluctant to embrace this principle for all Council decisions, because it might mean them having to accept some decisions which were fundamentally unacceptable to them. In practice, however, there is a 'consensus reflex' within the Council and therefore member states tend to seek compromises and seek to avoid negative votes being cast. A specific form of veto applicable to decisionmaking in CFSP was introduced by the ToA. Through a procedure known as the 'emergency brake', a member state may seek to block a CFSP decision for important and stated reasons of national policy (see Chapter 19, pp. 449 and 451). The ToN did not change this procedure. Arguably, another kind of veto, although without legal force, is the so-called 'Luxembourg compromise', deriving from a deal in the Council in 1966, to allow discussions to continue until a decision is reached on matters regarded by any member state as affecting its vital national interests. It has rarely been invoked (there were three threats to use it in the 1980s) and many analysts thought that voting provisions in the SEA effectively put paid to it. But in 1994, France threatened to use it in relation to the ratification of the GATT Treaty, although this threat was not carried out.

- **Simple majority.** Under this procedure, each member state has one vote and therefore in EU15, eight votes are required for a majority. It is restricted to minor procedural matters and to certain measures covered by the Common Commercial Policy (anti-subsidy and anti-dumping tariffs).
- **Qualified majority voting (QMV).** As a result of the SEA, the TEU and the ToA, this procedure now covers the vast majority of decisions taken by the Council. The ToN will extend it to about 35 additional aspects of policy (see p. 91). It is the main method used in the first pillar, although with some key exceptions for certain sensitive policy areas, and is also now used for some decisions in the other two pillars. Under Article 205 of the EC Treaty each state is given a number of votes, very roughly in accordance with population size. However, there is by no means an exact correlation between population size and voting strength. Under the current arrangements, Luxembourg has two votes, one for every 200,000 citizens whereas Germany has ten, one for every 8 million. A specific number of votes is required for a

positive decision. Until the fourth enlargement (which increased the number of Council votes to 87), 23 votes out of 76 were required to block proposals. Following the fourth enlargement, the adoption of acts requires 62 votes in favour, meaning that 26 votes are required to block legislation.

In Table 5.7 below, column A refers to the votes and percentage of votes required for qualified majority; column B refers to the minimum number of member states required for a qualified majority; column C refers to the minimum population required for a qualified majority; column D refers to the minimum number of states required for a blocking minority; and column E refers to the minimum population represented by a combination of votes constituting the smallest blocking minority. Column A shows that the percentage of votes required for a qualified majority has been fairly stable at about 71%. Column B shows that a qualified majority has always represented at least half of member states. Column C shows that a smaller minimum population is now required to secure a qualified majority. Column D shows that the proportion of states required for a blocking minority has fallen since 1958, from a third to one-fifth. Column E shows that the minimum population required for a blocking minority has remained fairly stable since 1973.

Table 5.7 QMV in Terms of Votes and Representativeness

Year	Members	Votes	A	B	C (%)	D	E (%)
1958	6	17	12 (70.59%)	3	67.70	2	34.83
1973	9	58	42 (72.41%)	5	70.62	2	12.31
1981	10	63	45 (71.43%)	5	70.13	3	13.85
1986	12	76	54 (71.05%)	7	63.29	3	12.12
1995	15	87	62 (71.26%)	8	58.16	3	12.05

Source: Commission (2000).

In March 1994, a serious dispute arose in the Council concerning a proposed change to the blocking threshold. At an informal meeting of EU foreign ministers in Ioannina in Greece, ministers discussed a proposal to change the number of votes required to block legislation from 23 to 27, to take account of the entry of four European Free Trade Association (EFTA) countries (Norway was then still in the running for entry). The UK, supported for a time by Spain, opposed these proposals, arguing that the change would weaken sovereignty, because the votes of more countries would be needed to block legislation. However, the British were forced to climb down, due to the resolute stance of ten other states and a threat from the EP to refuse to ratify the accession treaties unless the blocking threshold was increased. A deal known as the 'Ioannina compromise', was finally agreed, whereby if members representing between 23 and 26 votes expressed an intention to oppose a decision, the Council would do all in its power within a reasonable space of time to reach a satisfactory solution which could be adopted by at least 65 votes. A declaration annexed to the ToA renewed the Ioannina compromise until the next enlargement. The deal reflected the Council's penchant for consensual decisionmaking and conflict avoidance where possible.

In EU15, a QMV decision can be blocked by the three largest states acting together or by a group of the less populous states representing about 12% of the EU population. What these figures do not show, of course, is the subtle interplay of factors which determine actual voting patterns, such as the political complexions of national governments, bargains, trade-offs and informal alliances between states with perceived common interests (for example, poorer member states may seek budget increases, but richer states may join together to oppose this). As was discussed in Chapter 4, the ToN not only extends QMV to new areas, but also reallocates voting weights for a Union of 15 and of 27 (see Table 5.3 above). It also changes the criteria for a majority vote. The QMV threshold following these changes will be 71.31%, and will eventually rise to 73.91% when the Union's membership reaches 27.

○ The Council Presidency

The Council presidency is held for six months by each member state, beginning in January and July. The recent and forthcoming presidencies are: 1998: UK; Austria; 1999: Germany; Finland; 2000: Portugal; France; 2001: Sweden; Belgium; 2002: Spain; Denmark; 2003 (first half): Greece.

The presidency (in conjunction with the Commission and the secretary-general of the Council) organises Union meetings and plays a key role in setting the agenda for the six-month period. It has important external representation roles, acting as spokesman for the Union. Together with the Commission, it is required to keep the EP informed of CFSP developments. It is the representative of the Council in the EP and attends all plenaries. A foreign office minister from the country holding the presidency attends question-time at each plenary to answer questions from MEPs. Government ministers from member states holding the presidency frequently appear before EP committees. Although the presidency chairs Council meetings, it does not give the holder powers of executive decision. The holder is expected to play a constructive, 'consensus-building' role between member states and also to maintain good relations with the EP. Although it grants the holder no licence to blatantly push national interests, it nevertheless provides it with a periodic opportunity to set its stamp on the Union's development and to promote particular policies. There is prestige in running the presidency well, but few holders in recent years have escaped without criticism.

The role of the presidency has increased in importance in recent years, for several reasons: firstly, reform of the EU has been high on the EU's policy agenda in the last decade and the presidency is well placed to play a leading role in pushing the reform process forward. Secondly, the creation and development of the two intergovernmental pillars has given the presidency new responsibilities. Thirdly, as the Union's membership has expanded, the frequency with which each state holds the presidency has declined, which may mean that the presidency is now more highly prized. It has been suggested that some smaller states lack the resources to run an effective presidency (a problem which may increase with the next enlargements).

O Council Support Services

The Council has a General Secretariat based in Brussels with a staff of 2543 in 2000. It has a secretary-general, a legal service and seven directorates. There is a close working relationship between the Secretariats of the Council and Commission. The Council is supported in its work by the permanent representatives (the 'ambassadors') of the member states, collectively known as the Committee of Permanent Representatives and widely referred to by its French acronym COREPER. COREPER works behind the scenes by undertaking the groundwork necessary for Council decisions. Ambassadors are assisted by civil servants from their own countries (about half from foreign ministries and the rest from other ministries). Working on behalf of their governments, they seek to reach agreements with other representatives.

COREPER prepares the Council's agendas and organises each meeting of the GAC. The Special Committee on Agriculture (SCA) performs this role in relation to agriculture. There are also other committees covering various aspects of policy, for example, the Political Committee (PoCo), which deals with foreign and security policy; the Article 36 Committee (formerly the K.4 Committee), concerned with police and judicial co-operation; the Economic and Finance Committee (EFC); the Standing Committee on Employment; the 'Article 133' Committee (formerly the '113 Committee'), which deals with the Common Commercial Policy; the Energy Committee and the Committee on Education. There are also *ad hoc* groups of senior national officials, known as 'high-level groups', which are established to examine specific issues. The Council, COREPER and the various committees referred to above are assisted by a network of working parties and of committees made up of senior officials from government departments of the member states, although the standing committee on employment has both national officials and interest group representatives. About 270 working parties provide the committees with information and ideas (see Figure 5.2 below).

There are two groups within COREPER: 'COREPER 2' deals with 'high policy' and 'COREPER 1' with more technical policy subjects. COREPER 2 is attended by the ambassadors and COREPER 1 by their deputies. Another group, the *Antici Group* (named after the Italian official who created it in

1975), is made up of an official from each national ministry (usually the foreign ministry). Anticis help to prepare the ground for European Councils. Proposals usually start in working parties and committees. They are then referred to COREPER or the SCA. At Council meetings, items are listed as 'A' or 'B' points. A points have already been agreed and require only formal approval by ministers. B points require further consideration. About 80% of decisions are agreed at or below COREPER level.

Figure 5.2 The Council System

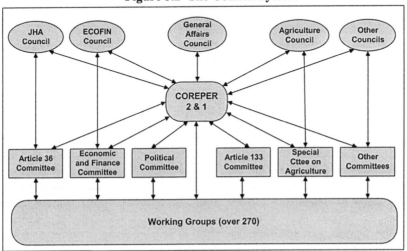

O The Main Strengths and Weaknesses of the Council System

The Council system provides a framework for governments to make binding collective decisions affecting EU citizens. It has a legitimacy which neither the Commission nor the EP yet possesses. Its decisions are likely to be financially realistic, because member states ultimately have to foot the bill for EU policies. In some respects, the Council's role has increased in recent years, due to the expansion of the Union's policy portfolio, the extension of QMV and the greater role now played by the Council in policy initiation. However, in at least two respects, its decisionmaking power has declined, due to the increasingly important role of the European Council in making key decisions and the introduction of the co-decision procedure, which has forced the Council to share legislative power with the EP.

The functioning of the Council has been criticised on three principal grounds, that is, excessive secrecy, poor continuity between Council presidencies and poor co-ordination.

- **Secrecy**. The Council is more transparent than it was, but arguably much less than it should be. In 1994 the *Financial Times* requested information about voting records on QMV decisions since 1989, but was informed that no such records had been kept. In October 1993, the Council, the Commission and the EP signed an *Interinstitutional Declaration on Democracy, Transparency and Subsidiarity*. The following December, the Council agreed new procedures to allow the publication of Council votes (although not the individual voting records of states). It also agreed a 'code of conduct' governing public access to documents held by itself or by the Commission. However, by majority vote, it inserted a catch-all clause into the code, allowing the institutions to refuse requests to disclose information.

Article 207 of the EC Treaty as revised by the ToA requires the Council, when acting in a legislative capacity, to make the results of votes and explanations of vote as well as statements in the minutes to be made public. But it is left to the Council to define when it is acting in this capacity and the stipulation does not extend to the Council's deliberations when acting in an executive capacity. The results of votes when the Council is acting in a legislative capacity are now published in the monthly bulletin of the EU. Most requests for access to Council documents have been granted. But the governments of member states have generally been reluctant to allow anything approaching full transparency, because it could mean that the views they have expressed in Council discussions would be open for full scrutiny by their domestic publics. A study by the human rights group Statewatch of Council voting records on appeals against refusal to give access to documents showed that the governments of some member states (in particular the Scandinavian countries, and to a lesser extent the Netherlands, the UK and Ireland) were more likely to vote in favour of access than the others (Statewatch, 2000).

The ToA (Article 255, ECT) required a new code on public access to documents to be agreed between the Council, the EP and the Commission by May 2001. The Council's proposals for these rules favoured retention of many exemptions to the right of public access. For example, in July 2000, the Council adopted the Solana decision to exclude whole categories of documents on foreign affairs from public access. In April 2001, the Council and EP finally agreed on a new code. It covers all official documents submitted to the Council, EP and Commission and requires EU institutions to prove that release of documents will be harmful. For the first time, citizens have a right of access to official documents with the support of the EC Treaty. The EU institutions will be obliged to establish a public register of official documents. Institutions must approve or refuse an application within 15 working days. When one is refused, applicants have a right of appeal to the ombudsman or to the ECJ. A transparency report will be produced annually. Critics of the new code argue that it has many loopholes and get-out clauses (for example for sensitive documents: see p. 180) and that it incorporates the much-criticised 'Solana decision' in a disguised form.

• **Poor continuity between presidencies.** The rotating presidency is obviously a threat to policy continuity, although *ad hoc* arrangements have been developed to facilitate the smooth running of the system. The previous, current and next presidencies of the Council work together on some matters to ensure continuity (the 'Troika' arrangement). Various solutions have been proposed to enhance continuity: for example, the duration of each presidency might be extended to one year; the automatic right of each country to hold the presidency might be removed (at present, small member states hold the presidency on the same basis as large ones); or 'team presidencies' might be introduced, whereby groups of states would jointly hold a presidency. In 1998, the alphabetical system of rotation was changed to ensure a more even balance between big and small states.

• **Poor co-ordination.** As we have noted, the Council is in fact made up of many specific Councils, supported by a complex network of supporting committees and working groups. The Council system as a whole has been criticised for lack of effective co-ordination between its various parts. In its report to the Helsinki European Council on reform of the Council system, the Commission recommended that the number of Council formations be reduced to no more than 15. It also recommended that the General Secretariat's role as advisor to the Council and the presidency should be strengthened.

● THE EUROPEAN COUNCIL

○ Main Functions and Roles

The European Council is the Union's supreme guiding body. It is concerned with shaping the EU's goals and giving strategic direction to the Union. It has frequently been the launching pad for new Union initiatives. Many landmark decisions in the EU's development have been taken at European Council meetings. It is essentially an executive summit meeting of Union heads of government (in the case of France and Finland, heads of state) and the Commission president. It has developed from informal fireside chats between government leaders to become, according to some assessments, the brains of the Union. The decision to formally establish the European Council was taken at the Paris summit in 1974. The first European Council took place in Dublin in March 1975.

The European Council was formally recognised in the Single European Act (Title I, Article 2), although the act did not define its powers. Nor were its powers comprehensively defined in the TEU. Article 4 of the TEU set out its role, although in general terms, that is 'to provide the Union with the necessary impetus for development and to define its general political guidelines'. It is referred to explicitly twice under Title VII of the EC Treaty, which gives it responsibility for deciding, on the basis of a report from the Council, the broad guidelines of the economic policies of member states and of the Community and gives it the right to receive the annual report of the European Central Bank. In an amendment to the EC Treaty, the ToA also requires the European Council to consider, and adopt conclusions on, the employment situation in the Community each year on the basis of a joint report by the Council and Commission (Article 128, ECT). Under the TEU, as amended by the ToA, it is required to define the principles of and general guidelines for the CFSP, including matters with defence implications (Article 13, TEU). The ToA also empowered it to decide on the possible integration of the Western European Union (WEU) into the EU (Article 17, TEU).

Article 7 of the TEU gives the Council 'meeting in the composition of the heads of state or government' a key role in determining serious and persistent breaches of human rights by a member state. Title VII of the EC Treaty gives the Council meeting in this composition key decisionmaking responsibilities with regard to appointments to the ECB and the transition to EMU (see Chapter 11). At first sight, these appear to be implicit references to the European Council. However, whereas the Commission president is a member of the European Council, he is not a member of the former and there are also differences in decisionmaking rules between the two formations.

O   **Operation**

A European Council is held at the end of each Council presidency, in June and December. Special meetings may also be held (for example, Tampere in October 1999). European Council meetings, which normally last two days, normally take place in the country currently holding the Council presidency. The meetings are attended by EU heads of government or state and their foreign ministers, plus the president and one of the vice-presidents of the Commission. They are accompanied by officials from the Commission and the Council Secretariat. The idea is to provide opportunities for face-to-face contact between governmental heads, unencumbered by armies of advisors. The Council and Commission presidents give press conferences at the end of each European Council. The European Council is a political, not a legislative body and therefore the implementation of European Council decisions is left to the Council and Commission. As mentioned above, some treaty provisions explicitly require the European Council to adopt decisions on certain subjects.

European Council meetings are big events and receive considerable media attention. Each becomes known by the place where it is held – for example,

'Maastricht', 'Amsterdam', 'Nice'. The European Council's work is prepared in the main within the Council: the GAC meets a few days before to examine issues likely to be discussed by the European Council. The Commission president holds preliminary talks with heads of government or state. A list of subjects to be discussed is circulated by the government of the member state holding the Council presidency a few days prior to the meeting. The president of the EP gives a speech and holds a brief discussion with members of the European Council before the start of proceedings. The European Council does not normally take votes and the tradition is to seek agreement by consensus.

The types of issue discussed at European Council meetings include the future direction and constitutional development of the Union; the situation of the Union in the world; major foreign policy issues; pressing issues of common concern to member states; and contentious issues which the Council has been unable to resolve. Some European Council meetings are damp squibs whereas others are of momentous importance. In recent years, there has been a growing belief that the symbolic value of holding European Councils in different locations is heavily outweighed by the logistic and administrative costs of this peripatetic arrangement. A declaration in the ToN requires half of the annual European Council meetings to be held in Brussels from 2002; and when the EU has 18 members, all are to be held there.

○ Evaluation

The European Council is firmly established as a heavyweight Union actor, with considerable power to guide and shape the direction of the Union. Its significance derives from the importance given to it by the heads of government of member states. Without it, the Union's overall coherence, and its capacity to make fundamental decisions concerning its future, would be seriously weakened. For example, landmark decisions on a wide range of policies and institutional questions have been taken at European Councils in recent years. Conversely, it constitutes an additional intergovernmental layer and therefore it has arguably weakened the importance of the Union's supranational elements. The Commission's policy initiation role is weaker in relation to the European Council than to the Council. Because of its decision-taking role, it has also (arguably) weakened the position of the Council, although it meets far too infrequently to usurp the Council's role. The EP has no say in setting European Council agendas and no control over the European Council, although the TEU does require the European Council to submit a report to the EP after each meeting, plus a yearly written report on the progress achieved by the Union. But it should be remembered that the SEA, the TEU and the ToA, each of which increased the power of the EP, were all agreed at European Council meetings.

● THE EUROPEAN PARLIAMENT

○ Origins

The EP has its origins in the appointed Assembly established in the ECSC Treaty. The term 'parliament', instead of 'Assembly', was first used in 1962.

○ The System of Election

The EP is the Union's only directly elected body. Until 1979, when the first direct elections were held, members were appointed from members of national parliaments. Elections take place every five years, in June. Under Article 190(4) of the EC Treaty, there is supposed to be a common electoral system, but this has still not been achieved. The first subparagraph of this article, as revised by the ToA, states that the EP is to draw up a proposal for elections by direct universal suffrage in accordance with a uniform procedure in all member states or in accordance with common principles. All countries now use proportional representation, but there is no uniform procedure: there are differences in voting rights and in electoral systems. The number of constituents per MEP also varies considerably between countries. The number of seats was increased from 518 to 567 for the 1994 elections. From January 1995, this rose to 626 following the fourth enlargement. The ToA set a limit of 700 MEPs following enlargement, although the ToN increased this to 732.

Turnouts tend to be significantly lower than in national elections. Less than half the European electorate voted in the 1999 elections for the EP. In each election since 1979, the turnout has been lower than on the previous occasion. This is ironic, since the powers of the EP have increased considerably in this period. It has frequently been argued that the EP needs to be given more power before it is taken seriously by the electorate. Evidence from recent polls seems to belie this assumption. In 1979, 63% voted in Euro-elections, but only 56.5% in 1994 (down from 58.5% in 1989) and only 49% in 1999, even though the SEA, the TEU and the ToA increased the EP's powers. Out of the 12 countries which participated in both the 1994 and 1999 elections, turnouts were lower in nine in 1999 than they had been in 1994 (Table 5.8 below). Euro-elections are widely viewed as a series of opinion polls on the performance of national governments. There appears to be little European consciousness among voters or even among national parties. There are still no 'Euro-parties' as such and national party battles remain paramount. Unlike national elections, Euro-elections provide voters with neither clear choices of governmental leadership nor of policies. Voters tend not to vote on European issues as such and there are elements of protest voting, suggesting that voters tend not to view Euro-elections as seriously as they do national elections.

It has been suggested that a form of direct democracy, through referenda on European issues, should be introduced to reduce the democratic deficit. But such referenda might tend in practice to be votes on the performance of national governments rather than on European issues as such. Another idea is to enable the EP to choose the commissioners. But there is no sign that governments are willing to forgo their role choosing nominees, or that they would be able to live with a Commission chosen by MEPs.

Table 5.8. Turnouts at Euro-elections: 1989–1999

	1999 (%)	1994 (%)	1989 (%)
Austria	49.0	–	–
Belgium	90.0	90.7	90.7
Denmark	50.0	52.5	46.2
Finland	30.0	–	–
France	47.0	53.5	48.7
Germany	45.0	58.0	62.3
Greece	70.0	71.9	79.9
Ireland	50.5	37.0	68.3
Italy	71.0	74.8	81.0
Luxembourg	86.0	90.0	87.4
Netherlands	30.0	35.6	47.2
Portugal	40.0	35.7	51.2
Spain	64.0	59.6	54.8
Sweden	38.0	–	–
UK	23.0	36.4	36.2

O Backgrounds of MEPs

Few MEPs are nationally known figures or heavyweights in their own parties. Their calibre is arguably lower than that of national MPs, possibly because MEPs cannot aspire to promotion to the 'government benches'. The parliament elected in 1999 included former Commission President Jacques Santer, former commissioner Emma Bonino, former Portuguese President Mario Soares and former Luxembourg Prime Minister Jean-Claude Juncker. But these 'big names' tend to be past their domestic political peaks. Moreover, a study of the attendance records of the 1999 intake showed that many 'big names' had poor attendance records. The June 1999 cohort included MEPs with backgrounds in education, law, business, finance, the media, trades unionism, science, engineering, medicine, the civil service and agriculture. Almost one-third of the 1999 intake are women. There has been a decline in the number of MEPs who also have seats in national parliaments. Some countries do not allow it. MEPs are not allowed to serve in the governments of member states. There is a mandatory register of MEPs' financial interests, but it is not widely distributed and has many loopholes.

○ Organisation and Procedures

The EP does not have a single headquarters: its plenaries are normally held in Strasbourg; its specialist committees normally meet in Brussels; its secretariat is in Luxembourg. A protocol inserted into the ToA specified that the EP will hold its 12-monthly plenary sessions, including the budget session, in Strasbourg, with additional plenaries in Brussels, with its committees meeting in Brussels and its secretariat remaining in Luxembourg. The division between Strasbourg and Brussels mattered far less when the EP was largely a talking shop. The argument for moving the EP to Brussels has been strengthened in recent years by the increasingly important role of the EP in the EU's legislative process. In addition to the costs of maintaining two sites, there are also the costs in money, time and energy in transporting people and documents. The 'Brussels–Strasbourg Euroshuttle' requires lorries to regularly transport documents and equipment 350 miles between the two cities. Arguably, the Strasbourg location marginalises the EP in the eyes of the public, who are likely to view Brussels as the EU's decisionmaking centre.

The EP sits from Monday to Thursday in plenary session in a 'hemicycle' (half-circle) chamber every month in Strasbourg, excluding August. Plenary sessions are also held in Brussels. The EP's debates are open to the public. The EP is not an adversarial debating chamber and lacks the clash of hot opinion to be found in the UK House of Commons. Most debates are poorly attended by MEPs. There are fixed allocations of speaking time and pre arranged lists of speakers. The fact that its business is conducted in 11 official languages is hardly conducive to the free flow of argument. The EP has a president (currently the Frenchwoman Nicole Fontaine), 14 vice-presidents and a college of five quaestors, elected by MEPs. Quaestors make administrative and financial decisions affecting MEPs' interests. Its secretariat, which provides support services, is organised on similar lines to the Council Secretariat. It had 3505 permanent and 616 temporary posts at the end of 2000. The cost of running the EP in 1999 was about €666 million, about one-quarter of which went on translation costs and another quarter on travelling between sites.

The ToN will introduce QMV into the procedure whereby the Council must approve the EP's proposals on regulations and conditions governing the performance of the duties of MEPs. But all rules or conditions relating to the taxation of MEPs will continue to require unanimity (Article 190(5) ECT). Co-decision will be introduced by the ToN for regulations governing political parties at European level, in particular rules on funding (Article 191, ECT). Shortly after the ToN was negotiated, the Commission put forward proposals under a different legal basis for a reform of party funding (see p.143), partly to prevent funds from the EU budget being used to subsidise national parties.

O **Political Groups**

MEPs sit in political, rather than national, groups. Current groups, together with details of the affiliations of British parties, are shown in Tables 5.9 and 5.10. Currently, to be recognised as a political group, one of the following minimum criteria must be met: 14 MEPs from at least four countries; 18 from at least three countries; or 23 from at least two countries (see p. 143 for proposed changes to these criteria). The parties comprising political groups have broad ideological similarities. But party relationships within groups tend to be loose and there is no common organisation outside the EP context. Some groups are little more than marriages of convenience. Although parties may agree on a common (usually very broad) manifesto at election times, the national dimension remains strong: MEPs derive legitimacy from national parties and national electorates which select them, not from the groups. There are currently eight groups. Each group determines its own working methods.

Table 5.9 Members of the EP, 1999–2004 (Situation in May 2001)

	EPP/ ED	PES	ELDR	Greens/ EFA	EUL/ NGL	EUN	TGI	EDD	IND	Total
Austria	7	7	–	2	–	–	–	–	5	21
Belgium	6	5	5	7	–	–	2	–	–	25
Denmark	1	3	6	–	1	1	–	4	–	16
Finland	5	3	5	2	1	–	–	–	–	16
France	21	22	–	9	11	3	5	9	7	87
Germany	53	35	–	5	6	–	–	–	–	99
Greece	9	9	–	–	7	–	–	–	–	25
Ireland	5	1	1	2	–	6	–	–	–	15
Italy	34	16	8	2	6	9	12	–	–	87
Lux.	2	2	1	1	–	–	–	–	–	6
Neth.	9	6	8	4	1	–	–	3	–	31
Portugal	9	12	–	–	2	2	–	–	–	25
Spain	28	24	3	4	4	–	–	–	1	64
Sweden	7	6	4	2	3	–	–	–	–	22
UK	36	30	11	6	–	–	–	3	1	87
TOTAL	**232**	**181**	**52**	**46**	**42**	**21**	**19**	**19**	**14**	**626**

Abbreviations

EPP/ED:	European Peoples' Party/European Democrats
PES:	Party of European Socialists
ELDR:	European Liberal, Democrat and Reform
Greens/EFA:	Greens/European Free Alliance
EUL/NGL:	European United Left and Nordic Green Left
EUN:	Union for a Europe of the Nations
TGI:	Technical Group of Independents
EDD:	Europe of Democracies and Diversities
IND:	Independents

Table 5.10 Political Groups of UK MEPs (Situation in May 2001)

Party	Group	Seats
Labour	PES	29
Conservative	EPP/ED	35
Liberal Democrats	ELDR	11
UK Independence	EDD	3
Green Party	Greens/EFA	2
Plaid Cymru	Greens/EFA	2
Scottish National Party	Greens/EFA	2
Social Democratic and Labour Party	PES	1
Ulster Unionist Party	EPP	1
Democratic Unionist Party	IND	1

There are two very big political groups: the European Peoples' Party and European Democrats (EPP/ED) and the Party of European Socialists (PES). The EPP/ED is a broad centre-right group of Christian Democrats, European Democrats and conservatives. The 1999 elections resulted in the centre-left PES losing control of the chamber for the first time since direct elections were held. The Greens/European Free Alliance comprises 'greens' and home rule and regionalist parties in the UK and Spain. The European United Left and Nordic Green Left (EUL/NGL) comprises left-wing and green parties from ten countries. The European Liberal, Democrat and Reform Party (ELDR) includes eleven British Liberal Democrats. The political charter of the Union for a Europe of the Nations states that the group favours the diversity of nations and opposes a Federal Europe. The Europe of Democracies and Diversities is a 'Eurosceptic' alliance of French pro-hunting and rural traditional interests, the UK Independence Party and Danish and Dutch parties opposed to deeper EU integration. A group of Italian, French and Belgian MEPs have registered as a 'Technical Group of Independents' (TGI) in order to enjoy group privileges. There are also 14 independents. Usually after an EP election, there are changes to party formations (the tendency being for parties to leave smaller groups to join larger ones, to avoid being marginalized).

There is a strong incentive for a party to join a group: there is definite strength in numbers, as the party is more likely to be allocated offices and also to be able to pursue its policy aims successfully by forming an alliance with others. Parties in the EP do not form pro-government and opposition parties, as they do in most democratic legislatures. Because the EP generally requires an absolute majority on legislation, the EPP/ED and PES frequently act together to enable decisions to be taken. In any case, most parties share a pro-European stance and view their real adversary as the Council rather than each other. The Eurosceptic parties are too small to form a powerful bloc.

Serving as an MEP is unlikely to lead to a post in the home government or in the Commission. Competition for advancement among MEPs within the EP centres on selection for specific committees and party leadership posts. The prospects for re-selection depend on national parties, not on the party groups, so it is with that constituency MEPs will primarily be concerned. However, national party selectors are likely to be impressed if the MEP gains an office such as the chairmanship of an important parliamentary committee. The leaderships of the party groups play the key role in allocating committee places and setting plenary session agendas. Committee chairmen are reallocated twice during each parliamentary term. These posts are allocated in proportion to the number of seats held by each party, with the EPP and PES getting the lion's share of chairmanships. The large number of parties (currently over 60) and groups renders it difficult for the EP to act cohesively.

In January 2001, the Commission proposed a statute which would, if adopted, introduce new eligibility criteria for the recognition and funding of European political parties: recognition criteria would include respect for democracy, fundamental rights and the rule of law, plus participation in a political group; funding criteria would include: elected members in the EP, national or regional parliaments in at least five member states or at least 5% of votes in five member states in the last EP elections; and at least 25% of the party's budget would come from its own resources. The proposal has been criticised by smaller parties for favouring larger groups and by 'Eurosceptics' for requiring parties to observe certain political principles. The legal basis upon which it is being introduced (Article 308, ECT) is also being challenged. In May 2001, the EP approved the Schleicher report on the proposal. The report, named after its rapporteur, German MEP Ursula Schleicher, advocated similar eligibility criteria to those in the proposal: it would also require a party to respect the Charter of Fundamental Rights. The Council has yet to decide on the Commission's proposal, which must be approved by a unanimous vote.

○ The Committee System

Much of the Parliament's work takes place in committee. There are 17 standing committees (Table 5.11 overleaf) and a small number of temporary committees and committees of inquiry. Some committees are far more popular than others (for example, foreign affairs and environment policy). Seats are divided on the basis of party group strength. Committee meetings take place two weeks a month in Brussels and are normally open to the public. Their key function is to examine legislative draft laws and policy issues in detail. Committee meetings are frequently attended by commissioners and other officials. Each MEP generally serves on two standing committees, as a full member of one and as a substitute for the other. Each committee is headed by a rapporteur (a committee member chosen by other members) who draws up the committee report. Committee minutes have to be translated into the 11 official languages. The committee structure was reorganised in 1999.

Table 5.11 Parliamentary Committees

- Foreign Affairs, Human Rights, Common Security and Defence Policy
- Budgets
- Budgetary Control
- Citizens' Freedoms and Rights, Justice and Home Affairs
- Economic and Monetary Affairs
- Legal Affairs and the Internal Market
- Industry, External Trade, Research and Energy
- Employment and Social Affairs
- Environment, Public Health and Consumer Policy
- Agriculture and Rural Development
- Fisheries
- Regional Policy, Transport and Tourism
- Culture, Youth, Education, the Media and Sport
- Development and Co-operation
- Constitutional Affairs
- Women's Rights and Equal Opportunities
- Petitions

Plus a small number of temporary committees and committees of inquiry

O   Interparliamentary Institutions

There is an ACP (African, Caribbean and Pacific)–EU Assembly on which over 70 MEPs serve. There are also inter-parliamentary delegations through which MEPs maintain relations with other parliaments and organisations outside the EU. The EP has 14 delegations to joint parliamentary committees and 20 interparliamentary delegations.

O   Main Functions and Roles of the EP

- **Legislative powers**. The EU's legislature is made up of the Council representing member states and the EP representing EU citizens. The EP is therefore the joint legislative arm of the Union. The EP is an integral element of the legislative process, but does not initiate legislation, which is the formal responsibility of the Commission. Since the ratification of the TEU, the EP may (under Article 192, ECT) by absolute majority request the Commission to submit a proposal where it is felt that a 'Community act is required for the purpose of implementing (the) Treaty'. However, this still does not give parliament the power to initiate legislation (although this depends on the interpretation of the word 'request'). Moreover, absolute majorities are difficult to obtain. It may issue 'own initiative' reports, but the Commission is not required to act on them. However, the informal influence it has on agenda setting and initiation is far from negligible.

Its legislative role used to be solely consultative. However, as a result of provisions in the SEA, the TEU, the ToA and the ToN, it now has substantial power to amend, and in some areas, veto legislation. About half of the EP's amendments to legislation are accepted. In July 1994 the EP used for the first time its limited powers of veto (the co-decision procedure introduced in the TEU and extended in the ToA) to reject a Council decision on the liberalisation of the voice telecommunications market. The ToA extended co-decision to 23 provisions: eight referred to new provisions and 15 to provisions previously covered by other procedures. It also streamlined the procedure, by eliminating the 'third reading', by which the Council could reaffirm its position: this means that the EP has equal weight with the Council in areas where co-decision applies. The ToN will extend co-decision, or in some cases allows for the possibility of its extension, to various other provisions (see pp. 171–2). But the EP's legislative powers, although now formidable, remain incomplete. For example, it is excluded from trade policy and the Common Agricultural Policy (CAP). Co-decision does not yet apply to all categories of legislation and all legislation still requires Council approval. Nor does the EP have to be consulted on Commission legislation.

• **The assent procedure.** The EP must consent to certain decisions before they can take effect. In some cases, the EP's assent requires a simple majority whereas in others it requires an absolute majority. The assent procedure was first introduced in the SEA and was extended by the TEU, ToA and ToN (see Table 5.12).

Table 5.12 Scope of the Assent Procedure (Post-Amsterdam and -Nice)

Article	Subject
18.2, ECT	Citizenship
105 (6) & 107.5, ECT	Monetary policy (powers of ECB)
161, ECT+	Structural Funds and Cohesion Fund
214.2, ECT	Appointment of Commission
190 (4), ECT	Uniform electoral procedure
300 (3), ECT	Some international agreements
Article 49, TEU	Accession of new member states
Article 7, TEU*	Fundamental rights
Article 11, ECT*	Enhanced co-operation (first pillar)

* Introduced in the ToN; + extended in the ToN

The TEU extended the scope of parliamentary assent considerably to cover a range of new issues, such as citizenship, the organisation of the structural funds, changes to the statute of the European system of central banks, the appointment of the Commission, and the uniform electoral procedure for European elections. The assent procedure gives the EP the last word on certain key decisions. It has no power to *amend* decisions under the procedure, but it can and does comment on them. Compared to co-decision, assent is a blunt weapon, but nevertheless a powerful one. The procedure does not cover all EU international agreements (for example, it only covers agreements establishing a specific institutional framework, or with budgetary implications or requiring the amendment of Community legislation under the co-decision procedure. It therefore, for example, excludes trade agreements reached under Article 133 of the EC Treaty). The EP has, however, used its assent procedure to block trade agreements with Turkey and Israel, (under Article 300.3) for alleged human rights violations.

• **Supervisory functions**. A basic function of any parliament is to oversee the work of the executive. However, within the Union, the Council, the European Council and the Commission each perform executive roles. Moreover, the rotating Council presidency, and the diversity of views within the European Council and the Council, means that the EP does not have a fixed or clear target upon which to focus. The EP's supervisory role is more apparent with regard to the Commission, which it has power to dismiss, rather than the Council. The EP does not appoint, nor can it dismiss, the Council or the European Council, the members of which are primarily answerable to the national parliaments of member states. Most EU policy is in any case implemented at national level and therefore it is difficult for the EP to supervise the execution of EU policy 'on the ground'.

There is little formal direct contact between the EP and the European Council, although the EP presidency is allowed to address the opening session of the European Council. The presidency of the Council (usually represented by the foreign minister) explains its programme to a plenary session of parliament at the start of each presidency. At the end of each presidency, the foreign minister returns to summarise the results achieved. Under Article 21 of the TEU, the presidency is required to consult the EP on the main aspects and basic choices of the CFSP and to ensure that the EP's views are taken into consideration, but there is scant evidence of its influence in this area so far. Members of the Council attend plenary sessions of the EP and are asked to reply to written and oral questions.

MEPs may put written questions to the Commission or Council. In 2000, MEPs addressed 5312 questions to the Commission and Council – 4163 written questions (3678 to the Commission and 485 to the Council), 145 oral questions with debate (89 to the Commission and 56 to the Council) and 1004 during question time (650 to the Commission and 354 to the Council). The EP can ask questions on subjects relating to any of the three pillars. It can ask the Court of Auditors to carry out special enquiries. It debates the Commission's annual work and legislative programmes and also the Commission's annual general report, but there is little evidence that these debates have much influence.

- **Budgetary functions**. Together with the Council, the EP is the budgetary authority of the Community. The EP has the right to propose modifications to compulsory expenditure (spending which arises from treaty obligations, mainly relating to the CAP) and the right to propose amendments to non-compulsory expenditure (that is, expenditure which is not a direct consequence of treaty obligations, such as spending on regional aid or research and technological development: RTD). The modifications it proposes cannot increase expenditure and the Council can reject them by QMV. The Council has the 'last word' on compulsory expenditure whereas the EP has the 'last word' on non-compulsory expenditure (currently accounting for around half of the total). The EP has campaigned consistently for the abolition of the distinction between compulsory and non-compulsory expenditure, but without success. In 1988, an interinstitutional agreement on budgetary discipline increased the non-compulsory elements of the budget. Under Article 272 of the EC Treaty, by majority vote and two-thirds of votes cast, it can reject the draft budget (as it has done on several occasions, although it subsequently has adopted revised budgets). Since 1977, the EP has had the exclusive right to grant a discharge of the general budget. However, this occurs after expenditure has been incurred. For example, on 17 December 1998, the EP refused to approve the EU's accounts for 1996.
- **Involvement in the appointment and dismissal of the Commission**. The EP can dismiss the Commission, by passing a censure motion requiring a two-thirds majority of votes cast, amounting to an absolute majority of members. However, the Council could simply re-appoint the same commissioners. Nor does the EP have the power to dismiss individual commissioners. However, the TEU gave parliament powers of approval in relation to the appointment of the Commission (the right of 'investiture'). It had a right to be consulted on the choice of president, that is, on the Council's nomination. It interpreted this as meaning it had a right to vote on the Council's nominee. It also holds Commission hearings, whereby nominees must explain themselves to an EU committee. A new Commission including a president must be approved by the parliament within six months of the election of a new parliament.

In 1994 and 1995, the EP sought to assert its new powers acquired under the TEU by engaging in several 'muscle-flexing' episodes, for example, by threatening to veto the Council's nomination for president-designate. Although MEPs were unhappy about the manner of his selection, Santer's nomination for the Commission presidency was endorsed by 260 votes to 238 with 23 abstentions. The vote was non-binding, but Council President in Office Klaus Kinkel said he would abide by the result. The EP questioned each of the nominees for the 1995–99 Commission (giving several a rough ride) but endorsed the new Commission on 20 January 1995. It passed votes of no confidence in two commissioners, Edith Cresson and Manuel Marin, but these were not legally binding. In 1998, it threatened the Commission with censure over food safety. In March 1999, it forced the resignation of the Santer Commission: although a censure motion was defeated on the issue of Commission mismanagement and fraud, the Commission nevertheless resigned. Following the resignation of the Santer Commission, the EP subjected the president-designate and the nominated commissioners to detailed scrutiny before granting its approval to the new Commission.

• **Participation in other appointments**. The EP is consulted on the appointment of the Court of Auditors and the European Central Bank, although not on appointments to the European Court of Justice (ECJ). It also appoints an ombudsman (see below).

• **Forum**. The EP holds discussions on many important issues and has provided a platform for many world statesmen, although the impact of this forum function is probably very limited.

• **Redress of grievances**. The TEU gave the EP formal powers in relation to the redress of grievances. Any citizen of the Union may petition the EP on any matter within the EU's field of responsibility, providing it affects the petitioner directly. The EP elects an ombudsman after each EP election to receive complaints from any Union citizen, or others resident in a member state, concerning maladministration in the activities of Community institutions, excluding the ECJ and the Court of First Instance acting in their judicial roles (Article 195, ECT). The ombudsman is completely independent and can only be dismissed by the ECJ at the request of the EP if he no longer fulfils the conditions required for the performance of his duties or if he is guilty of serious misconduct. The ombudsman acts either on his own initiative or on a complaint submitted to him direct or through an MEP, except in cases which are or have been the subject of legal proceedings. The ToA extended the ombudsman's remit to cover the PJCCM (third) pillar (Article 41, TEU). However, the treaty does not commit EC institutions to act on the ombudsman's findings.

• **Committees of inquiry** At the request of a quarter of its members, the EP may set up a temporary committee of inquiry to investigate alleged contraventions or maladministration in the implementation of Union law (Article 193, ECT). The result of its first inquiry, into the EU's transit system, was published in 1997. Its second inquiry, on BSE (bovine spongiform encephalopathy or 'mad cow disease'), has been said to have been influential in changing EU secondary legislation on veterinary medicine. In July 2000 it launched a third enquiry entitled 'Echelon', on electronic surveillance.

• **An agitator for EU 'Constitutional Reform'**. Throughout its history, the EP has been very active in calling for further institutional reform, particularly reforms which would push the Union forward in a 'federalist' direction. However, it has had no power to realise its aims. The EP had no formal input into the negotiations which led to the TEU. But two MEPs were appointed to the 'Reflection Group' established to prepare for the 1996/97 IGC and to IGC 2000, although no MEP has a place at the negotiating table when a new treaty is being decided. The EP is seeking a substantial increase in its powers, including extension of 'co-decision', the right to choose the Commission, the right to agree a five-year programme with the Commission, the right to monitor the Council and the right to raise revenue.

◯ National Parliaments and the European Union

Although EU legislation is scrutinised by national parliaments, the key issues have usually been decided before national parliaments have had an opportunity to consider them. This does not necessarily mean that national parliaments are of no consequence in EU affairs. For example, the Danish parliament, which has a powerful Common Market Relations Committee, initially voted against the SEA in 1986.

The relationships between the EP and national parliaments are currently weak, although both the TEU and the ToA seek to strengthen these links. Two declarations on the role of national parliaments were attached to the TEU. One sought to encourage closer contact between national parliaments and the EP and to improve the speed at which national parliaments received EU information. The other invited national parliaments and the EP to meet as a 'conference of parliaments'. The ToA annexed a new protocol to the EU treaties on the role of national parliaments in the EU. It confirmed that whilst scrutiny by individual national parliaments of their own governments in relation to the activities of the Union is a matter for each member state, the parties to the treaties sought to encourage greater involvement of national parliaments in Union activities. The protocol requires:

- all Commission consultation documents (green and white papers and communications) to be promptly forwarded to national parliaments;
- Commission proposals for legislation to be made available in good time, so that governments ensure that national parliaments receive them as appropriate; and
- a six-week period to elapse between a legislative proposal or a proposal for a measure adopted under the third pillar being made available to the EP and the Council by the Commission and the date when it is placed on a Council agenda for decision, subject to exceptions on grounds of urgency.

The EP has some formal contacts with national parliaments: there are annual meetings of the presidents of national parliaments and those of the EP; there is a Conference of European Affairs Committees (COSAC), which has met bi-annually since 1989 in the member state holding the Council presidency. It comprises representatives of relevant committees of national parliaments and of the EP, with a maximum of six MPs in each delegation. The ToA included a protocol on COSAC which allows it to make any contribution it deems appropriate for the attention of EU institutions, in particular on the basis of draft legal texts which representatives of governments of member states may decide by common accord to forward to it. COSAC can also examine proposals for legislative instruments relating to the area of freedom, security and justice which might have a direct bearing on the rights and freedoms of individuals. It may address to the EP, the Council and the Commission any contribution which it deems appropriate on EU legislative activities. However, COSAC has no formal decisionmaking powers and is a forum for the exchange of information. The IGC scheduled for 2004 will re-examine the issue of the role of national parliaments in the EU.

O EU Affairs and the UK Parliament

Ministers representing the UK in the Council and European Council are accountable to the UK parliament. Ministers in both the House of Commons and the House of Lords make statements on the outcome of Council and European Council meetings. Ministers may make statements on EU matters in the course of specific debates. In the UK, there are regular debates on EU affairs in both houses of parliament. Members of either house can ask written or oral questions on EU matters. There is a twice-yearly government white paper on developments in the Union, which is debated in parliament. There are also debates on the EU prior to European Council meetings in June and December. The big 'European' debates in the House of Commons tend to be of a general nature, providing Eurosceptic MPs with opportunities to assail the Union in general and British membership of the Union in particular.

Both houses of parliament have a select committee on European legislation. Such legislation is usually implemented through a statutory instrument laid before the UK parliament. In some cases however, the new legislation is included in a draft bill amending existing legislation. The select committee on European legislation in the Commons is known as the Scrutiny Committee and has 16 members, nominated for the duration of a parliament. It receives copies of Commission proposals, together with an explanatory memorandum prepared by the relevant government department. Any MP may take part in the committee's proceedings and may move amendments to motions, but only committee members may vote or be counted in the quorum. The scrutiny committee refers legislation to one of three European standing committees, (A, B or C), each with 13 members. Each deals with a different range of subjects. The committees may require a minister to make a statement or answer questions by members. The select committee in the House of Lords also examines proposals and produces reports.

○ **Evaluation**

The EP is clearly far more than a mere talking shop. Even though it does not have full control over the executive, its legislative and assent powers in particular now make it a force to be reckoned with. It also has a democratic mandate. However, unlike elections to the UK parliament, elections to the EP do not lead to the formation of a government. Nor can the EP vote the Council out of office. Nor does it yet have full legislative or budgetary powers. Its supervisory influence over the Council and the European Council remains weak. Its organisation on three sites is confusing and wasteful. Although it has frequently criticised the Commission for financial laxity and inefficiency, it has also been frequently accused of these failings. For example, a Court of Auditors' special report in 2000 (no. 6/ 2000) criticised the lax financial controls of spending by the political groups.

The EP also has a formidable public image problem: most European citizens remain ignorant or indifferent about the work of the EP. It attracts few top-flight politicians from member states. Its debates are seldom widely reported. It also lacks a 'parliamentary culture', perhaps due in part to the fact that new MEPS are often steeped in the traditions of their own national parliaments. Debates are dull. MEPs spend hours voting through technical amendments which they have not read or understood. The problem of MEP absenteeism has meant that it has been difficult to secure an absolute majority for some key votes. About a quarter of MEPs regularly fail to turn up for votes for plenary sessions. Arguably, this is at least partly due to the fact that the EP in Strasbourg is difficult to get to for many MEPs. In May 2001, MEPs voted to drop Friday meetings. It is widely accepted that reforms of the institution are needed in order for it to be able to fulfil its functions effectively. Examples of reform ideas are:

- granting the EP more power over legislation, finance and investiture;
- enabling the EP to concentrate more on 'big picture' debates rather than on the minutiae of legislation;
- replacing the EP with a bicameral system, by creating a second chamber in the form of a European senate, made up of MPs from national parliaments. This would provide a formal link between the EP and national parliaments. However, a second chamber might be hidebound to national interests and could create a conflict of democratic legitimacies, undermining the EP as a parliament in its own right;
- introducing 'constituency weeks' into the parliamentary calendar, to enable members to connect with their constituents more frequently;
- common salaries for MEPs, together with a common EU tax on these salaries. However, this proposal has found little favour with MEPs, some of whom would be worse off financially were it to be introduced.

● THE EUROPEAN COURT OF JUSTICE

○ Functions

The Court is the Union's judicial institution, with the task of ensuring that Union law is observed. It is also the authoritative interpreter and clarifier of Union law. This means that it ensures that member states fulfil their legal obligations under the treaties; that the institutions operate within the powers conferred on them by the treaties; and that the courts in member states interpret and apply Union law uniformly and correctly. Despite the fact that the vast bulk of 'Union law' relates to the Community treaties, the term 'Union law' rather than 'Community law' is used in this chapter because the Union as a whole is a legal order and because the ECJ now has (an albeit limited) remit in certain matters relating to the Union in addition to its remit over the Community. In its first 40 years, the ECJ made nearly 5000 judgments, including some of crucial importance to the Union's development. For example, the *Cassis de Dijon* judgment (1979) established the principle that goods fit to be sold in one member state are fit to be sold in them all (case 120/78). It is debatable whether the SEM programme would have been launched without this judgment. The Court cannot initiate cases, but makes judgments on cases referred to it by Union institutions, national governments, national courts, corporate bodies or individuals.

The ECJ is not to be confused with the European Court of Human Rights (ECHR), which is a Council of Europe institution based in Strasbourg. The ECHR derives from the Council of Europe's Convention for the Protection of Human Rights and Fundamental Freedoms signed in Rome in November 1950. Its role is to ensure the observance of the obligations entered into by the member states under the Convention. Article 6 of the TEU requires the Union to respect fundamental rights as guaranteed by this Convention, but human rights in the EU may only be enforced against EU legislation, acts of the EU institutions or acts of a member state in implementing Union law.

○ The Limited Jurisdiction of the ECJ

The remit of the ECJ does not extend to all facets of the Union. Union law has not supplanted the national law of member states (although it takes precedence if there is a conflict between the two). Nor does it extend to all judicial matters (for example, it excludes criminal law and has little involvement in areas where EU policy is relatively undeveloped, such as health and education). The ECJ can only act within the powers given it in the treaties. It is not a 'Supreme Court' on the US model, because the latter is part of a hierarchy of courts (district, state, federal). The ECJ, by contrast, has no formal connection with the courts of member states, each of which has its own legal traditions and judicial system.

Article 46 of the TEU as amended by the ToA specifies the treaty provisions which are subject to the exercise of the ECJ's powers. These powers apply to the amended EC, ECSC and Euratom treaties and to certain specified aspects of the TEU. The latter covers some aspects of Title VI dealing with police and judicial co-operation in criminal matters; to some aspects of Title VII dealing with closer co-operation; to Article 6.2 dealing with the requirement for the Union to respect fundamental rights; and to the TEU's final provisions, dealing with accession and treaty amendments. Article 46 therefore excludes the ECJ from jurisdiction over the CFSP pillar and from most of the PJCCM pillar. It also excludes it from jurisdiction over the Union's objectives (in the *Grau Gomis and Others* case (April 1995), the court held that it had no jurisdiction to interpret Article 2 of the TEU on the Union's objectives (case 167/94). The court's remit also excludes measures relating to the maintenance of law and order and the safeguarding of internal security. Its powers to give rulings on the interpretation of treaty provisions are also restricted. It has the right to review the legality of 'third-pillar' decisions, as well as to rule on disputes between member states, or between the Commission and member states: but neither the EP nor private actors can bring such cases to the court. In relation to the 'Communitarized' issues of free movement, asylum and immigration, preliminary rulings may only be sought by the highest courts of member states. Nor does the remit of the ECJ extend to the organisation and functions of the European Council.

○ Cases

The cases heard by the court are of two general types, *direct actions* and *indirect actions*. In direct actions, a party refers a dispute to the Court. Direct actions fall into six categories:
(1) proceedings for failure to fulfil an obligation;
(2) applications for annulment;
(3) proceedings for failure to act;
(4) actions for damages;
(5) cases brought by Community servants (staff cases); and
(6) appeals on points of law against judgments of the Court of First Instance (CFI).

In indirect actions, known as preliminary rulings, the court is requested by a court or tribunal in a member state to give a preliminary ruling on points of EU law. In addition, the ECJ's opinion may be sought on the legality of proposed international agreements. These cases are explained more fully below.

- **Direct actions**
  - *Failure to fulfil an obligation.* The Commission can bring an action to force a member state to comply with its obligations under the EC Treaty. Before the matter is brought before the court, the Commission delivers a reasoned opinion, giving the state concerned the right to respond and to comply (Article 226, ECT); a member state can bring an action against another member state for an alleged infringement of an obligation under the treaty. A reasoned opinion must be sought from the Commission before proceeding (Article 227, ECT). Most actions are brought by the Commission and most are settled without the need to be brought before the court. Actions by a member state against another member state are rare, perhaps because it might sour relations between the states concerned, leading to 'tit for tat' actions (although in 1978 France took the UK to court for introducing fish conservation measures without consultation. The court ordered the UK to repeal the measures (case 141/78)).
  - *Application for annulment.* Under Article 230, ECT, a member state, the Council or the Commission may apply to the court for the annulment of all or part of an item of Community legislation. Natural and legal persons may seek the annulment of a legal measure which is of direct and individual concern to them. The EP, the Court of Auditors and the ECB can bring actions to protect their prerogatives. Actions can be brought grounds of lack of competence, infringement of an essential procedural requirement, infringement of the EC Treaty or of any rule of law relating to its application or misuse of powers. Under Article 231, ECT, the ECJ can declare an act void if the action is well-founded. In the 1980 'Isoglucose judgment' (case 138/79), the court annulled an item of legislation because the Commission had failed to consult the EP when required to do so.
  - *Failure to act* (Article 232, ECT). Member states and the other institutions of the Community may bring an action against the EP, the Council or the Commission for failure to act. For example, in 1985, the court gave a judgment in a case brought by the EP against the Council for failing to introduce a common transport policy (case 13/83). Natural and legal persons may also complain to the court that a Community institution has failed to address to that person any act other than a recommendation or opinion.
  - *Actions for damages* (Articles 235, and 288, ECT). In an action for damages, the court rules on the liability of the Community for damage caused by its institutions or its servants in the performance of their duties. This includes member states in breach of Community law. For example, in *Frankovich* vs. *Italy*, the court ruled that the Italian government had failed to implement an EC directive on payment of wages by an insolvent employer (case 6 & 9/90).

- *Staff cases* (Article 236, ECT). The ECJ has jurisdiction in any dispute between the Community and its servants under the conditions laid down in the staff regulations or the conditions of employment
- *Appeals* (Article 225, ECT). The Court of Justice may hear appeals, on points of law only, against judgments given by the Court of First Instance in cases within its jurisdiction. Few such appeals succeed.

- **Indirect Actions.** These are *preliminary rulings* on references by national courts. Under Article 234 (ECT), national courts or tribunals seek judgments on cases brought to them which relate to any aspect of EU law. National courts have jurisdiction to review the administrative implementation of Union law, for which the authorities of member states are essentially responsible. The provisions of the treaties and secondary legislation (that is, regulations, directives and decisions) directly confer rights on nationals of member states which national courts must uphold. There is no appeal against the court's rulings. There has been a substantial increase in the use by national courts of preliminary rulings. The number of references for a preliminary ruling increased by about 85% between 1990 and 1998 and now account for over half of the new cases brought before the ECJ. Over 3,500 references for preliminary rulings have been submitted to the ECJ since it was first established.

In addition to the above, the court also gives opinions when requested to do so on the compatibility of international agreements with Union law (Article 300, ECT). Its opinions in such cases are binding. The Council, the Commission or a member state can request an opinion on proposed international agreements For example: in 1994, in response to a request for clarification from the Commission, the court ruled that the Commission and member states shared power to conclude agreements on trade in services and trade-related aspects of intellectual property (opinion 1/94 on the WTO Agreement).

The Commission has brought the most number of actions (which is hardly surprising given its role as guardian of the treaties) and has also been taken to the court more than any other body. The EP has taken the Council to the ECJ on a wide range of issues, such as transport (for failing to put into effect a common transport policy (case 13/83), 'comitology' (case 302/87), the draft budget (case 377/87), trade competence (case 360/93), road taxes (case 21/94) and visas (case 392/95). It has also brought actions against the Commission, for example, in 1994, the EP brought an action against the Commission on the issues of genetically modified micro-organisms (case 156/93) and frontier controls (case 445/93). In 1998, for the first time the ECJ was required to consider the question of citizenship of the Union, ruling that a national of a member state residing in another member state may rely on the TEU article dealing with European citizenship. In July 2000, the ECJ fined

Greece heavily for failing to comply with regulations governing the disposal of toxic waste. Greece was ordered to pay €20,000 a day until it complied with an earlier ruling to clean up a waste dump near a Crete holiday resort.

The ToA amended Article 46 of the TEU to enable the ECJ to give preliminary rulings on the validity and interpretation of framework decisions and decisions on the interpretation of conventions under the third (PJCCM) pillar. Its remit was also extended to provisions on closer co-operation under the third pillar.

⭕ Key Sources and Principles of Union Law

The sources of EU law are categorised in Table 5.13 below.

Table 5.13 Sources of Union Law

Primary legislation: that is, the treaties, including annexes, protocols and amendments to the treaties (although elements of the TEU are outside the ECJ's jurisdiction). It also includes treaties of accession.
Secondary legislation: adopted laws made by institutions in accordance with powers granted them by the treaties.
General principles of law (for example, 'proportionality' and fundamental human rights).
International law, to which the ECJ has referred in its judgments on issues with external implications.
Judicial interpretation (that is, 'case law' – the rulings of the ECJ).

The court operates on the basis of three fundamental principles, which were established before the UK joined the Union:

1. *Direct effect.* In the *Van Gend en Loos* judgment (case 26/62) the Court ruled that Community law creates rights for citizens which national courts must recognise and enforce. The principle applies to most treaty provisions and secondary legislation.

2. *Direct applicability.* Regulations (see below) are directly applicable in member states, without need for national legislatures to pass implementing legislation. It should be noted that the distinction between (1) and (2) is not always made and the terms are sometimes used interchangeably.

3. *The primacy of Union law over national law.* EU law cannot be overridden by domestic legal provisions (*Costa* v. *ENAL*, case 6/64). The ECJ can declare void any legal instruments adopted by the Commission, the Council or national governments which it deems incompatible with EU law. The European Communities Act (1972) gave legal force to EC law in the UK.

○ Structure and Working Methods

The court comprises one judge from each member state. Judges are chosen from persons whose independence is beyond doubt and who possess the qualifications required for appointment to the highest judicial offices. They are chosen from the legal and academic professions as well as from national judiciaries (few have been top flight judges in their home countries). All are appointed by common accord of the governments of member states for a renewable term of six years. Every three years there is a partial replacement of judges, with eight and seven judges being replaced alternately. One judge is elected president of the court by the others for a renewable term of three years. The court is assisted by advocates-general, who make reasoned submissions on cases brought before the court. The ToN stipulates that there shall be eight of these, although should the court so request, the Council may increase this number by unanimous vote. The advocates-general are partially replaced every three years, with four being replaced on each occasion. The court currently sits in chambers and plenary sessions. The chambers are comprised of three to five judges. The judges elect presidents of the chambers from among their number for 3 years (renewable once). When changes in the ToN are introduced, the court will also sit in grand chambers of eleven judges, which will deal with most of the cases currently dealt with in plenary session (see below). Grand chambers will not replace the smaller chambers.

There are two stages to the procedure before the ECJ and the CFI, a written stage followed by an oral stage. The written stage is generally viewed as the most important. At the written stage, there are differences in the procedures for direct and indirect actions (that is, preliminary rulings). Information relating to a case before the ECJ is gathered by an advocate-general and a judge-rapporteur, appointed by the president of the court to draw up a report for the oral hearing and a draft decision (there is normally no advocate-general for CFI cases). After the written stage, there is a public hearing, where lawyers of the parties involved make oral statements and are questioned by the judges and advocates-general. The advocate-general submits a report to the judge-rapporteur who, after considering the report, presents the court with a draft decision. After expressing their opinions, the judges take a vote by simple majority, although votes are always announced as unanimous. Sittings are held in public. The ECJ and CFI may use any of the official languages or Irish. The language is chosen by the applicant, but in references for preliminary rulings, it is the language of the national court making the reference. There is simultaneous interpreting at the hearing. Parties bringing direct actions are likely to use their own language. However, French is the common working language (judges deliberate without interpreters). Judgments and opinions are translated into all official languages.

○ The Court of First Instance

In order to enable the ECJ to cope with the large volume of cases, a *Court of First Instance* (CFI) was established under the SEA and began its work in October 1989. It is a second tier of judicial authority, established to enable the court to concentrate on its essential function, the interpretation of Union law. Each member state appoints a judge to the CFI for six years. It has four chambers. The CFI initially dealt only with administrative disputes within the institutions and disputes between the Commission and firms over competition rules or between the Commission and matters covered by the ECSC Treaty. From March 1994 jurisdiction in respect of trade protection measures was transferred from the ECJ to the CFI. In 1993 and 1994, the jurisdiction of the CFI was extended to cover all direct actions brought by natural or legal persons, but not those brought by the Community institutions or the member states. The ToN will extend the CFI's jurisdiction further to cover direct actions and also allows for judicial panels to be attached to the CFI in order to exercise competence in certain specific areas (see below). The CFI's judgments are subject to appeal to the ECJ on points of law. On issues of fact, the CFI's rulings are final. About a quarter of cases result in appeals. The ECJ and the CFI had 769 permanent and 241 temporary staff in 2000.

○ Reform of the ECJ and the CFI

As presently constituted, both the ECJ and the CFI are having difficulty in fulfilling their roles, due to the large increase in the number of cases. The court has a heavy caseload, made heavier by the need for documents to be translated. Between 1990 and 1998, there was an 87% increase in requests for preliminary rulings and a doubling in the number of CFI cases between 1992 and 1998. Whereas in 1975 the ECJ had 130 cases pending, on 1 January 2000 it had 896 and the CFI had 732. This workload is likely to increase further as a result of enlargement and various institutional and policy developments. Every enlargement increases the potential number of potential complainants. Every institutional or policy development creates new potential sources of dispute. The average time taken for cases to come to judgment has grown from six months in 1975 to 21 months for the ECJ and 30 months for the CFI in 2000. The number of preliminary reference proceedings is increasing as a result of the extension of the court's jurisdiction by the ToA to 'third-pillar' subjects, legislation relating to the introduction of the euro, the right conferred on the Court of Auditors and the ECB to initiate proceedings as well as similar rights of member states under Title VI of the TEU. The CFI is dealing with an increasing number of cases concerning trademarks and access to Union documents.

The court has therefore sought a revision of its organisational and procedural framework, to enable it to deal with the growing volume of cases. In a discussion paper entitled *The Future of the Judicial System of the EU* (ECJ, 2000), it proposed that it should be allowed to: amend its own rules of procedure; that a filtering mechanism to restrict appeals to the ECJ should be introduced, in cases which have already been initially reviewed before referral to the CFI; and that interinstitutional tribunals should be established to deal with staff cases; that the CFI should be enabled to hear certain actions for annulment brought by member states in certain fields; and that six fields of Union law be transferred to the CFI, namely: the common transport policy, competition rules applicable to undertakings, state aids, trade protection measures, decisions relating to Union funds and Commission decisions relating to clearance of accounts under the EAGGF. The proposals were controversial, because many of these fields raise politically sensitive issues.

In March 2000, the Commission submitted a document on reform of the ECJ and CFI (*The Future of the European Communities' Court System*, January 2000). The report noted that the courts were having increasing difficulty in fulfilling their roles and that this problem would increase with enlargement. The Commission's proposals for reform included ideas for clarifying the roles of the ECJ and national courts, to provide the latter with more scope for dealing with cases requiring preliminary rulings; transferring a large proportion of direct actions to the CFI, thereby limiting the ECJ's role to questions fundamental to the EU's legal order; and reducing the volume of certain types of cases. These ideas fed into the deliberations of the 2000 IGC and into the changes made to the courts in the ToN.

○ Reform of the ECJ and the CFI in the Treaty of Nice

The ToN contains substantial revisions of the EC Treaty's provisions on the ECJ and the CFI. The main changes made by the ToN are:
- **The Statute of the Court of Justice.** This is laid down in a protocol. The Statute's 64 articles stipulate the obligations and rights of the judges and advocates-general and the organisation and procedures of the ECJ and the CFI. Acting unanimously at the request of the ECJ, and after consulting the EP and the Commission or at the request of the Commission and after consulting the EP and the ECJ, the Council may amend the Statute, excluding Article 1, which states that it functions in accord with the provisions of the Union treaties;
- **The Grand Chamber.** It establishes the 'Grand Chamber', comprising eleven judges, including the president of the court and the presidents of the five-judge chambers, to deal with most cases currently dealt with in plenary session.

- **The CFI's jurisdiction.** A revision to Article 225 of the EC Treaty clarifies and widens the CFI's jurisdiction. It will become the judge in most direct actions or proceedings – that is, proceedings against a decision (Article 230); action for failure to act (Article 232); action for damages (Article 235) staff cases (Article 236) and regarding contracts concluded by the Community (Article 228) – with the exception of those assigned to a judicial panel and those reserved in the Statute of the Court of Justice. It will also have jurisdiction to hear and determine questions for a preliminary ruling under Article 234 in specific areas laid down by the Statute. The ECJ retains responsibility for other proceedings, in particular for Article 226 dealing with failure to fulfil an obligation, although the Statute provides for the possible extension of the CFI's jurisdiction. Decisions of the CFI on questions referred for a preliminary ruling may exceptionally be subject to review by the ECJ, where there is a serious risk to the unity or consistency of Community law. A declaration on Article 225 calls on the ECJ and the Commission to consider the division of competence between the ECJ and CFI and to submit proposals for examination by the competent bodies as soon as the ToN enters into force.
- **Judicial panels.** The ToN enables judicial panels to be attached to the CFI, which will spread the latter's workload. Article 225 states that the Council, acting unanimously on a proposal from the Commission and after consulting the EP and the court or at the request of the ECJ and after consulting the EP and the Commission, may create judicial panels to hear and determine at first instance certain classes of action or proceeding brought in specific areas (e.g. intellectual property). Members of the panels are chosen from persons whose independence is beyond doubt and who possess the ability required for appointment to judicial office. The panels will establish their rules of procedure in agreement with the ECJ, but these rules require approval of the Council acting by QMV. Panel decisions may be subject to a right of appeal on points of law only or, when provided for, a right of appeal also on matters of fact before the CFI. A declaration on Article 225a asks the ECJ and the Commission to swiftly prepare a draft decision establishing a judicial panel to deliver judgments on staff cases.
- **The judges.** The treaty changes Article 221, which states that the ECJ shall consist of 15 judges to: 'shall consist of one judge from each member state'. It states that the CFI shall comprise at least one judge from a member state, with the number of judges being determined by the Statute.
- **The right of the EP to bring actions under Article 230.** The treaty revises this article in order to allow the EP to bring actions on grounds of lack of competence, infringement of an essential procedural requirement, infringement of the treaty or any rule relating to its application or misuse of powers. In the existing treaty, only member states, the Council or the Commission can bring such actions.

○ **Evaluation**

The ECJ is undoubtedly a formidable institution. The cumulative impact of the ECJ's judgments has crucially influenced the shape and pace of EU integration. Eurosceptics tend to view the court as a centralising force, accusing it of 'judicial activism' and of a keenness to assert the dominance of Union law over national law. Eurosceptics tend to argue that it is biased in favour of European integration and therefore that it has political goals. It has undoubtedly fostered European integration through its decisions. It is hardly an impartial judge of the balance of powers between member states and the Union. It has been suggested that an additional judicial body should be created (a 'Union Court of Review') to adjudicate in cases involving disputes about the relative powers of the Union and member states. It remains to be seen whether the changes introduced by the ToN will enable it to cope with its ever increasing workload.

● THE ECONOMIC AND SOCIAL COMMITTEE

Based in Brussels, the committee is a consultative assembly, comprising representatives of employers, workers and other interests drawn from a wide variety of industrial and social sectors (the ToN amends Article 257 ECT to explicitly include consumers in this category). It was established to involve economic and social interest groups in the development of the Union and to be a formal channel for providing information and advice to the Commission and the Council. It puts forward opinions at the request of the Council, the Commission, and, since 1972, on its own initiative. Under the EC and Euratom treaties, in some cases it is mandatory, and in other cases optional, for the Commission or the Council to consult with the committee. The SEA and TEU extended the range of subjects for mandatory referral. The ToA extends the consultation role of the ESC to a new range of subjects relating to employment and social matters, including public health. In 1999, it adopted 140 opinions and two information reports. The committee's opinion was requested 52 times where this was compulsory and 59 times where consultation was optional; 29 were own initiative opinions. All opinions are published in the *Official Journal*. It can issue majority and minority opinions.

In EU15, the ESC has a membership of 220. The ToN introduces a limit of 350 on the future size of the ESC and also allocates national entitlements for an EU of 27 (see above). A new committee was appointed in September 1998 to serve until September 2002. Its members were nominated by national governments and formally appointed by the Council (following consultation with the Commission) for a renewable term of four years. The ToN introduces a requirement for the Council to act by QMV when adopting the list of members (Article 258, ECT). Although members are appointed as individuals, they tend to closely follow the views of the organisations they represent. Members are part-time and live in their own countries. They belong to one of three groups:

Group I: Employers (from industry, commerce, public enterprises and so on);
Group II: Workers (mainly from trade unions); and
Group III: Various interests (including agriculture, SMEs, the professions, public services and consumer groups).

It has a chairman and a bureau (elected by the members for two years) and a secretary-general. In 2000, it had 519 posts, of which 354 were in services shared with the Committee of the Regions. It is divided into six subject groups known as sections, namely:

- economic and monetary union and economic and social cohesion;
- the single market, production and consumption;
- transport, energy, infrastructure and the information society;
- employment, social affairs and citizenship;
- agriculture, rural development and the environment;
- external relations.

Section opinions are drafted by study groups with around 12 members, one of whom acts as a *rapporteur*. Each year there are about ten plenary sessions, 70 section meetings and 350 study group meetings.

The committee has produced many useful reports, particularly on technical issues, although its opinions do not have to be accepted by either the Council or the Commission. It brings together people from a wide range of occupations and organisations. It provides a vehicle for dialogue between the employers and trades unions. It may promote identification with Europe among various business and other groups. It may provide useful insights into national thinking on various issues. Although there is no constitutional link between the EP and the committee, there is frequent exchange of information between them. When the ECSC Treaty expires in July 2002, it seems likely that the ESC's remit will be extended to include the coal and steel sectors, entailing changes to the ESC's internal organisation and composition. The ESC does not have institutional status or right of appeal to the ECJ.

● THE COMMITTEE OF THE REGIONS

This is an advisory body established to ensure a stronger voice for the regions in the Union. It was established in the TEU, following a suggestion from Chancellor Kohl. Arguably, the establishment of the CoR was a prime example of 'gesture politics', signifying an acknowledgement of the importance of the regional dimension in EU affairs. The CoR is consulted on matters affecting regional interests and prior to the adoption of decisions on regional matters. It can also issue 'own initiative' opinions. It must be consulted on five policies: education, culture, public health, trans-European networks and economic and social cohesion. The ToA extended its role to include cases involving cross-border co-operation, if either the Council or the Commission consider it appropriate, and also specified that the CoR may be consulted by the EP. In 2000, the CoR adopted eight resolutions and 72 opinions, including 15 where consultation was mandatory, 19 in cases where it was consulted on the initiative of the Commission or the Council, 24 own-initiative opinions based on Commission documents and 14 other own-initiative opinions. In 2000, it had 226 posts, of which 111 were in services shared with the Economic and Social Committee.

The CoR's members (plus an equal number of alternate members) are currently appointed for four years by the Council acting unanimously on proposals from member states. However, the ToN introduces QMV for adoption of the list of members and alternate members. There are roughly equal numbers of regional and local government representatives. Members do not have to be elected representatives although most have political affiliations. Most members of the CoR are nominees of regional units, although in the UK it is the national government which nominates them. The ToN will make it a requirement for representatives on the CoR to either hold a regional or local authority electoral mandate or be politically accountable to an elected assembly, Article 263, ECT). The ToA specified that no member of the CoR may simultaneously be a member of the EP and that approval of the Council acting unanimously is no longer required for the adoption of the committee's rules of procedure. The CoR has a common organisational structure with the ESC, with which it shares premises and a secretariat. It is, however, independent of the ESC. The fact that the CoR, unlike the ESC, includes many seasoned regional and local politicians means that it has become more prominent than the ESC. However, it remains a consultative body and is but one of several channels available to regional and interests to express their views. Like the ESC, it does not have institutional status or right of appeal to the ECJ.

● THE COURT OF AUDITORS

The CoA is responsible for the external auditing of the Union's budget. It has extensive powers to examine whether receipts and expenditures have been collected and incurred in a sound and lawful manner. The TEU (Article 7, ECT) bestowed upon the CoA the status of a Community institution. It also gave the CoA more power to monitor the Union's accounts. The ToA (Article 248) gave it power to perform audits on the premises of any body which manages revenue or expenditure on behalf of the Union and in member states, including on the premises of any natural or legal person in receipt of payments from the budget. Its powers of control therefore now extend to all Union funds managed by external bodies, including the European Investment Bank (EIB). Other institutions of the Community are required to furnish the CoA with relevant documents. The ToA also gives it the power to take action against the other institutions before the ECJ in protection of its own prerogatives (Article 230, ECT).

The CoA assists the EP and Council in exercising their powers of control over the implementation of the budget. It provides the EP with valuable information to help it perform its supervisory functions. Based in Luxembourg, the CoA was established in 1975 and first met in October 1977. Members are appointed for six years, and may be reappointed, by the Council (currently by unanimous vote, but after ratification of the ToN by QMV) following consultation with the EP (the EP objected to two nominations in 1989, resulting in one state changing its nomination). In EU15, each state proposes one member for appointment. The ToN states that the CoA shall consist of one national from each member state (Article 247, ECT). Members must be qualified by virtue of their experience in auditing or in a closely related field. The auditors elect a president from their ranks for a three-year period. The CoA had 405 permanent and 142 temporary staff in 2000.

The CoA issues an annual report on the Union's institutions, divided into a financial audit and a financial management assessment. The report is published in the *Official Journal* at the end of each financial year. Its recent reports have included scathing accounts of financial irregularities concerning Union funds and of poor financial mismanagement by the Commission over many policy areas. Its reports have been particularly critical of the administration of the CAP and of the PHARE and TACIS programmes for Central and Eastern Europe. The CoA's critical reports provided the stimulus for the refusal of the EP in December 1998 to grant discharge on the 1996 budget, an action which subsequently led to the resignation of the Santer Commission. The CoA also produces reports on Euratom and the ECSC and special reports and opinions on specific subjects. An EU institution may ask it to submit an opinion. The Council must seek the CoA's opinion on a draft text when enacting a financial regulation. The ToN states that the CoA shall draw up its rules of procedure, which must be approved by the Council acting by QMV (Article 248, ECT).

It has frequently been argued that the CoA is too small to be able to cope effectively with the magnitude of its monitoring tasks. But the fact that questions of fraud and financial mismanagement are now prominent issues in the EU is at least partly due to the influence of CoA reports. The CoA's annual reports have frequently complained that the Commission has largely failed to achieve the level of financial control needed. However, after the debacle of the Commission's resignation in 1999, the Commission is likely to seek to respond more seriously to adverse CoA reports. A declaration in the ToN invites the CoA and national auditing institutions to improve co-ordination between them.

● THE EUROPEAN INVESTMENT BANK

Founded in 1958 and based in Luxembourg, the EIB is the Union's financial institution. It was established to finance capital investment projects which contribute to the 'balanced development, integration and economic and social cohesion' of member countries. It is both a Union institution and a bank. It is autonomous and has its own legal personality and an administrative structure separate from other EU institutions. It has about 800 staff. It has a board of governors, made up of ministers (usually finance ministers) of member states. It has a part-time board of directors nominated by the board of governors, plus a member nominated by the Commission. There is a full-time management committee, which controls all current operations. It was reorganised in 2000 to take account of the guidelines laid down by the Helsinki and Lisbon European Councils, which placed emphasis on preparing for enlargement and developing a knowledge-based society. Its lending departments were regrouped under a single directorate for lending operations, with a structure based on three operational zones (Western Europe; Central Europe and 'Partner Countries' in the Mediterranean, the Balkans, Africa, Caribbean, the Pacific, Asia and Latin America). A projects directorate is responsible for appraisal of projects submitted for financing.

Member states are the shareholders, and contribute to the bank's capital. It is self-financing. It raises its funds on the financial markets (mainly of member states) and re-lends money on a non-profit-making basis. Projects supported must be financially viable. It has the top credit rating (AAA) and therefore is able to raise and lend very substantial sums. It is the world's largest multilateral credit institution and, in terms of its equity base, is the largest bank in Europe. EIB loans may be given to either private or public sector borrowers. It provides funds up to half the cost of projects. Some projects are jointly financed with other EU funds (for example, with the European Regional Development Fund: ERDF).

Balanced regional development is a key priority of the EIB. About two-thirds of its funding is concentrated in regions lagging behind in development, or experiencing redevelopment problems. Trans-European networks and environmental protection are also current priorities. The bank has made contributions to many well-known projects, including high-speed train networks and the Channel tunnel. In 2000, the EIB granted loans of €36 billion in support of Union objectives, including €5.4 billion for development and co-operation aid policies with non-member countries. All EIB projects now have an environmental dimension. Individual loans for environmental protection amounted to €6.4 billion in 2000. Since 1988, over €20 billion has been granted to promote international competitiveness in various industrial sectors. As a result of decisions taken at the Edinburgh European Council, a *European Investment Fund* was set up in 1994. The fund assists the financing of trans-European networks projects and projects promoted by small and medium-sized enterprises (SMEs). It operates from within the EIB. Its board of directors consists of four members nominated by the EIB, two by the Commission and one by the financial institution shareholders. In 2000, it had outstanding guarantee operations of over €2 billion. The EIB is a low-profile, but solid, institution which has made a very significant contribution the development of the EU.

● OTHER INSTITUTIONS AND AGENCIES

The EU has a growing number of specialised functional institutions or agencies, most of which are of recent origin (Table 5.14 overleaf). The main justifications for creating these bodies are that they have a sharper focus than general-purpose organisations; that they may need to be independent of direct political influence (for example, the ECB and the European Police Office, Europol); that they take the workload off the Commission; and that they enable each member state to have its 'own' EU institution. The main criticisms of them are that they increase the complexity of the EU policy and implementation system and are insufficiently accountable. Location decisions have led to much horse-trading between member states.

These organisations are so diverse that they arguably have little in common apart from the fact that they are not directly run by the Commission. However, the diversity of these bodies suggests that some attempt at classification is needed. One basis of classification would be in terms of the powers and the profiles of these bodies. The ECB as a heavy-weight institution with a high profile needs to be placed in a category of its own, because of its sheer importance to the functioning of the Union (see Chapter 11). Europol is a body which is more controversial and has a higher profile than most. The ombudsman reports to the EP and is discussed earlier in this chapter. Some are low-profile institutions of which few citizens have even heard. Several are monitoring bodies with few powers.

Table 5.14 Other EU Institutions and Agencies

Community Plant Variety Rights Office (Angers): responsible for the regime of Community plant variety rights, patents and copyrights.

European Agency for Reconstruction (Thessaloniki): established in February 2000 to provide post-war aid to Kosovo, Serbia and Montenegro.

European Agency for Safety and Health at Work (Bilbao): improving working conditions with regard to safety and health.

European Central Bank (Frankfurt); (see Chapter 11).

European Centre for the Development of Vocational Training (now Thessaloniki, formerly Berlin): the promotion and development of vocational and in-service training (better known as CEDEFOP).

European Drugs Observatory (Lisbon): to analyse data on drugs.

European Environment Agency (Copenhagen): to provide objective, reliable and comparable information at European level (see Chapter 14).

European Food Agency: to be set up by 2002.

European Judicial Co-operation Unit (Eurojust) (Brussels): to facilitate co-ordination between national prosecuting authorities and support criminal investigations into organised crime.

European Medicine Evaluation Agency (London): provides scientific advice to Community institutions and member states concerning authorisation and supervision of medical products.

European Monitoring Centre for Drugs and Drug Addiction (Lisbon): to provide information at European level concerning drugs.

European Monitoring Centre on Racism and Xenophobia (Vienna): founded in 1998, it provides the Union and its member states with information at European level on racism, xenophobia and anti-Semitism.

European Police Office (Europol) (The Hague): to enable national police and customs to share information on international crime, drugs and terrorism (see Chapter 16).

European Training Foundation (Turin): to contribute to the development of the vocational training systems of Central and East European countries and Mediterranean partner countries and territories.

European Veterinary Inspection Agency (Dublin): to test animal health. Note: this is part of the Commission and is not a decentralised EU body.

Foundation for the Improvement of Living and Working Conditions (Dublin): to contribute to the planning and establishment of better living and working conditions through the dissemination of knowledge.

Office for Harmonisation in the Internal Market (Alicante): to implement Community law in relation to trade marks, designs and models.

Translation Centre for Bodies in the European Union (Luxembourg): to meet the translation needs of EU bodies and agencies, with the exception of the two bodies above.

● INSTITUTIONAL INTERACTIONS IN THE EU'S POLICY PROCESS

○ Principal Features of the EU's Policy Process

This process is very complex, comprising many different formal procedures and requirements. It is not immediately obvious which policy or aspect of policy is covered by which procedure. Figure 5.3 provides a preliminary insight into institutional interactions in this process.

Figure 5.3 Institutional Interactions

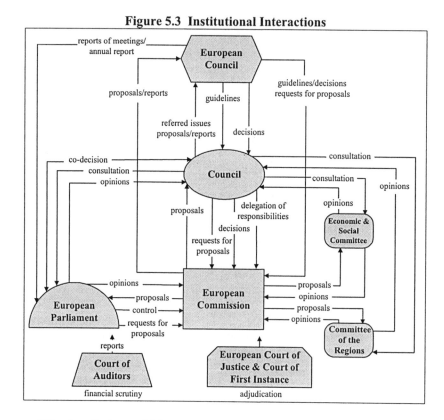

Other key features of this process are:
- the central role played by the Commission;
- legislative power is still unevenly distributed between the Council and the EP, although extension of co-decision has lessened the imbalance;
- the Council and the Commission constitute a type of 'dual executive' and share governmental responsibilities. According to Hix (2000), they have a

principal-agent relationship, whereby the initial holder of executive power (the Council) has delegated powers to the 'agent', that is, the Commission;

- the Commission, the Council and the EP need to work together closely in order to achieve their legislative objectives;
- policies do not necessarily take legislative form. For example, the CFSP and PJCCM pillars lie outside the Community legislative framework. The Council also issues non-legislative pronouncements (in the form of resolutions, declarations, agreements and so on);
- the European Council is not directly involved in the legislative process, but exercises considerable influence on policy, through its guiding and directing roles.

○ **The Legislative Process** embraces the following procedures.

- **The consultation procedure.** This was the earliest procedure, and was laid down in the Treaty of Rome. The role of the EP under this procedure is purely advisory, meaning that the Council takes into account the EP's opinion before voting on a Commission proposal. A draft is worked out in a Commission DG (in consultation with government officials and other interested parties). When completed, the Commission presents a proposal to the Council. The EP and, in some policy areas, the ESC and the CoR are then consulted for their opinions. The Commission considers the response of the EP, the ESC and the CoR and may make amendments in the light of their comments. The proposal is then re-submitted to the Council, which refers it to one of its working parties and to COREPER. After discussion in COREPER, the proposal is returned to the Council, which may adopt or reject it. The Commission tends to accept more of the EP's amendments than does the Council (which has the final say). The ToA included new provisions in the EC Treaty for consultation to cover closer co-operation between member states; combating of discrimination; visas, asylum and immigration; employment; the common commercial policy; social policy; and overseas territories; and police and . judicial co-operation in criminal matters. The ToN will extend consultation to Article 181a on economic and technical co-operation with third countries; aspects of visas, asylum and immigration from May 2004 (Article 66); and financial regulations from January 2007 (Article 279).
- **The co-operation procedure (Article 252, ECT).** The SEA effectively introduced a parliamentary second reading stage into the legislative process for measures relating to the SEM, social and economic cohesion and RTD. Some aspects of the SEM regarded as particularly contentious, such as value-added tax (VAT), were not subject to the procedure. But a broad range of legislative measures were within its scope. The TEU extended the procedure to a wide range of subjects. The ToA transferred most of the subjects

formerly dealt with under this procedure to the co-decision procedure, under which the EP has more power, with the exception of four aspects of economic and monetary union (EMU) (see Table 5.15). The Commission favours abolition of the procedure in the interests of clarifying the treaties and because it sees no justification for a distinction between EMU provisions and other EC Treaty provisions. But no changes to this were made in the ToN.

Table 5.15 Scope of the Co-operation Procedure

Article, ECT	Subject
Article 99(5)	EMU: multilateral surveillance procedure rules
Article 102(2)	Prohibition on overdraft facilities for Community institutions
Article 103(2)	'No bail out clause' for liability of other member states' debts
Article 106(2)	Harmonisation measures on circulation of euro coins

• **The co-decision procedure (Article 251, ECT).** First introduced in the TEU and extended and streamlined in the ToA, this procedure gives the EP roughly equal status with the Council in the adoption of legislation on specific subjects, although it does not apply to all legislation and does not extend to situations where the Council acts in an executive capacity. The co-decision procedure, which now applies to most areas of policy, means that the EP's views must be taken seriously by the Council because the final text of certain legislation requires the EP's approval (although all legislation still has to be approved by the Council). The Council and the EP therefore now share legislative power, although not on an equal basis. In some cases, EC Treaty articles require the ESC and/or the CoR to be consulted. In one case (Article 280), the CoA must be consulted. However, unlike the EP, none of these bodies has the power to block a proposal. This procedure (Figure 5.4) now involves between one and three stages, depending upon the ability of the Council and the EP to agree on a particular proposal, namely:

• *The one-stage procedure* (also known as the accelerated procedure). After receiving the EP's opinion on a Commission proposal, the Council adopts its common position, normally by QMV. If it approves the EP's amendments, or if none are proposed, the act is adopted.

• *The two-stage procedure.* If the Council does not approve the EP's amendments, it adopts a common position, by QMV. The Council's common position is then submitted to the EP for second reading. Within three months the EP can accept, amend, reject or fail to act on the common position. If it approves the Council's position or fails to act, the act is adopted. If the EP proposes amendments to the common position, the Commission delivers its opinion on these proposals and there is a second reading by the Council. If the Commission's opinion is positive, the Council can approve the proposed amendments by QMV. If the Commission's opinion is negative, it can approve the amendments by unanimity.

- *The three-stage procedure.* If the proposed amendments are rejected by the Council, a Conciliation Committee (CC) is convened by the presidents of the EP and the Council to facilitate agreement. The CC comprises an equal number of Council and EP representatives. Senior officials from national permanent representations to the EU usually represent the Council in the CC. The EP is represented by a mixture of MEPs from relevant parliamentary committees. The Commission participates in the proceedings, seeking to reconcile positions. The Committee has six weeks to achieve an agreed text. If agreement is reached, the amended proposal must be approved by the Council (by QMV) and by the EP (by absolute majority) within six weeks. If the CC fails to agree a joint text, the proposal is not adopted. If the CC approves a joint text, this is submitted to the EP and the Council for consideration. The proposal is adopted if both the EP (by absolute majority) and Council (by QMV) agree a joint text within six weeks. If either fail to agree on the joint text, the proposal is not adopted.

Until the entry into force of the ToA, if there was no agreement in the Conciliation Committee, the act could be adopted if the Council by QMV and (acting within six weeks of the expiry of the committee's six week period) confirmed its position, possibly with some of the EP's amendments, and the EP did not reject it (it could do so at this stage by absolute majority within six weeks of the date of confirmation by the Council). As a result of the ToA, in the event of non-agreement in the CC, a proposal cannot be adopted. The periods of three months and six weeks referred to above may be extended by one month or two weeks respectively, by accord of the Council and the EP.

The ToA considerably extended the scope of the procedure to new areas, such as social exclusion, public health and the fight against fraud. In 2000, the procedure covered over half of legislative proposals in the first pillar. Of the articles which the ToA made subject to co-decision, 11 had been under the co-operation procedure, two under consultation, one under assent and eight were new articles (either directly introduced by the ToA or transferred from the third pillar). The ToA also required co-decision to be automatically extended to measures on the crossing of external borders of member states, procedures and conditions for issuing visas and rules on a uniform visa. Most other measures in the EC Title on the free movement of persons, asylum and immigration were to be reviewed after five years, with the Council deciding by unanimity if all or part of these might be transferred to co-decision (these provisions were revisited by the ToN). The ToA also simplified the procedure, to make it speedier, more transparent and more effective. It did this by amending Article 251 so that a text may be definitively adopted at the end of the first reading, if the Council and the EP agree on an identical text.

The ToN will extend the scope of co-decision, although in some cases subject to deferrals and conditions. Articles 13.2, 65, 157.3, 159.3 and 191 will switch to co-decision and QMV as soon as the ToN is ratified (see Table 5.16 on p. 174). With regard to Articles 62.3 (free movement of third country nationals) and 63.3b (clandestine immigration), co-decision with QMV will apply from 1 May 2004, subject to a unanimous Council decision. Co-decision and QMV will also apply to Article 62.2a (checks at external borders) as soon as agreement has been reached on the scope of such measures, subject to a unanimous Council decision. With regard to Articles 63.1 and 63.2a (on asylum seekers and refugees) co-decision and QMV will apply when the Council, acting unanimously, has adopted legislation defining common rules and basic principles. Some of the changes to Articles 62 and 63 are made in a declaration on Article 67 attached to the ToN (see p. 381). The possible extension of co-decision and QMV to additional aspects of Article 137 (protection of sacked workers; co-determination and collective representation and defence of the interests of workers and employers; and conditions of employment of third-country nationals) is also subject to a unanimous Council decision. In their submissions to IGC 2000, the EP and the Commission proposed that a link be established between QMV and co-decision for all legislative decisions. However, no reference is made to this in the ToN. Nor does it extend co-decision to legislative measures in the fields of agriculture and trade, even though they are subject to QMV.

◯ The Council's Report on the Operation of the Co-decision procedure

Following a request by the Helsinki European Council, a report on the operation of the new co-decision procedure was presented to the Nice European Council by the presidency and the General Secretariat of the Council (Council, 2000). It noted that first and second reading agreements now account for about 75% of all co-decision dossiers (the breakdown being 25% for the first and 50% for the second reading). It tends to be the most politically sensitive dossiers which reach the conciliation stage, although not invariably. Almost half of the dossiers concluded during conciliation were concluded without a meeting of the Conciliation Committee. The report noted the importance of 'trialogues', that is, informal tripartite meetings between the Council, the EP and the Commission throughout the procedure. It found that the changes to the scope and mechanisms of the procedure had resulted in an increase in the number of conciliation proceedings, leading to a considerable increase in the workload of those involved. It recommended improvements in arrangements for timetables and deadlines; in the conduct of proceedings (to make them as speedy and as organised as possible); and in information flows between the actors. It also advocated a communications strategy to make co-decision more widely known among EU citizens (for example, by publishing information on co-decision dossiers on the institutions' websites).

Figure 5.4 The Co-decision Procedure under the ToA (Article 251)

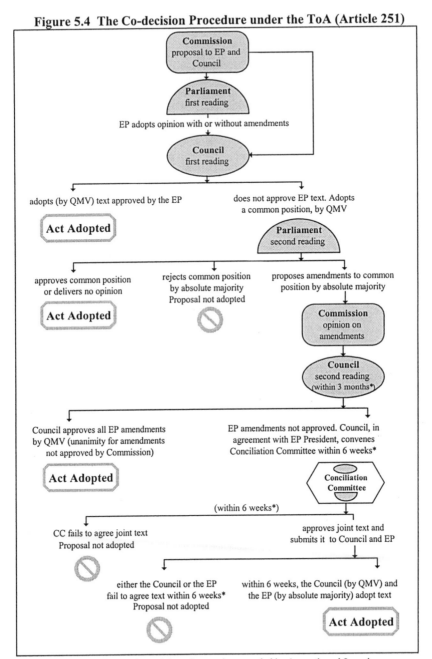

Note:* The periods of 3 months and 6 weeks may be extended by 1 month and 2 weeks respectively by mutual agreement of the Council and the EP.

Table 5.16 Areas of Co-decision Post-Amsterdam, Plus ToN Provisions

Article (ECT)	Subject
Post-Amsterdam	
12.2 qmv	Prohibition of discrimination
18.2 u → qmv in the ToN	Citizens' freedom of movement
40 qmv	Free movement of workers
42 u.	Social security arrangements for EU migrant workers
44 qmv	Right of establishment (internal market)
46.2 qmv	Treatment of foreign nationals
47.1 qmv	Mutual recognition of diplomas, certificates etc
47.2 u.	Provisions for the self-employed/the professions
55 qmv	Free movement of services
62.2*u. (qmv after 5 years)	Visa procedures, conditions and rules
71.1 qmv	Non-resident carriers of transport services
80.2 qmv	Sea and air transport
95 qmv	Internal market harmonisation
129 qmv	Employment incentives
135 qmv	Customs co-operation
137.2 qmv	Equal opportunities in employment (gender)
141.3 qmv	Equal treatment (gender)
148 qmv	European Social Fund
149 qmv	Education and youth policy
150.4 qmv	Vocational training
151 u.	Cultural policy
152.4 qmv	Public health inc. veterinary/phytosanitary policy etc.
153.4 qmv	Consumer protection
156 qmv	Trans-European networks – guidelines
162 qmv	ERDF
166.1 qmv	Research and technology framework programmes
172.2 qmv	RTD joint undertakings
175.1 qmv	Environment – actions
175.3 qmv	Environmental policy action programmes – objectives
179 qmv	Development co-operation
255 qmv	Transparency
280 qmv	Countering fraud
285 qmv	Production of statistics
286 qmv	Data protection
ToN Provisions	
13.2 qmv	Incentives to combat discrimination
65 qmv	Judicial co-operation in civil matters (not family law)
157.3 qmv	Industrial support measures
159.3 qmv	Economic and social cohesion outside structural funds
191.2 qmv	Statute for political parties at European level
62.3 qmv‡	Freedom to travel of third country nationals
63.3b qmv‡	Measures relating to illegal immigration and residence
62.2a qmv*	Checks on persons at external borders
63.1a,b,c,d and 63.2a qmv*	Asylum seekers and refugees
137 (certain aspects) qmv*	Various employment rights and conditions (see p. 172)

Notes: u.: unanimity in Council; qmv: qualified majority required in Council; → qmv: switch from unanimity to qmv in the ToN; ‡: switch to co-decision and QMV from 1 May 2004, subject to a unanimous Council vote.; *: switch to co-decision and qmv deferred and subject to conditions including a unanimous Council vote.

○ Types of Community Legislative Instrument

The following instruments apply to both the European Community and Euratom:

- *Regulations* are decisions which have direct legal force in all member states, with immediate effect. Most are concerned with technical decisions, particularly relating to the CAP. They are of general application, binding in their entirety and directly applicable (that is, they are not subject to national legislative processes) and come into effect as soon as they are published in the *Official Journal*. The main strength of the regulation is that it avoids many of the problems associated with the devolution of legislative responsibilities to national level (for example, foot-dragging and differences of interpretation). Its principal weakness (which explains why it is not used more frequently) is that it is rigid and does not take account of variations in national conditions.
- *Directives* set out the principles of legislation, but it is left up to the member states to implement the legislation through national law. The time limit for this to be done is usually set at two or three years. Regardless of the form and methods used to transpose directives into national law, they are nevertheless binding and are expected to have the same results in the member states to which they apply. They are not necessarily applicable to all member states, although they almost always are. They are usually more general than Regulations, although some are very specific (for example, in relation to technical standards and environmental protection). The merit of the directive is that it is a means of reconciling the *diversity* of national conditions and structures with the need to secure *uniformity* of Union law. Its principal weakness is that it may provide opportunities for 'policy erosion' at the implementation stage.
- *Decisions* are similar to regulations, but are addressed to governments, undertakings or individuals. They are binding upon those to whom they are addressed.
- *Recommendations and opinions* are not binding. They are used to provide additional information on specific issues.

The ECSC retains some distinctive institutional features, despite the partial institutional merger of the ECSC, the EEC and Euratom in 1967. Under the Paris Treaty, the Commission has more power within the ECSC than it does within other Union structures. The Commission has a wide range of decisionmaking powers in relation to the operation of the ECSC, which it may exercise without reference to the Council. The ECSC has its own Consultative Committee, comprising interested parties (producers, workers, consumers and retailers) in the coal and steel industries. When the current ECSC Treaty expires in July 2002, it will not be renewed and the coal and steel sector will be placed under the EC Treaty. The assets of the ECSC will be transferred to the European Community and the Commission will be entrusted with managing these assets. Net revenue will be used for coal and steel research.

❍ Committees in EU Policy Formation and Implementation

Committees and working parties assist Community institutions at all stages of the policy process: this applies to both the formulation and implementation stages of policy. Before drawing up new legislation, the Commission consults with advisory committees of experts. Committees and working parties also assist the Council. Some of these are provided for in the treaties and others are *ad hoc* committees. Most of the committees operate without any publicity. It is exceptional for a committee to receive much public attention (one such case was the Standing Veterinary Committee, responsible for considering the ban on British beef).

A peculiar feature of the Union is the system of committees set up to exercise supervision over the implementing powers delegated to the Commission by the Council, a system known as 'comitology'. The Council delegates a substantial amount of detailed rulemaking and individual decision taking to the Commission. This is necessary to prevent the Council from becoming bogged down in administrative and technical detail, thereby enabling it to concentrate on important policy matters (see Table 5.17). In addition to giving representatives of member states a means of exercising monitoring and supervision over the Commission's management of policies, they are also means through which national interests are represented, to ensure that member states receive their fair shares of funding. These committees were first used in the 1960s as management committees for the CAP, but soon spread to other fields. The ToA extended the comitology system to matters transferred from the third to the first pillar.

There are about 300 of these committees, although if sub- and temporary committees are included, there may be over 1000. They relate primarily to selection of projects for Community funding, harmonisation of technical standards and approval of rules drawn up by the Commission to achieve Council objectives. They comprise the representatives of national administrations of member states and are chaired by the Commission. The frequency of meetings varies: some meet often, some once or twice a year and some have never yet met. When a vote is taken, it is done by QMV of the national representatives. A declaration annexed to the SEA required the Community to adopt principles and rules on the Commission's powers of implementation. This resulted in the 1987 comitology decision, which had the effect of reducing the types of committee to three, that is, *advisory*, *management* and *regulatory*. The EP had no legal role in the comitology process (much to its chagrin). However, through an interinstitutional agreement, the Commission forwarded draft implementing measures to the EP for information (plus a procedure for adoption of safeguard measures).

Table 5.17 The Case For and Against Comitology

For

- it provides a vehicle through which the Commission and representatives from national administrations can work together;
- highly technical and specialised issues can be dealt with by experts;
- it is a vehicle through which conflicts may be resolved.

Against

- the system is clouded in secrecy: there is no comprehensive list of committees, functions or activities or membership. More transparency is needed, including a full list of committees and their activities;
- although enhanced by the 1999 reforms, the EP's role remains limited;
- a clearer distinction between legislation and implementation is needed, as recourse to these committees reduces the EP's influence;
- there are no clear criteria to distinguish between advisory, management or regulatory committees.

Declaration 31 of the ToA required the Commission to submit a proposal before the end of 1998 on amending the 1987 decision in order to simplify comitology procedures. The Commission's proposal, submitted in June 1998, sought to simplify and improve comitology by reducing the diversity of committees, enhancing monitoring procedures and setting criteria for guiding the choice of implementing procedure. In June 1999, the Council reached agreement on new procedures, to replace the 1987 decision. The new decision simplifies committee procedures (especially management and regulatory procedures), grants the EP a right of scrutiny over implementation of acts adopted by co-decision and increases transparency in comitology (for example, rules on public access applicable to the Commission are made applicable to committee documents).

O Lobbying in the EU

The number of pressure groups active at Euro-level is greater now than ever before. In the last twenty years, there has been a population explosion of groups active at Union level, possibly amounting to a ten-fold increase. Many professional lobbying firms are located in Brussels, including about 10,000 people who are exclusively engaged in lobbying the Commission, the EP and the Council. Over 130 non-EU countries also have representation in Brussels.

Many large European companies have units concerned with European issues in Brussels. Some subnational authorities (regional and local governments) also have permanent representation in Brussels. As the range of Union policies has become more diverse, so too has the range of groups active at Union level. Initially most represented industry and agriculture, but now these constitute less than half of the total. There has been a big growth in lobbying by local and regional councils and by environmental and social groups. There are also numerous subindustry groups (for example, the motor industry lobby). Many groups are represented in the Union's network of advisory committees. Many large multinationals have offices in Brussels. There are around 700 groups which represent members from several different EU countries ('Euro pressure groups') although these tend to have loose organisational structures.

The Commission has sought to foster the emergence of 'Euro pressure groups', such as UNICE (Union of Industrial and Employers Confederation of Europe), ETUC (European Trade Union Confederation), the European Environmental Bureau and the European Bureau of Consumer Unions, rather than those favouring exclusively national interests. Other groups include the Committee of Professional Agricultural Organisations (COPA); the Association of Chambers of Commerce and Industry (Eurochambres); the European Confederation of the Iron and Steel Industry (Eurofer); and the European Chemical Industry Foundation. However most 'Euro-groups' have weak structures. They tend to be too big and diverse to be able to reflect accurately a particular member's interests. Moreover, many national groups have representation in Brussels. For individual firms, direct approaches to the Commission seem to be more effective than going through a federation.

The EU policy range is very uneven and fragmented. Therefore some groups are more active at European level than others. Groups tend to pursue a dual strategy, by lobbying at both the national and European levels. The use of qualified majority voting removed the veto power from national governments on many issues, meaning that lobbying solely at national level is no longer adequate. As is true of pressure groups at national level, producer groups tend to have stronger representation than consumer groups. Each of the main EU institutions have codes of conduct for relations with lobbyists. These codes generally require lobbyists to be open and honest in their dealings and also to be careful in relation to employing former EU employees, or MEPs. The Commission bans lobbyists from its press conferences. The EP requires lobbyists to wear badges on EP premises. The Commission and Council keep a register of lobbying groups. But rules on lobbying are not legally binding and are by no means always observed. Some staff working for MEPs are believed to have outside interests. The ban on lobbyists attending Commission press conferences has frequently been breached.

Despite these ineffective rules, a lobbying pattern in the EU can nevertheless be discerned. As is the case with pressure groups operating within a state, there are both 'insider' and 'outsider' groups at EU level. The influential groups are likely to have bargaining counters in the form of knowledge and expertise. There have been many instances of direct action from groups excluded from the decisionmaking process, such as animal rights campaigners and certain farmers groups. Like national groups, Euro-groups seek to locate and influence the 'locus of power' and to both obtain and disseminate information. But in the Union system, power is more diffused than at national level and therefore groups have to adjust their activities accordingly. The EU's 'dual executive' system means that the Union has no clear government as such. The Commission is a primary lobbying target, because of its key roles in the policy process. It needs to collect information from groups in order to perform its policy initiation and monitoring roles. It may also need the support of groups in its attempts to persuade the Council to adopt its proposals. The EP has also become a major focus of lobbying, which is not surprising given its enhanced role in the legislative process. The Council is also subject to lobbying: indirectly through the permanent representations in Brussels and through the members of Council working groups, and more directly through national governments.

⭕ EU Institutional Reform Trends and Issues

Institutional reform is considered in some detail in the chapters on treaty reform as well as in this chapter. It might be useful, however, to summarise the trends of recent institutional reform and also to briefly list current reform issues which remain to be resolved (see Table 5.18 overleaf). It should be noted that the Council, the Commission and the EP have all so far proved resistant to radical institutional change. This may be partly due to the fact that organisational cultures, once embedded, tend to be resistant to radical reform. But it is also due to the difficulties involved in securing the agreement of all member states on institutional reform issues. The outcomes of institutional reform processes therefore tend to comprise a mixture of compromises, fudges, lowest common denominator solutions and postponed decisions.

The issue of transparency provides an example of institutional resistance to radical reform. The ToA commits the Union to taking decisions as openly as possible. The Commission, the Council and the EP were required to agree a new code on citizens' right of access to documents by May 2001, in accordance with Article 255, ECT. In January 2000, the Commission drafted proposals for a new law on public access to information. The EU ombudsman Jacob Söderman attacked the new proposals, arguing that the list of exemptions they contained was without precedent in the modern world.

(*European Voice*, vol. 6, no. 11, March 2000). He argued that the proposals meant that citizens would still be dependent on the goodwill of officials for access to documents. Various drafts of the proposed new code were formulated in 2000, and all came in for severe criticism from various civil rights pressure groups within the Union. A code was finally agreed between the Council and the EP in April 2001 but, according to its critics, contains many flaws (see p. 134 above). Under the code, sensitive documents to which access will be refused embrace a variety of subjects (public security, defence and military, international relations, financial, monetary or economic policy, privacy and integrity of the individual, commercial interests, court proceedings and legal advice, inspections, investigations and audits, unless there is an overriding public interest in disclosure).

Table 5.18 Institutional Reform Trends and Issues

Trends

- extension of supranational and 'tight intergovernmental' decisionmaking (extension of co-decision and of QMV);
- reweighting of votes and seats in EU institutions, necessitated by recent and future enlargement;
- a quickening of the pace of reform (more frequent IGCs and three treaties in 10 years);
- limited 'Communitarisation' of some policy areas in the third (particularly) and second pillars (albeit marginally);
- attempts to streamline the legislative process;
- attempts to reform the Commission;
- an increase in institutional types, due to the creation of new bodies;
- some increases in transparency (although with many exceptions).

Issues

- the impact of enlargement on institutional structures and ways of doing things;
- the increasing complexity of the EU's institutional machinery;
- the institutional balance (e.g., how much power for the EP relative to the Council and Commission?);
- how far should QMV be extended?
- the balance of representation between big and small states;
- the division of competencies between the EU and national and regional levels of government;
- the process of institutional reform (are IGCs and treaties the right mechanisms?);
- how to reduce the gulf between the institutions and EU citizens;
- increasing transparency: how open should the institutions be?

● CONCLUSION

Students of the EU cannot help but be struck by the complexity of the EU's institutional structures and processes. As organisations increase in size, they tend to become more complex. Enlargement is likely to exacerbate the Union's problem of institutional complexity. In the EU's case, institutional complexity is also a product of a search for acceptable compromises between member states and of the Union's piecemeal, *ad hoc* method of institutional change. We have noted that the Union has been virtually forced to give serious consideration to institutional reforms by the impending enlargement of a large group of small states. But there is little sign this will lead to a Union made easier for ordinary EU citizens to understand (indeed, the complexity of the Nice formula for QMV suggests that the reverse is more likely).

FURTHER READING

Commission (2000), *Adapting the Institutions to Make a Success of Enlargement*, COM (2000) 34.

Committee of Independent Experts (1999), *First and Second Reports on Allegations Regarding Fraud, Mismanagement and Nepotism in the European Commission*, www.europarl.eu.int/experts.

Cram, L. (1997), *Policy-making in the EU: Conceptual Lenses and the Integration Process*, Routledge, London.

Dehaene, J.-L., et al. (1999), *The Institutional Implications of Enlargement. Report to the Commission*, Brussels, October.

House of Lords Select Committee on European Communities (1999), *Delegation of Powers to the Commission: Reforming Comitology*, HL paper 23.

House of Lords Select Committee on European Communities (1999), *Enlarging the Jurisdiction of the Court of First Instance, 13th Report*, HL paper 82.

Hix, S. (2000), *The Political System of the European Union*, Macmillan, Basingstoke.

Levy, R. (2000), *Implementing European Union Public Policy*, Edward Elgar, Cheltenham and Northampton, MA.

Maurer, A. (2000), *(Co-) Governing after Maastricht: the EP's Institutional Performance 1994–1999*, European Parliament working paper, PE 168.625.

Nugent, N. (2000), *The Government and Politics of the European Union*, Macmillan, Basingstoke.

Nugent, N. (2001), *The European Commission*, Palgrave, Basingstoke.

Presidency and General Secretariat of the Council (2000), *Making the Co-Decision Procedure More Effective*, Council.

Spierenburg, D. (1979), *Proposals for the Reform of the Commission of the European Communities and its Services*, European Commission, Brussels.

Statewatch (2000), *Survey Shows Which EU Governments Back Openness, Which Do Not*, http://www.statewatch.org/secret/conformtable.htm.

Stevens, A. and Stevens, S. (2001), *Brussels Bureaucrats?*, Palgrave, Basingstoke.

Chapter 6

The Budget

● PRINCIPAL FEATURES

○ Budgetary Independence

The Union has its own budget, which is independent of the public finances of member states (strictly speaking, it is the European Community (EC), not the European Union (EU) as such, which has a budget, although for reasons of consistency, the term 'Union budget' is used throughout this chapter). Between 1958 and 1970, the Union was financed through national contributions, but since April 1970 it has been financed almost exclusively from its *own resources*. The EU has no tax-raising powers and its revenues are collected by member states. But states cannot withhold payment of these revenues, as the European Court of Justice (ECJ) has made clear. The budget is used to finance a wide range of policy commitments and activities. Although the Commission has responsibility for implementing the budget, about 85% of it is managed by member states (a fact which the Commission frequently points out).

○ Sources

The Union's own resources comprise four components: (1) agricultural duties and sugar and isoglucose levies; (2) customs duties; (3) a proportion of national VAT (the 'third resource'); and (4) GNP-based contributions (the 'fourth resource'). Items 1 and 2 are known as 'traditional own resources' or 'TOR'. A limit is imposed on the amount of budget revenue raised annually from member states. This is known as the 'own resources ceiling' and is derived from a percentage of the combined GNPs of member states (Union

GNP), set at 1.21% in 1995, rising to 1.27% by 1999 and beyond. Actual percentages are, however, likely to be below this ceiling. The 2000 budget amounted to 1.11% of Union GNP. Table 6.1 outlines the main features of the EU's 'own resources'.

Table 6.1 The Union's 'Own Resources'

1. **Agricultural duties and sugar and isoglucose levies:** agricultural duties are imposed on products from outside the EU. Sugar and isoglucose levies are paid by producers to cover market support arrangements and storage.
2. **Customs Duties:** levies on imports from non-member states, based on the Common Customs Tariff.
(Note: for items 1 and 2, member states retain 25% for collection costs)
3. **A Proportion of national VAT (the 'third resource':** a notional rate of VAT is applied to an identical range of goods and services in each member state, subject to a ceiling relating to the size of the state's GNP.
4. **GNP-based contributions (the 'fourth resource'):** the same proportion of the GNP of each member state. This was introduced in 1988, as a topping-up, or budget-balancing, resource to cover expenditure in excess of revenue raised by other means.

Yields from duties and levies (TOR) have been falling in recent years as a result of trade liberalisation, lower tariffs and the Union's increasing self-sufficiency in food. The TOR contribution to the budget fell from 29.1% in 1988 to 15.3% in 2000, although in absolute terms the amount raised through TOR has remained between €12 and 14 billion. The elements comprising TOR have been criticised for being inequitable and prone to fraud. Progressive capping of the VAT resource since 1988 has reduced its significance. VAT revenues as a share of the total declined from almost 70% in 1990 to 38% in 2000. A ceiling on the proportion of national VAT was set at 1% in 1970 and raised to 1.4% in 1985. From 1995 onwards, the ceiling was lowered from 1.4%, falling to 1% by 1999 (in 1999 it actually dropped to about 0.84%). In 1988, it was agreed that the VAT base should be limited to 55% of member states' GNP. This was lowered to 50% from 1995 for states whose GNP per head was below 90% of the EU average. For other states, it was reduced progressively, from 54% in 1995 to 50% in 1999. This means that the cap on the VAT base is now 50% of 1% of GNP for all member states. By its nature as a consumption tax, VAT is regressive, because poorer states have higher levels of consumption and lower savings rates. The GNP (or 'fourth') resource is taking on an increasingly important role, accounting for over two fifths of the budget, compared to 10% in 1988. Arguably, it is the most equitable and understandable of the means through which resources are raised, because it is directly related to the GNP of each member state. But assessing GNP is a difficult task (the statistical office of the EU has recently developed a new method of estimating GNP). Budgetary contributions are paid by member states in 12 monthly instalments. Figure 6.1 outlines the sources of EU budget revenue in 2000. Miscellaneous revenue refers to items such as interest on late payments, fines and surpluses from earlier years.

Figure 6.1 The Union Budget: Revenue in 2000

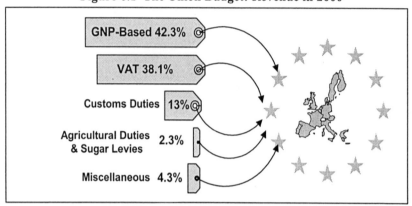

Table 6.2 Contributions to Budget Revenues for 2000 (€ Million)

	Ag. Duties & Sugar Levies	Customs Duties	VAT	GNP-Based	Total	%
Austria	42.8	200.6	958.4	906.0	2,107.8	2.4
Belgium	99.2	1,000.2	1,030.1	1,114.4	3,243.8	3.6
Denmark	44.0	250.1	657.2	731.1	1,682.4	1.9
Finland	16.1	113.8	529.4	559.2	1,218.5	1.4
France	348.2	1,126.5	6,494.7	6,286.3	14,255.8	15.9
Germany	444.4	2,714.5	9,263.7	9,176.4	21,599.0	24.1
Greece	19.9	166.7	611.4	564.5	1,362.5	1.5
Ireland	11.4	1,61.6	421.3	389.0	983.3	1.1
Italy	174.2	1,087.9	4,438.8	5,103.8	10,804.6	12.1
Lux.	0.6	19.7	90.6	83.7	194.6	0.2
Neth.	228.8	1,373.0	1,891.1	1,755.3	5,248.2	5.9
Portugal	42.9	142.3	526.8	486.4	1,198.5	1.3
Spain	72.7	722.1	2,845.9	2,627.8	6,268.6	7.0
Sweden	42.1	316.5	1,042	1,075.8	2,476.4	2.8
UK	451.0	2,269.9	3,247.3	6,945.3	12,913.5	14.4
Misc.					3,883.2	4.3
TOTALS	**2,038.3**	**11,566.4**	**34,048.7**	**37,805.1**	**89,440.7**	
%	**2.3**	**13.0**	**38.1**	**42.3**		**100.0**

Sources: Commission, *The Community Budget: The Facts in Figures*, 2000.

⊙ Imbalances in Contributions

There are wide variations in both the size and composition of member states' contributions to the budget, as Table 6.2 above shows. The UK contributes a disproportionate amount in customs duties because of its high level of imports. Poorer states are likely to pay disproportionate amounts in VAT contributions because of the consumption patterns of their citizens (they spend proportionately more than the Union average on VAT-rated items). The UK's VAT contribution, about 9.5% of total VAT contributions in 2000, is relatively low because of the substantial annual rebate negotiated by Mrs Thatcher at the European Council in Fontainebleau in 1984 (see below). VAT amounted to 25.1% of the UK's total contributions in 2000, compared with over 40% for most other member states. The contribution of some countries to TOR is significantly higher than their shares in GNP, due to their port facilities which serve as gateways for the entry of foreign goods into the EU.

⊙ Size

The 2000 budget was about €89.4 billion. This is still a relatively small sum, amounting to less than 1.11% of Union GNP, or around €4.57 a week for each citizen of the Union. According to the UK's National Audit Office, the UK's gross contribution to the 1999 budget amounted to €11.1 billion (£6.9 billion), or around €3.60 (£2.24) a week for each UK citizen. The UK's net contribution, that is, the difference between the amount paid in and received, was €5.3 billion (£3.3 billion), amounting to about €1.72 (£1.07) per week for each UK citizen. The national budgets of states are far larger (in the UK, public expenditure is well over 40% of GNP). Many Union policies do not impose heavy burdens on the budget, because they are regulatory in nature and member states are largely responsible for carrying them out. Moreover, a substantial amount of budgetary spending would have to be borne by member states if the budget did not exist. Nevertheless, the size of the EU budget has increased very substantially. Annual per capita expenditure has risen from €19 in 1970 to €238 in 2000.

As the EU's policy portfolio has expanded, so too have pressures on the budget (see Table 6.3). No EU policy is likely to be entirely cost free and some are very expensive. All 13 countries accepted as candidates for Union entry are likely to be net beneficiaries from the budget as presently constituted. Indeed, accession of these countries is hardly financially feasible without either a very substantial increase in budgetary resources or an agreement to restrict the access of the new members to these resources (see Chapter 20). Both deepening and widening of EU integration, therefore, have very significant budgetary consequences.

Table 6.3 Some Factors Accounting for the Expansion of the Budget

- the escalating costs of the CAP;
- the extension of the EU's policy responsibilities;
- the accession four poor countries (Ireland, Greece, Spain and Portugal);
- preparations for future enlargement ('pre-accession aid');
- economic recession (leading to expansion of regional and social aid);
- the cost of major integration projects;
- ineffective control mechanisms.

○ **Allocations**

As Figure 6.2 and Table 6.4 below indicate, *agriculture* takes the lion's share of the budget. The most significant trends in spending are the reduction in the proportion spent on agriculture (declining from over 80% in 1973 to less than half in 2000) and the increase in spending on structural operations (for example spending on regional economic regeneration and on employment training), which now amount to over one-third of the budget.

Figure 6.2 Breakdown of Budgetary Expenditure in 2000

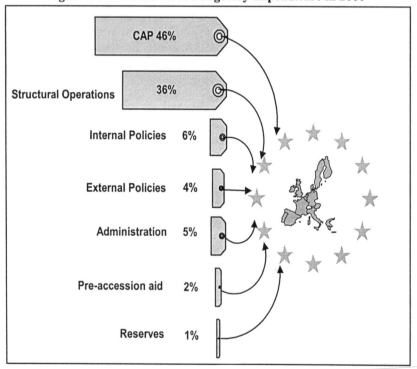

In 2000, €31.8 billion was spent on 'structural' operations (see Chapters 8 and 9), accounting for 36% of the EU's total financial commitments in this year, compared to 18.5% in 1988. These trends reflect deliberate policy to restrict the costs of the Common Agricultural Policy (CAP) and the increasing significance of other policies. Other internal policies, such as energy, transport, education, culture, the environment and consumer protection do not as yet account for a substantial proportion of the budget, although their budgetary significance is increasing. The amounts spent on external action and pre-accession aid have increased substantially. Apart from expenditure on the CAP, budgetary expenditures are largely directed towards investment in training, infrastructure, and research and technological development (RTD).

Table 6.4 The 2000 Union Budget (Payments)

	€ million	£ million	%
1. Common Agricultural Policy	**40,994**	**25,486**	**46**
2. Structural Operations	**31,802**	**19,771**	**36**
Structural Funds	29,002	18,030	
Cohesion Fund	2,800	1,741	
3. Internal Policies	**5,675**	**3,528**	**6**
Other agricultural operations	82	51	
Other regional operations	20	12	
Social and education policies	773	481	
Energy and environment policies	188	117	
Internal market & TENs	938	583	
Research and development	3,600	2,238	
Other internal policies	74	46	
4. External Action	**3,611**	**2,245**	**4**
Food aid & humanitarian aid	832	517	
Regional co-operation measures	2,293	1,426	
Other external actions	456	283	
CFSP	30	19	
5. Administration	**4,704**	**2,924**	**5**
Commission	2,923	1,817	
Other institutions	1,579	981	
6. Reserves and Repayments	**906**	**563**	**1**
Monetary reserve	500	311	
Emergency reserve	203	126	
Loan guarantee reserve	203	126	
Repayments	0	0	
Pre-accession aid	**1,696**	**1,054**	**2**
TOTAL	**89,387**	**55,557**	**100**

Sources: Commission; HM Treasury, *European Community Finances*, Cmnd 4771, July 2000.

The figures above relate to *payment appropriations* which are the amounts available to be spent during the year, taking into account commitments in the current year and preceding years. *Commitment appropriations* are the total cost of legal obligations which can be entered into during the current financial year for activities which will lead to payments in the current and future financial years (for 2000, commitment appropriations totalled €93,281). The difference between the two represents the balance of outstanding commitments. To 'balance the budget', revenue must equal payment appropriations. Surpluses are carried forward to the following year. Modest deficits can also be carried forward, but significant deficits require the adoption of a supplementary or amending budget.

In Berlin in March 1999, the European Council agreed on a financial perspective for Union activities for the 2000–06 period. Commitment appropriations were expected to be about €90 billion in 2000 and 2001 and about €100 billion for each year thereafter. The figures were based on the assumption that some candidate countries will join the EU in 2002, an assumption now widely viewed as overoptimistic. The draft budget for 2000 covered the first year of the 2000–06 financial perspective and took into account *Agenda 2000* (the Commission's blueprint for enlargement – see Chapter 20) and the conclusions of the Berlin European Council, which includes an agreement on reform of the CAP and structural funds. The EU's own resources are not expected to exceed 1.27% of GNP during 2000–06.

Not all EU financial operations are within the budget. The main source of aid to developing countries at EU level is the European Development Fund (EDF) to which members contribute directly. Nor does the budget cover the operations of the European Investment Bank or the European Investment Fund, both of which seek to boost the EU's economies through provision of investment finance. It also excludes the operations of the European Central Bank. Loans and guarantees have been provided to some non-member states, in particular transition economies. The EU has also, although infrequently, provided member states with assistance to overcome balance of payments problems. The European Coal and Steel Community (ECSC), which is to be wound up in 2002, has its own budget, derived from loans and a levy on coal and steel production: budgetary power is exercised by its High Authority.

● POWERS AND PROCEDURES

○ Powers

Formal power of decision in relation to the budget is shared between the Council and the European Parliament (EP), which together constitute the budgetary authority of the Union. The Commission plays a key preparatory and co-ordinative role in the budgetary process. The categorisation of budgetary responsibilities below should not be taken too literally: for example, there are qualitative differences in the powers of the Council and the EP as joint budgetary authorities, with the Council generally in the stronger position. Moreover, although the European Council is not formally part of the budgetary process, key financial decisions having major importance for the size and pattern of budgetary expenditure are being made more frequently at European Council meetings. In recent years, the European Council has adopted multiannual financial frameworks and perspectives outside the EU's formal budgetary process. Budgetary responsibilities can be roughly categorised as follows:

- Drafting   Commission
- Amendment   Council/EP
- Adoption and discharge   Council/EP
- Execution   Commission
- Control   Commission/Council/EP/Court of Auditors
- Audit   Court of Auditors

❍ Procedures

The tortuous process through which the budget is drafted, amended and adopted is known as the 'shuttle'. Budgetary procedures are laid down, although by no means exhaustively, in Article 272 of the EC Treaty and comprise the following stages (see also Figure 6.3 below).

• **The preliminary draft budget.** The Commission's DG for Budgets prepares a preliminary draft budget (PDB) for the following year, based on estimates submitted by the other DGs and by Community institutions. National representatives and interest groups also lobby to ensure that their concerns are taken into account in the PDB. The PDB must be agreed by all commissioners. It must fall within the framework of the current financial perspective agreed by the Council, the EP and the Commission (see below).

• **Council first reading.** The PDB is presented in April or May to the Budget Council comprising the finance ministers of the member states, who normally meet in July to agree the budget. This meeting is preceded by preparatory work undertaken by a budget committee of national officials and by the Committee of Permanent Representatives (COREPER). For example, the Commission adopted the 2001 PDB in May 2000, which amounted to €96.9 billion in commitment appropriations and €93.9 billion in payment appropriations. The Council usually cuts the PDB, but by only a fraction of the total amount. The PDB is also forwarded to the EP at the same time as to the Council. There are two broad categories of budgetary expenditure:

compulsory and *non-compulsory*, each of which now accounts for around half of the budget. Compulsory expenditure is necessary expenditure arising from the EC Treaty or from acts adopted in accordance with it (mainly spending on the CAP). The main non-compulsory items are social policy, regional policy, industry, energy and transport. The distinction is important, because although the EP can propose modifications to compulsory expenditure, the Council can reject them and the EP has no right to a further say on this element of the budget. Even before the EP's first reading, a conciliation procedure involving the president of the Budget Council, the chairman of the EP's Budget Committee and the Commissioner for Budgets may be established if a dispute seems likely over categorisation of compulsory and non-compulsory expenditure (the EP naturally wishes as much as possible to be included in the latter category).

- **EP first reading.** The draft as amended by the Council is then placed before the EP. Within 45 days of receiving it, the EP must complete its first reading. A key role in examining the draft is played by the EP's Budget Committee, although other parliamentary committees are also involved. Meeting in plenary session in October or November, the EP considers and votes on proposed changes to the budget. Proposed amendments to non-compulsory expenditure require approval of an absolute majority of Members of the European Parliament (MEPs) whereas proposed modifications to compulsory expenditure require a majority of votes cast.
- **Council second reading.** The Budget Council then considers the draft, as amended and modified by the EP. The Council has 15 days to react to the EP's amendments and proposed modifications. The Council can by qualified majority voting (QMV) modify amendments to non-compulsory expenditure and can reject modifications to compulsory expenditure. It frequently cuts proposed amendments and rejects proposed modifications. If it alters the amendments, it has 15 days to resubmit these to the EP for second reading.
- **EP second reading.** This normally takes place in December. The EP has 15 days to act on the Council's alterations. It can reinstate cuts made by the Council to non-compulsory spending, by a majority of MEPs and three-fifths of the votes cast. It cannot, however, propose further modifications or changes to compulsory spending. The budget is expected to be adopted no later than 20 December. If no agreement is reached, negotiations take place involving representatives from the Budget Council, the EP Committee on Budgets and the Budget Commissioner. The EP has the right to reject the budget as a whole (by a majority of its members and two-thirds of the votes cast) as it has done on several occasions. In these cases, the 'provisional twelfths' system comes into operation, a procedure by which spending is allowed on a monthly basis (based on the monthly figures of the last year's budget), until a new budget is agreed.

Figure 6.3 The EU Budgetary Process

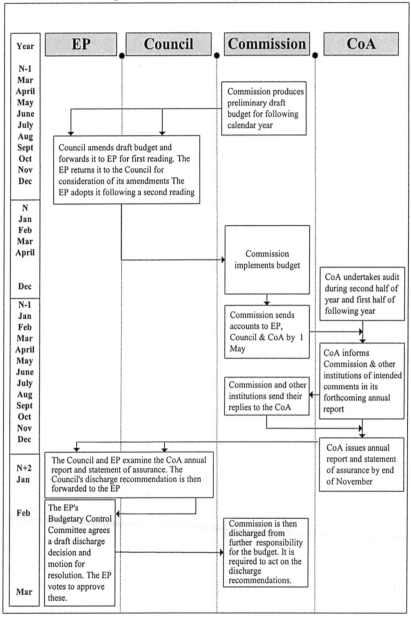

- **Control.** There is an elaborate, but by no means fully effective, system of budgetary control. The Commission has a system of internal financial control, which is the responsibility of a financial controller, charged with monitoring all budget operations. It also has an anti-fraud office, known by its French acronym OLAF (*Office de la Lutte Antifraude*), which is examined in more detail below. The Court of Auditors (CoA) is responsible for verifying the legality and regularity of Community revenue and expenditure. The court provides an annual statement of assurance on the reliability of the EU accounts and the legality and reliability of underlying transactions. The audits of the court, which are retrospective, are used by the EP in its examinations of the implementation of programmes. Auditors have a right of access to any document or financial information concerning financial management of departments or bodies subject to its examination The CoA has frequently presented scathing reports on the Commission's implementation of budgets, pointing to inadequacies in accounting, supervision and accountability.

● KEY ISSUES

The history of the Union budget is littered with conflicts and crises, many of which have centred on the following issues.

○ Institutional Powers

The budget has been at the centre of the EP's efforts to assert its powers *vis-à-vis* the Council and the Commission, by for example rejecting (or threatening to reject) the draft budget and by proposing budgetary amendments. A *conciliation procedure* has been established to facilitate agreement between the Council and the EP in respect of compulsory expenditure, but if no agreement is reached within the procedure the Council can reaffirm its position. The Council therefore has the 'last word' on compulsory expenditure. However, the EP has the last word on non-compulsory expenditure. It can formulate amendments on non-compulsory expenditure, up to a maximum rate of increase (based on the rate of Union GNP growth, the rate of inflation and the amount of government spending), and calculated by the Commission each year at the start of the budgetary procedure. Any increase in the maximum rate has to be agreed by both the Council and the EP. The EP has frequently proposed that the distinction between compulsory and non-compulsory expenditure should be abolished.

In recent years the establishment of formal and informal mechanisms for dialogue between the Council and the EP on budgetary questions has reduced the incidence of major interinstitutional budgetary conflicts. In particular, in 1988 an interinstitutional agreement on budget discipline was signed by the presidents of the Council, the EP and the Commission (see below). This committed the three institutions to *financial perspectives* for broad expenditure categories covering several years. The first perspective (1988–92) committed the institutions to an expansion of the budget, but also contained *ceilings* to ensure tight budgetary discipline (see below). The perspective for 2000–06 set out annual expenditure ceilings for seven broad expenditure categories (agriculture, structural actions, internal policies, external action, administrative expenditure, reserves and pre-accession aid).

○ **Inadequacy** (the failure of resources to keep pace with the demands made on the budget)

There have been many interinstitutional and intergovernmental disputes concerning the adequacy of budgetary resources. In some years, the budget has balanced only by carrying some expenditure items forward to future years. Within the Council, the main source of opposition to large budgetary increases has come from the net contributors among the member states. Conversely, the four poorest states have pressed for increases in support of policies aimed at narrowing the development gap between rich and poor states. The Single European Market (SEM) and the Treaty on European Union (TEU) resulted in substantial increases in the size of the European Social Fund (ESF) and the European Regional Development Fund (ERDF). In addition, the TEU established the Cohesion Fund for the four poorest states.

Budgetary issues figured prominently in the negotiations for the entry into the EU of Austria, Finland and Sweden. Spain, in particular, was adamant that wealthy potential entrants would have to agree to provide financial assistance for the poor 'southern' countries. All three 1995 entrants are net contributors to the budget and have provided additional support for countries seeking to limit budgetary growth. A distinction between *restrainers* and *expanders* also has an institutional dimension: whereas the Council (notwithstanding the views of its poorer members) has frequently sought to limit budgetary expenditure growth, the Commission and the EP have generally sought to expand it. Perhaps the most glaring example of imbalance between the EU's budgetary resources and its policy objectives is the current enlargement process: absorption of 13 new states into the EU, all with GNPs substantially below the EU average, obviously has major budgetary implications.

○ **Inequity** (disputes about fairness in revenue and allocation decisions)

Allocations are not based on the *just return* principle, by which states would obtain from the budget roughly what they pay in. Although gross contributions to the budget are now roughly proportional to member states'

GNPs, there are glaring disparities between member countries in the amounts paid in and received, as shown in Figure 6.4. below.

In the early 1980s, only Germany and the UK were significant net contributors. In recent years, France, Belgium, Luxembourg, the Netherlands, Denmark, Italy, Austria, Finland and Sweden have joined the 'net contributors' club': in 1999, 11 member states were net contributors. The UK, the fifth poorest member of EU15, has been a net contributor ever since it entered the Union. In 1980, West Germany was the richest country in the Union. By the early 1990s, Germany had slipped to sixth place (as a result of reunification and the recession), but it remains the largest net contributor, currently providing over twice as much as it receives from the budget each year. Within Germany, this has been a big issue during recent elections. The Netherlands, Sweden and Austria receive low returns from both the CAP and the structural funds. France's net contributions would be much greater were it not for the CAP. Italy's net contributions would also be significantly greater were it not for revenues received from the CAP and the structural funds. The largest net gainers are the four poorest members. In 1999, the net benefits received by these countries were: Greece, €3.6 billion; Portugal, €2.7 billion; Ireland, €1.7 billion; and Spain €6.7 billion – meaning that Greece and Portugal received over three times, and Ireland and Spain over twice, as much as they paid in. Ireland is likely to join the net contributors' club by 2006.

Figure 6.4 National Receipts From and Payments To the EU Budget (For 1999 in € Billion)

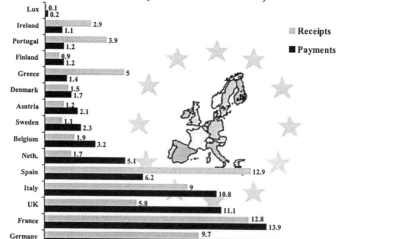

Source: National Audit Office (2001).

○ The UK's Budgetary Transfers

Because the UK has a relatively high degree of trade with other countries, it makes relatively high contributions to the budget (derived from high levels of agricultural imports from outside the EU and customs duties). Because it has a relatively small agricultural sector, it receives less from the CAP than several other member states. On the other hand, it has tended to receive more from the ESF than any other member state. The bulk of the moneys received by the UK derive from the CAP, the ERDF and the ESF. The size of the UK imbalance has fluctuated significantly, due to several factors, such as import costs, exchange rate fluctuations, adjustments to the UK's VAT rebate (see below) and adjustments to payments in previous years.

On joining the Union, the UK agreed to contribute to the budget on the basis of a fixed percentage of 8.78% of the total, rising to 19.24% in 1977. The incoming Labour government in 1974 sought to renegotiate these terms, on the grounds that the UK's low level of economic growth did not justify such high contributions. An agreement aimed at limiting divergences between contributions and ability to pay, involving partial repayment of VAT contributions (known as the 'clawback mechanism'), was reached at the European Council in Dublin in 1975 and implemented between 1976 and 1980. But the strict conditions governing repayment rendered it ineffective. The incoming Conservative government in 1979 sought to reduce the UK's contributions by £1 billion, but had to settle for £350 million. In 1983, the UK delayed payment of its contributions to the EU for a month, but the ECJ ruled this to be illegal.

At the European Council in Fontainebleau in June 1984, Mrs Thatcher succeeded in negotiating a substantial budget rebate for the UK, known as the Fontainebleau Abatement, which came into operation in 1986. The abatement is a refund based on a reduction of 66% of the difference between what the UK contributes to the budget and what it receives from it (in terms of grants and expenditure). The abatement, which is calculated by the Commission, is deducted from the UK's VAT contribution a year in arrears. The UK's contribution is calculated as though the entire budget was financed by VAT contributions. It excludes expenditure outside the Union, such as development aid (amounting to about 5% of the EU budget in 2000). Other states make up the difference (because of Germany's position as the main contributor to the budget, it pays only two-thirds of its 'share' – but this still amounts to the largest actual contribution). By the end of 2001, the cumulative value to the UK of the abatement is expected to reach £29 billion. Despite the abatement, the UK has continued to be a net contributor. According to the UK's National Audit Office, the UK contributed about €5.3 billion (£3.3 billion) more than it received in 1999, as Figure 6.5 below shows. The figure would be considerably higher were it not for the VAT abatement, which in 1999 amounted to about €3.6 billion (£2.2 billion). According to the UK Treasury, the annual underlying level of abatement is about £2.1 billion. The abatement is becoming harder to defend because several other countries (besides the UK and Germany) have become large net contributors. The Netherlands is now a larger net contributor than the UK, if the ratio of benefits to contributions is taken into account. Four other countries, that is, Germany, the Netherlands, Austria and Sweden, are currently seeking abatements.

**Figure 6.5 UK Payments To and Receipts From the EU Budget
(For 1999 in € Billion)**

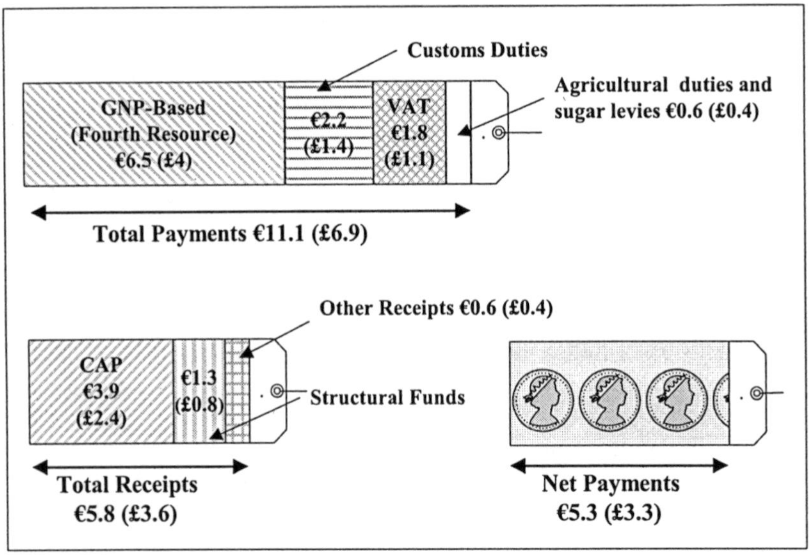

Source: National Audit Office (2001).

Successive British governments have refused to abandon the UK abatement, arguing that the UK still does relatively badly in terms of receipts from the budget, receiving less than any other member state per capita and as a proportion of GNP. Although the prosperity gap between the UK and some other net contributors has narrowed somewhat, the UK is still the fifth-poorest member of the Union. It is possible that the UK will agree to lose the abatement, but only as part of an overall budgetary reform package which addresses the issue of budgetary imbalances. At the Berlin European Council in March 1999, the UK government again refused to abandon it, despite pressure from several member states: an agreement was eventually reached enabling the abatement cost to be redistributed among the 14 other member states, which means that richer contributors will pay less than before.

● REFORMING THE BUDGET

○ Towards Greater Predictability

In recent years, attempts have been made to achieve tighter budgetary disciplines, a better balance between expenditure categories and vigorous action against fraud. The Delors Commission presented two major sets of proposals on budgetary reform, known as 'Delors 1' (1987–88) and 'Delors 2' (1992). In February 1988, the Council agreed principles of budgetary discipline based on 'Delors 1'. This set annual ceilings for categories of expenditure and ceilings for increases in the total budget. It capped increases in agricultural spending to 74% of average GDP growth. It doubled the amounts allocated to the structural funds. On the revenue side, it introduced the 'fourth resource'. These reforms formed the basis of an Interinstitutional Agreement on Budgetary Discipline and Improvement of the Budgetary Procedure reached between the Council Commission and the EP in June 1988. The agreement clarified the way the Council, the EP and the Commission exercised their budgetary responsibilities. It sought to increase the degree of predictability in relation to budgetary growth, by introducing a 'financial perspective' which outlined projected expenditures for 1988–92. It therefore sought to reduce the intensity of the annual conflicts concerning the size and composition of the budget.

The 'Delors 2' package focused on the financial implications of the TEU. It favoured orderly, but nevertheless substantial, increases in expenditure to match the objectives of the treaty. Unlike Delors 1, it included a category for external action. It proposed substantial increases in expenditure on structural policies and 'economic and social cohesion', of particular benefit to the four poorest member states. Richer states initially resisted these proposals, but eventually agreed to budgetary increases, based on the setting of ceilings on six categories of expenditure for the 1993–99 period. Since 1988, therefore, EU budgets have been developed within 'financial perspectives', which have time frames of several years and which breakdown projected expenditure into categories. In March 1999, a new financial perspective for 2000–06 was agreed by the Berlin European Council.

○ The Berlin Reforms

In March 1999, following growing concern among several member states about their budgetary contributions and about the implications of future enlargement, a special European Council meeting in Berlin agreed a package of budgetary reform measures. At this summit, each member state had interests to defend: the net contributor countries sought to reduce their contributions and net beneficiary countries sought to maintain their benefits. For example, Germany sought to reduce its contributions by €3 billion (but accepted a reduction of €700 million); the UK sought to defend its rebate; France sought to defend spending on agriculture; Spain defended its structural aid. The summit agreed on the following:

- a freeze on the EU budget at 1999 levels;
- the budget ceiling to be a maximum of 1.27% of GNP;
- VAT-linked contributions to be replaced by money raised as a proportion of the GNP of each member state;
- the UK rebate will remain, but its costs will be redistributed among the 14 other states;
- agricultural subsidies to be cut, but by less than some countries wanted;
- spending on the regions to be reallocated and marginally reduced;
- spending on trans-European networks to increase to €4.6 billion by 2006.

O The Fight Against Fraud

There has been considerable criticism of financial irregularity and fraud in relation to the budget, although their extent is difficult to gauge. The distinction between fraud and irregularity is that the former is intentional and is a criminal offence whereas an irregularity is an infringement of Union law resulting from an act or omission. CoA annual reports have repeatedly found unacceptable levels of error in budgetary payments and significant weaknesses in the management of the budget. In its 1998 annual report, the CoA found that over one in seven of the transactions examined in relation to the CAP was affected by a formal error. Errors in the structural funds accounted for over half the financial error found within the budget. It also found a high incidence of error in internal policies, particularly RTD. It found many cases where costs had been inflated. In 1998, member states notified the Commission of over 5000 cases of irregularity. The Commission estimates that about one in five of the cases of irregularity (mostly concerning revenue from customs and agricultural duties, sugar levies and the CAP) involves fraud. Only about 6% of the amounts involved in detected fraud cases is ever recovered. In recent years, there has been a growth in large-scale organised crime across national borders, for example, cigarette and alcohol smuggling.

The fight against fraud is made particularly difficult by five factors: firstly, the information upon which funding for agricultural and structural policies are based is often difficult to verify; secondly, the extreme complexity of legislation renders some funds, such as the European Agricultural Guidance and Guarantee Fund (EAGGF) (Guarantee section), vulnerable to fraud and difficult to control; thirdly, EU institutions do not have the resources to effectively monitor how allocated moneys are spent; fourthly, national and regional authorities of member states are responsible for paying out about 85% of Union funds to the final beneficiaries. These authorities are arguably likely to be less diligent in pursuing anti-fraud measures involving Union funds than they are in pursuing frauds on their own budgets. Member states are required to co-ordinate their actions in countering fraud and to take the same measures in countering frauds on the Community budget as they take in matters affecting their own direct financial interests (Article 280, ECT), but this is easier said than done; fifthly, the Commission has arguably been lax in seeking to develop a culture intolerant of fraud and irregularity. It thus took several major scandals to prompt the Commission's current interest in dealing effectively with fraud.

In 1998, in the light of the CoA's annual report, the EP postponed the decision to grant discharge to the Commission for the 1996 budget. The EP's committee on budgetary control recommended delay of discharge because the Commission had not responded adequately to its concerns about the budgets for tourism, the European Community Humanitarian Office (ECHO), regional aid and the CAP in particular. Although in November 1998 the Committee narrowly voted for discharge, calling on the Commission to institute radical reforms, in December 1998 the EP sent the issue back to the committee for reconsideration. In January 1999, the EP considered a motion of censure against the Commission, but did not obtain the two-thirds majority required. On 14 January the EP nevertheless appointed a committee of independent experts (known as the Middelhoek Committee) to investigate these allegations. The committee published two scathing reports on the Commission, in March and September 1999. The first report found instances where individual commissioners, or the Commission as a whole, bore responsibility for fraud, irregularity or mismanagement in their services or areas of responsibility. It found that even where commissioners were ignorant of these failings, this was indicative of a loss of control on their part. It identified a mismatch between resources and responsibilities; a failure of control mechanisms; inadequate anti-fraud mechanisms, weaknesses in administrative and disciplinary procedures; and a lack of clear responsibility. Following this damning report, the Commission had no choice but to resign, which it did in March 1999.

The second report of the committee was published in September 1999. It examined procedures for the award by the Commission of financial contracts and procedures for investigating allegations of fraud, poor management and nepotism. The report included 90 recommendations for improvement, including stronger arrangements for investigating fraud, establishment of an internal audit service reporting to the Commission president, establishment of a committee on standards in public life, clearer rules for whistle blowers and making directors-general responsible for all operational matters. In response, the Commission announced its intention to set up a new central financial service and internal audit service by May 2000. In April 2000, discharge of the 1998 budget was postponed by the EP. It was finally granted the following July, after the Commission had responded to various issues raised by the EP.

A House of Commons Select Committee of Public Accounts (29th report) session 98/99) also undertook an investigation of financial management and control in the EU and found that the Union's arrangements for combating fraud were ineffective. It stated that there was a lack of financial information on the performance of individual directors-general or expenditure programmes; that there needed to be much stronger accountability in member states for the payments made; that there was a cultural emphasis on devising policy without regard to effective management; that policies were adopted without due consideration of the resource implications, risks or financial controls needed; that financial statements were badly presented; that arrangements for investigating and prosecuting fraud were ineffective; and that the Commission has not responded effectively to the reports of the CoA.

The Commission's anti-fraud unit UCLAF (*Unité de coordination de la lutte anti-fraude*) was the target of considerable criticism. There were two categories of criticism of UCLAF: the first related to its efficiency and general functioning; and the second to its position within the Commission. A CoA report in 1998 (no. 8/98) was scathing in its criticisms of UCLAF, namely: inquiries by UCLAF were poorly defined or overcomplicated; security measures were frequently not correctly implemented; an excessive proportion of UCLAF's staff were temporary agents; electronic databases were neither fully operational nor effective; and management information on UCLAF's caseload was inadequate. The exposure of fraud and budgetary mismanagement, culminating in the resignation of the Commission, meant that UCLAF's days were numbered. A new anti-fraud office, OLAF, was set up in June 1999, replacing UCLAF. The new office is independent from the Commission and its director does not take instructions regarding its investigations from any EU institution or government. It is able to investigate all fraudulent or illegal activities at the expense of the EU budget and to conduct its investigations within member states as well as the European institutions. But OLAF does not have the power to conduct criminal investigations, which remains with member states.

In its 1999 annual report, the CoA recommended that the Commission should move away from a 'spending culture' and should make fundamental improvements in its internal controls and accountability. These included measures to ensure that departments do not accept additional responsibilities without adequate resources; strengthening internal audit and accounting systems; and setting clear measurable objectives for programmes and performance targets, focusing on outputs, outcomes and costs.

○ **Proposals for Further Budgetary Reform**

In recent years, the Union budget has already undergone substantial reform: for example, in the interests of predictability and budgetary discipline, financial perspectives and budget capping have been introduced. the proportions raised by specific budgetary resources and also the amounts spent on specific budget items have changed dramatically. However, it is widely accepted that further budgetary reform is needed, to cope with the pressures of future enlargement and to respond effectively to recent scathing criticisms of the EU's system of financial management. In 1998, a Commission report on the options for budgetary reform (*Financing the European Union*) examined the present system according to the criteria of adequacy, equity, financial autonomy, transparency/simplicity and cost effectiveness. It argued that although the current system had performed adequately in terms of sufficiency and in terms of equity (a very debatable point), it showed some shortcomings when judged against the criteria of financial autonomy, cost effectiveness and transparency.

- *Adequacy.* The system has generated sufficient revenue.
- *Equity*, meaning proportionality of gross contributions to income across the member states. This had improved, so that member states' contributions are now more closely correlated with national GNPs (although if the amounts paid in and received from the budget are introduced into the equation, the Commission's equity argument becomes much more debatable).
- *Financial autonomy.* It argued that TOR is the only true own resource of the EU and that its importance was diminishing. Moreover, member states collect these duties and tended to regard them as national contributions. The implications of this lack of financial autonomy were judged to be threefold: firstly, it has made the EU increasingly dependent on intergovernmental transfers, leading to budgetary conflicts and had encouraged member states to seek to maximise national benefits from the budget; secondly, EU financing issues were entangled with domestic policies, so that citizens lack knowledge of the EU-wide priorities at stake; thirdly, it obscured democratic accountability, because of the lack of a direct relationship between citizens and taxes paid to the budget.
- *Cost effectiveness.* The collection of TOR is very cumbersome. There are over 11,000 tariff positions and the Community customs code has over 400 articles. The Commission argued that member states were inclined neither to tighten the regulatory framework of the customs system nor to expend the necessary resources on collecting customs duties.
- *Transparency and simplicity.* The UK rebate added further complexity to an already complex system.

The Commission report also discussed options for reform of the system, such as the introduction of a 'correction mechanism', leading to an increase in redistribution of resources between member states. This would be likely to be fiercely resisted by the poorer member states, who would receive smaller net budgetary benefits as a result. It also discussed 'CAP co-financing', meaning that payments to farmers would only partly be made from the budget, with the rest coming from member states. This idea, however, is understandably very unpopular with countries which have large agricultural sectors.

O   Ideas for New Taxes

The Commission report also discussed possible use of new taxes, such as:

- *Withholding taxes.* These are taxes imposed on dividend or interest income derived by foreign and local investors in firms located in specific countries. They ensure that taxation authorities in the country get a share of this income. However, a drawback is that foreign investors get taxed twice (in their home countries and in the countries where they have investments). The Commission first proposed a withholding tax on interest income from savings in 1989, but this idea was rejected by the UK and Luxembourg, which attract considerable amounts of savings from other countries. It was argued that it would make European financial centres unattractive to foreign investors. It would create a more level playing field for investment, but it could lead to an outflow of funds from the EU and would probably not generate sufficient revenue to make it worthwhile.

- *A European corporation tax.* This could generate substantial revenue and would provide a more level playing field for business (currently corporation taxes are levied by individual member states and vary considerably). But some member states have an integrated system of corporation and personal tax and there are differences in definitions of corporate income. Moreover, as business profits fluctuate, so would the amounts raised. Nor does it score highly on the criterion of visibility to the individual taxpayer.

- *An energy or eco tax.* This idea was put forward by the Commission as early as 1978. It would involve taxation on use of energy, in particular on energy causing pollution In 1993, the Commission put forward a proposal for a carbon tax on fuel in order to stabilise CO^2 emissions. However, it was strongly opposed by several member states and also by various industrial groups. The main advantages of such a tax are that it would provide substantial revenue, it would foster the EU's environmental objectives and it would be an alternative to 'tax competition' between member states. Its main drawback is that it is not necessarily equitable, because of differences in energy production and use in member states.

- *Excise taxes on alcohol and tobacco.* These are levied by individual member states, so that many different rates apply. A Euro-tax on these commodities could generate substantial funds. It would be easy to collect, because member states already collect revenue on these items and revenues raised would be fairly stable. It would also foster the Union's health goals. However, it would be inequitable because consumption rates vary as between member states. These taxes are also regressive, in that people on lower incomes pay a relatively higher proportion of tax.

Each of these ideas has its drawbacks (as the Commission recognises), not least of which is the difficulty of getting all member states to accept it.

● CONCLUSION

Recent reforms of the budget have to some degree taken some of the heat out of 'getting and spending' debates within the EU. However, budgetary issues remain a source of conflict and it is highly likely that the next enlargements will exacerbate budgetary tensions. It remains to be seen whether the various pressures on the EU budget (in particular impending enlargement, exposure of budgetary inadequacies and the dissatisfaction of the net contributors with current budgetary arrangements) will result in thorough reform or more tinkering with an already highly complicated budgetary system.

FURTHER READING

Begg, I. and Grimwade, N. (1998), *Paying For Europe*, Sheffield Academic Press, Sheffield.

Commission (2001), *General Report on the Activities of the European Union 2000.*

Commission (1998), *Financing the European Union:* Commission Report on the Operation of the Own Resources System, COM (98) 560.

Committee of Independent Experts (1999), *First and Second Reports on Allegations Regarding Fraud, Mismanagement and Nepotism in the European Commission*, www.europarl.eu.int/experts.

Court of Auditors, Annual Reports.

HM Treasury (2000), *European Community Finances*, Cmnd 4771, HMSO, July.

House of Commons (1999), Committee of Public Accounts, 29th Report, *Financial Management and Control in the EU,* House of Commons, Session 1998–99.

House of Lords European Communities Committee (1999), Sixth Report: *Future Financing of the EU: Who Pays and How?*, Session 1998–99.

Laffan, B. (1997), *The Finances of the European Union*, Macmillan, Basingstoke.

National Audit Office (2001), *Financial Management of the European Union*, Report by the Comptroller and Auditor General, HC, Session 2000–2001.

Section 3

The Policies of the European Union

 # Introduction to Section 3

● THE EU'S POLICY PORTFOLIO AND POLICY STYLE

○ Overview and Key Characteristics

The rest of the book provides an introduction to the Union's current policy responsibilities. We shall begin with a short overview of the principal characteristics of the Union's policy portfolio and policy style.

• **Uneven development.** The EU's policy portfolio is both unbalanced and fragmentary. Some EU policies are of long standing and highly developed (notably the Common Agricultural Policy (CAP) and the Common Commercial Policy); some have developed mainly in the last two decades (for example, Regional and Social Policy); some are quite recent and relatively undeveloped (for example, Consumer Policy, Cultural Policy). There are several major policy areas where the EU has at most a minimal role (for example, health, social security) or where its remit does not yet extend (for example, domestic crime). Variations in national conditions, policy traditions and policy priorities render it difficult for the EU to develop 'full' policies in all areas. The range of subjects upon which the EU can justifiably be said to have a policy has nevertheless broadened considerably, as shown by the large number of policies explicitly referred to in recent EU treaties.

• **The extensive treatment of policy matters in the treaties** differentiates the EU from the constitutions of most federations. This does not mean that an EU policy requires a strong treaty basis before it can be developed: for example, progress was made in environmental policy from the 1970s, even though there was no explicit mention of the environment in the founding treaties. Similarly, a basis in an EU treaty does not mean that the policy *will* be developed: the Treaty of Rome stipulated a Common Transport Policy (CTP), but this area of policy remained dormant for decades. Policies were set out in great detail in the European Coal and Steel Community (ECSC) Treaty, but references to policies in the later treaties tend to be confined to policy principles (although the Treaty on European Union (TEU) outlines the policy on economic and monetary union (EMU) in great detail). Some policy provisions in the treaties give legal acknowledgement of *de facto* policy developments, such as references to 'European Political Co-operation' in the Single European Act (SEA).

• **The diversity of policy priorities.** Member states by no means have an equal commitment to a strong EU involvement in specific policy areas. For example, some member states are more committed to the development of a common foreign and security policy (CFSP) than others. The UK has traditionally been keen to develop trade policies, but otherwise has tended to be lukewarm about policies leading to deeper integration. EU budgetary allocations for policies are by no means evenly distributed among member states and therefore it is hardly surprising that states will have different preferences concerning the EU policy agenda. Both the Commission and the European Parliament (EP) have tended to favour extension of the Union's policy responsibilities. The Commission has played a dynamic role as a facilitator, energiser and source of ideas in relation to policy developments. Some Commissions (notably the Delors Commissions of 1984–94) have been far more proactive in this regard than others.

• **Types of policy.** Although there is some overlap between them, EU policies can be roughly divided into six categories, as set out in Table S.3.

Table S.3 Types of EU Policy

• **Regulatory policies** are primarily concerned with achievement of policy goals through the making and enforcement of rules (for example, setting out EU-wide standards). Examples are the rules governing the operation of the single market; competition and environmental policies.

• **Redistributive policies** are primarily concerned with the achievement of policy goals through the redistribution of resources (for example through the CAP and the structural funds).

• **Macroeconomic Stabilisation policies,** dealing with monetary and fiscal policies, such as managing currencies and countering inflation.

• **External policies** are concerned with the EU's relations with the outside world, for example trade relations and foreign policy.

• **Citizen's rights and judicial policies** are concerned with establishing, fostering and protecting the rights of EU citizens (for example, justice and home affairs and migration policies).

• **EU governance policies** are concerned with establishing and developing the EU's values, structures and procedures (for example, in relation to institutional goals, powers and ways of doing things).

The boundaries between these categories are by no means watertight. For example, EU directives on part-time working and equal pay are regulatory, but they are likely to have redistributive consequences. Similarly, trade relationships involve the imposition of regulatory measures. Asylum and immigration policies overlap into the external policy category and so on.

• **The type of EU involvement.** The Union's involvement in policy by no means fits into a homogeneous pattern. For example, CFSP and Police and

Judicial Co-operation in Criminal Matters are largely outside the EC policymaking framework. Some policies are referred to in the treaties as 'common' (agriculture, fisheries, commercial policy, transport, foreign and security policy) meaning that an agreed single policy is expected to replace national policies, at least with regard to major areas of policy. Some are costly to operate (notably the CAP) whereas others make only small demands on the EU budget. Some are based on a high degree of legal regulation (notably the CAP, fisheries, competition and common commercial policies).

- **Supranational and intergovernmental policymaking.** Some policy types are primarily subject to supranational decisionmaking procedures, meaning that, in addition to the Council, the Commission, the EP and the European Court of Justice (ECJ) have key roles in the policy process. Moreover, in these areas decisionmaking in the Council is likely to be by qualified majority voting (QMV). Most regulatory and redistributive policies fall into this category, whereas macroeconomic stabilisation falls more evenly across the (admittedly rather fuzzy) boundaries between supranationalist and intergovernmental procedures. External policies, citizens rights and judicial policies and EU governance policies are still very largely intergovernmental in character.

- **Policy style.** In some respects, the EU's policy system shares important characteristics with those of national policy systems in liberal democratic states: it is an *elite process*, in that in practice policy decisions are made by a relatively small group of actors; it is a *pluralist process*, in that policy decisions are the outcome of extensive bargaining and compromise between policy actors (principally governments, Union institutions and interest groups); it is *incrementalist*, in that EU policy is constantly adjusted and refined. The Union's policy system also has several distinctive features. It is more complex than policymaking at national level, in terms of its procedures and institutional framework. The formulation and implementation of EU policy involves several levels of government and a broader range of institutional actors than national systems. In many respects, the EU's policymaking system is probably more open than those of most national systems (notwithstanding the many flaws in EU policies on 'transparency').

- **Implementation remains largely a national function.** The national, regional and local governments of member states are largely responsible for carrying out EU policies. A factor often given insufficient consideration is the variation in the ability (and sometimes the will) of member states to implement policy effectively.

- **Citizens' knowledge of EU policies.** Most EU citizens probably have only the haziest knowledge of the EU's policy portfolio, or of the differences between EU and national policy responsibilities. The intermeshing of EU and national policies in a wide variety of fields means that perceptions of this distinction are likely to be increasingly difficult to make.

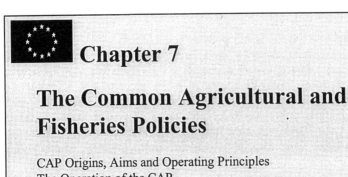

Chapter 7

The Common Agricultural and Fisheries Policies

● CAP ORIGINS, AIMS AND OPERATING PRINCIPLES

○ Origins and Aims

In most parts of the world, agriculture is regarded as a special industry, to be protected and subsidised. The volatility of agricultural markets and the need for security of food supplies has provided a plausible case for government intervention in this sector. The industry has also been widely viewed as part of a nation's cultural heritage. Prior to the creation of the Common Agricultural Policy (CAP), member states had their own policies for subsidising and protecting domestic agriculture. At the time of the CAP's formation, memories of food shortages during the Second World War were still fresh in many people's minds. The need to increase production and to ensure security of food supplies were therefore regarded as self-evidently desirable goals. Although in the 1950s, 'EU6' had a farming population of 17.5 million, it produced only 85% of its food requirements. The small size of most farms in EU6 (average farm sizes in the US were 20 times larger) was hardly conducive to efficiency.

The advantages of a common policy for agriculture were recognised by the Union's founders: it would enable agricultural problems common to all countries to be dealt with by collective action; market stability could be fostered through collective intervention in agricultural markets and through a common policy of external protection; it would provide farmers with new outlets for their produce; it would encourage regional specialisation in food products; it would offer consumers wider choice (see Table 7.1 below). The

CAP was formally established in the Treaty of Rome (Articles 38–47, now Articles 32–37). Its operational guidelines were agreed at the Stresa conference in 1958 and it came into operation in 1962. From the beginning, it has occupied a central (for many years a dominant) role in Union policy.

Table 7.1 The Objectives of the CAP (Article 33, ECT)

a. **to increase agricultural productivity** by promoting technological progress and by ensuring the rational development of agricultural production and the optimum utilisation of the factors of production, in particular labour;

b. **to ensure a fair standard of living** for the agricultural community, in particular by increasing the individual earnings of persons engaged in agriculture;

c. **to stabilise agricultural markets;**

d. **to ensure the availability of food supplies;**

e. **to ensure that supplies reach consumers at reasonable prices.**

○ Operating Principles

The CAP is based on the assumption that agricultural markets need to be *managed*. In a free market, the price of any product will rise and fall in accordance with the laws of supply and demand. The CAP was designed to modify the operation of this mechanism in the agricultural sector, through instruments such as price supports, production quotas, production subsidies and import barriers. Recent CAP reforms, for example modifications to price supports, introduction of direct income supports for farmers and incentives to 'set aside' land for non-agricultural uses, have not changed the system's essential character, which is 'market distorting'. In 1960, the Council adopted three principles upon which the CAP is based (see Table 7.2).

Table 7.2 Fundamental CAP Principles

- **Market unity:** free movement of agricultural produce within EU boundaries, meaning the abolition of cross-border barriers to agricultural trade.
- **Community preference:** protection from agricultural imports from outside the EU and promotion of EU agricultural exports, meaning that free trade in agriculture was *not* extended to states outside the Union.
- **Joint financial responsibility:** meaning that the costs of the CAP would be shared among member states and would not be based on the 'just return' principle (by which the financial benefits accruing to a member state would be equivalent to its contributions).

The seeds of the main controversies surrounding the CAP are contained within these principles, because each implies a disproportionate distribution of benefits and costs. For example, both consumers and producers should reap benefits from *market unity*. But it also exposes producers to cross-border competition. *Community preference* benefits some Union producers by shielding them from global competition. But it also restricts consumer choice and results in higher food prices. *Joint financial responsibility* means that producers in some countries probably receive greater financial benefit than they could obtain from their own governments if the CAP did not exist. But it also means that the citizens of some EU countries in effect subsidise the agriculture industries of others. The prime beneficiaries of the CAP, *producer interests*, have proved more powerful, and certainly better organised, than *consumer interests*. Because the costs and benefits of the CAP are distributed very unevenly between member states, some governments have a stronger interest in defending the system than others (although all are subject to strong pressure from producer interests).

● THE OPERATION OF THE CAP

○ Responsibilities

The Agriculture Council is the key decision-taker with regard to the CAP. Meetings of this Council are prepared by the Special Committee on Agriculture (SCA), not by the Committee of Permanent Representatives (COREPER). There is much horse trading within the Council, because each agriculture minister has national agricultural interests to promote and defend. The European Parliament's (EP's) powers of co-decision do not apply to agriculture, because it is classified as 'compulsory' expenditure, although the EP subjects the Commission's proposals to detailed scrutiny and suggests many amendments. In its report prepared for the 1996 intergovernmental conference (IGC), the EP recommended the extension of co-decision to agriculture. However, the Treaty of Amsterdam (ToA) did not change the EP's powers in this respect (nor will the Treaty of Nice).

The Commission has a deeper involvement in the implementation of the CAP than in most other policy areas. The directorate responsible for agriculture is the largest Commission directorate with policy responsibilities. The reorganisation of Commission departments in 1999 by the new Commission president, Romano Prodi, had important implications for the agriculture directorate. Responsibility for fisheries was transferred to this directorate, whereas public health and animal and plant health and activities associated with infringements of Union regulations in this area were transferred from it to the directorate for health and consumer protection. Responsibility for the co-ordination of agricultural research was transferred from agriculture to the research directorate. A central role in the management of the CAP is played by a network of management and regulatory committees, such as the management committees for cereals, milk and sugar and the Standing Veterinary Committee, comprising agricultural specialists in the Commission and in the agriculture ministries of member states.

○ Finance

The CAP is financed from the EU budget, through the European Agricultural Guidance and Guarantee Fund (EAGGF), which is divided into two sections:
• **The Guarantee section,** accounting for about 90% of EAGGF spending, finances the price and market support systems. It may take the form of intervention prices, production, aid, compensation for withdrawal of products from the market or income aid. It also funds some rural development activities, veterinary measures and information campaigns. Expenditure under the Guarantee section accounted for €40.97 billion in 2000. Under the 2000 draft budget, arable crops were set to account for 40.8% of Guarantee section spending, beef/veal for 11.5% and milk products for 6.5%. France takes the largest share: thus in 1999, France received 23.6% from the Guarantee section, followed by Germany (14.5%), Spain (13.2%), Italy (11.8%) and the UK (9.9%). Greece (6.5%) and Ireland (4.2%) were the next largest recipients, which, given their small populations, is indicative of the importance of the CAP to their economies.
• **The Guidance section** provides financial support for adjustment of agricultural structures. It finances rural development measures under Objective 1 and the Leader Plus initiative. Aid from this source is normally co-financed with member states. The European Investment Bank (EIB) and the Union's structural funds also contribute. In recent years, financing from this section has amounted to about €4 billion a year.

○ Market Intervention Instruments

The CAP has developed a complex array of rules, regulations and operating procedures. Each reform of the CAP has added new layers of complexity to the system. This section focuses on the 'traditional' CAP market intervention instruments, such as price supports and export subsidies, although within the last decade the importance of these in some sectors has been reduced by CAP reform. Other, increasingly important, instruments, such as income supports and 'set-aside', will be dealt with more fully in the section on CAP reform. The 'traditional' instruments used to implement the CAP are outlined below.

supports. The Agriculture Council sets price levels for a range of al commodities, after receiving proposals from the Commission. mission conducts reviews of the state of each agricultural sector and engage̱ in extensive consultations with various interests. The Commission relies heavily on a network of management, advisory and working groups. The Agriculture Council has about 25 working parties to assist in examining the Commission's proposals. Agriculture ministers are naturally under pressure from farming lobbies to set high prices, although as a result of recent reforms price levels for some commodities have been reduced (particularly for beef and cereals) in favour of income supports. A multiannual approach is now used for most pricing and the annual fixing of prices now covers only a few sectors (cereals, rice, aid for silkworms, sheep and pigmeat).

The price level which should be attainable under normal market conditions is generally referred to as the *target price*. If the price the farmer can obtain in the market is less than the target price, the produce may be sold to an *intervention agency*. These agencies, which operate in all member states, buy in the market when prices for certain agricultural products fall below a certain level. The *intervention* or *buying-in* price is the level at which the intervention agency will buy in the market. Conversely, when commodities are scarce, agencies release commodities on to the market. The main sectors covered by price supports are cereals, dairy products, rice, sugar, beef, veal, pigmeat, sheepmeat, certain fruit and vegetables and some fishery products. For some products, alternative forms of assistance are provided: for example, table wine receives aid for storage and distillation. For some fruits and vegetables, support for buying in by producer organisations is provided.

There are variations in the nomenclature used for these mechanisms. For example, the *guide price* is the target price for beef, veal, wine, fish and some other products; the *basic price* is the basis for calculating the buying-in price for pigmeat and fruit and vegetables; the *withdrawal price* is the level at which certain fruit, vegetables and fish are withdrawn from glutted markets. These operations, plus storage and depreciation costs, are primarily financed through the Union budget. *Threshold prices* are set for agricultural imports when the price of such imports would otherwise be lower than EU prices.

By creating false prices for certain agricultural products, the CAP system has provided farmers with incentives to increase production. This has led to the notorious problem of food surpluses (for example, 'milk lakes' and 'butter mountains'). Dairy, cereals and sugar producers have the worst records for surpluses. Mechanisms have been introduced to reduce support levels when certain production targets are reached. For example, *maximum guaranteed quantities* involve reductions in prices when production exceeds a certain quantity. Production quotas for milk were first introduced in 1984. *Co-responsibility levies* require producers in some sectors (principally milk and cereals) to bear a share of the costs of disposing of surplus production. Surpluses have been disposed of in several ways, such as subsidised sales to non-EU states and handouts to the EU 'needy'.

• **Direct subsidies.** A few products (for example, oilseeds, olive oil and tobacco) receive supplementary aid, covering a small proportion of production. Some marginal products (principally flax, hemp, silkworms and some seeds) receive flat rate aids by the hectare or quantity produced.

• **Import barriers.** 'Community preference' (a euphemism for protection) prevents prices for agricultural produce within the Union from falling to world levels. Levies on agricultural imports are imposed at Union frontiers and flow into the Union budget (minus the costs of collection, which accrue to national governments). Non-tariff barriers, such as import quotas, have also been used extensively. About 20% of products for which there is no regime of guaranteed prices (for example, eggs, poultry, some fruit and vegetables, quality wines, flowers) receive protection only from imports, via levies or customs duties. The Union has an extensive network of agreements with developing countries which allow these countries preferential access to EU markets. But, since the bulk of developing countries' agricultural exports consists of tropical products, these concessions offer little threat to the CAP.

• **Export subsidies (restitutions).** These are subsidies paid on some agricultural products exported from the EU, aimed at bridging the gap between Union prices and world prices. They encourage agricultural producers in member states to compete in external markets. Such subsidies are controversial, because they are viewed as a distortion of competition. Primarily as a result of World Trade Organisation (WTO) rules and limits, EU expenditure on export subsidies fell from 55% of the total value of EU agricultural exports in 1992 to 9.4% in 1998.

• **The 'agrimonetary system'.** Without an adjustment mechanism, the fluctuation in the values of Union currencies would defeat the CAP aims of uniform and stable prices. The agrimonetary system was designed to reduce volatility in the conversion rate applied to CAP support prices and payments. Until recently, although CAP prices were fixed in ECUs, EU farmers received payment in their own currencies, calculated at special exchange rates ('green rates') which did not change automatically in line with market exchange rates. Until they were abolished following a Council decision in December 1992, a system of *monetary compensation amounts* (MCAs) was used to cover the difference between 'green' and market rates. MCAs were designed to prevent distortions in trade due to differences between 'green' and market rates. Farmers in countries whose currency had risen were paid compensatory amounts on agricultural exports. Conversely, compensatory amounts were levied on agricultural imports. For countries whose currency had fallen, the reverse would happen (compensatory amounts would be granted on imports and levied on exports).

The MCA system was supposed to be temporary, but turbulence in the currency markets (combined with vested interests) prolonged its use. It is hardly surprising that a strong currency country such as Germany opposed its abolition. Not only was the system very expensive, it was also incompatible with the Single European Market, because in effect MCAs constituted a system of border taxes and subsidies. They were replaced by new agrimonetary arrangements, involving the periodic fixing and adjusting of 'green' rates by the Commission. From February 1995, new rules were introduced which allowed for some degree of currency fluctuation without revaluation of 'green' conversion rates. Another agrimonetary regime was agreed by the Agriculture Council in June 1995. The new regime introduced a dual green currency system, involving fixed rates for strong currency countries and ECU-linked rates for weak currency countries. It also increased the contributions of governments to farmers facing a reduction in farm payments due to currency movements. In July 1998, the Commission required the UK to pay agrimonetary compensation aid, following a significant drop in the agricultural conversion rate of the pound.

The agrimonetary system was complex to administer and constituted a potential distortion to trade, due to gaps in the value of green rates and market rates. The advent of the euro meant the abolition of green rates and their replacement by the market exchange rate. Within the eurozone, there is no justification for a special monetary system for agriculture. A new agrimonetary regime was adopted by the Council in 1998, in advance of the adoption of the euro. From 1 January 1999, green rates were abolished, including for the four countries not joining the euro area, and replaced by the market exchange rate. The implications of the euro for the agrimonetary system are shown in Table 7.3.

There are transitional measures for compensation to be given for losses of agricultural income resulting from a revaluation of the green rate following introduction of the euro. The euro therefore had immediate implications for the agrimonetary regime. By eliminating exchange risk and increasing price transparency, it should lead to greater competition, perhaps leading to greater rationalisation and concentration, in food processing and retailing.

Table 7.3 The Agrimonetary System and the Euro

- agricultural prices and aid are denominated and paid in euros;
- green exchange rates (i.e., agricultural exchange rates) were abolished;
- within the eurozone, there is no longer a need to convert prices into national currencies;
- for EU countries outside the eurozone, conversion is made using the real value of their currencies against the euro.

● BENEFITS AND COSTS OF THE CAP

○ Benefits

In some respects, the CAP is a victim of its own success, in that it has more than fulfilled some of its original objectives – in particular high agricultural productivity and regularity of food supplies. The Union is now self-sufficient in cereals, wheat, milk, butter, beef, veal, pork, poultrymeat and sugar. The Union is the second largest exporter of agricultural products. It is the world's leading producer of sugar beet and wine (accounting for about 60% of world production). Growth in productivity has been dramatic. Between 1973 and 1989, agricultural output in the Union rose by 29%. Arguably, however, this rise was due at least as much (if not more) to advances in agricultural technology than to the CAP, because dramatic productivity increases have also occurred in many other developed countries. Table 7.4 outlines key EU agricultural statistics for 1999.

Table 7.4 Key EU Agricultural Statistics for 1999

Member	Share of agriculture in GDP (%)	Output in agriculture sector € mn	Employment in 1000s & as % of civilian working population 1000s	%	Share of imports of food & ag. in imports %	Share of exports of food & ag. in exports %
Austria	1.2	5,246	229	6.2	6.8	5.4
Belgium	1.2	6,921	95	2.4	10.0	10.4
Denmark	2.0	7,722	90	3.3	10.2	18.8
Finland	0.9	3,533	148	6.4	6.9	2.4
France	2.4	62,929	968	4.3	8.3	11.9
Germany	0.9	41,612	1,034	2.9	8.8	5.0
Greece	7.1	11,285	669	17.0	13.2	28.8
Ireland	2.9	5,469	136	8.6	7.7	12.1
Italy	2.6	42,049	1,118	5.4	10.3	7.1
Lux.	0.7	251	3	1.7	10.2	6.4
Neth.	2.4	18,457	231	3.2	11.5	18.8
Portugal	3.3	6,309	611	12.7	10.9	6.0
Spain	4.1	33,344	1,020	7.4	9.0	13.6
Sweden	0.7	4,385	121	3.0	6.5	2.3
UK	0.9	24,147	424	1.6	9.0	6.0
EU15	**1.8**	**273,658**	**6,898**	**4.5**	**6.9**	**6.7**

Note: * in agriculture, forestry, hunting & fishing. *Source*: Commission, DG for Agriculture.

Its proponents argue that the CAP has prevented sharp price swings for agricultural products and has facilitated a fourfold increase in cross-border agricultural trade within the Union. They argue that, without it, both the agriculture industry and rural life within the Union would decline rapidly.

Although it has not prevented declines in the incomes of some groups of farmers in recent years, these declines would probably have been even steeper without it. Moreover, food prices have increased by less than consumer prices as a whole. The CAP may well have provided a useful 'cement' in the construction of the Union in the early phases of its development, by providing opportunities for mutually beneficial co-operation between member states in a key economic sector. However, the utility of the CAP as an 'integration cement' has lessened, for two reasons: firstly, the relative importance of agriculture in the economies of most member states has declined. Agriculture as a percentage of Union GDP declined from about 5% in 1973 (when the EU had nine members) to about 1.8% in 1999. The number employed in agriculture within the Union has fallen from 13.4 million in 1973 to about 6.9 million (about 4.5% of the Union's working population) in 1999. Secondly, enlargement has increased the degree of diversity within this sector, so that the agricultural interests of member states no longer easily converge into a common interest. There are wide variations in the relative importance of agriculture in the economies of the member states and in average farm sizes.

O   Costs

The CAP is an easy target for criticism. It is widely regarded as expensive, wasteful, bureaucratic and fraud-ridden. Not all of the criticisms below are entirely convincing. For example, although agricultural prices in the Union are generally higher than 'world prices', the latter provide an unreliable guide, because quantities traded on world markets are often small in comparison to total production. Moreover, many non-EU exporters also receive subsidies. The CAP is undoubtedly protectionist, but no more so (in some cases considerably less so) than the agriculture policies of many countries. The EU remains the world's largest importer of food. But the defenders of the CAP have, in recent years, found it difficult to present a plausible case against radical reform. The main criticisms of the CAP are:

• **It is an anachronism:** the conditions which led to its creation no longer exist. Food surpluses, rather than food shortages are now the major problem. Since 1973, consumption of agricultural produce within the Union has grown by only 0.5% per year whereas production has grown by about 2% a year.

• **It leads to a gross misallocation of resources,** through interference with market mechanisms.

• **It is very costly to operate** and places severe strains on the Union budget. Despite the 1992 reforms, guarantee section expenditure rose from €26.5 billion in 1990 to €39.9 billion in 1999 (almost half the EU budget). Although, as a percentage of EU GDP, Guarantee Section expenditure fell in the same period from 0.56% to 0.5%, this still amounts to a substantial sum.

- **Consumers pay dearly for the CAP,** through taxation and high prices.
- **It causes conflicts between member states,** because it benefits some states more than others. For example, France, the Netherlands, Denmark and Ireland with relatively inefficient agricultural sectors have done relatively well out of the CAP, but the UK, with a small but relatively efficient agricultural sector has not.
- **It is inherently inequitable:** according to some estimates, almost half of Union farmers' incomes derives directly or indirectly from subsidies and protection measures. Why should farmers be protected, but not coalminers or steel workers? CAP support is far greater for some agricultural products than for others. Moreover, some groups of farmers (particularly the bigger agricultural businesses) obtain more from the CAP than others. About 80% of CAP spending is directed towards about 20% of farmers.
- **It is a source of conflict with other countries:** the EU's principal trade disputes with the US have centred on the CAP. It is a barrier to penetration of the EU market by some of the poorest countries. Overproduction has led to dumping of agricultural products on world markets.
- **It is difficult to prevent CAP frauds:** the CAP has very complex operating procedures and there are an estimated three million farm-related cash transactions a year. National procedures for verifying claims have often been lax. These circumstances providing fertile conditions for fraud: for example, forgery of customs documents to evade customs duties; claims for non-existent produce, livestock or land; relabelling of imports as EU produce to obtain subsidies; or multiple claims for export refunds for the same goods. Almost half of all detected fraud on the EU budget relates to agriculture.
- **It has damaged the rural environment,** through encouragement of intensive farming and overproduction.

● REFORM OF THE CAP

○ Pressures For and Against Reform

Until 1992, reform of the CAP largely took the form of limited *ad hoc* adjustments to CAP mechanisms. Although many radical proposals had been made (most notably by Agriculture Commissioner Sicco Mansholt in 1968) these were blocked by powerful vested interests. The influence of entrenched and tenacious farming lobbies on government policies is often cited as a textbook example of 'institutional capture'. At Union level, farmers are represented by COPA (Committee of Professional Agricultural Organisations, comprising 31 farming unions and associations from all member states) and by more than 100 specialised groups. COGECA (*Comité Général de la*

Coopération Agricole de la Communauté) represents the interests of agricultural co-operatives and works closely with COPA. These are the only farming organisations recognised officially by the Commission. There are powerful farming lobbies at national level also. Conversely, consumer interests and animal rights lobbies are by no means as well represented in the corridors of power. BEUC (*Bureau Européen des unions de consommateurs*) the main consumers' organisation has fewer formal and informal contacts with the Commission than COPA. The food industry is represented by the CIAA (*Confédération des industries agro-alimentaires*) and various other specific coalitions. Environment groups (such as the European Environmental Bureau) also seek to exert influence, although for these groups agriculture tends to be part of a broader range of objectives.

In 1985, the Commission sought to place the issue of CAP reform firmly on the Union agenda in a Green Paper (*Perspectives for the Common Agricultural Policy*). A series of *ad hoc* reforms were introduced in the late 1980s. Their main thrust was towards efforts to align production more closely to consumption, through reducing price supports, introducing direct income supports and providing farmers with incentives to set aside land. The *set-aside* scheme adopted in 1988 provided financial assistance to farmers willing to take at least a fifth of arable land out of production for five years (it could be left fallow or used for other purposes, such as tree-planting). Schemes to encourage farmers and farm workers to seek alternative employment were also developed. In 1988, the Council introduced annual ceilings on the growth of agricultural expenditure (limiting it to 74% of GDP growth). Budgetary stabilisers were also introduced for agricultural products, which placed limits on the quantities for which money would be paid. Although in the beginning these reforms appeared to be working, they failed to prevent the accumulation of large surpluses of cereals, dairy products and meat. The reforms were too limited in scope and scale to be fully effective.

In the 1990s a combination of internal and external pressures proved too powerful for opponents of reform to resist. The main internal pressures were: the mounting cost of the CAP in a period when governments were struggling to control public spending; the demands made by the CAP on the Union budget inhibited the ability of the Union to develop other policy areas; an increasingly vocal environmental lobby pointed to the damage to the countryside wrought by overproduction; several food and livestock scares (most prominently bovine spongiform encephalopathy (BSE) or 'mad cow disease' and outbreaks of swine fever) gave prominence to the issues of food safety and animal welfare; exposure of CAP frauds tarnished the reputation of the Union as a whole. The main external pressures came from the US, which threatened trade sanctions against the Union unless it made major changes to the CAP; and from recognition of the major implications for the CAP of the entry of ten Central and East European countries (CEECs) into the Union in the next few years (see Table 7.5).

Table 7.5 Challenges to the CAP

- pressures to reduce the size of the agricultural budget;
- liberalisation of the world trade regime, leading to a more open and competitive world market;
- Eastern enlargement (CEECs have large farm sectors);
- the integration of environmental concerns into agricultural policies;
- greater concern over food safety and animal welfare.

O   The MacSharry Reforms

In February 1991, the Commission produced a Reflections Paper on CAP reform. It argued that the EU's self-sufficiency in many agricultural sectors raised questions concerning the need for production incentives. It favoured further reduction of price supports, an increase in income supports and expansion of accompanying measures, such as 'set-aside'. Six months later it produced more specific proposals, deriving from the Paper. The reforms proposed by Agriculture Commissioner Ray MacSharry in 1992 were based on the Commission's proposals and centred on the following objectives:

- to maintain the EU as a major agricultural producer and exporter;
- to bring production in line with demand;
- to concentrate support for farmers incomes where it is most needed;
- to maintain rural communities;
- to protect the rural environment;
- to develop the potential of the countryside.

The main points of the original MacSharry proposals were: a reduction in price supports for cereals, oilseeds and protein crops of 29% over three years; an increase in income supports, linked to the withdrawal of land from production (land set aside could be used for other purposes, such as afforestation or tourism); an early retirement scheme for farmers over 55; a compensation scheme for farmers, with small farmers being compensated in full and those with larger farms receiving less; greater emphasis on produce quality; subsidies for agriculture in less-favoured regions and mountain areas; and an environmental action programme, which recognised farmers' role as 'stewards of the countryside'. In addition, there would be measures to combat fraud, such as on-the-spot inspections by the Commission.

The proposals were not *qualitatively* different from the *ad hoc* reforms of the late 1980s. Moreover, they retained the basic features of the CAP. However, they were controversial, for two reasons: firstly, it was estimated that they would lead to 15% of land being taken out of production; secondly, the proposal that compensation arrangements should discriminate between small and large farms provoked strong opposition, not least from the UK. But after considerable wrangling, and some revisions (the compensation scheme was made available to all farm sizes), the plan was agreed by the Agriculture Council in May 1992. The reforms were not designed to effect an immediate cut in the CAP budget, but rather to introduce measures which in the long run should reduce (or at least contain) agricultural spending. The reforms partly shifted the means of subsidising agriculture from price supports to income supports. Income supports render the costs of the CAP more transparent and will be harder to justify or defend in the long run. This meant that the burden of supporting agriculture shifted somewhat from consumers to taxpayers. The reforms led to a reduction in public stocks in most of the affected sectors (that is, a reduction in food mountains). However, they have so far failed to halt rises in milk production and left some products (for example, sugar and wine) virtually untouched. Whereas in 1993 aid under the reform accounted for only 8.3% of the Guarantee fund, by 1999 this had risen to 50.6%. The corresponding figures for conventional market supports were 61.3% in 1993 and 28.9% in 1999 (the rest being accounted for by refunds). The reforms were an important first step rather than the end of the story in relation to CAP reform. They paved the way for the agreement on agriculture in the Uruguay Round of the GATT and also took account of environmental protection.

○ The GATT, the WTO and EU Agriculture

The GATT (General Agreement on Tariffs and Trade) was, until its replacement by the World Trade Organisation (WTO) in January 1995, a negotiating forum aimed at removing barriers to world trade. Its formal trade negotiations were known as 'rounds'. For most of its history, it focused on the issue of tariff barriers to trade in manufactured goods. However, the last GATT round (before the GATT was replaced by the WTO) also focused on barriers to trade in services and agriculture. Although EU member states are parties to the GATT and are members of the WTO, the Commission is mandated to negotiate external trade agreements on behalf of member states, in consultation with a committee appointed by the Council (Article 133, ECT). In the Uruguay Round of the GATT talks, the CAP was at the centre of the dispute between the Union, the United States and the 'Cairns group' of agricultural exporting countries (14 members, including Australia and New Zealand). The US farming industry stood to benefit greatly from the liberalisation of trade in agricultural products and US trade negotiators pressed hard for concessions from the Union. Unlike the Cairns group and the poor 'South', the US has a big stick to wield against the Union in the form of trade sanctions. US negotiators sought from the Union improved market and cuts in Union export subsidies for agricultural products.)

In 1992, the US threatened sanctions against Union agricultural export subsidies, by announcing its intention to introduce punitive tariffs on a range of Union food and agricultural products by December 1992. These sanctions were averted by a deal between the US and the Commission in November 1992, known as the Blair House Accord. The Accord went further than the MacSharry reforms in several respects: for example, it included sugar and involved 'tariffication' (conversion of protection measures into customs tariffs, which are easier to discern and compare than non-tariff barriers). In addition to 'tariffication', the main points of the deal were: the volume of export subsidies to be reduced by 21% over six years, compared with average annual volumes exported between 1986 and 1990; internal price supports to be reduced by up to 20% (from 1986–88 levels); a safeguard clause, to allow adjustments in tariffs if world market prices fell below the 1986–88 average; and a minimum access clause, allowing importers opportunities to take 3% of the domestic market (rising to 6% in six years). France vociferously opposed the deal. France is the EU's leading agricultural producer, accounting for over a fifth of EU output and is the world's second-biggest agricultural exporter. It has almost a million full-time farmers and powerful farm lobbies (although farmers now constitute only about 4.3% of France's working population and agriculture accounts for only 2.4% of French GDP). The lobbies argued that the deal would result in 30% of French farming land being taken out of production. But other EU countries were adamant that the Accord could not be renegotiated, as it would ruin the chances of the Uruguay Round being finalised. A GATT agreement was finally sealed in Geneva in December 1993, largely because France could not muster sufficient support within the EU to oppose US demands.

The GATT agreement on agriculture (based largely on the Blair House Accord) is legally binding and relates to export subsidies, import access and domestic support for agriculture. Under the agreement, import barriers were converted into import tariffs ('tariffication') and were reduced by an average of 36% between 1995 and 2000; agricultural subsidies and import barriers were to be cut over six years; ceilings were placed on export subsidies, meaning that the EU had to reduce expenditure on export refunds by 36% and the volume of subsidised exports by 21%. Without export refunds, some EU agricultural products (for example, sugar and milk) would be uncompetitive on world markets. Special safeguard provisions were allowed for import surges. Under the rules, the EU can activate the safeguard clause and apply supplementary customs duties when the volume of imports exceeds a threshold or when import prices fall below a threshold. For some products, in particular butter and sugar, there are special safeguard provisions.

The WTO arose out of the Uruguay Round of GATT. An agreement to set up the WTO was signed in Marrakesh in April 1994 and came into force on 1 January 1995. The inauguration of the WTO had major implications for EU agriculture. The WTO administers the GATT agreements, including various supplementary agreements with implications for agriculture. Unlike the GATT, the WTO monitors national agricultural policies. Because the WTO is a quasi-judicial system, members of the WTO find it more difficult to wriggle out of their obligations than was the case under the GATT.

The Uruguay Round agreement required WTO members to resume negotiations on agriculture by 2000, with the aim of continuing reforms to reduce supports and protectionism. In November 1999, a new round of trade talks began in Seattle. The Seattle talks broke up without an agreement, although this was only partially due to disputes over agriculture. EU tariffs on agricultural products remain high, even after the full implementation of the Uruguay Round agreement. Recent EU reforms of agriculture (MacSharry, *Agenda 2000*) have reduced some domestic support prices for agricultural products, but not tariffs. Indeed, some aspects of these reforms, such as increased direct payments for beef, cereals and dairy products, are opposed by the US. Agriculture has been a fertile source of conflict between the EU and US, for example over the EU's export subsidies, the EU's ban on hormone-treated beef and the EU's banana regime (see Chapter 17).

○ The Impact of Past and Future Enlargements

Each enlargement of the Union has exacerbated the range and complexity of the problems associated with the CAP. For example, enlargement has affected the size and composition of the Union's agricultural labour force. Greece had 935,000 engaged in agriculture in 1981; Spain 1,252,000 in 1986 and Portugal 942,000. The German total increased by about 180,000 following reunification. Although Austria, Finland and Sweden do not have large agricultural sectors, they nevertheless faced major problems in adjusting their agriculture to fit in with the CAP. Farmers in these countries tend to work in harsh or difficult environments. Levels of agricultural support and protection in the European Free Trade Association (EFTA) are generally higher than in the EU. The 1995 entrants agreed to transitional arrangements, involving the phasing out of subsidies which conflicted with the CAP and the introduction of supports for farmers working in remote or mountainous regions.

The issue of agriculture has loomed large in the negotiations for the entry of the ten candidate countries from Central and Eastern Europe (CEECs), because the latter tend to have large agricultural sectors. For example, Romania had over 4.8 million and Poland nearly 2.7 million people engaged in agriculture in 1999, which means that these two countries have more farmers than the whole of EU15. Poland has as many dairy farmers as the rest of EU15 put together. Whereas farming accounted for 1.8% of EU GDP and employed 4.5% of the EU working population in 1999, the figures for the ten CEECs were 5.1% for GDP and 22% for employment. In Bulgaria, the share of agriculture in GDP in 1999 was 17.6% and in Romania 13.9%. Labour productivity in agriculture in the CEECs, with the exception of Slovenia and the Czech Republic, is also much lower than the EU average. Although the candidate countries are insisting that they should be entitled to the same payments as existing members, direct aid to farmers in the new member states immediately after accession is not acceptable to current members. Recent independent studies have estimated that extension of the CAP to CEEC candidate countries would cost between €8 billion and €11 billion a year and would also lead to substantial increases in production (Deutsche Bank Research, 2001). There are also major issues concerning the quality of CEEC agricultural production. For example, less than a third of Polish milk currently meets EU health standards. Operational inefficiency, distribution, storage and marketing problems are currently blunting the export capacity of East European agriculture. Nevertheless, the EU currently accounts for over half of agricultural exports from the CEECs. Conversely, the CEECs offer good export markets for high-quality EU food products.

The Commission and the candidate countries have worked together on the screening of agricultural legislation, to analyse what needs to be done to adopt the *acquis* in relation to the CAP. The candidates are continuing to align their agricultural policies with the EU and are moving closer to the EU system of support, although payments given to their farmers are generally much lower. Pre-accession aid for CEEC agricultural and rural development is available through the Union's PHARE and ISPA programmes (see Chapter 20) and also through a Special Access Programme for Agriculture and Rural Development ('SAPARD'). SAPARD was created to support efforts by the applicant countries to prepare for their participation in the CAP after their accession. It provides funds for structural adjustment and rural development schemes and will run between 2000 and 2006, in accordance with the Berlin European Council's budget plans (see below).

○ *Agenda 2000* and the Berlin European Council Reforms

The MacSharry reforms were never intended to be the last word on the subject of agricultural reform. The Commission presented a new agricultural strategy to member states at the Madrid European Council in 1995, highlighting the need for further CAP reform, geared towards a stronger market orientation and further assistance for rural areas. But the most important development in CAP reform was *Agenda 2000*, the Commission's blueprint for Union reform in the light of enlargement. Agricultural

Commissioner Franz Fischler described Agenda 2000, published in July 1997, as heralding the widest-ranging CAP reform since the start of CAP in the 1960s. The aim of the *Agenda 2000* plan for agriculture was to increase the market orientation of the CAP and to reinforce its structural, rural and environmental elements. In March 1999, the special European Council meeting in Berlin agreed major budgetary reforms, including cuts in spending on agriculture, as part of *Agenda 2000*. The agreement continued the policy introduced in the MacSharry reforms of substituting direct aid (income supports) for price supports and of supporting rural development. Tougher ceilings for agricultural expenditure and reduction of price supports were introduced. At the Berlin summit, France vigorously resisted demands from several other countries for reductions in agricultural spending. A compromise deal was agreed, with agricultural spending reduced, but by less than some had hoped for: the agriculture budget will be restricted to an average of €38 billion for market policy and €4.3 billion for rural development measures between 2000 and 2006. The Berlin agreement also took account of the importance of food safety and the environmental impacts of agriculture.

The Berlin regulations came into force from the year 2000, with the exception of milk. Cereal subsidies are to be reduced by 15% in two equal stages between 2000 and 2002 and beef prices by 20% in three stages between 2000 and 2003. Beef producers will receive direct aid to compensate for 85% of their losses. There are also reforms to rationalise planting rights in the wine sector. Reform of the dairy sector was postponed until 2005/6 and the quota system renewed until 2008, with a review in 2003. Reform of the sugar sector was also postponed. The reform package includes:

- *lower support prices to encourage competitiveness* (ranging from 15% for cereals and 20% for beef, plus 15% for the milk sector from 2005/6);
- *a fair standard of living for the farming community* (price reductions will be partly offset by increases in direct income support, meaning decoupling aid from production);
- *strengthening the EU's international trade position*, through a stronger market orientation;
- *emphasis on food safety and quality*, taking into account consumer concerns over food quality, environmental protection and animal welfare;
- *integration of environmental goals into the CAP* and developing the role of farmers in managing natural resources and conservation;
- *a new policy for rural development*, to assure the future of rural Europe;
- *decentralised management*, by giving member states a bigger role in the allocation of resources from the EAGGF budget;
- *simplification of procedures*, for example, by streamlining regulations.

As the list above shows, what are referred to as non-trade concerns (food security, food quality, animal welfare, economic viability of rural areas and

national fishing interests (QMV also provides ministers with the excuse that, although they fought hard for national interests, they were outvoted in the Council). Although MEPs representing fishing regions are very active in the EP's Fisheries Committee, the EP so far has little influence on CFP decisions. Fishing lobbies are less well organised than their counterparts in agriculture.

○ The Objectives and Operation of the CFP

The objectives of the CFP are to stabilise fisheries markets, to ensure supply and reasonable prices, to protect and conserve fishing grounds and to obtain maximum economic benefits for fishermen. These objectives have proved far easier to define in broad terms than to achieve. The operation of the CFP can be divided into four main aspects:

• **Access to fishing waters, and conservation and management of resources.** Each year in December the Council sets total allowable catches (TACs) for more than 100 fish species for the following year. There are limits on the minimum size of fish caught. There is a 200 nautical mile Union fishing zone. TAC limits are heavily influenced by scientific advice concerning fish stocks, which is channelled through the conservation unit of the DG for fisheries. Quotas are then allocated between member countries, based on factors such as the size of fishing sector in each member state and the needs of specific fishing regions. Allocation of TACs between member states has been determined by historic exploitation of fish stocks, at levels pertaining to when the CFP was established or when new members joined. The principle of relative stability was adopted in 1980 to maintain quotas among member states at the then existing levels. However, there have been some departures from this principle. Union fishermen do not have completely free access to Union waters: when Ireland, Denmark and the UK joined in 1973, a 12-mile limit around national waters was allowed, initially for 20 years. The 1983 reform accepted the principle of 12-mile exclusion zones. The accession of Spain and Portugal (which doubled the number of EU fishermen and increased the EU's fleet tonnage by about 50%) led to further modifications: these countries were granted mutual access, with limits on allowable catches until January 1996. New rules allowing for access of Spanish and Portuguese vessels to the waters of other member states were agreed by the Fisheries Council in December 1994. They were, however, excluded from the North and Irish seas.

A Union Inspectorate is formally responsible for surveillance, although monitoring and enforcement of the CFP is the task of member states, which are required to provide the Commission with a record of fish landed at their ports. The Commission can, however, undertake spot checks at sea and in port and can demand inquiries and information on the application of EU regulations. However, there are major differences between member states in enforcement. UK fishermen have frequently complained that the UK authorities are more zealous in enforcement than their continental counterparts (in the UK, the Royal Navy undertakes inspections on behalf of the Ministry of Agriculture, Fisheries and Food (MAFF), at considerable cost. Fishing authorities in England and Wales and Scotland require all vessels over 20 metres to land catches at designated ports and times). A multiannual guidance programme (MAGP) sets targets for reductions in tonnage and motive power of fleets. The fourth MAGP, which ran from 1997-2000 required a 20% overall reduction in motive power. Some fishing businesses, particularly from Spain, have sought to overcome this by buying vessels in other EU countries (in particular, the UK, France and the Netherlands) and using available quotas in these countries. This practice of 'quota hopping' is the source of considerable adverse comment in the UK.

• **Common organisation of fishing markets,** to adjust supply to demand for fish and to guarantee, as far as possible, fair incomes to producers. There is a price support system, involving various intervention mechanisms: thus there is support for withdrawing unsold products from the market and for storing or processing fish products with the aim of returning them to the market when demand increases. Intervention mechanisms operate when the price of products placed on the market fall below withdrawal prices. There are annual guide prices fixed by the Council for each product, based on average prices over three years in representative ports. Compensation may be paid for catches withdrawn from markets, on a decreasing scale. These mechanisms are implemented by about 150 producer organisations located in member states, which receive financial support for carrying out these tasks, in the form of withdrawal prices, carry-over aid and private storage aid. There are common marketing standards for fish sizes and hygiene.

• **A programme to promote the fishing industry,** through measures to improve productivity, modernise of the fleet and promote of new activities. A structural fund for fisheries, known as the Financial Instrument for Fisheries Guidance (FIFG) was created in 1993. It supports various measures, such as adapting fishing to the demands of resource conservation, renovating and modernising the fishing fleet and developing aquaculture. Like other structural funds, it is based on a system of co-financing. Structural policy also seeks to encourage refurbishment and development of fishing infrastructure.

• **A common external tariff.** Although the Union gives priority to its own fish products, it imports nearly 60% of fisheries and aquaculture products. The Council sets minimum import prices for imports from third countries. Almost two-thirds of fish imports are covered by special rules. There are Union quotas for some products, such as canned tuna. The Commission has negotiated bilateral access agreements with many non-Union countries and there are special provisions under the Lomé Convention and the European Economic Area (EEA) and unilateral reductions under the Generalised System of Preferences (GSP) (see Chapter 17). The EU currently has 29 fisheries agreements with non-member countries. These embrace agreements allowing the EU partial access to fishing waters within a country's exclusive economic zone (EEZ) in return for benefits such as financial compensation; reciprocal access agreements; 'joint venture' agreements or development aid. The Commission conducts bilateral discussions with non-EU countries, including through international bodies such as the Northwest Atlantic Fisheries Organisation and the International Baltic Sea Fisheries Commission. There are 200-mile exclusive economic zones (EEZs) in northern waters of the EU. Jurisdiction over management of marine resources within EEZs lies with the coastal state concerned. Most of the Mediterranean is classified as high seas and therefore a 200-mile limit cannot be declared. Because the Mediterranean is not covered by an EEZ, it was exempted from TACs in 1983, although TACs were extended to it for blue fin tuna in 1998.

○ Problems

The EU fishing industry is currently in crisis, due to overcapacity, national rivalries, widespread rule-breaking and cheap foreign imports. Whereas the central CAP problem is 'too many farmers producing too much food', the central CFP problem is 'too many fishermen chasing too few fish', due to the growing capability of fleets and the depletion of fish stocks. Attempts to deal with this fundamental imbalance have involved input controls (such as reduction in fleets or use of fleets); output controls (reductions in catch sizes); and technical measures, such as minimum landing sizes and mesh sizes.

The CFP has not succeeded in conserving fish stocks, not least because of ineffective monitoring and enforcement by member states. There are wide variations in the degree of zealousness with which national inspectorates enforce CFP regulations, a situation which has done much to undermine the credibility of the CFP. EU fishermen have had difficulty in accepting that Union fishing grounds constitute a shared resource and have frequently accused each other of breaking the rules on TACs and of fishing illegally in 'national waters'. For example, in 1994, Spanish fishermen attempted to physically prevent British trawlers from fishing in the Bay of Biscay. TACs have tended to be set too high and even these limits have not been observed (there has been widespread misreporting of fish landings). The TACs system has also led to discarding of fish after quotas have been exceeded, with perhaps as much as 50% of catches by weight thrown back into the sea. Decommissioning schemes for vessels have not been very successful so far. In December 2000, the Fisheries Council agreed to further drastic cuts in

TACs, following independent scientific advice indicating that some key fish stocks, such as cod, hake and whiting, were in danger of collapse.

The problems besetting EU fishing have a major international dimension, due to the depletion of global fish stocks and the intensity of competition between the world's fishing fleets. About 16% of world fish stocks are regarded as being dangerously overfished. World production of fish increased from 17 million tonnes in 1950 to over 87 million tonnes in 1996. Whereas catches in non-EU countries rose sevenfold in this period, the total catches of EU countries less than doubled. The share of member states in world catches fell from 11 to 8% between 1971 and 1996. Between 1990 and 1997, employment in EU fishing fell by 19% in catching and by 10% in processing. Overexploitation of global fishing stocks has led to international disputes. In 1995, a serious dispute arose between Canada and the EU over access to Atlantic fishing grounds. A dispute over access to Norwegian fishing waters for EU vessels almost led to a Spanish veto on the EEA agreement. A compromise was agreed, granting the EU an access quota of Norwegian fish, with Spain and Portugal getting the lion's share. The vehemence of the protagonists in these disputes is indicative of an industry in crisis.

⭘ Reform of the Common Organisation of the Fisheries and Aquaculture Markets

Following a 1997 discussion paper on the future of the fisheries market, the Council adopted a new regulation on this market in 1999, covering the 2000–2006 period. The aims of the reform are to: encourage fishermen to fish only what can be sold, to avoid waste; strengthen industry organisations and make them more competitive; enable consumers to know what they are buying; ensure a better match between supply and demand; and protect employment in fish catching and processing.

These aims are being sought through encouraging producer organisations to take greater responsibility for regulation; improved planning to conserve fish stocks; aid for producers organisations; promotion of partnerships in various branches of the industry; reducing the volumes taken off the market which are eligible for compensation from 14 to 8% for most species; a new tariff regime in line with the needs of the market involving, for example, partial or total suspension of duties for certain products intended for the processing industry. The new common organisation will cost €20 million in 2000, rising to €22 million in 2002 and falling to €16 million by 2006. Despite these reforms, the EU fishing industry remains in crisis. Another looming problem is enlargement: although most CEECs do not have large fishing fleets, the accession of Poland and the Baltic countries will lead to a substantial increase in the size of the EU fleet. In March 2001, the

Commission produced its first Green Paper on the future of the CFP. It painted a dismal picture of the EU fishing industry and called for urgent change, in particular by reducing the fishing in EU waters in order to conserve fish stocks. Responses to the Green Paper were expected to help the Commission shape proposals for a revised CFP, to enter into force in 2003.

● CONCLUSION

Although the problems besetting the CAP and CFP are very different, both are subject to pressures for further reform. In the case of the CAP, these reform pressures continue to meet strong resistance from vested interests (countries and lobbies). A case could be made that substantial changes have already been made to the CAP regime. But recent CAP reforms are likely to prove inadequate to meet the challenges confronting EU agriculture (for example, in addition to enlargement, external pressures to liberalise the CAP regime; and mounting concerns over food safety and the rural environment). Despite the fact that many candidate countries have large farm sectors, agriculture is a subject not even mentioned in the Treaty of Nice. The central problem for the CFP is how a depleting resource can be managed in the least painful and most equitable way for the fishing industries of the member states.

FURTHER READING

Ackrill, R. (2001), *The Common Agricultural Policy*, Sheffield Academic Press, Sheffield.

Ackrill, R. (2000), 'CAP Reform 1999: A Crisis in the Making?', *Journal of Common Market Studies*, vol. 38, no. 2, pp. 342–53.

Commission (1999a), *28th Financial Report on the European Agricultural Guidance and Guarantee Fund*, COM (1999) 568.

Commission (1999b), *The EU Approach to the Millennium Round*, COM (1999) 331.

Commission (2001), *Green Paper on the future of the Common Fisheries Policy*, COM (2001) 135.

Deutsche Bank Research (2001), *Eastward enlargement of the EU endangered by agriculture?*, EU Enlargement Monitor, May, http://www.dbresearch.com

European Parliament (1999), *Glossary of the CAP and the Agenda 2000 Reform*, Working Paper, AGRI 118, June, Luxembourg.

Grant, W. (1999), *The Common Agricultural Policy*, Macmillan, Basingstoke.

Ingersent, K.A. and Rayner, A.J. (2000), *Agricultural Policy in Western Europe and the United States*, Edward Elgar, Cheltenham and Northampton, MA.

Payne, D.C. (2000), 'Explaining the Conservation Failure of the EU's CFP', *Journal of Common Market Studies*, vol. 38, no.2, pp. 303–324.

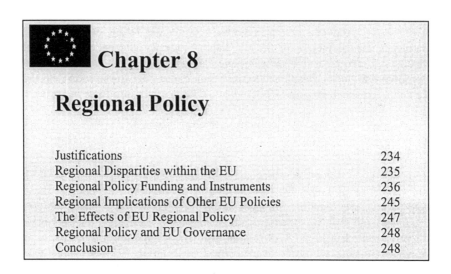

Chapter 8

Regional Policy

● JUSTIFICATIONS

Until the creation of the European Regional Development Fund in 1975, regional policy within the Union was very largely the prerogative of member states. Prior to the entry of the UK and Ireland, only Italy was really interested in a Union regional policy, because of its poor Mezzogiorno region. The number of countries with a strong interest in a Union regional policy increased again with the entry of Greece, Spain and Portugal. The accession of Spain and Portugal doubled the number of people living in regions with per capita incomes of less than 75% of the Union average.

In recent years, the case for a Union regional policy has also been strengthened by the decline of traditional industries concentrated in specific regions and by increasing recognition of the potential impact of other Union policies on regional disparities. Following the reunification of Germany in 1990, the Union gained an additional number of poor regions. Another factor has been the demand from 'regional Europe' (here meaning regional governments, and especially the German *Länder*) for a stronger voice in EU affairs. The Treaty on European Union (TEU) established the Committee of the Regions, to give the regions an institutional voice in the EU. The intergovernmental conference scheduled for 2004 will re-examine this 'levels of government' issue. The justifications for a Union regional policy can be summarised as follows:

• **The need for balanced development of the Union as a whole.** The notions of 'Community' and 'Union' imply the acceptance of some form of common interest, transcending the boundaries of member states. A Union policy can be justified on the grounds of *equity* (it is inequitable for living standards to vary so widely between regions) and *efficiency* (the Union's resources are being underutilised in poorer regions).

- **The multidimensional nature of regional problems.** Most Union policies have a regional dimension. Therefore, a Union-wide regional policy can contribute to the achievement of the Union's other policy objectives. The Commission now conducts regional impact assessments for each policy. There is also a need to counteract the tendency of some Union policies to exacerbate regional disparities (see below).
- **The magnitude of regional problems.** Although national regional policies are still operated within member states, national governments (especially in the poorer states) do not have the resources to tackle major regional problems by themselves.

● REGIONAL DISPARITIES WITHIN THE EU

Wide regional disparities exist not only within the Union as a whole, but also within many member states. Poorer regions tend to have fewer roads, rail lines, telephone lines or other services. According to a Eurostat report published in 2001 (based on 1998 data), there were 46 EU regions with a GDP per capita of less than 75% of the EU average, accounting for about one fifth of the EU's population (Eurostat, 2001a). This category included 11 of the 13 regions in Greece, five out of seven regions in Portugal, eight in Spain, five in Italy, seven in Germany (all in the new Bundesländer), four in the UK, four in France (the four overseas territories), one in Austria and one in Ireland. The report found that the region with the highest GDP per capita was inner London (243% of the EU average) and the region with the lowest was Ipeiros in Greece (42%), meaning that the richest EU region had about six times the GDP per capita of the poorest. Some countries have wider regional disparities than others. Spain, Italy, the UK and (since reunification) Germany have the most pronounced inter-regional variations. Some UK regions have a GDP per capita of one-third of inner London's. There are wide disparities between Italy's northern and southern regions and a four to one disparity between Hamburg and some regions in east Germany. Some Spanish regions have made substantial gains in recent years, whereas others continue to stagnate. Capital cities tend to be the richest regions within member states. Sweden has the least-pronounced interregional variations.

The Union includes an increasingly diverse range of regions – for example, industrial, urban, rural, border and peripheral regions. As a result of the 1995 enlargement, the Union gained some sparsely populated and remote regions in Finland and Sweden and an alpine region in Austria. Enlargement to the east will add to this diversity and will also result in a substantial increase in the number of poorer regions. Some regions are experiencing dynamic growth, whereas others (for example, many old industrial regions) are in decline. Some inner-city areas are experiencing severe deprivation. Some regions are industrially diverse whereas others are based on a narrow range of industries and others have never been industrially developed. Some are adjacent to national borders and have special problems arising from their geographical position. Although many of the poorest regions have high unemployment rates, some regions (mainly in Greece and Portugal) have comparatively low unemployment, even though incomes tend to be low. According to a 1998 Eurostat report, six of the top ten high-tech regions in the EU in 1995 were in Germany (Eurostat, 1998). The main regional problem in the UK is that of declining industrial areas. Some EU regions have declining populations, which usually have a higher than average proportion of elderly, and a smaller than average proportion of economically active, people. A strategy for the regions must therefore be flexible enough to address a very broad range of regional problems.

● REGIONAL POLICY FUNDING AND INSTRUMENTS

○ The European Regional Development Fund and other Structural Funds

The ERDF is the principal fund through which Union support for the regions is provided. The ERDF is one of the Union's *structural funds*, which, together with the *Cohesion Fund*, are the main financial instruments for pursuing greater economic and social cohesion within the Union. The structural funds comprise:
- the European Regional Development Fund (ERDF);
- the European Social Fund (ESF);
- the Guidance Section of the Agriculture Fund (EAGGF);
- the Financial Instrument for Fisheries Guidance (FIFG).

Because of its long experience in operating a regional policy, the UK played a key role in establishing the ERDF. Between 1975 and 1986, 95% of the Fund was administered on a quota basis, in order to ensure that all member states benefited in some way. The bulk went to Italy, France, the UK, Ireland and Greece. There was also a small non-quota section (5% of the total), which enabled the Union to offer assistance to any region in the form of specific measures or programmes. There were reforms of the funds in 1979, 1984, 1989, 1993 and 1999. The 1979 reforms introduced the non-quota section referred to above. Following reforms agreed in 1984, quotas were replaced by 'indicative ranges' (minima and maxima), which increased the degree of flexibility in the proportions allocated to each country. In the

1989 reforms, the Commission introduced four principles for implementing the structural funds, namely:

- *Concentration.* Measures would be concentrated on priority objectives, to ensure close co-ordination of structural policies.
- *Partnership.* between the Commission and the appropriate authorities at national, regional and local levels at all stages.
- *Additionality,* meaning that allocations should be additional to funding provided by national governments.
- *Programming,* meaning that the funds would be implemented through structured programmes targeted at specific problems over several years rather than through a multiplicity of national projects.

Each of the four principles above has proved difficult to fully reconcile with the national objectives and interests of member states. For example, the logic of *concentration* has been repeatedly challenged by the desire of national governments to get their regional and local areas included on funding lists, leading to resources being spread too thinly. *Partnership* (in particular the involvement of regional and local authorities in the planning and implementation of the funds) has in some cases led to tensions between national and subnational tiers of government and has proved difficult to implement in a uniform way because of differences in regional and local government structures. The *additionality* principle has by no means always been observed, because moneys allocated for ERDF programmes and projects have frequently been used for other purposes by national governments once ERDF finance has been secured. *Programming* for regional policy has resulted in elaborate and involved procedures, leading to repeated calls for simplification. Applications for ERDF moneys are channelled through national ministries. The ERDF has grown from 4.5% of Union spending in 1975 to about 13% in 2000 (it has risen as a proportion of the EU budget whereas CAP spending has been falling in relative terms).

○ The Common Objectives of the Structural Funds: 1994–99

From June 1993 until January 1995, there were six objectives. Following the accession of Sweden, Finland and Austria in January 1995, a seventh was added. These seven common objectives were:

- *Objective 1 (lagging regions)*: promoting the development of lagging regions. In 1993, following intensive lobbying, some additional regions were reclassified as Objective 1 regions. Prior to its extension, this category covered all of Greece, Portugal, Ireland and Northern Ireland, the Italian Mezzogiorno, ten regions in Spain, Corsica, France's overseas departments and the five east German Länder. Until recently, Objective 1 regions were expected to have a per capita income of less than 75% of EU GDP. Under the revised regulations, some regions not fulfilling this criterion were included (the Belgian Hainaut region; the French districts of Valenciennes, Douai and Avesnes; Cantabria; Flevoland; Merseyside and the Highlands and Islands of Scotland). These were mainly industrialised areas where decline in industrial activity was very severe. The UK had three Objective 1 regions. Austria's Burgenland also qualified for Objective 1 assistance.

- *Objective 2 (regions in industrial decline)*: the conversion of regions in industrial decline. In addition to well-established criteria (an unemployment rate higher than the Union average; a higher percentage of industrial employment than the Union average; a decline in industrial jobs) other more subjective criteria were added in July 1993, such as the need to rebuild inner cities. Some former Objective 2 regions were reclassified as Objective 1.
- *Objective 3*: combating long-term unemployment and facilitating the integration into work of women and of persons exposed to exclusion from the labour market.
- *Objective 4*: to combat unemployment by facilitating adaptation of workers to industrial change and changes in production systems.
- *Objective 5a*: modernisation and adjustment of agricultural structures.
- *Objective 5b*: adaptation of agricultural and fishery structures. Priority was given to developing jobs outside farming and fishing, such as tourism and small businesses.
- *Objective 6*: this category was established in 1995 to provide assistance to remote and sparsely populated regions in Sweden and Finland. It covered regions with very low population densities (less than eight inhabitants per square km). The regions covered had populations of 450,000 in Sweden (5.3% of the population) and 837,000 in Finland (16.7% of the population, mainly in Lapland and other areas bordering Russia).

The European Council in Edinburgh in December 1992 earmarked €141.5 billion for the structural funds between 1993 and 1999, with 74% going to Objective 1 regions, 11% to Objectives 3 and 4 and the rest distributed roughly evenly among other objectives. Only three of these objectives (1, 2 and 5b) were strictly regional. Including funding for the 1995 entrants, the total was increased to about €150 billion between 1994 and 1999. By 1999, the four poorest member states (Greece, Portugal, Spain and Ireland) had received about 54% of moneys allocated to the structural funds and the Cohesion Fund. The UK was the largest recipient of Objective 2 funding.

○ The Cohesion Fund

The fund was established at the Maastricht summit, due to strong pressure from the four poorest member states for additional financial support (not least to boost their prospects of meeting the convergence criteria for economic and monetary union (EMU). The fund applies to countries with a GNP per capita of less than 90% of the Union average (Portugal, Spain, Greece and Ireland, with a combined population of 63 million). Whereas the ERDF seeks to reduce *regional* disparities, the Cohesion Fund seeks to reduce disparities between *countries*. Moreover, the Cohesion Fund applies only to four states and is limited to transport and environment infrastructure projects. Fund disbursements are *project based*, whereas most ERDF funding is *programme based*. The Edinburgh European Council decided that €15 billion (at 1992 prices) would be allocated to the fund between 1993 and 1999, with 70% going to Objective 1 regions. The fund came into existence at the end of 1993 with an annual budget of €1.5 billion, rising to €2.6 billion by 1999. In 1999, commitments for financing Cohesion Fund projects amounted to €3.15 billion, covering between 80 and 89% of the cost of supported projects. €18 billion will be available for the fund between 2000 and 2006. There will be a mid-term review of the eligibility of the four beneficiaries in 2003.

Table 8.1 Cohesion Fund Commitment Appropriations 2000

	Environment		Transport		Total	Breakdown
	€m.	%	€m.	%	€m.	%
Greece	56.8	5.0	176.8	13.8	233.6	9.7
Spain	780.1	69.1	768.5	60.1	1,548.6	64.4
Ireland	137.0	12.1	89.5	7.0	226.5	9.4
Portugal	154.9	13.7	242.6	19.0	397.5	16.5
Total	**1,128.8**	**100***	**1,277.4**	**100***	**2,406.3**	**100**

Note: rounded to 100% *Source:* Commission *General Report* 2000 (2001a).

In the early 1990s, economic recession in the Union provided a powerful argument for increases in the amounts allocated to the problem regions. For example, disparities in unemployment rates between the ten worst-affected and ten least-affected regions became increasingly marked. In 1993, unemployment rates in the ten worst-affected regions were seven times greater than in the ten least-affected (Commission, 1994). The Commission's *Sixth Periodic Report* (Commission, 1999) showed that unemployment in the worst-affected regions had risen from 20 to 24%. In 1998, Andalucia in Spain had the highest unemployment rate (29.9%) and Centro in Portugal the lowest (2.1%) (Eurostat, 1999). Unemployment among under 25s in Calabria in Italy was 72.3% in 1998. The *Sixth Periodic Report* showed that between 1986 and 1996, the GDP per capita in the 25 poorest regions increased from 52 to 59% of the EU average. In this period, the GDP per capita in the four poorest *countries* increased from 65 to 76.5% of the EU average. Ireland, especially, but also Spain and Portugal, have benefited from substantial inflows of foreign direct investment (FDI), from both inside and outside the EU. It is not surprising that these countries are concerned about the effects of enlargement on their allocations from the structural funds.

○ The 1999 Reforms

Several ongoing and impending developments led to the reform of the structural funds in 1999. The potential impacts of EMU and of future enlargement on regional disparities were key factors, but other problems, such as rising unemployment and criticisms of the management and operation of the structural funds were also important.

The accession of Central and East European countries (CEECs), with an average income per head of about two-fifths of the EU average, obviously has major implications for the structural funds. The cost of bestowing Objective 1 assistance and Cohesion Fund assistance on the acceding CEECs is likely to be very high. A Eurostat report published in March 2001 (based on 1998 data) showed that of the 53 CEEC regions, 51 had a per capita GDP of below 75% of the EU average (Eurostat, 2001b). The lowest figure was for Yuzhen Tsentralen in Bulgaria (22%) and the highest was for Prague in the Czech Republic (115%) and Bratislava in Slovakia (99%). In *Agenda 2000* (June 1997), the Commission proposed that the Union should provide substantial amounts of pre-accession aid to the candidate countries and should also reform the structural funds in preparation for enlargement. It proposed pre-accession aid of about €7 billion beginning in 2000 and targeted in particular at infrastructure, the environment, the productive sector and human resources. After accession, the new entrants would be allocated about €38 billion between 2000 and 2006, accounting for around 30% of all EU structural funds by the end of the period. The amount for the structural funds was envisaged to increase, but the percentage as a proportion of Union GDP would remain roughly the same (that is, at 0.46%).

Also in *Agenda 2000*, the Commission recommended that the seven objectives of the funds should be replaced by three, comprising two regional objectives and a 'horizontal' objective concerned with human resources. The coverage of Objectives 1 and 2 would be decreased from 51% to between 35 and 40% by 2006, although about two-thirds of funding would continue to be spent on Objective 1 regions. It favoured a single multiannual programme for each region. The number of Community initiatives (see below) would be reduced to three (*Interreg*, *Equal* and *Leader*) and their share of structural fund allocations to 5% of the total. A fourth initiative, *Urban*, was later added. A further Commission proposal for reform of the structural funds in March 1998 was based on three priorities: more *concentration, decentralisation* and *strengthening of efficiency and control*. In addition to the existing four principles of the structural funds, that is, *concentration, partnership, additionality* and *programming*, a fifth, *efficiency*, would be introduced. Concentration meant the reduction of the number of objectives and initiatives, thereby reducing the size of the population covered but also freeing up more money for lagging regions. There would be transitional support for regions which would no longer meet the eligibility criteria. It also proposed increased involvement of local authorities and social and economic partners. It favoured simplifying the procedures for verifying additionality and also the introduction of a 'negotiated additionality' principle, involving negotiations between the Commission and each member state on structural expenditures for the programme period. It also sought simplification of the rules on eligible expenditure and favoured a mid-term performance reserve, to reward member states for using their funding allocations efficiently.

The proposals were clearly influenced by the perceived implications of the next enlargements and of monetary union. But they also reflected a widespread belief that structural fund resources had been spread too thinly and that the poorest regions required additional help. The thrust of the proposals was towards concentration of resources on a smaller proportion of the EU population and towards decentralisation, allowing member states to have a bigger role in specific decisions. These proposals provided the basis of the regulations adopted by the Council and the European Parliament (EP) in 1999 for the reform of the structural funds. These reduced the number of objectives from seven to three and the number of initiatives from 13 to four for the 2000-06 period. In March 1999 the Berlin European Council decided that for the 2000-06 period the resources available from the structural and cohesion funds will be €213 billion, of which around €195 billion is allocated to the structural funds and €18 billion to the Cohesion Fund. In addition, €7 billion will be provided by the structural funds for pre-accession aid under the ISPA programme for candidate countries. The average annual amount allocated will be €26.2 billion at 1999 prices: 69.7% of the structural funds will be allocated to Objective 1, 11.5% to Objective 2 and 12.3% to Objective 3. Objective 1 regions will account for 23% of the EU population and will receive €127.5 billion. Transitional support for regions taken off the Objective 1 list will amount to €8.4 billion. There will be a review of the eligibility of the four current beneficiaries of the Cohesion Fund in 2003. In exceptional cases, Objective 1 funding can rise from 75 to 85% of funding.

In July 1999, the Commission decided on the financial allocation for each member state as well as for Objectives 1, 2 and 3 and for the fisheries instrument outside Objective 1. The financial allocations for Objectives 1 and 2 were decided on the basis of eligible population, regional and national prosperity and the relative severity of structural problems, especially the level of unemployment. For Objective 3, allocations were fixed according to eligible population, the employment situation and the severity of problems, such as social exclusion, education and training levels and participation of women in the labour market. Member states were then asked to transmit their proposals for the list of areas eligible for Objective 2. The Commission also drew up the list of Objective 1 regions and the financial allocation for Interreg, Urban, Leader and Equal (see Tables 8.2 to 8.4).

Table 8.2 Structural Fund Objectives: 2000–06

Objective 1: lagging regions. Eligibility is restricted to regions with a per capita GDP of less than 75% of the EU average and to the previous Objective 6 regions (i.e. regions with an extremely low population density) in Sweden and Finland. There is additional support for regions with exceptionally high unemployment. Assistance from all four structural funds (ERDF, ESF, EAGGF and FIFG), totalling €135.9 billion (69.7% of SF assistance) is available for Objective 1. The EU will normally provide up to 75% of the funding for Objective 1 projects, although this can rise to 85% in exceptional circumstances.

This objective covers regions in eastern Germany (excepting east Berlin); the whole of Greece; ten Spanish regions; France's overseas departments; three Irish regions (Border, Midlands and the Western Seaboard); the Italian Mezzogiorno (excepting Molise); the Austrian Burgenland; Portugal (excepting Lisbon and the Tagus valley); six lowly populated regions in Finland and Sweden; and four areas in the UK, i.e., South Yorkshire, Merseyside, West Wales and the Valleys and Cornwall and the Isles of Scilly. There is phasing out support of up to six years for areas taken off the Objective 1 list.

Objective 2: regions undergoing economic and social conversion. It provides assistance to regions with major economic and social restructuring needs. This includes areas undergoing economic and social change in the industrial and service sectors, declining rural areas, urban areas in difficulties and depressed areas dependent on fisheries. It is financed from the ERDF, the ESF and the Guarantee section of the EAGGF. This objective covers up to 18% of the EU population, of which 10% will be allocated to industrial areas, 2% to urban areas, 5% to rural areas and 1% to fisheries-dependent areas. There is a four-year transition arrangement for former Objective 2 or 5b areas ineligible for Objective 2 status in 2000. €22.5 billion (11.5% of SF assistance) will be available from the ERDF, ESF and EAGGF-G for Objective 2. The EU will provide up to 50% of the funding for Objective 2 projects.

Objective 3: human resources. It supports the adaptation and modernisation of policies and systems of education, training and employment everywhere outside Objective 1 regions. Schemes chosen for Objective 3 funding must promote equal opportunities between men and women. It is not regionally based and therefore there are no Objective 3 regions as such. It serves as a reference framework for all human resource operations in the EU and takes account of the employment title in the Treaty of Amsterdam. It seeks 'dove tailing' with the national employment action plans It is financed by the ESF, which provides up to 50% of funding for selected projects. It amounts to €24.05 billion (12.3% of SF assistance).

Table 8.3 Structural Fund Allocations: 2000–06 (€ Million at 1999 prices)

Member State	1	Phasing Out 1	2	Phasing Out 2	3	Fisheries Instrument outside 1	Total
Austria	261	0	578	102	528	4	1,473
Belgium	0	625	368	65	737	34	1,829
Denmark	0	0	156	27	365	197	745
Finland	913	0	459	30	403	31	1,836
France	3,254	551	5,437	613	4,540	225	14,620
Germany	19,229	729	2,984	526	4,581	107	28,156
Greece	20,961	0	0	0	0	0	20,961
Ireland (1)	1,315	1,773	0	0	0	0	3,088
Italy	21,935	187	2,145	377	3,744	96	28,484
Lux.	0	0	34	6	38	0	78
Neth.	0	123	676	119	1,686	31	2,635
Portugal	16,124	2,905	0	0	0	0	19,029
Spain	37,744	352	2,553	98	2,140	200	43,087
Sweden (2)	722	0	354	52	720	60	1,908
UK (1)	5,085	1,166	3,989	706	4,568	121	15,635
EU 15	**127,543**	**8,411**	**19,733**	**2,721**	**24,050**	**1,106**	**183,564**

Notes: (1) Including PEACE (2000–2004); (2) Including special programme for Swedish coastal zones

Table 8.4 Average Annual Allocations: 1994–99 and 2000–06*

State	Period 1994–1999		Period 2000–2006	
	Annual Average € Million, 1999 prices	% of total	Annual Average € Million, 1999 prices	% of total
Austria	228	0.9	210	0.8
Belgium	293	1.2	261	1.0
Denmark	86	0.4	106	0.4
Finland	250	1.0	262	1.0
France	2,070	8.6	2,089	8.0
Germany	3,338	13.8	4,022	15.3
Greece	2,539	10.5	2,994	11.4
Ireland	1,021	4.2	441	1.7
Italy	3,440	14.3	4,069	15.5
Luxembourg	8	0.0	11	0.0
Netherlands	369	1.5	376	1.4
Portugal	2,539	10.5	2,718	10.4
Spain	5,671	23.5	6,155	23.5
Sweden	229	0.9	273	1.0
UK	2,022	8.4	2,234	8.5
EU15	**24,103**	**100***	**26,223**	**100***

Note: rounded to 100%. * Excluding Community Initiatives and Innovative Actions.
Source: Eurostat.

During the period 2000–06, the proportion of the EU population covered by Objectives 1 and 2 will be between 35 and 40% (it was about 51% during the 1994–99 period). Between 2000 and 2006, about 94% of the structural funds budget will be allocated to Community Objectives; about 5.35% to Community Initiatives; and about 0.65% to Innovative Actions (see below).

○ **Policy Instruments**

EU regional policy is implemented through various instruments, principally:

• **Objective programmes** (accounting for about 94% of the expenditure of the structural funds). Programming begins with the presentation of development or restructuring plans by the member states. For Objectives 1 and 2, the plans must be forwarded to the Commission not later than four months after the establishment of the list of eligible areas (unless otherwise agreed with the member states concerned). Each plan must include an analysis of the regional situation relative to the objective; an analysis of priority needs; the strategy and envisaged priorities for action; and an indicative financing plan. Responsible authorities from the member state draw up the plan, following consultation with relevant regional partners. The programmes are presented as single programming documents (SPDs) or as Community support frameworks (CSFs). The Commission establishes CSFs for all Objective 1 regions. The CSF defines the priorities of the policy to be implemented. Member states submit development plans to the Commission, presenting national and regional priorities. The Commission negotiates a support framework with national and regional authorities. Member states then submit operational programmes (OPs) for the priorities laid down in the CSF. Assistance under Objectives 2 and 3 takes the form of SPDs. SPDs are also prepared for operations of less than €1 billion in Objective 1 regions and for the fisheries sector. Generally, the Commission decides on structural fund contributions to CSFs and SPDs not later than five months after receiving the planning documents. Member states have general responsibility for operating and monitoring programmes. Each programme is under the responsibility of a managing authority at national or regional level and a monitoring committee.

• **Community initiatives (CIs).** Their aim is to encourage member states, regions and economic and social partners to co-operate in implementing measures of common interest to the EU. Until the 1999 reforms, CIs could target specific areas (for example, border or urban areas), industries (for example, textiles), groups (for example, the disabled) or subjects (for example, defence conversion). Almost 10% of the structural funds went on CIs between 1994 and 1999, compared with about 5.35% allocated to CIs between 2000 and 2006. Each CI is normally eligible for assistance from only one structural fund (see Table 8.5). Financial commitments for CIs (Interreg; Urban; Equal; and Leader) in 2000 amounted to €541 million.

• **Innovative actions,** for example pilot projects on regional problems such as urban regeneration. The Commission chooses and finances these actions. It also calls for proposals and selects the projects. About 0.65% of the total structural funds budget will be allocated to these actions between 2000 and 2006. In this period they will focus on the regional dimensions of e-Europe; technological innovation; and sustainable development, plus regional identity.

Table 8.5 Community Initiatives

1994–99 (about 10% of the structural funds)
Rechar II: economic and social conversion of coalmining areas.
Resider II: economic and social conversion of steel areas.
Retex: to promote economic diversification in areas reliant on the textile and clothing industry.
Interreg II: to promote co-operation between areas adjoining existing borders and completion of energy networks.
Regis II: to promote the development of the EU's most remote regions.
Employment and Development of Human Resources: to enhance employment growth and promote social solidarity. It embraced:
Now: a training initiative for women;
Horizon: improving access of disabled people to the labour market;
Youthstart: labour market integration of young people without qualifications.
Modernisation of the Portuguese Textile Industry.
SMEs: to assist SMEs to adapt to the SEM and to improve their international competitiveness.
Leader II: support for 'grass-roots' rural development networks.
Konver: the defence conversion scheme. The main beneficiaries are Germany, France and the UK.
Adapt: help for workers and firms adapting to industrial change.
Pesca: help for areas dependent upon fishing.
Urban: to tackle the problems of urban areas.
2000–06 (about 5.35% of the structural funds)
Interreg: Cross-border, transnational and interregional co-operation (ERDF) (€4.875 billion).
Equal: Transnational co-operation to combat all forms of discrimination and inequalities in the labour market (ESF) (€2.85 billion).
Leader: Local initiatives for rural development (EAGGF) (€2.02 billion).
Urban: Economic and social regeneration of cities and urban neighbourhoods (ERDF) (€700 million).

● REGIONAL IMPLICATIONS OF OTHER EU POLICIES

The effects, both positive and adverse, of other policies on the regions is potentially very great. For example:

• **The effects of the Single European Market programme:** although the precise effects of the SEM are difficult to measure, it is widely acknowledged that the benefits and costs of the programme have not been distributed evenly among the regions (see Chapter 10).

- **The effects of EMU.** EMU could exacerbate the economic problems of poorer regions, for several reasons. A common currency means that a member country can no longer use its exchange rate as a cushion against external competition. Prior to the formation of the eurozone, participating countries were required to make substantial adjustments to meet the EMU convergence criteria, including adoption of policies to reduce inflation (involving curbs on wages and prices) and budget deficits. Moreover, there is little labour mobility between regions to offset these shocks. The Cohesion Fund is too small to fully compensate for these adverse economic effects.
- **The challenge of enlargement.** Regional issues played an important role during the negotiations for entry into the Union of Austria, Sweden, Norway and Finland. The population density of the two Nordic entrants is only 16 people per sq. km, compared with 145 in EU12. Unemployment tends to be much higher in the northern regions of these countries. The emphasis in regional policy in the Nordic countries has been on maintaining population, employment and incomes in remote areas. In Austria, the aims have been more varied (for example, to protect the environment in alpine regions and to promote trans-frontier co-operation). The entry of the CEECs, Malta, Cyprus and Turkey will undoubtedly extend the range and complexity of the EU's regional problems. Given the scale of regional problems in candidate countries, the EU's current regional policy cannot be sustained without a very substantial increase in ERDF funding. The *Sixth Periodic Report* (Commission, 1999) estimated that the CEECs had a GDP per capita of about 40% of the EU average, although there were marked variations between CEECs, with the figure for Latvia being 27% and for Slovenia 68%. Even the Czech Republic and Slovenia have GDP per capita below that of Greece, the EU's poorest member. Prague and Bratislava were the only two CEEC regions with a GDP per capita above 75% of the EU average. Unemployment rates varied from 14% in Bulgaria to 5% in the Czech Republic. The €3.1 billion a year to be granted to candidate countries between 2000 and 2006 will not enable them to catch up to the EU average.
- **Trans-European networks (TENs).** The Union's aim to create Union-wide transport, telecommunications and energy networks obviously has a major regional dimension (see Chapter 13).
- **Subsidiarity.** The importance given to this principle in current Union thinking raises the fundamental question of where national regional policy ends and Union policy begins. Subsidiarity is reflected in the trend towards decentralisation in regional policy (that is, towards national, regional and local levels and away from the Commission). But the boundaries between these levels in regional policy remain fuzzy and difficult to discern. The issue of the delimitation of competencies between member states and the EU, reflecting the principle of subsidiarity, is one of the issues to be re-examined by the intergovernmental conference (IGC) to be convened in 2004.

● THE EFFECTS OF EU REGIONAL POLICY

The effects of EU regional policy are difficult to gauge, for several reasons: firstly, the impact of many programmes and projects, such as infrastructural improvements, can only be judged in the long term; secondly, regional economies, like national economies, are subject to a wide range of influences and it is difficult to assess the impact of specific factors; thirdly, it is difficult to isolate the effects of Union regional policies from those of national policies; fourthly, recipients of ERDF assistance arguably have a vested interest in overestimating its impact; fifthly, there has been little evaluation of the effects of this assistance.

EDRF money has undoubtedly become very significant for local and regional authorities. Commission reports on the regions point to evidence of real economic convergence in regional economic performance over the recent past. The *Sixth Periodic Report*, based on studies of the effects of the structural funds on the regions, estimates that they have added 0.5% or more to the growth of Objective 1 regions. By 1999, the cumulative effect of the funds was estimated to have increased the GDP of Greece, Ireland and Portugal by almost 10% and of Spain by over 4%. The report found that there has been a significant narrowing of disparities in income per capita between member countries, due mainly to the rise in income in the four poorest countries, Greece, Portugal, Spain and Ireland, which together saw their average per capita income rise from 65 to 76.5% of the EU average between 1986 and 1996. In this period, GDP per capita in the 25 poorest regions rose from 52 to 59% of the EU average.

However, the report also noted that there were still very significant regional disparities. Moreover *intra*regional disparities had widened rather than narrowed. Convergence is also a very slow process: some regions have indeed made progress, but others have stagnated or even declined. Moreover, the effects of Union spending on the regions have been muted to some degree by economic recession. Unemployment in the regions with the highest rate of unemployment increased in the period under study from 20% to nearly 24%. The Commission's second report on economic and social cohesion found that average income per head in the 10% of the population living in the most prosperous regions was 2.6 times greater than the bottom 10% in 1999. It found that although disparities between countries narrowed between 1988 and 1999, disparities between regions had narrowed by less, because the gaps between regions had widened in some member states (Commission 2001b).

Arguably, FDI has had a greater impact upon the economic development of specific regions than either national or European regional policy. FDI brings various benefits to the regions, such as injections of capital, 'know-how' and employment. For Spain, Portugal and Ireland, FDI has been greater in value than Union regional aid. Greece, however, receives twice as much from the structural funds as from FDI.

Union regional policy has been criticised on several grounds. The amount allocated to the ERDF has been very small, in comparison with the magnitude of the Union's regional problems. National spending on the regions has been substantially greater than ERDF spending. This reflects an unwillingness on the part of the more prosperous member states to agree to large increases in the ERDF. It has also been argued that ERDF moneys are spread too thinly, on too many projects. Another frequent criticism has been that ERDF programmes and projects have been poorly monitored. EU regional policies may (to a limited extent) have boosted incomes in recipient regions, but despite significant increases in ERDF funding, EU regional disparities remain very large. It remains to be seen if the 1999 reforms, with their emphasis on concentration and operational efficiency, will have the impact intended.

● REGIONAL POLICY AND EU GOVERNANCE

The development of EU regional policy has stimulated a lively academic debate concerning the nature of EU governance and policymaking (Bache, 1998; Sutcliffe, 2000). The key question addressed in this debate is: who are the key actors in EU policy? Some scholars (for example Marks, 1996) point to regional policy as an example of 'multilevel governance', in that it involves actors at supranational, national and subnational levels. The 'policy networks' approach has also been used to explain regional policymaking, in that a large group of interdependent actors constituting 'issue networks' or 'policy communities' are involved in the policy process. Some writers view the development of EU regional policy as a prime example of policy 'renationalisation', in that national governments are said to have wrested power back from the Commission. Bache argues that whilst there is multilevel *participation* in EU regional policymaking, this does not amount to multilevel *governance* because of the key 'gate-keeping' roles of national governments at all stages of the policy process. However, he argues that this gatekeeping role is flexible, in that it may change over time in accordance with the policy preferences of national governments. There is no single theory which can explain the development of EU regional policy.

● CONCLUSION

From small beginnings in the 1970s, EU regional policy has continued to grow in importance. The expansion of the Union and the pursuit of deeper integration have both provided powerful stimuli to the development of an EU policy for the regions. Moreover, the regional dimension of the Union's policy portfolio has drawn in local and regional actors into the EU policy process. EU regional policy has not solved the EU's regional problems (any more than have the regional policies pursued by member states). However, it is now firmly established as an integral element of the Union's policy portfolio. The three justifications of EU regional policy identified at the beginning of this chapter (that is, even development, the multidimensionality, and magnitude, of regional problems) will apply with even greater force in a greatly expanded and a more heterogeneous Union. The accession of the CEECs will result in a new category of EU region, that is, regions with a GDP per capita of below 40% of the EU average (Bulgaria, Romania, Poland, Estonia, Latvia and Lithuania: see page 471). The next enlargements are therefore likely to have profound consequences for EU regional policy, despite the best efforts of EU15's poorest member states to minimise this impact on their own shares of the structural funds.

FURTHER READING

Bache, I. (1998), *The Politics of European Union Regional Policy, Multi-level Governance or Flexible Gatekeeping?*, Sheffield Academic Press, Sheffield.

Button, K. and Pentecost, E. (1999), *Regional Economic Performance within the European Union*, Edward Elgar, Cheltenham and Northampton, MA.

Commission (1994), *Fifth Periodic Report on the Social and Economic Situation and Development of the Regions of the Community*, COM (94) 322.

Commission (1999), *Sixth Periodic Report on the Social and Economic Situation and Development of the Regions of the Community*, COM (99) 66.

Commission (2001a), *General Report on the Activities of the European Union (2000)*, Brussels.

Commission (2001b), *Second Report on Economic and Social Cohesion*, COM (2001) 24.

Eurostat (1998), '6 out of 10 High-Tech Regions in Germany', Eurostat memo no. 0598, Luxembourg.

Eurostat (1999), 'EU Regional Unemployment Ranges from 2.1% to 29.9%', Eurostat press release, no. 93/99, Luxembourg.

Eurostat (2001a), 'Regional GDP per capita in the EU in 1998', Statistics in focus, no.03/2001, Luxembourg.

Eurostat (2001b), 'Regional GDP in Central European Candidate Countries 1998', Statistics in focus, no.4/2001, Luxembourg.

Gidlund, J. and Jerneck, M. (2000), *Local and Regional Government in Europe*, Edward Elgar, Cheltenham and Northampton, MA.

Marks, G., Scharpf, F. and Schmitter, P. (eds) (1996), *Governance in the European Union*, Sage, London.

Sutcliffe, J.B. (2000), 'The 1999 Reform of the Structural Fund Regulations: Multi-level Governance or Renationalisation?', *Journal of European Public Policy*, vol. 7, no. 2, pp. 291–309.

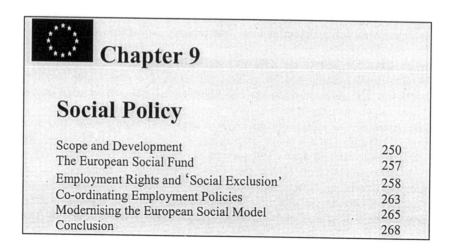

Chapter 9

Social Policy

● SCOPE AND DEVELOPMENT

○ Scope

At the outset of this chapter, a distinction needs to be made between 'European social policy' (meaning the social policies of member states plus those of the EU) and EU 'social policy'. A Commission Green Paper in 1993 took the term European social policy (ESP) to mean 'the full range of policies in the social sphere including labour market policies' (Commission, 1993). This definition encompasses social welfare policies as well as policies affecting employment. However, EU social policy (EUSP) is still largely centred on employment policies and working conditions. The social objectives of the EU, as revised by the Treaty of Amsterdam (ToA), are implicitly referred to in Article 2 of the EC Treaty as a high level of employment and social protection, equality between men and women, raising the standard of living and quality of life, and economic and social cohesion and solidarity among member states. The chapter on 'social provisions' in the EC Treaty (Articles 136–145) is almost exclusively concerned with employment-related issues. EU social policy remains in many respects undeveloped and lopsided.

Although the Union can claim to have policies affecting a wide variety of social groups (workers, the unemployed, women, the disabled) the social policies of national governments still have the biggest impact on the lives of EU citizens. EU expenditure on social policy is still a very small proportion of national spending on welfare and employment creation. National governments provide pensions, unemployment benefit and other welfare benefits. With the exception of the European Social Fund (ESF), which provides substantial funds for employment training, EU social policy is only marginally redistributive. However, although EUSP is largely regulative and focused on employment issues, some regulatory measures, such as the equal pay for equal work directive, have indirect redistributive consequences.

A full-blown EUSP (encompassing both substantive social welfare and labour market policies) is most unlikely to develop in the foreseeable future for several reasons, notably: the wide variations in the demographic and socio-economic characteristics of member states; the diversity of national social policy regimes; the reluctance of member states to relinquish control over social policy; the inherently contentious nature of many social policy issues and the budgetary transfers which a common social policy would require. Moreover, the next enlargements will increase the diversity of social policy regimes within the EU. Put bluntly, there is as yet no prospect of an 'EU welfare state'. As will be seen, however, many EU policies have implications for the welfare policies pursued by member states and therefore the EU dialogue on 'social policy' has tended to be broad-ranging in scope.

○ The Diversity of Social Policy Regimes

Various attempts have been made to classify the social policy regimes of member states: for example, distinctions have been made between the 'Bismarck' and 'Beveridge' traditions (the former financing social policy through employment insurance and the latter through general taxation). Similarly, a rough geographical demarcation has been discerned between the social policies of northern and southern member states (with the former tending to be far more generous). However, no distinction is watertight. There are wide variations between member states in the relative amounts contributed by governments, employers and individuals to social funding (see Table 9.1 below). There are wide variations in entitlements to, and amounts of, sickness benefit, pensions and family allowances (see Table 9.2 below).

Spending on social protection in 1997 ranged from 17.8% of GDP in Ireland to 33.6% in Sweden, with an EU15 average of 28.4% (see Table 9.3 and Figure 9.1 below). In most countries, old-age and survivors' pensions took the largest share, accounting for 45.4% of total benefits in EU15 in this year, although in Italy it accounted for 63.9%. Spending on health care and disability ranked second to spending on old age and survivors (34.6% of total benefits). Spending on families and children accounted for an average of 8.4% of total benefits. As a proportion of total benefits, unemployment benefit in 1997 ranged from 16.9% in Ireland to 2.9% in Italy, with an EU15 average of 7.6%. In Italy very low rates of unemployment benefit are paid as of right, but other forms of compensation are received. Unemployment benefit amounts to between 70 and 80% of GDP per capita in some northern member states, but to about 10% in Italy and about 12% in Greece. The next enlargements will lead to a marked increase in the diversity of the EU's social policy regimes. The legacy of communism has left Central and East European countries (CEECs) with extensive, underfunded and outdated social protection systems. Six of the ten CEEC candidates for EU membership currently have a GDP per capita of less than 40% of the EU average.

Table 9.1 Social Protection Receipts as % of Total Receipts in 1997

	Employers	Persons*	Government Contributions	Other
Austria	37.7	27.1	34.6	0.6
Belgium	49.2	23.1	24.9	2.8
Denmark	8.5	17.5	67.8	6.2
Finland	35.3	13.4	44.4	6.8
France	46.4	26.4	24.0	3.2
Germany	38.6	28.9	30.1	2.4
Greece	37.6	23.2	29.6	9.6
Ireland	22.8	13.7	62.5	1.0
Italy	50.9	16.9	29.9	2.3
Luxembourg	25.1	23.6	47.2	4.1
Netherlands	21.3	41.3	19.1	18.3
Portugal	28.6	18.1	43.3	10.1
Spain	52.2	17.5	27.1	3.3
Sweden	39.4	7.9	46.0	6.8
UK	25.2	15.3	47.3	12.3
EU15	**38.5**	**23.1**	**32.9**	**5.5**

Note: * e.g. employees, self-employed, pensioners. *Source*: Eurostat Yearbook 2001.

Table 9.2 Breakdown of EU Welfare Expenditure in 1997 (%)

	Health/ Disability	Old-age/ Survivors	Family/ Children	Unemployed	Housing	Social Exclusion
Austria	34.0	48.5	10.5	5.5	0.3	1.1
Belgium	32.7	43.0	8.8	12.7	–	2.7
Denmark	28.9	39.4	12.6	12.6	2.4	4.0
Finland	36.6	33.9	12.6	13.3	1.2	2.4
France	34.0	43.6	10.0	7.8	3.3	1.3
Germany	36.1	41.9	10.1	9.1	0.6	2.3
Greece	31.3	51.4	8.2	4.6	3.3	1.2
Ireland	40.2	24.6	13.0	16.9	3.3	2.0
Italy	29.6	63.9	3.5	2.9	0.0	0.1
Lux.	38.0	43.5	13.2	3.7	0.2	1.3
Neth.	37.2	39.4	4.5	8.6	1.5	8.7
Portugal	46.0	42.8	5.3	5.0	0.0	0.9
Spain	36.5	46.2	2.0	14.1	0.3	0.8
Sweden	33.7	39.5	10.6	10.4	2.6	3.2
UK	36.1	44.0	8.6	3.8	6.7	0.8
EU15	**34.6**	**45.4**	**8.4**	**7.6**	**2.2**	**1.8**

Source: Eurostat Yearbook 2001.

Table 9.3 EU Social Protection Spending by Member States in 1997

	Social Protection Spending As % of GDP	Social Protection Spending per capita in €
Austria	28.8	6486
Belgium	28.4	5988
Denmark	30.4	8577
Germany	29.9	6713
Greece	23.6	2376
Finland	29.3	6154
France	30.8	6539
Ireland	17.8	3318
Italy	26.3	4597
Luxembourg	24.8	8526
Netherlands	31.6	6463
Portugal	22.5	2037
Spain	21.4	2624
Sweden	33.6	7967
UK	27.8	5477
EU15	**28.4**	**5472**

Source: Eurostat Yearbook 2001.

Figure 9.1 Social Protection Spending by Member States in 1997

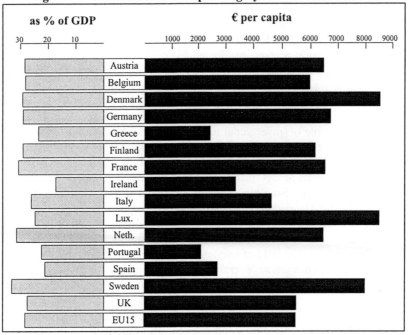

Source: Eurostat Yearbook 2001.

In EU15, about three-fifths of the total cost of these benefits is funded by social contributions by employers and persons (see Table 9.1 above), with tax-funded general government contributions providing almost one-third (the rest, accounting for 5.5% in 1997, comprises payments such as interest and dividends). Social contributions are highest in Belgium, France and Spain (about 70% or more of receipts), whereas Denmark and Ireland finance their social protection systems mainly through general government contributions (67.8% of receipts in Denmark and 62.5% in Ireland in 1997). Only about a quarter of Denmark's social expenditure comes from social contributions. Fear that entry into the eurozone would jeopardise the Danish welfare system was a contributory factor to the 'no' vote in the Danish referendum on the euro in September 2000. The Commission has repeatedly stated that there can be no question of fully harmonising social security systems, which derive from the traditions and cultures of member states. But four factors may be leading to a limited degree of convergence of national social policies:

• **Pressures on welfare budgets**. Member states are affected by common problems, such as ageing populations, changes in family structures, changes in work patterns and escalating social security and health-care budgets. Health and pensions account for about four-fifths of all social benefits. The capacity of governments to pay for welfare is declining. In all countries, therefore, there are pressures to control social spending and to re-examine the efficacy of social policy regimes.

• **Responses to globalisation.** The need for EU firms to compete successfully in world markets has forced EU countries to address the issue of how high levels of social protection can be reconciled with the need for greater labour market flexibility. The debate between those favouring social protection and those favouring labour market deregulation has by no means been resolved, not least because it raises contentious ideological issues concerning the role of government in modern market economies. In the early 1990s, economic recession and rising unemployment in the Union increased the intensity of this debate, which has focused on the issue of how to adapt the 'European social model' (see below) to a globalised economy.

• **The logic of the Single European Market (SEM).** The drive for the integration of EU markets, in particular as pursued through the SEM programme, has provided the rationale for attempts to introduce minimum common standards in EU labour markets. There is now a considerable body of EU legislation in the field of employment (see below).

• **EU-level acceptance of 'social rights'**, as enunciated for example in the 1989 Social Charter (see below), in the Charter of Fundamental Rights (see Chapter 4) and in the social provisions of the EC Treaty, as revised by the ToA, which provide legal bases for improvements in working conditions and for equal opportunities for men and women. The European Court of Justice (ECJ) plays a key role in ensuring that legislation in this area is enforced.

○ Development

EUSP has a long history, dating back to the formation of the European Coal and Steel Community (ECSC). Article 46 of the ECSC Treaty sought improvement of the living standards and conditions of workers in the coal and steel industries. A wide range of employment provisions were included in the Treaty of Rome. These covered, for example, free movement of workers, improvement in working conditions and in workers' living standards and equal pay for men and women. The treaty also established the ESF. The Economic and Social Committee (ESC) was established to provide the interests of business and labour (the 'social partners') with a vehicle for dialogue and a channel of influence on economic and social issues.

There have been both passive and active periods in the development of EUSP. Between 1957 and 1972 its main focus was on labour mobility. In the 1970s, it was expanded to address the growing problem of unemployment, resulting in a quadrupling of the ESF budget between 1973 and 1979. In 1972, member states agreed to establish a Social Action Programme, targeted at employment problems. From the mid-1980s, the notion of *Social Europe* has been promoted by the Commission. Jacques Delors sought to 'sell' the idea of the Single European Market (SEM) programme to European trade unions by insisting that the programme had a social dimension and was as much about creating a Europe for workers as for business people. The Single European Act (SEA) contains provisions to strengthen economic and social cohesion and introduced qualified majority voting (QMV) with regard to some aspects of social policy. The Treaty on European Union (TEU) introduced a wide range of social policy provisions. Before the treaty there was no specific legal competence in public health vested in the Union. The treaty gave the Union responsibility to take preventive action on public health. The TEU also introduced two sets of social policy provisions: those within the EC Treaty applicable to all member states and the 'Protocol on Social Policy' to which all member states except the UK subscribed. The ToA integrated these aspects of social policy into the Community pillar, following the UK's acceptance of the Social Chapter. It also extended co-decision to some key employment provisions. There is now therefore one set of social policy provisions for all member states.

A key factor in recent developments of social policy has been 'spillover' from other policy areas, such as the SEM, economic and monetary union (EMU) (which has put pressure on state budgets) and justice and home affairs (in relation, for example, to the 'social rights' of EU citizens living or working in other member states and of third-country nationals). Moreover, there has also been a degree of 'institutional spillover' into social policy, in that the ToA extended the co-decision procedure to some employment provisions, which enhanced the role of the European Parliament (EP) in this

ciao!

field. It also extended the use of QMV in the Council, which means that in some areas of employment policy individual member states may be forced to accept the majority decision. Jensen (2000) has argued that the spillover which has occurred in the field of EU social policy provides some support for the 'neofunctionalist' theory of integration (see Chapter 2).

Pressure for improvement in working conditions has tended to come from countries with high standards (whose firms would otherwise be disadvantaged in the SEM) and from the Commission, which has pursued an active role as a 'policy entrepreneur' in this field. In the 1990s, most EU governments were left-leaning and therefore tended to favour stronger employment measures, although in many cases the Commission's draft legislation has been watered down due to opposition to specific proposals by some countries and from some business interests. Not surprisingly, interest groups representing businesses and trades unions are very active in seeking to influence EU policy in this field. Some employment measures (for example, the working-time directive) are highly controversial and receive considerable attention in the media. Another important source of influence on employment policy has been the ECJ, which has played a key role in clarifying and establishing EU employment law (having made judgments in over 600 cases). Its rulings in key employment cases have frequently been cited as a good example of 'judicial activism'. However, although member states have agreed to extend EU competence in the field of EUSP, they have also set limits on it. Some member states continue to oppose extension of co-decision and of QMV to some aspects of employment policy (certain matters such as pay and the right to strike were explicitly excluded from EU decisionmaking procedures in the ToA). The effects of EU employment legislation have been weakened by patchy implementation and 'foot dragging' by member states.

○ The European Company Statute

In December 2000, EU social affairs ministers agreed on legislation for a European Company Statute. This will enable a company with a European dimension to set up as a single company under EU law, with a unified set of rules, management and reporting system. while safeguarding workers' rights. The statute lays down rules on worker consultation and participation. According to Commission estimates, this could lead to savings of €30 billion a year. A directive concerning worker involvement in these companies (which will be known as 'Societas Europaea', or SE) was also agreed. Member states had been trying to reach agreement on this statute since 1970, so the deal represented a significant breakthrough. It was made possible by an opt-out secured by Spain on worker participation aspects and by the fact that the decision to set up an SE is optional. If approved by the EP, the legislation will enter into force in 2001.

● THE EUROPEAN SOCIAL FUND

The fund was established by the Treaty of Rome and was set up in 1960, to promote employment and the geographical and occupational mobility of workers. The bulk of the ESF is now spent on measures to combat unemployment, through the provision of finance for vocational training, resettlement and job creation. The fund is administered by the Commission, in accordance with guidance by the Council. There is also an advisory committee (the Social Fund Committee) comprising national officials, employers and trades union representatives. The *additionality principle* applies to projects supported by the ESF. In other words, public authorities in member states are required to provide at least as much funding as that sought from the ESF. In the UK the ESF is administered through the Department of Employment. The budget for the ESF is small, relative to the size of the unemployment problem. It has nevertheless increased markedly in both absolute terms and in relation to its share of the Union budget.

In 1983, it was agreed that 75% of the fund would be directed towards alleviation of unemployment among the under 25s. The other main group assisted are over 25s unemployed for more than 12 months. About 40% of the fund is reserved for the most deprived regions and areas experiencing industrial decline. The scope of the fund was widened in 1993, following decisions taken by the European Council in Edinburgh in December 1992. Objectives 3 and 4 of the structural funds were grouped together to form a single new Objective 3, which was extended to cover those exposed to long-term unemployment. A new Objective 4 was created, to facilitate adaptation of workers to industrial change. Between 1994 and 1999, 9% of ESF appropriations were earmarked for initiatives to enhance employment opportunities for disadvantaged groups. A European Employment Services Agency (EURES) has been established to act as a European employment agency and to provide a discussion forum on employment.

The ESF was adapted in the late 1990s to take account of growing EU unemployment. The new ESF has been developed within the context of the employment title introduced into the EC Treaty by the ToA; the European Employment Strategy (EES) launched at the Luxembourg European Council in November 1997; and the Council's 1997 employment guidelines (based on the themes of *employability, entrepreneurship, adaptability* and *equal opportunities* and reflected in annual national employment action plans). The new ESF provides support in five policy fields, namely:

- developing and promoting active labour market polices;
- promoting equal opportunities;
- promoting and improving training, education and counselling;
- promoting a skilled, trained and adaptable workforce;
- improving women's access to and participation in the labour market.

A frequent criticism of ESF spending has been that resources have been spread too thinly on too many projects, a problem which the 1999 reforms of the structural funds sought to address (see Chapter 8). The new ESF seeks greater concentration, by focusing on a more limited number of priority objectives than its predecessor, namely: supporting local initiatives on employment, harnessing the job potential of the information society; and ensuring equal opportunities for men and women.

● EMPLOYMENT RIGHTS AND 'SOCIAL EXCLUSION'

In addition to the right to work in any member state, EUSP seeks to promote a wide range of other employment rights. These embrace provisions on health and safety at work, working conditions, information and consultation of workers, equal opportunities for men and women and integration of persons excluded from the labour market (Articles 136 and 137, ECT). Examples of measures in the field of working conditions in recent years are the directives on working time, on protection of pregnant women at work, and on the rights of part-time workers. Various directives, dealing both with general health and safety at work and with rules for specific industries, have been passed. There is a European Agency for Safety and Health at Work.

The decision procedures used for legislation in the field of employment rights remain very complicated. In some cases, the co-decision procedure, and in other cases the consultation procedure, applies, whereas some matters are explicitly excluded from the EU's provisions. In one case (Article 42 on co-ordination of social security), the co-decision procedure is combined with unanimity rather than QMV in the Council. The more sensitive the issue for member states (not least in terms of impinging on the question of sovereignty) the less likely it is that it will be covered by co-decision and QMV. Indeed, some issues (for example, pay and the right to strike) are explicitly excluded from the social provisions in the EC Treaty. Thus no minimum wage is set at EU level. In EU15, nine countries (Belgium, Spain, Greece, France, Luxembourg, the Netherlands, Portugal, the UK and Ireland) have national minimum wages. But the minimum varies considerably, for example, being about three times higher in the Netherlands and Luxembourg than in Portugal. The ToA requires implementing measures in the employment field to take account of 'diverse forms of national practices, in particular in the field of contractual relations, and the need to maintain the competitiveness of the Community economy' (Article 136, ECT).

Article 136 outlines the objectives of the Community and member states in this field (for example employment promotion, improved living and working conditions, proper social protection) and Article 137 lists the activities to be used in support of these objectives. Some items listed under

Article 137 (which the Treaty of Nice (ToN) re-worded) are covered by QMV and co-decision (for example, improvement of the working environment (137.1a); working conditions (137.1b); information and consultation of workers (137.1.e); and integration of persons excluded from the labour market (137.1.h). In four cases unanimity applies (social security and social protection of workers (137.1c); protection of workers where their contract is terminated (137.1.d); representation and collective defence of the interests of workers and employers, including co-determination (137.1f); and conditions of employment for third-country nationals (137.1g).

The ToN will not substantively alter Article 137, although it includes a provision enabling the Council to decide by unanimity, following a proposal from the Commission and after consulting the EP, to render QMV and co-decision applicable to three of the four cases mentioned above, the exception being social security. The provisions of Article 137 do not apply to pay, the right of association, the right to strike or the right to impose lockouts (135.5). The ToN sets a further explicit limit on the provisions of Article 137 by stipulating that these provisions shall not affect the right of member states to define the fundamental principles of their social security systems.

○ The Social Charter ('The Community Charter of the Fundamental Social Rights of Workers')

A key development in the promotion of employment rights in the EU was the adoption of the Social Charter. The Charter reflected the continental approach to industrial relations, based upon the enunciation of employment rights and upon collaboration between 'social partners' (business leaders and trades unions). In 1985, Jacques Delors had sought a new social dialogue between the Commission, the Union of Industrial and Employers' Confederations of Europe (UNICE) and the European Trade Union Confederation (ETUC) – the 'social partners' – by arranging a meeting at Val Duchesse, a Belgian chateau. The process which ensued became known as the Val Duchesse Social Dialogue, leading to proposals for strengthening Union employment policies. In 1988, the Marin Report on Social Policy advocated a 'social charter'. The Commission published the first draft of the charter in May 1989. This was amended largely as a result of British objections, but even the revised draft was unacceptable to the UK government. The draft was adopted in December 1989 by all member states except the UK. Although enthusiastically welcomed by UK trade unions and by the Labour and Liberal parties, the charter was regarded by the UK's Conservative government as an attempt to introduce socialism by the back door.

At the Maastricht summit, the UK government reaffirmed its opposition to the charter and therefore this aspect of social policy formed a separate protocol of the TEU. The protocol did not exempt the UK from other commitments on social policy made at Maastricht, or from social policy provisions in the EC Treaty or in the SEA. Social policy was therefore in the unusual position of having two legal bases: that forming an integral part of the *acquis communautaire* (applicable to all member states) and that deriving from the protocol (applicable to all except the UK). This created considerable confusion. A Commission communication of December 1993 stated that where possible, social proposals would continue to be presented within the terms of the EC Treaty and the SEA, in order to make them binding on all members. The Commission set out criteria to determine which procedure would be used for proposals. It was not until June 1994 that an employment law (European Works Councils) was passed under the terms of the protocol.

Table 9.4 Social Charter 'Rights'

- the right to work in the EC country of one's choice;
- the freedom to choose an occupation and the right to a fair wage;
- the right to improved living and working conditions;
- the right to social protection under prevailing national conditions;
- the right to freedom of association and collective bargaining;
- the right to vocational training;
- the right of men and women to equal treatment;
- the right of workers to information, consultation and participation;
- the right to health and safety at work;
- protection of children and adolescents;
- a decent living standard for the elderly;
- improved social and professional integration for the disabled.

Opponents of the charter argued that its provisions conflicted with the global trend towards more flexible labour markets and would increase non-wage labour costs, thereby making the goods of EU firms uncompetitive in world markets. Conversely, the proponents of the charter argued that there could hardly be a level playing field for business if wide divergences in labour market conditions existed between EU countries. They argued that without social protection and agreed minimum standards, there could be widespread *social dumping*. This was defined by Padraig Flynn, the social policy commissioner as: 'the gaining of unfair competitive advantage within the Community through unacceptably low social standards' (*Frontier Free Europe*, January 1994), an accusation frequently levelled at the UK because of its rejection of the Social Charter. The social policy protocol was abrogated as a result of the UK Labour government's acceptance of the Social Charter and its provisions were incorporated by the ToA into Title XI (ex VIII) of the EC Treaty, so that social policy measures now apply to all member states. Chapter 1 of this title, which deals with social provisions, explicitly refers to 'fundamental social rights' such as those set out in the 1961 European Charter and the 1989 Social Charter. A key (and controversial) element of the Charter of Fundamental Rights (CFR) declared by the Nice European Council is that it contains references to a range of 'social rights' (see Chapter 4). The influence of the Social Charter on the social aspects of the CFR seems clear.

○ Equal Opportunities

The principle that men and women should receive equal pay for equal work was laid down in Article 119 (now 141) of the Treaty of Rome. This article has been reinforced by various judgments of the ECJ - for example, the *Defrenne* vs. *the Belgian State* judgment on equal pay (1976) and by various directives for example, on equal pay (1975), on equal treatment (1976) and on eliminating discrimination in occupational pension schemes (1986). However the Commission has frequently expressed its dissatisfaction with levels of compliance with these directives. The EU also operates equal opportunities 'action programmes'. The ToA strengthened the Union's commitment to equal opportunities, especially with regard to gender equality. It introduced QMV and co-decision into Article 141, ECT, concerning equal pay for equal work or work of equal value. It also allows for member states to pursue policies of positive discrimination with regard to gender in vocational and professional activities (Article 141.4). The European Social Agenda approved by the Nice European Council calls for various measures for promoting gender equality, including gender impact assessments, equality on pay, and the establishment of a European Institute for gender issues.

Several EU organisations are concerned with gender equality. For example, within the Commission, the Equal Opportunities Unit monitors the application of directives and compliance with the action programmes; the Women's Information Service provides information about developments affecting women; the Advisory Committee on Equal Opportunities represents equal opportunities organisations in member states. The EP also has a very active Women's Rights Committee. The Commission produces an annual report on equal opportunities for men and women in the EU.

○ Management–Labour Dialogue and Workers' Participation

The goal of 'social partnership' between management and labour can be traced back to the beginning of the EU. Article 136 of the EC Treaty requires both the Community and member states to pursue dialogue between management and labour. Article 138 specifically requires the Commission to promote the consultation of management and labour at European level and also to consult with both before submitting proposals in the social policy field. Forms of employee participation exist in several Union countries. In the 1970s, the Commission proposed several draft directives on company organisation, including workers' participation: the draft *Vredeling* directive of 1972 sought to introduce information and consultation procedures for workers in larger companies, but this was not accepted by the Council. In 1980 and 1983, the Commission drafted directives on worker consultation, but these were blocked by opposition from the UK. In 1994, after 13 years of discussion, a directive on worker consultation in EU-wide companies was approved by all member states, excluding the UK. Because of its social policy opt-out (which it subsequently relinquished), the UK did not vote on this proposal. The directive requires companies with 1000 employees or more and 150 staff in a minimum of two member states to consult employees on cross-border decisions. It allows for considerable flexibility in application and only applies to large companies. In June 2001 the Employment and Social Policy Council agreed a new directive on worker consultation which will require EU companies to inform and consult with their employees about decisions affecting their jobs. A company with 50 employees or more will also be required to inform employees about its financial situation. For small companies, some aspects of the directive will be implemented over seven years in the UK and Ireland and over three years in other member states.

○ Social Exclusion

This is the EU term for poverty and marginalization. The Commission estimates that in the EU about 18% (65 million) of the population live in low-income households. Poverty is a problem largely dealt with at national level, although between 1975 and 1994, the Commission operated three token poverty programmes (running from 1975–80, 1984–88 and 1989–94). Although the 'Poverty 3' budget was twice that of 'Poverty 2', it still only amounted to €121 million, largely because of the reluctance of the richer member states to countenance expansion of the EU's financial responsibilities in this area. In its proposal for a fourth programme, the Commission reiterated that responsibility for fighting social exclusion lay mainly with member states, but affirmed the EU's contributory role. In 1995, adoption of a fourth programme was blocked by the UK and Germany, which argued that this policy area was a national responsibility.

The EU has also developed policies for the disabled. About 38 million people in the EU have some form of physical or mental handicap. Although member states have primary responsibility for action in this field, the Union has a disability strategy aimed primarily at improving the access of disabled people to jobs and facilities. In the employment field, support is provided through the European Social Fund and the Community initiative EQUAL. The Commission has established a high-level group of member states' representatives on disability. It has also instituted a European Day of Disabled People. It provides support to the European Disability Forum, in which most disability organisations in member states participate.

Following ratification of the ToA, under the Article 13 of the EC Treaty the Community can take action to combat discrimination based on gender, race, ethnic origin, religion or conviction, disability, age or sexual orientation. The ToN allows the co-decision procedure to apply to Community incentive measures to support action by member states in pursuit of Article 13 objectives. The DAPHNE programme has sought to combat violence and sexual abuse of children, adolescents and women. The ToA requires a high level of human health protection to be ensured in the definition and implementation of all Community activities and policies, although it also stipulates that Community action in the field of public health shall fully respect the responsibilities of member states for the organisation and delivery of health services and medical care (Article 152, ECT). The European Social Agenda requires member states to develop national action plans for combating poverty and social exclusion by June 2001 and also to develop action during the European Year of Disabled Citizens (2003).

● CO-ORDINATING EMPLOYMENT POLICIES

The issue of employment in the EU loomed large throughout the 1990s and is high on the Union's current policy agenda. The EU performance on employment has continued to lag very significantly behind the US and Japan. Whereas the US and Japan both had unemployment rates of 4.4% in February 1999, the rate for EU15 was almost 10% (Eurostat, 1999). The EU also has a lower *employment* rate, of about 60% of the active population (compared with 70% in the US) and a serious problem of long-term unemployment. The US success in generating new jobs is frequently attributed to its flexible labour markets. Although the EU has in recent years sought to foster increased labour market flexibility, this has not been sought at the price of abandoning the relatively higher levels of social protection in the EU. Instead, strong emphasis is placed upon the need for member states to co-ordinate their employment policies, to introduce incentive measures and to encourage local employment initiatives (for example, through 'territorial employment pacts' involving co-operation between local economic actors). As a result of a Swedish initiative, the ToA added a title on employment to the EC Treaty (Title VIII), the key elements of which are:

- member states and the Community must work towards developing a co-ordinated strategy for employment;
- member states shall regard promoting employment as a matter of common concern;

- the objective of a high level of employment is to be taken into account in the formulation and implementation of Community policies and activities;
- it establishes a framework for multilateral surveillance procedures, based on annual employment guidelines; national implementation reports and a joint employment report, submitted annually to the European Council;
- the Council may, on recommendation from the Commission, issue specific recommendations to member states for urgent action;
- it introduces a legal base for the promotion of incentive measures for employment;
- it establishes a new employment committee, to play an active part in these processes and to serve as a forum for debate.

Concern over unemployment led to the first jobs summit, a special meeting of the European Council held in Luxembourg in November 1997, at which the EES was launched. At this summit, a co-ordinated strategy for employment, known as the *Luxembourg Process*, was agreed. This involves the formulation of commonly-agreed employment guidelines and annual national action plans, built around the four pillars of employability, entrepreneurship, adaptability and equal opportunities. The Council approves these guidelines each year, based on a proposal from the Commission. Each country then draws up a national action plan, describing how these guidelines will be put into practice. The Commission and Council examine each action plan and present a joint employment report to the December European Council. The Council if necessary makes recommendations to governments, on the basis of QMV following a proposal from the Commission and consultation with the EP, the Economic and Social Committee (ESC) and the Committee of the Regions (CoR). Member states are required to bring their employment policies in line with the employment guidelines and to implement the reforms outlined in the national action plans.

At the Cardiff European Council, member states agreed to pursue a comprehensive approach to structural reforms of goods, services and capital markets (the *Cardiff Process*). Following a German proposal, an 'employment pact' was launched at the Cologne European Council in June 1999. It is meant to facilitate dialogue and confidence building between all actors concerned with macroeconomic policy, with the aim of stimulating growth and employment. This process, known as the *Cologne Process*, is channelled through the Commission's twice yearly economic forecasts and through the annual broad economic policy guidelines. Critics of these 'processes' argue that they result in many vague declarations and statements of intent, but few concrete policies. They argue that their role is largely symbolic rather than substantive, in that they are a means of demonstrating that member states are working together on employment. Nevertheless, they provide formal mechanisms for the formulation, development and review of co-ordinated strategies for tackling unemployment.

● MODERNISING THE EUROPEAN SOCIAL MODEL

Despite the differences between national social policy regimes within the Union, it is widely accepted that there is a 'European social model', which in particular distinguishes European social policy from that of the United States. The European model presumes a strong commitment to public social support, strong social safety nets and universal social protection systems. In the EU, the proportion of social expenditure funded through taxation is significantly higher than in the US. A debate is currently raging in all modern societies concerning the future of public welfare and employment policies. In the EU, the superior performance of the US economy has raised the question of whether the European social model is fully compatible with labour market flexibility and global competitiveness.

In 1993, the Commissioner for Social Affairs and Employment published a Green Paper (Commission, 1993) on the options for the Union in field of social policy, with the aim of stimulating a debate on the future of ESP. The escalating costs of social protection and the growing problem of unemployment made this debate both urgent and necessary. The Green Paper was published at roughly the same time as the Delors White Paper on *Growth, Competitiveness and Employment* (see Chapter 10). Both papers addressed the issue of unemployment. In 1994, the EU had an unemployment rate of about 11%, compared with 6% in the US and 3% in Japan. Both papers rejected the 'option' of abandoning EU social protection policies in order to compete with low-wage economies in the Far East. But both accepted the need for greater flexibility and mobility in EU labour markets, without abandoning the EU's standards. The Green Paper advocated a move away from detailed prescriptive employment laws. Correctly, it predicted that the incoming European Free Trade Association (EFTA) countries would seek to improve minimum standards of social protection.

Following receipt of 594 comments on the Green Paper from interested parties such as Union institutions, governments, unions, employers and voluntary organisations, the Commission published a White Paper on ESP (Commission, 1994). The paper noted the tension in reactions to the Green Paper between those criticising the EU's high labour costs and those arguing that high labour standards are an integral part of the formula for achieving competitiveness. It observed that there was a core of opinion recognising a 'European social model' and supported the need to set minimum standards for labour in order to avoid social dumping. But it also asserted that subsidiarity was a guiding principle in social policy and that ESP legislation had to be more flexible and less detailed than hitherto. Moreover, it also recognised the need to reconcile high social standards with the capacity to compete in world markets. This approach, labelled the *new realism*, was further developed in the Commission's 5th Social Action Programme (1995–

97) launched in April 1995, which gave top priority to job creation and has been reiterated in many other subsequent pronouncements on social policy.

It has generally been accepted that social protection systems within the Union need to be modernised, not least to cope more effectively with demographic and employment trends such as the growth in the number of elderly people, the increased participation of women on the workforce and increased long-term unemployment. In 1997 the Commission presented a communication on 'modernising and improving social protection in the EU' which argued that there was an urgent need for modernisation and adaptation of social protection systems, by making better use of available resources. A further communication by the Commission in July 1999, entitled *A Concerted Strategy for Modernising Social Protection*, proposed a strategy centred on four objectives, namely:

- *to make work pay and provide secure income.* This would necessitate changes in tax and benefit systems; new working arrangements; income bridges to fill temporary gaps between jobs; a contribution to reconciling work and family life; and the need to provide systems with adequate resources, avoiding negative impacts on employment and taking account of the need for budgetary discipline;
- *to make pensions safe and pensions systems sustainable*, for example by measures to discourage early withdrawal from the labour market;
- *to promote social inclusion*, including effective safety nets and active rather than passive measures;
- *to ensure high quality and sustainability of health care.*

This communication was endorsed by the Council in December 1999. In its recommendation for the broad economic policy guidelines for 1999, the Commission invited member states to review pension, health-care and taxation systems and to promote other active labour market policies. The 1999 employment guidelines refer several times to ideas for making social protection systems more employment friendly, for example by providing incentives to the unemployed to seek work. Reconciling these objectives however remains an extremely formidable task.

○ The European Social Agenda and the Social Protection Committee

In June 2000, the Commission adopted a European Social Agenda set around strategic guidelines in all social policy areas for the period 2000 to 2005. The Agenda was approved by the Council in November and subsequently by the Nice European Council. It reflects commitments made by the Lisbon European Council in March 2000, which affirmed the need to promote an inclusive 'knowledge economy' and to reconcile high levels of social protection with market friendly and competitive labour policies. The Agenda defines the European social model as being 'characterised in particular by systems that offer a high level of social protection, by the importance of the social dialogue and by services of general interest covering activities vital for social cohesion'. It requires studies to be undertaken of national strategies for guaranteeing secure and viable pensions and of how a high and sustainable level of health protection can be guaranteed. Every spring, the European Council will look at how the Lisbon agreements are being implemented. The first review took place at the Stockholm European Council in March 2001. On the basis of the Lisbon agreements, the Stockholm summit examined the issues of employment, economic reform, research and innovation in the knowledge economy and social cohesion (especially effective social protection for an ageing population). The summit set targets for employment rates of 67% overall and 57% for women by January 2005. For older men and women, it agreed a target of 50% by 2010. It also agreed steps to encourage labour mobility and to combat social exclusion. However, the supposed focus on the European social agenda was diluted by the attention given to other issues, such as events in the Balkans and the foot and mouth crisis. The summit was also marred by the failure of member states to agree on several major market liberalisation measures (gas, electricity, air transport). Moreover, the Stockholm conclusions in the social and employment field were rather vague and it remains to be seen how they will be translated into actual policies.

The ToN provides the legal basis for a Social Protection Committee (SPC). A new article (144, ECT) states that the SPC will be an advisory body, set up to promote co-operation between member states and with the Commission on social protection policies. Its tasks will be to monitor the social situation and the development of social protection policies in member states and the Community; to promote exchanges of information, experience and good practice between the member states and the Commission; and to prepare reports, opinions or undertake other work at the request of the Council, Commission or on its own initiative. Each member state and the Commission will appoint two members.

❍ The European Social Model and the CEEC Candidate Countries

The European social model presents problems for the acceding Central and East European countries (CEECs). When they accede, their economies may be subject to stronger competitive pressures which may increase unemployment. This will place additional strains on their limited budgets and overstretched welfare regimes. Some support is available through PHARE and the structural funds to assist the CEECs to meet the requirements of the Union's social *acquis communautaire*, which they are required to accept. However, this is likely to be a fraction what is needed for social modernisation in the CEECs. The European Social Agenda approved by the

Nice European Council calls for regular exchanges of views on all aspects of social policy linked to enlargement, in conjunction with the social partners and measures to help candidate countries to take on board the European Employment Strategy.

● CONCLUSION

The distinctive feature of EU social policy has been and remains the strong emphasis upon employment-related issues. However, it has been broadened to encompass a diverse range of subjects. The diversity of national social policy regimes and disparities in wealth between member states rule out the possibility of a common EU welfare regime. The next enlargements will make this prospect even more unlikely. However, the existence of a 'European Social Model', which in particular distinguishes the EU from US values and practices, is widely acknowledged. A key challenge for the EU is how this model can be modernised, so that it contributes to, rather than impedes, the competitiveness of European industry in global markets.

FURTHER READING

Buti, M. Franco, D. and Perch, L.R. (eds) (1999), *The Welfare State in Europe*, Edward Elgar, Cheltenham and Northampton, MA.

Commission (1993), *Green Paper on European Social Policy*, COM (93) 551.

Commission (1994), *European Social Policy – A Way Forward for the Union*, COM (94) 333.

Commission (1997), *Modernising and Improving Social Protection in the EU*, COM (97) 102.

Commission (1999), *A Concerted Strategy for Modernising Social Protection*, COM (99) 347.

Commission (2000) *Report on Social Protection in Europe 1999*, COM (2000) 163.

Commission (2000), *Social Policy Agenda*, COM (2000) 379.

Commission (2000), *Building an Inclusive Europe*, COM (2000) 79.

Commission (2000), *Towards a Barrier-Free Europe for People with Disabilities*, COM (2000) 284.

Eurostat (1999), Statistics in Focus, *Regions*, no. 5/99, Luxembourg.

Eurostat (2000), *Eurostat Yearbook. A statistical eye on Europe*, Luxembourg.

Faulkner, G. (1998), *EU Social Policy in the 1990s: Towards a Corporatist Policy Community*, Routledge, London.

Hine, D, and Kassim, H. (eds) (1998), *Beyond the Market: The EU and National Social Policy*, Routledge, London.

Jensen, C. (2000), 'Neofunctionalist Theories and the Development of European Social and Labour Market Policy', *Journal of Common Market Studies*, vol. 38, no. 1, pp. 71–92.

 **Chapter 10**

Strategies for Economic Regeneration: From the Single Market to '*e*-Europe'

● INTRODUCTION

From its earliest days, the European Union project has been underpinned by the belief that the pursuit of economic integration between member states will deliver concrete benefits to EU citizens. In this sense, the Union's policies for economic growth and regeneration transcend economics and are closely bound up with the Union's attempts to legitimise itself through 'good works'. In recent decades, the faltering economic performance of the Union's economies (when measured against that of the United States) and the perceived opportunities and threats posed by globalisation have provided the impetus for a series of major policy initiatives aimed at the economic transformation of the Union, namely:

- the Single European Market (SEM) programme (from 1985);
- economic and monetary union (EMU) (from 1991);
- the strategy for growth, competitiveness and employment (from 1993);
- the European Employment Strategy (EES) (from 1997); and
- the '*e*-Europe' initiative (from 1999).

The sheer number of these policy initiatives is indicative of the intractability of the economic regeneration problem they seek to address. The ambitious nature of these initiatives is also indicative of the Union's penchant for setting itself formidable development goals. The EES was considered in the previous chapter and EMU will be examined in Chapter 11. This chapter therefore focuses on the SEM programme, the strategy for growth, competitiveness and employment and the '*e*-Europe' initiative.

● ORIGINS AND PRINCIPAL FEATURES OF THE SEM

○ Eurosclerosis and the Single Market Prescription

In the mid-1980s, the term 'Eurosclerosis' gained wide currency as a description of an illness afflicting the economies of the EU member states. Its principal symptoms were economic stagnation, industrial decline, poor productivity, rising unemployment and poor competitiveness in world markets. This perception of weakness was justified by reference to a number of 'gaps' between the performance of the EU economies and those of Japan and the US, namely: a *trade gap*, a *productivity gap*, an *employment gap*, an *investment gap* and a *technology gap*. The solution adopted to restore the EU to economic health was the Single European Market programme, an ambitious project to abolish remaining trade barriers between member states. The central assumption underpinning the programme was that non-tariff barriers to trade between member states were major causes of Eurosclerosis. These barriers included differences in technical standards for products; fiscal barriers (for example, excise duties and VAT); restrictions on the ability of EU firms to operate in other member states; and restrictions on cross-border movement. The EU's performance gap was thus attributed by the programme's proponents to the fragmentation of the EU economy: whereas the US and Japan each had one market, in 1985 the EU had ten markets, with diverse technical standards, business laws and industrial policies.

On 1 January 1993, the 'completion' of the SEM programme was officially celebrated with bonfires and fireworks displays all over the EU. The previous month in Edinburgh, the European Council declared that the programme had been completed in all essential respects. However, this was something of an anti-climax, because the gaps between the economic performance of Japan and the US on the one hand and the EU on the other were as wide (if not wider) in 1993 than in 1985 when the programme had been launched. As further evidence that the programme was no miracle cure for Eurosclerosis, by the end of 1993 the Commission launched another major strategy to deal with the EU's problems of poor growth, rising unemployment and unsatisfactory international competitiveness.

With hindsight, the assumption that the EU's relatively poor economic performance in this period was *largely* attributable to the effects of cross-border trade barriers seems highly questionable. It is also now apparent that 'completing' the programme by establishing a framework of laws was insufficient to create an SEM, partly because of omissions in the programme and partly because of incomplete or faulty implementation. But without the hype associated with the programme, it is debatable whether it would ever have been launched.

○ Relaunching the Union

Several other major developments contributed to the adoption of the SEM programme. The landmark *Cassis de Dijon* ruling by the European Court of Justice (ECJ) in 1979 (which established the principle that if a product was fit to be sold in one member state, it was fit to be sold in them all) provided a juridical underpinning for an ambitious programme of market opening. Member states were resorting to technical barriers to protect their industries, resulting in an increase in cases taken to the ECJ. In the early 1980s there was stronger support amongst governments of member states for a programme of market-oriented economic liberalisation than hitherto: the Conservative Party was returned to power in the UK in 1979; in 1982, a CDU-dominated coalition came into office in West Germany; in the early 1980s, the Mitterrand government in France largely abandoned its socialist programme. Although the UK government was opposed to forms of integration which would erode sovereignty, it viewed the SEM programme favourably, as being fully in accordance with its free trade principles. Business interests, notably the Union of Industrial and Employers' Confederations of Europe (UNICE) and the leaders of some of Europe's largest corporations (who in 1983 had formed the 'European Round Table of Industrialists') added their voices to the call for removal of restrictions on cross-border business. The Commission, enthusiastically supported by the European Parliament (EP), was in the vanguard of this mounting pressure for a major attack on market fragmentation. The SEM programme therefore was made possible by a confluence of interests (national governments, the Commission, the EP and business), although the governments of member states, as the key gatekeepers and decision takers, probably had the decisive influence because they had power to make or break plans for the SEM.

The appointment of Jacques Delors to the presidency of the Commission in 1984 was also an important contributory factor. Delors' energy and vision secured him a key role as a change agent in the integration process: his initial idea was to pursue the goal of monetary union rather than an SEM. However, in the mid-1980s, this seemed a rather impractical goal (not least because Mrs Thatcher would not have agreed to it). It became clear that Delors saw the SEM as a means of accelerating European integration. The SEM programme is frequently characterised as an effort to *relaunch* the Union. By the mid-1980s, it was widely felt that European integration had stalled. A fundamental aim of the Treaty of Rome, to create a common market, had not been achieved because many barriers to the free cross-border movement of goods, persons, services and capital remained. The SEM programme was therefore designed to kill two birds with one stone: to enhance the EU's economic performance and (more controversially) to kick start the integration process.

○ Justifying the Single Market Prescription

The Commission produced a wealth of statistics to prove that internal trade barriers were costing the Union dearly in terms of competitiveness, efficiency and jobs. The expected benefits of the SEM were exhaustively elaborated in the officially commissioned Cecchini Report on the 'costs of non-Europe' published in 1988: according to the report, stronger competitive disciplines would force 'flabby' companies to become more efficient by means of a 'supply-side shock'; economies of scale would be reaped, as firms expanded into other EU countries; EU firms would be fitter to compete in global markets. The report, based on a survey of 11,000 firms, estimated that creation of an SEM could have positive results, as itemised in Table 10.1.

Table 10.1 The Benefits of the SEM (Cecchini Estimates)

- a 4.5% increase in GDP (possibly amounting to €200 billion);
- an increase in employment of between 1.8 million and 5 million (job losses would be more than offset by job gains);
- lower prices (of between 4.5% and 6.1%);
- more choice for consumers at more competitive prices;
- an improvement of the external trade balance by 1% of GDP.

The Cecchini Report was widely criticised for being too optimistic in its assessment of the benefits of the SEM (Grahl and Teague, 1990). It was also criticised for giving insufficient weight to the strong possibility that SEM benefits would be distributed very unevenly among member states, regions and industries. With the benefit of hindsight, the report's main weakness was that it underestimated the difficulties involved in realising SEM objectives and this led it to overestimate the likely benefits of the programme.

○ The Main Features of the SEM Programme

The Commission's White Paper entitled *Completing the Internal Market* was approved by the European Council in Milan in June 1985. In December of that year, the Single European Act (SEA) (which amended the Treaty of Rome) was also approved by the European Council in Luxembourg. The act was ratified by all national parliaments and came into force on 1 July 1987. The Danish parliament initially rejected the act, but later accepted it following a referendum. The act defines the SEM as 'an area without internal frontiers in which the free movement of goods, persons, services and capital is ensured' (these became known as the *four freedoms*). A commissioner from the UK, Lord Cockfield, a former chief executive of 'Boots' and a former UK trade and industry minister, was put in charge of drafting the SEM programme. It embraced 289 legislative proposals, many coming into effect at different times, but structured around clear timetables for completion. The legal and institutional framework of the SEM was sought through:

• **Removal of technical barriers,** to enable EU producers to sell their products in any member state, without need to modify these products to conform to different national technical requirements. Given the wide disparities in national regulations and standards within EU12, it was clearly impossible to suddenly replace these with uniform standards. Two strategies were adopted in relation to technical barriers: firstly, *mutual recognition* of existing national standards, providing essential requirements are met. Each member state is required to accept on its territory products and services legally produced and/or sold in other member states; secondly, *harmonisation*, through stipulation of Union-wide 'essential requirements' such as minimum safety, health and environmental standards, in order to simplify technical regulation in Europe. Instead of product by product harmonisation, which is impractical, products are placed into categories, through use of 'new approach' directives. Three bodies have been involved in creating these harmonised standards, namely: CEN (European Committee for Standardisation); CENELEC (European Committee for Electrotechnical Standardisation); and ETSI (European Telecommunications Standards Institute). A 'CE' marking (known as a passport for products in Europe) has been introduced to show that products conform with essential requirements and can be sold anywhere in the Union.

• **Removal of fiscal barriers.** Differences in indirect taxes, in particular value-added tax (VAT) and excise duties, were regarded as major obstacles to cross-border trade. Given the wide disparities in tax systems within the Union and the political sensitivity of taxation, full tax harmonisation was not a realistic goal. Nevertheless, new systems for the collection and control of VAT and excise duty payments have been introduced. It proved impossible to reach full agreement within the Council on approximation of VAT (a minimum rate of 15% has been agreed, with various exceptions, but no maximum rate). Excise duties have traditionally been collected by the country where the goods are consumed, not where they originate, leading to substantial differences in prices paid by consumers in different EU countries. Excise duty is now payable when goods are released to retail outlets for consumption. In general, citizens can buy goods in any member state without having to pay extra taxes, providing that they are for personal use and have been bought 'duty paid'. They have the right to buy substantial quantities of alcohol and tobacco for personal consumption. 'Duty free' shops should be meaningless in a borderless Union. However, following intensive lobbying by affected business interests, a decision was taken in 1991 to allow a long transition period. The transition did not affect citizens' rights with regard to cross-border shopping, because they were still able to buy goods for their own personal use without having to pay additional taxes or excises on their return home. Despite strong pressure from duty free sales operators to maintain duty free, the transition period came to an end on 30 June 1999.

- **Removal of physical barriers.** For example, abolition of customs forms and formalities. A single administrative document for goods transported across EU internal borders was introduced on 1 January 1988, replacing over 150 previous documents. From 1 January 1993, even this was abolished. Liberalisation of transport services has been a key element of the programme, for example, removal of quota restrictions on road haulage.

- **The right to work in other member states.** Nationals of any member state have the right to seek and obtain employment anywhere in the Union and to enjoy the same treatment as nationals of the host state in matters of pay, working conditions and trade union rights, subject to certain restrictions (see Chapter 15), although there is still considerable ignorance among EU citizens concerning their right to work and reside in other member states.

- **Opening up of the professions.** Professionals in many occupations (for example, doctors, architects, engineers) now have the right to have their *vocational* qualifications recognised in other member states.

- **Opening up of financial services.** Cross-border restrictions on the operation of financial services sector businesses, such as banking, securities and insurance, have been largely eliminated. National financial markets have opened, subject to some national measures and derogations. Financial firms can obtain 'financial passports' to operate in any member state. Arrangements for free movement of capital now apply throughout the Union.

- **Opening up of telecommunications.** For example, open competition in telecommunications equipment, voice telephony and the supply of infrastructure and provision of services in fixed and mobile telephony (however, voice telephony was not introduced until 1998, and even then with derogations for countries with less developed systems).

- **Opening up of air transport.** The opening up of domestic markets, through various measures to promote 'freedom of the skies' (see Chapter 13).

- **Opening up of electricity supply,** following a 1996 directive to liberalise electricity markets over nine years (although this has been proceeding more slowly than envisaged).

- **Opening up of gas markets** (although progress has so far been slow).

- **Opening of 'public procurement' markets.** According to Commission estimates, public purchasing amounts to up to 15% of Union GNP. Various public procurement directives, enabling firms to compete for public sector contracts throughout the Union, have now been introduced. Public procurement has proved to be one of the most difficult markets to open up.

● THE WIDER IMPLICATIONS OF THE SEM AND AN EVALUATION

○ The SEM is Not Solely about Trade

The programme is a pivotal event in the development of the Union and has had major internal and external consequences. The Single European Act embraced highly significant institutional and policy changes which went far beyond technical issues of trade. Partly, this was due to the realisation that internal trade barriers could not be effectively removed without substantial changes in other areas of policy and in the way the Union reached its decisions. The act therefore involved various flanking (or 'side') measures, for example, in the fields of social policy and the environment. In recognition of the danger that removal of barriers would exacerbate the problems of the 'periphery' of the EU, by leading to a further shift of business activity towards the more prosperous industrial regions (the 'golden triangle' of London, Paris and the Ruhr), policies to develop the economies of peripheral regions were to be introduced.

The main institutional changes were the extension of majority voting in the Council and increased powers for the European Parliament, which under the co-operation procedure was able to amend or reject proposals (although under conditions which made this difficult). Mrs Thatcher doubted the commitment of some governments to full-blooded trade liberalisation and therefore favoured the use of majority voting in relation to SEM measures. For this reason, she has subsequently been criticised for signing away British sovereignty. However, it is clear that she expected the use of majority voting to be strictly limited to SEM measures. But the broad focus of the SEM programme meant that majority voting covered a wide range of policy areas. 'Integrationists' in the Commission and the Council naturally favoured a broad interpretation of the areas to which it applied (although given the Council's consensual decisionmaking style, votes are by no means always taken). The act also contains references to co-operation between member states in foreign policy, known as 'European Political Co-operation' (EPC).

○ Fortress Europe?

Initially, the EU's leading partners (the US, Japan, and the European Free Trade Association: EFTA) were fearful that the SEM could lead to the creation of a 'Fortress Europe', protecting EU countries from competition from outside the EU. The EU has consistently denied that the SEM is protectionist, and this view has come to be generally (if not universally) accepted. At the European Council in Rhodes in December 1988, the Council explicitly rejected the term Fortress Europe and instead adopted the term 'Partner Europe'. Foreign firms seeking to sell their products in EU markets have benefited from the removal of technical barriers to trade, because their products need to conform to one set of trade and technical standards rather than many. The SEM has also provided the basis for conclusion of mutual recognition agreements (MRAs) for product standards with some countries outside the EU (see Chapter 17). It has also led to the replacement of national trade regimes with an EU trade regime for cars. However, an anticipated effect of the SEM was that it would result in increased intra-EU trade at the expense of EU trade with other countries – the *trade diversion* effect. Fears of adverse trade effects provided a stimulus for non-EU companies and countries to seek closer ties with the Union, in order to circumvent potential barriers and thereby gain access to the Union's big market. Circumvention strategies have included foreign direct investment (establishing production bases within the EU); attempts to negotiate new formal relationships with the EU (for example, the EEA agreement and association agreements); and applications for full EU membership.

○ The European Economic Area (EEA)

The SEM programme provided a powerful stimulus for EFTA countries, which have strong trading links with the Union, to secure continued access to EU markets and to avoid loss of exports through 'trade diversion'. This led to the formation of the EEA, essentially a vehicle for extending the SEM to EFTA countries. Negotiations for an EEA were set in motion by Jacques Delors in a speech to the EP in January 1989. Delors offered EFTA 'a more structured partnership with common decisionmaking and administrative institutions'. This offer was enthusiastically accepted by EFTA. If Delors' overture was designed to discourage EFTA states from applying for full membership of the Union (by offering them an attractive alternative) it backfired: the Commission's tough negotiating stance in the EEA negotiations probably accelerated the decision of several EFTA countries to apply for full EU membership. Doubts about the ultimate purpose of the EEA hung over the negotiations. Thus the EEA could be viewed either as a transitional arrangement leading gradually but inexorably to EU enlargement or as a free-standing structure. The EEA Treaty was signed in Opporto in May 1992 and was due to come into force on the same day as the SEM. However, the rejection of the treaty by the Swiss in a referendum in December 1992 delayed the timetable by a year.

The legal basis of the EEA is the EEA Treaty, plus Community legislation appended to it. The EEA is the world's largest free trade zone, accounting for more than two-fifths of world trade. It is a free trade association, not a customs union and therefore there is no common external tariff. It does not embrace political or monetary union and also excludes agricultural and fisheries policies. The main features of the agreement are: the 'four freedoms' (that is, free movement of goods, services, capital and persons); a competition regime based on EU competition rules; co-operation between the EU and the other signatories in a wide variety of fields, that is, education, research, environmental co-operation protection, social policy, statistics and consumer protection; an EFTA financial support mechanism for poorer EU countries; and new institutions to administer the agreement. The EFTA signatories to the agreement gained access to the SEM, excluding agriculture and fisheries (with the exception of veterinary matters). The EFTA signatories participate in export and advisory committees to the Commission, but are excluded from the Council framework.

By the time the EEA came into being on 1 January 1994, its future was already in doubt as a result of the decision by several EFTA countries to apply for full EU membership. But its formation can still be regarded as an important development, for two principal reasons: negotiations for the EEA served as an important economic and psychological preparation for the fourth enlargement; it offers the remaining EFTA countries an alternative to EU membership. Moreover, it may yet in the long run serve as the framework for a pan-European trade zone embracing both Western and Eastern Europe (and possibly including those East European countries unlikely to be admitted into the Union for the foreseeable future, such as Russia or Ukraine).

❍ Evaluation of the SEM: A Qualified Success or a Damp Squib?

It is difficult to disentangle the effects of the SEM programme from other influences on the economies of member states. The global economic recession weakened the positive effects of market opening, because many companies were not strong enough to expand into other EU markets. Moreover, the full impact of the programme will only be apparent when SEM legislation is comprehensively embedded. In December 1996 the Commission presented an detailed review of the SEM, entitled *The Impact and Effectiveness of the Single Market* (COM (96) 520), to the Dublin European Council. The main positive effects of the SEM identified in the review, based on a large number of commissioned studies, are outlined in Table 10.2. But the report also pointed out many flaws, gaps and implementation deficits in the programme.

Ultimately, any project must be judged in relation to its effectiveness in realising its goals. Despite the tangible achievements listed below, the SEM programme has so far not had the transformative impact on the Union that its architects intended and it is widely acknowledged that much more remains to be done before the SEM is complete.

Table 10.2 Positive Effects of the SEM (The Commission's 1996 Study)

- an increase in employment (300,000 and 900,000 new jobs);
- an increase in Union GDP of between 1.1 and 1.5% by 1994;
- intra-EU manufacturing trade had increased by 20–30%;
- increased FDI (with 44% of global FDI entering the EU in the early 1990s, compared with 28% in the mid-1980s);
- growing competition between companies in manufacturing and services;
- a wider range of products available to consumers at lower prices;
- faster and cheaper cross-frontier deliveries;
- greater mobility between member states for both workers and others;
- confirmation of economic convergence and cohesion between regions;
- substantial gains in efficiency and significant cost reductions in the distribution sector;
- conflicts between 100,000 sets of national technical specifications has been largely overcome;
- abolition of customs documents resulting in savings of €5 bn a year;
- cross-border public procurement purchases increased from 6% in 1987 to 10% in 1994;
- prices of telecommunications equipment decreased by 7% between 1985 and 1995 as a result of SEM measures;
- a 25% increase in the freedom of capital movements since 1990;
- elimination of road haulage quotas and border delays had led to average savings of 5–6% on a typical 1000 km journey;
- 800 new licences to operate in the air transport sector had been granted;
- the number of cross-border bank branches increased by 58% between 1993 and 1995 following introduction of the second banking directive.

Source: Commission (1996)

The Union still suffers from poor competitiveness and productivity relative to the US and higher structural employment. US manufacturing output grew twice as fast as that of the EU between 1980 and 1992. Moreover, from 1992, the US economy had eight years of continuous growth, with expansion of over 4% a year, inflation below 2% and unemployment less than 5%. By contrast, the EU's growth rate in the same period was roughly half the US figure, whereas its unemployment rate was over twice that of the US. There are two possible reasons for the muted impact of the programme so far. It could be due to weaknesses in implementation or to the possibility that the programme was at best a partial solution to the problem of Eurosclerosis. Implementation has certainly been incomplete. The implementation of SEM measures in some key sectors, such as intellectual property and public procurement has been generally poor. Temporary deferrals have also contributed to slow implementation (for example, until July 1994 insurance companies were not able to set up and do business anywhere in the EU; stockbrokers were not able to operate anywhere in the EU until 1996; vocational qualifications were not valid throughout the Union until June 1994; liberalisation of basic telephone services was postponed until 1998). The service sector, now the largest source of employment and output, has proved difficult to deregulate. Even when legislation has been passed by governments, it has by no means always been fully implemented. Removal of non-tariff barriers to trade is hardly sufficient if major impediments to cross-border movement, such as transport and energy bottlenecks, remain.

In recent years, the emphasis in the SEM programme has shifted towards more effective implementation and 'enforcement. In June 1993, the Commission published its *Strategic Programme for the Internal Market*, which gave priority to monitoring, enforcement and evaluation. The Commission's 1995 work programme included a new SEM offensive, aimed at stricter monitoring and enforcement. The Commission has also launched initiatives to develop closer links between national enforcement bodies: for example, the MATTHAUS and KAROLUS programmes involve vocational training and exchanges of officials engaged in implementation of SEM programmes. In 1996, an initiative for simpler legislation for the internal market (SLIM) was launched. A new Commission action plan for the single market (based on recommendations in the December 1996 report on the impact and effectiveness of the SEM) was endorsed by the Amsterdam European Council in June 1997. The action plan outlined details of the priority actions needed to improve the functioning of the SEM by 1 January 1999 and defined four strategic targets: making SEM rules more effective through simplification and enforcement; tackling key market distortions, such as taxation barriers and anti-competitive behaviour; removing sectoral obstacles to market integration (for example, in energy and electronic commerce); and enhancing the social dimension of the SEM by ensuring high levels of health, safety and environmental protection. These actions were to be implemented under a three-phase timetable: *phase 1*: short-term or urgent actions, such as elimination of delays in transposing single market directives; *phase 2*: rapid adoption of a number of existing proposals, such as the European Company statute; and *phase 3*: attaining maximum possible agreement on remaining measures by 1 January 1999

As a result of a proposal in the 1997 Action Plan, a 'Single Market Scoreboard' is now presented to the Council by the Commission every six months. The scoreboard contains a review of the remaining deficits in implementation of SEM measures and also includes feedback from citizens. The scoreboards have repeatedly exposed uneven implementation of single market policies across all sectors within member states. The scoreboards have also highlighted gaps in implementation of legislation in many sectors, including telecommunications, transport, intellectual property, public procurement and the environment. The May 2001 scoreboard (Commission, 2001a) showed that, although the situation was improving, 11.5% of all single market directives had still not been transposed into national law by all member states. Greece, France, Ireland and the UK had the worst records for transposing directives into national law. Conversely, Sweden, Denmark, Finland and Spain had the best records. The scoreboard found that the number of formal infringement proceedings opened by the Commission against member states under Article 226 of the EC Treaty for failure to apply single market rules had increased by 7% since November 2000. Moreover, most infringement cases which eventually end up in the European Court of Justice take at least three years to resolve and many take far longer.

Table 10.3 SEM Implementation Deficits: the May 2001 Scoreboard

	Commission Infringement Proceedings (Totals)	Recent Directives Not Transposed On Time* (%)	Deficits in Transposing SEM Directives (%)
Austria	90	66	3.2
Belgium	123	68	2.4
Denmark	37	79	1.2
Finland	43	82	1.4
France	254	55	3.5
Germany	185	61	2.8
Greece	151	32	4.8
Ireland	119	58	3.3
Italy	251	60	2.6
Lux.	35	70	2.0
Neth.	70	64	2.0
Portugal	78	47	2.7
Spain	208	68	1.8
Sweden	46	77	0.5
UK	93	62	3.3
EU15	1783		11.5+

Note: * % of directives with a transposition date in 2000 actually transposed in that year; + % of directives not transposed by all member states. *Source*: Commission, 2001a.

Commission opinion surveys have also repeatedly shown that few citizens are aware of the extent and limits of their single market rights (leading to considerable misunderstanding on issues such as recognition of qualifications, rights of residence, retirement abroad, health-care entitlements and social security). The Commission has identified a raft of difficulties people have in exercising these rights, due to excessive bureaucracy and misapplication of rules by authorities within member states. The Commission's 1999 review of the internal market strategy (Commission, 1999a) pointed out a familiar catalogue of gaps in the SEM: for example, a fully integrated European financial market had still not been achieved; state aids were still too high; there were still barriers to trade in services; no agreement had been reached on a European Company statute (although member states did finally reach an agreement on this statute in December 2000 – see Chapter 9); there was still no measurable impact on public procurement markets; and tax competition still distorted the functioning of the single market. In November 1999, the Commission set out a new strategy for the SEM over the next five years. The strategy seeks to enhance the efficiency of product and capital markets, improve the business environment and exploit achievements of the internal market. It incorporates the financial services action plan agreed in May 1999 and measures to combat unfair tax competition. But the Commission's drive against tax competition (Table 10.4 below) is proving to be an uphill struggle.

It is clear that much remains to be done to fully embed and apply SEM rules. Fifteen years after the launch of the SEM programme, the Lisbon European Council asked for liberalisation in fields such as energy, transport and postal services to be speeded up. However, the Commission's 2001 review of the internal market strategy criticised member states' failure to agree on further liberalisation measures in any of these three sectors. It also criticised the failure to develop a Community patent. It noted that of the 36 SEM actions scheduled to be achieved by June 2001, only 20 were expected to be completed on time (Commission, 2001b). At the Stockholm European Council in March 2001, member states again failed to agree on a Community patent or a date for full liberalisation of the gas and electricity markets.

Nevertheless, the SEM has been a powerful force for the de-regulation of markets in the EU, through the removal of barriers to cross-border competition. However, it has also been a powerful force for the *re*-regulation of these markets, through the imposition of EU-wide regulations, for example, by setting common standards for products. The programme proved that member states could develop and carry through an ambitious collaborative project. It created the world's biggest single market, 40% larger than the US market and three times larger than the Japanese market. It provided the momentum for the proposals for European Union agreed at Maastricht, in particular for economic and monetary union. It has been a major stimulus to the removal of barriers to the cross-border movement of EU citizens. It has loomed large in accession negotiations for the Central and East European countries, because candidate countries are required to accept and conform to all SEM legislation (a formidable hurdle). In this sense, the SEM programme provides some support for the 'neofunctionalist' explanation of EU integration, in that the pursuit of deeper market integration has spilled over into other areas, such as EMU, enlargement and employment policy.

Table 10.4 Tax Competition in the European Union

Taxation is usually regarded as a core function of states and therefore is bound up with questions of sovereignty. Each member state has its own system of taxation. There are wide variations between member states in corporation taxes, personal income taxes and indirect taxes. For example, a single person on an average wage may pay income tax at 7.2% in Portugal and 38.3% in Denmark. There is a minimum normal rate of VAT of 15% but no maximum rate. In 1999, the normal rate varied from 15% in Luxembourg to 25% in Denmark and Sweden. Examples of aspects of tax systems which may distort competition include tax havens, double taxation of corporate and personal incomes and exemption from taxation of non-residents' savings income. There is competition by authorities offering tax incentives for investment, even though this may breach Union rules. As capital has become more mobile, tax has also become an important factor in location decisions for multinational corporations. With the removal of other barriers to cross-border trade, including the elimination of exchange rate risk as a result of introduction of the euro, differences in national tax systems become more visible. The complexity and diversity of tax regimes within the EU also increases the possibility of tax avoidance and evasion.

In October, 1996 the Commission outlined the forms of tax competition detrimental to the SEM in a report entitled *Taxation in the European Union, Report on the Development of Tax Systems* (COM (96) 546). The following year it proposed a package of measures to deal with harmful tax competition, including a code of conduct for business taxation (which would not be legally binding), measures to eliminate distortions in taxation of capital income; measures to eliminate withholding taxes on cross-border interest and royalty payments between companies; and measures to eliminate significant distortions in indirect taxation (see *Towards Tax Co-ordination in the EU: A Package to Tackle Harmful Tax Competition* (COM (97) 495). However, it encountered considerable resistance on the part of some member states to these proposals.

The UK and Luxembourg have rejected proposals for a withholding tax, because they want exemptions for certain investments such as Eurobonds. At the Feira European Council, an alternative to the withholding tax was agreed. Under the new plan, the EU has two years to agree an exchange of information on overseas savings accounts in all international financial centres. Only if that is agreed will the EU enter a seven-year transitional period in which countries can either levy the tax or exchange information on savers. After that, all EU countries will exchange information. At the 2000 IGC concluded in Nice, the UK, Luxembourg and Ireland refused to allow extension of QMV to taxation. However, it seems likely that further attempts will be made to address the issue of tax competition.

● THE STRATEGY FOR GROWTH, COMPETITIVENESS AND EMPLOYMENT

In the early 1990s, Eurosclerosis led to a search for other possible causes of the EU's continuing economic malaise such as low investment, poor infrastructure, high labour costs, low labour market flexibility and technological backwardness. It also led to a search for appropriate solutions, such as labour market deregulation, reskilling, increased investment, lower taxes and protection from 'unfair' competition. At the European Council in Copenhagen in June 1993, the Commission was asked to prepare a White Paper on the EU's jobs crisis. The White Paper, *Growth, Competitiveness and Employment*, was adopted by the European Council in Brussels in December 1993. The paper put forward a strategy (which became known as the Delors growth strategy) to create 15 million new jobs by the year 2000, thereby reducing EU unemployment rates from the current 10.4% to 5%. The White Paper rejected various solutions, including a resort to protectionism; a 'dash for growth' (meaning a big increase in government spending and consequent inflation); a generalised reduction in working hours and job sharing; or drastic cuts in wages. It argued that there was no way the EU could reduce its labour costs to the level of Eastern Europe or China. It put forward many specific proposals, such as measures to improve the EU's infrastructure; more research and technological development (RTD) investment; employment incentives and more investment in training. Its key proposal in relation to external trade was that European firms should be encouraged to 'trade up' to higher added value activities, such as the information technology and biotechnology industries. The strategy lacked the coherence of the SEM programme. But it contained measures to address many deficiencies in the EU's economic performance (see Table 10.5).

The strategy would be financed through mixtures of private sector funding and public sector loans, via the EU budget, the European Investment Bank (EIB) and 'Union bonds' issued by the Commission on behalf of the EU. The Union bonds proposal (which would have given the Commission its own fund-raising powers) was vetoed by the European Council, because it would have increased public spending and might have undermined the EIB's role. The European Council did, however, accept the broad thrust of the Delors growth strategy. It also agreed to the creation of a new financial institution, known as the European Investment Fund (EIF) to bring together investors from the public and private sectors. But it has proved difficult to find adequate finance for large infrastructure projects, such as trans-European networks (TENs). Although spending on RTD has increased, the technology gap between the EU and the US, particularly with regard to high-tech industries, remains wide.

Table 10.5 The Delors Growth Strategy: Specific Measures

- new incentives for part-time work;
- tax incentives for small firms to create jobs;
- training schemes for unqualified school leavers;
- switching some labour costs from employers to general taxation;
- non-wage social security costs to be made more progressive, to encourage more jobs for the less skilled;
- enabling social security to 'top up' income from work;
- greater wage flexibility;
- promoting training and 'know-how';
- increased investment in industry and in infrastructure;
- a higher investment rate of 23–24% of GNP (from about 19%);
- a target of 3% of GNP to be spent on RTD;
- reorienting government support for industry towards growth sectors;
- increases in spending on transport and energy networks;
- the creation of 'information highways' for telecommunications;
- new environmental projects;
- a network of European science parks.

The strategy contained a variety of proposals, some of which were problematic from the outset. For example, some proposals had high price tags (requiring substantial new investment and new policy commitments); some raised contentious ideological issues, not least concerning the role of government in business; and some raised questions concerning how national and Union-level policies could be reconciled. In some key ways, therefore, the Delors growth strategy was overambitious (particularly with regard to the financing of TENs). In any case, the strategy was to some extent overtaken events, as the focus of the Union's decisionmakers shifted more towards the launch of EMU and preparations for enlargement. For example, some of the elements of the strategy were at odds with the squeeze on public sector budgets, due not least to pressures to meet the Maastricht convergence criteria for EMU and the budgetary reforms proposed in *Agenda 2000*. Delors' retirement from the Commission presidency was also detrimental to the plan, because the next incumbent was less closely associated with it.

Nevertheless many of the elements of the strategy, in particular the need for more investment in high-tech industries, training and infrastructure, are reflected in current policies. Although some TENs projects have run into difficulties due to lack of finance, others are on target for completion or have already been finished. The Delors targets for increasing industrial investment have not yet been realised (between 1960 and 1998, levels of investment in the EU fell from about 22% to about 18% of GDP). By the end of the decade, there was increasing realisation that the EU's economies needed to adapt to rapid changes in technology in order to boost growth and employment, in particular to cope with the challenges of electronic commerce. The Treaty of Nice will extend qualified majority voting (QMV) and co-decision to measures supporting the action of member states in the industrial sphere (Article 157, ECT), but explicitly excludes tax provisions or provisions relating to the rights and interests of employed persons.

● THE 'e-EUROPE' INITIATIVE: PANACEA OR TRENDY GIMMICK?

The e-Europe initiative was launched by the Commission in December 1999 in a communication entitled *e-Europe – An Information Society for All* (Commission, 1999b). The initiative was motivated by a growing realisation of the importance of digital technologies for growth and employment. The initiative was approved by the Helsinki European Council and further developed by the Lisbon and Feira European Councils. A progress report on the initiative considered by the Lisbon European Council pointed out a number of advantages of e-commerce, such as lower input prices, lower inventories, reduced time to market, lower transaction costs, greater global reach and lower market entry costs. It predicted that e-commerce would grow 40 times between 1998 and 2003. The report recognised that the EU was lagging behind the US in internet-driven business in most sectors. It estimated that there were 2.3 million internet-related jobs in the US in 1999 (there were no comparable statistics for the EU, but it conceded that these were likely to be significantly lower). It noted that penetration of the internet into US households was 2–3 times higher than in Europe, with the exception of Nordic countries.

A directive on electronic commerce was approved by the Council in February 2000 and by the EP in May 2000. Member states have up to 18 months to implement the directive into national law following its publication in the EU's *Official Journal*. The directive establishes harmonised rules for the supply and receipt of information society services throughout the EU. The directive covers all information society services and prohibits member states from imposing special authorisation schemes and obliges member states to remove prohibitions or restrictions on the use of electronic contracts. It applies the principle of mutual recognition, so that services provided from another member state are not restricted, except to protect the public interest (for example, on grounds of bigotry, hate, public health or security).

The Commission's draft action plan on e-Europe presented to the Feira European Council in June 2000 set out ideas to increase use of the internet in the EU and also to make it cheaper, faster and more secure. A high-level group concerned with the 'Employment and Social Dimension of the Information Society' (ESDIS), and comprising member state representatives, annually monitors the actions set out in the plan and contributes to the assessment of its impact on employment. But, as the EU's previous 'transformation strategies' have shown, it is one thing to recognise the importance of major economic or industrial trends: developing effective policies to reap the benefits of these trends is quite another.

● CONCLUSION

Since the mid-1980s, the Union has launched a series of initiatives designed to deal with its sluggish economic performance (when measured in particular against its major rival in the global economy, the United States). So far, none of these initiatives has succeeded in enabling the Union to match the US in terms of growth, competitiveness and employment creation. Some analysts argue that the principal reasons for this are that the real causes of the Union's relative economic weaknesses (such as rigidities in labour markets, insufficient market deregulation and lack of investment) have not been fully addressed because of the difficulties involved in securing the agreement of all member states on effective measures to deal with these issues.

FURTHER READING

Armstrong, K.A. and Bulmer, S.J. (1998), *The Governance of the European Single Market*, Manchester University Press, Manchester.

Cecchini, P. (1988), *The European Challenge: 1992 The Benefits of a Single Market*, Wildwood House, Aldershot.

Commission (1985), *Completing the Internal Market*, COM (85) 310.

Commission (1993), *Growth, Competitiveness and Employment*, COM (93) 700.

Commission (1996), *The Impact and Effectiveness of the Single Market*, COM (96) 520.

Commission (1999a), *Review of the Internal Market*, COM (99) 464.

Commission (1999b), e-*Europe – An Information Society for All*, COM (99) 687.

Commission (2000), e-*Europe Action Plan*, presented to the Feira European Council.

Commission (2001a), *Internal Market Scoreboard*, no. 8, May 2001

Commission (2001b), *2001 Review of the Internal Market Strategy*, COM (2001) 198.

Darmer, M. and Kuyper, L. (eds) (2000), *Industry and the European Union*, Edward Elgar, Cheltenham and Northampton, MA.

Grahl, J. and Teague, P. (1990), *1992: The Big Market*, Lawrence & Wishart, London.

Chapter 11

Economic and Monetary Union

● BACKGROUND

On 1 January 1999, 11 member states effectively replaced their national currencies with a single European currency, the euro. In January 2001, Greece became the twelfth member of the 'eurozone'. Although euro notes and coin will not begin to be issued until the autumn of 2001, in all other respects the euro already exists as a real currency. On 28 February 2002, the national notes and coin of the participating states will cease to be legal tender, being fully replaced by the euro. Already in its short life, the euro project has shown a capacity to confound both pessimistic and optimistic predictions concerning its future. For example, 'Eurosceptic' assertions that the euro project would be abandoned before it was even launched and 'Europhile' assertions that the new currency would soon rival the dollar as an international reserve currency have both proved wide of the mark.

The ultimate goal of economic and monetary union (EMU) is the replacement of the currencies of all member states by a single currency. EMU is undoubtedly the most ambitious, far-reaching and controversial integration project ever undertaken by the Union. It is also perhaps the riskiest. If it succeeds, it could well lead to a substantial deepening of political and economic integration in the Union. If it fails, the Union project could well be seriously damaged. For Euro-integrationists, a single currency is viewed as a logical corollary of the SEM programme and as an essential feature of a fully developed Union. For Eurosceptics, EMU constitutes a nightmare scenario, confirming their worst fears about the threat to state sovereignty of deeper European integration. It is perhaps not surprising that Euro-integrationists have pursued the goal of EMU with such dogged determination, or that

Eurosceptics remain resolutely opposed to it.

There have been many previous examples of monetary unions, some of which have succeeded and some of which have not. For example, we can cite monetary union between England and Scotland (1707); the monetary unification of Italy (1861); the Scandinavian currency union (1873–1920); monetary union between Belgium and Luxembourg (1923); the Soviet Union (1917–1993); the West African franc zone (1948); and the post-cold war monetary unification of west and east Germany (1990). However, EMU is fundamentally different from any previous monetary union in its scale and implications: never before have so many countries voluntarily relinquished their own currencies or ceded sovereignty in the monetary field to a supranational body, the European Central Bank (ECB). Moreover, the euro is a *stateless currency* and there is no prior example of a lasting monetary union which has not been anchored to a state.

Most previous attempts at monetary union were undertaken for political rather than economic reasons (most recently German reunification) and many have failed also for political reasons. Similarly, EMU also has underlying *political*, as well as economic objectives. For example, former Chancellor Helmut Kohl of Germany said on many occasions that the project would help to underpin post-war peace and stability in Europe. German governments have consistently argued that political union must accompany monetary union, implying an element of sacrifice in the decision to replace the Deutschmark (DM) with the euro. Indeed, if economic reasons were the sole drivers of EMU, then it is likely that EMU either would not yet have been launched (because of the fact that the EU is far from being an optimal currency area) or alternatively would have been confined to a smaller club of states, that is, those with similar business cycles.

The Treaty of Rome did not refer to the goal of a single currency, or indeed to a system for co-ordinating monetary policy. But from the late 1960s, the need to secure greater monetary stability became increasingly apparent, following recurring crises in the international monetary system. The 'Bretton Woods' system of fixed exchange rates finally collapsed in 1971. In 1969, the Commission proposed the Barre Plan (named after the commissioner who produced it) for greater co-operation and mutual assistance in financial crises. The following year, the Werner Report (named after its main author, the prime minister of Luxembourg) proposed a phased economic and monetary union by 1980. But this was an idea ahead of its time, not least because of the low priority accorded by member states to deeper integration in this period. An agreement to restrict fluctuations between member currencies within a range of ±2.25%, known as the 'Snake', was introduced in 1972. But the Snake was a venomless beast, quite unable to cope with the turmoil in global currency markets. Nevertheless, efforts to enhance monetary co-operation between member states continued. Following decisions taken by the Brussels European Council in December 1978, a European Monetary System (EMS) was established in March 1979. The EMS was designed to create a zone of monetary stability, by reducing fluctuations in the exchange rates of member currencies. It also sought to impose greater disciplines on members by inhibiting resort to unilateral devaluations.

Table 11.1 Some Key Events on the Road to EMU

- **1970: the Werner Report,** advocated a 3-stage plan for EMU (including centralisation of tax policy) by 1980. It was not adopted;
- **1979: the European Monetary System (EMS),** aimed to create a 'zone of monetary stability in Europe'. This included the *Exchange Rate Mechanism* (ERM) for exchange rate stabilisation;
- **April 1989: the Delors Report** advocated a 3-stage plan for EMU, without centralisation of tax policy;
- **June 1989: the Madrid European Council** accepted the Delors Report and convened an intergovernmental conference (IGC) on EMU;
- **July 1990:** start of stage 1 of EMU (lifting of capital controls);
- **December 1991: Conclusion of the IGC on EMU** and negotiation of the TEU at the Maastricht European Council. Much of the TEU concerns provisions for EMU. It laid down strict 'convergence criteria' required for countries to qualify for participation in the final stage of EMU;
- **January 1994:** start of stage 2. European Monetary Institute established;
- **December 1995: the Madrid European Council** decided on the timetable for changeover and the name 'euro';
- **June 1997: the Amsterdam European Council** agreed on a Stability and Growth Pact and a new version of the ERM (ERM 2);
- **May 1998:** the Council meeting as heads of state or government decided which countries could participate in the final stage of EMU; set bilateral conversion rates; and chose the ECB president and Executive Board;
- **July 1998:** ECB and System of Central Banks set up;
- **January 1999:** start of stage 3. Launch of the euro: exchange rates of participating states irrevocably fixed; foreign exchange operations in euros; execution of single monetary policy;
- **25 September 2000:** 'G7' intervention to halt falling value of the euro;
- **28 September 2000:** Danish referendum on the euro;
- **January 2001:** Greece becomes the 12th member of the eurozone;
- **from 1 January 2002:** general circulation of euro notes and coins (banks and large retailers issued with euros in late 2001);
- **by 28 February 2002 at the latest:** all national banknotes and coins removed from circulation.

● THE EUROPEAN MONETARY SYSTEM

The EMS comprised: the European currency unit (ECU), the Exchange Rate Mechanism (ERM) and – from 1 January 1994 – the European Monetary Institute (EMI). The EMI took over the tasks of the European Monetary Co-operation Fund (EMCF) which had operated since 1973.

○ The ECU

The ECU was introduced in 1975, replacing the book-keeping unit known as the 'European Unit of Account'. It was a nominal currency, made up of a basket of all EC currencies, weighted according to the strengths of the economies of member states. These weights were defined in units per ECU. The currency composition of the ECU was reviewed every five years, but was 'frozen' when the Treaty on European Union (TEU) came into effect. The ECU was not legal tender and did not exist in note or coin form. In other respects it was regarded as a currency and could be used in settlements between organisations or individuals. It was the unit of account for the EU budget. It was traded on foreign exchanges and there was a substantial ECU bond market. It was used far more in financial settlements than in trade transactions (only about 1% of trade transactions were settled in ECU). Individuals could buy travellers' cheques, unit trusts and mortgages in ECU because it was recognised by EU banks, although these uses were very limited. In December 1995, the Madrid European Council opted for the title 'euro' instead of ECU as the name of the future single currency, signalling the demise of the ECU.

○ The European Monetary Co-operation Fund

The EMCF was established in 1973 to facilitate currency transactions between member states. EMCF credit facilities were used to settle obligations deriving from interventions in the foreign exchange markets by the central banks of member states. Participants deposited 20% of their gold reserves and 20% of their dollar reserves in return for ECUs of the same value. In accordance with the TEU's provisions for Stage 2 of EMU, the EMCF was dissolved and its tasks taken over by the EMI.

○ The Exchange Rate Mechanism

The ERM was established in 1979 as a mechanism for reducing fluctuations in the relative values of member currencies. It operated on the basis of mutual support and collective action by the central banks of the member states. The central banks intervened in the currency markets, by buying or selling member currencies to influence their value. Intervention was based on the laws of supply and demand: when a currency rose or fell in value to above or below an agreed level (known as a fluctuation margin or band) the central banks were expected to act to restore the value of the currency to within the prescribed limits. At the time of the ERM crises in the summer of 1992, the ERM had ten members. Spain joined in June 1987, the UK in October 1990 and Portugal in April 1992. Greece never participated (its economy was too weak) and Luxembourg based its franc on the Belgian franc. The ERM was based on a parity grid system, meaning that each member currency was allowed to fluctuate by a limited amount from a fixed par value with regard to every other currency in the system. An ECU central rate was determined for each currency, which enabled the central rates between all currencies to be calculated. When the upper or lower limit between two currencies was reached, the bank with the strong currency sold its own currency in exchange for the weak currency and vice versa. The most common measure of divergence was deviation from bilateral DM central rates, because of the strength of the DM.

Before the crises of 1992–93, ERM members kept their currencies within a set margin of fluctuation against a central rate established for each currency: ±2.25% within the normal (or narrow) band, or ±6% within the wide band. These rates were agreed at meetings of the ECOFIN Council (comprising the finance ministers of member states). The wide band was regarded as provisional, in that all countries were expected to enter the narrow band as soon as circumstances permitted. The UK, Spain and Portugal were in the wide band in August 1992. Italy had moved from the wide to the narrow band in January 1990. In practice, interventions took place before currencies reached their upper or lower bands. Divergence indicators signalled that a currency was deviating too much from the average and were designed to provoke a timely response before a currency reached its permitted limit. Currencies could also be realigned by common agreement. There were 12 realignments of central rates between 1979 and 1991, although most of these were in the early years of the system. In the later years, realignments were fewer and smaller in scale. This served to further strengthen confidence in the soundness of the mechanism.

The ERM came into operation in the year Mrs Thatcher came to power in the UK. She opposed the ERM on the grounds that it distorted market forces and limited the capacity of governments to make decisions appropriate to domestic conditions. However, by the late 1980s, there was a strong groundswell of opinion in the UK in favour of entry, not least because the ERM was widely perceived to have played a key role in securing monetary stability and low inflation within the ERM zone in the 1980s. By contrast, the

UK experienced wide sterling fluctuations throughout this decade. The critical mass of support for entry proved too strong for Mrs Thatcher to resist. Chancellor John Major took the UK into the ERM in October 1990. The main benefits of entry for the UK were perceived to be counterinflationary discipline and reduction in currency risks for UK businesses. The DM was the linchpin of the ERM, because of the strength of the German economy and the reputation of the Bundesbank for financial prudence. Ironically, the UK entered in the month when Germany was reunified, an event which placed severe strains on the mechanism. Sterling entered the wide band of the system at a rate of DM 2.95, which most analysts now agree was too high to sustain in the long term because of the weakness of the UK economy.

○ The Faultlines in the ERM Exposed: 'Black Wednesday'

The crises of 1992–93 (leading to two withdrawals, five realignments and a move to 15% fluctuation bands) ended 13 years of stability within the ERM. Because the ERM was widely regarded at the time as fundamentally sound, it figured prominently in the Maastricht blueprint for monetary union. However, on 16 September 1992 ('Black Wednesday'), sterling and the lira were forced out of the ERM by currency speculation: the Spanish peseta was devalued by 5%, and by another 6% in November, together with the Portuguese escudo (also by 6%). The Irish punt, the Danish krone and the French franc also came under attack from speculators. By the end of 1992, sterling and the lira had depreciated by about 15% and 16%, respectively. Between January and July 1993, ERM currencies came under renewed speculative attack, forcing a move to broader fluctuation bands of ±15% on 2 August 1993 for eight currencies (the exceptions being the DM and the Dutch guilder). Other than as a face-saving exercise, and as a symbol of a refusal to admit that the ERM was effectively suspended, the bands were so wide as to appear meaningless.

Why did these crises occur? Apprehension over the future of the TEU (following the outcome of the first Danish referendum and the looming French referendum) has been cited as a precipitating factor of the 1992 crisis. But this does not explain why the mechanism proved too fragile to withstand uncertainties concerning the TEU. German economic and monetary policy was widely regarded as a fundamental cause of the 1992–93 crises. Because the DM was the linchpin of the system, the fate of the ERM was greatly influenced by developments in the German economy. In order to finance reunification, the German government chose a policy of borrowing rather than raising taxes or revaluing the DM. The Bundesbank was determined to maintain a tight monetary policy. To stem rising inflation, German interest rates were kept high. To prevent their currencies depreciating against the DM, the interest rates of other members had to be maintained at a high level.

According to British Eurosceptics, the consequences of the UK's ERM membership were high interest rates, economic stagnation, bankruptcies and higher unemployment (although the underlying weakness of the UK economy obviously pre-dated UK entry into the ERM). The cause of the crises in 1992–93 was also attributed to insufficient co-operation between member countries and to the inflexible manner in which the mechanism was operated. It has been argued that parities ought to have been adjusted more frequently. By contrast, Eurosceptics argued that the very principle of the ERM, which centred on government intervention to counteract market forces, was fundamentally flawed. Arguably, global currency markets are now far too large to be 'bucked', even by collective intervention: over €1.7 trillion is traded daily on world currency markets, which is estimated to be about 2.5 times the official reserves of the ten leading industrialised nations.

○ The Effects of Black Wednesday

The near collapse of the ERM threatened the plan for EMU as laid down in the TEU. Although the day of the UK's exit from the ERM was dubbed 'Black Wednesday', it enabled the UK government to lower interest rates by half in order to boost economic recovery. Sterling was also devalued, making British exports cheaper. But the UK's exit from the ERM was no unmixed blessing, because it made its imports more expensive and increased foreign exchange risks for UK businesses. After the move to wide fluctuation bands in August 1993, turmoil in the ERM subsided. The new bands were so wide that speculators had no clear target at which to aim. There were no dramatic currency adjustments in the following year. The French and Belgian francs and the Irish punt were soon back within the narrow bands. But in March 1995, the peseta and the escudo were devalued by 7% and 3.5%, respectively.

Suggestions for reform of the ERM centred on the need for greater operational flexibility and for new mechanisms for action before crises develop ('fire prevention' rather than 'fire fighting'). But the move towards the single currency in the late 1990s rendered this debate far less important than it had been: an ERM is only required when countries have separate currencies. However, four out of the 15 EU countries did not participate in the launch of the euro on 1 January 1999. Arguably therefore, until all EU countries move to the euro, there remains a need for an ERM to foster currency stability between remaining national currencies and the euro (see Table 11.2 below). A 'post-EMU' version of the ERM, known as 'ERM2' was launched in 1999, although of the four countries outside the eurozone, only two (Greece and Denmark) joined it. It involves intervention by the ECB and the central banks of the participating countries when exchange rates move outside ±15% of the central rate. As Greece and Denmark signalled their wish to join the eurozone by 2001, the primary function of ERM2 as a staging post for entry into the eurozone became clear (despite the 'no' vote in the Danish referendum in September 2000). Indeed, according to Article 121 of the TEU, a qualification for entry is that applicants must have observed the normal fluctuation margins provided by the ERM for at least two years. It remains to be seen how strictly this requirement will be adhered to.

Table 11.2 The ERM Debate

Advantages of ERM1
(as frequently mentioned by its proponents prior to the 1992–93 crises)
- a more stable financial environment: it provided a semi-fixed exchange rate system which reduced the risks faced by businesses;
- collective action: countries did not have to rely solely on their own efforts to maintain the relative value of their currencies;
- it imposed counterinflationary disciplines, by limiting the extent to which a currency was allowed to depreciate. If firms in one member country raised their prices above those of competitors in other EU countries, they would not have been able to sell their goods.

Weaknesses of ERM1
(according to its detractors)
- it was based on the dubious assumption that currency values could be maintained through collective government intervention, that is, that governments could buck the market;
- it was based on the equally dubious assumption that, when the chips were down, central banks would defend other countries' currencies;
- it was a fair-weather system: there was a long period when it seemed to work (currencies were relatively stable and inflation was relatively low), but it could not cope with the consequences of German reunification;
- it provided rich pickings for speculators, who had a guaranteed buyer of weak currencies in the system – the central banks of member countries;
- loss of monetary sovereignty: governments could not set interest rates to meet national economic requirements, because the economic policies of weak currency countries are dominated by those of the strongest.

The Aims of ERM2
- to help ensure that participating member states outside the euro area have stability-oriented policies;
- to provide these countries with a reference for the conduct of sound economic policies in general and monetary policy in particular;
- to foster convergence as countries prepare for entry into the eurozone;
- to help to protect them from pressures in the foreign exchange market.

● ENTER THE EURO

The gestation of the momentous decision to adopt EMU in many ways typified the Union's policymaking style: firstly, it involved bargains, compromises and trade-offs between member states (by no means all of whom were committed to the project from the outset); secondly, it involved the formation of coalitions of interests (in particular certain governments, supported by the Commission); thirdly, the European public was hardly involved. The French government was principal instigator of the EMU initiative, which it saw as a means of obtaining greater influence over European monetary policy (the strength of the German economy and of the DM meant that existing arrangements were perceived as unduly influenced by German domestic concerns). France received strong support from the Commission and Italy, which had a history of monetary weakness. Germany, with a post-war history of monetary strength, was unenthusiastic but was persuaded to support it in return for commitments to pursue parallel political union and for a strong influence on the EMU model. The UK Conservative government was strongly opposed. Poorer countries sought commitments to financial transfers, to offset the potentially negative effects of the transition to EMU. The outcome was that France obtained a clear EMU timetable; Germany obtained a Bundesbank model of EMU, commitment to strict convergence criteria and to pursuit of political union; the four poorest states obtained the Cohesion Fund; and the UK, and later Denmark, obtained formal opt-outs. Table 11.3 below outlines the main arguments for and against EMU.

○ The Delors Report on EMU

In June 1988, the Hanover European Council instructed Commission President Delors to head a committee to work out a plan for EMU. The committee included the 12 governors of the national central banks. Its remit was to focus on practical issues. The committee's report (*Report on Economic and Monetary Union* or the Delors Report), presented in April 1989, favoured a phased approach to EMU based on three stages. It recommended creation of a European system of central banks and emphasised the need for greater co-ordination and convergence of economic and monetary policies. It did not go so far as to *explicitly* recommend a single currency, but its idea for a currency area in which exchange rate parities would be irrevocably locked was a small step from this goal. The UK strongly opposed its main recommendations, on the grounds that they threatened sovereignty. The Madrid European Council in June 1989 reached a compromise: the date for the start of the first stage was set for 1 July 1990. An intergovernmental conference (IGC) was convened to consider the later stages.

Table 11.3 Arguments For and Against Monetary Union

For

- **completion of the single market:** 'one market needs one money';
- **faster and cheaper monetary transfers:** elimination of currency conversion costs and insurance against fluctuating currency values (estimated by the Commission to be 0.3–0.4% of EU GDP);
- **reduction of business risk** for trade and investment through elimination of exchange rate fluctuations. Businesses can quote prices for goods to be sold elsewhere in the EU without the risk of profits being wiped out by currency movements;
- **transparency of prices:** consumers can know how much the same goods cost in each member state; firms and individuals will recognise the need for wage and price discipline;
- **monetary discipline:** governments will no longer be able to use currencies as instruments of economic policy, for example, by printing more money or devaluing, to avoid tough and unpopular measures;
- **lower inflation,** due to the disciplines imposed on EU economies;
- **the merger of financial markets** could lead to economies of scale;
- **increased efficiency and higher economic growth,** due to increased cross-border competition and a more stable financial environment;
- **international clout,** giving the EU greater weight in the international monetary system;
- **it will foster the goal of political union,** by establishing an additional common link between citizens of the EU;
- **the alternatives are worse:** for example, floating rates are inimical to the goal of a single market; the ERM has serious flaws.

Against

- **loss of national sovereignty over monetary affairs** (for example, the power of national governments to change interest rates);
- **loss of flexibility:** the ability of governments to insulate their countries from adverse economic trends in other countries will be weakened;
- **EU economies are too dissimilar for EMU to make sense:** convergence of business cycles and of living standards in the EU is needed before a move to monetary union becomes feasible;
- **the EU is not an optimum currency area,** because it lacks wage flexibility, high labour mobility and sufficient fiscal transfers. It could lead to more unemployment, because the effects of poor competitiveness can no longer be cushioned by a depreciating currency;
- **divisiveness:** it will divide the EU into 'insider' and 'outsider' countries;
- **costs:** the effort and expense of monetary union is simply not worth it.

○ The Maastricht Schedule for EMU

The outcome of the IGC on EMU, together with the Delors Report, formed the basis of the agreements on EMU reached at Maastricht. The main thrust of the TEU's references to economic and monetary policy was towards ever closer integration. The treaty set out a timetable towards monetary union, an institutional framework for the Union's central bank and its system of central banks, and a set of convergence criteria for the economies of member states. It defined the respective roles of the ECB and the Council (that is, ECOFIN) in monetary policy. It also set out EMU's goals: the importance of prudent financial management, price stability and sound public finances constitute an underlying theme of the TEU programme for EMU. According to the treaty, full EMU was expected to be achieved in three stages:

- **Stage 1** (1 July 1990 to 31 December 1993). The central elements of the first stage had been agreed prior to Maastricht. It embraced the abolition of remaining restrictions on capital movements, completion of the SEM, reduction of exchange rate fluctuations and greater co-ordination of economic and monetary policies. In March 1990, the Council agreed a convergence framework, involving adoption of an annual economic report and multilateral surveillance over member states' economic policies. Member states were required to regard their economic policies as a matter of 'common concern', and to co-ordinate them within the Council (Article 99, ECT). Closer co-ordination and convergence of the economic performance of member states was monitored through the surveillance procedure, involving submission of reports from the Commission to the Council. If the economic policies of a member state were judged inconsistent with broad economic policy guidelines set by the Council, the Council could by qualified majority voting (QMV) on a recommendation from the Commission make recommendations to the state concerned. Before the start of Stage 2, the Council was also required (on the basis of a Commission report) to assess progress with regard to economic and monetary convergence and implementation of the Single European Market.

- **Stage 2** (from 1 January 1994). This transition period embraced closer alignment and convergence of member states' economies, moves towards independence by the central banks and establishment of the European Monetary Institute. The EMI, based in Frankfurt, started operations on 1 January 1994. The EMI Council consisted of an independent president plus the governors of the national central banks (NCBs), one of whom was vice-president. The EMI was responsible for strengthening co-operation between the NCBs; strengthening co-ordination of monetary policies; monitoring the functioning of the EMS; facilitating use of the ECU and laying the foundations for later stages of EMU. Its resources consisted of contributions from the central banks based on a weighting of 50% population/50% GDP.

During this stage, the Commission and the EMI reported to the Council on progress made on economic and monetary convergence, with particular reference to quantitative reference targets or 'convergence indicators' (Article 121, ECT), as shown in Table 11.4.

Table 11.4 The Numerical Convergence Indicators

- **low inflation** (an average of not more than 1.5% higher than that of the three best-performing states in the year prior to examination);
- **low long-term interest rates** (no more than 2% higher than the three best-performing states in the year prior to examination);
- **a budget deficit of no more than 3% of GDP**;
- **a public debt ratio of no more than 60% of GDP**;
- **two years' currency stability within the ERM** (a member's currency would have to be in the normal fluctuation margins of the ERM and without being devalued on its own initiative against the currency of any member state for at least two years).

The reports of the Commission and the EMI were also required to take into account other factors, such as results of the integration of markets, balances of payments, unit labour costs and other price indices. Only states meeting the necessary conditions could join Stage 3. On the basis of reports from the Commission and the EMI, the Council acting by QMV assessed whether member states meet these conditions. The Council recommended its findings to the Council 'meeting in the composition of heads of state or of government' (which also received the opinion of the European Parliament: EP). The TEU required the Council meeting in the composition of heads of state or of government to decide by QMV no later than 31 December 1996 whether a majority of members fulfilled the conditions for the adoption of a single currency and whether it was appropriate to begin Stage 3 in 1997 (the 1997 date was later ruled out). If the date for beginning Stage 3 had not been set by 31 December 1997, the TEU required this stage to begin on 1 January 1999, regardless of whether a majority of members met the criteria. The UK and Denmark had separate protocols allowing them a choice on participation in Stage 3.

- **Stage 3.** This involved a move to irrevocably fixed exchange rates and to a single monetary policy for participating member states, leading to adoption of a single currency. In Stage 3, the Council would be able to impose sanctions on member states running excessive deficits. The European Central Bank was created on 1 July 1998, taking over the tasks of the EMI.

The Maastricht blueprint for EMU was therefore based on the strategy of a phased transition, with qualifying criteria, stages and deadlines.

○ Meeting the Convergence Criteria

The Maastricht schedule clearly did not allow for the crisis in the ERM, or for the severity of the economic recession in the early 1990s. In this period, the disparities between the convergence criteria and the economic performance of most member states raised serious doubts concerning the feasibility of the Maastricht schedule. The importance of adherence to the rules governing progress towards EMU was confirmed by the German constitutional court prior to the ratification of the TEU. This tough stance was subsequently repeatedly reaffirmed by the German government.

According to some analysts, the convergence criteria were devised for political rather than economic reasons, that is, to demonstrate countries' commitments to 'fiscal chastity', or, more cynically, to confine monetary union to a select club. Strict interpretation of the criteria could also be justified on grounds of economic rationality, that is, the closer the eurozone resembled an optimum currency area, the more likely it would be to succeed. The poorer states sought to meet the criteria through austerity programmes and by agitating for additional compensatory funding in support of convergence. Due to an upturn in its economy, Ireland had an easier task in meeting the criteria than either Spain or Portugal. But the adverse effects of efforts to meet the criteria were no means confined to poorer countries. The austerity programme introduced in France in the winter of 1995, leading to a wave of public sector strikes, was widely viewed as being at least partly attributable to efforts by the French government to meet convergence targets.

On 2 May 1998 in Brussels, the Council meeting in the composition of heads of state or government agreed that 11 out of the 15 EU countries qualified to participate in the final stage of EMU. Of the excluded countries, only Greece was keen to join and therefore was the only country to be disappointed by the decision. There was an element of fudging on the debt criterion, which most member states failed to meet. Although Italy and Belgium had much higher debt ratios than the reference value of 60% of GDP, they were judged to be approaching this target at a satisfactory pace. The UK met all numerical targets, but not the criterion of central bank independence or the two years' membership of the ERM requirement. In order to prevent governments from reneging on their commitments to maintain tight control over their finances, a Stability and Growth Pact was launched at the Dublin European Council in December 1996. This was meant to secure budgetary discipline in Stage 3, by avoiding excessive government deficits. It commits member states to medium-term budgetary objectives of close to balance. The Commission is required to present reports opinions and recommendations. The Council can impose sanctions if a member state fails to take the necessary steps to end the excessive deficit situation.

○ Technical Preparations and Name

In May 1995, the Commission produced a Green Paper on the practical measures needed for a changeover to a single currency, within four years of the decision to launch it. The paper rejected a 'big bang' approach, in favour of a gradualist strategy, which divided the changeover into three phases:

- *Phase A. Launch of EMU* (1 year maximum duration), commencing between the end of 1996 and July 1998. In accordance with TEU provisions, the decision would be taken to move to a single currency. It would be decided which countries qualify to participate. The European System of Central Banks (ESCB) and the European Central Bank (ECB) would be established. There would be intense preparation in the banking and financial sectors. Production of notes and coin would begin.
- *Phase B. Transitional Phase* (three years' maximum duration): the effective start of EMU and the emergence of a critical mass of activities. There would be irrevocable fixing of currency parities by the ECB, which would begin to operate a single monetary policy. National currencies would remain in circulation, as the new currency was introduced, first for banking and other large transactions and then for the general public. A critical mass of users would thereby be created. An information campaign would explain the benefits of a single currency and how it would work.
- *Phase C. Final Changeover* (several weeks' duration): national notes and coins would be phased out and the new currency would become the sole legal tender in the participating states.

The Commission's paper on the changeover was approved by ECOFIN and by the Cannes European Council in June 1995. The Madrid European Council in December 1995 agreed that EMU would begin on 1 January 1999 and outlined the definitive blueprint for the introduction of the new currency. Following modifications to the changeover schedule, euro notes and coins will enter general circulation on 1 January 2002 and by 28 February 2002 (at the latest) national notes and coin will be withdrawn from use. Figure 11.1 below outlines the timetable for the changeover.

Figure 11.1 Timetable for the Changeover to the Euro

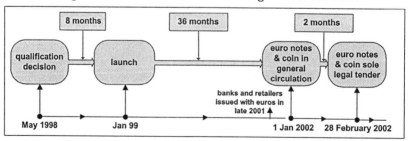

Financial institutions and large retailers will be issued ('frontloaded') with euros in late 2001, although participating states have their own schedules. For example, in Ireland and Germany, frontloading will begin in September 2001 whereas in the Netherlands and Finland it·will not begin until December. Until 1995, it was generally thought virtually inevitable that the new currency would be called the. ECU. In 1995 the German government and the Bundesbank challenged this assumption by suggesting the alternative name 'Franken'. The value of the ECU had fallen substantially against the DM between 1979 and 1995 and the name ECU inspired little confidence in Germany. The Franken idea found little favour. Other names were suggested, such as 'Euro-Mark', 'Ducat', 'Florin' or 'Monnet'. This issue was settled at the Madrid European Council, which decided on the name 'euro'.

On 25 May 1998, the members of the Executive Board of the ECB were appointed by the ministers of finance of countries adopting the single currency and the ECB was established on 1 June 1998. The EMI was then wound up. A serious dispute between France and other member· states over the choice of governor for the ECB had threatened to stall the whole process. France favoured French Finance Minister Jean Claude Trichet, president of the Banque de France, for the post, but other members wanted Wim Duisenberg of the Netherlands. The dispute was resolved only by an informal agreement that Duisenberg may 'voluntarily' give up his post after four years, leaving Trichet to serve the other half of the ECB governor's eight-year term. This agreement was heavily criticised for being little more than a shabby fudge and Duisenberg has subsequently reaffirmed his right to serve out a full term. The finance ministers and the governors of the NCBs of the countries adopting the single currency agreed that the then ERM bilateral central rates of the participating states would be used to determine the irrevocable conversion rates for the euro. (See Table 11.5.)

Table 11.5 Euro Conversion Rates

One euro equals			
40.3399	Belgian francs	1.95583	German marks
166.386	Spanish pesetas	6.55957	French francs
0.787564	Irish punt	1936.27	Italian lire
40.3399	Luxembourg francs	2.20371	Dutch guilders
13.7603	Austrian schillings	200.482	Portuguese escudos
5.94573	Finnish marka	340.750	Greek drachma

○ The European System of Central Banks

The ECB and the national central banks together form the European System of Central Banks (Figure 11.2 below). The central banks of non-participant countries are members of the ESCB, but do not take part in the decisionmaking with regard to the single monetary policy for the euro area or implementation of these decisions. The primary objective of the ESCB is to maintain price stability (Article 2 of the ESCB and ECB statute), although no figures are mentioned in the treaty and therefore the ECB has scope for interpretation for an inflation target. More specifically, its tasks are:

- to define an implement the monetary policy of the Union;
- to conduct foreign exchange operations;
- to hold and manage the official foreign reserves of participating states;
- to promote the smooth operation of payments systems;
- to contribute to the smooth conduct of policies relating to the prudential supervision of credit institutions and the stability of the financial system.

The ESCB is independent and neither the ECB nor a national central bank may seek or take instructions from any external body when performing ESCB related tasks. Although basic responsibilities of the ESCB includes conduct of foreign exchange operations and the management of the foreign exchange reserves of member states, the final word in the determination of exchange rate policy is the responsibility of ECOFIN.

Figure 11.2 The European System of Central Banks

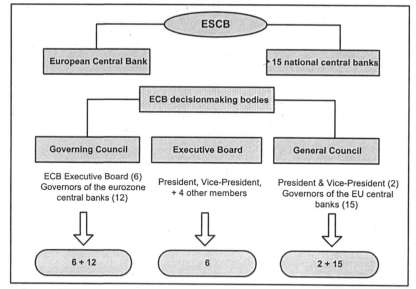

Source: ECB.

- **The ECB.** Monetary policy is adopted by the ECB and then implemented by the central banks participating in the single currency. It is independent, and does not take orders from EU institutions or member governments. It does not lend to national governments or to Commission organisations. It has exclusive right to authorise the issue of bank notes within the eurozone. The NCBs are the sole subscribers to and holders of the capital of the ECB. Subscription of capital is based on EU member states' respective shares of GDP and population of the EU. Key issues concerning its representation in international bodies have yet to be settled. But the ECB already participates in the work of the G7, the G10, the Bank for International Settlements and the Organisation for Economic Co-operation and Development (OECD). It has observer status at the International Monetary Fund (IMF).

- **The Governing Council** is the supreme decisionmaking body of the ECB. Its main responsibilities are to adopt the guidelines and make decisions necessary to ensure the performance of the ESCB's tasks and to formulate the monetary policy of the Union. It comprises six members of the executive board of the ECB and the central bank governors of the 12 countries participating in monetary union. There is a minimum renewable term of office for governors of five years. It operates on a one member one vote principle, except for decisions on the ECB's subscribed capital, which are weighted according to the shares of the national central banks. The six members of the executive board are not allowed to voted on these issues. Arguably, the Governing Council contains too many members and it has been suggested that a rotation system for NCB governors could be introduced.

- **The Executive Board** comprises the president, vice-president and four other members. They are appointed by the European Council on a recommendation from the Council after it has consulted the EP and the ECB Governing Council. The main responsibilities of the executive board are to implement day-to-day monetary policy in accordance with the guidelines and decisions laid down by the Governing Council and in so doing to give the necessary instructions to the NCBs. There is a non-renewable term of office for members of the executive board of eight years. Removable from office is only possible in the event of incapacity or serious misconduct.

- **The General Council** consists of the president and vice-president of the executive board plus the governors of the national central banks of all member states. It has an advisory role and also enhances co-operation between the NCBs and supervises ERM2. It has no role in making monetary policy and was established as a means of giving NCBs of 'pre-in' countries a means of contributing to the work of the ESCB.

- **The Role of ECOFIN and of the 'Euro-12 Group'**. European finance ministers, meeting as ECOFIN, remain responsible for general economic policy and for the determination of exchange rate policy. ECOFIN gives priority to the co-ordination of the macro economic policies of member countries. The president of the ECB may attend ECOFIN and send two representatives to the economic and financial committee of officials established in 1999. The ECOFIN chairman and the Commission president may attend meetings of the ECB governing council. Whereas the ECB is a supranational institution, ECOFIN is intergovernmental.

'Euro-12', also known as the 'euro-group' or 'euro-x', comprises the finance ministers of the members of the eurozone. The group meets prior to the ECOFIN Council to discuss policies relating to the euro. The idea for such a group came from the French government, which sought to reassert some kind of political control over the operation of EMU. However, the idea initially ran into two kinds of opposition: firstly, from those who regarded it as a threat to the power and independence of the ECB; and secondly from the UK government, which feared, as a non-participant in the final stage of EMU, exclusion from discussions on key issues (that is, it feared that these would be decided in this group rather than in ECOFIN). The French government sought to expand the range of topics with which the group is concerned during the French presidency of the EU in the second half of 2000. The group also became more visible by holding press conferences after its meetings. In the Treaty of Nice, a declaration on Article 111 of the EC Treaty states that procedures must enable all member states in the euro area to be involved in each stage of preparing the position of the Community at international level as regards issues of particular relevance to EMU. The treaty will also introduce QMV for Council decisions on EMU issues and representation at international level (Article 111(4), ECT). Clearly, governments have by no means surrendered all instruments of economic policy to the ECB. ECOFIN and the euro-12 group have a major say in key areas of economic policy. The Council can devalue the euro, increase or decrease the budget and change taxation policies. It could even do away with the Stability and Growth Pact.

○ Euro notes and coin

ECOFIN decided that the largest value coin would be €2 and that notes would range from €5 to 500. The notes are identical on both sides and are the same for all member states. Each note denomination is a different colour and a different size. To prevent counterfeiting, the notes contain fluorescent fibres, security threads and foils. In some countries the notes are being printed by the national central banks and in others by private or public companies. There are eight coins, from 1 cent to €2. One side of each coin is common to all countries whereas the other reflects national identity. Some countries have the same design for all eight coins. Some have divided them into three groups of different designs. Austria and Italy have chosen a different design for all eight coins. Monarchies have put their monarch on some or all of the coins (Belgium, the Netherlands and Spain). Others have national symbols and others national figures (Mozart in Austria and Dante in Italy).

● IMPACT AND EVALUATION

Before examining the performance of the euro since January 1999, it will be useful to contrast pessimistic and optimistic forecasts concerning its future.

○ Optimistic Forecasts

These can be summarised as:

• **The commitment to monetary discipline:** the goals of monetary discipline and of price stability are central to the EMU project and will be rigorously pursued and enforced. The ECB will safeguard the stability of the currency and will pursue a very cautious monetary policy.

• **The size and strength of the eurozone:** the eurozone is to a large extent self contained and, given its size, is capable of absorbing external shocks.

• **EU economies are becoming more integrated**, due to the combined effects of the SEM, increased trade and investment flows and developments in communication. EMU is helping to foster a single European capital market, stimulating corporate restructuring and boosting growth. These factors, together with the same interest rate, are likely pull business cycles together.

• **The euro is likely to be popular with citizens** in the long run, when euros are used for cross-border travel and purchases. Citizens will benefit from low inflation (good for those on fixed incomes); lower interest rates (meaning cheaper borrowing for businesses and cheaper mortgages for housebuyers); and savings on cross-border travel.

• **The architects of EMU have too much invested in it to fail** and therefore will go to great lengths to ensure the success of the project (not least because failure could, according to some, lead to the unravelling of EU integration).

○ Pessimistic Forecasts

The arguments of 'euro-pessimists' generally fall into three categories (which are often conflated into a generalised attack on the project by Eurosceptics).

• *Economic unsuitability*, that is, that the economies of the EU are too diverse for the eurozone to constitute an optimal currency area and therefore the euro project is fundamentally unstable.

• *Unacceptable political costs*, that is, the euro project requires a massive transfer of sovereignty to the European level, which EU citizens are not ready to accept.

• *Implementation flaws*, that is, that regardless of its intrinsic merits, the project has been badly executed.

1. The economic unsuitability argument is presented in Table 11.6 below.

Table 11.6 Launching EMU in a Suboptimal Currency Area

The EU currently does not meet the conditions for an optimal currency area. An 'optimal' currency area would have a high degree of cross-border mobility of capital and labour; it would have high wage and price flexibility; it would allow for fiscal transfers, where tax revenues are redistributed to areas in recession; the business cycles of participating states would be compatible.

- **The problem of labour market rigidities.** Workers in the EU are reluctant to move to other EU countries in search of employment. Because of welfare entitlements, they are reluctant to work in low-paid jobs. Regulations on working conditions and wages also inhibit labour market flexibility. For uncompetitive countries, when the effects of competition begin to bite, wages are unlikely to fall and workers are unlikely to move. Within the euro-zone, devaluation of the currency will no longer be an option. Real wages are unlikely to fall to levels at which these adverse effects are reversed. The result may be *higher unemployment* in these countries. The EU does not have sufficient budgetary resources to cope and there is no mechanism for fiscal transfers from richer to poorer countries. For this reason, Eurosceptics argue that EMU stands for 'even more unemployment'.

- **The problem of incompatible economies.** Some argue that member states' economies are too dissimilar for EMU to make sense, namely:
  the danger of 'asymmetric shocks' – e.g., if country A is a net importer and country B is a net exporter of a product, changes in the world price of this product will have opposite consequences for these countries. Similarly, consumers in some countries borrow more and are therefore more sensitive to interest rate fluctuations (e.g., housing finance in the UK). The exchange rate will no longer cushion asymmetric shocks;
  the problem of incompatible business cycles: countries may have different business cycles, meaning that one country may be in a growth phase and another in a phase of decline or stagnation. If there is a boom in one country and a recession in another, the same monetary policy is not appropriate for these countries. For example, if the UK entered the euro with high inflation relative to other euro members, its businesses would be uncompetitive, resulting in higher unemployment.

Within the eurozone, member states can no longer set their own interest rates or use the exchange rate as a tool of economic policy: moreover, none of the alternative adjustment mechanisms, that is, migration, wage levels, capital movements, fiscal policy, fiscal transfers or direct aid are likely to work well within the eurozone. There are language and cultural barriers to labour mobility, so people are unlikely to move from depressed to richer areas.

Large fiscal transfers, cuts in wages and direct aid are unacceptable on political grounds. The ECB manages the money supply and sets short-term interest rates for the eurozone as a whole. The interest rate, however, might be too high for some countries (experiencing stagnation and high unemployment) and too low for countries with economies in danger of overheating. For example, in 2000, it was argued that the interest rate set by the ECB was too high for Germany and too low for Ireland. In December 2000, Ireland's inflation rate reached 7%. But instead of responding by raising taxes and cutting public spending, the Irish government lowered taxes and raised public spending. This earned the Irish government a formal rebuke from the Commission for flouting the eurozone's broad economic policy guidelines.

2. Unacceptable political costs. According to this argument, the single currency requires *a single economic government*, necessitating the transfer of key policy responsibilities (such as fiscal and taxation policy) from national governments. In other words, the euro project can only work if it is accompanied by political union, which is currently unrealistic. The argument that the euro project requires a massive transfer of national sovereignty has frequently been advanced by British Eurosceptics and also figured prominently (perhaps decisively) in the Danish referendum on the euro.

3. Implementation flaws. The argument that the implementation of EMU has been deeply flawed (see Buiter, 1999) has several strands, namely:

- *the division between monetary and fiscal authority*: the eurozone has a single monetary, but not a single fiscal, authority. Monetary policy is centralised, but fiscal policy remains a national responsibility;
- *the unclear relationships between the ECB, ECOFIN and 'euro-12'*, which leads to confusion and lack of clarity in policy towards the euro;
- *internal monetary policy is not well co-ordinated with external exchange rate policy,* leading to confusion concerning policy objectives. The ECB is responsible for maintaining the internal purchasing power of the euro, but its external value is the primary responsibility of EU governments;
- *there is no single external representative for the eurozone in international monetary organisations.* For example, the president of euro-12 and the president of the ECB represent the eurozone in meetings of the G8;
- *lack of openness and accountability*: for example, the ECB Governing Council does not publish minutes of its meetings or make public the voting records of its members. It has been argued that there is a culture of secrecy within the ECB (although this is rejected by Issing, 1999);
- *the size of the ECB governing council,* which is arguably too large for effective decisionmaking, with 17 members;
- *the system is undemocratic and therefore lacks legitimacy,* not least because monetary authority has been transferred to an unelected and insufficiently accountable central bank.

◯ The Performance of the Euro since Its Launch

It will be useful to distinguish between how the euro has performed *internally* (that is, inside the eurozone) and how it has performed *externally* (that is, against other currencies and as a potential international reserve currency).

- **The internal performance of the euro.** The main criteria against which the euro's internal performance can be measured are:

  - *Has it contributed to price stability within the eurozone?* The head of the ECB has repeatedly affirmed that his primary responsibility is to maintain domestic price stability, defined as an inflation rate of less than 2% within the eurozone. But in spite of the monetary and fiscal disciplines imposed on member states by EMU, eurozone inflation rose to 3.4% in April 2001, about twice the previous year's figure. This has been attributed to rising energy and food prices and to the low external value of the euro.

  - *Is the transition to the euro going smoothly?* It is almost certain that the switch to euro notes and coin will occur in 2002. Given the sheer magnitude of the undertaking, this will be a major achievement. But many companies and also the public remain unprepared for the changeover.

  - *Has it had a catalytic effect on the eurozone economies?*. It is difficult to isolate the economic and business effects of EMU from other factors. According to the Commission, it is deepening integration of financial markets and is providing a stimulus for businesses to refocus their activities. Mergers within the eurozone has increased and unemployment has fallen slightly, but these are not necessarily due to EMU. In the early part of 2001, growth within the eurozone appeared to be slowing, raising the spectre of 'stagflation' (stagnation, combined with inflation).

  - *Are EU citizens in favour of the euro?* A *Eurobarometer* survey (no. 54) undertaken in Autumn 2000 found that 55% of EU citizens supported the euro project and 37% opposed it. Public support for the euro was highest in Italy at 79% and lowest in the UK (21%), Sweden (26%) and Denmark (41%). In Germany only 47% supported it. Ironically, opposition to the project in Germany appears to be strongly influenced by a belief that it is inflationary, whereas in some other countries it is viewed as deflationary, due to the imposition of a tight monetary policy. The EU public was not involved in the decision to launch the euro and still appear to have little knowledge of it. Arguably, citizens may warm to the euro once they are actually using euro notes and coin, but this is by no means certain.

The euro has not yet stimulated the rapid and robust economic growth, or generated the public support, predicted by some of its more ardent proponents, but neither has it been the unmitigated disaster predicted by some eurosceptics. However, these are early days and it is still too early to predict how it will perform in the long term.

• **The external performance of the euro.** In its first two years (from January 1999 to December 2000), the value of the euro against the dollar fell by about a quarter (from an opening value of $1.1743). It also fell substantially against the yen and sterling. In the first half of 2001 it had an average dollar value of $0.9011. Some explanations for the euro's fall in external value are given in Table 11.7. The main short-term positive effect of this fall was that it made exports from the eurozone cheaper, leading to booms in export sales in some sectors. But it also made eurozone imports more expensive, fuelling inflation. This poor external performance has undoubtedly damaged the prestige of the euro project and has made nonsense of predictions that the euro would soon develop into a currency capable of rivalling the dollar for global supremacy.

Table 11.7 Some Explanations for the Fall in the Euro's External Value

• the strength of the dollar (although the euro has fallen in value against the yen and pound also);
• the relatively strong performance of the US economy: e.g., the US is a more attractive investment location (in 1999, the US attracted $125 bn. of net FDI, whereas the eurozone recorded net outflows of $150 bn.);
• higher interest rates in the US and UK than in the eurozone;
• misleading signals on policy from the ECB and national governments;
• lack of international confidence in the euro project;
• fiscal laxity by some eurozone countries;
• rigidities in eurozone economies;
• it was overvalued at launch.

Some economists contend that the eurozone is so large that the external value of the euro does not matter very much. Like the US, the EU is a relatively closed economy, because intra-EU trade amounts to a much larger proportion of GDP than extra-EU trade. External trade accounts for only about 10% of EU member states' income (about 12% for the eurozone). But economic conditions inside the eurozone are significantly affected by the euro's value against other major currencies, which is why a policy of indifference (or 'benign neglect') towards its external value is unlikely to be sustained. On 25 September 2000, the central banks of the 'G7' sought to halt the slide in the euro's value by intervening in the currency markets.

In some quarters, notably in France, the goal of promoting the euro as an international reserve currency has been regarded as an important aspect of EMU. The dollar is used in over 80% of global foreign exchange transactions and accounts for 56% of all reserves. About half of international trade is currently invoiced in dollars, as against less than a third for the euro. The benefits to the US of reserve currency status include *seigniorage* (the profit from issuing dollars outside the US); reduction of exchange risk in trade and increased influence in international monetary organisations. Arguably, the sheer size of the eurozone, combined with the eurozone's trading and investment relationships, will mean that the euro will eventually make significant inroads into the dollar's position as an international currency (see Table 11.8). EU15 has a similar GDP and a similar share of global trade to the US. The eurozone has a population of about 300 million and a GDP of about 80% of US GDP. In the inter-war period, the dollar replaced sterling as the international currency. However, Britain was then economically exhausted whereas the US economy is currently strong. In the long run, what may emerge (although this is by no means certain) is a bipolar financial regime in which the dollar and the euro each account for about 40% of foreign exchange transactions. This transition is unlikely to happen quickly and is dependent on the relative performances of the EU and US economies and on many other factors. The official policy of the ECB is that it will neither foster nor hinder the development of the euro as an international currency.

Table 11.8 What May Facilitate Use of the Euro?

- the sheer size of the eurozone;
- firms trading with the EU will be expected to pay and invoice in euros;
- the conversion of assets currently held in European currencies into euros means that over a third of the world's currency portfolio is held in euros;
- the EU's trading and political relationships (e.g., close links with CEECs, Africa and the Mediterranean);
- the policy of monetary stability pursued by the ECB;
- the euro is creating a more integrated financial market in the eurozone.

○ **Partial Monetary Union and the 'Insider/Outsider' Problem**

The EU is currently a partial monetary union, in that not all member states are members of the eurozone. It has long been recognised that a limited currency zone could lead to friction between zone 'insiders'and 'outsiders'. Insiders may be suspicious that outsiders will seek to use their currencies to gain competitive advantage (for example, by devaluing in order to boost trade and investment). In the autumn of 1995, various ideas for dealing with the insider/outsider problem were canvassed, including the idea of a monetary pact between the two groups and the idea that outsiders should be obliged to participate in a revamped ERM. Greece was admitted to the eurozone in January 2001, after it was judged to have met the convergence criteria. The three remaining outsiders could probably be admitted to the eurozone quickly should they choose to do so. However, the result of the Danish referendum in September 2000, the low public support for the euro and the weak performance of the euro against the dollar have increased the probability that the UK, Sweden and Denmark will remain outside the eurozone for the foreseeable future. Denmark participates in the new exchange rate mechanism (ERM2), whereas Sweden and the UK do not. The 'no' campaigners in the Danish referendum argued that a 'yes' vote would dilute Danish sovereignty and threaten its welfare state. Danish voters rejected entry into the eurozone (by a margin of 53% to 47%) even though the five main Danish parties, the business community and the press all favoured entry. Although Sweden does not have a formal/legal opt-out on the euro, its decision to hold a referendum on the issue amounts to a *de facto* opt-out. The earliest date for a Swedish referendum is after the next general election in September 2002 (Swedes are currently even less enthusiastic about the euro project than the Danes).

The next group of countries to enter the EU will not qualify immediately for participation in the eurozone. At an ECB-sponsored high-level seminar held in Vienna in December 2000, it was made clear to the governors of the central banks of the 12 acceding countries that entry into the eurozone will be based upon strict interpretation of treaty obligations, including fulfilment of the convergence criteria (ECB Press Release, 15 December 2000). It is possible that some, for example Poland, Hungary Slovenia, Estonia or the Czech Republic, will be admitted before the UK, Denmark or Sweden (Estonia and Bulgaria already peg their currencies to the euro). The EU's monetary landscape would then comprise the eurozone, willing outsiders and unwilling outsiders (with some outsiders in ERM2 and others not).

● THE DEBATE ON UK ENTRY

Within the UK, the largest 'outsider' country, the issue of entry is fiercely contested. The Labour and Liberal-Democratic parties both favour entry in principle. The Labour government elected in June 2001 intends to hold a referendum on the issue as soon as economic conditions are judged to be favourable to UK entry (which could in fact take a long time). Under the leadership of William Hague, the Conservative party's policy was strongly opposed to UK entry. The policy of 'keeping the pound' did not, however, reap electoral dividends for the Conservatives at the 2001 general election and William Hague resigned as party leader shortly afterwards. At the time of writing, the party had yet to elect a new leader and therefore the repercussions of Hague's resignation on the party's European policies were not known. A survey by the *Financial Times* on 1 December 1999 showed a more or less even split between business firms favouring entry and those opposed. Firms with large business operations in the EU appear to be most in favour of joining as soon as possible whereas smaller companies tend to be against early entry. Two Reuters surveys conducted in 2001 found that whereas 62%

of larger companies favoured UK membership, almost 58% of smaller companies said they would not benefit from it (*Financial Times*, 21 June, 2001). Most British citizens currently oppose entry, with only 21% in favour in the Autumn of 2000 (*Eurobarometer*, no. 54). Pressure groups are active on both sides (for example, the Business for Sterling group on the 'no' side and the European Movement on the 'yes' side: see p. 500 for their websites).

The entry debate in the UK has crystallised around the issues of sovereignty (relinquishing control of its currency) and the consequences of staying out for the economy. Those against entry on economic grounds argue that the differences between the British and eurozone economies are currently too large for entry to make sense. Examples frequently cited are: differences in business cycles and trade patterns; the greater sensitivity in the UK to short term interest rates, as a result of the greater proportion of housing mortgage debt; and the greater dependence of companies on equity finance in the UK, meaning that the UK is more sensitive to stock market volatility. In October 1997, Chancellor Gordon Brown stated in parliament that the UK would not join the single currency before *five economic tests* were met (see Table 11.9).

Table 11.9 Gordon Brown's 'Five Economic Tests'

- Are business cycles and economic structures compatible so that the UK and others could live comfortably with euro interest rates permanently?
- If problems emerge, is there sufficient flexibility to deal with them?
- Would joining EMU create better conditions for firms making long-term decisions to invest in Britain?
- What impact would entry have on the competitive position of the UK's financial services industry, particularly the City's wholesale markets?
- Will joining promote higher growth, stability and a lasting increase in jobs?

These 'tests' are actually rather vague and subjective, so it will be a matter of opinion as to whether they are met. British 'Europhiles' tend to argue that the UK largely meets them already, whereas British Eurosceptics contend that wide economic divergences still exist between the UK and the eurozone. It should also be remembered that according to the convergence criteria, candidates must have respected 'the normal fluctuation margins provided by the ERM' for at least two years. It is not clear if the UK will be required to join the ERM2 prior to entry. An issue of vital importance is the exchange rate at which the UK joins. Perhaps the most important test will be that of persuading the British public, which remains generally hostile to the euro. One of the supposed negative effects of the UK's opt-out is that foreign companies may seek alternative destinations for their investments, because the currency barrier between the UK and the eurozone constitutes a major business risk. Some major foreign companies, including Toyota, Nissan, Honda, Fujitsu, Siemens, BMW and Vauxhall have voiced fears about the possible consequences if the UK decides to stay out of the eurozone. In June 2000, the president of Nissan stated that the future of the Nissan plant in Sunderland was in doubt because of the strong pound. The strength of sterling was a major reason given for the decision of Ford to shift part of its production from Dagenham to Cologne; for Toyota to build a new plant in France rather than in the UK; and for BMW to sell its Rover subsidiary.

However, the UK's relatively investment-friendly environment (it has relatively flexible labour markets, skilled labour, the English language and a favourable regulatory environment) appears so far to have outweighed negative impacts on investment. Between March 1999 and March 2000, foreign direct investment (FDI) into the UK increased by 23% (*Financial Times*, 6 June 2000). In 1999, the UK attracted three times as much FDI as Germany and twice as much as France. The City of London has maintained its market share since the launch of the euro. But there is a time lag between location decisions and actual investment, so optimism concerning the UK's attractions as an investment location may be premature (see Table 11.10).

Table 11.10 Should the UK Join the Eurozone Now?

Arguments for Not Joining Now
- the UK's business cycle is out of 'sync' with those of most of the countries in the 'eurozone';
- the success of EMU is by no means certain. There is no provision in the treaties for leaving the eurozone and therefore it is an irrevocable step. It might be best to adopt a 'wait and see' approach;
- only a small minority of UK citizens currently favour entry;
- the UK business community is split on the issue and only a minority of British companies favoured *immediate* entry.

Arguments for Joining as Soon as Possible
- to not do so will repeat the UK's past mistake of 'missing the boat' with regard to European integration projects;
- the eurozone accounts for almost half UK exports and over 40% of FDI;
- the UK may lose out on future inward investment;
- some firms operating in the UK may relocate to the eurozone;
- the UK may lose markets, due to increased *intra*-eurozone trade;
- staying out may weaken London's position as a major financial centre;
- British exporters are likely to price their goods in euros anyway;
- even if firms operate mainly in the UK, if they provide goods or services to multinationals they might be forced to deal in euros;
- many large companies investing in the UK favour entry.

● CONCLUSION

The launch of EMU is undoubtedly a major event in the history of European integration, with implications which go far beyond the fields of economics and finance. Indeed, it has become increasingly clear that the EMU project involves questions of political as well as economic union. Some critics of the project argue that it was unwise to launch on such an ambitious project before the Single European Market was fully complete, before the absorption into the Union of the countries of Central and Eastern Europe, before EU citizens had been persuaded of its merits and before deeper political integration had been achieved. They also argue that there is no successful prior example of a 'stateless currency'. However, the EU is unique in the depth of integration it has already achieved, so previous experience may provide a misleading guide to the euro's future.

FURTHER READING

Buiter, W.H. (1999), 'Alice in Euroland', *Journal of Common Market Studies*, vol. 37, no. 2., pp. 181–209.

Commission (1995), *One Currency for Europe – Green Paper on the Practical Arrangements for the Introduction of the Single Currency*, COM (95) 333.

Commission (2001), *Eurobarometer*, no. 54, http://europa.eu.int/comm/dg10/epo.

Crouch, C. (ed.) (2000), *After the euro*, Oxford University Press, Oxford.

De Grauwe, P. (2000), *The Economics of Monetary Integration*, Oxford University Press, Oxford.

Edmonds, T. (2000), *The Euro-zone: Year One*, House of Commons Research Paper, 00/34.

Eijffinger, C.W. and De Haan, J. (2000), *European Monetary and Fiscal Policy*, Oxford University Press, Oxford.

European Central Bank, http://www.ecb.int.

European Parliament (1998), *The Single Currency Background Brief*, PE166.162.

European Union euro site: http://euro.eu.int.

House of Commons, Select Committee on Treasury (2000), Eighth Report, *Economic and Monetary Union Since 1999.*

Issing, O. (1999), 'The Eurosystem: Transparent and Accountable or Willim in Euroland', *Journal of Common Market Studies*, vol. 37, no. 3, pp. 503–19.

Martin-Das, J.C. (2001), *The European Monetary Union in a Public Choice Perspective,* Edward Elgar, Cheltenham and Northampton, MA.

OECD Observer (2000), *EMU One Year On*, February.

Padoa-Schioppa, T. (2000), *The Road to Monetary Union in Europe*, Oxford University Press, Oxford.

Temperton, P. (2001), *The UK and the euro*, John Wiley and Sons, Chichester.

UK Government euro site: http://www.euro.gov.uk.

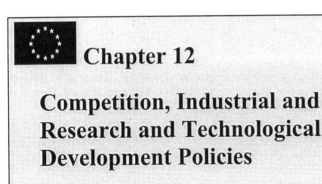

Chapter 12

Competition, Industrial and Research and Technological Development Policies

The Union's competition, industrial and RTD (research and technological development) policies are perhaps best examined in conjunction for several reasons: developments in any one of these policies are likely to have major repercussions for the others. Each constitutes an important component of the European business environment. Each has implications for the ability of European firms to compete successfully in world markets. Each has been accorded a central role in the Union's strategy for economic growth, competitiveness and employment. Each has stimulated an ideological debate concerning the role of government in business and industry. In each case the problem of reconciling national- and Union-level policies has loomed large.

● COMPETITION POLICY

The Treaty of Rome established competition rules designed to prevent or remove anti-competitive practices deemed incompatible with the common market. The Commission and the European Court of Justice (ECJ) are the key actors. The distinctive features of the Union's competition policy are:

- *it has a strong treaty basis* (Articles 81–89, ECT);
- *it has not replaced the competition policies of member states*: however, there is now a tendency for the latter to be aligned to or modelled on the EU's rules (the UK's 1998 Competition Act is an example of these 'look-alike' rules);
- *Commission dominance*: the Commission has considerable autonomy in this sphere: it regulates, investigates, decides, enforces and if necessary punishes (although its decisions can be challenged in the ECJ);

- *it is a regulatory regime*, based on the formulation and enforcement of rules of conduct);
- *it has played a pivotal role in the Single European Market (SEM) programme*, which would be unsupportable without a strong competition policy to underpin and drive it forward (for this reason, it is often cited as an example of integration 'spillover');
- *it tends to be a high-profile policy*, due to the controversial nature of many competition cases;
- *it is a 'busy' policy*: the volume and complexity of EU competition cases has increased substantially in recent years, due for example to the development of the SEM; the increase in cross-border business; industrial restructuring; the rise of new industries; and the impact of globalisation on business environments. In 2000, the Commission dealt with 1206 new competition cases, comprising 297 antitrust cases, 345 merger cases and 564 state aid cases;
- *it is unique*, being the only successful example of a cross-border competition regime.

The main features of EU competition policy are outlined below.

○ Anti-competitive Agreements

Article 81 of the EC Treaty prohibits agreements between undertakings which may prevent, restrict or distort competition, such as agreements which:
- directly or indirectly fix purchase or selling prices;
- limit or control production, markets, technical development or investment;
- share markets or sources of supply;
- apply dissimilar conditions to equivalent transactions with other trading parties;
- make conclusion of contracts subject to acceptance of supplementary obligations.

Article 81 only applies if the agreement has a significant effect on competition within the Union. Exemption may be given if the agreement contributes to an improvement in production or distribution of goods or promotes technical or economic progress, or if it benefits consumers. For example, in September 1999, the Commission approved an agreement between 16 European postal operators on compensation for the cost of distributing cross-border mail, on the grounds that it was part of the restructuring and liberalisation of the sector. Exemptions have also been given on the grounds that agreements strengthen European industry in global markets. Most of the workload of the Commission's Competition Directorate is concerned with Article 81 cases. The Commission has the power to order parties to terminate conduct illegal under Article 81 and can impose large fines of up to €1 million or 10% of the world-wide turnover of the group to which the infringing firm belongs (whichever is the larger). In December 1999, the Commission imposed fines totalling €99 million on eight manufacturers of seamless steel tubes and pipes for operating a restrictive agreement respecting each other's domestic market.

The cornerstone of the system for implementing Article 81 is regulation 17/62, which lays down the Commission's powers with regard to notification, consultation procedures with governments, investigative powers and ability to levy fines. Proceedings for the application of Article 81 may be started by the Commission on its own initiative, as a result of an application for approval or exemption by an undertaking, or on receipt of a complaint by a third party. National authorities in the member state concerned are consulted and assist with the investigation in an advisory capacity. But although representatives of member states are consulted in advisory committees, the Commission has the final say in granting exemptions. An undertaking can apply to the Commission for a 'negative clearance', that is, confirmation that an agreement is exempt from Article 81. Exemptions will only be granted once the Commission has been notified. The Commission does not have the resources to deal with all notifications under Article 81. In an effort to increase the speed and to reduce the cost of decisions, 'comfort' letters, '*de minimis* notices' and 'block exemption' regulations are currently used. Comfort letters set out the Commission's view of a particular agreement or practice. Although these letters are not legally binding, it is most unlikely that an agreement will be rejected after a comfort letter has been issued. *De minimis* notices set out criteria to assist undertakings to decide whether their agreement is likely to fall within the scope of Article 81. Block exemption regulations set out categories of agreement which are exempt from Article 81. Agreements will not breach Article 81 if:

- market share as a result of the agreement is less than 5% of the total market in the area affected by the agreement;
- aggregate annual turnover of the undertakings is below € 200 million.

Commission decisions on competition can be challenged in the ECJ (although the Court has a tendency to support the Commission in such cases). Most Article 81 cases are excluded either by block exemptions or by comfort letters. But the increasing volume of such cases has forced the Commission to propose a radical overhaul of the system (see below).

○ Dominant Positions

Dominant positions may enable firms to put pressure on suppliers or buyers. The ECJ has defined dominance as 'the ability to act to a significant extent independently of competitors, customers and ultimately of consumers' and has stated that an indication, even presumption, of dominance exists once a company achieves a 50% market share. Article 82 of the EC Treaty concerns abuse of a dominant position by one or more undertakings, through activities such as:

- the imposition of unfair selling or purchase prices;
- limiting production, markets or technical development to the prejudice of consumers;
- applying dissimilar conditions to equivalent transactions with other trading parties;
- making the conclusion of contracts subject to supplementary obligations.

Procedures for investigation and decision follow the same pattern as for Article 81 cases (regulation 17 covers both Articles 81 and 82). There must be a cross-border dimension before the Commission can act. It has been difficult for the Commission to prove that a dominant position has been abused and the first referral under Article 82 did not occur until 1971. There have been about 15 times as many Commission decisions under Article 81 as under Article 82. However, in 1999, the Commission adopted four prohibition decisions under Article 82: three involved airline operators offering discriminatory discount schemes and the other the French organising committee of the 1998 football World Cup for discriminatory ticket sales.

○ Reforming Articles 81 and 82 Competition Rules

The current surveillance regime for Articles 81 and 82 has frequently been accused of being excessively bureaucratic, slow, outdated, secretive and ineffective. Much of the Commission's time has been tied up in procedures for dealing with routine cases rather than the battle against serious cartels. Moreover, enlargement will make it more difficult for a centralised system of detection and prosecution to operate. The Commission is currently seeking to decentralise and simplify the competition regime, by allowing for national competition authorities and courts to take on a greater share in the application of Articles 81 and 82 (although the Commission would retain overall control). In April 1999, the Commission published a White Paper on modernisation of the rules implementing Articles 81 and 82 (Commission, 1999). The White Paper proposed abolition of the current notification and authorisation arrangements in favour of a directly applicable exception system, which could be applied by the Commission or by any national authority or court. The Commission could then refocus its activities on the most serious infringements and devote more resources to cartel busting. Decentralisation is consistent with the principle of subsidiarity. But a common criticism of decentralisation is that it would lead to a loss of legal certainty and would place undue reliance on national authorities, with the strong possibility of inconsistency in the way EU competition law is applied. At the time of writing, these reform ideas were still under discussion. In its submission to the 1996–97 intergovernmental conference (IGC), the German government favoured an independent cartel office, which it argued would be less subject to political pressures than the Commission. This idea found little favour with the Commission or with other governments.

O Merger Control

The Treaty of Rome did not contain a specific provision dealing with mergers. Articles 81 and 82 (formerly 85 and 86) of the treaty proved inadequate to deal with mergers, even though in 1972 the ECJ ruled that Article 82 could be used to block a merger if it created a dominant position in a particular market. A wave of merger activity in the 1980s led to pressure to develop specific merger legislation. The Merger Control Regulation introduced in September 1990 prohibits cross-border mergers which would create or strengthen dominant positions. It gave the Commission power to block large-scale cross-border mergers and take-overs where: (a) aggregate world-wide turnover is over €5 billion; and (b) aggregate EU-wide turnover of at least two of the undertakings exceeds €250 million, unless one has more than two-thirds of its aggregate EU-wide turnover in one member state.

Such high thresholds have meant that many mergers have escaped scrutiny at EU level. In 1997, Council Regulation 1310 introduced rules to cover mergers involving three or more member states, but lower turnovers. Firms are required to notify the Commission of their intention to merge if an EU dimension is involved. The 1990 regulation gave the Commission investigative powers and powers to fine undertakings which fail to notify a merger or which supply incorrect information. In 1999, for the first time the EU imposed fines on several notifying parties for providing incomplete or misleading information. Of nearly 2000 merger proposals considered by the Commission between 1990 and December 2000, only 13 were vetoed, even though the number of proposals the Commission reviews annually has increased fivefold (from 63 in 1991 to 345 in 2000). But whereas between January 1990 and August 1999 only ten prospective mergers were blocked, in the following six months the Commission blocked two (see Table 12.1) and another (Alcan and Pechiney) formally withdrew a notification after Competition Commissioner Mario Monti signalled his intention to veto it. In July 2001, Monti vetoed a merger between General Electric and Honeywell International (both US companies). In 2000, the Commission received 345 notifications under the merger regulation. Most were cleared within a month; in 19 cases an investigation lasting a further four months was undertaken; nine investigations were carried over from 1999. Of these 28 cases, three were approved unconditionally and 12 conditionally; two were banned; in six cases the merger was abandoned and in five a decision was deferred until 2001. The Commission has the final say on deals it reviews. Companies can appeal to the ECJ, but it usually takes at least two years to reach a verdict.

Table 12.1 Mergers Blocked by the Commission: 1990–2000

Proposed Merger	Market	Date
Aerospatiale/Alena/De Havilland	Aircraft manufacture	October 1991
MSG/Media Service	Pay TV	November 1994
Nordic Satellite Distribution	Satellite TV	July 1995
RTL/Veronica/Endemol	TV	September 1995
Gencor/Lonrho	Platinum	April 1996
Kesko/Tuko	Consumer goods	November 1996
St. Gobain/Wacker Chemie/Nom	Silicon carbide	December 1996
Blokker/Toys 'R'Us	Toys .	June 1997
Deutsche Telekom/Betaresearch	Digital TV decoders	May 1998
Bertelsmann/Kirch/Premiere	Digital Pay TV	May 1998
Airtours/First Choice	Foreign package holidays	September 1999
Scania/Volvo	Heavy goods vehicles	March 2000
MCI WorldCom/Sprint	Telecommunications	June 2000

Source: adapted and up-dated from *European Voice*, 23–29 March, 2000, p. 21.

The wave of European merger activity gained considerable momentum in the late 1990s, due for example to the globalisation of markets, introduction of the euro and the continuing development of the SEM. Mergers have increased not only in number but also in complexity. A substantial number now involve different sectors and different countries. Since 1990, the Commission's Competition Directorate has had a Merger Task Force. It had only 47 members in September 2000, which is arguably too small to cope with the magnitude of its tasks. The tight deadlines the Commission imposes in investigations have frequently been criticised. The current competition commissioner, Mario Monti, is seeking to streamline investigations, for example, by simplifying procedures for 'run of the mill' deals.

O   Regulating Services of General Economic Interest

Article 86 (formerly 90) of the EC treaty requires EU competition rules to be applied to undertakings entrusted with the operation of services of 'general economic interest' or having the character of revenue-producing monopolies, providing they do not obstruct the performance of the tasks assigned to them. Although this article dates back to the Treaty of Rome, it was not used until the late 1980s, when the logic of the SEM brought it to life. Examples of such services are utilities, such as rail, energy, telecommunications and postal services. A level playing field in these sectors is hardly possible if some undertakings are protected and subsidised and others are not. Starting in 1988, the Commission has used Article 86 primarily to foster competition in telecommunications. The slow pace of liberalisation in the other sectors (indeed, rail transport has remained largely unaffected) has meant that regulatory activity in this field has so far had a rather narrow focus, although as energy and postal service liberalisation proceeds, this is likely to change.

○ State Aids

State aids are government subsidies to enterprises, such as direct payments, 'soft loans', debt write-offs, tax breaks, or guaranteed borrowing. Between 1995 and 1997, an annual average of €95 billion was granted in state aid by member states to the manufacturing, agricultural, fisheries, coal-mining, transport and financial services sectors. There are wide variations in the scale and pattern of state aids between EU countries. The Commission's 8th annual survey of state aid published in April 2000 showed that aid volumes were falling in Germany, Italy, Belgium, Spain and Portugal but rising in the ten other member states (Commission, 2000a). In terms of value added, the UK (0.7%) and Sweden (0.8%) granted least aid, whereas Greece (4.9%) and Italy (4.4%) granted most. In Italy, aid as a percentage of value in the manufacturing sector is six times higher than in the UK. Aid in terms of euros per person employed is highest in Italy, Luxembourg and Ireland and lowest in Sweden and the UK.

State aids which distort, or threaten to distort, competition by favouring certain undertakings or the production of certain goods are banned by Article 87 of the EC Treaty (the coal and steel industries are covered by Article 67 of the ECSC Treaty). Article 87 covers aid granted by a member state or through state resources which provides a firm with an economic advantage which it would not otherwise have and which is capable of affecting trade between member states and therefore is incompatible with the common market. However, Article 87 contains many exemptions, such as:

- aid having a social character;
- aid to alleviate natural disasters or other exceptional occurrences;
- aid to promote the economic development of areas where the standard of living is abnormally low or where there is serious underemployment;
- aid to promote important projects of common European interest;
- aid to facilitate the development of certain economic activities or areas;
- aid to promote culture and heritage conservation;
- other categories decided by the Council (by qualified majority voting: QMV) following a Commission proposal.

These exemptions are so varied as to provide the Commission with considerable discretionary powers. Article 88 sets out the procedures for decisions on state aids. The rules on aids apply equally to the public and private sectors (in the case of the former, aid should not be given to state-owned companies if a private investor would not do so, given the same circumstances). An aid may be suppressed or modified by the Commission, subject to appeal by interested parties to the ECJ. The Commission has formulated three principles to guide decisions on aid: it should be part of a restructuring package; it may be used as a breathing space for industries with major social problems; it should not lead to an expansion of capacity.

In recent years, governments have come under pressure to provide rescue packages for troubled industries, although they have also been under pressure to cut state budgets. Under Article 88(3), national authorities are obliged to notify the Commission of any plans to grant aid or alter existing aid measures. All aid, other than assistance of up to €50,000 over three years to any one firm, must be notified to the Commission. In 2000, the Commission received 812 notifications of new aid schemes or amendments to existing schemes and registered 133 un-notified schemes. It raised no objections to 623 cases and initiated proceedings in 76. Of these, only 38 were rejected. The Commission's policy on state aids has arguably been lax. It has tended to approve restructuring packages without much scrutiny. Control of aids has proved difficult for several reasons: it is often difficult to ascertain the true level of aid or to compare levels between countries; the number of Commission staff involved is small; unlike anti-trust control, there is no parallel body to control state aids at national level.

The Commission, with the support of the Council, has sought to modernise state aid control, for example by implementing a procedural regulation on application of Article 88 which set out established practices and the case law of the ECJ regarding aid. It also gave the Commission additional powers, for example with regard to the recovery of illegal aid. The regulation, which came into force in April 1999, also seeks to speed up procedures. In December 2000, the Commission approved block exemption regulations concerning state aid to SMEs, aid for education and training and the *de minimis* rule, to enable it to concentrate on the most important cases. In March 2001 it set up a state aid register, which provides details on state aid cases. The register is published on the Competition Directorate's website.

○ EU Competition Policy: Principal Criticisms and Reform Trends

The main criticisms levied against EU competition policy are that there is a mismatch between the Commission's responsibilities and its resources; that the Commission's procedures for dealing with cases are slow and bureaucratic; that the Commission's judgements in competition cases are not adequately explained; that the Commission is insufficiently accountable; and that the competition regime has failed to adjust to changes in the business environment (which is increasingly global rather than regional or national).

The reform trend in EU competition policy seems to be towards *decentralisation*, that is, towards shifting the burden of competition work to national competition authorities, thereby allowing the Commission to concentrate on big competition cases. Under reforms proposed by the Commission, Articles 81 and 82 could be applied by any national authority or court as well as by the Commission (the 'parallel powers' approach). But decentralisation could lead to inconsistency, due to the fact that more bodies will be enforcing rules. Competition Commissioner Mario Monti is also seeking to explain the implications of competition policy decisions for citizens and to develop closer relations with consumer groups. The effects of globalisation increasingly means that competition policy is throwing up issues that have to be dealt with in a global, not a regional context. Large international mergers (for example between US and EU undertakings) are likely to be investigated by more than one competition authority, giving rise to jurisdictional conflicts and inconsistencies. This is leading to pressure for closer international co-operation. The EU would like the issue of competition policy to be included in the next World Trade Organisation trade round.

● INDUSTRIAL POLICY

○ Goals and Development

In its broadest sense industrial policy embraces all government policies affecting industry (including, environmental, energy and competition policies). However, it now tends to be defined more narrowly, to refer to government policies to foster and protect European industries, through:

- restructuring packages for ailing industries;
- support for 'sunrise' industries;
- support for small and medium-sized enterprises (SMEs);
- support for RTD programmes;
- protection of industries against 'unfair' foreign competition.

Elements of industrial policy can be discerned in both the European Coal and Steel Community Treaty, which includes references to intervention in the coal and steel industries, and the Treaty of Rome, which contains a reference to government support for industry. But neither treaty spelt out an industrial policy as such. The 1950s and 1960s were decades of economic growth in member states and industrial policy was not regarded as a key priority.

The need to support Europe's industries became more widely recognised in the 1970s, as traditional industries declined and the competitive position of EU firms in world markets worsened. The perception of significant gaps between the industrial performance of the Union and of its principal competitors was a major factor precipitating the development of a European industrial policy in the 1980s. It also became widely accepted that some key industrial problems could only be effectively dealt with at European level. The importance of EU industrial policy is shown by the fact that an industry chapter was added to the EC Treaty (Title XVI) in the Treaty on European Union (TEU). The title refers to actions in this field, to be taken at EU and national levels, aimed at speeding up adjustment of industry to structural changes; encouraging an environment favourable to initiative and the development and co-operation of undertakings (particularly SMEs); and fostering better exploitation of the industrial potential of policies of innovation, research and technological development. These actions are required to accord with the obligations of the EU and member states to ensure conditions necessary for the competitiveness of the Union's industry. They do not therefore provide a basis for the distortion of competition (Article 157, ECT). The Treaty of Nice will extend QMV and co-decision to measures taken under Article 157 but explicitly excludes measures containing tax provisions or provisions relating to the rights and interests of employed persons. EU support for industry is channelled through various mechanisms, such as the structural funds, the European Investment Bank and the RTD framework programmes.

❍ A Contentious Policy

The operation of an industrial policy is fraught with problems. For example, government intervention could do more economic harm than good. Financial aid might be given to prop up economically unviable enterprises. There will always be lobbies calling on governments to bail out ailing firms. It is by no means self-evident which industries or firms should be supported. The records of governments in 'picking industrial winners' has been poor. One strategy might be to encourage the emergence of large *Eurochampion* firms, able to take on the US and Japanese manufacturing giants in global markets (there are fewer very large businesses in the Union than in the US). This might be sought through encouraging mergers between EU firms or through financial support to boost firm size. Arguably, the Eurochampion strategy has several flaws: it could reduce competition within the EU, by reducing the number of firms; it means that some firms (the potential Eurochampions) will be given preferential treatment; it could have a negative effect on the efficiency of Eurochampions because they may become reliant on subsidies.

There is by no means unanimity of view concerning the purpose of industrial policy and the extent to which it is compatible with other policy objectives (for example, reconciling support for industry with the creation of a level playing field for business). There are significant variations in the industrial philosophies of member states. France has tended to favour an 'interventionist' industrial policy, involving commitment to national planning and assistance. By contrast, Conservative governments in the UK severely curtailed industrial subsidies. Industrial policy has caused fierce debates within the EU between those advocating state intervention and those arguing that industrial growth is best achieved through the operation of market forces. In recent years, the balance has shifted towards the latter but advocates of intervention have fought a spirited rearguard action. In the 1990s, Commission and Council statements on industrial policy have tended to have three interrelated emphases: firstly, on the need to promote industrial competitiveness and innovation in order to compete successfully in global markets: see, for example, *An Industrial Competitiveness Policy for the EU* (Commission, 1994); secondly, on the need for the Union's industries to pursue high-tech, high value-added activities: see, for example, the White Paper on *Growth, Competitiveness and Employment* (Commission, 1993) and the conclusions of the Lisbon European Council in March 2000; and thirdly, on the need to respond to the challenges of the knowledge-driven, 'new economy'. In April 2000, the Commission adopted a multiannual programme on enterprise and entrepreneurship for the 2001–05 period (COM (2000) 256) aimed at assisting businesses (particularly SMEs) to respond to the challenges of the new economy. RTD Policy has been assigned a crucial role in fostering the Union's current industrial policy goals.

● RTD POLICY

○ The EU's 'Technological Lag'

In January 2000, a Commission communication entitled *Towards a European Research Area* identified *technological lag* as a major factor accounting for the EU's poor economic performance relative to its major competitors (Commission, 2000b). Both the Cecchini Report (1987) and the Commission's 1993 White Paper on *Growth, Competitiveness and Employment* had made similar observations. The EU has lagged behind in the development of high-tech industries, which tend to create more jobs than other industries. It has also had a large negative trade balance in high tech products in recent years, averaging €20 billion a year in the decade ending in 1998. The main reasons often cited to account for this technological lag are:

● **Low investment:** In 1998, only 1.8% of EU GDP was spent on research, compared with 2.8% in the US and 2.9% in Japan. Moreover, this gap appeared to be widening: the spending gap on research between the US and Europe was €12 billion in 1992 and €60 billion in 1998. In 1998, the EU had 2.5 researchers for every thousand of the industrial workforce, compared with 6.7 in the US and six in Japan. In Japan and the US, private sector investment in research accounted for over three times as much as the public sector, whereas in the EU it accounted for less than twice as much. Moreover, expenditure on RTD by the private sector was increasing faster in the US and Japan than in the EU. There were also wide variations in the amounts devoted to research within the EU. In 1998, investment in RTD in the EU ranged from 3.85% of GDP in Sweden to 0.5% in Greece. Moreover, there were also wide variations in the breakdown of research expenditure between the public and private sectors: for example, whereas in Greece the public sector accounted for over three times as much research as the private sector, in Sweden the reverse was true. The next enlargements of the Union are likely to exacerbate the relatively poor performance of the EU with regard to RTD spending because candidate countries spend substantially lower amounts on RTD than the EU average, as Table 12.2 below shows.

• **Poor application:** Both the US and Japan are currently better at producing tangible research outputs in the form of saleable products. Europe is stronger in pure science than in applied research and commercial applications, despite the fact that EU researchers produce more than three times as many scientific papers as their counterparts in Japan. In high-tech sectors, European countries accounted for 9% of patents applied for in the US in 1998, whereas the US accounted for 36% of patents in high-tech sectors in Europe (the corresponding figures for Japan were 3% and 22%). This has been attributed to poor links between universities and businesses and to over-emphasis on basic research rather than product development.

• **Fragmentation:** Duplication of research and failure to reap economies of scale have frequently been cited as major deficiencies. National RTD programmes predominate, with EU programmes accounting for less than 17% of total public spending on European research. EU research has tended to be additional to, and overlap with, that of the 15 member states. Another example of fragmentation is the cumbersome European patients system, involving translation requirements and legal disputes between national courts. The average cost of registering a patent in Europe is €50,000, five times higher than in the US. The Feira European Council in June 2000 called for a Community patent to be introduced in 2001. But at the Stockholm European Council in March 2001 no agreement was reached on this.

Table 12.2 RTD Investment in the EU and Candidate Countries, 1998

EU	% of GDP	Candidate Countries	% of GDP
Greece	0.50	Latvia	0.4
Portugal	0.65	Turkey	0.5
Spain	0.86	Lithuania	0.5
Italy	1.03	Bulgaria	0.6
Ireland	1.43	Romania	0.6
Belgium	1.58	Estonia	0.6
Austria	1.63	Hungary	0.7
UK	1.87	Poland	0.7
Denmark	1.91	Malta	1.0
Netherlands	2.12	Slovakia	1.2
France	2.20	Czech Republic	1.2
Germany	2.32	Slovenia	1.5
Finland	2.92		
Sweden	3.85		
EU15	1.80		

Source: Commission (2000b).

The Development of RTD Policy

The idea of a European technological community was part of Jean Monnet's 'Action Committee for a United States of Europe' programme in the 1950s and 1960s, but was not adopted. The development of the civilian nuclear power industry was boosted by the signing of the European Atomic Energy Community (Euratom) Treaty in 1957. But it was not until the late 1970s, when the problems of poor competitiveness and industrial decline in the Union became manifest, that the issue of RTD in the non-nuclear field began to be addressed seriously. In 1979, Vicomte Étienne Davignon, who had been appointed Commissioner with responsibilities for RTD in 1977, produced a document which criticised the fragmentation of the Union's research effort and which advocated an explicit industrial strategy for the Union. Davignon invited the heads of Europe's top electronics and information technology (IT) companies to a round-table discussion on this issue in 1979. Davignon's ideas provided the underpinning for the European research programmes created in the 1980s.

The need to address the Union's technology gap was reflected in the Single European Act (SEA), which placed a strong emphasis upon the need for cross-border collaboration in RTD and gave the Commission the task of improving co-ordination of member states' RTD programmes. As a result of the TEU and (particularly) the Treaty of Amsterdam, qualified majority voting and co-decision now apply to most areas of RTD policy. Union RTD programmes have several distinctive features. The idea behind all programmes is to encourage firms to 'think European': they support collaborative projects, involving partners from different member states; they are undertaken on a shared cost basis (the EU being responsible for up to half of total costs); research grants are awarded on a competitive basis (there are no national research quotas). In principle only projects involving fundamental research at the 'pre-competitive' stage are eligible for assistance. Product development and marketing remain the responsibility of private industry. This principle was established to prevent firms receiving research support from reaping unfair competitive advantages. But when research support is pre-competitive, it is difficult to judge its impact. Because of the problem of poor application, there is a trend towards support for more market-oriented projects. The EU has its own joint research centre, located on sites in Italy, Germany, the Netherlands, Belgium and Spain.

By no means all European collaborative RTD projects are confined to member states. For example, EUREKA, the European Research Co-ordination Agency, ESA (the European Space Agency), DIANE (Direct Information Access Network for Europe, a database), CERN (European Centre for Nuclear Research), the European Science Foundation, COST (co-operation on scientific and technical research) and JET (the Joint European

Torus programme aimed at harnessing fusion energy) are pan-European ventures, involving EU and non-EU countries. The Anglo-French Concorde project and the Airbus project (involving companies from France, Germany, the UK and Spain) were developed outside the EU framework. EUREKA was established in 1985, with the aim of improving Europe's performance in producing high-tech goods and services for world markets. It was proposed by President Mitterrand as a response to the US 'Star Wars' programme. It is not an EU body and its membership now comprises 29 countries. However, it is managed by the Commission. EUREKA projects are proposed and run by industrial firms. EUREKA's critics argue that it has a poor record in producing results in the form of commercially successful products, although its annual impact reports paint a far more positive picture (see for example its 2000 report at http://www3.eureka.be). The Commission provides an information service on the EU's RTD activities (CORDIS, the Community Research and Development Information Service).

The weaknesses and gaps in the EU's RTD performance (particularly in relation to that of the US) led the Commission to launch a major new RTD initiative in January 2000. It noted that Europe was continuing to lag behind the US in RTD spending (the US spent €70 billion more than Europe on RTD in 1999). Moreover, the gap appeared to be widening in the field of the new technologies required to develop the new economy and the knowledge-based society. It therefore proposed the creation of a *European research area* (ERA), in order to remove the compartmentalisation of national public research systems and to improve co-ordination in implementation of national and European research policies. This would involve forging closer links between the EU's research activities and those of member states, so that they reinforce, rather than duplicate, each other. It called for a concerted effort by policymakers and researchers in Europe and identified priority targets for creating a coherent and barrier-free research area (Commission, 2000b).

The ERA proposal was endorsed by the Lisbon European Council in March 2000 and a progress report on its implementation was submitted to the Stockholm European Council in March 2001. In May 2001, the Commission proposed a sixth research framework programme, with a budget of €17.5 billion for the period 2002 and 2006, built around the goals of the ERA (see below for more information on the framework programmes). The programme will focus on seven sectors: biotechnology and genomics; information society technologies; nanotechnologies; aeronautics and space; food safety and health risks; sustainable development and global change; and citizens and governance in the knowledge-based economy. It will also provide financial support for researcher mobility within the ERA. It remains to be seen if the ERA initiative will have the transformative effect intended. Previous RTD initiatives have also sought to reduce the fragmentation of the EU research effort and to boost RTD investment, with limited success.

○ **The RTD Framework Programmes**

Since 1987, as a result of the SEA, EU RTD activities have been co-ordinated under framework programmes. These programmes are accorded a central role in the Union's RTD policy and provide insights into current RTD priorities. Their principal aims are : to ensure that there is sufficient expertise in main technologies; to enable European firms to reap economies of scale in RTD; to facilitate co-ordination of national RTD efforts, to avoid duplication; and to narrow gaps in RTD spending between member states.

The third programme (1990–94) was worth €6.6 billion and the fourth (1994–98) €13.16 billion. The fourth reflected many ideas for 'technological awakening' contained in the Delors White Paper. The programme sought improved transfer of technologies from universities to companies, through better dissemination and utilisation of research results, with particular emphasis on benefiting SMEs. It sought to boost the Union's research effort in newer technologies, such as IT, biotechnology and eco-technology, and better integration of national, Union and pan-European research activities. The fifth programme was adopted by the Council and the European Parliament in December 1998 and became operative from the beginning of 1999. The programme, which has a budget of €14.96 billion (see Table 12.3 below), recognises that the major challenge to the EU is employment, which depends increasingly on use of new technologies. It differs from its predecessors in a number of respects. The aim is to move away from pure research towards research focusing on 23 current socio-economic problems, known as key actions. These account for over two-thirds of the funding under the programme and cover all types of RTD, from basic research to demonstration activities. Technical advice is provided by 17 external advisory groups. Researchers from candidate countries, plus Norway, Iceland, Liechtenstein, Israel and Switzerland also participate, subject to contributions from these countries to the EU budget.

Table 12.3 The 5th Framework Programme Budget: 1999–2002

5th EC & Euratom Framework Programmes	€ m.
5th EC Framework Programme	**13,700**
Quality of life and management of living resources	2,413
User-friendly information society	3,600
Competitive and sustainable growth	2,705
Energy, environment and sustainable development	2,125
Confirming the international role of Community research	475
Promotion of innovation and encouragement of SME participation	363
Improving human research potential & socioeconomic knowledge	1,280
Direct actions (Joint Research Centre)	739
5th Euratom Framework Programme	**1,260**

Source: Commission.

● CONCLUSION

Key roles have been assigned to competition, industrial and RTD policies in the EU's strategy for economic regeneration and global competitiveness. Recognition of the EU's relatively poor economic performance when measured against that of the US has provided a stimulus for reform in each of these policy areas. But in each case progress has been impeded by the difficulties involved in reconciling the interests and philosophies of member states. Moreover, the impact of these policies on the EU's overall economic health is hard to assess. For example, the effect of EU RTD policy is difficult to evaluate, not least because the EU is but one of several sources of funding for research projects and because of difficulties in measuring research impacts. The Commission's annual reports on the EU's RTD activities tend to highlight the benefits of the framework programmes for competitiveness, employment and regional development (see, for example, Commission, 2000c). However, a five-year assessment of the programmes by a panel independent experts (known as the Majò report after its chairman) concluded in 2000 that these were not enough to achieve the EU's RTD goals and needed to be adapted and supplemented (Commission, 2000d). By itself, RTD policy is unlikely to solve the problem of the EU's 'technological lag'. But it is firmly established as a key aspect of the EU's policy portfolio and, given the EU's commitment to the promotion of high-tech, high value-added industries, seems set to grow in importance.

FURTHER READING

Bangemann, M. (1993), *Meeting the Global Challenge: Establishing a Successful European Industrial Policy*, Kogan Page, London.

Cecchini, P. (1988), *The European Challenge: 1992 The Benefits of a Single Market*, Wildwood House, Aldershot.

Cini, M. and McGowan, L. (1999), *Competition Policy in the EU*, Macmillan, Basingstoke.

Commission (1993), *Growth, Competitiveness and Employment*, COM (93) 700.

Commission (1994), *An Industrial Competitiveness Policy for the EU*, COM (94) 319.

Commission (1999a), *White Paper on Modernisation of the Rules Implementing Articles 81 and 82 of the EC Treaty*, COM (99) 101.

Commission (2000a), *8th Survey on State Aid in the EU*, COM (2000) 205.

Commission (2000b), *Towards a European Research Area*, COM (2000) 6.

Commission (2000c), *RTD Activities of the EU*, Annual Report, COM (2000) 284.

Commission (2000d), *Comments of the Commission on the conclusion of the RTD Framework Programmes 5-Year Assessment*, COM (2000) 659.

Darmer, M. and Kuyper, L. (eds.), *Industry and the European Union. Analysing Policies for Business*, Edward Elgar, Cheltenham and Northampton, MA.

 **Chapter 13**

Trans-European Networks

● WHAT ARE TRANS-EUROPEAN NETWORKS?

The Union is currently according high priority to the promotion of trans-European networks (TENs) programmes in the fields of transport, energy, telecommunications and environmental infrastructure. These programmes seek to connect the networks of member states, in order to create integrated, Union-wide networks. The importance of TENs to the aims of integrating the economies of member states and to economic growth was acknowledged in both the Treaty on European Union (TEU) and in the Commission's 1993 White Paper on *Growth, Competitiveness and Employment.* In December 1993, the Brussels European Council established two TENs working groups, one on the subjects of transport and energy (headed by Commissioner Henning Christopherson and comprising high-ranking officials from member states) and the other on telecommunications (headed by Commissioner Martin Bangemann and comprising industrialists). In June 1994, the Corfu European Council extended the mandate of the Christopherson group to include environmental infrastructure. At Corfu, over 40 TENs projects were agreed.

The EU is performing guiding and co-ordinating roles in TENs programmes, although only a small proportion of the finance for TENs projects is coming from the EU budget. The bulk of funds for these projects is expected to be provided by the private sector and by national governments, although the European Investment Bank (EIB) and the European Investment Fund have important roles. This chapter focuses on transport networks, although it also deals briefly with energy and telecommunications networks. The EU transport, energy and telecommunications sectors share several characteristics: each has developed largely within a national rather than an EU context; EU policy for these sectors has been rather slow to develop; the logic of the Single European Market (SEM) has provided a powerful stimulus to EU policy in each sector.

● THE COMMON TRANSPORT POLICY

○ The Slow Development of the Common Transport Policy

The goal of a Common Transport Policy (CTP) was set out in Title IV (now V, ECT) of the Treaty of Rome. Article 71 (formerly 75) outlines the substance of the CTP, that is, common rules applicable to internal transport affecting member states; conditions for permitting non-resident carriers to operate within member states; and measures to improve transport safety. Article 80 specifies that the title applies to rail, road and inland waterways, but that the Council acting by qualified majority can extend its provisions to air and sea transport (which the Council did in 1986). The CTP is one of only three common policies mentioned in the treaty (the others being the Common Agricultural Policy and the Common Commercial Policy). However, unlike the other two common policies, the CTP lay virtually dormant until the 1980s. The CTP has proved difficult to develop for several reasons:

- *the diversity of national systems*: each member state has developed its own transport system within a national context and there are wide variations in the pattern and quality of national networks. For example, railway and motorway networks are dense in some countries but sparse in others. Belgium has the densest rail and motorway networks whereas Greece, Portugal, Spain and Ireland are relatively poorly served by road and rail links. In the rail sector, there are different sizes of rolling stock and of power supply. Several countries have no inland waterways;
- *costs*: the enormous expense involved in developing a common transport infrastructure (for example, building roads, tunnels, railtracks and airports);
- *burden-sharing*: the 'who pays?' problem (should the financial burden fall primarily on the states directly affected by transport projects or should costs be borne by all EU members?);
- *vested interests*: the domination of some transport sectors by national carriers, which have an interest in defending near-monopoly positions.

Although the Commission made several attempts in the 1970s to kick start the CTP, it was not until the 1980s that it began to show signs of life. In 1983, the European Parliament (EP) took the Council to the European Court of Justice (ECJ) for failing to carry out its obligations with regard to transport under the Treaty of Rome: in a complex judgement in 1985 (case 13/83), the court ruled that, although references in the Treaty to the CTP were too vague to identify clearly what the Council's obligations were, the treaty had nevertheless been infringed. The court ruled that inland transport of goods and passengers should be open to all Union firms and recommended that the Council work towards a CTP.

○ **Factors Shaping the CTP**

From the mid-1980s, the CTP has been shaped and energised by a combination of factors:

• **The impact of the Single European Market.** The SEM programme includes a wide range of measures to reduce barriers to the cross-border movement of goods and people and to increase cross-border competition in transport. It was recognised that peripheral regions could lose out on the benefits of the SEM because of poor transport links to prosperous regions (justifying investment in transport infrastructure via the EIB and the Union's structural funds). The impact of the SEM on the CTP is arguably another good example of 'integration spillover'.

• **Trans-European networks.** Underlying the TENs programme is a recognition that a barrier-free Europe cannot be achieved without measures to remove the problem of physical barriers, such as transport bottlenecks, missing links and poor infrastructure.

• **Environmental policy.** Transport is never environmentally neutral. A key feature of the EU's current transport policy is the extent to which it has become intertwined with environmental policy. Transport represents around a quarter of CO_2 emissions and is set to become the biggest contributor to greenhouse gas emissions in the EU. The themes of environmentally friendly transport and of *sustainable mobility* are now integrated into the CTP.

• **Traffic congestion,** due for example to increases in car ownership, cross-border trade, citizens' leisure time and international travel. In the last two decades, intra-EU traffic has grown by 3.1% a year for passengers and by 2.3% a year for goods. Road transport is now the predominant mode of transport for passengers and freight. In 1998, the 169 million cars on EU roads accounted for about 79% of passenger transport compared with 9% for buses and coaches, 6% for railways, 1% for trams and metro and 5% for air. Road accounted for about 80% of goods transported (in tonnes), compared with 7% for rail, 3% for inland waterways, 6% for sea (intra-EU) and 4% for pipelines. Air traffic, in terms of passengers carried, has more than tripled in the last two decades whereas both rail and waterway transport have declined as a proportion of total transport use.

• **The growing importance of the transport industry.** In EU15, transport accounts for about 8% of Union GDP, 40% of public investment, 30% of energy consumption, and 10% of all persons employed (about six million in transport services, about two million in transport equipment and about six million in closely related sectors, such as vehicle repair and car rental).

• **Enlargement.** The geographical expansion of the Union as a result of enlargement, and the Union's closer links with Eastern Europe, have increased the need for a pan-European approach to transport policy. As a

of the information society in Europe. In 1997, the Commission published a Green Paper on the convergence of the telecommunications, media, information and technology sectors (Commission, 1997). But given the rapid pace of technological change in these fields, the appropriateness and effectiveness of EU measures to promote the information society remain to be seen. Moreover, telecommunications is a global industry and therefore EU policies for this sector are likely to be developed increasingly within a global rather than an exclusively European or national framework.

● CONCLUSION

The EU's trans-European networks policy derives from the logic of deeper integration, in that a Single European Market could never be entirely complete if each member state has its own transport, telecommunications and energy policies and infrastructures. However, the development of EU policies in these fields has been impeded by the fact that each policy has been developed within a national context. The heavy price tags involved in pursuing transport projects has encouraged member states and the Commission to favour 'public–private partnerships' as a means of securing adequate funding. But much remains to be done before the EU has fully integrated networks in transport, telecommunications and energy.

FURTHER READING

Johnson, D. and Turner, C. (1997), *Trans-European Networks*, Macmillan, Basingstoke.

Commission (1992), *White Paper on the Future Development of the Common Transport Policy* , COM (92) 0494.

Commission (1994a), *Europe's Way to the Information Society*, COM (94) 34.

Commission (1994b), *Green Paper: For a European Energy Policy*, COM (94) 659.

Commission (1994c), *Green Paper on the Liberalisation of Telecommunications Infrastructure and Cable TV Networks*, COM (94) 440 and 682.

Commission (1995a), *The Common Transport Policy Action Programme 1995–2000*, COM (95) 0302.

Commission (1995b) *Trans-European Networks*, The Group of Personal Representatives of the Heads of State or Government Report.

Commission (1996) *White Paper: A Strategy for revitalising the Community's Railways*, COM (96) 421.

Commission (1997), Green Paper on *Convergence of the Telecommunications, Media and Information Technology Sectors*, COM (94) 623.

Commission (1998), *The Common Transport Policy – Sustainable Mobility: Perspectives for the Future*, COM (98) 716.

 **Chapter 14**

Environmental Policy

● DEVELOPMENT

○ The Main Factors Shaping EU Environmental Policy

The Treaty of Rome contained no provision for a Union environmental policy. Indeed, the initial impetus for the development of the Union was towards rapid industrial and agricultural growth, aims which might be perceived as potentially incompatible with environmental protection. However, since the beginning of the 1970s, the EU has developed an extensive range of policies on environmental issues and has launched six environmental action programmes. All EU policies are now required to take into account the environmental dimension (a requirement known as 'environmental mainstreaming'). Environmental concerns are accorded high priority, for example, in the EU's policies on transport and agriculture. Environmental policy is now a key issue in enlargement negotiations and in the EU's assistance programmes for Central and Eastern Europe. Environmental considerations play important roles in projects financed by the European Investment Bank (EIB). The EU is also a major participant in international fora on global environmental issues. It has established a European Environmental Agency (EEA) to monitor the state of the European environment. The EU has already enacted over 700 environmental laws and has also adopted numerous opinions, recommendations, declarations and other non-binding statements on the environment.

The growing importance of EU environmental policy in the last two decades can be attributed to a combination of factors, such as the rise of the 'green' movement in Western Europe; acceptance of the need for cross-border collaboration on environmental problems because 'pollution knows no frontiers'; and recognition that 'level playing field' measures are needed to ensure that member states do not use national environmental standards as

343

barriers to trade within the Single European Market (Commission, 1999a). The development of EU environmental policy has, however, been constrained and shaped by several other key factors, namely:

• **The wide variations in environmental standards within the EU.** For example, Austria, Denmark, the Netherlands, Finland, Sweden and Germany have much higher environmental standards than Greece, Portugal or Spain. In recent years, there has been a trend towards greater flexibility in the application of Union environmental protection measures, providing that minimum requirements are met. The fourth enlargement increased pressure for high environmental standards in the EU, because Sweden, Finland and Austria generally have higher environmental standards than the EU average. The accession of Central and East European countries (CEECs), all of whom currently have lower standards than the EU average, may slow down the pace of further developments in EU environmental policy, perhaps leading to a focus on consolidation rather than upon higher standards.

• **The fuzzy boundary between national and EU policies.** Some environmental matters (for example, the environmental consequences of domestic road projects) are restricted in their effects to a specific territory whereas others affect several countries and some have global implications, such as the emission of chlorofluorocarbon (CFC) gases. Those opposed to deeper EU integration have tended to argue that the EU had no right to be involved in every nook and cranny of domestic policy and that domestic governments should decide on the environmental implications of projects with no cross-border dimension.

• **Environmental policy has often proved difficult to implement.** Environmental law remains the most frequently ignored aspect of EU legislation. The majority of member states have been admonished by the European Court of Justice (ECJ) for failing to apply EU standards with regard to environmental legislation. The EU's chief legislative instrument for the implementation of environmental policy has been the directive which provides member states with some leeway in relation to when and how EU laws are transposed into national law. Moreover, even when directives have been transposed, they have not necessarily been fully complied with. In 1999, the Commission produced its first annual survey on the application of EU environmental law: this report showed that in 1997, it referred 37 cases to the ECJ and sent 69 reasoned opinions to member states, mainly concerning hazardous waste, conservation and the labelling of dangerous materials. In five cases, the Commission imposed daily fines ranging from €26,000 to €246,000 per day for persistent non-compliance (Commission, 1999b). By May 2001, almost a third of the Commission's infringement proceedings against member states concerned the environment sector.

• **Environmental problems shows no signs of abating.** In June 1999, the EEA produced a detailed report on the state of the environment in the EU, plus environmental forecasts for the year 2010. The report argued that there was no room for complacency and that the EU environment will continue to be subject to pressure from industrial production, transport, energy, agriculture, tourism and household consumption. Waste increased by 10% from 1990 to 1996 and was expected to continue to increase at roughly the same rate; between 1995 and 2010, the EU's energy consumption was expected to increase by 15%; passenger car transport by 30%; freight transport by 50%; and international tourist numbers by 50%. The report foresaw no indication of significant eco-efficiency gains in transport and agriculture up to 2010 (EEA, 1999).

• **Reconciling environmental priorities with other policies.** The adverse environmental consequences of some Union policies (for example, commitment to industrial growth, the Common Agricultural Policy or transport projects) are by no means easy to eliminate. This has often led to tension between the commissioner for the environment and other commissioners. The White Paper on *Growth, Competitiveness and Employment* (Commission, 1993), however, argued that the pursuit of high environmental standards (reflected, for example, in the development of new, cleaner technologies) could enable European industry to 'trade up' to higher value-added activities. It stressed the need to exploit positive synergies between industrial competitiveness and environmental protection.

• **Burden-sharing.** Environmental improvements can be very costly: this raises the question of how much member states are prepared to contribute to environmental renovation in countries other than their own. EU environmental policy is primarily regulatory rather than redistributive: nevertheless, the European Regional Development Fund, the Cohesion Fund and the EIB all provide assistance for environmental projects. In some cases, the price exacted by some of the poorer states for acceptance of higher environmental standards has been the agreement by other states to support increases in funding for environmental infrastructure projects (for example via the Cohesion Fund).

O The Key Actors in EU Environmental Policy

The Commission, the member states and (as a result of enhancement of its legislative powers) the European Parliament (EP) are the key actors. The ECJ plays a key role in the enforcement of EU environmental law and has made many important judgments in this area. Having responsibility for policy formulation and by being at the centre of a dense network of environmental and industrial lobbies, the Commission exerts considerable influence over the substance and direction of environmental policy. However, its proposals are subject to amendment and approval by the Council and (in most cases) the EP, which have their own agendas. Within both the Council and the

Commission, environmental policy is subject to competing interests and influences. For example, within the Council there is a recurring 'tug of war' between member states seeking higher environmental standards (such as Germany, the Netherlands, Austria and the Scandinavian countries) and those resisting such proposals (generally the poorest member states). Generally speaking, however, instead of a 'lowest common denominator effect', there has been a tendency for the 'less green' countries to be pulled towards acceptance of higher standards. There is also the problem of reconciling the goals and interests of the Environment Council with those of other sectoral councils such as transport or enterprise. Similar sectoral conflicts occur between directorates within the Commission. The EP's legislative role in environmental policy was considerably enhanced by the extension first of the co-operation and then of the co-decision procedure. The EP, through its large and well-established Environment Committee, has been strongly and consistently supportive of higher environmental standards. However, the ability of the EP to shape environmental policy effectively has been weakened by its lack of technical expertise and support staff.

In addition to the formal institutional actors mention above, the EU's environmental policy networks also embrace a complex web of organised interests and advisory groups. The Commission supports the European Consultative Forum on the Environment and Sustainable Development, (comprising representatives from business, trade unions, non-governmental organisations (NGOs) and public bodies) which provides it with advice on environmental matters. Green pressure groups, such as the European Environmental Bureau (which includes various NGOs), Friends of the Earth, the World Wildlife Fund and Greenpeace also operate at EU level. The first three are financially supported by the Commission. At the European level, green groups are still outgunned in resources by well-organised and well-funded industrial lobbies. It seems likely that green groups are able to exert greater influence on policy at the national rather than the European level.

Although the Commission is formally responsible for implementation, in practice environmental policy is carried out by national and subnational authorities. The Commission does not have sufficient resources to enable it monitor the implementation of environmental policy effectively. Even when environmental policies are adopted, there is no certainty that they will be fully and promptly implemented. For example, in March 2001, Environment commissioner Margot Wallström complained, in a 'name and shame' seminar on city sewage, that most member states had still not fully implemented the urban waste water directive adopted ten years earlier and that 37 large cities were still discharging untreated waste water into the environment. 'Implementation deficits' in environmental policy result from many factors, including foot-dragging by member states; the vagueness of some environmental directives; unanticipated costs involved in implementing some legislation (such as the directives on water standards); the Commission culture (widely regarded as weak on managerial ability); and the large number of actors involved in implementation on the ground. There is now an EU network for the implementation and enforcement of environmental law (IMPEL), involving national enforcement authorities who meet twice yearly. In 1998, CEECs became involved in this network, through the formation of a network entitled AC-IMPEL. Although they are not empowered to complain directly to the ECJ, pressure groups and individuals play an important role in notifying the Commission about non-compliance by member states.

◯ The Impact of the SEA, the TEU and the ToA

The Single European Act (SEA) marked a watershed in the development of EU environmental policy, by providing the Union with an explicit statutory mandate in this field. Prior to this, EU environmental policy had to be legitimised through a liberal interpretation of certain general provisions in the Treaty of Rome (such as the preamble which refers to the goal of improving living and working conditions). The SEA added a title on the environment to the Treaty (Title XVI, now XIX, ECT), declaring its objectives to be:
- preserving, protecting and improving the quality of the environment;
- protecting human health;
- prudent and rational utilisation of natural resources.

The title stated that the Union would act when these objectives could be attained better at Union level than at national level, an implicit reference to the 'subsidiarity' principle. It also stated that environmental protection requirements would be a component of other Union policies, an implicit reference to 'environmental mainstreaming' (see below). It allowed member states to adopt more stringent measures providing they are compatible with the Treaty (Article 176, ECT), meaning in effect that they should not be used to restrict trade and are subject to the Commission's approval. The Treaty on European Union (TEU) further strengthened the Union's role in environment policy and also made the nature of this role more explicit. It added a fourth policy objective, namely:
- promoting measures at international level to deal with regional or world-wide environmental problems.

The TEU also stated that a task of the Union is the promotion of 'sustainable and non-inflationary growth respecting the environment' (Article 2, ECT). It committed the Union to aim for a high level of environmental protection, taking into account regional diversity (Article 174, ECT). Prior to ratification of the TEU, Council decisions on environmental policy were based on the 'unanimity' principle. The TEU provided for qualified majority voting on most environmental issues, although in some areas, such as fiscal measures, town and country planning and measures significantly affecting choices between different energy sources, the unanimity principle still applies (Article 175, ECT). The TEU also established the Cohesion Fund, which finances environmental and transport projects in the four poorest member states.

The Treaty of Amsterdam (ToA) introduced the concept of 'sustainable development' and also includes a declaration on environmental impact assessments, requiring the Commission to prepare such assessments when making proposals which have significant environmental implications. Sustainable development is referred to in the preamble and in Article 2 of the revised TEU, which states that one of the tasks of the Union is the promotion of 'harmonious and balanced and sustainable development of economic activities' and 'a high level of protection and improvement of the quality of the environment'. Article 6 of the EC Treaty requires environmental protection to be integrated into the definition and implementation of Union policies and activities (environmental mainstreaming, see below). The EP is granted powers of co-decision on most aspects of environmental policy, excluding environmental taxation, land use planning, management of water resources and energy supply.

◯ The Mainstreaming of Environmental Policy

The aim of mainstreaming is to ensure that environmental considerations are part of any new initiative in all policy sectors. Put bluntly, environmental mainstreaming is an attempt to force Union policymakers to 'think green'. The Commission is seeking to ensure that environmental requirements are fully taken into account as soon as Union policies are conceived. Each of the Commission's Directorates-General is required to choose an official charged with the task of ensuring that the environmental effects of legislative proposals are taken into account. They are also required to provide an annual report on the environmental dimension to their activities. Any project liable to have an environmental impact is now subject to a *strategic environmental impact assessment*. At the Cardiff European Council, in June 1998, the Commission presented a communication entitled *Partnership for Integration*, which outlined guidelines for the integration environmental dimension into all policies. The Cardiff summit agreed a strategy for the integration of environmental objectives into all Community policies and actions. At the Helsinki European Council in December 1999, the integration strategies of six sectoral councils – agriculture, transport, energy, industry, internal market and development – were presented and agreed.

However, as the European Environment Agency's forecasts for the state of the European environment in 2010 have shown (EEA, 1999), environmental protection is an uphill struggle: far more than lip-service will need to be paid to 'mainstreaming' if the EU's environmental objectives are to be achieved.

● PROGRAMMES AND POLICIES

○ The Environmental Action Programmes

From 1973, the Union has adopted a series of environmental action programmes. The programmes are indicative rather than legally binding. However, many items contained in the programmes are eventually translated into Union law, although often after considerable argument, refinement and delay. The first action programme set out to: foster environmental awareness in member countries; conduct impact studies; prevent or reduce pollution and noise nuisances; introduce measures for the management of waste; and promote clean technologies. It also led to the establishment in 1975 of the principle that those guilty of polluting the environment should be made to pay (*the 'polluter pays' principle*), which was given legal force in the SEA (Article 174, ECT). The second and third programmes consolidated and developed the ideas contained in the initial programme. The fourth (1987–92) was closely linked to the environmental policies in the SEA.

The fifth programme, for 1993–2000 (Commission, 1992), signalled a shift in emphasis in EU environmental policy in several ways: it emphasised that policy should be geared towards prevention rather than correction of environmental damage; it favoured a shift from the traditional 'top-down' (or command-and-control) approach based on regulatory environmental legislation towards a 'bottom-up' approach. The new approach had two essential features: it sought to involve a broader range of actors and to employ a broader range of policy instruments, including economic incentives to promote 'environmentally friendly' products and improved information and education. It focused on five target sectors: industry, energy, transport, agriculture and tourism. It had seven themes: climate change; acidification and air quality; the urban environment; coastal zones; waste management; management of water resources; and protection of nature and bio-diversity.

The sixth programme, for 2001–2010 (Commission, 2001), seeks the active involvement of all sections of society in the search for innovative, workable and sustainable solutions to environmental problems. It identifies four priority areas: climate change; nature and biodiversity; environment and health; and natural resources and waste. Improvements in these areas are to be sought through five key approaches: ensuring implementation of existing legislation; integrating environmental concerns into all relevant policy areas; working closely with business and consumers; ensuring better and more accessible information for citizens; and developing a more environmentally conscious attitude towards land use. Arguably, there has been a tendency of the Commission to set targets for these programmes which are too ambitious. But without a strong element of exhortation and the setting of guidelines, it is arguable whether so much in this field would have been achieved.

○ The European Environment Agency

The European Environment Agency is the successor to the 'CORINE' programme (1985–90), which was an experimental project on the collection and collation of information on the state of the environment and natural resources within the Union. The agency is based in Copenhagen and has been operational since 1994. It was established to collect and publish comparative data on environmental conditions in member states. It publishes a report on the state of Europe's environment every three years. It also prepares reports on the EU's environmental action programmes. It carries out its functions in co-operation with the European Information and Observation Network (Eionet), which comprises national networks. In addition to EU countries, Norway, Iceland and Liechtenstein are also members of the EEA. The agency also works closely with CEECs. It has a management board comprising one representative from each member state, two from the Commission and two designated by the EP. Its work focuses on several priority areas, including air and water quality, waste management, noise emissions, hazardous substances and coastal protection. A 'state of the environment' report was published by the agency in March 1999 (EEA, 1999). The EP wanted the agency to have an enforcement role, but the Council would not agree to this. Its functions may be extended to include involvement in the monitoring of EU environmental legislation and preparation of criteria for the award of environmental labels. However, its staff is arguably too small to take on wider responsibilities.

○ Examples of Specific Environmental Policies

• **Water.** Measures have been introduced in relation to drinking water quality, sewage treatment and the discharge of dangerous substances into rivers and seas. In 1980 the EU established strict standards for the quality of drinking water, through the drinking water directive. Several member states (including the UK) have been taken to the ECJ because of alleged breach of this directive. The urban waste water directive requires competent authorities to ensure that all areas with over 2000 inhabitants have adequate sewerage systems and/or treatment plants by 2005. A considerable proportion of the UK's water industry investment programme is directed towards meeting EU standards on water and sewage treatment. There are still major marine pollution problems, particularly in relation to the North Sea, the Mediterranean and the Baltic Sea. Various measures against marine pollution have been introduced, for example, in relation to bathing water quality and promotion of clean beaches. EU legislation prohibits discharge of dangerous substances into EU waters. The EU publishes an annual report on EU bathing water standards. A blue flag is awarded to the cleanest EU beaches.

- **Waste.** The reduction, processing and recycling of waste is now regarded as a key priority. In the EU alone, over 100 million tonnes of municipal waste and over 27 million tonnes of hazardous waste are produced each year. The first directive on waste recycling was adopted in 1975. A new directive on the disposal of hazardous waste was adopted in December 1991. There are standards relating to the classification and labelling of dangerous substances and a voluntary scheme for labelling environmentally less-harmful products. EU-wide rules for the disposal of end-of-life vehicles were agreed in 1999, requiring manufacturers to pay the cost of disposal of all vehicles put on the market from 2001 and all older cars from 2006. In 1999, the Council adopted a directive to reduce the effects of landfill on the environment.

Over 80% of packaging waste in the EU is currently dumped. In December 1994, the Council adopted a directive on packaging waste, to promote its recovery and recycling. The 'eco-labels' scheme launched by the Commission in 1992 gives a seal of approval to producers meeting environmental criteria, to encourage manufacturers to make products which are less environmentally damaging and to encourage consumers to buy environmentally friendly products. It has been awarded to over 200 products, such as refrigerators, washing machines, light bulbs and computers. It coexists with national eco-labels. The fifth action programme sought to stabilise waste production at the 1985 level by 2000. LIFE, a programme first established in 1996, funds specific actions on the environment, such as projects to promote clean technologies. LIFE III runs from 2000 to 2004.

- **Air.** Atmospheric pollution is a main cause of 'global warming' and 'acid rain'. Policies on air quality include: the limitation of atmospheric pollution by industrial plants and by motor vehicles; a ban on the use of CFCs in aerosols; and measures to promote use of unleaded petrol. Carbon dioxide (CO_2) emissions, from the use of coal and petrol, contribute to 'global warming' through the so-called 'greenhouse effect'. The EU aimed to stabilise CO_2 by 2000 at 1990 levels. Air quality limits have been set for many air-polluting substances, such as nitrogen dioxide, sulphur dioxide and lead. In 1996 the EU adopted a directive on ambient air quality. Several directives seek to control motor vehicle emissions. In 1999, the Commission concluded an agreement with the European Automobile Manufactures Association for the reduction of CO_2 emissions from passenger cars. In December 1999, the Council and EP adopted a directive providing consumers with information on the fuel economy of passenger cars.

The Commission has on several occasions proposed a carbon/energy tax (commonly known as an *eco-tax*) with the combined aims of increasing energy efficiency and reducing pollution. The tax would be weighted towards fuels with the highest carbon content. Renewable or non-polluting energy sources would be exempt from the tax. However, although it has been strongly supported by some member states, notably Denmark, the proposal has run into determined opposition from several others, principally on the grounds that it would handicap European industry and would be very unpopular with EU citizens. None of the eco-tax proposals put forward so far has managed to gained the acceptance of all member states (being regarded as too strong by some and as too weak by others). Eco-taxes have been strongly opposed by Spain, Ireland, Portugal, Greece and the UK. In 1999, the German presidency of the Council managed to get approval of all but two states (Spain and Ireland) for an eco-tax, even though it would have allowed them to set very low rates.

• **Noise.** Maximum noise levels have been set for cars, lorries, motor cycles, subsonic aircraft, tractors, plant machinery and lawnmowers.

• **Biotechnology.** In the 1990s, the issue of the release of genetically modified organisms into the environment has risen to prominence. The EU has adopted a directive on monitoring and control of genetic engineering and has introduced legislation on labelling of genetically modified raw materials.

• **Funded projects.** The Commission operates various environment projects: for example, SAVE II (special actions for vigorous energy efficiency) promotes energy efficiency and reduces energy consumption through various measures. ALTENER promotes exploitation of renewable energy resources. There are various research and technological development projects concerned with the environment, including the TELEMATICS environment programme; the environment and climate programme; the MAST (marine science and technology) programme; the non-nuclear energy programme and the nuclear fission safety programme.

● THE INTERNATIONAL DIMENSION

○ The Pan-European Dimension

Because pollution knows no frontiers, it is essential that EU environment policy has a wider European dimension. In the 1990s, there were four pan-European environmental conferences, involving environment ministers of both EU and non-EU European countries. The first conference in 1991 led to the Commission being asked to prepare a report on the state of the environment for the whole of Europe. This report, known as the Dobris Assessment, was produced by the European Environment Agency (EEA) and presented to the third conference held in Sofia, Bulgaria, in October 1995. A second assessment, also produced by the EEA, was presented to the fourth conference, held in Aarhus, Denmark in June 1998. These reports have provided the basis for an Environmental Programme for Europe, which sets out pan-European environmental priorities.

The EU is assisting environmental renovation programmes in Eastern

Europe in various ways. Environmental renovation and protection are integral components of the Union's aid programmes for the region. Association agreements signed with CEECs also contain environmental provisions. Although all candidate countries are required to accept the environmental *acquis*, full compliance will probably take a long time and they will struggle to meet the EU's required standards. *Agenda 2000* suggested a strategy for the adoption and implementation of the environmental *acquis* by candidates, combined with pre-accession assistance. Candidates are required to draw up long-term strategies for alignment before accession, particularly in relation to water and air pollution. But EU finance for these strategies is very limited.

O The Global Dimension

The EU (meaning here the member states and the Commission acting collectively as a negotiating bloc) is a leading global player in developing policies in relation to global environmental issues, such as climate change, depletion of the ozone layer and deforestation. It is an active participant in the UN's Commission on Sustainable Development and other international environmental fora. The Council has confirmed its commitment to implementing 'Agenda 21', a non-binding UN action plan for sustainable development into the 21st century, agreed at the UN Conference of the Environment and Development held in Rio de Janeiro in June 1992. Account is taken of Agenda 21 in the EU's Environmental Action Programmes.

At the third conference of the UN Framework Convention on Climate Change, held in Kyoto in December 1997, the EU made a binding commitment for a reduction in greenhouse gas emissions by 8% by 2012 from 1990 levels. At Kyoto, the EU favoured more ambitious targets than the US, which was persuaded to accept a reduction target of 7% in return for inclusion of 'flexible' mechanisms such as tradable quotas (Commission, 1999c). However, at the sixth conference held in the Hague in December 2000, the EU was at loggerheads with the US on a range of environmental issues and no agreement was reached. Moreover, at the conference there was an open disagreement between the British and French delegations. In April 2001, President George W. Bush announced that the US was giving up its Kyoto commitments on the grounds that implementation of the Kyoto protocol would place too heavy a burden on US industry. This decision was widely condemned within the EU. At the Gothenburg European Council in June 2001 member states agreed to press on with ratification of the Kyoto protocol. The Treaty of Nice includes a declaration affirming a determination by the contracting parties to see the EU play a leading role in promoting environmental protection in the EU and at global level, using all possibilities offered by the EC Treaty, including use of market-oriented incentives and instruments. However, many of these instruments are highly controversial.

● CONCLUSION

From small beginnings in the 1970s, the EU's environmental policy has developed considerably in scope, depth and diversity. It is now required to be an integral element of all Union policies. However, environmental problems show no signs of abating and there is no room for complacency. The problem of the Union's 'implementation deficit' with regard to environmental policy has by no means been solved. Indeed, future enlargement is likely to exacerbate this problem. Given the lower environmental standards in candidate countries, it may become more difficult for member states in an enlarged and more diverse Union to reach agreement on environmental legislation. The need for greater flexibility in environmental policy as a result of the EU's increasingly diverse membership may lead to a shift in emphasis in EU environmental policy from reliance on command-and-control techniques based on regulation towards more flexible, market-oriented techniques, such as fiscal instruments (for example, taxes and charges). It also seems likely that the Union's role as a global player in international fora on environmental issues will continue to increase.

FURTHER READING

Andersen, M.S. and Liefferink, D. (1997), *European Environmental Policy: The Pioneers*, Manchester University Press, Manchester.

Barnes, P.M. and Barnes, I.G. (2000), *Environmental Policy in the European Union*, Edward Elgar, Cheltenham and Northampton, MA.

Commission (1992), *The 5th Environmental Action Programme*, COM (92) 23.

Commission (1993), *Growth, Competitiveness and Employment*, COM (93) 700.

Commission (1998), *Partnership for Integration*, COM (98) 333.

Commission (1999a), *The Single Market and Environment*, COM (99) 263.

Commission (1999b), *Survey on the Application of Environmental Law*, Luxembourg.

Commission (1999c), *Preparing for Implementation of the Kyoto Protocol*, COM (99) 230.

Commission (2000), *White Paper on Environmental Liability*, COM (2000) 66.

Commission (2001), *The Sixth Environmental Action Programme*, COM (2001) 31.

European Environment Agency (1999), *Environment in the European Union at the Turn of the Century*, Luxembourg.

Golub, J. (ed.) (1998), *Global Competition and EU Environment Policy*, Routledge, London.

Jordan, A. (1999), European Community Water Policy Standards: Locked In or Watered Down?, *Journal of Common Market Studies*, vol. 37, no. 1, pp. 13–37.

Lowe, P. and Ward, S. (1998), *British Environmental Policy and Europe*, Routledge, London.

Scott, J. (1998), *EC Environmental Law*, Longman, Harlow.

Zito, A. (2000), *Creating Environmental Policy in the EU*, Macmillan, Basingstoke.

Chapter 15

A 'People's Europe'

● THE GAP BETWEEN THE UNION AND ITS CITIZENS

Although it is demonstrably true that European integration has touched the lives of all citizens of the European Union, in the vast majority of cases it has yet to touch their hearts and minds. It is probable that only a tiny minority of European citizens have an awareness of the impact of Union policies on their lives, or even a basic understanding of how the Union operates. Although the Commission and the European Parliament (EP) launched a joint campaign to encourage Europeans to vote in the elections to the EP in June 1999, voter turnout at 49%, was the lowest of the five direct elections held since 1979. The lack of public involvement in, and understanding of, Union affairs has been attributed to many causes, such as:

● **The domination of European affairs by political and technocratic elites.** European integration is still widely viewed as the concern of governments rather than of ordinary people. Eurosceptics attribute this to a desire of these elites to monopolise policy processes, or to deliberately hide their 'federalist' intentions from the European electorates. Euro-federalists, on the other hand, contend that levels of popular participation could and should be increased, by strengthening Union democracy and by increasing citizens' perceptions of the importance of the Union to their lives.

● **Lack of information about European affairs.** Although thousands of documents emanate from the Union every year, very few ever reach ordinary citizens. People are generally aware only of the aspects of the EU which affect them directly, such as cross-border shopping and the euro.

● **The Byzantine complexity of rules and procedures.** The Union's policymaking and implementation system, comprising a complex network of institutions and a vast web of technical rules and arcane procedures, is undoubtedly difficult to understand.

• **'Euro-jargon'.** The Union has developed a large vocabulary of technical terms (including more than 1300 acronyms) which all but the most determined are likely to find off-putting.

• **The resilience of national identities.** Although the EU is seeking to encourage citizens to feel a sense of European identity, Europeans tend to think of themselves as citizens of a particular state rather than as European citizens *per se*. For example, national, rather than European, issues still largely determine how people vote in elections to the EP.

• **Poor image.** If ordinary people think of the EU at all, they are likely to associate it with bureaucracy and waste. The forced resignation of the Commission in 1999 for mismanagement, and disclosures about lax financial controls within the EP, have done nothing to foster a favourable image of the EU. This poor image has been reinforced by a tendency of national politicians and the tabloid media to blame 'Brussels' for all national ills. Many national problems are falsely attributed to the EU. 'Euromyths' and 'Euroscares' constitute a staple diet of stories about the EU in the British tabloids. The real significance of such stories is not that they are demonstrably untrue, but that they derive from and reinforce the popular cartoon image of 'Brussels' as a rule-obsessed, profligate bureaucracy (see Table 15.1).

Table 15.1 Recent British Euromyths and Euroscares

• EU fishermen must wear hairnets;
• Brussels may ban mushy peas and British cheese;
• rhubarb must be straight and strawberries must be oval;
• charity shops are to be banned from selling second-hand toys;
• Europe is set to ban lethal bathtime ducks;
• the UK must abandon British toilets in favour of continental versions;
• children's swings must be moved if they face the wrong way;
• an EU ban on food waste means swans cannot be fed;
• EU grants have funded IRA arms bunkers;
• the Queen's crest on UK passports will be replaced by the EU stars;
• the British army is to be absorbed into an EU army.

The Commission conducts twice-yearly surveys of public opinion in the EU known as 'Eurobarometers': the 54th *Eurobarometer*, conducted in November and December 2000 among 16,000 EU citizens, was published in April 2001. It showed that only 50% of those surveyed thought that their country's membership of the EU was a good thing and only 47% thought that their country had on balance benefited from EU membership (Commission, 2001). There is considerable variation in public attitudes towards the EU between member states. *Eurobarometer* no. 54 showed that whereas 79% of people in Luxembourg, 75% in Ireland and 71% in the Netherlands thought that their country's membership of the EU was a good thing, only 28% in the UK, 34% in Sweden, 38% in Austria and 39% in Finland thought so (Commission, 2001). Many factors affect levels of support for the EU within member states, such as whether the member state is a net beneficiary or a net contributor to the budget; perceptions of the pre- and post-entry performance of a domestic economy; the popularity or unpopularity of national institutions; whether or not entry is perceived as a means of rejoining Europe after a period of isolation (Greece, Spain and Portugal); and the role of the domestic media (which in the UK tends to be more critical about EU developments than is the case in other countries). In response to these problems of limited understanding, limited participation and low popularity, the EU has sought to bring the Union closer to its citizens by promoting the goal of a People's (or Citizens') Europe.

● THE PROMOTION OF A 'PEOPLE'S EUROPE'

○ The Goal of a People's Europe

The notion of a Citizens' (or People's) Europe was endorsed at the European Council in Fountainebleau in June 1984. Following this meeting, a committee comprising representatives of heads of government and the Commission president, and headed by Pietro Adonnino, was appointed to explore ways of narrowing the gap between 'Europe' and the citizen. The Adonnino Committee's two reports were approved by the European Council in 1985. The reports advocated a raft of measures to foster the goal of a People's Europe, such as greater freedom of movement, promotion of European cultural, educational and sporting links, extension of citizens' rights and promotion of a European identity. The need to bring European integration closer to ordinary people has been endorsed by several European Council meetings and has also figured prominently in recent intergovernmental conferences (IGCs). It has also been incorporated into the Treaty on European Union (TEU) and the Treaty of Amsterdam (ToA). The TEU stated that the treaty marked a new stage in the process of creating an ever closer Union among the peoples of Europe, in which decisions are taken as closely as possible to the citizen. The ToA added the words as *openly as possible* to this statement (Title 1, ex A), signifying a stronger emphasis on transparency. The sheer variety of specific proposals has hardly served to clarify the notion of a People's Europe, which has remained rather vague and fuzzy. Promotion of a People's Europe is usually taken to comprise six elements, namely:
- *promoting a European identity*, through the use of European symbols and the creation of a European citizenship;

- *promoting citizens' rights*, such as the freedom to live and work in other member states and promotion of equal opportunities. Initially, this focussed on economic rights, but is now being broadened to embrace social, political and human rights;
- *enhancing public understanding of the EU policy system*, by simplifying and opening up the decisionmaking process and also by providing more information about EU institutions and policies;
- *increasing the involvement of EU citizens in EU affairs* through, for example, measures to encourage citizens to express their views on specific EU topics;
- *strengthening the European dimension of policies and activities*, through collective action on common problems and encouragement of cross-border links;
- *protecting EU citizens* from cross-border crime, terrorism and illegal immigration (see Chapter 16).

These subjects encompass most of the Union's activities in one form or another and are dealt with also in other chapters. In particular, policies relating to freedom of movement and the protection of EU citizens are examined more fully in the next chapter on justice and home affairs. Measures to promote a People's Europe might also be categorised on the basis of their underlying strategy. Firstly, some measures, such as promotion of a European identity, are designed to create a greater sense of European consciousness among EU citizens (the *'we feeling' strategy*); secondly, other measures are designed to demonstrate to EU citizens that they reap benefits from the Union's activities (the *'good works' strategy*); and thirdly, some measures seek to enhance EU citizens' sense of involvement in Union affairs (the *'enhanced participation' strategy*). This strategy seeks to enhance the legitimacy of the Union by addressing the problem of the democratic deficit. An additional distinction has been made between *'output legitimacy'*, that is, measures which focus on enhancing legitimacy through policy outputs (or good works) and *'input legitimacy'*, that is, measures which seek legitimacy through involving citizens at the policy input stage.

There are problems with each of these strategies: EU citizens already have strongly entrenched national and regional identities, rooted in history, culture and language, therefore it is difficult to superimpose a meaningful 'European' identity onto these. If EU citizens have a sense of 'Europeanness', that is, a 'we feeling' which distinguishes them in their own minds from Americans, Africans or Asians, it is not one which they are likely to associate with the EU as such. The 'good works' strategy is also problematic, in that given most Union policies are implemented by the governments of member states, EU citizens are unlikely to associate the EU with policies of benefit to them. Moreover, governments of member states tend not to be slow in claiming credit for beneficial policies or in blaming the EU for policy failures.

Similarly, 'bad works' make better news stories than 'good works', thereby reinforcing the negative image of the EU in the eyes of its citizens. The role of the EU as a vehicle for preserving peace in Europe might also be included in the 'good works' strategy. But most EU citizens were born after the Second World War and seem unlikely to base their support for the EU on its role in securing post-war peace. Arguably, as fear of another European civil war has declined, the policy benefits motive has become more significant.

Enhancing EU citizens' sense of involvement in EU affairs has proved to be no less problematic: the vast majority of EU citizens seem to have no desire to become more directly involved in the European integration project. Moreover, as the Union has developed and expanded, it has become more complex and difficult for ordinary people to understand. Few Europeans are willing to devote the time and energy required to make sense of it all. It might also be argued that, despite their rhetoric to the contrary, the EU elites would not really welcome increased participation by citizens in EU affairs. At best, perhaps, they favour providing EU citizens with more information and opportunities to put forward their views (that is, greater consultation, as distinct from greater participation).

○ Promoting a European Identity

The EU already has many symbols of identity. The *European flag* was chosen by the Council of Europe in 1955. It was not adopted by the Union until 1986. According to the Council of Europe, the number of stars was chosen as a 'symbol of perfection'. It will remain at 12, however many countries join the EU. The *European anthem* (adopted in 1972) is the prelude to the 'Ode to Joy' from Beethoven's 9th Symphony. *Europe Day* (9 May, the date of the Schuman Declaration) was chosen by the European Council in Milan in 1985. The TEU established citizenship of the European Union (Article 17, ECT). The most obvious and tangible 'badge' of this citizenship is the common EU burgundy-coloured passport. Under a non-binding agreement between member states, EU passports are supposed to be of the same size, colour and shape, although they vary somewhat and still include national symbols. In November 2000, several UK newspapers reacted with outrage to an alleged Commission plan to replace national symbols (such as the Queen's crest) on passports with an EU logo. Other symbols of identity include the forthcoming EU driving licence and the euro currency. However, although most Europeans could probably identify the European flag, very few would have knowledge of the European anthem or 'Europe Day'. Having a standardised passport has not so far engendered a 'we feeling' among EU citizens. It remains to be seen whether use of euro notes and coins within the eurozone will have a greater effect (moreover, if the euro project is perceived as not working well, it could engender an anti-'we feeling').

○ Promoting Citizens' Rights

Rights conferred on EU citizens by EU treaties include:

• **Freedom of movement,** that is, the right to move freely within the territory of member states (Article 18, ECT), subject to the limitations and conditions laid down in the EC treaty and secondary law. The notion of a People's Europe is probably most visibly manifested in the Union's policies on freedom of movement. Freedom of movement of individuals was one of four integration objectives mentioned in the Treaty of Rome. Substantial progress has been made on abolishing controls of the movement of EU citizens across the borders of member states (see Chapter 16). EU passports have replaced national passports. There are special channels for EU citizens at air and sea ports. There has been mutual recognition of driving licences since 1983. A directive in force from July 1996 abolished the need for EU citizens to change driving licences when residing in another EU country. But for various reasons, governments have been reluctant to scrap intra-Union border controls altogether. The UK government argues that passport checks are the only effective way of distinguishing between EU citizens and others. Under the EC Treaty, member states can refuse entry to EU citizens whom they regard as posing a threat to national security, public health or public policy. EU citizenship laws do not prevent countries from expelling EU citizens from other countries whose presence is deemed undesirable, as the mass expulsion of English 'football hooligans' by the Belgian authorities during the Euro 2000 football championships showed.

• **The right to work and live in other member states.** About five million EU citizens reside in a member state other than their own. Article 48 of the Treaty of Rome (now Article 39, ECT) gave European workers the right of freedom of movement and to work in any member state, although Article 39(4) specifies that this does not extend to public service employment. The European Court of Justice (ECJ) ruled in 1980 that this clause applies only to certain public posts, such as those conferring responsibility for safeguarding state interests (for example, the police, judiciary, army or diplomatic service). The Single European Act introduced measures to abolish various impediments to free movement for workers, such as qualifying periods for eligibility for employment. Those working in another member state require a residence permit valid for five years and renewable on request (they can only be refused a permit on the grounds of public policy, security or health). This right is extended automatically to the person's family. Citizens may stay to look for work in another member state for a 'reasonable' period (up to six months). They may continue to receive unemployment benefit from their home countries for up to three months, providing they register as jobseekers in the host country. They must possess an identity card and forms E303 (issued by the body responsible for paying unemployment benefit) and E119 issued by the health insurance authority.

It is now easier for EU citizens to move within the Union without losing benefit entitlements. Insurance contributions paid in another member state are taken into account when benefits are being assessed in the host country. Citizens may also receive certain benefits from the home country whilst living in another member country. Retired people may reside permanently in a member state in which they have lived for three years or have worked for one year. Citizens on short visits to other member states (of up to one year) are entitled to urgent medical and dental treatment at free or reduced cost, providing they obtain an E111 form. Students have a right to live in any member state, providing they can support themselves financially and are not a charge on the host country's social security system. EU citizenship rights do not apply to nationals of non-EU countries residing in the EU, known as 'third-country nationals' (or TCNs), even if they are married to EU citizens.

- **Electoral rights.** EU citizens residing in another EU country have the right to vote and stand as candidates in elections to the EP and in municipal elections (Article 19, ECT). A directive adopted by the Council in December 1994 set a deadline for the transposition of this right to vote in local elections at 1 January 1996 and limited candidature in local elections to office lower than mayor/deputy mayor. This right was not transposed into national law in all member states until January 1999. In March 2001, for the first time, 79 British expatriates (together with hundreds of other non-French citizens) stood in French local elections. Luxembourg has a derogation authorising it to apply a minimum residence requirement.

- **Access to means of redress**, through the right to apply to the EU's ombudsman, a right to petition the EP and the right to lodge a complaint with the Commission. EU citizens have the right to raise cases of maladministration by any EU institution with the ombudsman (Article 21, ECT). The first ombudsman, Jacob Söderman from Finland, was elected by MEPs in June 1995 and was re-elected in 1999. The EP's Petitions Committee examines complaints by citizens of discrimination by national authorities against EU citizens from another country. The ToA added a new paragraph to Article 21, stating that any EU citizen may write to any of the institutions and to the ombudsman in any of the official Union languages (including Irish) and receive an answer in the same language. The ombudsman's annual report for 1999 (Ombudsman, 2000) recorded a high percentage (about 70%) of inadmissible complaints, pointing to considerable misunderstanding about the ombudsman's powers. Any person or business may lodge a complaint with the Commission about an alleged violation of Union law by a member state. The Commission then decides whether to take up the complaint, within a year of the complaint being registered.

- **Stronger diplomatic protection**. Citizens have access to diplomatic and consular facilities of a member state other than their own in a third country where their own countries are not represented (Article 20, ECT).

• **Non-discrimination.** The ToA strengthened the provision in the EC Treaty, which prohibits discrimination on grounds of nationality (Article 12, ECT), by enabling the Council, acting unanimously on a Commission proposal and after consulting the EP, to take appropriate action to combat discrimination based on sex, racial or ethnic origin, religion or belief, disability, age or sexual orientation (Article 13, ECT). The Treaty of Nice (ToN) will amend Article 13 to enable Community incentive measures in support of actions in this field by member states to be taken by qualified majority voting and co-decision.

• **The European Charter of Fundamental Rights.** Following much discussion and deliberation, this charter was 'declared' by the European Council in Nice in December 2000 (see Chapter 4).

◯ Is 'EU Citizenship' really 'Citizenship'?

Some observers see Union citizenship as the beginning of a 'post national' citizenship. However, Union citizenship is *complementary* to national citizenship. The ToA amended Article 17 of the EC treaty to explicitly state that Union citizenship complements and does not replace national citizenship. Arguably, Union citizenship largely falls into the category of 'concessions to foreigners' rather than genuine citizenship. It might also be argued that it is an attempt to create something artificially which can only develop naturally. Moreover, Europeans might even perceive EU citizenship as a threat to their national identities. In any case, only a very small minority of EU citizens live and work in another member state. Moreover, there remains a disturbing gap between the ideal and the reality in relation to Union citizens' rights. The Commission's second report on citizenship of the Union (Commission, 1997) assessed the application of provisions relating to citizenship of the Union between 1994 and 1996. It noted that some member states had still not implemented the directive granting citizens the right to participate in local elections. The report noted that citizens still faced difficulties when seeking to exercise their rights of free movement and residence. It noted that the right to reside in another member state is still subject to different provisions applicable to different categories of citizens, as secondary Community law is made up of two regulations and nine directives. Transposition of directives into national law, particularly on the right of residence of retired persons, students and persons having ceased work, has left much to be desired.

◯ Public Understanding of the EU Policy System

A long-standing criticism of the Union is that it is remote from ordinary people and that its operational procedures are too complex and obscure for people to understand. The Cardiff European Council stated that: 'a sustained effort is needed by the member states and all the institutions to bring the Union closer to people by making it more open, more understandable and more relevant to daily life'. However, similar statements had been made many times before and much remains to be done before this aim is realised.

At the European Council in Edinburgh in December 1992, it was agreed that measures should be introduced by the Union to improve its openness, to simplify its procedures and to encourage dialogue with the public. This resulted in the adoption of a 'new approach' to information and communication policy and subsequent measures to increase the openness or 'transparency' of decisionmaking. In December 1993, the Council and Commission approved a code of conduct establishing general rules on the right of access to information from Union institutions. The code, reviewed every two years, sets out minimum requirements governing applications for information. The ToA introduced new provisions on transparency into the EC Treaty (Article 255), which allow any Union citizen and any natural or legal person residing or having its registered office in a member state, right of access to Council, Commission and EP documents, subject to some limitations. However, the devil is in the detail. The ToA's provisions on transparency leave much to be desired, for two principal reasons: firstly, they make no specific reference to Union institutions other than the Council, EP and Commission. Secondly, they leave leeways which in effect enable the Council, the EP and the Commission to limit access to information. Each of the three institutions referred to above is allowed to elaborate in its own rules and procedures regarding access to its documents. The Council still meets behind closed doors. The outcome of decisions taken by the Council are published afterwards, but it retains the right not to publish the results of votes. Excessive secrecy surrounding Council deliberations has been repeatedly criticised by the EU ombudsman.

The Commission's current information strategy for a People's Europe centres on the need to make information more widely available and easier for citizens to understand. In November 1996, the Commission launched 'Citizens First', with the aim of increasing people's awareness about the rights and opportunities they have in the Union. There is also a Citizens First 'signpost service' for those with specific practical problems. The Commission is encouraging 'active participation' of European citizens, by, for example, greater use of green and white papers, public hearings and conferences. The Commission is currently negotiating an accord with the EP to give the latter greater access to internal Commission documents (a factor which contributed to the ouster of the Commission in 1999). The Commission has sought to exclude all papers relating to infringement and competition cases. In May 2000, Commission President Prodi declared his intention to allow political groups in the EP access to sensitive papers, but not to minutes of internal inquiries or disciplinary proceedings against officials (*European Voice*, 11 May 2000). The Commission was accused of excessive secrecy by the EU ombudsman in respect of an investigation into a major competition case (*European Voice*, 27 April 2000). The ombudsman also criticised the Commission's draft law on access to documents for containing too many 'get-out' clauses. In April 2001, in accordance with Article 255, the Council, the Commission and the EP agreed a new code on access to EU documents. But the new code has been criticised for containing many loopholes and by no means guarantees complete access (see p. 134).

○ Increasing the Involvement of EU Citizens in EU Affairs

The EU is not a 'participatory democracy' in that the extent of public involvement in the EU policy process remains stubbornly low. The EP is the only directly elected EU institution and turnouts for EP elections have been low (less than half the electorate voted in the June 1999 elections to the EP). A key problem is that in order to have a genuine 'European' democracy, you need a European political consciousness which hardly exists among EU voters. There are no European parties as such and voters in EP elections find it difficult to believe that their votes will have a direct impact on the way they are governed. Arguably, the population of the EU is also too large and diverse, the EU system too complex, and citizens' knowledge of the EU too limited, for a truly democratic European polity to emerge.

Following the chastening experience of the TEU ratification process, the Commission sought to encourage wider participation in the discussions preceding the 1996/97 and 2000 IGCs than took place prior to Maastricht. It launched a European dialogue to involve citizens and businesses in the 2000 IGC, setting up web sites for this purpose (http://europa.eu.int/citizens and http://europa.eu.int/business). Although such 'opening' measures are undoubtedly useful, particularly to pressure groups, researchers and students, they seem unlikely to have much direct impact on the public. More radical measures for reducing the democratic deficit have been suggested, such as:

- *stronger powers for the EP*, through, for example, extension of co-decision and by increasing the EP's role in appointments. But this could weaken the EU's democratic legitimacy, by weakening the power of the Council (which comprises the representatives of elected governments);
- *stronger involvement of national parliaments*. For example, a second EP chamber made up of representatives from national parliaments could be established. But this could weaken the powers of the EP;
- *holding EU-wide referenda on specific issues*. This raises key questions: what would be the issues and what would be done with the results?
- *directly electing the Commission president*. Although the Commission president is a big fish in Brussels, his profile among European citizens is

currently low. It has been argued that directly electing the Commission president would give the Commission a more prominent public face and would also strengthen the legitimacy of the EU, because it would mean that voters would be involved in two European elections. But an elected Commission presidency could be viewed as a threat to the Council's position and could create a 'dual mandate' problem. Moreover, it is not clear how candidates for the presidency would be chosen or who by.

○ Strengthening the European Dimension of Policies and Activities

Virtually all EU policies are expected to contribute in some way to the realisation of a People's Europe. Arguably, tangible policies are likely to have a bigger impact upon citizens' perceptions of the EU than symbols or information campaigns. The TEU and the ToA extended the range and depth of the Union's involvement in various policy fields, such as education, culture, consumer policy, migration and environmental protection. Examples of the partial 'Europeanisation' of policies are given below.

● EDUCATION POLICY

There is no mention of education policy in the Treaty of Rome, although it does refer to 'training'. Although education remains primarily a national responsibility, the Commission has sought to promote the incorporation of a 'European dimension' into the education systems of member states. The main emphasis of Union 'education policy' is on voluntary co-operation. The TEU espouses educational objectives for the Union, but these are rather vague and are qualified by an explicit acknowledgement of member states' responsibility for the content of teaching and the organisation of education systems (Article 149, ECT). EU education policy has centred on the promotion of inter-university co-operation programmes (of which there are currently over 2500) and the injection of a 'European dimension' into teaching. Substantial progress has been made on the mutual recognition of qualifications. University degrees and higher education diplomas awarded after at least three years' study are now recognised in all member countries (although in some cases aptitude tests are taken). There are other rules for more specialised diplomas and qualifications.

Until January 1995, when the SOCRATES and LEONARDO programmes came into force, there were six main EU education programmes: ERASMUS (cross-border interuniversity co-operation and student exchanges), LINGUA (language learning); COMETT (training in advanced technology through co-operation between universities and enterprises); FORCE (promotion of continuing vocational training in the EU; PETRA (an action programme for the vocational training of people under 28) and EUROTECNET (promotion of innovation in vocational training and technological change). In June 1994, the Council agreed that these would be regrouped into two five-year action programmes: SOCRATES (action linked to universities, schools and higher education establishments) and LEONARDO for vocational training. From 1995, all EU education programmes were open to participation by countries in the European Economic Area.

SOCRATES promotes co-operation between educational institutions and provides funds for students to study at institutions outside their own countries. It supports actions in three spheres: higher education (a minimum of 55% of the budget); school education (a minimum of 10%) and 'horizontal actions' relating to language teaching, open and distance education and exchanges (a minimum of 25%). In addition to taking over the work of ERASMUS and LINGUA, it added a third strand, COMENIUS, which extended cross-border educational co-operation to schools, at nursery, primary and secondary levels, although the budget for school education is so far small. It also took over two other programmes: EURYDICE (promoting information exchanges on education systems) and ARION (study visits for educational specialists). In 1998, SOCRATES facilitated the mobility of 200,000 students and 35,000 teachers. The four primary objectives of the SOCRATES programme for 2000–04 are: to strengthen the European dimension; to promote co-operation in all sectors and levels; to remove obstacles to such co-operation; and to encourage innovation.

LEONARDO embraces three strands: support for vocational training systems and policies; promotion of innovation in training programmes; and support for language skills in vocational training. It covers activities supported by the COMETT, PETRA, FORCE and EUROTECNET programmes. In addition, the Union also operates *Youth For Europe,* which promotes exchange projects between young people between 15 and 25. A third of the Youth For Europe budget is earmarked for those not having access to the other education programmes. For the 2000–04 period. funding of €3 billion is being allocated to the education, vocational training and youth programmes (€1.4 billion for the second phase of SOCRATES; 1 billion for the second phase of LEONARDO; and €600 million for *Youth For Europe*). The Commission also operates TEMPUS, an education co-operation scheme for Central and East European countries.

Union educational programmes, particularly in the fields of inter-university co-operation and student exchanges, have become established features of the education sectors of member states. But these remain essentially adjuncts to national educational systems rather than serious threats to them. A host of factors (not least the diversity of educational traditions, the enormous cost of education and 'subsidiarity') seem likely to ensure that education remains primarily a national responsibility.

● CULTURAL POLICY

The Union's cultural policy has two principal objectives: to foster regional and national traditions and to reinforce a sense of European identity. Article 151 of the EC Treaty requires the Union to contribute to the flowering of the cultures of the member states, while respecting their national and regional diversity and at the same time bringing the common cultural heritage to the fore. Cultural aspects must be taken into account in its action under other provisions of the treaty (Article 151(4)). The ToA clarified this requirement by adding the phrase 'in particular in order to respect and promote the diversity of its cultures' to Article 151(4).

The *Culture 2000* programme is a framework programme for the 2000–04. period It aims to treat cultural activity as a European policy in its own right by grouping all Community activity in this field together. It refers to the Union as a common cultural area and supports cultural co-operation and projects with a high symbolic value, such as the European City of Culture and cultural exchanges. Specific programmes include KALEIDOSCOPE (support for artistic and cultural activities with a European dimension); ARIANE, to support books and reading; the MEDIA II programme, which aims to promote a more integrated European audio-visual industry; and RAPHAEL, a cultural heritage programme. There is also a European Union youth orchestra. The Cultural Capitals of Europe programme is hosted by different European cities each year, for example: Copenhagen, 1996; Thessaloniki, 1997; Stockholm, 1998; Weimar, 1999; nine cities in 2000; Porto and Rotterdam, 2001; Bruges and Salamanca, 2002; and Graz, 2003. In order to promote links with the wider Europe, a programme of European 'cultural months' was established in 1990 (for example, St Petersburg, 1996; Ljubjana 1997; Linz and Valetta, 1998; Plovdiv, 1999; and Basel and Riga in 2001). Some critics question the need for a European cultural policy, arguing that cultural developments should be left to the market or to the public sectors of member states. Nor is there unanimous agreement on the purpose and direction of cultural policy: for example, not all states share France's enthusiasm to counter American domination of the film industry.

● PUBLIC HEALTH AND CONSUMER POLICIES

Public health and consumer protection policies affect citizens directly and tangibly, and therefore are important aspects of the goal of bringing the EU closer to is citizens. Public awareness of food safety issues has recently been raised by food scares concerning dioxin, growth hormones, BSE (bovine spongiform encaphalopathy) and other possible dangers to health. The EC Treaty contains chapters on both public health and consumer protection.

○ Public Health

The ToA amended Article 152 of the EC Treaty to state that a high level of human health protection shall be ensured in the definition and implementation of all Community policies and activities. It also contains a specific provision with regard to pursuit of this objective through adoption by the Council of measures setting high standards of quality and safety of organs and substances of human origin, blood and blood derivatives, no doubt with the Aids (acquired immune deficiency syndrome) and BSE crises in mind.

The Commission produces reports on the integration of health protection requirements in Community policies. There are Community action programmes on various health issues, such as health promotion and monitoring; cancer; the prevention of drug dependence; prevention of Aids and other communicable diseases; rare diseases; injury prevention and pollution-related diseases. The budgets for these programmes are, however, very small. In April 1998, the Commission outlined possible future strategies for the EU with regard to public health policy, in line with ToA provisions. It focused on three strands of action: improving information; swift reaction to threats to health; and tackling determinants through health promotion and disease prevention. In 1998, the Commission set up a network for the surveillance and control of communicable diseases in the EU. In May 2001, the Council and EP agreed legislation on the labelling and content of tobacco products. In this month, the Commission proposed a new directive on tobacco advertising and sponsorship (a previous directive had been ruled unlawful by the ECJ on the grounds that it was incompatible with single market rules).

○ Consumer Policy

There was no specific mention of consumer policy in the Treaty of Rome. Although a consumer protection unit within the Directorate-General for Competition was established in 1968, consumer policy nevertheless remained undeveloped, due primarily to differences in national approaches, technical standards and product regulations. Several factors led to greater emphasis on consumer policy: the growth of the consumer movement in member states; the entry of the UK and Denmark, both of which had strong consumer traditions; and increasing recognition that the free market approach was insufficient to ensure high consumer standards.

The principal aim of the Union's consumer policy is to *complement* rather than replace national policies and to encourage co-operation between member states in this field. In 1975, the Council agreed a programme for a consumer protection and information policy, based on five fundamental rights: protection of consumers' health and safety; protection of consumers' economic interests; the right to information and education; the right to redress; and the right to consumer representation and participation. It envisaged action to safeguard consumers' interests in foodstuffs, textiles, toys, credit and advertising. The second programme, launched in 1981, recognised two other objectives: the inclusion of the interests of consumers in all EC policies; and the promotion of dialogue between representatives of consumers, producers and distributors. The third programme was launched in 1986 to coincide with the White Paper on the single market. This programme introduced the 'new approach' doctrine, meaning that essential requirements would be specified in general terms, leaving the details to be developed by the standardisation bodies. An independent Consumer Policy Service was created by the Commission in 1989. European consumer 'infocentres' have been established in areas where there is significant cross-border traffic. The Commission has a consumer committee, comprising representatives from national consumer organisations and public bodies, to advise it on consumer policies. In 1998, the Commission adopted a new consumer policy action plan (1999–2001), the central objectives being: to give consumers a greater say in consumer matters; to guarantee high levels of health and safety for consumers; and to respect consumers' economic interests. It also launched an information campaign on food safety and consumer health protection.

The amended Article 153 of the EC Treaty states that in order to promote the interests of consumers and to ensure a high level of consumer protection, the Community shall contribute to protecting the health, safety and economic interests of consumers, as well as promoting their right to information, education and to organize themselves in order to safeguard their interests. The ToN will alter Article 257 of the treaty to include an explicit requirement for the Economic and Social Committee to include consumers' representatives. Article 153(2) states that consumer protection requirements be taken into account in defining and implementing other Community policies and activities. A member state may maintain or introduce stricter consumer protection measures than are required by the Community, providing they are compatible with treaty provisions and providing the Commission is notified. The Commission's White Paper on food safety (Commission, 1999) identified 80 gaps in legislation in food safety which needed to be plugged. The White Paper identified many weaknesses in the present system, such as inadequacies in monitoring and surveillance, gaps in the rapid alert system and lack of co-ordination of scientific co-operation and analytical support. It envisaged the establishment of a European Food Authority (EFA) by 2002, to be concerned primarily with risk assessment and risk communication. This proposal has been accepted by both the Council and EP and the EFA is currently being set up. The White Paper also proposed an action plan covering all aspects of food products from 'farm to table'. The commissioner responsible for health and consumer protection now has overall responsibility for all elements of the food chain.

Each member state has its own policies for dealing with public health and consumer protection issues. However, the rapid pace of European integration in recent years, in particular the implications of the Single European Market, have provided the impetus and rationale for the development of EU-wide public health and consumer protection policies. Candidate countries have lower standards of public health and consumer protection and are being required by the EU to meet the *acquis communautaire* in this field.

● CONCLUSION

The gap between the Union and its citizens identified at the beginning of this chapter currently shows no signs of narrowing, despite the launch of many People's Europe initiatives, about which vast majority of EU citizens remain stubbornly unmoved. In March 2001, Commission president Romano Prodi, in a speech marking the opening of a debate on the future of Europe acknowledged that EU citizens found the Union 'increasingly opaque and incomprehensible'. It is inevitable that the EU will increase in size, with enlargement: it is also highly probable that it will increase in complexity, with the introduction of 'multispeed' arrangements. The perceived distance between the Union and the citizens may well therefore increase rather than decrease, despite current efforts to streamline the Union's policymaking machinery. This does not mean that the efforts to promote a People's Europe should be abandoned. Indeed, as the Union's impact on the lives of EU citizens continues to increase in range and depth, People's Europe policies are also likely to increase in importance. This may require a fundamental re-evaluation of such policies, leading perhaps to more emphasis on substance (that is, seeking to make the connection in citizens' minds between EU policies and their impacts) and less on token gestures and symbolism.

FURTHER READING

Anderson, P. and Weymouth, A. (1999), *Insulting the Public? The British Press and the EU*, Addison-Wesley Longman, London.
Commission (1997), Second Report on Citizenship of the EU, COM (97) 230.
Commission (1999), *White Paper on Food Safety*, COM (99) 719.
Commission (2001), *Eurobarometer no. 54*, http://europa.eu.int/comm/dg10/epo.
Ombudsman (2000), *1999 Annual Report*, http: www.euro-ombudsman/report99.
Scharpf, F. (1999), *Governing in Europe: Effective and Democratic?*, Oxford University Press, Oxford.
Statewatch (2000), *Survey Shows Which EU Governments Back Openness, Which Do Not*, http://www.statewatch.org/secret/conformtable.htm.

Chapter 16

Justice and Home Affairs Policy

● SCOPE AND DEVELOPMENT

○ Scope

Each member state has its own legal traditions and its own judicial and policing system. Within the EU there is no common European legal zone, penal code or police force. Nevertheless, from small beginnings, very significant progress has been made in recent years in developing EU justice and home affairs (JHA) policies, embracing the following:

- *judicial co-operation* between the justice administrations of member states, in both criminal and civil matters. 'Criminal matters' includes extradition and mutual legal assistance and mutual recognition of judicial decisions; 'civil matters' includes issues such as mutual recognition in child custody or divorce cases where at least two member states are involved and efforts to harmonise certain types of civil law;
- *customs co-operation* between customs administrations of member states, to ensure compliance with EU law on customs matters and to combat trafficking in drugs, weapons, cultural goods and dangerous materials;
- *police co-operation* between the police forces of member states, and through the European Police Office (Europol), to combat international terrorism, drug trafficking, football hooliganism and other forms of crime;
- *migration issues*, involving co-operation between member states on issues of immigration and external borders; and decisionmaking through the European Community framework with regard to visas, asylum, immigration and other policies relating to the free movement of persons.

Because most of these fields impinge on matters which have been regarded as the prerogative of states, involving inherently contentious and sensitive issues, JHA policies have been slow to develop and were initially based on intergovernmental agreements outside the Community framework.

○   **The Phases of JHA**

Co-operation between EU member states in the field of justice and home affairs can be roughly divided into three phases:
• **The first phase** covers the period prior to the Treaty on European Union (TEU), that is, before the creation of the JHA or third pillar. In this first phase, co-operation between governments in JHA was largely *ad hoc* and lacked a formal institutional framework. It was initially focused on issues of freedom of movement of workers within the common market established by the Treaty of Rome, although the bulk of migration policies were outside the Community framework. However, in 1975, the TREVI group was established by ministers of home affairs of the member states, in order to combat the growing problem of international terrorism. TREVI (a French acronym for 'terrorism, radicalism, extremism and international violence' and also the name of the Rome fountain near where its first meeting was held) involved the exchange of information between national authorities. These meetings were conducted on an *intergovernmental* basis, involving ministerial meetings every six months and did not involve European Community decisionmaking procedures. The work of the TREVI group was later expanded to include international organised crime and football hooliganism. Working parties of national officials examined questions of terrorism, immigration, drugs and related matters. In June 1990, TREVI ministers agreed to establish the European Drugs Unit, the precursor of Europol. In 1990, concern about migration from outside the EU led to the signing of the Dublin convention on asylum (see below). But in this phase co-operation between member states on issues of migration, terrorism and crime was largely reactive and piecemeal.

From the mid-1980s, attempts to remove restrictions on cross-border movement within the Union led to further developments in JHA. In June 1985 in Schengen (Luxembourg), France, Germany and the Benelux countries agreed a radical agenda to remove remaining restrictions on the movement of people across their borders (although progress on implementing the Schengen Agreement was to prove tortuously slow). Freedom of movement of people across the borders of member states was one of the 'four freedoms' pursued in the Single European Market (SEM) programme.
• **The second phase** covers the period between ratification of the TEU and the Treaty of Amsterdam (ToA). The TEU brought JHA policies within a formal institutional structure by creating the JHA or third pillar. The TEU was supposed to mark a major step forward with regard to political union, not least with regard to foreign and security policy and justice and home affairs. However, the governments of member states were reluctant to relinquish control over these sensitive policy areas, by allowing them to be fully integrated into Community decisionmaking institutions and structures.

Instead, they favoured more co-operation and co-ordination between governments in these fields (that is, the 'intergovernmental method' as distinct from the 'Community method'). It was agreed that the common foreign and security policy ('CFSP') and justice and home affairs would respectively form the second and third pillars of the Union's institutional structure. Both pillars were 'intergovernmental' in that they were outside the Community's decisionmaking framework. A distinctive feature of the JHA pillar was the large and heterogeneous range of subjects it covered. The establishment of the JHA pillar to some extent brought within a formal institutional framework policy areas which had formerly been regarded as the exclusive preserve of nation states. It also provided the stimulus to co-operation between national authorities on a wide range of issues, such as organised crime, drugs, immigration and asylum seeking. The Maastricht formula for JHA, a product of messy compromises and fudges, did not work well, because decisions on JHA proved difficult to reach and implement.

• **The third phase** began with the ToA, which made substantial changes to the third pillar, in particular by transferring responsibility for visas, asylum, immigration and other policies relating to the free movement of persons from the third to the first pillar. It also introduced the objective to maintain and develop the Union as an 'area of freedom, security and justice'. It increased the involvement of the ECJ and the Commission in the remaining third pillar, which was renamed 'Police and Judicial Co-operation in Criminal Matters' (PJCCM). This phase has also been marked by initiatives to reduce the implementation deficit in JHA, for example by holding a special European Council on JHA subjects at Tampere in October 1999; by initiatives to enhance collaboration between police and judicial authorities; and by the launch of a scoreboard to review progress on the creation of an area of 'freedom, security and justice'.

○ **Pressures Fostering the Development of JHA**

The principal driving forces behind the development of the Union's JHA policies have been: firstly the perceived inadequacy of national solutions to the growing problems of migration pressure, cross-border crime, football hooliganism and terrorism; and secondly the removal or relaxation of border controls between member states, which have exacerbated the difficulties involved in attempting purely national solutions. For example, due to recognition that no EU country can tackle these problems on its own, there has been a trend towards transnational collaboration, leading to the partial 'Europeanisation' of JHA issues. Moreover, it has become increasingly clear that purely 'intergovernmental' solutions to these problems are also inadequate. We can distinguish between '*bottom-up*' and '*top-down*' approaches to the formation of EU policy. In the bottom-up approach, member states develop bilateral and multilateral policies which eventually become EU law. In the top-down approach, rules are set at European level through Community decisionmaking procedures. The EU's JHA policy has so far largely been based on the bottom-up approach. The problem with this approach is that it tends to lead to grindingly slow decisionmaking and patchy implementation. Recognition of these flaws led to the partial 'Communitarisation' of JHA, in that the ToA allows for certain aspects of JHA policy to be subject to Community decisionmaking procedures. These influences will now be considered in more detail.

- **The Single European Market project.** The influence of the SEM on the development of JHA policies might be regarded as providing evidence for neo-functionalist explanations of European integration, in that the logic of the SEM led to 'spillover' effects into JHA. In particular, the aim of the SEM project was to ensure freedom of movement of goods, capital, services and people within the EU, by removing impediments to cross-border movement. This raised key questions concerning how illegal cross-border activities, such as illegal immigration, drug-trafficking, smuggling and money laundering, are to be policed. By facilitating cross-border movement, the SEM programme also increased the possibility of citizens becoming involved in civil disputes in other member states (for example, over house purchases, divorce or child custody). The SEM programme also raised important questions concerning the rights of 'third-country nationals' (TCNs), that is, people residing, and often working, in the EU who are not citizens of a member state. There are over 12 million TCNs in EU15. Each EU country has its own citizenship laws, meaning that it is more difficult for some TCNs to gain citizenship than others. Although few will be returning to their countries of birth, the rights of TCNs are very restricted (for example, they currently do not have the right to live and work in another member state).
- **Migration pressures from outside the EU.** In June 2000, the discovery by UK customs authorities in Dover of the bodies of 58 Chinese illegal immigrants who had suffocated to death in a Dutch truck provided horrific evidence of the strength and scale of migration pressures. People from outside the EU seeking to migrate to EU countries are generally divided into three categories: *asylum seekers* (refugees from war or oppression); *economic migrants* seeking legal permanent residence (that is, those seeking to improve their economic situation); and *illegal immigrants*. In addition, large numbers of people from outside the Union seek to work for a limited period in the EU. Economic migrants are no longer welcome in any EU country and the growth in asylum seeking led to the attempted imposition of strict curbs. Growing recognition that EU countries face similar migration problems, combined with efforts to remove the EU's internal borders, led to greater intergovernmental co-operation in this field. However, immigration policies and citizenship laws have been developed more or less independently by each

member state, meaning that transition from national to EU-wide immigration policies is fraught with difficulties.

The problem of developing a common EU migration policy is compounded by several factors: immigration is a much bigger problem in some EU countries (for example, Germany or the UK) than others (for example, Portugal); the point at which illegal migrants enter is not necessarily their chosen destination; the problem of organised smuggling gangs seems to be growing; and there is the problem of what to do with the illegal migrants when caught. In recent years we have seen a trend from national measures to interdependency and partial 'Europeanisation' in the field of migration policy, deriving from recognition that member states must work together in order to achieve effective results.

- **The attention given to specific law and order problems**, such as organised crime, drug trafficking, football hooliganism and terrorism. Each of these problems has a cross-border dimension which has encouraged police and judicial authorities in member states to co-operate with each other and to develop a network of interinstitutional links. Such co-operation is now viewed as a necessity rather than a luxury.
- **The end of the cold war** in 1989/90 led to new, non-military threats to the security of the member states of the EU. Many of these threats are perceived to derive from the effects of the collapse of communism in Eastern Europe, such as the rise in the number of illegal immigrants, war refugees, asylum seekers, economic migrants and an increase in international organized crime. Not all of these security threats of course derive from Eastern Europe: for example, the problems of international drug trafficking, money laundering, counterfeiting and terrorism have many sources.
- **The pursuit of EU 'deepening' and 'widening'.** 'Deeper' European integration embraces not only economic integration but also political integration. The development of JHA has partly resulted from the aim to pursue deeper political union, that is, to develop the Union as a political and not just an economic formation; and partly because of the logic of economic integration. Economic and financial integration has forced authorities to give greater attention to the problem of cross-border counterfeiting and money laundering. Moreover, the enlargement of the Union also raises important issues concerning the control of crime and migration.
- **The failure of intergovernmental solutions.** The TEU also unintentionally exposed the inadequacy of purely intergovernmental solutions to JHA problems, because it was increasingly recognised that its JHA provisions were deeply flawed. These provisions, based on voluntary intergovernmental co-operation, were incapable of dealing with the growing problems of illegal immigration, asylum seeking and organised crime. But as will be seen, recognition of the weakness of intergovernmental solutions has not meant that 'supranational' solutions have been grasped with open arms.

○   **The Weakness of the Maastricht Treaty's JHA Provisions**

By establishing the third pillar, the TEU agreed at Maastricht put JHA formally within the EU framework. Under this framework, the Council was the sole decisiontaker in JHA and decisions required the unanimous agreement of the governments of member states. Instead of Community instruments, intergovernmental instruments were used to carry out policy. The roles of the Commission, the European Parliament (EP) and European Court of Justice (ECJ) in JHA were limited, as shown in Figure 16.1.

Figure 16.1 Decisionmaking in JHA under the Maastricht Treaty

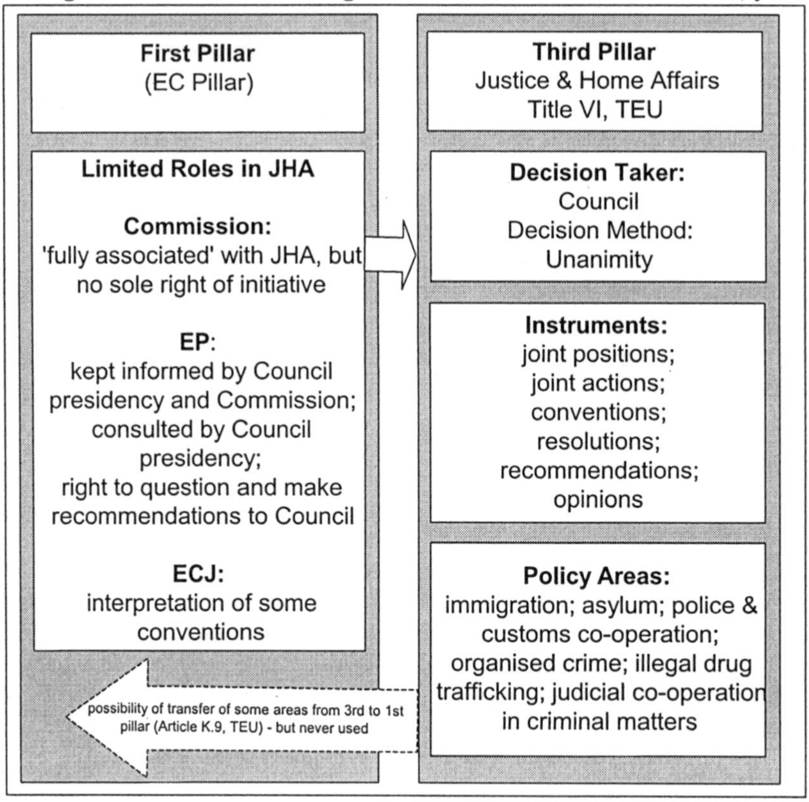

First Pillar (EC Pillar)	Third Pillar Justice & Home Affairs Title VI, TEU
Limited Roles in JHA **Commission:** 'fully associated' with JHA, but no sole right of initiative	**Decision Taker:** Council Decision Method: Unanimity
EP: kept informed by Council presidency and Commission; consulted by Council presidency; right to question and make recommendations to Council	**Instruments:** joint positions; joint actions; conventions; resolutions; recommendations; opinions
ECJ: interpretation of some conventions	**Policy Areas:** immigration; asylum; police & customs co-operation; organised crime; illegal drug trafficking; judicial co-operation in criminal matters

possibility of transfer of some areas from 3rd to 1st pillar (Article K.9, TEU) - but never used

Most of the criticisms about the operation of the Maastricht third pillar centred on its inadequacy and ineffectiveness, due in large measure to its intergovernmental and voluntary character. In particular:
1. *Decisionmaking difficulties.* Because decisions generally required the unanimous agreement of all member states, it was difficult to make

progress. In the five years after ratification of the TEU, the JHA Council agreed only one joint position and five joint actions in migration policy.

2. *Weak policy instruments.* Because JHA was outside the Community framework, there were no strong instruments to implement policies once agreed. Thus the JHA pillar did not use the legal instruments of the first pillar, such as directives and regulations. Instead it used other instruments, such as common positions, joint actions, resolutions, recommendations and conventions. Adoption of 'common positions' to define the Union's approach on a particular question required approval of all member states and tended to result in broad guidelines rather than unambiguous policies. Many JHA meetings led only to resolutions and recommendations, that is, 'soft law', with no binding effect. Conventions (that is, the Europol convention or the control of external frontiers convention) took years to negotiate and ratify.

3. *The limited roles of European Community institutions in JHA.* The TEU gave the ECJ, the EP and the Commission only a limited role in JHA. The Commission's right to initiate proposals was limited to certain areas and was shared with member states. The EP had for most things only to be kept informed. The Court of Justice also had a very minor role. JHA decisionmaking therefore remained almost entirely intergovernmental.

4. *The overlap between European Community and JHA policies.* For example, third-pillar immigration issues were difficult to separate from cross-border movement issues in the first pillar.

5. *Shifting JHA priorities*, due to the fact that the presidency of the Council largely set the JHA agenda (for example, leading to an emphasis on combating drugs during the 1996 Irish presidency and on combating illegal immigration during the 1998 Austrian presidency).

Although the Maastricht formula for JHA had many shortcomings, it provided the impetus for further reform and increased co-operation between national authorities, such as police and customs bodies, in this field.

● REFORMS OF JHA IN THE ToA AND THE ToN

○ Background

The 1996/97 intergovernmental conference devoted considerable attention to the issue of JHA reform. There was a broad consensus among member states that the EU's JHA policies needed to be strengthened, if the growing problems of asylum seeking, illegal immigration and international crime were to be addressed successfully. Germany and the Netherlands in particular pushed hard for radical changes to the Maastricht formula for JHA, although this provoked resistance from the UK and France. As had been the case at

Maastricht, the results of these differences were some messy compromises and fudges at the Amsterdam European Council at which the ToA was agreed. Nevertheless, the ToA introduced major changes to JHA, namely:

- it seeks to maintain and develop the Union as an 'area of freedom, security and justice';
- it transplants visa, asylum and immigration policy from the third to the first pillar;
- it incorporates the Schengen Agreement into the Union framework;
- it introduces important changes to JHA decisionmaking procedures;
- it revises the content and title, of the third pillar, as shown in Figure 16.2.

Figure 16.2 Decisionmaking in JHA under the ToA

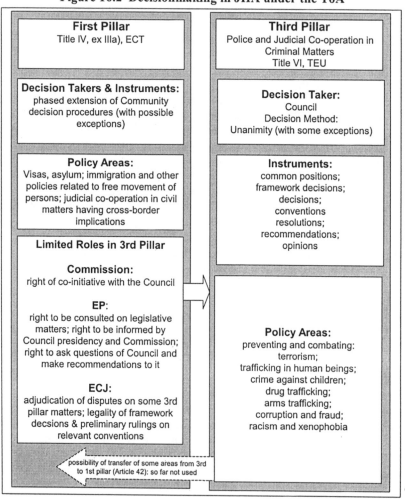

○ The EU as an Area of Freedom, Security and Justice

This objective is explicitly referred to in Articles 2 and 29 of the TEU as amended by the ToA. Article 29 states that:

> Without prejudice to the powers of the European Community, the Union's objective shall be to provide citizens with a high level of safety within an area of freedom, security and justice by developing common action among the member states in the fields of police and judicial co-operation in criminal matters and by preventing and combating racism and xenophobia.

It goes on to state that the objective will be achieved by preventing and combating crime, organised or otherwise, in particular terrorism, trafficking in persons and offences against children, illicit drug trafficking and illicit arms trafficking, corruption and fraud. It further explains that the means used to pursue these objectives will be through closer co-operation between police forces, customs authorities, judicial authorities and other competent authorities in member states and through Europol. There will be approximation where necessary of rules on criminal matters in member states. Article 61 of the EC Treaty lists specific measures in relation to visas, asylum, immigration and other policies related to free movement which the Council is required to adopt in order to 'establish progressively an area of freedom, security and justice'. The EU is a patchwork of diverse national judicial and policing systems and it is unrealistic to expect that these aims will lead to the establishment of a homogeneous EU legal zone. Instead, they are being sought through collaboration and setting of minimum standards.

○ Transplanting Visa, Asylum and Immigration Policies

The ToA transplanted most non-criminal matters from the third to the first pillar. The effect of this has been to separate asylum and immigration issues from police and judicial co-operation issues, thus linking the former with freedom of movement issues. The treaty introduced major provisions in relation to migration from outside the EU. The new Title IV of the EC Treaty encompasses visas, asylum, immigration and other policies related to free movement of persons. This means that the Commission, the EP and the ECJ have a bigger role in these areas of policy. The ToA allows for *phased*, *selective* and *controlled* extension of qualified majority voting (QMV) and co-decision to these areas, with a five year transition period after its entry into force (the period ending 1 May 2004). It states that after this date, the Council, acting unanimously after consulting the EP, may decide to introduce co-decision for all areas under this Title. The Treaty of Nice (ToN) reworks Article 67 to allow for deferred QMV and co-decision in this field after certain conditions are met. The ToA's provisions are outlined below.

- **Checks at external borders and visas**. Within a supposedly border-free zone, it makes little sense for member states to have different external border-checking and visa policies. The objective of a common visa policy has proved difficult to achieve, primarily because of entrenched differences in national practices and disagreements between member states concerning the list of third countries to which visa requirements are to apply.

The ToA sought to establish common rules on checks at external borders and visas, with phased extension of QMV in these areas (Article 67, ECT), namely: (1) standards and procedures to be followed in carrying out checks at external borders (62.2a); (2) the list of third countries whose nationals must be in possession of visas (62.2bi); (3) a uniform format for visas (62.2biii). Note: since the ToA came into force measures (2) and (3) are taken by the Council acting by QMV on a proposal from the Commission and after consulting the EP; (4) procedures and conditions for issuing visas (62.2.bii); (5) rules on a uniform visa (62.2biv). Note: measures (4) and (5) are taken by the Council acting unanimously. Article 67 states that within five years of the treaty entering into force, such measures will be taken by co-decision; (6) conditions for travel of third country nationals (62.3). In March 1999, the Council agreed a common visa regulation, defining the non-EU countries whose nationals must possess a visa on crossing the EU's external borders.

- **Asylum policy**. The number of people seeking asylum in EU countries has soared in recent years, leading to pressure to stem the flow of asylum seekers and also to develop fair and effective ways of assessing asylum applications. The Dublin Convention, signed in 1990, requires asylum seekers to apply for asylum in the first EU country they enter, to prevent asylum seekers from shopping around the EU for asylum (this requirement however has by no means been rigorously applied by member states). Member states have agreed on common policies on the legal definition of 'refugee'; on unfounded asylum claims; on safe third countries; on safe countries of origin and on many minimum guarantees for asylum applicants.

Article 63 (ECT) states that within five years after the entry into force of the ToA, the Council is required to adopt: criteria and mechanisms for determining which member state is responsible for considering an asylum application (63.1a); minimum standards on the reception of asylum seekers (63.1b); minimum standards with respect to the qualification of third country nationals as refugees (63.1c); minimum standards on procedures on member states for granting or withdrawing refugee status (63.1d); minimum standards for giving temporary protection to displaced persons from third countries and those needing international protection (63.2a); measures to promote a balance of effort between member states in receiving and bearing the consequences of receiving refugees and displaced persons (63.2b) – this was not made subject to the five-year provision. An interesting aspect of the ToA's protocol on asylum is that it forbids asylum applications *between* member states, perhaps thereby implicitly bestowing a quasi federal status on the EU.

• **Immigration policy.** In some cases within five years of the ToA entering into force the Council is required to adopt measures within the following areas: conditions of entry and residence and standards for issue of visas and residence permits (63.3a). This was not made subject to the five-year provision); illegal immigration and illegal residence, including repatriation of illegal residents (63.3b); and definition of the rights and conditions under which third country nationals may reside in another member state (63.4). This was not made subject to the five-year provision. The Council may also adopt, by QMV on a Commission proposal, provisional measures for emergencies in which there is a sudden inflow of nationals of non-member countries (64.2).

• **Judicial co-operation** in civil matters having cross-border implications (65a,b,c); and co-operation between judicial administrations (66).

○ The Treaty of Nice and Changes to Decisionmaking in JHA

The ToA's approach to changes to decisionmaking in JHA was rather cautious and tentative and it is hardly surprising that this subject was revisited in the ToN. The ToN makes the ToA's phased, selective and controlled shifts to QMV and co-decision in JHA somewhat more concrete, but again a cautious approach is adopted. The provisions affected are: judicial co-operation in civil matters, except family law (65) – QMV and co-decision as soon as the ToN comes into force; co-operation between administrations (66) – QMV with consultation from 1 May 2004; free movement of third country nationals (62.3) and clandestine immigration (63.3b) – QMV and co-decision from 1 May 2004, subject to a unanimous Council decision; checks at external frontiers (62.2a) – QMV and co-decision as soon as there is unanimous agreement on the scope of the measures (the changes to Articles 62.3. 63.3b and 62.2a were included in a declaration on Article 67, which also stated that the Council would endeavour to make co-decision applicable from 1 May 2004 or as soon as possible thereafter to other areas covered by Title IV or parts of them); standards and procedures for receiving asylum seekers and refugees (63.1a,b,c,d) and minimum standards for temporary protection to refugees (Article 63.2a) – QMV and co-decision as soon as the Council by unanimity lays down common rules and basic principles. The ToN will also extend QMV to the enhanced co-operation procedure in JHA.

If the ToA's and the ToN's provisions are fully implemented, EU migration policy will become partly 'supranationalised' (that is, subject in part to Community decisionmaking procedures). But current treaty arrangements are extremely complicated and subject to various deferrals and qualifications. Through protocols attached to the ToA, the UK, Ireland and Denmark are not bound by Title IV provisions (see below). It remains to be seen how far states are willing to loosen their grip on this policy area.

○ Incorporating the Schengen Agreement into the EU

This Agreement is a good example of how a 'vanguard' integration project, involving a group of EU states can become an official EU policy. Until the ToA, the agreement was separate from, but complementary to, EU policy to abolish border controls. It seeks to remove all impediments to the movement of EU citizens (such as passport controls) across the borders of member states. Common travel areas within Europe are not uncommon (for example, the Nordic common travel area; the common travel area between the UK and Ireland; and the Benelux common travel area). However, the Schengen system is unique in the number of participant countries (currently 13). The Schengen Agreement originated from the Saarbrucken Agreement between France and Germany in July 1984, which sought to abolish frontier controls between the two countries. The Benelux countries soon became involved and an agreement was signed by these five countries in Schengen in June 1985. Italy signed in November 1990 and Spain and Portugal in June 1991. The UK was sceptical about the ability of Schengen to achieve tight external frontiers and refused to participate. The UK's position is an obstacle to the entry of Ireland, because if Ireland joined and the UK did not, it could mean extra border controls between the two countries.

The Schengen Convention and decisions adopted under it form the heart of the Schengen *acquis*. The Convention was signed in June 1990 and sets out the rules concerning common treatment of non-EU nationals and the measures needed to replace internal border controls with a system of common controls. The main features of the Schengen convention are:

- it establishes the institutional framework for the abolition of border controls between the Schengen countries. Internal borders become external frontiers of the Schengen zone for non-Schengen countries;
- freedom of movement: once a person is allowed entry into the Schengen area, they are free to move throughout all Schengen countries, subject to EU law. For non-EU nationals, this freedom is limited to three months. If a person is refused entry to one Schengen state, s/he must be refused entry to all. The Convention exempts third country nationals from visa requirements for visits up to three months. But they do not have the right to freely settle in other member states. This raises the question of whether or not the EU's 'area of freedom, security and justice' applies to them;
- police co-operation, involving mutual assistance between police authorities in the Schengen countries to prevent and detect crime;
- other forms of co-operation such as extradition and the transfer of the enforcement of criminal judgments;
- the Schengen information system (SIS) is a computerised information system enabling Schengen states to exchange data in order to maintain security. Each Schengen state maintains a national computer system with

a Schengen-wide data base, for example, on undesirable aliens, persons suspected of committing or likely to commit extremely serious offences, stolen vehicles, firearms, bank notes or official documents;

- data protection: all Schengen countries must adopt national laws on data protection which are at least as good as those provided for in the 1981 Council of Europe convention for the protection of individuals with regard to the automatic processing of personal data;
- there are provisions on measures to facilitate cross-border movement of goods and to enhance co-operation between customs authorities.

The Schengen executive committee comprises one minister from each Schengen country. It takes decisions by unanimity and has a six-month rotating presidency. Senior officials prepare the committee's work. Implementation of the Schengen Convention was delayed for five years because of various disagreements between the signatories. The main problems centred on mechanisms for effective co-operation between police and immigration authorities, doubts about the effectiveness of external controls around 'Schengenland' and differences in domestic policies. The Convention eventually came into force on 26 March 1995. Seven countries agreed to participate (Belgium, the Netherlands, Luxembourg, Germany, Portugal, Spain and France), but in June 1995 France temporarily suspended full participation due to concerns about internal security. Greece and Italy initially did not participate, due to problems concerning the control of coastal frontiers and delays in preparing for exchange of data between police forces. Austria's participation began in 1997.

A protocol attached to the ToA integrated the Schengen Agreement into the framework of the EU. The legal basis of Schengen is currently divided between Title IV of the EC treaty and Title VI of the TEU, that is, between the first and third pillars, depending on the issues involved. In 1999, the Council defined the Schengen *acquis* and also allocated the legal bases to its various parts (this demarcation had been delayed by disagreements between member states). Another ToA protocol on the position of the UK and Ireland exempts these countries from participation, although they may opt to do so, subject to certain conditions. In July 1999, the Commission approved a request by the UK to participate in certain Schengen provisions. Denmark also has an 'opt-in' arrangement, of a different kind. Unlike the UK or Ireland, Denmark has signed the Schengen Convention and therefore is committed in law to adopt many measures agreed under Title IV. Iceland and Norway also formally co-operate with the Schengen countries. There are separate agreements between Iceland and Norway and the 13 Schengen countries and also between Iceland and Norway and the UK and Ireland, to cover the implications of the UK and Irish exemptions. Full implementation of the Schengen *acquis* by Denmark, Norway and Iceland commenced on 25 March 2001.

○   **JHA Decisionmaking in the First and Third Pillars**

• **First-pillar procedures.** At Amsterdam, the 'Communitarisation' of EU migration policy was only possible through the insertion of various get-out clauses and delaying measures into Title IV (ex IIIa). For the first five years after the entry into force of the ToA, the Council will take Title IV decisions unanimously on proposals for measures put forward by the Commission or a member state and after consulting the EP (with exceptions for two aspects of visa policy, which required QMV as soon as the treaty entered into force). The ToA states that after five years, the Council, acting unanimously after consulting the EP, shall decide whether to make all or parts of Title IV subject to QMV and co-decision (Article 67). The ToN allows for partial transition to QMV and co-decision in respect of judicial co-operation in civil matters as soon as the treaty enters into force; for some other areas once the Council by unanimity has adopted legislation laying down common rules and principles; for some other areas by 1 May 2004; and for other areas either by 1 May 2004 or as soon as possible. In the case of judicial co-operation between administrations, QMV with consultation will apply from 1 May 2004. Although Article 68 gives the ECJ jurisdiction on migration policies, this jurisdiction is subject to various limitations. As a result of a protocol in the ToA, the UK and Ireland will not take part in measures under Title IV of the EC Treaty and will not be bound by them. However, if they wish to participate in these measures, they can do so by informing the president of the Council within three months of a proposal or initiative being submitted. They are also free to adopt measures after they have been adopted by the Council. A separate protocol also gives Denmark an 'opt in' arrangement.
• **Third-pillar procedures.** Unanimity remains the rule for Council decisionmaking under the third pillar. However, the ToA changed the third pillar decisionmaking system in the following ways:

  • it removed the instrument of 'joint action' established in the TEU;
  • it established binding 'framework decisions' for the approximation of laws and regulations of the member states without direct effect;
  • the Council may adopt binding decisions for any other purpose, excluding the approximation of the laws and regulations of member states. Measures to implement these decisions will be adopted by QMV;
  • conventions can come into force when adopted by half the member states, in those states;
  • the Council is required to promote co-operation through Europol;
  • the Commission has the right of co-initiative with the Council in all policy areas under the third pillar;
  • it gives the ECJ a greater role in the third pillar, for example, with regard to the adjudication of disputes on some third-pillar matters, the legality of framework decisions and preliminary rulings on relevant conventions;

- the EP has to be consulted on legislative measures, including conventions. The presidency and the Commission must regularly inform the EP of discussions in the areas covered by Title VI. The EP may ask questions of the Council or make recommendations to it.

Framework decisions and decisions (Title VI, TEU) replaced *joint actions* once the ToA entered into force. More binding and more authoritative than joint actions, they should serve to make action under the reorganised third pillar more effective. Framework decisions are used to approximate the laws and regulations of the member states. They may be proposed on the initiative of the Commission or a member state, and must be adopted unanimously. They are binding on the member states as to the result to be achieved but leave to the national authorities the choice of form and methods. Decisions are used for any purpose other than the approximation of the laws and regulations of the member states. They are binding and the measures required to implement them at Union level are adopted by the Council acting by QMV. The Commission is fully associated with work in the third pillar (Article 36, TEU). Unlike its role in relation to Community policies, under the provisions of the TEU, the Commission did not have sole initiative in JHA. However, its role was extended by the ToA to cover all Title VI fields. In the case of the third pillar, this right of initiative will be shared with the member states for the first five years following the treaty's entry into force, after which it will become an exclusive right. Article K.9 of the TEU allowed for the possibility of certain third-pillar matters to be transferred to the first pillar, subject to unanimity in the Council and ratification by member states. Under Article 42 of the ToA, this 'bridge' provision is retained, so that third-pillar matters may be transferred to the first pillar, providing the Council first consults the EP. However, the bridge has so far never been used.

○ The JHA Council System and JHA Collaborative Programmes

The Justice and Home Affairs Council is made up of the justice and home affairs ministers of the member states. Each Council presidency organises one or two Council meetings on JHA. Directorate-General H of the Council's Secretariat assists the Council presidency in JHA matters. The JHA Council's work is prepared by the Committee of Permanent Representatives (COREPER 2). Issues are forwarded to COREPER 2 by three specialist committees of national officials, that is, by the Article 36 Committee (dealing with police, customs and judicial co-operation); the strategic committee on immigration, frontiers and asylum; and the committee on civil law matters. The Article 36 Committee derives its name from the article in the TEU which requires a co-ordinating committee of senior national officials be established to assist the Council on third-pillar matters. Its tasks are to give opinions for the attention of the Council, either at the Council's request or on its own initiative and to contribute to the preparation of the Council's discussions on police and judicial co-operation in criminal matters. It normally meets once a month in Brussels except for one meeting every six months which takes place in the country holding the presidency. The other two committees have been established to deal with areas formerly under the third pillar. In addition to the above, there are about 20 working groups of national officials, on specific subjects. For example, there are working parties on police co-operation, Europol, illicit drug trafficking, terrorism and customs co-operation. There are also high-level expert groups on organised crime, drugs and Schengen (see Figure 16.3 below). The Commission takes part in meetings of the Council, COREPER, the three JHA committees and all working parties. However, it has a limited role in policy initiation. The Council rather than the Commission has driven the development of JHA. Many initiatives on JHA derive from member states rather than from the Commission.

Figure 16.3 The JHA Decisionmaking System

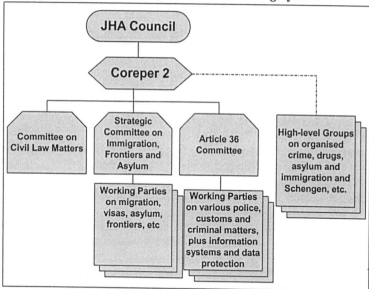

A diverse range of collaborative programmes involving national authorities and agencies has also been established: for example, *Grotius* promotes incentives and exchanges for lawyers; *Stop* is an exchange programme for those seeking to combat trade in human beings; *Oisin* involves co-operation between law enforcement bodies; *Odysseus* is a training and exchange programme in the field of asylum and immigration; *Falcone* seeks co-operation between those responsible for actions to combat organised crime; the *European Judicial Network*, inaugurated in September

1998 and administered by the General Secretariat of the Council, seeks to improve standards of co-operation between judicial authorities in criminal matters. It originated from a 1997 action plan to combat organised crime. A European Judicial Co-operation Unit, *Eurojust*, has been set up in Brussels, composed of national prosecutors or police officers of equivalent competence drawn from each member state and having the task of facilitating co-ordination between national prosecuting authorities and of supporting criminal investigations in organised crime (Article 31, TEU, as amended by the ToN). Eurojust is expected to work closely with the European judicial network and with Europol (see below). A *European Refugee Fund* has been established to ensure improved reception of refugees in member states. The *European Monitoring Centre for Drugs and Drug Addiction* (EMCDDA) is a monitoring agency based in Lisbon. Its collects, analyses and disseminates information on illegal drug use in the EU. *Reitox*, a European information network, collects information on national drug situations for the EMCDDA annual report. A draft action plan to combat drugs during 2000–04 was agreed at the Helsinki European Council. But action to combat drugs is still fragmented between member states.

○ The Content and Title of the Third Pillar under the ToA

The policy areas remaining in the third pillar are police and judicial co-operation in criminal matters (PJCCM), plus a new policy in relation to racism and xenophobia.

• **Police Co-operation** (Article 30, TEU) comprises common action decided by the Council and through Europol (see below). It includes operational co-operation between the competent authorities in relation to the prevention, detection and investigation of crime; collection, storage, processing, analysis and exchange of relevant information; co-operation and joint initiatives in training; and evaluation of investigative techniques relating to serious organised crime.

• **Judicial co-operation in criminal matters** (Article 31, TEU). Common action on judicial co-operation in criminal matters includes: facilitating and accelerating co-operation between competent authorities; facilitating extradition between member states; ensuring compatibility of rules applicable in the member states to improve such co-operation; preventing conflicts of jurisdiction between member states; progressively adopting measures establishing minimum rules relating to criminal acts and to penalties in the fields of organised crime terrorism and drug trafficking.

• **Common action by member states to prevent and combat racism and xenophobia** (referred to in Article 29, TEU). This embraces both police and judicial co-operation. A European Monitoring Centre on Racism and Xenophobia opened in Vienna in April 2000.

- **Europol** (Article 30, TEU). As a result of an initiative by Chancellor Kohl of Germany, Europol was established in the TEU, with the aim of improving co-operation between member states in the areas of drug trafficking, illicit trafficking in radioactive and nuclear substances; crimes involving clandestine immigration networks; illicit vehicle trafficking; trafficking in human beings; illegal money-laundering activities; terrorism; and other serious forms of international organized crime. An international convention on Europol was drafted in 1993 and 1994, setting out the areas with which Europol would be concerned and its operational characteristics. After considerable controversy, it was agreed that terrorism would be included in Europol's functions. The creation of Europol required the agreement on a convention which was signed by representatives of member states on 26 July 1995, ratified by all member states in June 1998 and came into force on 1 October 1998. Europol, which is based in The Hague, did not become fully operational until 1 July 1999, following ratification of certain protocols by member states. Europol supports member states by:
  - facilitating the exchange of data (personal and non-personal), between Europol liaison officers seconded by member states;
  - providing operational analyses in support of member states' operations, general strategic reports and crime analyses;
  - providing expertise and technical support for investigations and ongoing operations carried out by law enforcement agencies of the member states under the supervision and legal responsibility of the states concerned.

Europol has a substantial degree of operational independence. It is responsible to a management board representing the JHA Council. The management board, comprising one representative from all member states, has the overall task of supervising its activities. Each member state has a Europol national unit and a Europol liaison officer. Europol is funded from contributions by the member states according to their GNP. The Council is required to promote co-operation through Europol and within a period of five years after the entry into force of the ToA to enable Europol to facilitate and support the preparation, co-ordination and implementation of specific investigative actions by the competent authorities of the member states; adopt measures allowing it to ask the authorities of member states to conduct and co-ordinate investigations; promote liaison between prosecuting/investigating officials in the fight against organised crime; and establish a research, documentation and statistical network on cross-border crime.

The establishment of Europol led to some rather fanciful speculation that the EU was developing an organisation on the lines of the US FBI (Federal Bureau of Investigation). However, Europol is a police *office*, not a police force and it has not been set up to overrride the authority of national police forces. Many civil rights groups, and Eurosceptics, are highly suspicious that Europol's powers will increase to the point where, in all but name, it becomes an operational police force. Eurosceptics see in the creation of Europol the thin end of an expanding wedge, in that they fear that it will be given ever more resources and power. Some of the criticisms of the existing powers of Europol are: under Article 10, Title III of the Europol Convention, Europol officers have the power to open files on victims of crime and witnesses or others who might provide relevant information; Europol officers will not be compelled to testify in court and will be immune from prosecution for acts they perform in the exercise of their official functions. This means, according to Europol's critics, that citizens will lack adequate safeguards against actions of Europol officers; unlike the US FBI, which is accountable to Congress, Europol lacks accountability to the EP (the director of Europol answers to a management board under the Council). However, Europol officers cannot make arrests or search houses. Rather, they provide technical support to national police authorities. But, in September 2000, EU justice ministers agreed to give Europol the power to initiate criminal investigations.

○ **The Action Plan for Implementation of ToA Provisions on Freedom, Security and Justice**

The Cardiff European Council called on the Council and Commission to present to the Vienna European Council an action plan on how best to implement the provisions of the ToA with regard to the area of freedom and security and justice. The Commission's action plan was approved by the Vienna European Council and contains many specific proposals to foster police and judicial co-operation and to combat crime. It favoured an extension of Europol's powers and consideration of the arrangements under which a law enforcement service from one member state could operate in the territory of another. It also sought to establish an overall migration strategy, using the experiences gained in the Schengen framework. In the field of asylum and immigration the Vienna European Council recognised the need for an overall migration strategy. A high-level working group was established in December 1998 to examine migration and asylum policy. It submitted its final report to the Tampere European Council in October 1999.

The Tampere European Council was a special meeting devoted exclusively to the creation of an area of freedom, security and justice in the EU. Its recommendations focused on identifying the main elements of a common immigration and asylum policy (through, for example, partnership with countries of origin; developing a common asylum procedure and managing migration flows); developing a common area of justice (for example, through mutual recognition of judicial decisions, improved access to justice in cross-border cases and greater convergence in civil law); minimum standards for the protection and rights to compensation of the victims of crime; and reinforcing efforts to combat cross-border crime through developing co-operation between police and judicial authorities. It called for the setting up of joint investigative teams to deal with drug trafficking, terrorism and similar matters. It called for the establishment of a European Police Chiefs Operational Task Force and the creation of a European Police College (the task force had its first meeting in Lisbon in April 2000; the college is being set up as a network of existing institutes and will be operational from 2001). It called for the setting up of Eurojust (see above). Tampere set a deadline for December 2000 for adoption of a programme on mutual recognition. Mutual recognition means that decisions taken in one member state should be accepted as valid in any other member state and put into effect on a reciprocal basis. It was also agreed at Tampere that court judgments, rulings or orders (for example, arrest warrants) in one country should be enforceable throughout the EU. But much remains to be done to bring the different legal systems closer together through harmonisation of certain types of civil law and mutual recognition. Human rights groups such as *Statewatch* and *Fair Trials Abroad* have expressed concerns that such measures could lead to injustices of various kinds.

The Tampere European Council also asked the Commission to monitor the progress achieved by the Union in creating an area of freedom, security and justice by means of a scoreboard. The scoreboard agreed at Tampere focuses on three areas: asylum and immigration policies; a European area of justice; and the fight against organised crime. The Commission produced the first such scoreboard in April 2000 (Commission, 2000). For each objective relating to the three areas, it listed the action needed, the institutions responsible, the timetable for adoption of the action and progress made in achieving the objective). In March 2000, the Council approved a new action plan on organised crime, including recommendations for strengthening Europol and the investigation of organised crime. The ToN will insert a new section on enhanced co-operation into Title V of the TEU, with the aim of enabling the EU to develop more rapidly into an area of freedom, security and justice (see Chapter 4). It will also introduce co-decision for aspects of incentive measures in support of anti-discrimination actions taken by member states (Article 3, ECT). These developments in JHA suggest an attempt to narrow the 'implementation deficit' which has dogged this area of policy.

O   The CEECs and Police and Judicial Co-operation

There remains considerable concern in the EU about the competence of police authorities and judicial systems in the Central and East European country (CEEC) applicant states, particularly because central and eastern Europe is a source of considerable international crime and is a conduit for illegal immigration from Russia and other CIS (Commonwealth of Independent States) countries. In accession negotiations, the EU is requiring applicant countries to ratify EU and international justice treaties and conventions and is seeking to ensure that these policies are put into practice on the ground. Candidate countries are expected to accede to the *acquis* of the Union in the field of JHA. For example, they must all sign all conventions signed by member states in this field, such as the conventions on asylum and the Europol convention. The EU is assisting in the reform of their police and judicial systems, through the PHARE and other programmes. Negotiations with the 'first-wave' applicants on JHA issues opened in May 2000.

● CONCLUSION

The development of the EU's JHA policies provide useful insights into why and how member states pursue the paths of co-operation and integration. JHA policy, which embraces many sensitive issues concerning national sovereignty, has been considerably strengthened and broadened in recent years principally because member states recognise that JHA problems cannot be tackled in isolation. The development of JHA provides some support for the 'spillover' theory of integration in that, from small beginnings, co-operation in JHA has led to further co-operation. However, the development of JHA is also indicative of the difficulties of pursuing deeper integration where important issues of sovereignty are concerned. These difficulties, not least the reluctance of member states to fully 'Communitarise' this aspect of policy, has meant that progress has often been slow and fragmentary. It also helps to explain why JHA is still extremely complicated, because decisions on JHA have resulted from fuzzy compromises and 'fudges'. Nevertheless, the pace at which the EU's JHA policy is developing has undoubtedly increased in recent years and seems set to increase further.

FURTHER READING

Commission (2000), *Scoreboard to Review Progress on the Creation of an Area of Freedom, Security and Justice in the EU*, COM (2000)167, Brussels.
Geddes, A. (2000), *Immigration and European Integration. Towards Fortress Europe*, Manchester University Press, Manchester.
Guiraudon, V. (2000), 'European Integration and Migration Policy', *Journal of Common Market Studies*, vol. 38, no. 2, pp. 251–272.
House of Lords Select Committee on European Communities (1999), *Schengen and the United Kingdom's Border Controls*, 7th Report, HL Paper 37.
Monar, J. (2001), *Justice and Home Affairs in the European Union*, Macmillan, Basingstoke.
Stetter, S. (2000), 'Regulating Migration: Authority Delegation in Justice and Home Affairs', *Journal of European Public Policy*, vol. 7, no. 1, pp. 80–103.

 **Chapter 17**

The EU in the Global Economy

● TRENDS IN THE GLOBAL ECONOMY

○ Why Global Economic Trends Are Important to the Union

The European Union is the world's largest trading entity and has the world's largest market. It has less than 7% of the world's population but accounts for about a quarter of world GDP and for about a fifth of world trade (indeed, two-fifths if trade between EU members is included). It is the world's largest exporter and the world's second largest importer of goods (after the USA). It is the largest importer of many goods, including agricultural products, textiles and clothing. In 1998, it accounted for about 20% of exports of goods, compared with 16% for the US and 9% for Japan. The corresponding figures for imports were 18% for the EU, 21% for the US and 6.5% for Japan. It is also the world's largest exporter and importer of services, which now account for about a quarter of the EU's total trade.

Access to the EU's big market is therefore of crucial importance to many countries outside the Union. But the economic health of the Union also depends upon the ability of Union countries to compete successfully in world markets. Many millions of jobs in the EU depend directly on the export of goods and services. The EU economies are currently facing major challenges of adaptation, as a result of structural changes in the global economy – for example, growing international economic interdependence, rapid technological change, the decline of traditional industries, the emergence of new 'sunrise' industries, the e-commerce revolution and the rise of new economic 'growth poles', particularly in Asia. Within the Union, there is currently a lively debate about how best to rise to these challenges. It will be useful, therefore, to examine the Union's external trading position in the context of global economic change.

○ Key Global Economic Trends

Perhaps the most fundamental trend in the global economy is towards the internationalisation of production, finance and markets (Table 17.1).

Table 17.1 Key Developments in the Global Economy

- **Unprecedented growth:** in international trade, in foreign direct and indirect investment and in world production.
- **Increasing international interdependence,** manifested in (1) and also in the growth of transnational production chains.
- **Globalisation,** manifested in (1) and (2). The concept also embraces the notions of global markets, industries and products.
- **Rapid industrial change,** manifested for example in the decline of traditional, and the rise of new, industries and production systems.
- **The communications revolution,** manifested for example in high-tech telecommunications networks and in 'e-commerce'.
- **The emergence of new 'growth poles',** particularly in the Far East.
- **The spread of market-based economic systems,** for example, integration of former communist states into the global economy and the global privatisation revolution.
- **The 'new protectionism':** for example, the widespread use of non-tariff barriers to international trade.
- **The growth of regional economic co-operation:** for example, attempts to create regional trading formations in North America, South America, Asia and Europe.
- **The rise of the Green movement,** which constitutes a challenge to growth-oriented ideologies. It is affecting patterns of energy use, production processes and products.

A central role in the globalisation process is being played by foreign direct investment (FDI) by multinational companies (MNCs). These are companies which locate productive assets, such as factories or retail outlets, in more than one country. MNCs now control about one-third of the world's private sector productive assets, with a turnover greater than the total of world exports. A finished product is increasingly likely to contain components manufactured in several countries. The cross-border production chains operated by many MNCs offer many examples of 'international sourcing' of this kind. Increased FDI flows in recent years are due to a combination of factors, including the removal of barriers to trade and investment; technological change, improved transport and communications and the rise in the number of countries capable of producing high-quality manufactured goods. This has led to greater integration in the global economy. For example, the EU and US economies are becoming increasingly intermeshed through cross-investment (Table 17.2). The EU is the second-largest recipient and source of FDI, after the US. In recent years, the EU has been a net exporter of FDI (Table 17.3), due in large measure to the attraction of the US as an investment location. Countries entering, or about to enter, the EU are likely to attract additional inward investment. For example, US manufacturing investment trebled in Ireland in the five years after Ireland's accession and in the four years after Spain's accession. The largest form of FDI in the EU, however, is cross-border investment (that is, from one EU country into another). In recent years there has been a cross-border merger and acquisition boom within the EU, amounting to over $200 billion in 1998. The amount of FDI which member states attract varies considerably. For example, in 1998 the UK attracted 43% of all US investment into Europe and held 22% of the stock of inward FDI in the EU. 'Indirect' or 'portfolio' investment (investment of money abroad) has also increased dramatically.

Table 17.2 FDI Stocks Held Abroad in 1997 (€ Billion)

EU15		US		Japan	
Total Extra-EU	658.6	World	783.8	World	245.9
of which to:		*of which to:*		*of which to:*	
US	298.2	EU15	337.4	US	92.5
Switzerland	52.4	Canada	87.0	EU15	47.6
Australia	29.5	Brazil	31.8	China	19.2
Canada	24.4	Japan	30.5	Australia	10.6
Brazil	24.2	Switzerland	28.5	Singapore	9.9
Singapore	15.5	Australia	27.1	South Korea	8.0
Japan	12.0	Mexico	21.9	Hong Kong	7.5
Hong Kong	10.7	Hong Kong	17.4	Indonesia	7.1
Norway	10.5	Singapore	16.2	Thailand	5.2
Argentina	8.8	Argentina	9.1	Brazil	5.0

Source: Eurostat (1999).

Table 17.3 EU FDI Flows: Manufacturing and Services (€ Billion)

	1992	1993	1994	1995	1996	1997	1998
Total FDI outflows	17.8	24.2	24.1	45.6	47.4	90.1	190.5
Of which Manufacturing	7.5	7.4	16.8	19.8	17.8	30.9	55.8
Services	9.5	13.4	4.2	22.8	27.7	47.2	69.6
Total FDI inflows	22.8	21.5	21.8	37.2	31.8	38.2	89.3
Of which Manufacturing	8.3	7.9	5.3	15.2	6.5	10.3	27.9
Services	12.4	12.6	13.5	18.2	22.3	23.2	53.1

Note: excluding reinvested earnings. *Source*: Eurostat (1999).

International trade, often described as the engine of economic growth, has increased faster than world output in almost every year in recent decades. Since 1951, world trade has increased seventeenfold, world production fourfold, and world per capita income has doubled (Commission, 1999). The growth in world trade is partly attributable to *trade liberalisation*: tariffs on goods have fallen from 40% at the end of the Second World War to less than 5%, although these falls have been significantly offset by the increase in *non-tariff* barriers to trade, such as import quotas and technical regulations. The geographical distribution of world production is very uneven. The EU, the US and Japan account for about 15% of the world's potential labour force but produce about 70% of world GDP. But East Asia has become an increasingly important 'growth pole', despite the severe crisis in emerging markets in Asia in the late 1990s. The economies of Hong Kong, South Korea, Taiwan and Singapore have grown considerably faster than those of Western developed economies in the past two decades. There is now a new generation of 'Asian Tigers' (Thailand, Malaysia, the Philippines and, most importantly, China). Integration of the transition countries in Central and Eastern Europe (the CEECs) into the global economy is also highly significant, particularly for the EU which, for geographical and historical reasons, has assumed special responsibilities for this region: moreover, ten of these countries are currently negotiating entry into the EU. Global economic change is also occurring at an increasingly rapid pace, due not least to the information technology revolution and the rise of high-tech industries. Firms, indeed whole societies, must therefore adapt to change more readily than hitherto.

● EU TRADING PATTERNS

○ The Structure of EU Trade

The structure of EU trade falls into two categories: firstly, trade between EU countries (*intra-EU trade*) and secondly, trade between EU countries and the outside world (*extra-EU trade*). EU membership is likely to result in a substantial increase in the proportion of a country's trade accounted for by 'intra-Union' trade. Intra-EU trade, at about 62% of total EU trade (Table 17.4), is significantly greater than intraregional trade in other parts of the world. For example, just over a third of Japan's exports go to the Asia Pacific region and about a third of US exports go to North and South America. The expansion of intra-EU trade has largely been due to *intra-industry trade* (for example, where two countries both import and export machinery) rather than to increasing specialisation (for example, where one country would specialise in manufacturing and the other in food products).

Table 17.4 Exports to and Imports from EU Countries in 1998

	Imports from EU as % of total national imports	Exports to EU as % of total national exports
Austria	73.3	62.9
Belgium/Lux	70.9	75.8
Denmark	70.3	67.1
Finland	65.7	56.1
France	67.6	62.4
Germany	58.3	56.4
Greece	65.1	50.7
Holland	57.7	78.8
Ireland	61.5	70.1
Italy	61.6	56.2
Portugal	77.2	81.6
Spain	68.5	70.5
Sweden	69.2	57,9
UK	53.3	58.0
EU15	**62.5**	**62.9**
Iceland	56.2	65.0
Norway	67.7	76.9
EEA	62.5	63.2
Switzerland	76.7	62.4
US	19.3	22.0
Canada	9.5	5.0
Japan	13.9	18.5

Source: Eurostat, *Yearbook*, 2000.

Prior to the fourth enlargement, the European Free Trade Association (EFTA) was the EU's leading trading partner, accounting for almost a quarter of the EU's external trade. Trade with EFTA has been relatively harmonious, probably because it is roughly balanced 'intra-industry' trade. The US is the EU's single most important trading partner, accounting for about one-fifth of the EU's trade in goods and for about a third of its trade in services. There have been a series of protracted trade disputes between the EU and the US, but these have not yet resulted in an all-out trade war. Whereas the EU's trade with the US has tended to be broadly balanced (despite recent EU surpluses), for years the EU has had a substantial trade deficit with Japan (Figure 17.1 and Table 17.5). Almost all of the EU's imports from Japan are manufactured goods.

The EU both exports to and imports from a more diverse range of countries than does the US or Japan. EU trade with developing countries consists largely of the export of manufactures and the import of raw materials, agricultural products and low-tech manufactures. The EU currently has a trade surplus with many developing countries and with many transition economies in Central and Eastern Europe (the EU's fastest growth in trade in recent years has been with this region). As an integral element of its external aid policy, the EU grants varying degrees of preferential access to EU markets for developing and transition countries. There are significant variations in the trading patterns of trade of EU countries: for example, the UK has very large export markets in the US and the developing world. About three-quarters of EU exports consists of manufactures, including machinery and vehicles. The EU is a substantial net importer of energy and raw materials (Table 17.6).

Figure 17.1 Trade and FDI between the EU, the US and Japan (€ bn)

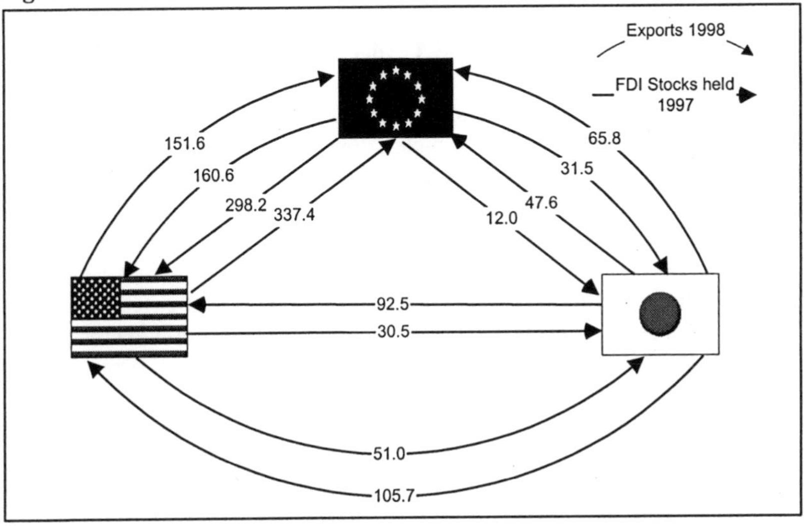

Source: Eurostat (1999).

Table 17.5 World Trade in Goods in 1998 (€ bn)

	Exports			Imports		
	1988	1998	1998* (%)	1988	1998	1998* (%)
EU15	343.4	731.6	19.7	368.7	712.4	18.4
US	270.1	606.9	16.3	388.8	842.6	21.7
Japan	224.1	346.1	9.3	158.5	250.9	6.5
Canada	98.5	188.5	5.1	93.1	177.7	4.6
Hong Kong	53.4	154.9	4.2	54.0	164.7	4.2
China	40.3	163.9	4.4	46.8	125.2	3.2
Rest of World	667.4	1520.1	41.0	684.6	1607.4	41.4
World	1697.2	3712.0	100.0	1794.5	3880.9	100.0

Note: * share of world total. *Source*: Eurostat (1999).

Table 17.6 Share of EU15 Exports and Imports of Goods by Product

	Exports (%)			Imports (%)		
	1988	1998	Growth 1988–98	1988	1998	Growth 1988–98
Food and drink	7.1	6.0	+80	9.8	7.0	+38
Raw materials	2.6	2.0	+63	9.1	5.9	+26
Energy	2.2	1.9	+82	13.9	9.1	+27
Chemicals	12.0	13.1	+132	6.4	7.8	+134
Manufactured goods	31.8	27.7	+86	25.7	29.6	+123
Machinery & vehicles	38.9	47.0	+157	27.8	37.4	+160
Other	5.4	2.3	-8	7.3	3.2	-16

Source: Eurostat (1999).

O The EU's Position as a World Trader

The EU currently has a problem of poor global competitiveness in many manufacturing sectors, such as vehicles, textiles and electronics. The EU's trading position would be much worse were it not for Germany's success as an exporter of manufactures. Germany has consistently had a trade surplus with most other countries, including the US and Japan, whereas several (including the UK) have had substantial trade deficits in recent years. EU imports of high-tech products have been growing at almost twice the rate of EU exports of such products. Conversely, the proportion of low-tech goods in EU exports has increased. Germany accounts for a substantial proportion of high-tech goods produced by the EU. The EU's poor external trade performance has been attributed to a variety of possible causes, for example, to high labour costs, over-regulated labour markets, poor productivity, technological lag and 'unfair' competition from low-wage economies. In 1996, average labour costs in the EU were €20.2, compared with €17.4 in the US and €19.7 in Japan (Commission, 1999). The US and Japan spend less on welfare per capita, but higher proportions of their GDP on research and technological development (RTD), than the EU. The US continues to outperform the EU in labour productivity (about 20% higher than in the EU) across all sectors. This disparity is especially marked in manufacturing. There are wide variations in manufacturing productivity between member states, with Germany and Italy having the highest productivity (Commission, 2000).

The White Paper on *Growth, Competitiveness and Employment* (1993) argued that EU industry must enhance industrial competitiveness by trading up to higher value-added activity in new high-tech industries rather than by trading down, meaning drastically reducing the wages of EU workers to the levels pertaining in Asian Tiger economies. This would not only be politically impossible, but would make no economic sense as the White Paper recognised. Another possible solution is that of *protectionism* (thereby insulating the EU economy from external economic pressures). For various reasons, however (see below), this 'solution' would probably be worse than the disease. Another 'solution' involves state aid for industry, in particular through financial support for ailing firms or for firms selected for their growth potential ('Euro-champions'). But state aids are not only costly to the taxpayer, they also cushion subsidised industries from market disciplines.

● EU TRADE POLICY AND TRADE RELATIONSHIPS

○ Responsibilities

EU trade policy derives from the Common Commercial Policy (CCP) established in Article 113 of the Treaty of Rome (now 133, ECT), which transferred tariff and general trade policy from the national level. The CCP embraces a common tariff regime, common trade agreements with third countries and uniform application of trade policy instruments.

Responsibility for trade policy can be roughly divided into three aspects: proposals; negotiations and decisions. The Commission proposes and negotiates trade policy (in close consultation with the Council) but decisions are taken by the Council. Article 133 requires the Commission to submit proposals to the Council for implementing the CCP. When agreements with non-member countries need to be negotiated, the Commission makes recommendations to the Council, which then authorises the Commission to open and conduct these negotiations, in consultation with a committee of the Council (the '133 Committee') comprising national officials and permanent representatives. EU foreign ministers in the General Affairs Council (GAC) determine the negotiating mandate. Although trade ministers approve the results of negotiations it is the GAC which has the final say. The Council takes decisions on trade policy mainly by qualified majority voting (QMV), although the tendency is to seek agreement by consensus. Multilateral trade rounds fall in the category of shared competence (that is, between member states and the Community) and must be decided by unanimity by member states. Anti-dumping and countervailing duties decisions are decided by simple majority; association agreements (negotiated under Article 310, ECT) require unanimity.

Several Commission DGs are involved in trade policy, in particular the DGs for external economic relations, agriculture, development and competition. This has sometimes led to confusion concerning the EU's negotiating position. In the early 1990s, the Commission was engaged in seven sets of external trade negotiations: the Uruguay Round of the General Agreement on Tariffs and Trade (GATT); the fourth Lomé Convention (aid and trade to 77 developing countries); the fourth multifibre agreement (MFA); the reform of the Generalised System of Preferences (GSP); negotiation of the European Economic Area (EEA) agreement with EFTA; negotiation of association agreements with East European countries; and negotiations with Japan over market access. EU countries undoubtedly benefit in terms of 'clout' from this collective approach to external trade negotiations. It seems reasonable to argue that the larger the EU becomes, the more clout it will have. But the interests of member states in external trade are by no means easy to reconcile, a problem which increases with every enlargement. For example, some member states have car industries to protect, whereas others do not; there have been fierce disagreements between EU countries over trade negotiations with the US and over the extent of market access to be granted to the transition economies in Central and Eastern Europe.

The EU does not as yet have a fully common commercial policy, because member states still pursue national trade policies in some key areas. For example, export promotion is still largely a national responsibility. Member states can also apply for deviations from the CCP. The extent to which responsibility for external trade policy has been transferred from the national level is still not fully clear, despite a ruling by the European Court of Justice (ECJ) in 1975 that the CCP covers all trade instruments. From 1980 the Commission negotiated on behalf of all member states in the GATT forum, even though it was the member states, not the EU, which were the contracting parties to GATT. EU states signed the GATT agreement in Marrakesh in April 1994 separately, and in accordance with the alphabetical order of GATT. The GATT deal had to be ratified by the Council, the European Parliament (EP) and national legislatures. The Commission also negotiates on behalf of all member states in the World Trade Organisation (WTO), the successor to GATT. There is constant dialogue between the Commission and member states during negotiations, especially through the 133 Committee.

As a result of its dissatisfaction with the agreement reached by the Commission in the Uruguay Round of GATT, France disputed the Commission's right to negotiate on trade on behalf of all members. Germany was dissatisfied with the agreement on bananas and Italy and Portugal with the Commission's deal on textiles and clothing. In April 1994, the Commission asked the ECJ to examine the issue of responsibility. The Court gave its opinion the following November, ruling that the Community had exclusive powers in relation to trade in goods and in the cross-border supply of services. It confirmed that the Community had exclusive powers in the areas of trade in services and goods covered by intellectual property rights where Community legislation had achieved complete harmonisation or where there are provisions relating to the treatment of nationals of non-member countries. But in relation to other issues concerning services and intellectual property, it decided that responsibility was shared between the Community and member states. In the 1996/97 intergovernmental conference, the Commission argued that services and intellectual property should be within the exclusive competence of the EU. The Treaty of Amsterdam amended Article 133 to allow the Council to decide, by unanimity, to extend the CCP's scope to international negotiations and agreements on services and intellectual property. The Treaty of Nice will extend QMV to the negotiation and conclusion of agreements relating to trade in services, and commercial aspects of intellectual property, but (at French insistence) excludes agreements relating to trade in cultural and audio-visual services, educational services and social and human health services. A 'logic of parallelism' can be discerned in these changes, in that extending QMV to trade in services and commercial aspects of intellectual property brings these subjects into line with use of QMV on internal market directives on the same subjects. The treaty inserts a sentence into Article 133.3 stating that the Council and Commission shall be responsible for ensuring that agreements negotiated with other countries and international organisations are compatible with internal Community policies and rules. It also requires the Commission to report regularly to the 133 Committee on the progress of negotiations.

Parliamentary accountability in relation to trade policy is weak, both at EU and national levels. This is partly due to the fact that trade negotiations tend to be abstruse and protracted. But it is also due to the EP's weak formal powers in this policy area. The EP has no automatic right to be consulted on trade agreements concluded under Article 133, although it is kept informed and its views on these agreements may be taken into account. Its assent is, however, required for 'association' (Article 310) and 'trade and co-operation' (Article 300) agreements.

○ Is the EU Protectionist?

The EU's posture towards the world is described in Commission literature as being 'open to the world and in solidarity with it'. However, the EU by no means practices open trade in relation to non-EU countries, as the list of protectionist instruments and preferential agreements below shows. The EU is hardly unique in practising 'managed trade' (a euphemism for protectionism). Moreover, the use of protectionist instruments has not prevented substantial import penetration of EU markets by Japan and the newly industrialised countries (NICs). It has often been argued that collective decisionmaking in relation to the CCP has a protectionist bias, because member states tend to support each other's protectionist demands on a *quid pro quo* basis: one country will agree to support protection of the car industry, if another will agree to support protection of footwear and so on. Nevertheless, some countries are less protectionist than others. The EU 'trade liberals' have tended to be the UK, Germany, the Netherlands, Luxembourg, Denmark and Belgium. Sweden, Finland and Austria have pursued protectionist policies in services and agriculture, but less so in industrial products where they have a strong comparative advantage. Spain, Portugal, Italy and France have tended to be the most protectionist. Protectionist industrial lobbies are active both in Brussels and in member states. One measure of openness to trade is the ratio of imports to GDP: on this criterion, the EU, with a ratio of 12% in 1998, was more open than Japan (9%) but less open than the US (13.5%) in this year.

The principal protectionist argument is that free trade is not fair trade, because foreign competitors have unfair advantages, such as subsidies and lower labour costs. The consequence of opening EU markets to 'unfair' competition, according to the protectionists, is the destruction of European industries. The protectionist case is often buttressed by the 'breathing spell' argument that European industries need to be shielded from foreign competition until they are fit to compete. It has also been argued that EU policies of 'social protection' can only work if cheaper foreign goods (produced in countries where social protection is minimal) are kept out of EU markets. The problem with protectionist solutions to adverse trade balances is that domestic industries have little incentive to become more efficient or to engage in restructuring, because they are shielded from external competition. Protectionism has certainly contributed to Eurosclerosis and at least partly explains why the EU has fallen behind its main competitors in production of high-tech goods. Protectionist measures are likely to provoke retaliation, leading to a spiral of tit-for-tat actions. Moreover, enrichment of developing regions through trade could create new opportunities for EU exporters.

O Instruments

The EU has an armoury of instruments to facilitate 'managed trade', namely:
- **The Common External Tariff**. The CET imposes a system of harmonised tariffs (about 10,500 tariff lines) on exports from outside the Union. Once the tariff has been paid in one EU country, an additional tariff does not have to be paid if the good is then moved to a second EU country.
- **Quantitative restrictions**. Under the original Article 115 of the Treaty of Rome (now Article 134, ECT), a member state was able to impose quantitative restrictions on imports from outside the EU, even if these imports had already entered the EU via another member state. If goods were free to circulate, then Japanese car manufacturers could attack the French car market via Denmark (which has no car industry to protect). The launch of the SEM meant the end of national restrictions and their replacement by Union-wide measures. In 1994, all national quantitative restrictions maintained by

member states were removed and EU-wide quotas were introduced on seven product categories (the EU maintained 209 quotas on textiles and clothing from 21 countries in 1998). A member state can still request the Commission to authorise a temporary suspension of certain products from EU treatment.

• **Anti-dumping measures.** 'Dumping' is (1) the export of goods below the cost of production or (2) charging different prices in different markets (below the price charged in the exporter's home country). Union-wide anti-dumping measures were introduced in 1990. A new anti-dumping regulation came into force on 1 January 1995 and was updated in March 1996. A decision on coal and steel products came into force on 2 December 1996. Within the EU there are about 100 complaints against dumping each year. The most affected sectors have been chemicals and electronics, but steel, cars, typewriters, photocopiers, printers, textiles, cement, fork-lift trucks and flowers have all been subject to duties. Industries must provide evidence of dumping and of its effects. Anti-dumping applications should normally be made by a trade organisation or by a company acting on behalf of a substantial proportion of producers (national or Union-wide) amounting to 50% of the sector concerned or by a member government. The Commission may then investigate and may recommend to the Council that anti-dumping duties be imposed. Many investigations are terminated following price undertakings. Anti-dumping measures, which may consist of duties or undertakings concluded with exporters, normally remain in force for five years and are subject to interim and expiry reviews. In accordance with the anti-dumping regulation and decision of 1996, anti-dumping duties can be imposed following three 'tests', namely:

• *there is a finding of dumping*: the price at which the product is sold in the EU is shown to be lower than the price in the producer's home market;
• *a material injury to EU industry*: the imports have caused or threaten to cause damage to a substantial part of the industry within the EU, such as loss of market share;
• *the 'Union interest' test*: the costs for the EU of taking measures must not be disproportionate to the benefits.

The Commission investigates complaints and assesses whether or not they are justified. It can also impose provisional measures and definitive measures for coal and steel products. For other cases, it is the Council which imposes definitive anti-dumping duties. When an EU industry considers that dumping is causing it material injury, it may forward a complaint to the Commission, either directly or through its national government. The Commission then has 45 days to examine the complaint, and decide whether or not there is enough evidence to warrant a formal investigation. Investigations must be completed within 15 months and normally take less than a year. The Commission may impose provisional duties within 60 days to nine months. After the full investigation is complete, it may impose definitive duties (after further consultation with member states). A regulation imposing anti-dumping duties may be challenged in the Court of First Instance (CFI) and the WTO disputes procedure may be used to settle disputes between WTO signatories.

- **Anti-subsidy actions.** A subsidy is a financial aid from a government which confers a benefit to producers or exporters (for example, grants, tax exemptions or preferential loans). The regulation on protection against subsidised imports provides for imposition of countervailing duties on goods which have been subsidised by the governments of non-EU countries, and whose import into the Union causes or threatens injury to EU producers of the same product. Anti-subsidy measures can be taken where aid has been given for the production, export, sale or transport of goods. They have been used far more sparingly than anti-dumping measures. At the end of 1999, the EU had 156 anti-dumping and anti-subsidy measures in force, covering 63 products and 35 countries. Five of the measures related to anti-subsidy proceedings. In 1999, the Commission imposed definitive countervailing duties on imports of stainless steel wire and on polyethylene terephthalate from India and initiated proceedings against imports of various products from the Far East, South Africa and India. Procedures for investigation and imposition of penalties are similar to those governing anti-dumping actions.

- **Safeguard clauses.** That is, the imposition of restrictions on imports for a temporary period when exports are seriously injuring, or threatening to seriously injure, domestic industry. The threshold of injury is usually higher than in anti-dumping cases. In safeguard cases, a Commission decision can be referred for Council review within 90 days. It is limited to the duration of the injury or threat. The main products affected have been textiles, steel, machinery consumer electronics and vehicles. EU-wide measures were introduced in 1990, with a new safeguard regulation coming into force in January 1995. Only a member state and not the affected industry as such may ask the Commission for a safeguard measure.

- **Local content rules**, also known as 'rules of origin', relating to the extent to which a product has been locally manufactured (as distinct from being imported). For example, France initially refused to recognise the Nissan Bluebird produced in Sunderland as a British car, because it did not have a high enough 'local content'. The internationalisation of production is making it increasingly difficult to determine the origin of goods. The EU has formulated a complex set of regulations concerning rules of origin.

- **Regulatory policy** is often a byproduct of other objectives: for example, in relation to health or environmental standards.

- **Sanctions.** These may take the form of an embargo or boycott, an increase in tariffs, imposition of quotas; suspension of preferences; freezing of financial assets; suspension of cultural, technical and scientific co-operation;

or transport bans. In recent years, trade sanctions of various kinds have been applied to the former republic of Yugoslavia, Iraq, Libya, Angola, Sierra Leone, Togo, Burma, Haiti and Cuba.

• **The Trade Barriers Regulation (TBR).** This came into effect in January 1995 and provides a means for EU firms and industries to act against trade barriers affecting their access to markets outside the EU. The Commission investigates complaints and may seek redress through retaliatory measures, through the WTO dispute settlement procedures or through bilateral agreement. It is an offensive rather than a defensive instrument, in that a firm or industry can lodge a complaint with the Commission in respect of trade barriers restricting their access to third-country markets. The Council must approve an application of the TBR by QMV. A market access database (http://mkaccdb.eu.int) lists all trade barriers affecting EU exports by sector and country. It also provides information about customs, taxation and import formalities in target markets.

• **Mutual recognition agreements (MRAs).** These allow manufacturers to have their products assessed for conformity with the import regulations of other countries, by bodies within their own countries. They are easiest to negotiate between countries with broadly similar regulations and standards. The EU currently has MRAs with the US, Canada, Australia, New Zealand, Switzerland, Israel and Japan. A joint committee oversees implementation of each MRA. Protocols on European Conformity Assessment (PECAs) are being negotiated with acceding countries. These are similar to MRAs, but are firmly based on the *acquis communautaire*.

○ Trade Relationships

The bargaining power of the EU in trade negotiations with other countries varies considerably: the US has considerable negotiating strength, because it is a huge export market for the EU. The US was the EU's major protagonist in the Uruguay Round of GATT and eventually forced the EU to make concessions with regard to agricultural exports. It is currently the EU's major protagonist in the WTO 'Millennium Round' which began in Seattle in November 1999. The EU's adverse trade balance with Japan has enabled it to negotiate agreements with Tokyo without fear of retaliation. The EU's trading relationship with EFTA countries has been the closest of all and has been based on reciprocal free trade agreements (the mutual elimination of tariffs and quantitative restrictions on manufactures), although the EU holds most of the aces in trade negotiations with EFTA. The European Economic Area Treaty extended this relationship, but its significance was soon overtaken by the decision of several EFTA countries to seek entry to the Union. Developing countries are too weak and divided to exert much clout in trade negotiations with developed countries.

The EU operates an elaborate system of preferential trading arrangements, based on a *hierarchy of discrimination*, or *pyramid of privileges*, in relation to market access. Thus trade barriers are applied selectively, depending on the country (or group of countries) concerned. Many of these arrangements embrace far more than trade objectives. For example, the trade aspects of the African, Caribbean and Pacific (ACP) partnership agreements with the EU (see Chapter 18) are part of the EU's development policy for the Third World. The association agreements signed with ten CEEC candidates for EU membership are integral elements of the enlargement process. The 'trade and co-operation' and 'partnership and co-operation' agreements signed by the EU with countries of the former Soviet Union each contain references to political co-operation. 'Carrot and stick' trade weapons (withdrawal or extension of trade privileges) have been used to foster foreign policy objectives. An agreement leading to a customs union with Turkey was concluded by the EU–Turkey Association Council in March 1995. The EP made its approval (required under the assent procedure) conditional upon improvements in Turkey's human rights record. The EP finally approved the agreement by 343 votes to 149 in December 1995. In 1995, the EU held up a trade agreement with Russia because of Russia's actions in Chechnya.

The Union has concluded a bewildering variety of trade treaties: some involve specific states and others groups of states; some are largely or entirely confined to trade matters, whereas others embrace additional forms of co-operation; some are fully reciprocal, whereas in other cases the EU offers more trade concessions than it receives. In agreements with developing and 'transition' economies, the EU usually offers technical and financial assistance in addition to trade concessions. A key feature of the structure of international trade in Europe is the existence of a complex network of regional trading agreements (RTAs) between European countries, of which there are currently over 90. All but four are bilateral agreements, for example between the EU and non-member states or between two non-member states. The EU's trading relationships with other European countries are based on 'hub and spoke bilateralism' in that the EU has preferred to develop bilateral trading links with non-member countries rather than through multilateral trade agreements with groups of these countries. The big exception to this has been the EEA agreement signed with three members of EFTA.

The European multilateral RTAs are: the EU; EFTA; CEFTA (the Central European Free Trade Area – Bulgaria, the Czech Republic, Hungary, Poland, Romania, Slovakia and Slovenia); and the Baltic Free Trade Area (Estonia, Latvia and Lithuania). The EU is a customs union and the others are free trade areas: in customs unions, participating states have the same import duties on trade with other states; in free trade areas, participating states have zero duties between each other but are free to set their own duties with other states. The patchwork of multilateral and bilateral trading arrangements in Europe is extremely complex and inherently discriminatory. Sapir (2000) has suggested that possible solutions might be to forge a Pan-European Free Trade Area (PEFTA) or even a Pan-European Customs Union (PECU).

The main types of agreement offered by the EU are: trade agreements (*Article 133, ECT*); trade and co-operation agreements (*Article 300, ECT*); and association agreements (*Article 310, ECT*). However, there are variants within, and some overlaps between, these categories. In general, Article 310 agreements offer the closest and broadest relationships with the EU, involving reciprocal rights and obligations, trade privileges, co-operation and institutional links. Article 133 agreements tend to offer the least privileges.

○ Examples of EU Agreements Involving Trade

These can be roughly divided into agreements with European non-member countries and agreements with countries outside Europe.

- **Agreements with European non-member countries**
  - *The European Economic Area agreement* (see Chapter 10). This is the EU's only multilateral trade agreement with other European countries and provides for the reciprocal free movement of goods, services, capital and people between the EU and Iceland, Liechtenstein and Norway. It also embraces co-operation in many non-economic fields.
  - *Customs Union agreements*, with Cyprus, Malta, Turkey, Andorra and San Marino.
  - *'Europe' agreements*. These are association agreements involving reciprocal rights and obligations, common action and special procedures. They grant privileged, although by no means full, access to EU markets for the partner country, plus various forms of co-operation with the EU. Signatories tend to view these agreements as stages on the way to Union membership rather than ends in themselves. Indeed, these agreements now routinely contain a reference to the goal of EU membership.
  - *Co-operation agreements*. 'Trade and co-operation' and 'partnership and co-operation' agreements have been signed with individual transition countries: for example, partnership and co-operation agreements with Russia and some other members of the Commonwealth of Independent States (CIS). They offer trade privileges and various forms of assistance, but tend to be less generous than association agreements.
- **Agreements with countries outside Europe.** Unlike the agreements it has concluded within Europe (which, with the exception of the EEA, are *bilateral*), the EU has tended to favour a mixture of multilateral *and* bilateral agreements with countries outside Europe. The principal multilateral

agreements are:

- *The ACP-EU Partnership agreements.* These are agreements between the EU and 77 former colonies of member states in Africa, the Caribbean and the Pacific (the 'ACP' countries (see Chapter 18). The latest was signed in Cotonou in Benin in June 2001. Under the agreements, ACP countries have been granted almost duty-free entry on industrial exports and agricultural exports on a non-reciprocal basis. Some agricultural products have guaranteed access. The agreements have also provided technical and financial assistance. Despite these concessions, the share of ACP countries in EU imports has fallen in recent years.

- *The Euro-Mediterranean Partnership* was established by a conference of foreign ministers Barcelona in November 1995, at which the Barcelona declaration was signed. The partnership, comprising the EU and 12 Mediterranean countries (Algeria, Morocco, Tunisia, Egypt, Israel, Jordan, Lebanon, Palestine, Syria, Turkey, Cyprus and Malta) refers to the objective of a free trade zone between the EU and these countries by 2010 (although both Cyprus and Malta are European countries and will probably be full EU members by this date). This involves the progressive elimination of tariff and non-tariff barriers on manufactured products and progressive liberalisation of trade in agriculture and services. 'Euro-Mediterranean' association agreements are being negotiated with individual countries (although at the time of writing, only three had been concluded). There are also annual Euro-Mediterranean conferences.

- *Agreements with regional groupings in Latin America.* The Union has three framework co-operation agreements with Latin American countries, the main one being the Interregional Framework Co-operation Agreement with Mercosur (Argentina, Brazil, Uruguay, Paraguay, plus Bolivia and Chile as associate members), of December 1995 which includes provision for the future establishment of a free trade area. There are two other such agreements, one with the Andean Pact (1992) and the other with the Central American Isthmus, that is, Costa Rica, El Salvador, Guatemala, Honduras, Nicaragua and Panama (1993).

Multilateral links of this kind have several advantages over bilateral arrangements: firstly, it is easier for the EU to negotiate with a bloc of states than with each state individually; secondly, the groups are composed of states with many common interests with regard to their relationship with the Union. For the groupings themselves, a key advantage might be strength in numbers, in that collectively they might have more clout in negotiations with the EU than they would individually. Some individual agreements signed with developing countries under Article 133 also include financial and technical assistance. In addition, the Generalised System of Preferences involves generalised reductions of import duties, without reciprocity, for imports from developing countries (subject to quantity ceilings). Most relate to industrial goods. They are less generous than Lomé agreements and are of value only to developing countries excluded from other arrangements. In February 2001, the Council agreed an 'everything but arms' policy of duty-free access to EU markets by 2005 for the world's 48 least-developed countries (see p. 428).

○ The Implications for the EU of GATT and the WTO

Until its replacement by the World Trade Organisation in January 1995, the General Agreement on Tariffs and Trade was essentially a forum established to facilitate the liberalisation of world trade. GATT operated on the 'most favoured nation' principle of *non-discrimination*, which obliged GATT signatories to offer the same trade concessions to all members, although in practice there are many exceptions to this principle. GATT negotiations proceeded through forums known as 'rounds'. The seven rounds prior to the Uruguay Round led to tariff reductions on manufactures of the major industrialised countries from approximately 40% to about 4.7%. The Uruguay Round was generally regarded as the most ambitious and wide-ranging of all GATT rounds. It sought to deal with the issues of agriculture, textiles, services, intellectual property and other sensitive sectors. It also grappled with the issue of the *new protectionism* (non-tariff barriers to trade, or NTBs), whereas previous rounds concentrated primarily on tariff reduction. NTBs now constitute a more formidable obstacle to trade liberalisation than tariffs.

The Uruguay Round was deadlocked for years, principally because of conflicts of objectives. For example, there were bitter disputes between the US and the EU over the liberalisation of trade in agriculture and services. The US threatened trade sanctions against EU countries unless they agreed to remove trade-distorting export subsidies from agricultural exports. The dispute over agriculture threatened to destroy the facade of unity between EU countries in the GATT negotiations, because France was less willing to make concessions on agriculture than other member states. After several periods of deadlock, a deal was eventually agreed, much to the chagrin of the French farm lobby, which accused the Commission of conceding too much. However, it is widely thought that the GATT deal was beneficial to the EU as a whole. The final act of the Uruguay Round of GATT was signed in Marrakesh in April 1994. It led to the EU reducing tariffs by about 37%. The Uruguay Round consisted of about 60 agreements and separate commitments.

The WTO has a more comprehensive brief and also more powers of enforcement than were available to GATT. The WTO currently has 134 members, covering over 90% of world trade. Over three-quarters of WTO members are developing or least-developed countries. Unlike GATT, it is an organisation rather than a negotiating forum as such. It involves regular meetings of ministers and has a dispute settlement mechanism, which serves to clarify and enforce the commitments and obligations of WTO members entered into in multilateral trade negotiations. It has comprehensive sets of rules governing international trade and has concluded new agreements on information technology products, telecommunications and financial services. The EU was involved in about three-fifths of the 175 dispute settlement cases between January 1995 and July 1999. Many of these involved disputes with the US, the most prominent being over bananas and hormone-treated beef.

O   Battle in Seattle: The Millennium Round

A third WTO ministerial conference was held from 30 November to 3 December 1999 in Seattle, with the aim of launching a new round of trade talks, known as the 'Millennium Round'. The agenda at Seattle was for negotiations to further liberalise agriculture and services, from the end of 1999. The EU sought a comprehensive round, conducted as a single undertaking and concluded in three years. US negotiators in Seattle favoured a more limited round, embracing agriculture, services, tariff liberalisation, labour standards and environmental protection. As had been the case in the Uruguay Round, the EU was on the defensive over agriculture, with the US pressing for further concessions. Developing countries focused on issues of fairness in the trading system and favoured exclusion of issues such as labour standards or the environment, which could make their products less competitive in world markets. However, the Seattle talks broke down and the participants were unable to issue even a joint statement.

O   EU–US Trade Relations

The EU and the US are both global economic superpowers. Together they account for about 30% of world trade and for about 60% of industrialised countries' GDP. The US and EU economies are increasingly intermeshed. Far from being a US economic satellite, the EU is increasingly the source of investment flows into the US, accounting for the bulk of FDI and of RTD activities by foreign firms with production operations in the US. The US accounts for the bulk of FDI and RTD activities by foreign firms in the EU. In each, about 3 million jobs depend on these investments. The EU is the largest importer of US farm products. The US and the EU share the same fundamental values of democracy and free markets. However, despite these similarities and interdependencies, the EU and the US have been involved in a series of trade disputes covering a wide range of specific issues, such as bananas, hormone-treated beef, aerospace, mobile telephone standards, data privacy and cultural products. In early 2001, a new trade dispute over alleged subsidies for the European airbus project appeared to be looming.

Despite sharing fundamental values, there are significant differences in the US and EU economic systems. The US has more-flexible labour markets; stronger growth; superior industrial competitiveness, lower inflation and a larger capital market. It is also continuing to lead the EU in most industries requiring advanced technology, such as computer software, semiconductors, biotechnology, defence, telecommunications and consumer electronics. But the gap between the US and the EU is narrowing. Thus in some sectors, such as mobile telecommunications, heavy electrical equipment, transportation equipment and in some pharmaceutical subsectors, industries in the EU currently have the edge. In recent years, strong economic growth in many EU economies, and the strong performance of key industrial sectors, suggests that this gap is set to narrow further. In any case, the growth in transatlantic FDI and of strategic alliances means that the benefits of technological innovation are now reaped on both sides of the Atlantic. 'Intermeshing' does not mean that the US and EU economies will become carbon copies of each other. The EU remains committed to what it terms the 'European social model', which means a commitment to welfare, such as generous unemployment benefits, subsidised health care, and labour market regulation. But it is also committed to tight fiscal discipline and to promotion of more-flexible labour markets than have traditionally been operated in Western Europe.

It remains to be seen whether the dominant relationship between these two economic superpowers will be that of partnership or rivalry (in practice it is likely to be a dynamic mixture of both). Attempts are being made to forge closer transatlantic links. For example, there have been EU–US presidential summits since 1990. The Transatlantic Declaration of 1990 sought to define EU-US relations following the collapse of communism. The Transatlantic Business Dialogue (TABD), launched in 1994, was established to promote co-operation between the US and the EU, with particular regard to the issue of competitiveness in order to boost economic growth and job creation. In December 1995, the New Transatlantic Agenda was signed in Madrid, committing the two sides to work together to promote peace, democracy, stability, economic growth and liberalisation. It also included an action plan which commits the two sides to co-operate in 150 policy areas and which involves bi-annual consultations at various levels, including between the US president and the Council and the Commission. A Transatlantic Economic Partnership (TAEP) was launched at the EU–US summit in May 1998. The TAEP aims to deal with trade issues through discussion and co-operation. It encourages dialogues, for example between legislators; business groups; consumer groups; and groups concerned with the environment. There has even been speculation about the possible emergence of a Transatlantic Free Trade Area (TAFTA), as a replacement for or extension of NAFTA.

● CONCLUSION

The EU has the world's largest market and is also the world's largest trading entity in the global economy. It has developed an array of trade policy instruments and a complex web of trading relationships with other countries. The size and strength of the EU as a trading bloc is a fundamental attribute of the EU's status as an economic (but not yet a political or military) superpower. However, although the EU is undoubtedly a formidable player in the global trading system, it is by no means all-powerful, not least because member states have their own interests and concerns in trade matters. Member states recognise the value of arrangements which enable the Union to speak with one voice in trade matters, but they have been reluctant to give the Commission *carte blanche* in trade negotiations.

FURTHER READING

Bayne, N. (2000), 'Why did Seattle Fail? Globalisation and the Politics of Trade', *Government and Opposition*, vol. 35, no. 2, pp. 131–151.

Commission (1999), *The EU Approach to the WTO Millennium Round*, COM (99) 331.

Commission (2000), *European Competitiveness Report*, SEC (2000), 1823

Fagerberg, J., Guerrieri, P. and Verspagen, B. (eds) (2000), *The Economic Challenge for Europe*, Edward Elgar, Cheltenham and Northampton, MA.

Eurostat (1999), *The European Union. Figures for the Seattle Conference*, News Release, 18 November.

Financial Market Trends (1999), *Recent Trends in FDI*, no. 73, June, pp. 109–126.

Gavin, B. (2001), *The European Union and Globalisation*, Edward Elgar, Cheltenham and Northampton, MA.

Hanson, B.T. (1998), 'What Happened to Fortress Europe? External Trade Policy Liberalisation in the EU', *International Organisation*, vol. 52, no. 1, pp. 55–86.

Johnson, M. (1998), *European Community Trade Policy and the Article 113 Committee*, Royal Institute of International Affairs, London.

Meunier, S. and Nicolaidis, K. (1999), Who Speaks for Europe? The Delegation of Trade Authority in the EU, *Journal of Common Market Studies*, vol. 37, no.3, pp. 477–501.

OECD (1998), *The EU's Trade Policies and their Economic Effects*, Economics Working Paper 194, OECD, Paris.

Sapir, A. (2000), 'Trade Regionalism in Europe: Towards an Integrated Approach', *Journal of Common Market Studies*, vol. 38, no. 1, pp. 151–62.

Young, A.R. (2000), 'The Adaptation of European Foreign Economic Policy: From Rome to Seattle', *Journal of Common Market Studies*, vol. 38, no. 1, pp. 93–116.

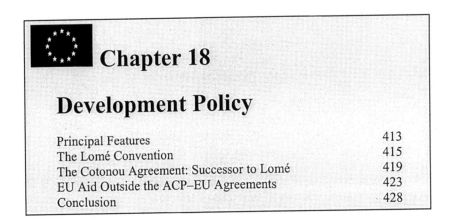

Chapter 18

Development Policy

● PRINCIPAL FEATURES

The Union and its member states together provide about 55% of total international development assistance and over two thirds of grant aid to developing countries. This is more than the combined total for the US and Japan. However, less than a fifth of EU aid is channelled through EU institutions. The Commission and the European Investment Bank (EIB) managed about 17% of international aid provided by the EU and its member states in 2000. *Bilateral* aid remains the principal form of aid provided by EU countries to developing countries. Only Greece gives more aid via the EU than bilaterally. The EU's development policy is nevertheless of long standing (dating from the Treaty of Rome) and embraces agreements with well over 100 countries. It is implemented through instruments such as trade preference, development finance and humanitarian aid.

The EU's total external aid (in commitments) has almost tripled from €3.3 billion in 1990 to €9.6 billion in 2000, of which about €7 billion was earmarked as development assistance. Given budgetary pressures, it seems unlikely that there will be a large increase in the EU aid budget. However, the EU and its member states rank favourably in relation to other developed economies in relation to aid. For example, in 1998, total development assistance amounted to 0.23% of the GNP of all OECD countries: the EU provided 0.34% of its GNP, whereas the figure for non-EU countries was 0.18%. Nevertheless, the EU falls a long way short of the UN target for development assistance of 0.7% of GNP.

EU development policy derives from a mixture of enlightened self-interest and altruism. The developing world accounts for about a third of world imports and exports and is the EU's biggest export market, taking over a third of EU exports. The EU is dependent upon developing countries for a wide

413

range of food products and raw materials, such as tropical fruits, coffee, bananas, rubber, tin, copper, manganese and uranium. It obtains about 90% of its oil from the developing world. Moreover, a substantial amount of EU development aid returns to the EU in the form of contracts for EU firms. About three million jobs in the EU depend upon exports to developing countries. EU development policy also provides the EU with levers of influence in the world arena. Until the 1980s, EU development policy was shaped in very large measure by Europe's imperial past. Four of the six original members of the Union (France, Belgium, the Netherlands, Italy) had colonial or ex-colonial links with territories outside Europe. At the time of the Union's formation, France was anxious to retain special relationships with its overseas colonies and advanced the idea of 'association' between the Union and these territories. Articles 131–6 of the Treaty of Rome (now Articles 182–88, ECT) outlined this concept of association, which embraces trade concessions and development assistance. It was formalised in the 'Yaoundé Convention' (signed in 1963 and 1969), a programme mainly directed at former French and Belgian colonies in Africa. Largely as a result of the accession of the UK, which has post-colonial ties with many developing countries, the Yaoundé Convention was superseded by the Lomé Convention in 1975, an agreement between the EU and a large group of countries in Africa, the Caribbean and the Pacific (known as 'ACP' countries).

The external assistance policies of the EU now have a global scope and are no longer focused almost exclusively, or even mainly, on ACP countries. About two-thirds of EU external aid goes to non-ACP countries in Central and Eastern Europe, the Middle East, the Mediterranean, Asia and Latin America. The EU's external assistance policies have both 'regional' and global dimensions: the regional dimension embraces wide-ranging agreements with specific groups of developing countries (see below). Since the fall of communism, the EU has been very active in provision of assistance to the Central and East European countries (CEECs). The global dimension embraces agreements affecting most developing countries. EU external assistance has also widened to embrace a much broader range of policies and programmes than formerly, such as aid for reconstruction, environmental renovation, humanitarian aid, institution-building, democracy and human rights. The Treaty on European Union (TEU) introduced a title on development co-operation (now Title XX) into the EC Treaty. This title set out the main objectives of EU policy in relation to developing countries, namely: sustainable economic and social development; smooth and gradual integration into the world economy; the campaign against poverty; and developing and consolidating democracy, the rule of law and respect for human rights and fundamental freedoms.

Article 178 of the EC Treaty requires the EU to seek to ensure that the objectives of its development policy are taken into account in the policies that it implements which are likely to affect developing countries. The Council is the key decisionmaker and the Commission the proposer, negotiator and implementer of policies. Unlike many EU spending programmes, external assistance is directly managed by the Commission. The importance of the European Parliament's (EP's) role varies in relation to which particular aspect of development policy is being considered and the legal basis under which a proposal is introduced. The EP's assent is required for certain types of external agreement with developing countries (for example, for co-operation and association agreements). However, the European Development Fund (EDF), the main source of finance for development aid to ACP countries, lies outside the Union budget and therefore the EP's influence on this source of funding is limited. Since 1973, the EP has repeatedly sought to integrate the fund into the Union budget (the goal of 'budgetisation'), but so far without success. Member states remain reluctant to lose control over the size of their EDF contributions. The EP takes a very active role in development policy, notably through its Committee on Development Co-operation, and has contributed to many initiatives. The EP has repeatedly agitated for the transfer of national development policies to the EU level. Article 180 of the EC Treaty requires the EU and member states to co-ordinate their policies on development co-operation and to consult each other on their aid programmes. In recent years, attempts have been made to develop mechanisms for co-ordination between national and EU policies, in order to achieve 'complementarity' between them. The TEU allows the Commission to take initiatives to promote such co-ordination. The Council adopted a resolution on complementarity in June 1995, but the process of co-ordination has not yet developed very far.

● THE LOMÉ CONVENTION

○ Origins and Development

This convention was once the centrepiece of the EU's development policy. It came to an end in February 2000 and a replacement regime, the Cotonou partnership agreement (see below) is being phased in. Although the Union has an elaborate network of aid policies for other developing countries, the signatories to the convention are at the top of the EU's pyramid of privilege in terms of aid and trade benefits. The convention was a formal, comprehensive and binding set of aid agreements between the EU and developing countries in Africa, the Caribbean and the Pacific (the ACP countries). The first Convention was signed in 1975 in Lomé, capital of Togo in West Africa, between the Union and 46 developing countries. There are now 77 ACP countries, 48 in Africa, 15 in the Caribbean and 14 in the

Pacific. Thirty-eight of these are in the United Nations list of the 48 least-developed countries. Of the 77 ACP countries, only Liberia and Ethiopia are not former colonies of a member state. Not all former colonies of European countries are included in the ACP category. For example, India and Pakistan, although formerly part of the British empire, are excluded. ACP countries tend to have relatively small populations, the big exception being Nigeria. Because of its relative trading strength and wealth, South Africa was offered only partial Lomé membership and has a separate agreement with the EU. In addition to the 77 ACP countries, both the Convention and the Cotonou agreement include 20 overseas countries and territories (OCTs) for which specific member states (mainly the UK and France) are still responsible. The main beneficiaries of Lomé aid have been sub-Saharan African countries.

Under Lomé a broad range of instruments, embracing financial, technical and trade co-operation were developed. The EU emphasised that Lomé was based on partnership and dialogue. To facilitate this dialogue, three joint institutions were established: an ACP–EU Council of Ministers, comprising ministerial representatives of EU and Lomé states, plus a Commission representative; an ACP–EU Committee of Ambassadors, comprising the permanent representative of each member state, a representative of the Commission and the heads of mission to the Union of each ACP state; and an ACP–EU Joint Assembly, comprising one elected representative from each Lomé country and an equal number of Members of the European Parliament (MEPs). The ACP–EU Council is the decisionmaking body; the Committee undertakes advisory, preparatory and monitoring work on behalf of the Council; the Assembly is a consultative body and meets twice yearly, alternately in an EU and an ACP country.

Between 1986 and 1998, the EU committed nearly €30 billion of aid to ACP countries, 77% of which (€22.8 billion) was provided under Lomé. The other 23% of EU aid for ACP countries comprised 16% from the EU budget (mainly food and humanitarian aid) and 7% in the form of concessional loans from the EIB. This amounted to two-fifths of all aid committed by the EU in this period. Lomé 1 and 2 had a bias towards promotion of industrial development, whereas Lomé 3 focused more on promoting self-sufficiency and food security. Lomé 4 came into force in September 1991. It lasted for ten years, double the period of previous conventions, divided into two five-year cycles. The main emphases of Lomé 4 were on long-term development, in particular upon private investment, promotion of small businesses and environmental protection, plus promotion of democracy, good governance and human rights. It also placed greater emphasis upon monitoring. A mid-term review of Lomé 4 in 1994 and 1995 led to several amendments: for example, respect for human rights, democracy and the rule of law became essential and explicit elements of the Lomé regime. A performance-related element to Lomé funding was also introduced.

Tables 18.1 and 18.2 outline the structure of EU aid to the ACP countries.

Table 18.1 Regional Distribution of EU Aid to the ACP (€ million)

	Commitments		Disbursements	
	1998	1986–98	1998	1986–98
Sub-Saharan Africa	2,480	23,204	1,476	17,762
Caribbean	150	2,144	222	1,583
Pacific	56	974	60	828
Regional	–6	1,732	9	1,164
Unallocable	173	1,645	185	2,988
Total	**2,853**	**29,698**	**1,952**	**24,326**

Table 18.2 Sectoral Distribution of EU Aid to the ACP
Commitments in € Million and % of Total Aid

Commitments	1998		1986–98	
	€ mn	%	€ mn	%
Programme aid	872	30.6	7,543	25.4
Structural adjustment	720	25.2	3,484	11.7
STABEX (see p. 418 below)	152	5.3	3,444	11.6
SYSMIN (see p. 419 below)	1	0	616	2.1
Food aid (development)	138	4.8	2,643	8.9
Humanitarian aid	179	6.3	2,156	7.3
Aid to NGOs	65	2.3	487	1.6
Natural resources	137	4.8	1,835	6.2
Agriculture	123	4.3	1,521	5.1
Forestry	4	0.1	184	0.6
Fisheries	9	0.3	129	0.4
Other productive services	95	3.3	2,404	8.1
Industry, mining, construction	22	0.8	1,987	6.7
Trade	42	1.5	251	0.8
Tourism	30	1.1	163	0.5
Investment promotion	–	0	3	0.0
Economic infrastructure & services	847	29.7	5,597	18.8
Transport & communications	622	21.8	3,605	12.1
Energy	98	3.4	1,650	5.6
Banking, finance & bus. services	127	4.5	342	1.2
Social infrastructure & services	321	11.2	2,216	7.5
Education	69	2.4	556	1.9
Health & population	92	3.2	636	2.1
Water supply	141	4.9	789	2.7
Other	19	0.7	235	0.8
Governance & civil society	86	3.0	509	1.7
Multisector/crosscutting	62	2.2	2,653	8.9
Unallocable by sector	51	1.8	1,657	5.6
Total	**2,853**	**100.0**	**29,698**	**100.0**

Source for Tables 18.1 and 18.2: Commission (1999).

○ The European Development Fund

The European Development Fund, which was central to the operation of Lomé and which is also accorded a key role in Lomé's successor, was established in 1958, as a result of provisions in the Treaty of Rome. It is the principal vehicle for the provision of EU assistance to the ACP countries. The fund is outside the EU budget and is financed directly by member states. Separate EDFs were established for each Lomé Convention (for example, the 7th and 8th for Lomé 4). The 8th EDF amounted to €13.1 billion. The 9th EDF (for 2000–05) is endowed with €13.5 billion, plus €1.7 billion in EIB loans. Funds for Lomé development projects were channelled through the EDF mainly in the form of grants (which, unlike loans, do not have to be paid back). Ninety per cent of the funds allocated to Lomé 4 were in the form of EDF grants (compared with about 70% for Lomé 3) and the rest in the form of loans and risk capital from the EIB. EDF resources comprise both *programmable aid*, based on an indicative programme agreed with each ACP country or OCT, and *non-programmable aid*, which is not earmarked for any specific state. Five specific funds have operated through the EDF: STABEX, SYSMIN, emergency aid for disaster relief, refugee aid and structural adjustment aid. There has been considerable wrangling between member states over their EDF contributions. The Lomé 4 mid-term review exposed serious differences between EU states on future contributions, with France, supported by the Commission, seeking an increase of 30% in the fund's size and several members (the UK and Germany in particular) opposing increases. Contributions by member states to the 8th EDF ranged from 23.26% for Germany to 0.29% for Luxembourg (the UK contributed 12.69%).

○ The Main Policies and Instruments of Lomé: note: some of these are being phased out as a result of the new ACP–EU agreement (see below).

• **Trade co-operation.** About 92% of ACP exports have duty- and quota-free access to EU markets. Agricultural products account for an additional 7% of ACP exports and these are subject to a tariff quota with zero duty. Less than 1% of ACP agricultural exports are covered by the Common Agricultural Policy (CAP) (arguably CAP protectionism deters ACP countries from producing CAP products). More than 95% of EU imports from ACP countries are primary products. These trade concessions are not reciprocal, but ACP countries must agree to grant member states trade provisions no less favourable than the World Trade Organisation (WTO) regime. A derogation for the Lomé trade regime was obtained from GATT in 1994.

• **STABEX** (stabilisation of export earnings). The commodities exported by many ACP countries are subject to dramatic price fluctuations in world markets. STABEX provides a cushion for eligible ACP states when their export earnings are reduced due to adverse market conditions, by guaranteeing them a minimum revenue from their exports of basic commodities to the EU. It offers grants for the least-developed countries and interest-free loans for the others. Under Lomé 3, STABEX funds totalled ECU 925 million. Coffee accounted for about one-third of STABEX funds. Prior to Lomé 4, products covered must have accounted for at least 6% of the country's average earnings from the EU for the last four years (1.5% for the least-developed countries). Under Lomé 4, dependency thresholds were lowered to cover products constituting 5% of an ACP country's total export earnings (1% for the least-developed, landlocked or island countries). It covers about 50 products. STABEX has not always been adequate to cover drops in earnings, even though Lomé 4 increased its size by 62%. Under the post-Lomé agreement, STABEX is being phased out.

• **SYSMIN** is similar to STABEX, but related to countries dependent upon a specific mineral (accounting for at least 15% of export earnings over four years). Loans have been given to countries suffering a drop in export earnings or production capacity. The main products covered are copper, cobalt, phosphates, manganese, tin, bauxite, alumina, iron ore, uranium and (in certain circumstances) gold. The bulk of SYSMIN aid has been co-financed with other agencies (principally the EIB, the World Bank and the African Development Bank). Like STABEX, SYSMIN is being phased out.

• **The sugar protocol** requires the EU to undertake to purchase specific quantities of cane sugar from ACP states at guaranteed prices, above world prices. The protocol covers 1.3 million tonnes of ACP sugar, representing about two-thirds of ACP sugar exports. ACP signatories to the sugar protocol are each given a quota. It is continued in the post-Lomé agreement. The EU's highly protectionist sugar regime has so far escaped radical reform and is the target of considerable criticism (a Court of Auditors special report in 2000 (no. 20/00) estimated that it cost EU consumers over €6 billion a year).

• **Technical and financial co-operation,** to assist industrialisation and rural development. It is financed through the EDF and the EIB. The structural adjustment facility was the main innovation of Lomé 4. It provides financial support to assist countries undergoing economic reforms.

● THE COTONOU AGREEMENT: SUCCESSOR TO LOMÉ

Following long and tortuous negotiations, a new partnership agreement between ACP countries and the EU was signed in Cotonou in Benin in June 2000. The agreement replaces the Lomé regime which had existed for a quarter of a century. Table 18.3 below outlines the arguments for and against Lomé. During the negotiations, there was no intention simply to scrap the ACP–EU partnership, but rather to develop and adapt it.

Table 18.3 The Case For and Against Lomé

For
• it committed the EU to a long-term and comprehensive programme of development assistance;
• it established formal mechanisms for dialogue on development issues between the EU and ACP countries;
• it provided a vehicle for dialogue and collaboration between EU member states on development issues;
• the ACP countries benefited from negotiating as a bloc;
• it had fewer strings attached than bilateral aid programmes;
• no ACP country left the Lomé scheme.
Against
• it was an agreement among unequals; despite the EU's rhetoric about partnership, ACP states have weak negotiating power;
• the Commission lacked the analytical capacity to prepare strategic development programmes for over 70 countries;
• the distinction between ACP and other developing countries is arbitrary;
• it perpetuated a 'dependency culture';
• the ACP share of EU trade has fallen under Lomé;
• Lomé funds failed to keep pace with ACP population growth;
• for many ACP countries, debt rescheduling could make a bigger contribution to their development needs than Lomé;
• rates of disbursement of aid under Lomé have been slow;
• projects tended to be insufficiently adapted to local conditions;
• Lomé projects were inadequately monitored and evaluated;
• the development records of many ACP states have been poor.

The main factors which led to the replacement of Lomé were:

- *Lomé's inherent deficiencies*. It was generally acknowledged by both the EU and the ACP countries that Lomé had serious deficiencies. It seemed to be increasingly anachronistic and had certainly not achieved the development goals of its architects. For example, although the ACP countries are granted preferential access to EU markets, they have not done as well in trade terms as many non-ACP countries in Asia and Latin America. Some ACP countries have little in the way of exports and therefore trade concessions are largely irrelevant. Sixty per cent of ACP exports are confined to only ten products. The ACP share of the EU market declined from 6.7% in 1976 to 2.8% in 1999, despite the preferential access granted to ACP exports. ACP is a large and diverse group and Lomé was not flexible enough to cope with this diversity. Although the EDF has kept up with inflation, it has not expanded to match the growth in population in many ACP countries. Lomé nevertheless resulted in considerable financial aid for these countries.

- *Changes in the global trading system.* The value of preferential trade arrangements under Lomé has declined, due to trade liberalisation. There was increasing incompatibility between WTO rules and Lomé trade preferences. For example, the banana dispute (see below) has its origins in the trade preference provision under Lomé.
- *From a post-imperial to a global development policy.* EU aid policy had become more 'global' in that it embraces many countries outside the ACP. It has evolved from being an aspect of post-colonialism to a wider and more diverse system. This has been due to a combination of factors, including changes in the scope of the international EU's role; the end of the cold war; and EU enlargement: the accession of Greece, Spain and Portugal increased pressure to expand aid to the Mediterranean region; none of the 1995 entrants had colonies outside Europe and therefore had no reason to support the 'ACP bias' in EU development policy.

In the negotiations for a replacement for Lomé, ACP countries sought to maintain as much of the current preferential arrangements as possible, viewing the WTO as biased against smaller and weaker states. The EU sought to link the new agreement to broader political and economic objectives, such as good government, human rights and sound and sustainable economic policies. It also favoured the encouragement of free trade agreements between developing countries in specific regions and greater participation of non-state actors within ACP countries. The Cotonou agreement has been concluded for 20 years, with a revision and a financial protocol every five years, although some aspects may be reviewed annually. The deal involves a package of trade and aid measures, including preferential access to EU markets; an increase in the size of the EDF; and efforts to work towards regional free trade agreements. The ACP countries are expected to take measures to deal with issues concerning the EU, such as illegal economic migration. The ratification process for the new deal is expected to take up to 18 months. The present trade regime will be maintained between 2000 and 2008. STABEX and SYSMIN will be relinquished and new arrangements will be introduced to deal with the financial impact of drops in export earnings. Starting in 2000, essentially all imports from less-developed countries will be liberalised on the basis of the Generalised System of Preferences (GSP) (see Chapter 17 and also below) although the protocols on sugar, beef and veal will be maintained and reviewed in negotiations for new trading arrangements. The aim is to lead to a fully WTO-compatible regime. The ACP states and the EU have asked the WTO for a waiver allowing them to keep the present preferential arrangements during the preparatory period.

The new ACP–EU partnership is based on five interdependent pillars, namely: *a political dimension* (political dialogue, peace-building, respect for human rights and good governance); *participation* (greater involvement of non-state actors, such as economic and social groups, as well as governments); *a poverty reduction strategy*; *a new framework for economic and trade co-operation* (in particular to promote the gradual integration of ACP countries into the world economy); and *reform of financial co-operation*. This involves a change to EDF instruments, which were judged to be too complex and rigid. There will be two new instruments, one for providing grants and the other risk capital and loans to the private sector.

○ The EU's Banana Import Regime

The issue of the EU's banana import regime provides useful insights into the EU's external development and trade policies. It shows, for example: (1) the potential conflict between these two policies; (2) the power of the US as an adversary in trade disputes; (3) the tensions between member states on trade policy issues; (4) the role of WTO dispute mechanisms; and (5) the difficulties in resolving such disputes in ways satisfactory to all parties.

The Union's banana regime offers preferential access to EU markets for exports of bananas from former colonies of member states in ACP countries. Initially, the regime included three sets of tariff arrangements: duty-free imports for ACP countries under the Lomé Convention's banana protocol for exports to France, the UK and Italy; duty-free imports to Germany from any source; and duties on exports to other EU countries. In 1993, a new system was introduced, whereby ACP bananas entered the EU duty free, but Latin American bananas were subject to a two-tier tariff and quota arrangement designed to discourage Latin American producers from increasing their market share. This led several Latin American producers to file a complaint with the GATT, which ruled in their favour. The EU responded by raising quotas for four Latin American producers, thereby upsetting other Latin American producers and also US banana companies. The banana regime is inherently discriminatory, because ACP banana producers are given preference over banana producers in Latin America. Latin American bananas (known as 'dollar bananas') have tended to be cheaper than those from ACP countries. But if ACP producers competed on equal terms with the more efficient Latin American producers, their markets would be in danger of collapsing. As ACP banana producing countries tend to be very poor, and because they are highly dependent on banana exports, abolition of favourable treatment in EU markets could prove disastrous to their economies. About half the bananas entering the EU now come from ACP countries and the other half mainly from Latin America. Spain produces bananas, as do to a lesser extent Portugal and Greece. Historical links with ACP countries and also producer interests have tended to determine member states' views on reform of the banana regime. For example, Germany, with no colonial links to ACP banana producers, favours duty-free access from any source. France and the UK have been reluctant to abandon the current regime because of the impact of this upon producers in their former colonies in Africa and the Caribbean. Several large US multinational companies such as Dole and Chiquita are involved in the production, packaging and sale of South American bananas, which is why the US has become so heavily involved in the dispute (in 1997 Dole unsuccessfully sued the Commission for damages in the ECJ, claiming loss of market share. In February 2001, Chiquita launched a similar action).

In 1997, the WTO dispute settlement body ruled that the EU's banana regime discriminated unfairly against non-ACP producers. In response, in January 1999 the EU introduced arrangements which altered the tariff quota and tariff rates for non-ACP producers. However, in April 1999, the WTO ruled that the new regime was still discriminatory and did not comply with WTO rules. The WTO also authorised the US to take retaliatory action in the form of 100% increases in customs duties on imports of specific European products, to the value of $191 million. In November 1999, the Commission drew up a new two-stage plan for the reform of the banana regime. It sought to retain existing import quotas, before moving to a single tariff within six years, providing that the US and the four Latin American countries which challenged the regime agreed not to contest the new rules in the WTO. During the six-year phase, there would be three quotas, with preferential access for ACP countries, followed by the introduction of a flat-rate tariff. There would be accompanying support measures to improve the efficiency of ACP producers. However, this plan proved to be contentious both among member states and also between ACP banana producers. Following further negotiations and disagreements, a deal to resolve the dispute over bananas was finally agreed between the US government and the Commission in April 2001. The deal provides for a transition, to a tariff-only banana regime, commencing in July 2001 becoming fully operational by July 2006. During the transition, import licenses will be distributed to banana producers on the basis of past trade. The US government has agreed to support the EU's request for WTO authorization for the new regime. The result of these changes will be a dilution of Community preference for ACP producers.

● EU AID OUTSIDE THE ACP–EU AGREEMENTS

Outside the ACP–EU framework, the EU has an extensive range of trade and aid agreements with developing countries and with the transition economies of Central and Eastern Europe. Among developing countries, some of the largest recipients of EU aid (for example, Egypt, Bangladesh and Turkey) are not ACP countries. Co-operation agreements between the EU and non-ACP developing countries outside Lomé tend to be less generous than those offered to the ACP. Of non-ACP developing countries, the Mediterranean countries in North Africa and the Middle East have been the most favoured. These embrace the 'Mahgreb' group (Algeria, Morocco, Tunisia, Libya and Mauritania) and the 'Mashreq' group (Egypt, Jordan, Lebanon and Syria). Agreements with these countries offer restricted, but non-reciprocal access to EU markets, plus financial and technical assistance. The Euro-Mediterranean partnership based on the 1995 Barcelona Declaration signed by the EU and 12 Mediterranean countries (see Chapter 17) offers the latter non-reciprocal duty-free access to the EU for industrial products and limited preferential access for some agricultural products. Association agreements are also being negotiated with several of these countries. The results of the Barcelona process however have so far been meagre. The EU has also concluded bilateral agreements with many Latin American countries and multilateral agreements with 'Mercosur', the Andean Pact and the Central American isthmus. A wide range of programmes are now funded through the EU budget, for example aid for the Mediterranean, Asia, Latin America and the transition economies (see Chapter 20). As Table 18.4 shows, the proportion (although not the absolute amount) of EU aid given to ACP countries has fallen whereas the proportions given to Mediterranean and transition countries (including CEECs) has risen markedly. In 2000, aid from the EU budget (about €5.3 billion) exceeded aid from the EDF (€4.3 billion).

Table 18.4 Regional Distribution of EU Aid: 1988–1998

	1988 (€ mn)	%	1998 (€ mn)	%	1998 as % of total
ACP (including South Africa)	2,899	69.4	2,983	43.6	34.7
Asia	226	5.4	617	9.0	7.2
Latin America	159	3.8	485	7.1	5.6
Mediterranean	309	7.4	1,368	20.0	15.9
CEECs	1	0.0	614	9.0	7.1
NIS	–	0.0	243	3.6	2.8
Not Attributable	582	13.9	534	7.8	6.2
Total ODA	**4,176**	**100**	**6,843**	**100.0**	79.4
Other Aid to Transition countries	20		1,771		20.6
Grand Total	**4,196**		**8,614**		100

Note: CEECs: Central and East European Countries; NIS: most countries of the former Soviet Union); ODA: Official Development Assistance. *Source*: Commission, 1999.

The main forms of aid applicable to developing countries outside Lomé (some of which also apply to ACP countries) are:
• **The Generalised System of Preferences (GSP)** allows developing countries outside Lomé to export most of their industrial and other processed products to the Union, free of customs duties. However, the quantity of goods is subject to quotas and some products are largely excluded. GSP is also

administratively very complex. The effects of GSP have in fact been very limited because exports from many Third World states are not competitive anyway. The main beneficiaries of GSP have been China, Brazil and the Asian Tigers rather than the poorest developing countries. The significance of GSP has been further reduced by the lowering of customs duties as a result of GATT agreements. In March 1998, the Council extended GSP coverage to all least-developed countries not party to the 4th Lomé Convention.

- **Development projects** in more than 100 countries, embracing for example aid for public health, poverty alleviation, transport and environmental infrastructure, Aids prevention and food distribution networks.
- **The EC Investment Partners (ECIP)** scheme was set up in 1988 to assist EU private businesses to invest in developing countries in Asia, Latin America and the Mediterranean through joint ventures and other means. ECIP is currently being wound up (Commission, 2000a).
- **Humanitarian Aid.** Humanitarian aid constitutes about one-fifth of the EU's total assistance to poorer countries, in the form of food and finance. It covers food aid and emergency aid, deriving from disasters such as drought, famine and human conflict. It is financed through both the EDF and the Union budget. The EU also channels humanitarian aid through UN agencies, such as UNRWA (the United Nations Relief and Works Agency) and UNHCR (the United Nations High Commission for Refugees) and through international non-governmental organisations (INGOs). About 60% of EU food aid is given to non-ACP countries and is mainly supplied through international agencies and INGOs. Budget allocations for food aid amounted to almost €530 million in 1998. ECHO, the European Community Humanitarian Office, was set up in April 1992 to provide a single service to manage all emergency humanitarian aid. There has been a tenfold increase in the amount of humanitarian aid disbursed through the EU since 1985.
- **The Role of the EIB.** Although the EIB's primary responsibility is to provide development finance for projects within the EU, it also provides loans to developing countries and to the CEECs, as shown in Table 18.5.

Table 18.5 EIB Financing Outside the EU in 2000 (€ million)

Area	Total	Own Resources	Risk Capital*
CEEC Applicants	2,948	2,948	
Western Balkans	154	154	
ACP/OCT	401	186	215
South Africa	140	140	
Euro-Mediterranean Partnership countries (excluding Cyprus and Malta)	1,214	1,193	21
Asia and Latin America	532	532	
TOTAL	5,389	5,153	236

Note: * From EU or member states' budgetary sources. *Source*: EIB.

○ **Pressures for Change and Reform**

Pressures for change in EU development policy are emanating from both inside and outside the EU. *Internal pressures* include the fallout from various negative reports by the Court of Auditors on the management of the EU's external assistance programmes and also a growing recognition that the EU needs to improve co-ordination of its external actions in order to enhance its impact as an international actor. *External pressures* include WTO trade liberalisation processes (which seek to prohibit discriminatory trade arrangements) and demands to assist transition processes in CEECs. Since the end of the cold war, there has been a tendency for aid donors (for example, the World Bank, the International Monetary Fund (IMF), the EU and developed states) to add conditions to aid, such as promotion of good governance, human rights and prudent economic management. Although fear of a 'big switch' in EU aid in absolute terms from developing countries to CEECs has not proved well-founded, the end of communism increased demands on EU aid resources. The current enlargement process has led to a big increase in aid to CEECs, which now account for a large proportion of EIB loans to non-EU states. The EU's development policy is easy to criticise. Its main flaws, identified in various official reports, have been:

- *it is too complex and fragmented.* The rapid growth in the geographical and functional scope of the EU's external aid activities has not been matched by the pace of administrative change in the Commission, leading to serious flaws in the management and implementation of EU aid policy. There have been different policies for different regions and over 70 different financial instruments and programmes;
- *inadequate staffing,* both in Brussels and on the ground. For example, in 2000, for every €10 million of aid, there were 2.9 Commission staff compared with 4.3 in the World Bank and between four and nine in member states. This has been due primarily to failure to match staffing levels to aid volumes and to the increasing complexity of the EU's aid portfolio, leading to reliance on subcontracting through 'Technical Assistance Offices', although these are being phased out (see below);
- *sluggish and unresponsive delivery.* There have been long delays in delivering aid projects. including a backlog of unfinished projects. Between 1995 and 2000, the average delay in the disbursement of committed funds increased from three to 4.5 years (much longer for some programmes). By 2000 the EU had about €20 billion in unpaid commitments and a backlog of 1200 uncompleted projects;
- *inadequate monitoring and financial control of projects,* a common criticism of official reports on the EU's development policy. The control authorities of the EP, the member states and the Court of Auditors are many and varied (embracing management committees, Council groups, EP

committees) and this leads to duplication of effort;

- *lack of coherence* between development policies and other EU policies, such as trade and the environment. It has also been argued that the EU's potential to influence events through aid is not being fully exploited;
- *poor targeting*. For example, aid has been spread too thinly on too many projects. In 1999, the Commission was responsible for managing 14,500 committed and 30,000 contracted projects. A Court of Auditors report in 2000 (no. 18/00) severely criticised the EU's food programme for Russia for being based on dubious information about the Russian food situation;
- *poor co-ordination* between member states' bilateral development programmes and EU programmes and also between EU departments and agencies responsible for delivering aid. Development policy now affects several portfolios, including trade, external relations and the environment.

○ Current Reform Plans and Changes in EU Development Policy

In April 2000, the Commission unveiled proposals for an overhaul of development policy in an attempt to make it more coherent and effective (Commission, 2000b). The proposals focussed on the twin aims of alleviating poverty and integrating developing countries into the global economy. It argued that development policy should centre on the aim of poverty reduction and that aid should be targeted on priority areas such as trade, health, education, transport, food security, rural development and good governance. It argued that a better division of labour was needed with member states' bilateral development programmes and that economic, trade and political aspects of development co-operation should be better integrated. This initiative was welcomed by the Council in May 2000. Between May and November 2000, various other reform ideas were advanced by the Council, the Commission, the EP and the Economic and Social Committee (Commission, 2000a). In May, the Commission announced a major reform of the management of the EU's external aid (2000c). The reform embraced: radical changes to programming, to better reflect development objectives; the creation of a single body to be responsible for project implementation; the delegation of more responsibility to missions abroad; improvements in financial controls; and the elimination of old or dormant commitments.

Current changes in EU development policy can be categorised into four types: firstly, the radical overhaul of the management of external aid, with an emphasis on improved co-ordination and effective implementation. A 'EuropeAid Co-operation Office' was established in January 2001, with a staffing level of 1200, to manage about 80% of the EU's external assistance programmes, thereby bringing external assistance projects under a single structure. New administrative responsibilities are being delegated to the 128 Commission offices around the world and the technical assistance offices are being dismantled; secondly, shifts in the orientation of aid programmes. There are signs that EU aid programmes are following similar patterns to those of other international donors, such as the World Bank and the IMF, in that there is a stronger emphasis than hitherto on political dialogue, good governance, performance measurement and sustainable development; thirdly, efforts to enhance the compatibility of the EU's development policies with WTO rules; fourthly, a new market-opening strategy aimed at the poorest countries: in September 2000, the Commission proposed 'everything but arms' duty-free access to EU markets for the 48 least-developed countries by 2005 (the existing regime excludes about 10% of the EU's tariff lines and 1% of total trade flows). Bananas, sugar and rice would be included in three stages over three years. 'Everything but arms' was agreed by the Council (after considerable argument) in February 2001. Critics of the scheme argue that it will 'rob Peter to pay Paul', in that the trade benefits to the 48 may be at the expense of other LDCs who are not much better off. Moreover, the economies of many of the 48 may be too weak to take advantage of the deal.

● CONCLUSION

The scope and diversity of EU development policy have expanded markedly, particularly in the last decade. It remains to be seen whether current plans for reforming the EU's rather ramshackle system of external aid will be sufficient to deal with the problems of complexity, fragmentation, incoherence and poor implementation identified above. It seems unlikely that national aid programmes will be superseded by EU programmes in the foreseeable future. Nevertheless, the need for greater co-ordination between the aid policies of the EU and of member states is increasingly recognised. Because development policy is an aspect of the EU's external relations, the emergence of a stronger common foreign and security policy would also enhance the prospects for the convergence of EU and national aid policies.

FURTHER READING

Commission (1999), *Financial Information on the European Development Funds*, COM (99) 323.
Commission (2000a), *General Report on the Activities of the EU 2000.*
Commission (2000b), *The EC's Development Policy*, COM (2000) 212.
Commission (2000c), *The Reform of the Management of External Assistance,* SEC 16052000.
Cox, A. and Koning, A. (1997), *Understanding EC Aid*, Overseas Development Institute, London.

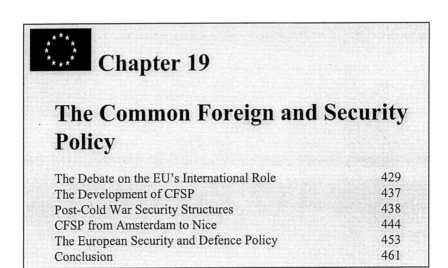

Chapter 19

The Common Foreign and Security Policy

● THE DEBATE ON THE EU'S INTERNATIONAL ROLE

○ From Civil Power to Superpower?

In some respects, the EU is already a formidable international actor, although in ways which do not qualify it for superpower status. Characteristics of 'actorness' include an identity, a capacity to take decisions and to put them into effect, plus recognition by other actors. The EU has an identity and is recognised as an actor on the world stage. It has a foreign policy in all but name in the realm of economic affairs. It has considerable economic weight in the world arena, being the world's largest trading power and the largest provider of aid. It has an extensive network of relationships with other international actors. About 150 states have diplomatic missions accredited to the EU and the Commission also operates about 120 external delegations. The EU has observer status at the United Nations and in some UN institutions, such as the Economic Commission for Europe, the Conference on Trade and Development (UNCTAD) and the Educational, Scientific and Cultural Organisation (UNESCO). In addition to its central role in external trade negotiations, the Commission is a key actor in the EU's relations with developing countries and with transition economies in Central and Eastern Europe. Although most of these relationships are linked to economic matters, they also tend to have a strong political dimension: political conditions tend to be attached to EU trade and aid relationships.

However, despite this formidable portfolio of external relationships and instruments, the EU is still widely regarded as essentially a *civil power*, with an international role primarily concerned with external economic relations (that is, as an economic giant and political pygmy). Its weight in international affairs derives largely from the economic carrots and sticks at its disposal. Moreover, the Commission's external delegations have not replaced the bilateral diplomatic missions between member states and other countries. In the fields of foreign policy and defence, the EU has frequently been accused of not punching its weight and of an inability to translate bold words into effective deeds. Recent events in Bosnia, Kosovo and the Middle East provide ample evidence of the tendency of the EU to be sidelined in major international crises, even when they occur on its own doorstep. In the military conflicts in Bosnia and Kosovo, EU countries found themselves reliant on the US for satellite intelligence, logistics and military hardware. The EU is still widely regarded as a lightweight in international conflicts, incapable, according to the US Senate's Foreign Relations Committee head Jesse Helms, of fighting its way out of a wet paper bag.

The continuing ability of member states to behave independently on the world stage, combined with the extent of disagreements on a common foreign and security policy (CFSP) (on institutional and procedural issues as well as on substantive questions of policy) has been repeatedly demonstrated in recent years. Each state within the EU retains primary responsibility for the conduct of foreign affairs and for its own defence. Moreover, each state has its own distinctive network of external relations, based on history, physical geography and perceived national interests. Spending on defence by EU countries would need to be considerably increased before the combined military capacity of EU15 was on a par with that of the US. Average spending on defence by EU members is below 2% of GDP and in total amounts to around 60% of the US figure of 3.1%, but the EU has far less to show for it in terms of military capability. Eight member states (Austria, Belgium, Denmark, Finland, Germany, Luxembourg, Ireland and Spain) currently spend 1.6% or less of their GDP on defence. In 1993, Hill (1993) argued that a dangerous gap had opened up between EU capabilities and expectations in relation to CFSP, leading to unrealistic external policies.

Proponents of a stronger CFSP tend to lay blame for slow progress upon the governments of member states, who are accused of resorting to vacuous statements of intent and elaborate procedural formulae as an alternative to the development of a CFSP with real substance. According to this view, it is a failure of collective will rather than a lack of collective capacity which explains the slow development of CFSP. However, at least in the short to medium terms, *failure of will* can be no less immovable as an obstacle to change than a *deficiency in capacity*. Current CFSP 'deficits' are summarised in Table 19.1 below.

Table 19.1 Current CFSP 'Deficits'

- **a deficit of collective will**, i.e., the problem of commitment to the development of CFSP among EU members;
- **an institutional deficit**, i.e., the problem of cumbersome and complex decisionmaking procedures;
- **a capability deficit**, i.e., the problems of inadequate means to achieve CFSP objectives;
- **an identity deficit**, meaning that the EU lacks a clear face and a coherent policy with regard to CFSP;
- **a reputation deficit**, in that the Union in that in foreign policy terms, the EU is still widely regarded as a lightweight.

Both the Treaty on European Union (TEU) and the Treaty of Amsterdam (ToA) sought to address the issue of these deficits, although with limited results due to disagreements between member states on CFSP reform. However, in 1999, with the war in Kosovo fresh in people's minds, the Cologne and Helsinki European Councils set out operational measures for a European Security and Defence Policy (ESDP) and for an EU rapid reaction force (RRF) (see below). The ESDP has not replaced the defence policies of member states: nor is the RRF a 'European army'. Nevertheless, the EU is developing a military capability of a kind. These developments suggest that the pace of CFSP reform may be quickening. However, at present it seems more realistic to expect a partial and incremental narrowing of these deficits rather than their sudden and complete elimination.

A combination of external and internal developments has increased the urgency with which member states have needed to address the issue of the EU's external role. The end of the cold war confronted the Union with major foreign and security policy challenges: by unfreezing cold war institutional structures, it transformed Europe's geopolitical landscape and placed the EU's relations with Eastern Europe on an entirely new footing; it created new conflicts in Europe, deriving from ethnic and border disputes in and between former communist states; it provided the EU with opportunities to play a major role in reshaping the European continent; it raised fundamental questions concerning the EU's status in a post-cold war international order; it raised major issues concerning the future pattern of the EU's relations with the United States; it led to the emergence of new security threats of a qualitatively different kind from the well-defined and conventional military threats of the cold-war era; it also made the pattern of the EU's external relations more complex and uncertain. Pursuit of deeper integration also has implications for the EU's external policy: for example, removal of restrictions on the movement of EU citizens across the borders of member states requires agreement on common approaches to questions of migration.

○ CFSP and the Nature of the EU

The issue of CFSP raises fundamental questions about the nature of the Union. Is the EU likely to remain essentially a *civil power*, with an external role largely confined to the economic sphere, that is, a lop-sided, one-dimensional superpower? Is the ultimate aim of CFSP to transform the EU into a 'superpower', capable of intervening in global crises and of competing with the US for global leadership? Do member states have the desire or capacity to transform the EU into a major political and military force in the international arena? Although in some EU circles there is considerable enthusiasm for a major strengthening and extension of the EU's external role, the arguments over CFSP issues which preceded the signing of the TEU and the ToA clearly demonstrated that this aspiration is not shared by the governments of all member states. The civil power image of the EU is implicitly rejected in the TEU (Article 17), which defines CFSP to include all questions relating to the security of the Union, including the progressive framing of a common defence policy, which might lead to a common defence, should the European Council so decide. But although in terms of its economic and military *potential*, the Union may have the capability to develop into a major international power in its own right, much still needs to be done to transform aspiration into reality.

The power and clarity of the Union's voice in international affairs has been crucially affected by the absence of consensus among the governments of member states as to the practical meaning of CFSP. CFSP remains a hotly contested field of ideas, ranging from the maximalist vision of European federalists to the minimalist position favoured by intergovernmentalists. The maximalist conception implies a unified, supranational foreign policy, with the EU eventually having its own foreign ministry and its own defence forces under a single command. The minimalist conception, based on a state-centric model of intra-Union relations, would limit CFSP to co-operation between the governments of member states on matters of mutual interest. If it became a reality, maximalist CFSP would mean transformation of the EU into a fully developed superpower, competing with the US for world leadership. At present maximalism is highly unrealistic, because most member countries have no interest in pursuing it. In any case, the EU currently lacks the ability to forge a superpower presence for itself in the international arena. Because of these elementary facts, 'minimalist' views on CFSP have tended to be in the ascendant in discussions on CFSP, although this does not mean that more-ambitious CFSP goals have been abandoned.

Despite the maximalist hue with which Union statements on CFSP are sometimes tinged, the current aim of CFSP is to enhance the ability of the governments of member countries to reach agreement on foreign policy positions and, where feasible, work together more effectively on the international stage, through institutional structures and procedures designed specifically for these purposes, The solutions which tend to recur in the prescriptions for a strengthened CFSP are, for example, measures which would make CFSP less declamatory and more operational; which would enhance the profile and presence of the Union in world affairs; which would limit the capacity of member states to engage in independent action; which would streamline CFSP decision-taking processes; which would enable the Union to react quickly and decisively to international events (including through use of military force); and which would add to the credibility of the Union as an international actor.

In recent years, the concept of 'European security' has been broadened to embrace economic security as well as political and military security. The former, for example would embrace security against non-military threats such as migration pressures, drugs, terrorism and pollution. In the context of the EU, does 'European security', mean simply the sum total of the securities of the member states? Does it embrace the whole of Europe, or is it concerned with the defence of the EU's borders? Does it embrace a concept of the EU as being greater than the sum of its parts, so that it has its own distinctive security identity and concerns? It may be that territorial definitions are inadequate to explain the nature of the EU's security, which may embrace defence of the EU project itself. This 'defence of the Union' motivation can certainly be discerned in some official pronouncements on CFSP, but these also tend to be larded with more conventional definitions of security, embracing defence against specific threats to the wellbeing of the states and peoples of the Union.

○ The Case For and Against a Strengthened CFSP

An underlying assumption in many political and academic commentaries is that a much strengthened CFSP is inherently desirable. Indeed, many commentators go further and argue that it is essential for the Union, in terms of its internal health and its external security in an uncertain post-cold war world. Although the case for strengthening CFSP hinges on several inter-related arguments, these can be divided into three categories, namely:

1. **'Health of the Union' arguments.** These comprise two strands:
   - *The need to maintain the momentum of the EU's development.* This view rests on the assumption that unless the EU continues along an upward integration path, it will stagnate or even unravel. An example of the momentum theory is the bicycling analogy, frequently used in relation to the Single European Market and economic and monetary union, that is, that there must be fast pedalling in order to avoid a falling off in

integration activity. This argument, the logic of which derives from the neo-functionalist idea of integration 'spillover', undoubtedly has considerable force in relation to economic policy and arguably has been the underlying driving force between many EU developments in the fields of economic and social policy. A key issue, however, is whether the bicycling analogy is applicable to the realm of external affairs.

Deeper Union integration is undoubtedly having an impact on the Union's external policy: thus the removal of internal borders necessitates the development of a common approach to questions of migration from outside the Union. But the forces which have energised economic integration may not be as strong in the field of foreign and security policy. It might be argued that the idea that member states are reluctant to surrender sovereignty in these fields is bogus, because many already do so through participation in the North Atlantic Treaty Organisation (NATO). But this argument might also be used as a partial explanation of why 'spillover' into CFSP has proved difficult, that is, if the hard security needs of member states are satisfied through NATO, then the logic of deeper integration within Union structures may have reduced potency.

- *A strong CFSP is needed to ensure a balanced, complete Union*, that is, that, without a more credible and effective international role, the EU will be incomplete, because it is a political, as well as an economic formation. A counter argument to the above is that a great leap forward in CFSP under current conditions is more likely to be divisive rather than unifying. Given that several member countries of the EU are neutral, could the Union's CFSP be truly representative of the Union as a whole? It can be argued that this does not really matter, as long as the neutrals remain in a small minority. Even so, the development of a partial CFSP can hardly be conducive to the Union's cohesion and could establish a precedent for *à la carte* Europe.

2. **'Sleeping Giant' arguments.** The view that the EU is underperforming internationally, that is, not making effective use of its tremendous potential as an international actor, underpins much of the argument in favour of a strengthened CFSP. A distinction might be made between arguments in favour of harnessing the EU's economic strength in the service of external policy and arguments in favour of realising the Union's potential in the field of foreign and defence policy. The former argument assumes that, because most EU policies have an international dimension, the EU has the potential to influence international developments through economic levers. Although the EU already makes use of these levers (for example, by building human rights criteria into its enlargement and aid programmes), arguably there is scope for further use of such instruments in other areas of external policy.

The latter argument rests on the assumption that, in terms of its military capability, the EU has the potential to become a global superpower, vying with the United States for world leadership. But even if there is no major conflict leading to high casualties, a fully developed CFSP is still likely to require increased military spending. Are EU citizens willing to accept significant increases in taxation for defence, at a time when several member states are actually cutting defence budgets? It might be argued that, once they realise the price of superpower status, most EU citizens would prefer to let the 'sleeping giant' remain sleeping.

3. **'New security agenda' arguments.** In recent years, it has seemed reasonable to assume that the demise of cold-war structures and certainties provides rich opportunities for a fundamental recasting of the contemporary security order. The end of the cold war was perceived in some quarters as creating 'vacancies' for new kinds of security organisation in Europe. In Western Europe, the potential hard security threat from the East was perceived as emanating primarily from an unstable, but still militarily formidable, Russia and from the prospect of wars deriving from ethnic or territorial disputes between transition countries. Threats to the EU's economic security were perceived as deriving from various forms of border spillage from the East, such as immigration, crime and pollution. As a product of the cold war, the appropriateness of NATO as the core security institution in Europe came into question in some quarters, as did the resolve of the US to maintain a strong European presence. These challenges required, it was argued, a more *proactive* policy and fresh thinking by the EU if it was not to be buffeted by unforeseen external events to which it was ill-prepared to respond.

Few if any of the threats identified above have so far materialised. Fears of a hard security threat from the East were based on misjudgements of Russia's capabilities and intentions. The problem of 'border spillage' from Eastern Europe has so far not approached the magnitude of the nightmare scenarios envisaged by the pessimists. Far from being an inflexible, cold-war anachronism, NATO has proved itself to be remarkably adaptable to post-cold war circumstances. For example, since the end of the cold war, NATO has re-defined its objectives (adding new missions of crisis management, peacekeeping and peace enforcement); it has demonstrated an ability to act effectively in major international crises; it has launched initiatives designed to establish relationships with non-member countries, such as the Euro-Atlantic Partnership Council and the Partnership for Peace (PFP) Programme. It has launched an enlargement process, in response to the strong desire for membership expressed by many Central and East European countries. The US has repeatedly reaffirmed in word and deed its commitment to a strong European presence (whilst calling on European countries to bear a greater share of the defence burden and whilst remaining suspicious of European initiatives which might threaten the alliance). The 'security vacuum' theory has tended to underestimate the attraction of NATO membership to former Warsaw Pact countries. The argument that NATO is inappropriate to Europe's needs because it is neither a purely European organisation nor an EU organisation is questionable, because in an increasingly interdependent world, security cannot be defined in strictly regional terms, even if we could agree a definition of Europe's boundaries.

Table 19.2 summarises the main arguments in the CFSP debate.

Table 19.2 Arguments For and Against a Stronger CFSP

For	Against
• Collectively, EU countries will be able to exercise greater clout in international affairs.	• Differences in foreign policy interests, deriving from geography and history.
• The EU needs a political and military capability to match its economic strength.	• Europe has a 'security surfeit' rather than a 'security deficit'; a strengthened CFSP is not needed.
• The development of the EU is creating common international interests among its members.	• Foreign and security policy are core functions which governments are reluctant to relinquish.
• It is a logical phase in the development of the Union.	• The EU's decision-taking style is unsuited to the realm of foreign policy.
• If the EU is not to remain incomplete and unbalanced, an effective CFSP is essential.	• There are major problems in co-ordinating foreign policy positions.
• The potential for instability in post-cold-war Europe requires a common approach.	• Several member states are at best lukewarm about CFSP.
• The US may not always be willing to play the leading role in international crises.	• Desire for a stronger CFSP may derive from a desire to share burdens rather than to 'beef up' capability.
• The need for a strong CFSP is shown by the EU's weak responses to international crises.	• NATO has shown itself to be capable of effective action in international crises.
• The EU can contribute something distinctive to the resolution of international disputes.	• CFSP difficulties are likely to be exacerbated by the next EU enlargements.

● THE DEVELOPMENT OF CFSP

○ From European Political Co-operation to CFSP

Member states have operated a formal, albeit very loose, system of co-operation in foreign policy for over three decades. In 1969, an EC heads of government meeting in The Hague requested EC foreign ministers to consider ways of enhancing co-operation between member states in the field of foreign policy. As a result, European Political Co-operation (EPC) was established in 1970, without a treaty basis. EPC was a framework for concerted action by EC countries in the field of foreign policy, involving intergovernmental communication, consultation and mutually agreed common action. It was a limited step towards a common foreign policy rather than a great leap forward. The system developed in an *ad hoc* way and operated outside the EC's institutional structures and legislative processes, on the basis of consensus between governments. There was no voting and its provisions were non-binding. Nor did it cover military aspects of security.

EPC was given recognition in Title III of the Single European Act, which stated that member states would endeavour jointly to formulate and implement a European foreign policy. EPC largely resulted in a plethora of vaguely worded declarations (usually after key events had occurred) and little action. The absence of a defence component also weakened the credibility of EPC. EPC never opened a dialogue with communist Eastern Europe. The Gulf crisis of 1990–91 exposed wide differences in the contributions member states were prepared to make to the military campaign to oust the Iraqi army from Kuwait. EPC was formalised and extended in the TEU, but was subsumed under the heading of CFSP (effectively replacing the term EPC).

A Union CFSP was formally established by Article J.1 (now 11.1) of the TEU, as one of the EU's three pillars. The TEU requires member states to co-ordinate their action in international organisations and to uphold common positions in international forums. Article 11.2 requires member states to support the Union's external and security policy actively and unreservedly in a spirit of loyalty and mutual solidarity. As under EPC, CSFP is based on intergovernmental co-operation. The main differences between EPC and CSFP are that CSFP covers defence issues and strengthens the EU's commitment to the development of *joint action* in foreign and security policy. According to its many critics, the CFSP established by the TEU resulted in a foreign and security policy which was essentially faceless (or so hydra-headed as to appear faceless), feeble and confusing. The ToA made many changes to the TEU's provisions on CFSP. The Nice European Council adopted the Council Presidency's report on the European Security and Defence Policy. The pace of reform in CFSP therefore appears to be quickening (see below).

● POST-COLD WAR SECURITY STRUCTURES

○ Key Questions

The end of the cold war raised several fundamental issues concerning European security. Firstly, what was to be the function of NATO following the demise of the Soviet threat? Secondly, could the EU develop its own defence capability, either distinct from, or in partnership with, NATO? Thirdly, how could members of NATO respond to requests for membership by former communist countries? Fourthly, to what extent could the EU assume a 'trouble-shooter' role in relation to the ethnic and border disputes resulting from the collapse of communism? There are two ways in which a security system appropriate to a post-cold war environment might be built: existing institutions can be adapted to suit new conditions, or new 'purpose-built' organisations can be created. In the security field, there has been a tendency to make use of existing institutions, in particular NATO, the Western European Union (WEU) and the Organisation for Security and Co-operation in Europe (OSCE), formerly known as the Conference on Security and Co-operation in Europe (CSCE). This *ad hoc* approach has meant that security policy currently involves a complex web of institutions with overlapping functions and memberships. This approach can also be discerned in the functions and resources assigned to the EU's new rapid reaction force, which will make use of NATO assets and capabilities and which will take over key crisis management and peacekeeping functions formerly performed by the WEU. Table 19.3 provides an insight into post-cold war security structures in Europe. It is not exhaustive. For example, it does not include initiatives such as the *Eurocorps*, formed in 1995, which comprises one French and one German division plus contingents from Belgium, Spain and Luxembourg. In 2001, the Eurocorps was being transformed into an EU rapid reaction corps, that is a crisis management asset at the disposal of the EU.

A system of *complex interdependence* has emerged, linking security structures. Two key issues are, firstly, whether these organisations duplicate or complement one another; and secondly, whether or not they are all needed. In organisational terms, it might be argued that there is a security surfeit rather than a security deficit in Europe. Arguably, each of these institutions contributes something distinctive and useful to European security. These security networks may help to avoid a 'we' and 'they' syndrome which could be both divisive and dangerous. But there is always the danger of overlap, duplication and sheer confusion about the roles of these diverse organisations and instruments. A central question relating to the organisation of security in Europe, therefore, centres on the quality and forms of co-operation in order to maximise organisational synergies and minimise duplication.

Table 19.3 'Variable Geometry' in Europe's Security Architecture

	NATO	EAPC	WEU	RRF	OSCE	CE
Belgium	y	y	y	y	y	y
France	y	y	y	y	y	y
Denmark	y	y	o	n	y	y
Germany	y	y	y	y	y	y
Greece	y	y	y	y	y	y
Ireland	n	y	o	y	y	y
Italy	y	y	y	y	y	y
Luxembourg	y	y	y	y	y	y
Netherlands	y	y	y	y	y	y
Portugal	y	y	y	y	y	y
Spain	y	y	y	y	y	y
UK	y	y	y	y	y	y
Austria	n	o	o	y	y	y
Finland	n	o	o	y	y	y
Sweden	n	o	o	y	y	y
Iceland	y	y	am	n	y	y
Liechtenstein	n	n	n	n	y	y
Norway	y	y	am	n	y	y
Switzerland	n	y	n	n	y	y
Cyprus	n	n	n	n	y	y
Malta	n	n	n	n	y	y
Turkey	y	y	am	n	y	y
Albania	n	y	n	n	y	y
Armenia	n	y	n	n	y	n
Azerbaijan	n	y	n	n	y	n
Belorus	n	y	n	n	y	n
Bosnia-H	n	n	n	n	y	n
Bulgaria	n	y	ap	n	y	y
Croatia	n	n	n	n	y	n
Czech Rep.	y	y	ap	n	y	y
Estonia	n	y	ap	n	y	y
Georgia	n	y	n	n	y	n
Hungary	y	y	ap	n	y	y
Kazakhstan	n	y	n	n	y	n
Kyrgyzstan	n	y	n	n	y	n
Latvia	n	y	ap	n	y	y
Lithuania	n	y	ap	n	y	y
Macedonia	n	y	n	n	o	o
Moldova	n	y	n	n	y	y
Poland	y	y	ap	n	y	y
Romania	n	y	ap	n	y	y
Russia	n	y	n	n	y	y
Slovakia	n	y	ap	n	y	y
Slovenia	n	y	n	n	y	y
Tajikistan	n	y	n	n	y	n
Turkmenistan	n	y	n	n	y	n
Ukraine	n	y	n	n	y	n
Uzbekistan	n	y	n	n	y	n
Yug. Fed.	n	n	n	n	y	n
US	y	y	n	n	y	n
Canada	y	y	n	n	y	n

Organisations

NATO = North Atlantic Treaty Organisation

EAPC = Euro-Atlantic Partnership Council

WEU = Western European Union

RRF = Rapid Reaction Force

OSCE = Organisation for Security and Co-operation in Europe

CE = Council of Europe

Note: the WEU's peacekeeping functions are being transferred to the EU. Non-EU countries may participate in RRF operations, although the formal relationships between these countries and the RRF have not yet been worked out.

Categories

European Union

EFTA

'Mediterranean' States

Ex-Communist States

North America

Abbreviations

y = yes

n = no

o = observer status

am = associate member

ap = associate partner

Note: Andorra and San Marino are members of the OSCE and CE; Monaco and the Vatican are members of the OSCE.

○   NATO and the EAPC

We have already noted how NATO has flourished in the post-cold war era: it played decisive roles in the conflicts in the Gulf and the Balkans; it is widely acknowledged to be the cornerstone of collective security in Europe; it has expanded its membership from 16 to 19 (the Czech Republic, Poland and Hungary were admitted to NATO in 1998) and is likely to admit other countries in the future. It has also established formal relationships with non-members. In October 1991, US Secretary of State James Baker and German Foreign Minister Hans-Dietrich Genscher proposed that a 'North Atlantic Co-operation Council' be formed, to institutionalise East European participation in the non-military activities of NATO. The NACC came into existence in December 1991. In May 1997, the NACC changed its name to the Euro-Atlantic Partnership Council (EAPC). The Council consists of the foreign ministers or other representatives of member states, meeting at least once a year. The EAPC oversees relations between NATO and its partners. It meets twice a year at both foreign and defence ministers level and normally at ambassadorial level in Brussels very month.

At the NATO summit in Brussels in January 1994, President Clinton launched the *Partnership for Peace* initiative, based on the idea of a more extensive degree of collaboration between NATO and other countries than envisaged in the EAPC agreements. Invitations to negotiate PFP agreements were sent to all former Warsaw Pact countries, including Russia and other former Soviet republics. Twenty-seven countries have now joined PFP, which involves bilateral relationships between NATO and each PFP partner. The PFP retains its own separate identity within a consultative forum which facilitates co-operation within the framework provided by the EAPC. PFP does not offer security guarantees, but PFP signatories are able to consult with NATO if they feel their security is threatened.

○   The Western European Union

The WEU is an example of a low-profile institution revitalised (albeit temporarily) as a result of the end of the cold war. With hindsight, the post-cold war role of the WEU has been to serve as a makeshift organisation, whilst new EU defence structures were being developed. The WEU has its origins in the Brussels Treaty of 'Economic, Social and Cultural Collaboration and Collective Self-Defence' (March 1948), concluded between Belgium, France, the Netherlands, Luxembourg and the UK, when the main concern of its signatories was the prospect of German rearmament. The exercise of the military responsibilities of the treaty were transferred to NATO in 1949. The Treaty was subsequently modified by the Paris agreements of October 1954, which enabled Germany and Italy to join (following the refusal of the French National Assembly to ratify the European Defence Community Treaty). The Paris agreements introduced the 'Western European Union' title and explicitly referred to the promotion of European integration as a WEU goal. Between 1954 and 1973, the WEU helped to integrate the Federal Republic of Germany into the Atlantic alliance. There was a slowing down of its activities between 1973 and 1984. But the potential of the WEU to play a more important role in European security was recognised in various proposals for 'deeper' European integration which emerged in the 1980s. The US decision in 1983 to launch the 'Star Wars' programme without consulting Europe encouraged EU countries to consider the need for a stronger European dimension to European security. The WEU was relaunched in Rome in 1984, at a meeting of WEU foreign and defence ministers. In October 1987, the WEU ministerial council set out the WEU's future programme, based around giving European integration a security dimension.

The declaration on the role of the WEU agreed at Maastricht viewed the WEU as both strengthening the European pillar of NATO and as the defence component of the future EU. At Maastricht, member states outside the WEU were invited to join or become observers. The WEU's 'variable geometry' embraces the following: *members* (all are also members of NATO and the EU); *observers* (members of NATO and/or of the EU); *associate members* (NATO but not EU members); and *associate partners* (neither NATO nor EU members). The WEU is currently made up of ten countries: the UK, France, Germany, Italy, Spain, Portugal, Belgium, the Netherlands, Luxembourg and Greece. Austria, Denmark, Finland, Ireland and Sweden are observers. Observers may attend WEU Council meetings and are invited to working-group meetings where they may, on request, speak. Norway, Iceland and Turkey are 'associate members'. Associate members may take a full part in Council meetings and working groups. They may associate themselves with the decisions of member states and can take part in WEU military operations. Nine Central and East European countries became 'associate partners' in May 1994. Associate partner status involves various forms of consultation and co-operation.

The WEU has a Council of Ministers (the WEU Council) and a Permanent Council. The Permanent Council, chaired by the WEU Secretary-General and supported by a Secretariat is responsible for day-to-day management. The WEU has a parliamentary assembly established in 1954 (consisting of members of national parliamentary delegations to the Council of Europe's Consultative Assembly). The WEU played a role in co-ordinating member states' naval units deployed in the Gulf (Operation *Cleansweep*). Ships and aircraft under the control of the WEU helped to monitor the UN embargo on

Serbia-Montenegro and the WEU has been active in the EU's administration of Mostar in Bosnia. But actions by the WEU have been overshadowed by those of NATO, the world's most powerful military alliance.

In the 1990s, the WEU's main role changed from collective defence to crisis management, peace support and humanitarian missions. In June 1992, the foreign and defence ministers of the WEU met in Petersberg (near Bonn) in order to define the role and tasks of the WEU. This resulted in the 'Petersberg Declaration', outlining the guidelines for the WEU's future development. The declaration reaffirmed NATO's responsibility for collective self-defence and defined its own tasks as those of peacemaking, peacekeeping, crisis management and protection for humanitarian operations. The Petersberg tasks are included in the ToA. The WEU has never had forces of its own or permanent command structures. However, it was given a Planning Cell, a Satellite Centre and a Military Committee (consisting of the Chiefs of Defence staff) to facilitate performance of its 'Petersberg tasks'. It was also given 'Forces Answerable to WEU' (FAWEU), comprising national units plus several multinational formations, such as the Eurocorps (Germany, France, Belgium, Luxembourg and Spain) and EUROFOR, a rapid deployment force comprising France, Italy, Portugal and Spain.

During the early post-cold war years, there was considerable discussion about the potential effect of the WEU (an exclusively European organisation) upon NATO and therefore upon transatlantic relations. NATO was established in 1949 as an alliance against the threat of a Soviet attack on Western Europe. Four EU states are outside NATO and six NATO states are not in the EU. In October 1991, prior to the Maastricht summit, France and Germany and the UK and Italy produced contradictory proposals on European defence: the Franco-German proposal sought to downgrade NATO by beefing up the WEU, whereas the UK–Italian proposals for the WEU were based on continuation of a strong NATO role. After much argumentation, it was agreed that any changes to the WEU would not undermine NATO.

A substantial degree of co-operation between the WEU and NATO has developed. In 1994, a NATO summit called for a European Security and Defence Identity (ESDI) involving both organisations. A formula for ESDI involving institutional co-operation between the WEU and NATO was adopted by NATO foreign ministers in Berlin in June 1996 and was further elaborated at further NATO summits. ESDI allows NATO's assets and capabilities to be made available for WEU operations, on a case-by-case basis. Ideas are being developed for combined joint task forces (CJTFs), involving both NATO and WEU military capabilities. The first ever joint WEU/NATO crisis management exercise (CRISEX 2000) based on a peace support mission scenario took place in February 2000. But the WEU has very much been a junior, dependent, partner in these relationships. The WEU could not muster a peacekeeping force to deal with the collapse of civil order in Albania in 1997, although it is involved in police assistance operations through MAPE (Multinational Police Advisory Element).

The ToA includes a declaration on enhanced co-operation between the Union and the WEU, with a view to the possibility of the WEU's eventual integration into the Union. The idea that the WEU should be merged into the EU was rejected at Amsterdam by the UK and several other countries. However, some countries, not least Germany and France, continued to press for merger. The Council's High Representative for CFSP, Javier Solana, is also now Secretary-General of the WEU, which is another indication of the close links between the WEU and the EU. The decision was taken at the Cologne European Council to transfer most or all the WEU's operational resources to the EU. The Helsinki European Council confirmed that the WEU's crisis management role would be taken over by the EU. The rapid reaction force, scheduled to be operational by 2003, will take over the WEU's crisis management functions. In November 2000, the WEU Council of Ministers decided in Marseilles that the WEU will continue to be used for collective defence as outlined in Article V of the Brussels Treaty. There will be a new WEU structure by July 2001. The WEU parliamentary assembly will continue to function and the WEU will continue to provide support for the Western European Armaments Group (WEAG). Some analysts regard the collective defence aspect of the WEU as largely irrelevant, because collective defence is now sought through NATO. The ESDP is now emerging as the European pillar of NATO, not the WEU (see below). The Treaty of Nice (ToN) excised most of the references to the WEU from the TEU. Although therefore, for a period in the 1990s, the WEU's future looked bright (as the prospective defence arm of the EU), there is a distinct possibility that it will sink back into obscurity or even be wound up.

○ The Rapid Reaction Force

This is examined in more detail in the section on the European Security and Defence Policy below.

○ The Organisation for Security and Co-operation in Europe

The OSCE (known as the CSCE until January 1995) is the only current pan-European institution to which all European countries belong. It was created in the early 1970s to promote East–West dialogue, during the period of *détente* between the West and the Warsaw Pact countries. The OSCE now has 55 members, comprising all European states plus the US and Canada. The cold war was formally wound up at a CSCE summit in Paris in November 1990, which led to the signing of the Paris Charter for a New Europe. The Charter established the Council of Foreign Ministers of the CSCE, together with a Committee of Senior Officials, a Secretariat in Prague, a Conflict Prevention Centre in Vienna and an Office of Democratic Institutions and Human Rights (ODIHR) in Warsaw. The OSCE is essentially a forum which provides regular opportunities for members to discuss, and co-operate on, security issues. It established preventive diplomacy missions in Estonia and Latvia and also has missions in Kosovo, Sanjak and several other trouble spots. It has been involved in withdrawal of Russian troops from the Baltic; in crisis management in Moldova; in conflict resolution in Nagorno-Karabakh and Chechnya; and in sanctions assistance missions in the Balkans. Its main asset is its pan-European and pan-Atlantic membership. Its main drawback is that it is viewed as little more than a talking shop. Its decisions have to be unanimous, limiting its scope for effective action.

○ The Council of Europe

Based in Strasbourg, the Council was established in May 1949, following the Hague Congress (see Chapter 1). Its principal aims are to maintain the basic principles of human rights, pluralist democracy and the rule of law and to enhance the quality of life for European citizens. It is not a military organisation and its statutes do not allow it to become involved in defence issues. It nevertheless has an important contribution to make to stability in Europe through its promotion of democratic values and human rights. It has a Committee of Ministers and a Parliamentary Assembly. The Council has concluded about 140 intergovernmental conventions and agreements, including the Convention on Human Rights. Several former communist states have now been admitted to the Council, including Russia (in January 1996), despite misgivings about Russia's actions in Chechnya.

● CFSP FROM AMSTERDAM TO NICE

○ CFSP and the Treaty of Amsterdam

The deliberations of the 1996–97 intergovernmental conference were influenced by several factors: general acknowledgement that references to CFSP in the TEU left much to be desired; the ineffectiveness of CFSP in response to the crises in the Balkans; entry into the EU of three neutral countries in January 1995; and the predicted implications of future enlargement. The IGC provided clear indication of the wide divergences of viewpoint between member states, the European Parliament (EP) and the

Commission on CFSP questions. Although it was generally agreed that CFSP needed improvement, there were many views as to how this could be done. Some countries advocated the WEU's integration into the EU; some favoured more use of majority voting, some advocated the establishment of a secretary-general for CFSP. These divergences explain why agreement could only be achieved through resort to circumlocutory phraseology, equivocation and 'get-out' clauses. They also explain why the IGC focused more on forging CFSP tools (institutional relationships and procedures) rather than on substantive issues of policy. At Amsterdam, the intergovernmentalist spirit reigned (almost) supreme on CFSP matters. Most member states opposed abolition of the CFSP intergovernmental pillar, with France and UK the most adamant. Conversely, Germany favoured abandonment of CFSP's intergovernmental character and advocated qualified 'Communitization' of CFSP, through its integration into the EC pillar. Germany received some support from Belgium, which criticised the intergovernmental emphasis in CFSP. Given these differences, it is hardly surprising that the ToA's CFSP reforms were of an *incremental* character.

- **Objectives and instruments.** The ToA changes the first subparagraph of Article 11 of the TEU which outlines the objectives of CFSP, that is, to 'safeguard the common values, fundamental interests, independence and *integrity* of the Union, *in conformity with the principles of the UN Charter*' (the words in italics above and below are new: all the italics are added by the author). The phrase '*integrity of the Union*' is not, however, explained, leaving a huge question mark over the meaning of 'Union integrity'. Nor is it clear how or by whom this integrity might be challenged. It might be argued that the phrase reflects a conception of the Union as an entity in its own right, but in terms vague enough to be acceptable to member states unenthusiastic about a stronger CFSP. Article 17 states that CFSP covers all questions relating to the security of the Union, including the '*progressive* framing of a common defence policy...*which might lead* to a common defence, *should the European Council so decide*'. The objective of preserving peace and strengthening international security is extended to include external borders, but this is not explicitly linked to the 'integrity' clause. The second sub-paragraph of Article 11 is changed from 'to strengthen the security of the Union and its member states in all ways' to 'strengthen the security of *the Union* in all ways'. The language used here is vague enough to permit various interpretations. The Petersberg tasks are specifically included in Article 17. The ToA is more explicit on how CFSP objectives are to be pursued (Article 12), that is, by defining the principles of and general guidelines for CFSP; deciding on common strategies; adopting joint actions and common positions and strengthening systematic co-operation between member states in the conduct of policy. Table 19.4 below provides a snapshot of the changes to

CFSP contained in the ToA. It also provides an indication of the many omissions in the treaty.

Table 19.4 What the ToA Does and Does Not Do in Relation to CFSP

What the ToA Does (or Seeks to Do)

- it seeks to makes CFSP more coherent, by clarifying its objectives;
- it establishes the role of High Representative for the Union's CFSP, thus giving CFSP a clearer and more coherent 'face';
- it strengthens the role of the European Council in defining CFSP principles and guidelines;
- it introduces the concept of 'common strategy' and clarifies the concepts of joint actions and common positions;
- the Commission is fully associated with drafting CFSP and at the Council's request may submit proposals for implementation of joint actions;
- it allows for adoption of decisions which are not unanimous in certain cases (that is, 'opt-outs' through constructive abstention) thus freeing the Union from paralysis in CFSP;
- it improves CFSP planning capabilities, by establishing a policy planning and early warning unit ('PPEWU');
- it allows the Union to carry out missions based on the Petersberg tasks;
- it includes a clause requiring members to co-ordinate their activities and uphold common positions within international organisations and international conferences;
- with important exceptions (see below) administrative and operational expenditure of the CFSP is to be charged to the EU budget.

What the ToA Does Not Do

- it does not integrate CFSP into EC decisionmaking structures;
- it does not grant the EU a legal personality or legal competence;
- it does not integrate the WEU into the Union;
- it does not include a European defence or military policy;
- it does not really address the implications of enlargement for CFSP;
- it does not grant the Commission parity with the Council in CFSP;
- it does not substantially enhance the role of the EP in CFSP;
- it does not replace unanimity by QMV as the principal means of
- decisionmaking in CFSP;
- it does not remove the possibility that a proposed CFSP action might be paralysed by a national veto (in certain circumstances it allows decisions to be blocked on grounds of 'important national policy').

- *Common strategies* are a new instrument, added to joint actions and common positions. The European Council defines the principles and general guidelines of CFSP, including matters with defence implications. It decides on common strategies to be implemented by the EU in areas where member states have important interests in common. The Council takes the decisions necessary for defining and implementing CFSP on the basis of the European Council's general guidelines. It recommends common strategies to the European Council and also implements them.
- *Joint actions* (Article 14). The Council has the power to adopt joint actions for specific situations where operational action by the EU is deemed to be required. The Council may request the Commission to submit CFSP proposals, to ensure implementation of a joint action.
- *Common positions* define the approach of the Union to a particular matter of a geographic or thematic nature (Article 15).

The concept of CFSP instruments is therefore in theory clarified by the ToA. However, there are semantic and practical difficulties involved in distinguishing between 'strategies', 'actions' and 'positions'.

- **Consistency and clarity.** The ToA aims to improve overall consistency of CFSP through clarification of the role of the European Council, the Council and the European Commission in decision-making. It also requires member states to inform and consult one another within the Council on any matter of foreign and security policy of general interest (Article 16). Member states must refrain from any action contrary to the interests of the EU or which is likely to impair its effectiveness as a cohesive force in international relations (Article 11.2). They must co-ordinate their action in international organisations and international conferences and uphold common positions in such fora (Article 19). The Council is charged with ensuring the unity, consistency and effectiveness of action by the Union (Article 13.3). Member states must ensure that national policies are in conformity with these common positions. Any member state may refer to the Council any question relating to CFSP and may submit proposals. Where a rapid decision is required, the presidency, whether on its own or at the request of the Commission or a member state, may convene an extraordinary Council meeting within 48 hours (less in emergencies). But the stress on consistency is weakened by exemptions and opt-outs from CFSP operations (see below).

The treaty addresses the issue of responsibility for presenting and explaining CFSP. The problem of the absence of a clearly identifiable and prominent figurehead to explain the CFSP is exacerbated by the EU's system of rotating Council presidencies and by diffusion of responsibility for various aspects of external policy. The EP's request to give the Commission the task of responsibility for external policy was not accepted. Instead, the Secretary-General of the Council is established as High Representative for the CFSP, keeping this function firmly in intergovernmental hands. The ToA states that the presidency shall represent the EU in CFSP matters, assisted by the Secretary-General of the Council, designated as the High Representative. The Secretary-General's administrative tasks have been transferred to his deputy. The High Representative is required to assist the Council in matters within the scope of CFSP. At the request of the presidency and on behalf of the Council, the High Representative may conduct political dialogue with third parties. In October 1999, Javier Solana, formerly NATO Secretary-General of NATO, was appointed to the post. He was also appointed Secretary-General of the WEU, signalling the EU's aims to ensure *de facto* integration of the WEU into the EU. Regardless of Solana's calibre, the post is not equivalent to, say, that of the UN Secretary-General. The Council presidency is still responsible for external representation of the EU and is *assisted* by the High Representative. There is also a commissioner for external relations (currently Chris Patten). Moreover, member states retain their foreign and defence ministries. It is hardly surprising therefore that the ToA's efforts to give the EU a clearer external face and voice have so far yielded modest results.

• **Reacting more quickly to international events.** A weakness of post-Maastricht CFSP has been the inability of member states to react to international events in a timely and co-ordinated way. A reason often given for this failing has been the absence of sufficient information and analysis. The ToA seeks to fill this gap, by establishing a new planning unit, to provide decisionmakers with timely information and advice. Known as the 'Policy Planning and Early Warning Unit' (PPEWU), it is located in the General Secretariat of the Council, under the authority of the Secretary-General. It is staffed from the General Secretariat, the member states, the Commission and the WEU. Its tasks are: monitoring and analysing developments in areas relevant to the CFSP; providing assessments of the EU's CFSP interests; providing timely assessments and early warning of events or situations likely to have significant repercussions for CFSP; and producing policy options papers at the request of the Council, the presidency or on its own initiative. The unit could provide a useful source of additional information for decisionmakers. But this depends on the quality of its advice, the credibility of its advisors and the willingness of decisionmakers to make use of it

• **Decisionmaking.** The ToA seeks to make the CFSP more coherent, streamlined and efficient. It allows for the possibility of clearer decision-making, through the formulation of common strategies by the European Council. Although the TEU and the ToA formalised the role of the European Council in CFSP agenda setting (requiring it to define the principles, guidelines and common strategies for the CFSP), it is the Council (in the form of the General Affairs Council) which is the principal CFSP decisionmaking body. The Council is empowered to adopt common positions, which define the EU's approach to a matter of a geographical or thematic nature and to decide on matters which are to be the subject of joint actions.

The ToA requires decisions under CFSP to be taken by the Council acting unanimously, although by derogation it may act by qualified majority (see below). However, the treaty allows for *constructive abstention*, in that a state may choose not to apply a decision taken by the Council, but must nevertheless accept that the decision commits the Union, so that adoption of the decision is not blocked. In a spirit of mutual solidarity, the member state concerned is required to refrain from any action likely to conflict with or impede Union action based on the decision and the other member states must respect its position. A member may make a formal declaration when abstaining. However, if the members of the Council qualifying their abstention in this way represent more than a third of the votes weighted in accordance with Article 205(2) of the EC Treaty, the constructive abstention mechanism does not apply and the decision is not adopted. Even where constructive abstention is allowed, it will take over a third of weighted votes to block a decision. However, abstention may send the wrong signals to other countries that the Union is divided on specific issues.

A derogation allows the Council to act by QMV when adopting joint actions, common positions or taking any other decision on the basis of a common strategy or when adopting any decision implementing a joint action or a common position. But a vote will not be taken if a member state declares that for important and stated reasons of national policy, it intends to oppose the adoption of a decision by qualified majority voting (QMV). In these cases, the Council may, by QMV, request that the matter be referred to the European Council for decision by unanimity. The treaty therefore introduced an 'emergency brake' procedure, which allows any member state to oppose the adoption of a decision by the Council for important and stated reasons of national policy. Since the European Council operates by consensus, countries unwilling to agree to decisions are likely to seek to have matters referred upwards. QMV does not apply to decisions having military or defence implications. The ToA's 'devil in the detail' therefore affords potentially powerful escape and blockage mechanisms for states opposed to the majority view. For procedural questions, the Council acts by simple majority.

- **Defence.** Article 17 (formerly J.7) of the Maastricht TEU stated that CFSP includes questions relating to 'the eventual framing of a common defence policy which might in time lead to a common defence', whereas the ToA revises Article 17, to state that CFSP includes the progressive framing of a common defence policy '*which might lead* to a common defence, *should the European Council so decide*'. The European Council is therefore explicitly given the task of deciding on the issue of a common defence. The Cologne, Helsinki and Nice European Councils have subsequently taken key decisions to establish a European Security and Defence Policy.

• **Financing.** Although the ToA includes some improvements to the financing of CFSP (Article 28), under-resourcing of CFSP is likely to remain a key issue. The administrative and operational expenditure of the CFSP, with the exception of military expenditure and other expenditure decided unanimously by the Council, is charged to the EU budget as non-compulsory expenditure, as the EP had wanted. In other cases, expenditure will be charged to member states, based on GNP, unless the Council acting unanimously decides otherwise. Member states deciding not to participate in operations with military or defence implications are not obliged to participate in financing such operations. There is a consultation procedure between the EP and Council on the amount and distribution of CFSP expenditure.

• **CFSP and other external policies.** The Union's external policy remains fragmented between CFSP and other aspects of the Union's external relations. Although the provisions on CFSP are included in the TEU, various aspects of external economic relations are dealt with in the EC Treaty. It might be beneficial to bring all aspects of external policy together, not least because of the clout which the Union exercises in international affairs currently tends to be economic rather than military. Given that 'security' now embraces a wide range of subjects, in the interests of policy coherence and synergy there is a strong case for bringing these aspects together within a single framework. However, this would have major implications for the demarcation of policy portfolios, both within the Council and the Commission.

○   **CFSP and the Treaty of Nice**

The ToN will not alter the basic framework of CFSP as developed by the ToA. However, it will make a number of significant changes. It amends the following articles in the TEU: Article 17, by deleting the provisions defining relations between the EU and WEU; Article 23 to allow the Secretary-General and special representatives to be chosen by QMV; Article 24 (conclusion of international agreements in the CFSP and JHA areas for which QMV is required); Article 25, by changing the name of the Political Committee to 'Political and Security Committee' (PSC) and by enabling the Council to authorise the PSC to take appropriate decisions under the second pillar to ensure the political control and strategic leadership of a crisis management operation; and Article 27, by introducing the possibility of establishing enhanced co-operation in CFSP for the implementation of joint actions or common positions (excluding issues which have military or defence implications). The Council will authorise such co-operation after receiving the opinion of the Commission. The Council will decide by QMV, but each member state may request that the matter be referred to the European Council for a unanimous decision (the 'emergency brake' procedure referred to earlier). A declaration on European security and defence policy is also attached to the ToN, stating that the objective of the EU is for ESDP to become operational quickly and that a decision to that end will be taken as soon as possible in 2001 on the basis of existing TEU provisions (that is, entry into force of the ToN does not constitute a precondition).

○ Institutional Roles and Relationships in CFSP

The institutional framework of CFSP is largely determined by the intergovernmental character of this field of EU policy. The dominant roles in CFSP are played by the Council and the European Council. The Commission plays a supporting role in CFSP. The EP's role is weak and the European Court of Justice (ECJ) is excluded. The European Council sets principles and guidelines and decides on common strategies. However, it meets too infrequently to take day-to-day decisions, which is the responsibility of the Council. The main decisionmaking body is the General Affairs Council (GAC), comprising EU foreign ministers. The GAC expands to include defence ministers when dealing with the ESDP. CFSP includes the military aspects of ESDP and is governed by the GAC. The Council presidency rather than the Commission represents the Union on CFSP issues and is responsible for the implementation of common measures.

The Council is assisted in its CFSP role by a network of supporting groups: the Council Secretariat provides the framework for co-ordination and administrative support. The Council Secretary-General is the High Representative for CFSP and assists the Council in CFSP matters; works closely with the Council Presidency and with the Commission; and assists the presidency in the external representation of CFSP. Special representatives with mandates on specific policy issues may also be appointed by the Council (Article 18). Other bodies involved are: the *Committee of Permanent Representatives* (COREPER), which meets weekly to prepare Council meetings and decisions; the *Political and Security Committee* comprising senior foreign officials from member states who prepare CFSP work for COREPER and the GAC; the *Correspondents Group* (other foreign ministry officials who perform liaison and preparatory work not dealt with initially by the PSC); the *CFSP Counsellors*, who are officials who examine legal, institutional and financial aspects of CFSP on behalf of the PSC and COREPER; and about 25 *CFSP working groups*, comprising high-ranking diplomats and Commission representatives, who prepare discussions on specific subjects for the Political and Security Committee.

Although the Commission is 'fully associated' with CFSP, it does not have the exclusive right to initiate proposals. However, it may submit CFSP issues and proposals to the Council and therefore shares initiative rights with member states. The external relations commissioner co-ordinates the external relations activities of the Commission (there are also commissioners for trade, enlargement, development and monetary affairs which form a team of external relations commissioners) and liaises with the High Representative for CFSP. The External Relations Directorate is responsible for the Commission's relations with most areas of the world and with international organisations. The Commission is involved in the diplomatic and economic measures preceding or following EU military missions and is involved in the non-military aspects of crisis management (a new crisis management unit has been set up in the Commission). The presidency must consult the EP on the main aspects and basic choices of the CFSP (including financial implications of CFSP for the EU budget) and must ensure that the views of the EP are considered. The EP can ask questions of, and make recommendations to, the Council on CFSP issues. It holds an annual debate on progress in implementing CFSP. The EP's role in CFSP decisionmaking was not substantively enhanced by the ToA or ToN, due to the strong preference of most member states to retain CFSP's intergovernmental nature. However, the role of parliaments in foreign policy tends to be limited. In some ways, the EP has more power with regard to external policy than many national parliaments (for example, it has rights of assent with regard to accession treaties).

○   CFSP and Enlargement

Aspirants for EU membership have been left in no doubt that they must accept CFSP as defined in the EU treaties. Prior to entry, Austria, Finland and Sweden accepted that their accession should strengthen rather than weaken the EU's capacity to act effectively in foreign and security policy. But all three have post-war traditions of neutrality which inhibit them from taking a central role in CFSP. Conversely, some Central and East European countries, when admitted to the EU, might prove to be enthusiastic participants in CFSP. No state has joined the EU with the primary purpose of participating in CFSP. This does not mean that broader security motivations are not important in decisions to seek EU entry. However, these are likely to fit more into the category of 'soft' security (that is, economic and societal security) rather than 'hard' (or military) security. As far as it applies to 'hard security', this motivation might be satisfied through NATO membership. The 'rejoining Europe' motive does not have to be pursued through affiliation to a 'hard' security organisation: neutral European countries feel no less 'European' than those which participate fully in European defence structures. Mechanisms are however being developed which will enable candidate countries to participate in operations involving the EU's rapid reaction force (see below).

● THE EUROPEAN SECURITY AND DEFENCE POLICY

○ The EU's Faltering First Steps as a European Trouble-Shooter

The will and ability of the EU to develop a credible CFSP has been put to severe test in post-cold war Europe, no more so than in the Balkans, where arguably EU diplomacy was tried and found badly wanting. Defenders of CFSP's record can point to a number of specific activities in which CFSP could be shown to be something more than a pipe dream. Joint actions by EU countries have included humanitarian aid for Bosnia; supply of observers to Russian elections; support for the democratic process in South Africa; support for the Middle East peace process; and preparations for the Conference on the Non-Proliferation Treaty. The WEU helped to co-ordinate member states' naval forces during the Gulf crisis and also assisted in the monitoring of the UN embargo on Yugoslavia. In May 1994, the EU Council agreed to a request of the Bosnian Federation to administer the Bosnian town of Mostar. The EU played a key role in developing the 'Stability in Europe' pact. The pact, monitored by the OCSE, is primarily designed to contribute to peace and stability in Central and Eastern Europe.

But these achievements seem somewhat paltry when measured against the EU's failure to prevent or halt the civil wars in ex-Yugoslavia and their attendant horrors of 'ethnic cleansing'. In 1991, the foreign minister of Luxembourg, Jacques Poos, one of a 'troika' of EU foreign ministers charged with the task of resolving the developing crisis in Yugoslavia, optimistically referred to this crisis as 'Europe's hour'. The Bosnian imbroglio provided a graphic demonstration of the EU's inability to develop effective crisis management and crisis resolution mechanisms. The EU made earnest efforts to mediate between the warring factions: it organised several peace conferences and played a major role in drafting peace plans. Each of these plans collapsed, due to failure to secure agreement of the warring sides. By the autumn of 1995, and in particular following acceptance by the belligerents of a US-brokered peace plan for Bosnia (the Dayton Accord), the EU had effectively been relegated to a supporting role in the conflict resolution process. The conflicts in Bosnia and Kosovo proved Europe's inability to solve its problems on its 'own' (meaning without the military and diplomatic muscle of the US). It also exposed the limitations of the WEU, which was relegated to a minor role in these conflicts, whereas NATO's role became paramount. With hindsight, the conflict in ex-Yugoslavia exposed flaws in the EU's capacity to act effectively in international affairs, namely:

- *the pursuit of independent policies by EU countries*, which weakened the coherence and purpose of CFSP. German unilateral recognition of Croatia and Slovenia gave an impression that Germany was determined to pursue its own goals (an example of 'chain gang diplomacy', where one state takes unilateral action, virtually forcing others to follow suit);

- *the unwillingness or inability of the EU to back tough words with tough action*: the Bosnian crisis in particular showed that there is a fundamental difference between tough talk and determined action. EU countries could agree on broad declarations of principle, but lacked the will or ability to transform words into effective action;
- *conflicts of interest and viewpoint*: there were serious differences of view between EU countries on what to do about Bosnia and Kosovo. For both historical and geographical reasons, Germany and Greece have dissimilar, and conflicting, perspectives on Balkan questions which shaped their views on the crises in Bosnia and Kosovo; Greece refused to countenance the recognition of Macedonia unless it changed its name.

Arguably, the EU's floundering performance as peacemaker in ex-Yugoslavia had as much to do with the complexity and intractability of the problem as with the EU's own shortcomings. Nor should we underestimate the importance of the EU's role in the Balkans. For example, all but 11,000 of the 68,000 troops currently in Bosnia and Kosovo are European (and most are from the EU). The EU played a key role in supporting the democratic opposition in Serbia during the Milosovic regime and is very active in supporting Serbian reconstruction. Perhaps the most important lesson arising from recent EU involvements in international crises is that EU objectives need to be more precisely defined and matched more closely with capabilities. The development of the EDSP and the RRF are in large measure a response to perceived weaknesses of the EU as an actor in European crises. These initiatives seem to be based on a 'new realism' which takes into account the limitations of the EU's capabilities as well as their strengths.

○ The ESDP Takes Shape

Even before the war in Kosovo in 1999 exposed once again the weakness of the EU as an actor in international crises, moves were afoot to strengthen CFSP in ways which went beyond the ToA's provisions. At the EU summit in Poertschach in October 1998, Tony Blair called for 'fresh thinking' on European security, a potentially important development given the UK's erstwhile opposition to many of the ideas for CFSP reform. The defence ministers of EU countries held their first meeting in Vienna in November 1998, with the aim of improving crisis management mechanisms and of strengthening military capabilities. In December 1998, the French and British governments issued the 'St. Mâlo Declaration' which outlined the need for a stronger European defence capability, which would enable Europeans to act without the US (without jeopardising the transatlantic alliance). This initiative was particularly significant because France has tended to favour 'European' defence initiatives whereas the UK has been (and is) strongly committed to 'Euro-Atlanticism' (meaning that that all such initiatives would either involve or have the support of the US). The experience France and the UK gained in collaborating with each other in the Gulf and Balkans may have contributed to a willingness to develop a joint position on defence. The Vienna European Council welcomed the St. Mâlo Declaration and stated that the CFSP must be backed by credible operational capabilities. It invited the German presidency to pursue these aims, for consideration at the Cologne European Council.

A declaration by the Cologne European Council in June 1999 on security and defence resolved to give the EU the necessary means and capabilities to assume its responsibilities on security and defence, including a capacity for autonomous action, backed up by credible military forces, but without prejudice to NATO actions. The Helsinki European Council in December 1999 took several major decisions with regard to CFSP, notably agreeing measures to develop a temporary bureaucratic framework for an ESDP, to create conditions for the Union to eventually run its own military missions and to independently respond to and manage crises (see Table 19.5). In addition to developing military capabilities, it is also developing capabilities in the civilian aspects of crisis management, for example, 5000 police officers by 2003. The Helsinki European Council approved a presidency report on non-military crisis management, which aimed to make more effective use of instruments, such as civil police and medical teams. The High Representative for the CFSP was asked to work on a study to establish a rapid reaction capability for non-military responses to crises.

Table 19.5 The Main Features of the ESDP

- it will give the EU a crisis-management and conflict prevention capability;
- it establishes new political and military structures for EU security and defence (to work with, and in subordination to, existing EU bodies);
- the WEU's crisis management and conflict prevention tasks, plus its Institute for Security Studies and Satellite centre are transferred to it;
- a 60,000 strong EU Rapid Reaction Force (RRF) will be introduced by 2003 (with some elements ready by the end of 2001);
- the RRF is not a European army and contributing states decide on their own deployments;
- the EU intends that RRF operations will be able to draw on NATO assets and capabilities;
- it is viewed as complementary to, but not a rival of, NATO;
- other countries may be invited to participate in ESDP operations.

○ **The New Political and Military Bodies for ESDP**

New political and military bodies have been established within the Council in order to increase the effectiveness of decisionmaking procedures for the day-to-day management of ESDP operations. This new structure is outlined in Figure 19.1.

Figure 19.1 The EU's Crisis Management Command Structure

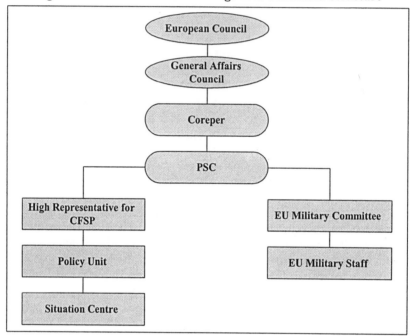

• **The Political and Security Committee (PSC).** This comprises national representatives of senior/ambassadorial level. It deals with all aspects of CFSP, including the ESDP. In the case of a military crisis management operation, it exercises, under the authority of the Council, the political control and strategic direction of the operation. It also forwards guidelines to the military committee and receives military advice from it. The PSC keeps track of the international situation in the areas within the CFSP, helps define policies by drawing up opinions for the Council, either at the request of the Council or on its own initiative, and monitors implementation of agreed policies. It maintains a special link with the High Representative for CFSP and the special representatives. It co-ordinates, supervises and monitors discussions on CFSP and ESDP issues in various working parties, to which it may send guidelines and whose reports it may examine.

- **The EU Military Committee**, comprising chiefs of defence. The EUMC gives military advice, makes recommendations to the PSC and provides direction to the EU military staff. It is the highest military authority within the Council. It has a chairman who is of four-star general rank. In March 2001, Gustav Hägglund, a Finnish general, was chosen to head this committee.
- **The EU Military Staff,** which provides military expertise and support to the ESDP, including the conduct of EU-led military crisis management operations and early warning, situation assessment and strategic planning for Petersberg tasks. Its main operational functions are early warning, situation assessment and strategic planning. Under the direction of the EUMC it provides military expertise to EU bodies, in particular the High representative for CFSP. It also establishes permanent relations with NATO. It identifies and lists European national and multinational forces for EU-led operations co-ordinated with NATO. Its first commander is General Klaus Schuwirth, from Germany, and his deputy Major-General G. Messervy-Whiting, from the UK.

The High Representative for CFSP, Javier Solana, is responsible for developing new structures in the EU and links with NATO.

○ The Rapid Reaction Force

The Cologne, Helsinki and Feira European Councils laid the groundwork for the development by the EU of a capacity to launch and conduct military operations in response to international crises. The Helsinki European Council stated that member states must be able, by 2003, to deploy military forces of up to 50–60 thousand troops within 60 days, sustainable for at least one year and capable of the full range of Petersberg tasks. It stated, however, that this did not imply creation of a European army, a comment which is now routinely reaffirmed in official EU statements. At Helsinki it was agreed that where NATO is not directly involved in a military operation, the EU should have recourse to NATO's assets and capabilities, requiring full co-operation and collaboration between them. It was also agreed that non-EU European NATO members and other interested states might contribute to EU crisis management. Non-EU European NATO members can participate if they so wish in the event of an operation requiring recourse to NATO assets and capabilities. On a decision by the Council, they will be invited to take part in operations where the EU does not use NATO assets. Accession candidates may also be invited by the Council to participate in EU-led operations. There will be arrangements for consultation and participation by other potential partners. To facilitate the association of third countries wishing to be involved in EU military activities, such countries may appoint an officer accredited to the EU military staff to serve as contact.

At the Feira European Council, plans for a 60,000-strong rapid reaction force were approved. All European members of NATO were invited to participate. On 20 November 2000 in Brussels, member states held a Capabilities Commitment Conference, to work out the size and structure of the RRF. All member states with the exception of Denmark agreed to provide troops for the RRF (see Table 19.6), placing 100,000 troops, 400 combat aircraft and 100 ships at the EU's disposal. The UK has pledged 12,500 troops, 18 warships and 72 aircraft, plus various combat support units. Denmark drew attention to protocol no.5 annexed to the ToA, which enables it to opt out of decisions and actions of the Union with defence implications. These commitments will not result in additional military capability. Although the EU can meet the numerical target of 400 aircraft and 100 ships, it is still deficient in heavy lift aircraft, strategic sea transport, satellite intelligence and precision guided munitions. French defence minister Alain Richard predicted that the EU would develop global security responsibilities. However, others saw a more limited role for the RRF, which according to the British defence secretary, Geoff Hoon, would be largely confined to Europe and its immediate backyard (*Times*, 21 November 2000).

Table 19.6 Troop Contributions Offered to the EU Rapid Reaction Force

State	Contribution	State	Contribution
Germany	13,500	Finland	2,000
UK	12,500	Sweden	1,500
France	12,000	Portugal	1,000
Italy	6,000	Belgium	1,000
Spain	6,000	Ireland	1,000
Netherlands	5,000	Luxembourg	100
Greece	3,500	Denmark	Nil
Austria	2,000		

The goals of the EDSP are likely to be difficult to achieve, for several reasons: firstly, the resources to be made available by member states for the EDSP are likely to be inadequate; secondly, there are widely differing capabilities among member states, meaning that the larger member states are likely to dominate decisionmaking; thirdly, 'variable geometry' in this field (not all EU members are NATO members or full members of the WEU) will add further complexities on to an already complex field; fourthly, not all member states are likely to show the same will or readiness to act.

○ The Implications of ESDP for NATO and EU–US Relations

Despite repeated reassurances, some critics of ESDP argue that it could have a disruptive or debilitating effect on NATO. However, the Presidency report presented to and approved by the Nice European Council stated that:

> In developing this autonomous capacity to take decisions and, where NATO as a whole is not engaged, to launch and conduct EU-led military operations in response to international crises, the EU will be able to carry out the full range of Petersberg tasks as defined in the TEU, viz. humanitarian and rescue tasks, peacekeeping tasks and tasks of combat forces in crisis management, including peacemaking. This does not involve the establishment of a European army. The commitment of national resources by member states to such operations will be based on their sovereign decisions. As regards the member states concerned, NATO remains the basis of the collective defence of its members and will continue to play an important role in crisis management. The development of the ESDP will contribute to the vitality of a renewed transatlantic link. This development will also lead to a genuine strategic partnership between the EU and NATO in the management of crises with due regard for the two organisations' decision-making autonomy.

However, the development of ESDP has already shown a capacity to create tension with NATO and in particular with the US and Turkey. US governments have been supportive of policies which would mean that the EU would take on more of the burden of defence, but has been suspicious of anything smacking of an independent European military force detached from NATO, that is, of European 'go it alone' strategies. The US criteria for approval of EU initiatives in the field of defence have been based on the 'three Ds': that is, *no duplication* of assets or capabilities; *no decoupling* from NATO structures; and *no discrimination against non-EU members of NATO*. A similar formula (espoused, for example, by the current NATO Secretary-General, Lord Robertson) is that the European security and defence identity should be based on the three 'I's': *inclusiveness* of all NATO allies; *indivisibility* of the transatlantic link; and *improvement* of capabilities.

On 5 December 2000, US Defense Secretary William Cohen warned that a badly thought out European defence initiative could turn NATO into a 'relic'. The tension with the US over ESDP has arisen in part because of a lurking suspicion that France would like to loosen transatlantic links in favour of an exclusively European defence capability. Although a NATO member, France is outside NATO's military and command structure. There has been a long history of suspicion between France and the US (and indeed the UK) over NATO. The current French government has repeatedly asserted that collective defence remains a NATO responsibility. But it is far more likely that NATO will be called upon for peacekeeping activities than for collective defence, leading to a potential confusion between its roles and those of the RRF. There are still many issues concerning the place of the RRF in European defence structures which still need to be clarified, such as the potential problem of duplication or overlap with NATO. Thus it is envisaged that military planning for operations will largely be carried out by NATO, with the RRF reliant on

NATO for information. It was agreed by the Nice European Council that planning for large-scale operations will be carried out by NATO's Strategic Headquarters Allied Powers Europe (SHAPE). It still not fully clear under what circumstances the RRF would act rather than NATO; or how the relationship between the two organisations will work in practice. At the first joint meeting of EU and NATO foreign ministers in December 2000, Turkey would not agree to allow the EU guaranteed access to NATO military assets and capabilities. Turkey, a staunch NATO member, took strong exception to being excluded from the new defence force. Turkey is seeking to be involved in EU decisionmaking and does not wish to be fobbed off with mere consultations. Plans for the establishment of the RRF have also caused disquiet in some CEECs because of its implications for NATO. The key issues in the ESDP/RRF debate are presented in Table 19.7.

Table 19.7 Arguments For and Against the ESDP and RRF

For

- it will enable the EU to play its role fully on the international stage and to assume its responsibilities in the face of crises;
- it may result in improved co-ordination between member states on peacekeeping operations;
- it will reduce the need to rely so heavily on US military might;
- it enables neutral EU countries to participate in EU peacekeeping operations without compromising their neutrality;
- the EU was ill-prepared to respond to conflicts in Bosnia and Kosovo: this must never happen again.

Against

- it could place severe strains on the NATO alliance and could worsen relations with the US, Turkey and some other European countries;
- it may cause intra-EU conflicts, over the relationship with NATO;
- when 'push comes to shove', will the EU member states deliver on their commitments?
- it will not result in the generation of new military resources;
- it does not really address the US complaint about burden sharing within NATO;
- it is unlikely to conduct operations independent of NATO so what is the point?
- the idea to utilise NATO resources is tantamount to 'asset stripping';
- NATO is already over-stretched and it will add additional resource strains on NATO;
- Europe already has enough, indeed a surfeit of, security organisations.

● CONCLUSION

Both optimists and pessimists can find evidence to support their views on the future of CFSP. Optimists can cite major decisions taken at St Mâlo, Cologne, Helsinki and Nice. They can also point to the establishment of new political and military structures supportive of the ESDP and of the agreement to establish a rapid reaction force. Pessimists might point out that these initiatives may not amount to very much unless there is a will to make them work. Although, in material terms, the Union may have the economic and military *potential* to transform itself into a fully-fledged, post-cold war superpower, it has a long way to go before the chasm of credibility between potential and reality is bridged. The Union's CFSP is likely to continue to be marked by conflict over objectives, variations in commitment, resource inadequacy and over elaborate procedures. Moreover, it still has many 'faces' (the Council presidency; the High-Representative; the commissioner for external relations and the foreign ministers of member states). With regard to CFSP, the ToA and ToN primarily addressed issues centring on improvements to institutional machinery and procedures. But CFSP machinery remains cumbersome and complicated. Moreover, machinery is not an end in itself: commitment to operate the machinery must also be present. Furthermore, if the gap between expectations and capabilities is to be narrowed, the member states will have to increase their defence expenditures.

FURTHER READING

Eliassen, F. (1998), *Foreign and Security Policy in the EU*, Sage, London.

Hill, C (1993), 'The Capability–Expectations Gap, or Conceptualizing Europe's International Role', *Journal of Common Market Studies*, vol. 31, no. 3, pp. 305–28.

Hoffmann, S. (2000), 'Towards a Common European Foreign and Security Policy?', *Journal of Common Market Studies*, vol. 38, no.2, pp. 189–98.

Lodge, J. and Flynn, V. (1998), 'The CFSP After Amsterdam. The Policy Planning and Early Warning Unit', *International Relations*, vol. 14, no. 1, pp. 7–21.

Monar, J. (1997), 'The European Union's Foreign Affairs System After the Treaty of Amsterdam', *European Foreign Affairs Review*, no. 2, pp. 437–454.

Nuttall, S. (2000), *European Foreign Policy*, Oxford University Press, Oxford.

Peterson, J. and Sjursen, H. (1998), *A Common Foreign Policy for Europe?*, Routledge, London.

van den Broek, H. (1996), 'Why Europe Needs a Common Foreign and Security Policy', *European Foreign Affairs Review*, vol. 1, no. 1, pp. 1–5.

Waever, O. (1996), 'On European Security Identities', *Journal of Common Market Studies*, vol. 34, no.1, pp. 103–48.

Council, (2000), *Presidency Report on the European Security and Defence Policy*.

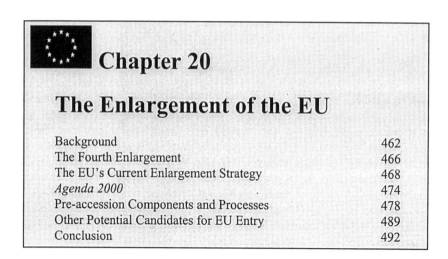

Chapter 20

The Enlargement of the EU

● BACKGROUND

○ Why Are So Many Countries Seeking Entry?

Under the terms of Article 49 of the Treaty on European Union (TEU), any European state which respects the principles of liberty, democracy, respect for human rights and fundamental freedoms and the rule of law may apply for membership of the European Union (although the article does not define what a 'European' state is). Until recently, enlargement could be dealt with by the EU at a fairly leisurely pace: the first enlargement did not occur until 1973, when the UK, Ireland and Denmark acceded. Greece acceded in 1981 and Spain and Portugal in 1986. In each case, there had been long preparatory periods before entry. Greece signed an association agreement in 1961 and applied in 1975. Spain signed an association agreement in 1970 and applied in 1977. Portugal was a member of the European Free Trade Association (EFTA) and also applied in 1977. The accession of Austria, Finland and Sweden in January 1995 was preceded by shorter preparatory periods (see the section on the 'fourth enlargement' below).

By the end of the 1990s, 13 other countries had been accepted as candidates for EU membership and all, with the exception of Turkey, are expected to join in the first decade of this century. Several countries in the Western Balkans which are not yet eligible, were offered the 'perspective' of future membership at the Balkans summit held in Zagreb in November 2000. The EU will eventually, therefore have a membership of more than double that of EU15, with a population of well over 500 million. The next enlargements are likely to be unprecedented in scale, complexity and pace.

Never before has the EU been confronted with the task of absorbing such a large and diverse group of countries in so short a time. Table 20.1 outlines the reasons which have frequently been suggested to explain the rush to join.

Table 20.1 Why Are So Many Countries Seeking Entry into the Union?

- **The removal of cold war prohibitions.** The end of communism removed a barrier to the entry of CEECs. Neutrality was a formidable obstacle to the entry of Austria and Finland during the cold war.
- **The disappearance, or receding attraction, of the alternatives.** Comecon, the communist regional economic bloc, was one of the first casualties of the collapse of communism. EFTA is attracting no new members and is widely regarded as a 'rump' organisation.
- **Fear of marginalisation** and isolation from major developments in Europe. In Central and Eastern Europe, the entry motive is often expressed as part of a wider aspiration to 'rejoin Europe'.
- **Panic of the closing door.** Fear of being left behind in the rush to join.
- **Guaranteed access to EU markets.** Although the EU denies that the SEM has protectionist objectives, removal of trade barriers between EU countries tends to boost intra-EU trade at the expense of trade with the outside world. Non-EU firms, therefore, could lose business through *trade diversion*. Association agreements give countries preferential access to EU markets, but do not give them complete, unqualified access.
- **Insider participation.** Only members are allowed to participate in the EU's decisionmaking processes. Non-members with substantial trading links with the EU have no right to a say in EU decisions of vital concern to them.
- **Access to resource transfers.** When admitted, the CEECs, Malta, Cyprus and Turkey will be net beneficiaries from the EU budget.
- **EU entry is likely to boost inward investment.** The large volume of FDI received by Hungary, the Czech Republic and Poland have no doubt been influenced by their leading positions in the race to join the EU.

The collapse of communism in 1989/90 precipitated a wave of applications for membership from Central and East European countries (CEECs). Even if communist countries had been willing or able to apply for EU membership, they would have been deemed ineligible on political and economic grounds. The collapse was so sudden and unexpected that little prior attention had been given by the EU to the question of its future relationship with the CEECs in a post-cold war world. During the communist period, official contacts between the EU and the Soviet bloc had been minimal, due to ideological hostility and low levels of trade. With the exception of Yugoslavia and Romania (which had trade agreements with the

Union), communist European countries were at the bottom of the EU's system of trade preferences. The EU employed a phalanx of tariff and non-tariff barriers to keep out goods from these countries. The changes brought about by Mikhail Gorbachev resulted in the signing of bilateral trade and economic co-operation agreements of modest scope between the EU and several CEECs between 1988 and 1990.

Following decisions taken at the 'G7' summit in Paris in July 1989, the Commission was given responsibility for co-ordinating Western aid to Poland and Hungary, through the PHARE programme (see below). PHARE was later extended to other former communist European countries, although it excludes all former Soviet republics with the exception of Latvia, Lithuania and Estonia. A separate EU programme, known as 'TACIS' (see below) was set up in July 1992 to provide aid to former Soviet republics in the Commonwealth of Independent States (CIS). The EU's assumption of a special relationship with CEECs can be justified in terms of enlightened self-interest: for reasons of geographical proximity, the EU would find it difficult to insulate itself from the consequences of economic collapse and political instability in the region. EU15 shares land borders with several CEECs (Finland with Russia; Germany with Poland and the Czech Republic; Austria with the Czech Republic, Slovakia, Hungary and Slovenia; Italy with Slovenia). Moreover, from the beginning of the post-communist era, it was apparent that most CEECs were not interested in a 'special relationship' with the EU: instead they sought full EU membership. On 1 April 1994, Hungary became the first ex-communist country to formally apply for EU entry. Nine other CEECs – Poland, Romania, Slovakia, Estonia, Latvia, Lithuania, Bulgaria, the Czech Republic and Slovenia – subsequently applied.

The EU also had suitors from the south as well as the east. Cyprus and Malta applied for membership in 1993. Malta subsequently withdrew, then re-activated, its application and was reaccepted as a candidate in February 1999. Turkey's application was rejected in 1989. Turkey continued to press for membership and in December 1999 the Helsinki European Council added it to the list of candidates, although with stringent conditions. The current candidates therefore comprise ten CEECs and three Mediterranean states (Cyprus, Malta and Turkey). Questions relating to the next round of enlargements can be divided into *Who, When, How* and *What if?*:

- *'Who'* has largely been settled, for the time being (although the issue may soon be raised again in relation to countries in the Western Balkans).
- *'When'* has still to be firmly and unequivocally decided.
- *'How'* has been addressed by various Commission and Council statements and by launch of a formal accession process.
- *'What if'* (that is, the implications of enlargement) still raises many unanswered questions.

and rising unemployment encouraged Finland to take a clos
Union. Norway previously applied in 1969 and was accepted fo
in 1972. However, it withdrew its application following :
Norway has done well economically since its decision not to j
1972. Therefore, fears of missing the EU boat were still widely regarded as
unfounded. Referenda on entry were held in each of the applicant countries in
1994. The votes in favour of entry were: 66.4% in Austria, 56.9% in Finland
and 53.1% in Sweden. Only the Norwegians rejected entry, albeit by a narrow
margin, with 52.2% voting against. The accession of Austria, Finland and
Sweden increased the EU's population by about 6%; its GDP by about 7%, its
GDP per capita by about 1% and its area by about 37%. It extended the
boundaries of the EU to the Arctic Circle and to the borders of Russia. There
were several important institutional and policy implications of the fourth
enlargement. It increased the number of working languages from nine to 11;
the number of votes in the Council from 76 to 87 and the number of votes
needed to block decisions based on qualified majority voting (QMV) from 23
to 26. The 1995 entrants currently have 11 Council votes out of 87, over
twice as many as they would be entitled to if votes were allocated strictly in
accordance with population size.

The 1995 entrants are net contributors to the EU budget, although by less
than was originally estimated. There was a rebate on entrants' budgetary
contributions for the first three years of membership (amounting to €3.6
billion between 1995 and 1998), in order to offset the effects of alignment of
the entrants' higher farm prices to EU levels. A regional aid programme was
introduced for the remote and sparsely populated regions of the Nordic
countries and for Austria's Burgenland region. The entrants were required to
phase out subsidy programmes which conflicted with the Common
Agricultural Policy (CAP). They sought to ensure that entry would not be at
the price of lowering their standards in relation to the environment, consumer
safety and other policies. A deal which in effect enabled the new entrants to
maintain their high environmental and safety standards was therefore agreed.
The entrants indicated that the TEU provisions on common foreign and
security policy were broadly acceptable. Austria's application in 1989 was
made on the understanding that Austria would maintain its neutral status. But
the concept of neutrality has changed in the post-cold war era and all three
1995 entrants have observer status in the Western European Union and have
agreed to participate in the EU's rapid reaction force (see Chapter 19).

Sweden, Finland and Austria have made their presence felt in the EU. For
example, they have tended to align themselves with other rich 'northern'
states in opposing increases in resource transfers to poorer EU members.
None has fundamentally altered its neutralist stance. Nordic traditions of open
government and of financial probity may have contributed to an increased

constitution did not allow such referendums. The Commission and the European Parliament (EP) have generally been supportive of enlargement, although the candidate countries have frequently complained of the Commission's tough negotiating stance in enlargement talks.

The debate between those wishing to give priority to pursuit of deeper integration between member states and those wishing to give priority to widening the EU's membership intensified following the end of the cold war. The main arguments in this debate are outlined in Table 20.3. A key issue between wideners and deepeners has been that of *motive*: for example, deepeners have accused wideners of pursuing a hidden agenda, aimed at slowing down processes of deepening and at transforming the Union into a loose confederation. Conversely, wideners have accused deepeners of insularity – that is, of failing to adjust to post-cold war realities and of perceiving 'Europe' to mean 'Western Europe'.

Table 20.3 Deepening versus Widening

The Case for Deepening

- the momentum of integration must be maintained, otherwise the whole process will stall;
- it is better to create strong foundations for the EU before other countries are allowed in;
- premature entry of CEECs would impose a burden on the EU budget;
- precipitate widening could make the EU more inward looking and preoccupied with problems arising from its heterogeneous membership;
- extensive widening would exacerbate conflict within the EU, by increasing the number and range of problem issues.

The Case for Widening

- it is inevitable that many other European states will join the EU. It therefore seems reasonable to delay further deepening, so that new members can play a full role in the EU's development;
- not to widen would be to betray the principles on which the EU was founded (that is, it is open to any democratic European state);
- the EU would no longer be confined to Western Europe, and would become a truly European formation;
- not to widen would be to miss a historic opportunity created by the end of the cold war to end the division of Europe once and for all.

As a means of reconciling these positions, another possibility mooted in the early 1990s was that applicants could be asked to join a separate organisation, closely linked to the EU, as a necessary prelude or preparation for full entry (the *waiting-room approach*). The European Economic Area was often cited as having the potential to perform this function. Another suggestion was that East European countries could be encouraged to set up their own 'Economic Union', with the possibility that the Western and Eastern 'Unions' would merge once disparities in economic performance and wealth between them had narrowed (the *parallel integration approach*). It was also suggested that some countries might be offered *partial membership* (for example, entailing exclusion from the CAP and structural funds and from provisions on migration). Aspirants were unenthusiastic about these options, because they were wary of being fobbed off with forms of second-class membership. But ideas for a 'waiting room', parallel integration, or partial membership may have value when considering future relationships between the EU and states which are unlikely to be admitted for the foreseeable future. (for example, Russia, Ukraine, Moldova, Belarus, Georgia and Armenia).

Both sides in the 'widening versus deepening' debate can claim some victories, because both widening and deepening are on the EU's current agenda. Indeed, the either/or debate was effectively ended by an emerging consensus that the EU must both deepen *and* widen. The decision to enlarge the Union is now irrevocable and therefore the current enlargement debate is concerned with the practicalities, timing and implications of enlargement rather than its inherent wisdom. Recent enlargements have actually quickened the pace of deepening rather than slowing it down.

- **Tensions between the applicants and the EU.** Although the candidate countries are naturally keen to accede as quickly as possible, the EU has repeatedly stated that the quality of enlargement preparations will not be sacrificed for speed. It has therefore insisted that the candidates embark upon thorough and comprehensive entry preparations. Moreover, the EU now recognises that it must also make adjustments in order to prepare itself for the next enlargements. The perceived unreadiness of the applicants for membership and concerns about the 'absorption capacity' of the EU have combined to ensure that the applicants will be admitted only after meeting very stringent political and economic conditions. Without adequate preparatory measures, a greatly enlarged, more heterogeneous EU could slow down the pace of integration, by making the objectives of political, economic and monetary union more difficult to achieve. Without reforms of key EU policies and without transition arrangements (meaning that new entrants may not be granted immediate access to certain EU policies and funds) entry of the CEECs and Turkey would require a massive expansion of the EU budget.

Many candidate countries have a GDP per capita of less than half of the EU average and most have small populations. In Chapter 8 we noted that 51 out of the 53 CEEC regions have a per capita GDP of below 75% of the EU average (see p. 240). A recent Eurostat study estimated that, if all ten CEECs were admitted, GDP per capita in the EU would fall to about 87% of the EU15 average (Eurostat, 1999). Table 20.4 below provides some indication of the implications of the accession of the 13 candidate countries. It shows that the GDP per head in these countries is considerably below the EU average and that most have very large farm sectors which would strain an unreformed CAP to breaking point. Within the ten CEECs, GDP per capita is about 2.6 times lower than in the EU. Turkey is both poor and has a large population. Future enlargement also raises crucial issues of effective Union governance, an issue which the Treaty of Nice (ToN) seeks to address.

Table 20.4 The Candidate Countries: Economic Indicators, 2000

(1) Country	(2) Pop. (m.)	(3) €/ Inhabitant (PPS)	(4) (3) as % of EU av.	(5) Av. inflation	(6) FDI net inflow % of GDP	(7) Employed in agriculture (%)
Bulgaria	8.3	4,700	22	2.6	6.1	26.6
Cyprus	0.7	17,100	81	1.3	2.1	9.3
Czech R.	10.3	12,500	59	2.0	9.1	5.2
Estonia	1.4	7,800	36	4.6	4.6	8.8
Hungary	10.1	10,700	51	10.0	2.9	7.1
Latvia	2.4	5,800	27	2.4	5.8	15.3
Lithuania	3.7	6,200	29	0.8	4.5	20.2
Malta	0.4	n.a.	n.a	2.1	3.4	1.8
Poland	38.7	7,800	37	7.2	4.3	18.1
Romania	22.5	5,700	27	45.8	2.4	41.7
Slovakia	5.4	10,300	49	10.6	3.7	7.4
Slovenia	2.0	15,000	71	6.1	0.2	10.2
Turkey	64.3	5,900	28	64.9	0.4	41.3

Source: Commission, *Enlargement Strategy Paper* (2000).

- **Tensions between the EU and 'excluded' European countries.** Until Turkey was finally accepted as a candidate in December 1999, the EU's rejection of Turkey's desire for membership placed considerable strain on relations between Turkey and the EU. Strains are also discernible in the EU's relations with 'outsider' countries such as Russia, Ukraine and Belarus, even though they have not applied for EU membership. The EU may be impelled to offer these countries a special relationship which falls short of membership but which is meaningful enough to defuse 'outsider resentment'.

○ **General Principles Underpinning the Enlargement Strategy**

The unprecedented scale of applications for EU entry in recent years has forced the EU to give serious consideration to the development of a coherent strategy to replace its erstwhile *ad hoc* approach to enlargement. This strategy was developed and refined between 1993 and 2000. The evolution of this strategy was marked by key decisions taken at various European Councils and by publication of major Commission reports, notably *Agenda 2000* (Commission, 1997). *Agenda 2000* outlined the broad perspectives for the development of the EU and its policies beyond 2000 and the impact of enlargement on the EU as a whole.

Table 20.5 Key Events in the Current Enlargement Process

June 1993: Copenhagen European Council set the criteria for entry.

December 1995: Madrid European Council decided that negotiations would commence after the conclusion of the 1996 IGC.

June 1997: Amsterdam European Council. ToA agreed.

July 1997: *Agenda 2000*, the Commission's blueprint for enlargement.

December 1997: the Luxembourg European Council endorsed *Agenda 2000* and announced an *accession process* involving all CEEC applicants plus Cyprus, to be launched on 30 March 1998.

30 March 1998: negotiations begin for 'first-wave' countries.

October 1999: Commission proposal for a 'multispeed' accession process;

December 1999: Helsinki European Council adds Turkey to the list of candidate countries, under stringent conditions.

February 2000: negotiations begin for 'second-wave' countries.

December 2000: IGC agrees institutional arrangements for an enlarged Union and incorporates these into the ToN.

The Union's enlargement strategy seeks to address four central issues:

- **Financial and institutional implications.** Consideration of the implications of future enlargement centre on the EU's capacity to absorb such a large, diverse and largely poor group of candidates without straining the EU's financial resources and institutional framework to breaking point.
- **Conditions for membership.** The EU has repeatedly affirmed that applicant countries must accept the *acquis communautaire* and that enlargement must not jeopardise the 'forward movement' of EU integration. This means that the applicant countries must meet stringent economic and political conditions, such as compatibility with the SEM, political stability, maintenance of democracy and respect for human rights. These conditions were spelt out at various European Councils (in particular, Copenhagen, June 1993 and Madrid, June 1995), in the Treaty of Amsterdam (ToA) and in *Agenda 2000*. The Copenhagen European Council marked a watershed in EU policy because it accepted that the CEECs would join the EU and focused on the conditions for membership. It stated that membership presupposed the candidate's ability to take on the obligations of membership, including adherence to the aims of political, economic and monetary union. Another

key consideration was the capacity of the EU to absorb new members, while maintaining the momentum of integration.

• **Preparations for membership.** The Commission has drawn up detailed plans to help candidate countries prepare themselves for entry. In June 1994, the European Council in Corfu instructed the Commission to prepare a report outlining an accession strategy for associated CEECs. The report, presented to the European Council in Essen in December 1994, accorded the association agreements a central role in the accession process. In May 1995, the Commission published a White Paper on the subject of Eastern enlargement, focusing on the measures thought necessary to adapt the economies of the CEECs to the SEM (Commission, 1995). Its *pre-accession strategy* for associated CEECs included proposals for economic alignment, requiring CEECs to take measures to bring their standards and administrative structures in line with EU practice. The White Paper did not, however, include a specific timetable for membership. Nor did it deal with the problems of agriculture, environmental or social policy, except where these were directly related to SEM issues. The strategy was accepted by the European Council in Cannes in June 1995. *Agenda 2000*, published in July 1997, provided a more comprehensive analysis and strategy for enlargement.

• **Time-scale and sequencing.** The current enlargement strategy is based on the principle of *differentiation*, meaning that each application will be treated on its merits and therefore candidate countries may well enter the Union at different times, although it seems likely that most will be admitted in waves. The EU has insisted that applications must involve separate negotiations. But although the fourth enlargement also involved separate negotiations with each applicant, these took place in parallel. The same approach is being adopted in relation to the current accession negotiations.

The *wave approach* is a variant of the 'concentric circles' model of enlargement once advanced by Jacques Delors. In 1997, applicant countries were divided by the Commission into two groups, which became known as the 'first wave' and the 'second wave': first-wave countries were deemed to have made most progress in meeting entry requirements and were placed on a fast negotiations track; second-wave countries had made less progress and therefore the process towards entry would proceed more slowly for these countries. However, this approach caused considerable resentment among 'second-wave' countries, and arguably engendered complacency among countries included in the first wave. Following a recommendation from the Commission, the 'two-wave' approach was, at least formally, abandoned by the Helsinki European Council in December 1999 in favour of the principle that each application would be judged on its merits. The Nice European Council confirmed that countries lagging behind could catch up with the front runners. But it remains likely that applicants will accede in groups rather than

at these groups are likely to closely resemble the Commission's
d second wave categories (although Malta, which reapplied in
ced in the second-wave category but is making good progress
towards accession). Turkey is currently excluded from either category.

● *AGENDA 2000*

○ Background to the Commission's 'Blueprint for Enlargement'

In July 1997, the month following the Amsterdam European Council which
agreed the ToA, the Commission submitted *Agenda 2000* to the Council and
EP, together with opinions on each membership application. The document
was the Commission's response to a request by the Madrid European Council
to submit a paper on enlargement after conclusion of the 1996/7
intergovernmental conference (IGC). It was based on recognition that
enlargement had major implications for EU spending and for major policies,
such as the CAP and regional and social policy. *Agenda 2000* continues to be
the nearest thing to a blueprint for enlargement which the Union has yet
produced. It contains the Commission's recommendations for Union finances
for the 2000–06 period in the light of the Union's spending policies and
future enlargement. The main thrust of these recommendations was that,
before accession, candidate countries needed to prepare themselves by
adjusting their policies to those of the EU. It was made clear that the basis of
accession would be the *acquis* of the EU as it existed at the time of
enlargement. It recognised that meeting the *acquis* would be a difficult and
costly process, requiring investment in a broad range of policy fields and
restructuring and upgrading of infrastructures. In its interim report on
enlargement to the Madrid European Council, the Commission had stated that
transition arrangements might be needed in some areas such as agriculture
and the movement of persons, but that these transition periods would be
limited in scope and duration.

The Commission stated that the timetable for accession would depend
primarily on the progress made by individual countries in adopting,
implementing and enforcing the *acquis*. It sought also to reinforce the pre-
accession strategy by bringing together the various forms of support provided
by the EU into a single framework and by familiarising the applicants with
EU policies and procedures, through their participation in some EU
programmes. There would also be pre-accession financial assistance, for
agricultural development (€500 million a year) and for structural aid (€1
billion). During the accession negotiations, the applicants' progress in
adopting the *acquis* would be regularly reviewed on the basis of Commission

reports. In *Agenda 2000*, the Commission also proposed the establishment of a *European Conference*, to provide an opportunity for consultations on a broad range of issues in relation to a common foreign and security policy (CFSP) and justice and home affairs. It would provide a forum for all applicant states, including Turkey, and the EU, to discuss matters of common concern, such as relations with CIS countries and European security, the fight against organised crime and illegal immigration. The conference meets at either ministerial or at heads of state or government level. The fourth conference, held at ministerial level, was held in Sochaux, France in November 2000. It was attended by all ministers from EU15, all applicant states, plus Switzerland. A fifth conference, held at heads of government or state level, was held in Nice in December. The Nice European Council proposed that countries in the Western Balkans and also EFTA countries should be invited to attend future conferences.

○ The *Agenda 2000* Impact Study

The *Agenda 2000* impact study favoured a *gradual* process of adaptation as the only realistic way, given the difficulty of absorbing so many CEECs. It also argued that candidate countries had to shoulder the main effort required during the pre-accession period, although some technical and financial assistance would be provided by the EU. It further argued that progress should also be linked to the gradual opening up of EU markets, which would be preferable to having long transitional periods after accession. Some previous enlargements have involved long transition periods for new entrants (for example, Greece, Spain and Portugal were not fully integrated into the CAP. There were quotas on Iberian iron and steel for seven years and restricted migration rights for five years). However, previous entrants were given full access to the structural funds. Exclusion of CEEC countries from access to the structural funds and the CAP would, in the light of the EU's aim to narrow regional imbalances within the Union, be a glaring anomaly: it would mean that whereas poor regions in Western Europe would receive regional aid, eastern regions would not.

- **Institutional implications.** *Agenda 2000* recognised that the institutional reforms introduced in the ToA would be insufficient to cope with the next enlargements. At the Amsterdam European Council at which the ToA was agreed, key institutional issues were avoided or postponed, such as the weighting of the votes in the Council and the future size of the Commission. A protocol on the institutions with the prospect of enlargement was attached to the ToA, requiring the member states to resolve the issue of the weighting of votes prior to the next enlargement. It also stated that at least one year before EU membership exceeded 20, a further IGC would be established to comprehensively review the composition and functioning of the institutions. It recognised that the increase in the number of small states would have significant institutional implications and argued that if EU decisionmaking was not to be paralysed, there was a need to extend QMV and to alter the basis on which votes are allocated in order to avoid 'small-state dominance'. It also favoured a review of appointments and seats on EU bodies.

• **Policy implications.** *Agenda 2000* recognised that the development of some EU policies might be impeded by the difficulties likely to be experienced by some acceding countries in attempting to meet the EU's standards. It argued that enlargement was likely to result in more flexible approaches to EU environmental regulation with a stronger emphasis on implementation and enforcement. It also examined the effects of enlargement on various structural policies. It stated that with enlargement, economic and social cohesion should be taken into account more than ever in the formulation and implementation of EU policies. It recognised that 'adjustment strains' from exposure of the candidate countries to competition could be considerable in the agricultural sector, leading to the shedding of labour in these countries. It also recognised that extension of the CAP in its present form to these countries would create difficulties, not least by stimulating surplus production. It argued that enlargement would increase the Union's pool of labour and could place a downward pressure on employment, due to increased competition. It recognised that economic and monetary union (EMU) created a major challenge to acceding countries, as they would be expected to implement the *acquis* in this area, even though most would not initially participate in EMU. In relation to justice and home affairs, it argued that enlargement would provide opportunities to address common problems.

• **Financial implications.** *Agenda 2000* noted that if existing criteria for eligibility for structural aid were to be applied to acceding countries, it would mean a large shortfall in the EU budget. However, it further noted that in the light of the proposed reform of the structural funds, and taking into account that the new members would be gradually integrated into the structural aid system and have limited absorptive capacity, increases in funding would be sustainable without a major impact on the total level of structural aid to existing member states. It noted that massive investment in the acceding countries would be required, in public utility sectors and by enterprises. With regard to other internal policies (for example, research and technological development (RTD), education and training, trans-European-networks, environmental policy and so on). It argued that there was a danger that funding would be spread too thinly. Therefore, finance should be concentrated on fewer programmes of proven benefit. Even so, these areas would require more than proportional increases in expenditure, in relation to the size of the acceding countries. *Agenda 2000* estimated that extension of the CAP could add about €11 billion a year to the EU budget. However, fisheries would not be seriously affected, because the candidate countries have small fisheries sectors. It also estimated that there could be an increase in administrative expenditure for the institutions, resulting from the introduction of new languages and the increase in administrative tasks. In addition to identifying possible costs, it also pointed out some possible positive economic effects of enlargement, such as expansion of the SEM and an increase in the EU's pool of human and natural resources.

○ The Candidates' 'Readiness for Entry'

The Commission's opinions in *Agenda 2000* utilised the Copenhagen criteria in judging the candidate's readiness for entry. In April 1996, the Commission sent out identical questionnaires, comprising over 1000 questions, to each of the candidate countries. The Commission judged that none fully satisfied all of the Copenhagen criteria. It noted that nine of the ten CEEC candidates satisfied the *political* criteria (the exception being Slovakia), while certain countries had made progress towards satisfying the *economic* criteria. The Copenhagen economic criteria comprised an assessment of progress in establishing a functioning market economy and the capacity to cope with competitive pressures inside the EU. None met all the economic criteria, although Hungary and Poland were closest, with the Czech Republic and Slovenia not far behind. Although none would be likely to meet the criteria for EMU, this was not regarded as an obstacle to accession. The report also identified weaknesses in the judicial and administrative capacities of the candidate countries. It recommended opening negotiations with the CEEC candidates in early 1998, together with Cyprus. The Commission would report regularly to the European Council on the progress made, with the first report being submitted at the end of 1998 and annually thereafter.

○ The Response to *Agenda 2000*

The Luxembourg European Council in December 1997 endorsed *Agenda 2000* and launched an accession process for 11 countries, in accordance with the Commission's recommendations (Malta had not yet applied and Turkey had then not been accepted as a candidate country). This meant opening accession negotiations with six countries initially (Hungary, the Czech Republic, Poland, Slovenia, Estonia and Cyprus) and at the same time preparing for negotiations with the other five (Romania, Slovakia, Latvia, Lithuania and Bulgaria). It also opened up some EU programmes (for example, education, training and research) to applicant states, on a case-by-case basis. The report was naturally greeted favourably by the six countries placed in the fast track for accession and with disappointment by the other five. The main criticisms of the report were that it divided the applicant states into two groups; that it did not fully address the issue of institutional reform of the EU; and that the budgetary implications of enlargement were not given their due weight.

The Luxembourg European Council also addressed the issue of Cyprus. Cyprus has been divided since 1974 into Greek and Turkish zones and at present there seems little possibility of an end to the division of the island. Put bluntly, Greek Cyprus favours a united Cyprus with a single sovereignty whereas Turkish Cyprus favours a confederal Cyprus, with Greek and Turkish sovereign entities. The choice facing the EU therefore is whether or not to admit a divided Cyprus or to delay its admission until the problem is solved. The Luxembourg European Council affirmed that accession negotiations would contribute positively to the search for a political solution to the Cyprus problem and requested that the government of Cyprus include Turkish Cypriot representatives in the accession negotiating delegation. The Helsinki European Council in December 1999 stated that if no settlement was reached by the completion of accession negotiations, this would not be a precondition for entry. This decision was no doubt influenced by the threat of the Greek government to veto CEEC accessions if the accession of Cyprus is delayed. At the time of writing, Greek- and Turkish-Cypriots had made little progress towards a settlement. Some Turkish Cypriot leaders were threatening to seek integration of the Turkish part of the island with Turkey if Greek Cyprus was admitted to the EU on its own.

● PRE-ACCESSION COMPONENTS AND PROCESSES

○ **Components**

The main components of the Union's pre-accession strategy are:
- accession partnerships;
- association agreements;
- financial and expert assistance;
- participation of the candidates in Union programmes and agencies;
- structured dialogue between the EU and the candidates; and
- regular Commission reports on the candidates.

● **Accession partnerships**. As a result of the Luxembourg European Council, a new legal instrument known as the *accession partnership* (AP) was created for each applicant country. The current accession partnerships were adopted in December 1999 for the ten CEECs and in March 2000 for Cyprus and Malta. The Council agreed an accession partnership for Turkey in

December 2000. Each AP sets out priority areas for further work identified from the Commission's opinions and the financial assistance from the EU available to solve these problems. This means close bilateral links with each CEEC. Accession partnerships involve: firstly, precise commitments on the part of the applicant country, relating in particular to democracy, macro-economic stabilisation and nuclear safety as well as a National Programme for the Adoption of the *acquis* (an NPAA). Each candidate country prepares an NPAA, which indicates the resources and timetable needed to meet accession priorities. The Commission assesses each NPAA in its regular reports on candidate countries; and secondly, mobilisation of resources available to the EU for preparing applicant countries for accession. The Commission reports regularly to the European Council on the progress made in fulfilling the individual AP targets and also makes recommendations concerning when accession negotiations should start.

- **Association agreements**. It was agreed at the special European Council in Dublin in April 1990 that association (or 'Europe') agreements should be offered to certain CEECs. These are also known as *second-generation* agreements because they replace the agreements signed between 1988 and 1990. These offer more generous terms than the earlier agreements and also contain explicit political provisions. In each of the Europe agreements, the CEEC's aspiration to join the EU at some unspecified date is explicitly recognised. The EU has signed Europe agreements with all ten CEEC candidates. Each is valid for ten years. Such agreements have to be ratified by the EP and by the national parliaments of the member states. They consist of four elements: (1) promotion of freer trade between the signatories; (2) industrial, technical and scientific co-operation; (3) financial assistance; and (4) a mechanism for political dialogue. To foster implementation of the agreements, three sets of institutions have been established: association councils; association committees and joint parliamentary committees (JPCs). Association councils are composed of EU foreign ministers and representatives from the applicant state plus the enlargement commissioner. Their principal function is to ratify agreements and position papers worked out by the association committees, which comprise Council representatives, and representatives of the associate countries and of the Commission. The committees meet once or twice a year. Each JPC consists of 15 MEPs and an equal number of MPs from the associated country. JPCs meet twice a year.

The agreements grant the CEECs free trade in industrial goods over ten years. Market access provisions are weighted in favour of the CEECs in that the EU has agreed to reduce its import barriers more quickly than the CEEC signatory. Negotiations for the agreements led to fierce haggling over details, due to pressure by EU industrial and agricultural lobbies. The lobbies argued that the lower labour costs and lower environmental standards in the CEECs give these countries unfair trade advantages. In the agreements, sensitive industrial sectors are subject to transitional arrangements. The agreements also contain safeguards against disruption of EU markets. Mainline agricultural items (cereals, beef, lamb, dairy products) remain protected by the CAP. The European Councils held in Copenhagen and Corfu both endorsed a more rapid opening of the EU's market than anticipated in the agreements and favoured early-warning mechanisms before anti-dumping or similar measures were introduced.

• **Financial and expert assistance.** Programmes financed through the EU budget embrace technical assistance, infrastructure investment and humanitarian and emergency aid. The PHARE programme is the principal mechanism through which the EU has supported the transition of the CEECs to democracy and the market economy. It is also now the main financial tool of the pre-accession strategy for the CEEC applicants (see Table 20.6). PHARE (Poland and Hungary: Aid for Economic Restructuring) has kept its original name, even though it now includes 13 CEECs (that is, the ten candidate countries, plus Albania, Bosnia and Macedonia (FYROM)). It is now viewed largely as *accession-driven*, focusing on institution building, investment support and assisting the candidates to implement the *acquis*.

Table 20.6 PHARE Expenditure: 1990–1998 (€ million)

Country	Commitments	Contracts	Payments
Albania	493	348	316
Bosnia	282	207	152
Bulgaria	747	518	479
Czech Republic	390	246	196
Estonia	163	117	95
FYROM (Macedonia)	167	128	94
Hungary	864	587	567
Latvia	207	150	115
Lithuania	272	197	146
Poland	1,732	1,386	1,251
Romania	972	676	598
Slovakia	253	149	133
Slovenia	131	96	78
Ex-Czechoslovakia	233	229	229
Multicountry	881	701	545
Horizontal programmes	1,105	964	594
Total	**8,891**	**6,697**	**5,589**

Source: PHARE Programme Annual Report 1998, COM (2000) 183, March 2000.

Institution building embraces participation in some EU programmes, technical assistance and twinning (e.g., the secondment of EU practitioners to institutions in the candidate countries). Investment support accounts for about

70% of the PHARE budget in the candidate countries. For 2000–06, PHARE funding will be about €11 billion. PHARE operates through indicative programmes agreed between the Commission and the government of the recipient state. The operation of PHARE has been widely criticised for being slow and bureaucratic, with long gaps between applications and disbursements. During 1997, 69 monitoring and assessment reports on PHARE programmes were issued, covering 22 sectors and 119 programmes. These assessment reports pointed to the need for improvements in programme and project design, for simpler management structures and for more clearly defined ownership of projects. In 1999, a Court of Auditors report (no. 5/99) on the PHARE cross border co-operation programme cited poor co-ordination, over-centralised management and low rates of disbursement to explain the rather modest impact of the programme at project level. Table 20.7 outlines the main strengths and weaknesses attributed to PHARE.

Table 20.7 Strengths and Weaknesses of PHARE

Strengths

- it is the single largest source of know-how transfer to CEEC candidates;
- it has made a particular contribution to areas of little interest to other aid donors, such as the development of national statistical services and customs offices; cross-border and multicountry programmes;
- it has developed a flexible approach to programming, allowing it to adapt to changing political and economic circumstances.

Weaknesses

- priorities and criteria for selection of programmes have been too broadly defined, meaning that resources have been stretched too thinly;
- the fragmentation of PHARE's efforts has limited its performance;
- spending pressures have led to a strong emphasis on financial and procedural control rather than on substantive performance;
- poor implementation has led to the weakening of the impact of programmes.

The new focus of PHARE is leading to changes in operational management, towards greater decentralisation, transparency and concentration of funds. Decisions on PHARE projects are increasingly being taken in the candidate countries. In each of the ten candidate countries, a central financing and contracting unit has been established to handle tendering, contracting and payments. New procedures have also been introduced to make funding procedures more rigorous. Other new measures to improve implementation include attempts to avoid the spread of funds over many agencies. Fewer but larger projects are now being financed, with a minimum size of €2–3 million. The accession-driven nature of PHARE has meant emphasis on new policy priorities, such as justice and home affairs, which was one of four sectors identified as priorities for support under twinning (the others being finance, agriculture and the environment). A new PHARE cross-border co-operation programme was established in December 1998. New forms of pre-accession aid came into effect at the start of 2000, entitled ISPA (instrument for structural policies for pre-accession) with a budget of €1 billion a year and SAPARD, which provides support of €500 million a year for sustainable agriculture and rural development. There is also a European Investment Bank pre-accession facility. In 2000, EIB loans to CEEC applicants totalled €2.9 billion. Other mechanisms for providing financial and expert assistance apply to Cyprus, Malta and Turkey. In Berlin in March 1999, the European Council laid out new financial perspectives for the EU for 2000–06, which contain financial commitments to new member states: €22 billion is to be allocated for pre-accession support in this period.

• **Participation in Union programmes and agencies.** The applicants are given opportunities to participate in Union programmes, for example in the fields of education, vocational training, youth, culture, research, energy, environment, SMEs and public health, as they progressively adopt the *acquis*. This serves to familiarise applicant countries and their citizens with EU policies and working methods. However, it does not give applicants decisionmaking power with regard to these policies.

• **The structured dialogue.** The structured dialogue includes regular multilateral meetings between ministers from candidate countries and the European Council and Council. Heads of state or government of the candidate countries are invited to attend the second day of European Council meetings; there are twice yearly meetings with EU foreign ministers on the second day of the General Affairs Council; and annual joint ministerial meetings between EU and candidate country ministers on specific policy fields.

• **Regular reports.** In these reports, the Commission evaluates progress on political and economic reform in the candidate countries, using the yardstick of the Copenhagen criteria. It evaluates the capacity of each candidate to implement the *acquis* and prepares composite papers for the Council, containing a synthesis of the reports and a series of recommendations, plus updates on the negotiations. All the candidates (with the exception of Turkey) have been judged to have met the political criteria (although in some cases with the qualification that more progress needed to be made in protecting human rights and minorities). Meeting the economic criteria, however, is proving a more daunting task for most candidates.

The Commission's 1999 report noted that some second-wave countries, notably Slovakia, had made good progress since the 1998 report, whereas some 'first wave' countries (especially the Czech Republic) had lost momentum (Commission, 1999). The report argued that in 2000 negotiations should be opened with all candidates that met the political criteria for membership and that were proved ready to take the necessary measures to comply with the economic criteria, although it also argued that the opening of negotiations with Bulgaria and Romania should be conditional: in Bulgaria's case on further economic reform and reform of its nuclear power industry; in Romania's case on reform of childcare institutions. The report argued that transition periods in relation to the single market should be few and short, but in areas requiring considerable adaptation and important financial outlays (such as the environment, energy and infrastructure), transition arrangements could be much longer, providing that candidates demonstrated their commitment to catching up in these areas. It also argued that the Helsinki European Council should commit itself to be ready to decide from 2002 on the accession of candidates fulfilling all the necessary criteria.

The Commission's proposal was accepted by the Helsinki European Council in December 1999, which affirmed that the accession process now comprises 13 candidate countries within a single framework and that candidates should participate in the process on an equal footing and would be judged on their own merits. It decided to begin negotiations with Romania, Slovakia, Latvia, Lithuania, Bulgaria and Malta on the conditions for their entry into the EU. It stated that candidates now brought into the negotiating process would have the possibility to catch up with those already in negotiations if they have made sufficient progress. It expected to be in a position to welcome new member states from the end of 2002.

The Commission's November 2000 report judged that all candidates except Turkey continued to meet the political criteria. It also noted some positive developments regarding treatment of minorities, although the Roma continued to face widespread discrimination. It noted that, with few exceptions, the economic performance of the candidates had improved since 1999. Although the differentiation between first and second waves of entrants has now been officially abandoned, Table 20.8 below shows that the countries once designated as likely to be in the first wave of candidates to enter the EU are still making better progress than those once designated as second wave, with the exception of Malta. However, progress towards accession is a highly dynamic process and it is by no means certain that all first-wave countries will enter the Union at the same time. In the 2000 report, for the first time, Lithuania and Slovakia were judged to be market economies. Three second-wave countries, Malta, Latvia and Slovakia, received favourable reviews, which suggests that that they might be included in the first group of countries to join. The report noted that economic growth was generally higher and inflation lower, although there had been an overall increase in unemployment. However, it noted that corruption and fraud were still widespread in most candidate countries and that most were weak in judicial and administrative capacity. It argued that with few exceptions, adoption of the *acquis* in the social policy and employment sector had been slow. It argued that agriculture required major structural reform in several CEECs. It noted that Romania had met none of its short-term priorities and its economy was still very weak. Bulgaria was doing better, but was still lagging behind the first-wave countries. In relation to the economic criteria, it asked the two questions which had also been asked in *Agenda 2000*, namely, (1) is the candidate a functioning market economy; and (2) will it be able to cope with competitive pressures and market forces? Table 20.8 provides a snapshot of its findings.

Table 20.8 Commission Report on the Candidates: November 2000

Country & 'Wave'	Political Criteria	Functioning Market Economy?	Ability to cope with competitive pressures?
Bulgaria (2)	yes	not yet, but some progress	not yet
Cyprus (1)	yes	yes	yes
Czech R. (1)	yes	yes	in the near term*
Estonia (1)	yes	yes	ditto
Hungary (1)	yes	yes	ditto
Latvia (2)	yes	yes	in the medium term*
Lithuania (2)	yes	yes	ditto
Malta (2)	yes	yes	yes
Poland (1)	yes	yes	in the near term*
Romania (2)	yes	not yet, little progress	not yet
Slovakia (2)	yes	yes	in the medium term*
Slovenia (1)	yes	yes	in the near term*
Turkey	no	no	no

Note: (1) = 'first wave'; (2) = 'second wave'; (NB: officially candidates are no longer grouped into 'waves'); * providing reforms continue. *Source*: adapted from Commission (2000).

○ **Processes**

The principal stages in the enlargement process are: (1) submission of an application to the Council; (2) the Commission gives an opinion on the application and submits it to the Council; (3) if the opinion is favourable, negotiations open; (4) completion of negotiations: a draft accession treaty is submitted to the Council, which must approve it unanimously and to the EP, which must approve it by absolute majority. The results of the negotiations are incorporated in a draft accession treaty, requiring the approval of the Council and the assent of the EP. The accession treaty must then be ratified by the member states and by the applicant country; (5) the accession (all previous accessions have occurred on 1 January of the year of entry). Table 20.9 below outlines the principal actors in the enlargement process.

Table 20.9 Actors in the Accession Process

Member states are the parties to the accession negotiations on the EU side. Each member state must ratify the treaties of accession.

The Council Presidency: puts forward negotiating positions agreed by member states and chairs negotiating sessions at ministerial level.

The General Secretariat of the Council and the applicant countries provide the secretariat for the negotiations.

Applicant countries. Each country draws up its position on each of the 31 chapters of the EU *acquis* and engages in negotiations with the member states. Each applicant appoints a chief negotiator, supported by experts.

The Commission conducts screening exercises with applicants and draws up draft negotiating positions for member states. It communicates regularly with the applicant countries in order to seek solutions to problems in the negotiations. The Commission established a *Task Force for the Accession Negotiations* (TFAN) on 21 January 1998. The TFAN liaises with all Commission services, holds talks with the negotiators of the applicant countries and presents to member states the Commission's proposals for positions to be taken in negotiations. It prepares draft negotiating positions; drafts and revises legal texts; examines applicant countries' laws, to determine compliance with EU laws; represents the Commission in Council discussions and deliberations on enlargement; and co-ordinates with the Council presidency and secretariat.

The European Parliament is kept informed of the progress of the negotiations and gives its assent to the resulting accession treaties.

Formal negotiations with all candidate countries except Turkey are now well under way. On 31 March 1998 negotiations opened with Hungary, Poland, Estonia, the Czech Republic, Slovenia and Cyprus. On 15 February 2000, negotiations opened with Malta, Romania, Slovakia, Latvia, Lithuania and Bulgaria. Negotiating sessions are conducted with each applicant country separately and are held at the level of ministers or deputies, that is, permanent representatives, for the member states, and ambassadors or chief negotiators for the applicants. Whereas the Commission proposes common negotiating positions for the EU for each chapter relating to matters of Community competence, the Council presidency, in close liaison with member states and the Commission, makes proposals on the chapters concerning CFSP and JHA.

Screening of the applicants involves examination of the *acquis* with the candidate countries (*multilateral screening*) and identification of problem areas to be dealt with in individual negotiations (*bilateral screening*). A detailed presentation on each of the chapters of the *acquis* is made by Commission experts to the applicants in a multilateral meeting, followed by bilateral sessions with each applicant. At bilateral meetings, applicants are asked if: (1) they can accept the relevant chapter of the *acquis*; (2) they intend to request transitional arrangements in the chapter; (3) they have already adopted laws necessary to comply with the *acquis* and if not, when they intend to adopt such laws; (4) they have the administrative and other capacity to implement and enforce EU laws and if not, when these structures will be put in place. Written and oral answers to these questions help the Commission and the applicant country to identify issues that may arise during the negotiations. The Commission reports to member states on the problems likely to arise in the negotiations with each applicant for each chapter of the *acquis*. The Council then decides by unanimity whether or not to open detailed negotiations on particular chapters of the *acquis*. The candidates are also required to dismantle a range of subsidies for specific agricultural sectors. The Commission has registered over 170 requests for transitional measures for candidates in fields other than agriculture and over 340 in agriculture. Some of these have been deemed acceptable, others negotiable and others unacceptable. Some candidates sought permission to increase agricultural production by the time of their accession to close to the levels of the communist era. The Commission has turned down these requests. It has also turned down requests for special measures against sudden increases in imports from other EU countries. When agreements are reached, they have to be ratified by all member states, which could take up to 18 months.

⭕ The Nice and Gothenburg European Councils and Enlargement

The Nice European Council in December 2000 was one of the most important EU summits for the enlargement process for several reasons. Firstly, the 2000 intergovernmental conference (IGC) concluded its work at Nice and agreed the Treaty of Nice (ToN), which is largely about adoption of practical solutions to the institutional problems of enlargement. The protocol on the Enlargement of the EU attached to the ToN has already been considered in some detail in Chapters 4 and 5 and so will not be repeated here. Secondly, the Nice European Council endorsed the General Affairs Council's conclusions of 4 December on the Commission's strategy for enlargement. The Commission had prepared a 'road map' for enlargement for the following 18 months. All 29 chapters of the negotiations had been opened up with Cyprus, Estonia, Hungary, Poland, the Czech Republic and Slovenia and on 17 chapters with Malta, 16 with Latvia, and Slovakia, 11 with Bulgaria and nine with Romania. The 'differentiation principle', meaning that each application would be judged on its own merits, and which allows countries scope to catch up with other candidates, was reaffirmed. Thirdly, it stated that this strategy, together with the completion of the 2000 IGC, would place the EU in a position to welcome those new member states which are ready from the end of 2002, in time for the next EP elections in 2004. Fourthly, it took note of a Council report on candidate countries' exchange rate strategies, which confirmed that new entrants would be required to participate in the ERM before adopting the euro. Fifthly, it welcomed the Council's recent agreement on an accession partnership for Turkey and requested Turkey to submit its national programme for adoption of the *acquis*. Sixthly, it proposed that countries in the Western Balkans and in EFTA should be invited to attend the European Conference as prospective members.

The Gothenburg European Council in June 2001 announced that the ratification process for the ToN would continue, despite the 'no' vote in the Irish referendum (see p. xxviii). It stressed that the enlargement process was irreversible for all candidates. It reaffirmed that accession negotiations should be completed by the end of 2002 for candidates that are ready, the objective being to enable them to participate in the 2004 EP elections as members of the Union. Although no candidates were given specific entry dates the leading countries in the accession race were therefore given clearer targets to aim at.

O   Turkey: The Lagging Candidate

The Helsinki European Council in December 1999 stated that Turkey is a candidate country destined to join the Union on the basis of the same criteria as applied to other candidates. The Union's decision to add Turkey to the list of candidate countries was an important stage in Turkey's long and bitter battle to gain entry into the Union. Turkey's association agreement (1973) contained a reference to eventual Turkish membership of the Community, but without specifying a date. Turkey is generally recognised as being the most secularised of all Muslim countries. It formally applied for membership in April 1987. In December 1989, the Commission issued a negative opinion on Turkey's application, on the grounds that Turkey would be a major institutional, political and financial burden to the Union, at least for the foreseeable future. Turkey has been regarded as an unappealing prospect for several reasons: it has a large population; it has a GDP per capita of less than half of the EU's poorest member; it has a very large agricultural sector; it has a poor human rights record (particularly in relation to its treatment of its Kurdish minority); and it has an unresolved dispute with Greece over Cyprus.

The Commission's 1989 opinion nevertheless recognised Turkey's geopolitical importance and favoured appropriate steps to 'anchor it firmly within the future architecture of Europe'. Since 1973, there has been duty-free access of Turkish industrial goods, excluding textiles. A customs union between the EU and Turkey, which excluded services and agriculture, came into effect on 1 January 1996. Turkey continued to press its case for membership of the Union. Underpinning its overtures for entry was a sense of exasperation concerning the Union's willingness to enter into accession negotiations with 12 other countries. The Union sought to reassure Turkey that it would be considered for membership, if it met the entry criteria. The Luxembourg European Council in 1997 outlined a strategy for Turkish accession by bringing it closer to the Union in every field, including intensification of the customs union, implementation of financial co-operation, approximation of laws and adoption of the Union *acquis* and participation in certain programmes and agencies. It offered Turkey the opportunity to participate in the European Conference, but did not add it to the list of candidate countries. It stated that the strengthening of Turkey's links with the EU depended on Turkey's pursuit of political and economic reforms, improvements in human rights, establishment of satisfactory relations with Greece and support for a political settlement in Cyprus. Turkey criticised the European Council's statements and complained that it had not been treated fairly. It rejected the offer to participate in the European Conference and criticised the decision to start negotiations with Cyprus. It attended the European Conference for the first time in November 2000.

In its enlargement report of October 1999, the Commission argued that Turkey should be considered a candidate for membership, but that it could not open negotiations for entry until it met the political criteria, due to concerns over human rights and the role of the military in the political system. It favoured an 'enhanced political dialogue' with Turkey to consider these issues and also an accession partnership, focusing on aligning Turkey's laws and policies with those of the EU. It argued that it should be considered for full participation in all EU programmes and agencies. The Helsinki European Council accepted these recommendations. It favoured a pre-accession strategy for Turkey and stated that an accession partnership should be drawn up, combined with a national programme for the adoption of the *acquis*.

In its enlargement report on Turkey in November 2000, the Commission stated that Turkey had not met the political criteria, having shortcomings regarding respect for human rights, the rights of minorities and the role of the military. It stated that Turkey was slow in implementing institutional reforms needed to guarantee democracy and the rule of law; that it needed to translate its intentions concerning human rights into concrete policies; and that it had to start making substantial progress in alignment with the *acquis* and in other fields. A severe economic crisis hit Turkey in February 2001. But despite these unpropitious circumstances, Turkey signed an accession partnership (AP) with the EU in March 2001. The AP outlines the reforms Turkey is required to undertake before accession negotiations can begin. Turkey swiftly announced a reform programme aimed at meeting these requirements. However, the adequacy of this programme is questionable and Turkey's road to accession is likely to be very long and hard.

● OTHER POTENTIAL CANDIDATES FOR EU ENTRY

The European countries which are neither EU members nor on the list of candidate countries are a diverse group, comprising:

- *EFTA countries* (which currently do not wish to join the EU);
- *Balkan 'outsiders'* (which have been offered the 'perspective' of future membership, but currently are far from meeting the EU's entry criteria);
- *European members of the Commonwealth of Independent States*: Russia, Ukraine, Belarus, Moldova, Georgia and Armenia have very poor entry prospects although one perhaps should never say never.

Map 20.1 The Enlargement of the EU: Future and Potential Members

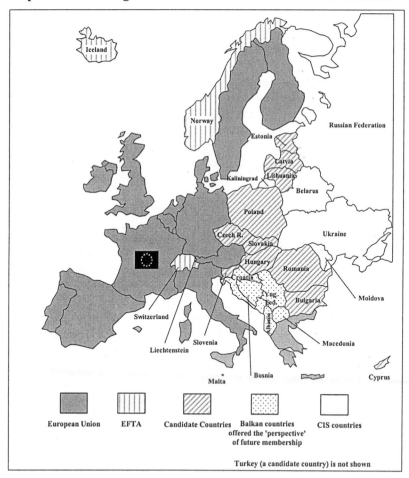

○ EFTA Countries

Norway, Switzerland and Iceland could probably enter the EU quickly, if they opted to do so, as they already meet the Union's membership criteria. The result of the Norwegian referendum in November 1994 effectively ended the possibility that Norway would join the EU in the near future. A 'no' vote in the Swiss referendum on the EEA in December 1992 had the same effect in Switzerland. Switzerland has a very long history of avoiding European entanglements. Its economy is already highly intermeshed with the EU economy (being the EU's third-largest trading partner). Large companies and banks tend to favour entry (Swiss banks and insurance companies already have many subsidiaries in the EU, and all major EU banks have branches or subsidiaries in Switzerland) but there is strong opposition to entry from some other groups, including farmers. In a referendum in March 2001, no less than 76% of Swiss voters voted against EU entry. An opinion poll in Norway in March 2001 found that 56.2% of Norwegian voters opposed, and only 35.6% favoured, entry (*Nationen*, 30 March 2001). If Norway opted to join, Iceland might be pulled towards entry via a Nordic 'domino effect' and in order to secure the same access as Norway to the EU's market for fish (Iceland depends upon fishing for about 80% of its exports). EU membership is currently opposed by all main parties. Liechtenstein (population 30,000) is too small to join as a full member. It may be satisfied with membership of the EEA, which it joined in May 1995. As long as the EFTANs continue to do well economically, EU entry pressures will probably remain weak.

○ The Balkan 'Outsiders': Soon to be Insiders?

The countries in the Balkans which may be added to the list of candidates at some point, that is, Albania, Croatia, Bosnia, Macedonia and Yugoslavia (Serbia and Montenegro) have been offered the perspective of future membership, if they work with the EU and among themselves to implement a strategy of regional stabilisation. The EU's relations with these countries have been dominated by recent conflicts in the Balkans. The end of the wars in Bosnia and Kosovo, combined with the election of new Western-oriented governments in Croatia in 1999 and Serbia in 2000 radically improved the entry prospects of these Balkan outsiders. The Feira European Council in March 2000 agreed that all Balkan countries are potential candidates. The framework for the EU's policy in the Balkans is a stabilisation and association process, regarded as the 'road to Europe' for these countries. It provides for political dialogue, trade liberalisation, financial assistance and other forms of co-operation. But the Balkan outsiders currently fall far short of the political and economic criteria for EU membership.

O **European Members of the Commonwealth of Independent States**

The CIS comprises newly independent states of the former Soviet Union (excluding Latvia, Lithuania and Estonia) and includes states which are generally accepted as being European countries (Russia, Ukraine, Belarus, Moldova, Georgia and Armenia) as well as central Asian countries (for example, Uzbekistan and Azerbaijan). As the TEU states that any European country can apply for EU membership, countries in the former category might be viewed as potential candidates. However, the chances of entry for countries in this category currently seem very remote. Most are too poor and many too politically unstable for serious consideration. Most will probably have to settle for alternatives to membership, such as preferential trading agreements or association agreements containing only the vaguest reference to future entry. Russia and Ukraine (with populations of 147 million and 51 million respectively), would be very difficult to absorb, even if they made substantial progress in reform. Other CIS countries are also currently unacceptable on political and economic grounds. All CIS countries have found it difficult to successfully make a successful transition from communism to the market and democratic stability. For example, in Russia, corruption, crumbling economic infrastructure, poverty, alcoholism and disease are major problems.

The EU is nevertheless seeking to develop closer relationships with its eastern neighbours, not least because enlargement will create new EU borders with these countries. Indeed, after the accession of Poland and Lithuania, Kaliningrad will become a Russian enclave within the EU. EU assistance to the CIS centres on strengthening democracy and the rule of law, nurturing the private sector and economic development. The former focuses on promotion of good governance and support for key policymaking institutions. The latter seeks to promote a fully functioning market economy and integration of the CIS into the world economy. The EU is the most important trading partner of the CIS. Partnership and co-operation agreements (PCAs), embracing trade, economic and political matters, have been signed with Ukraine and Russia. A PCA falls somewhere between a trade and co-operation agreement and a Europe agreement, in that there is explicit reference to political co-operation. Its main components are: trade co-operation; economic co-operation; political dialogue; institutional links (for example, a ministerial co-operation council); and co-operation in justice and home affairs. In addition to PCAs, the EU has developed a new instrument, known as the 'common strategy', to extend its partnerships with Russia and Ukraine. The common strategy focuses on developing and implementing policies in priority areas, such as consolidation of democracy, European security, crime and environmental issues. It is also encouraging regional co-operation, through frameworks such as the Barents

Euro Arctic Co-operation Council, the Council of Baltic States and Black Sea Economic Co-operation.

The TACIS (Technical Assistance to the CIS) programme was formally established in July 1991 and is the largest provider of technical assistance to the CIS. Unlike the PHARE programme, it is not a vehicle to facilitate accession. Between 1991 and 1997, about €3.3 billion was allocated to the TACIS programme. Since the end of 1998, TACIS has included a performance incentive scheme to reward the best-performing beneficiary countries. The amounts provided, however, have been small. A common criticism of TACIS has been that it has been too inflexible to respond to the changing needs of the partner countries. In December 1998, the Commission adopted a proposal for overhauling assistance to the CIS, with an emphasis on promoting democracy and stimulating investment.

Each of the European members of the CIS know that there is, for the foreseeable future, no point in formally applying for EU membership. However, this has not prevented some leading politicians in these countries from voicing an aspiration to join the EU, even though this is currently not a realistic prospect.

● CONCLUSION

The unprecedented scale and character of the next enlargements will inevitably mean that the EU will not only be bigger, but also different. How different remains to be seen. We still do not know if the EU's preparations for enlargement will be adequate to cope with the financial and institutional implications of absorbing such a large and diverse group of countries. The continuing capacity of enlargement to cause strains in relations between member states was evident in the informal weekend meeting of EU foreign ministers held in Nyköping, Sweden, in May 2001 (attended on its second day by foreign ministers from the candidate countries). At Nyköping, several member states sought to defend specific national interests from perceived threats from the next enlargements. Germany and Austria sought a seven-year restriction on the free movement of workers from the new entrants (a deal was later agreed which will prevent workers from CEEC countries from seeking jobs in the present EU for two years after their country accedes: each EU country can then restrict access for a further three to five years); Spain sought to protect its aid money from the structural and cohesion funds; France was concerned to ensure that future enlargement will not jeopardise its aid from the Common Agricultural Policy. The enlargement negotiations on regional aid and CAP funding scheduled for 2002 are likely to be very difficult. Some of the thorniest enlargement issues, therefore, remain to be dealt with.

But even when all of the current 13 candidate countries have acceded, the EU will still not be able to close the book on enlargement. Countries in the Western Balkans are already knocking on the EU's door, requesting entry. The EFTAN outsiders may not wish to remain outsiders for ever – despite the resounding 'no' vote in the March 2001 Swiss referendum. At some point in the future (although not for the foreseeable future), the prospect of the entry of at least some CIS countries may be given serious consideration.

Even if no other potential candidates apply, this does not necessarily mean that there will be a clear demarcation between an enlarged Union and the rest of Europe. It seems more likely that the EU and European countries outside it will become increasingly intermeshed in pan-European ventures of various kinds, such as trans-European networks and research and technological development programmes. Moreover, the agreements signed between the EU and non-associated European countries are recognised to be stages on the road to deeper co-operation, perhaps leading eventually to a free trade zone encompassing virtually the whole of Europe. Intermeshing could well mean that the Union's boundaries will become increasingly rough-edged and fuzzy.

FURTHER READING

Avery, G. and Cameron, F. (1998), *The Enlargement of the European Union*, Sheffield Academic Press, Sheffield.

Commission (1995), *Preparation of the Associated Countries of Central and Eastern Europe for Integration into the Internal market of the Union*, COM (95) 163.

Commission (1997), *Agenda 2000: For a Stronger and Wider Union*, COM (97) 2000.

Commission (1999), *Enlargement Composite Paper. Reports on Progress towards Accession by Each of the Candidate Countries*, COM (99) 500.

Commission (2000), *Enlargement Strategy Paper. Report on Progress towards Accession by Each of the Candidate countries*.
http://www.europa.eu.int/comm/enlargement/report_11_00/index.htm.

Commission (2001) Enlargement Homepage,
http://www.europa.eu.int/comm/enlargement/index.htm.

Eurostat (1999), *Regional GDP in the Central European Countries*, Luxembourg.

Hafner, D.F.(1999), 'Dilemmas in Managing the Expanding EU: The EU and Applicant States' Points of View', *Journal of European Public Policy*, vol. 6, no. 5, pp. 783–801.

Mayhew, A. (1998), *Recreating Europe: The European Union's Policy towards Central and Eastern Europe*, Cambridge University Press, Cambridge.

McLaren, L.M. (2000), 'Turkey's Eventual Membership of the EU: Turkish Elite Perspectives on the Issue', *Journal of Common Market Studies*, vol. 38, no.1, pp. 117–29.

Nugent, N, (2000), 'EU Enlargement and "the Cyprus problem"', *Journal of Common Market Studies*, vol. 38, no.1, pp. 131–50.

Bibliography and Internet Sources

● OFFICIAL PUBLICATIONS

A vast range of information is published by the Union on virtually every aspect of its activities. The Office for Official Publications of the European Communities (OOPEC) based in Luxembourg is the principal source of official information, but most EU institutions also disseminate material. Information leaflets of various kinds are available (usually free) from Commission and EP offices in member countries. A more comprehensive range of publications is held in European documentation centres. There are about 40 EDCs in the UK, mainly in University libraries. EDCs receive copies of all publications issued by OOPEC. A newsletter, *EUR-OP News*, is published four times a year by OOPEC. OOPEC also publishes a guide to EU information sources. The library of the European Commission compiles a monthly bibliography of recent EU publications.

EUROPA, the European Union's Internet server, can be found at: http://europa.eu.int. Most official publications, and also the websites of each of the Union's institutions, can be accessed from this server.

The following list, which is far from comprehensive, contains information about some of the most widely used official publications and sources.
Bulletin of the European Union: published ten times a year by the Secretariat-General of the Commission, it provides an account of the Union's recent activities. Supplements to the *Bulletin* are published on significant issues;
CELEX: the official data base of Community law (see also Eur-Lex);
COMEX: external trade statistics of the EU and member states;
Commission documents are generally known as COM documents. These set out the Commission's viewpoint on Union matters and include proposals for legislation, plus analytical reports of various kinds;
Competition Policy Newsletter, published quarterly by the Commission;
The Courier, reports on EU relations with ACP countries;

Court of Auditors produces special reports;

Court of Justice. Legal Bibliography of European Integration (annual);

Directory of Community Legislation in Force, published twice yearly;

Economic Report, published annually by the Commission;

EP News, newsletter published by the European Parliament;

ESC Opinions and Information Reports, published in the C section of the *Official Journal* (*OJ*). There is a monthly *ESC Bulletin*;

Eurobarometer reports on public opinion in the EU (twice yearly);

Eur-Lex: a website containing the complete L and C series of the *Official Journal*. The *Official Journal* is displayed free of charge for 45 days, after which it is available for a fee in Eudor, Celex or on CD ROM;

European Economy: published quarterly, by the Commission;

European Parliament Briefing, published by the European Parliament;

Eurostat: the Statistical Office of the European Communities provides statistical information for the Commission and all the citizens of Europe. For example, it produces *Basic Statistics, Europe in Figures* (annual) and *Rapid Reports* (about 50–55 issues a year on a variety of subjects). There is a Eurostat Information Office in Luxembourg and a data shop in Brussels;

Eudor: a website containing nine million pages of official documents (fees are charged);

Factsheets on the European Parliament and the Activities of the European Communities, published by the European Parliament;

General Report on the Activities of the European Union, published annually by the Commission, provides summaries of institutional and policy developments;

Official Journal of the European Communities (*OJ*) is published on most working days, divided into the following sections: *L series*: Legislation containing the full text of all legislation and acts the EU is obliged to publish and information on other legal acts; *C series*: Communications, Information and Notices. It covers proposals for legislation; written questions put by parliament; euro exchange rates; reports on cases before the ECJ; EU job vacancies and other official notes; *S series*: Supplements, containing notices of public works and public supply contracts open to competitive tender; *Annex*: debates in the EP. The ToN requires the name of the OJ to be changed to the *Official Journal of the European Union*;

Panorama of EU Business (formerly Panorama of EU Industry) is a detailed annual review by the Commission of the situation of business in the EU;

Review of the Council's Work, published annually by the Council;

Scad Bulletin: a weekly bibliographic guide to principal EU publications and documents;

Social Europe: published thrice yearly by the Commission;

Treaties are published by the OOPEC.

● OTHER SOURCES

○ Independent Guides to EU Activities

Various guides are produced, for example:

Agence Europe, daily reports, Agence Internationale d'information pour la Presse, Brussels.

Annual Report on the Activities of the European Community, published by the *Journal of Common Market Studies*, Blackwell, London.

Annual Review of European Community Affairs, Brassey's, London.

Annual Review of European Community Affairs, Centre for European Policy Studies, Brussels.

European Access (bimonthly), Chadwyck-Healey, Cambridge.

European Trends, Economist Intelligence Unit, London.

The European Companion, published annually by Dod's, London.

○ Journals and Other Sources

Many academic journals in the social and legal sciences publish articles on European affairs. The following have a specific European focus:

Common Market Law Reports, Sweet & Maxwell, London.

Common Market Law Review, Kluwer, Dordrecht.

Euromoney, Euromoney, London.

European Journal of Sociology, Cambridge University Press.

European Law Review, Sweet & Maxwell, London.

European Urban and Regional Studies, Longman, Harlow.

Journal of Common Market Studies, Blackwell, Oxford.

Journal of European Public Policy, Routledge, London.

Journal of European Social Policy, Longman, Harlow.

West European Politics, Frank Cass, London.

European Voice, published by the Economist Group, London, is a weekly newspaper on the EU. *The Economist* and *Financial Times* also have excellent regular coverage of EU developments.

○ Books

Ackrill, R. (2001), *The Common Agricultural Policy*, Sheffield Academic Press, Sheffield.

Armstrong, K.A. and Bulmer, S.J. (1998), *The Governance of the European Single Market*, Manchester University Press, Manchester.

Bache, I. (1998), *The Politics of European Union Regional Policy, Multi-level Governance or Flexible Gatekeeping?*, Sheffield Academic Press, Sheffield.

Barnes, P.M. and Barnes, I.G. (2000), *Environmental Policy in the European Union*, Edward Elgar, Cheltenham and Northampton, MA.

Burgess, Michael (1989), *Federalism and European Union*, Routledge, London.

Chryssochoou, D.N. (1998), *Democracy in the European Union*, Taurus Academic Studies, London.

Church, C. and Phinnemore, D. (1994), *European Union and the European Community: A Handbook and Commentary on the Post-Maastricht Treaties*, Harvester Wheatsheaf, Hemel Hempstead.

Cini, M. (1996), *The European Commission: Leadership, Organisation and Culture in the EU Administration*, Manchester University Press, Manchester.

Cini, M. and McGowan, L. (1999), *Competition Policy in the EU*, Macmillan, Basingstoke.

Cram, L. (1997), *Policy-making in the EU: Conceptual Lenses and the Integration Process*, Routledge, London.

Darmer, M. and Kuyper, L. (eds) (2000), *Industry and the European Union*, Edward Elgar, Cheltenham and Northampton, MA.

De Grauwe, P. (1997), *The Economics of Monetary Integration*, Oxford University Press, Oxford.

Eijffinger, C.W. and De Haan, J. (2000), *European Monetary and Fiscal Policy*, Oxford University Press, Oxford.

Fagerberg, J., Guerrieri, P. and Verspagen, B. (eds.) (2000), *The Economic Challenge for Europe*, Edward Elgar, Cheltenham and Northampton, MA.

Faulkner, G. (1998), *EU Social Policy in the 1990s: Towards a Corporatist Policy Community*, Routledge, London.

Galloway, D. (2001), *The Treaty of Nice and Beyond*, Sheffield Academic Press, Sheffield.

Gavin, B. (2001), *The European Union and Globalisation*, Edward Elgar, Cheltenham and Northampton, MA.

George, S. (1994), *An Awkward Partner, Britain in the European Community*, Oxford University Press, Oxford.

Golub, J. (ed.) (1998), *Global Competition and EU Environment Policy*, Routledge, London.

Grant, W. (1999), *The Common Agricultural Policy*, Macmillan, Basingstoke.

Haas, E.B. (1958), *The Uniting of Europe*, Stanford University Press, Stanford, CA.

Hendriks G. and Morgan, A. (2000), *The Franco-German Axis in European Integration*, Edward Elgar, Cheltenham and Northampton, MA.

Hine, D. and Kassim, H. (eds.) (1998), *Beyond the Market: The EU and National Social Policy*, Routledge, London.

Hix, S. (1999), *The Political System of the European Union*, Macmillan, Basingstoke.

Keohane, R.O. and Hoffman, S. (1991), *The New European Community*, Westview Press, Boulder, Colo.

Laffan, B. (1997), *The Finances of the European Union*, Macmillan, Basingstoke.

Levy, R. (2000), *Implementing European Union Public Policy*, Edward Elgar, Cheltenham and Northampton, MA.

Lieshout, R.H. (1999), *The Struggle for the Organisation of Europe*, Edward Elgar, Cheltenham and Northampton, MA.

Lipgens, W. (1986), *The History of European Integration* (2 vols), Oxford University

Press, London.

Lowe, P. and Ward, S. (1998), *British Environmental Policy and Europe*, Routledge, London.

Lundestad, G. (1998), *'Empire' by Integration: The United States and European Integration, 1945–1997*, Oxford University Press, Oxford.

Marks, G., Scharpf, F. Schmitter, P. and Streeck, W. (1996), *Governance in the European Union*, Sage, London.

Mayhew, A. (1998), *Recreating Europe: the European Union's Policy towards Central and Eastern Europe*, Cambridge University Press, Cambridge.

McKay, D.(1999*), Federalism and European Union,* Oxford University Press, Oxford.

Meeusen, W. (ed.) (1999), *Economic Policy in the European Union*, Edward Elgar, Cheltenham and Northampton, MA.

Milward, A.S. (1987), *The Reconstruction of Western Europe 1945–51*, London, Methuen.

Milward, A.S. (1992), *The European Rescue of the Nation-State*, Routledge, London.

Monar, J. (2001), *Justice and Home Affairs in the European Union*, Macmillan, Basingstoke.

Moravcsik, A. (1998), *The Choice for Europe: Social Purpose and State Power from Messina to Maastricht*, Cornell University Press, Ithaca, NY.

Neunreither, K. and Wiener, A. (2000), *European Integration After Amsterdam*, Oxford University Press, Oxford.

Nugent, N. (2000), *The Government and Politics of the European Union*, Macmillan, Basingstoke.

Nuttall, S. (2000), *European Foreign Policy*, Oxford University Press, Oxford.

Peterson, J. and Bomberg, E. (1999), *Decision-making in the EU*, Macmillan, Basingstoke.

Peterson, J. and Sjursen, H. (1998), *A Common Foreign Policy for Europe?*, Routledge, London.

Preston, C. (1997), *Enlargement and Integration in the European Union*, Routledge, London.

Rosamund, B. (2000), *Theories of European Integration*, Macmillan, Basingstoke.

Sandholtz, W. and Stone Sweet, A. (1998), *European Integration and Supranational Governance*, Oxford University Press, Oxford.

Scharpf, F.(1999), *Governing in Europe: Effective and Democratic?*, Oxford University Press, Oxford.

Siedentop, L. (2000), *Democracy in Europe*, Allen Lane, London.

Smith, K.E. (1999), *The Making of European Union Foreign Policy: The Case of Eastern Europe*, Macmillan, Basingstoke.

Stirk, P.M.R. (1996), *A History of European Integration Since 1914*, Pinter, London.

Vanthoor, W.F.V. (1999), *A Chronological History of the European Union*, Edward Elgar, Cheltenham and Northampton, MA.

Wallace, H. and Wallace, W. (eds) (2000), *Policy Making in the European Union*, Oxford University Press, Oxford.

Weatherill, S. and Beaumont, P. (1999), *EU Law*, Penguin, Harmondsworth.

Westlake, M. (1999), *The European Union Beyond Amsterdam: New Concepts of European Integration*, Routledge, London.

O   Internet Sources

The EU's main website at: http://www.europa.int is a good starting point for information on the Union. The EU's institutions and agencies also have their own sites. A small selection of key official sites is shown below. I also include a small selection of other sites from the vast range now available. The academic sites in particular provide extensive links to other EU-related sites.

•   Some Official EU Sites

Commission's home page: http://europa.eu.int/comm
Council of the European Union: http://ue.eu.int (the Council Presidency and the European Council can also be accessed for this site).
European Parliament: http:www.europarl.eu.int
European Court of Justice: http://curia.eu.int
European Investment Bank: http://eib.eu.int
Court of Auditors: http:www.eca.eu.int
European Central Bank: http://ecb.int
European Ombudsman: http://www.euro-ombudsman.eu.int
Economic and Social Committee: http://www.ces.eu.int
Committee of the Regions: http://www.cor.eu.int
'Futurum' (debate on the future of Europe site): http://www.europa.eu.int/futurum

•   Some Academic Sites

http://www.keele.ac.uk/depts/por/eubase.htm (Keele University).
http://wu-wien.ac.at/erpa (European Research Papers Archive).
http://www.pitt.edu/~wwwes (West European Studies: University of Pittsburgh).
http://www.uni-mannheim.de/users/ddz/edz/net/enet.html (University of Mannheim).
http://www.ecsanet.org/euinfo.htm (European Community Studies Association).
http://www.rewi.hu-berlin.de/WHI/english/index.htm (Walter Hallstein Institute at the Humboldt University in Berlin).
http://www.lib.berkeley.edu/GSSI/eu.html (University of Berkeley).

•   News Sites Focusing on Current Developments in the EU

http://www Euractiv.com (stated aim: 'to serve the community of EU actors').
http://www EUbusiness.com (online business information service about the EU).
http://www European-Voice.com (website of the *European Voice* weekly newspaper).
http://EUObserver.com (latest news, covering 'Eurosceptic' and other viewpoints).

•   Some 'Eurosceptic' and 'Federalist' Sites

http://www.eusceptic.org (links to Eurosceptic sites and resources).
http://www.eurocritic.demon.co.uk (website of the Bruges group).
http://www.no-euro.com (Business for Sterling group).
http://www.eurplace.org ('Grand-Place Europe': European federalist site).
http://www.euromove.org.uk (European Movement: pro-European membership site).
http://www.euraction.org (Campaign for a European Federal Constitution).
http://www.cix.co.uk/~fedtrust (the Federal Trust: think tank and research centre).

Index

Note: Institutions and organisations are listed under their abbreviations or acronyms when these are well known. A full list will be found on pp. xiv–xix.